W9-BCK-558

North Carolina Hiking Trails

4th Edition

The State's Most Comprehensive Trail Guide

Allen de Hart

NEW HANOVER COUNTY
PUBLIC LIBRARY
201 CHESTNUT STREET
WILMINGTON, NC 28401

APPALACHIAN MOUNTAIN CLUB BOOKS
BOSTON, MASSACHUSETTS

To the volunteers who design, construct, and maintain
the hiking trails in North Carolina.

Cover photograph: Kevin Adams
Book design: Amy Winchester and Eric Edstam
Cover design: Kala Sabel
Cartography: Ken Dumas
All interior photographs by Allen de Hart

North Carolina Hiking Trails: The State's Most Comprehensive Trail Guide
Copyright © 1982, 1988, 1996, 2005 by Allen de Hart. All rights reserved.
Published by the Appalachian Mountain Club, 5 Joy St., Boston, MA 02108.
Distributed by the Globe Pequot Press, Guilford, CT

All rights reserved. No part of this publication may be reproduced or transmitted in
any form or by any means, electronic or mechanical, including photocopying and
recording, or by any information storage or retrieval system, except as may be
expressly permitted by the 1976 Copyright Act or in writing from the publisher.
Requests for permission should be addressed in writing to Appalachian Mountain
Club Books, 5 Joy St., Boston, MA 02108.

Library of Congress Cataloging-in-Publication Data
De Hart, Allen.
North Carolina hiking trails / Allen de Hart.—4th ed.
p. cm.
Includes index.
ISBN 1-929173-47-4 (alk. paper)
1. Hiking—North Carolina—Guidebooks. 2. Trails—North Carolina—Guidebooks.
3. North Carolina—Guidebooks. I. Title.

GV199.42.N66D4 2005
917.56—dc22
2004015364

The paper used in this publication meets the minimum requirements of the American
National Standard for Information Sciences—Permanence of Paper for Printed
Library Materials, ANSI Z39.48–1984.

Due to changes in conditions, use of the information
in this book is at the sole risk of the user.

Printed on recycled paper using soy-content inks.
Printed in the United States of America.

10 9 8 7 6 5 4 3 2 1   05 06 07 08

Contents

Acknowledgments

The fourth edition of this book has been made possible by the assistance of many resource personnel of the forests and parks, professional outdoor sports and recreation specialists, hikers, and college and university students. Those who assisted me in accumulating data, double-checked research material, planned the logistical needs, and spent relentless days of field work deserve grateful acknowledgment. Our work was mitigated by having the original research manuscripts and maps from the 1980–1981 research of Kay Scott, former state trails coordinator, and her supervisor, Jim Hallsey, assistant chief of planning and special studies section of the Division of Parks and Recreation. Although since retired, their work was the foundation on which the second, third, and fourth editions of this book depended.

By 1986 an additional library of trail information had been accumulated for the second edition. Recognition of faithful hiking friends such as Alan Householder, Todd Shearon, and Kevin Bighannitti was made at that time. Additional information came from the Division of Parks and Recreation by Susan Currie, trails coordinator; Bynum Riggsbee, visitor service director; Mike Dunn, interpretive and education director; and Jim Hallsey again, who had been promoted to chief of operations. Others whose work became part of the second edition were Harry Baker, landscape architect for the Blue Ridge Parkway; Melinda Waldrep, landscape architect of the national forests in North Carolina; and Joseph Smith, assistant chief ranger of the Cherokee area of the Great Smoky Mountains National Park. Major assistance in the third edition was Melinda (Waldrep) MacWilliams of the USFS headquarters; Karen Wade, superintendent of the Great Smoky Mountains National Park; Will Orr, landscape architect of the Blue Ridge Parkway; Darrell McBane, state trails coordinator of the Division of Parks and Recreation; and Burt Kornegay of the Bartram Trail Society.

From USFS headquarters staff in Asheville for the fourth edition are John Ramey, forest supervisor; Holly Hixson, graphic information systems specialist; Terry Seyden, public affairs officer; Pat Momich, interpretive specialist; Julie Trzeciak, assistant public affairs officer; Mary Noel, staff officer; and

Steve Hendricks, recreation planner. For district staff of Croatan NF: Lauren Hillman, ranger; Dennis Foster, recreation assistant; and Johnny Morris, forestry technician. In Nantahala NF's Cheoah Ranger District: R.E. Vann, ranger; Laney Cutshaw, fire management officer; Frank Findley, other resources assistant; Jay Orr, support service assistant; and Tim Solesbee, recreation technician. In Highlands Ranger District: Erin Bronk, ranger; Chad Boniface, operations manager; Grant Keener, recreation technician; and Christina Thomas, forester trainee. From Tusquitee Ranger District: Charles Miller, ranger; Bill Champion, operations forester; Horace Mitchell, archaeologist; and David Stiles, forestry technician. In Wayah Ranger District: Mike Wilkins, ranger; Grey Brooks, trails and wilderness technician; Sally Browning, resources assistant; and Dale Holland, development/recreation technician. From Pisgah NF's Appalachian Ranger District at Hot Springs Station: Linda Randolph, operations assistant and silviculturist; and Darlene Huntsinger, support services assistant. At the Burnsville station: Paul Bradley, district ranger; Derek Ibaruguen, outdoor recreation planner; and David McFee, operations assistant. In Grandfather Ranger District: Miera Crawford, ranger; Dean Karlovich, forester; and Debbie Thomas, forestry technician and recreation. From Pisgah Ranger District: Randy Burgess, ranger; Diane Bolt, outdoor recreation supervisor; Ronnie Carnes, fire management officer; Pat Lancaster, wilderness ranger; and Jim Spenser, volunteer. In Uwharrie NF: Tom Horner, ranger.

Information and assistance from the Appalachian Trail Conference was from Laurie Potteiter, information services coordinator, and Brain King, public affairs director. From the Blue Ridge Parkway: Dan Brown, superintendent; and Larry Hultquist, resident landscape architect. Among the Great Smoky Mountains National Forest: Donna Losson, administrative officer; George Minnigh, park ranger and backcountry operations specialist; Tom Robbins of Oconalufftee Visitor Center, and Eric Kreuksch, archaeologist. From some of the private trail areas (open to the public) are Steve Miller of Grandfather Mountain, Robert E. Wyatt of Highlands Biological Station, and Wayne Horton for mapping of Sauratown Trail.

From the county and city parks and recreation was assistance from Marek Smith, environmental education supervisor, of Mecklenburg County; Candice Bruton, assistant trails director, of Greensboro; and Ed McNeal, marketing coordinator of Winston-Salem. For a multi-county rail-trail project, assistance was provided for the American Tobacco trail by Bill Bussey, president of the Triangle Rails-to-Trails Conservancy.

Those who hiked many days with me in hot and rainy weather or endured freezing nights on long journeys or provided shuttle service or trail measurements or trail maintenance and construction are Ray Benedicktus, Bob Benner, Jeff Brewer, Tony Butler, Wendell Burton, Josh Carpenter, Travis Combest, Lacy Desist, Natalie Foster, Greg Gillette, Colleen Haney, Graham Hildreth, Alan Householder, Steven Joines, John Jaskolka, Glenn McLeroy, Jason Mason, John Naylor, Guillermo Ochoa, Dennis Parrish, Ronnie Price, Jason Ryan, Martin Sweat, Dwayne Stutzman, David Straw, Tim Straw, Marc and Kristi Trinks, Morgan and Tegan Warfield, Jonathan Weary, Harold White, Matt White, and Bruce Wisely.

I express my special appreciation to the editorial staff of Appalachian Mountain Club Books: former editor Arlyn Powell (who suggested and worked with the first edition); his successors, and the current editorial staff: Laurie O'Reilly, marketing manager; Belinda Thresher, production manager; and Sarah Jane Shangraw, editor-in-chief.

How to Use This Book

This completely revised fourth edition is divided into sixteen chapters that cover the national forests (Croatan, Nantahala, Pisgah, and Uwharrie); the national parks and refuges; the state parks, forests, and historic sites; city and county parks; private and college properties; and an introduction to the Mountains-to-Sea Trail (MST). At the beginning of each chapter is a map and a brief listing of trail locations. An appendix offers suggestions for challenging trails, for family day trips, and for the physically disabled. Each chapter and section has an introduction to acquaint you with the location of and access to the properties, addresses and telephone numbers for information, and the nearest support services. If not in the main introduction, this information will be shown in a specific section where trails are concentrated. An appendix provides names and addresses of agencies that can assist you with more information. It is recommended that allied maps be secured in your advance planning and that some familiarity be developed with the topography of the area to which you are going. This will enable you to plan better for your transportation, seasonal needs, and hiking and camping supplies. This book is designed to be carried in a side pocket of your backpack or in a large pocket of your clothes.

Format for Trail Descriptions

The trails are described either numerically (all USFS trails are described from the lowest to the highest number, the official method of USFS inventories), alphabetically, or from a grouping of trails with proximity. In the national forests the descriptions may be described in any direction, but in the Smokies the description is from the NE to the SW. Exceptions are made when trail proximity or connections are an advantage to your planning options.

Title and Number

The trail name is from the most current source, but references may indicate that it was formerly known by another name. Some trails will carry a double name because they run jointly for a distance. An example is where the Mountains-to-Sea Trail runs jointly with an original trail. The first number nearest the title is the USFS trail number, listed in parentheses, the official number assigned by the USFS on its trail inventories and maps. It is significant because it is on all the US Geological Survey (USGS) maps modified for USFS use—the topo map you should use in the national forests. This is the same number that you will see on special maps (examples are the Linville Wilderness or Joyce Kilmer/Slickrock Wilderness) created by the USFS. Additionally, you may see the trail number on commercial maps such as the National Geographic Topographic Maps. If the number is absent, the USFS has not assigned a number or the number may have been deleted from its inventories. Each district or national forest should have its own group of numbers, but unfortunately you will find that the assignments in North Carolina are set at random (with trail inventories from 1 through 700). The exception is the Croatan National Forest, with all numbers in the 500 range. A few major or interstate trails will carry the same number through all districts, regardless of the national forest. Examples are the Appalachian Trail (#1), the Bartram Trail (#67), and the Overmountain Victory Trail (#308). Following the USFS number, or the trail name outside the national forests, are capital letters to indicate trail traffic: foot (F), bike (B), horse (H), wheelchair (W), interpretive (I), or other (O). These are the official USFS codes used on its transportation inventory. The second number on the page, at the outside margin in bold type, is a numeric assignment by the publishers of this book for the purpose of matching trail numbers in the index and maps.

Mileage

The trail length is always within the nearest 0.1 mile (with the exception of short trails that may be described in yards or feet). All numbers followed by "mi" (mile/s) indicate the distance from one trailhead to another. If the mileage is followed by "round-trip" or "backtrack," it means the distance is a loop (perhaps using a road route) or doubled by returning on the same route. When a group of trails is used for a combined or connecting mileage, the length will be followed by "combined" to indicate the total mileage of multiple routes. I used a 400 Rolatape measuring wheel (which registers each foot), a GPS system, or both on all the trails.

How to Use This Book

Connecting Trails

Where a single trail is listed with a number of connecting trails, some of the trails may be covered in more detail under another heading. If so, they will be enclosed in parentheses. Although reading about a connecting trail may create a temporary break in your train of thought, a return to the main description usually will start with the words "to continue" or "continuing ahead." The objective is to give you flexibility on how far you wish to hike before backtracking, making a loop, or staying on the main trail. If continuing, you can ignore the paragraphs in parentheses, but the information will be available if you change your mind.

Difficulty

Trails are described as easy (meaning the trail has a gentle grade, may be short, and does not require a rest stop); moderate (with a greater change in elevation or rough treadway that requires some exertion and likely rest stops); or strenuous (with the need for some skill over rough treadway, high or steep elevation change, exertion, and perhaps frequent rest stops). Elevation changes on strenuous trails are usually listed.

Special Features

Some of the trails have features that are more distinctive, unique, unusual, rare, or outstanding than trails in general. This listing will follow "Length and Difficulty" or "Connecting Trail" and will precede "Trailhead and Description." The word "scenic" is frequently used as synonymous with impressive, bucolic, unspoiled, panoramic, or pleasant to experience. I have made an effort to avoid using superlatives for every trail, even when I may have felt it was deserving. I found beauty in all the trails; you probably will also, but I have left some mystery for your judgment.

Trailhead

Where possible, access to a trailhead is described from the North Carolina official highway map. More specifically, I have used county and city maps. Because the USGS or the USGS-FS (Forest Service) topographic maps are not as easily or quickly attainable, they are not emphasized but are listed either after the introductory paragraphs or at the end of the trail description. The nearest city, town, or community is usually cited; otherwise roads by title and number and their junctions are listed. If the trailhead has more than one access option, the easiest and nearest is described first.

Description

Trail descriptions are determined by trail length, usage, features, history, connective value, difficulty, and book space. Most of the trails are described as *main* or *primary* (blazed, marked, or maintained), *alternate* or *connector* (usually with the same goal). Some are *primitive* (the opposite of primary), and others are as follows: *side* or *spur* (a shorter route or to a point of interest); *multiple* or *multi-use* (used by equestrians, bicyclists, hikers, or vehicles); *ATV routes* (mainly old forest or hunting roads); *manway* or *wilderness* (exceptionally primitive, grown up, or obscure); *special* (used for special populations, such as the physically disabled). A *gated* trail may be a *foot* trail for pedestrians during a protective season for wildlife that is open to both hikers and vehicles at other times, and a *seeded* trail is usually a former logging road planted with grass for soil stabilization. There are numerous paths used by hunters and fishermen that may be called *fisherman's* trails or *hunter's* trails in both public and private game lands. Some of the mountain trails are used as *ski* trails in wintertime. Other trails may be described as *recreational* (jogging, exercise, fitness); *historic* (emphasizing heritage, historic districts, historic sites); *nature* (interpretive, botanical, kiosk displays); *social* (unofficial trails by users to points of personal interest); or *greenways* (asphalt, concrete, granite, screening, recycled materials, crush and run, grassy).

Address and Access

The addresses, telephone numbers, or fax numbers are your most immediate source of additional information about the trail area and trail conditions. They are listed at the end of an introduction or description. The access explains how to arrive at either the address trailheads or at campgrounds, parks, or special places administered by the address source.

Support Facilities

To assist you in planning for your food supply, gasoline and vehicle services, and accommodations, the nearest stores are listed at large or major groupings of trails. The nearest (or most amenable to hikers) commercial campgrounds are listed, particularly in areas where public campgrounds do not have full services or hot showers. Motels are listed for some areas.

Maps

The maps in this book are meant to orient you to the region of the state covered in each section and to help you locate trailheads. The maps will assist you in planning your hikes. You should bring a state or county road map with you as well. And remember that although you may be familiar with an area, you may need to give someone clear directions about where you will be or how you are to be picked up after a long hike. State highway maps are available at service stations, Chambers of Commerce, and free from the North Carolina Department of Transportation, PO Box 25201, Raleigh, NC 27611; 919-733-7600. Detailed county maps are available from county courthouses, local Chambers of Commerce, and statewide from the N.C. Dept of Transportation for a nominal cost. Of course, city maps are available for purchase at city newsstands and bookstores—and Chambers of Commerce as well. Additionally you may wish to contact the state's Division of Travel and Tourism, N.C. Dept of Commerce, 430 N. Salisbury St, Raleigh, NC 27611; 919-733-4171 (in Raleigh) or 800-847-4862 for information on county or city vacation attractions and services.

Make sure to use a detailed trail map of the area in which you are hiking. If you plan to hike in a wilderness area, take a topographical map and compass with you. They could save your life in a crisis or if you are lost. The best source for acquiring USGS-FS maps (which show the forest boundaries and the trails with numbers) is National Forests of North Carolina, 160-A Zillicoa St., (P.O. Box 2750), Asheville, NC 28802; 828-257-4200. Also ask for a revised list (most recent dates of publication) of the USFS forest and wilderness maps. To mail order topo maps, write to: Branch of Distribution, USGS, Box 25286 Federal Center, Denver, CO 80225. Because you must pay in advance, write for a free N.C. Map Index and order form. Allow two to four weeks for delivery. For immediate needs contact a local outdoor-sports store or blueprint company for topo maps.

State parks and county and city parks also have maps of their areas. Contact the main offices (addresses in chapters 10, 11, 12, and 13). For a map of the Great Smoky Mountains National Park, contact the main office address listed in chapter 7.

Signs, Blazes, and Markers

It would be ideal if all trails were signed and blazed. Because they are not, it is suggested that you carefully follow the directions in this book. If there are signs, they are usually at the trailheads, and blazes are usually painted on trees at eye level at irregular intervals. An exceptionally large number of trails in the national forests have neither. One district, Grandfather, in the Pisgah National Forest has 200 mi of trails, none of which (except the MST) are blazed. (District plans improvement of trail identification.) As a result, I have described the trails with emphasis on other landmarks—rock formations, flora, bridges, streams, and unique points of interest. (Do not expect to see signs or markers in any of the wilderness areas. That is in keeping with the wilderness milieu.) Vandalism results in the loss of numerous signs. You will find more signs in the Great Smoky Mountains National Park (GSMNP) and state parks than in the national forests. The USFS trail numbers and the assigned numbers in this book for the map references will not be seen on trail posts, trees, or other markers. The AT blaze is a white 2x6-in. vertical bar, with same-size blue blazes indicating a spur (often to water) or an alternate route. The Bartram Trail blaze is yellow, the same size as the AT, and the MST blaze is a white dot, three inches in diameter. Alternate MST trails may be blue. You will see a wide range of other colors where there is a color-coded trail system, such as the Pisgah district in chapter 3, section 3. The USFS boundary line has bright-red markings (usually circling a tree), and some trees for timbering may have blue, white, green, or yellow markings.

Abbreviations

In an effort to save space in this book, abbreviations are used wherever possible. The majority are part of everyday usage.

AMC	Appalachian Mountain Club
AT	Appalachian National Scenic Trail
ATC	Appalachian Trail Conference
ATV	all-terrain vehicle
B	bicycle trail
BRP	Blue Ridge Parkway
BMT	Benton MacKaye Trail
BT	Bartram Trail
ca.	circa
CCC	Civilian Conservation Corps
CMC	Carolina Mountain Club
DENR	Department of Environment and Natural Resources
E	east
elev	elevation
F	foot trail
fac	facilities
FMST	Friends of Mountains-to-Sea Trail
FR	forest road
FS	Forest Service
ft.	foot/feet
GSMNP	Great Smoky Mountains National Park
GPS	Global Positioning System
H	horse trail
I	interstate highway
jct	junction or intersection
L	left
mi	mile/s
mil	million
mp	milepost (usually on the BRP)
MST	Mountains-to-Sea Trail
Mt.	Mount (used in proper names)

Mtn.	mtn/s Mountain, mountain/s
N	north
NC	state primary road
NE	northeast
NF	National Forest
NP	National Park
NPS	National Park Service
NW	northwest
OHV	off-highway vehicle
OVT	Overmountain Victory Trail
R	right
Rd	Road (used in proper names)
rec	recreation/al
RR	railroad
RS	ranger station
S	south
SC	South Carolina primary road
sec	section
SE	southeast
SR	state secondary road
sta	station
svc	service/s
SW	southwest
tel	telephone
TIS	Transportation Information System
topo	topographic map
TVA	Tennessee Valley Authority
US	federal highway
USFS	United States Forest Service
USGS	United States Geological Survey
USGS-FS	United States Geological Survey-Forest Service
W	west
YACC	Young Adult Conservation Corps
YCC	Youth Conservation Corps
yd.	yard/s
4WD	four-wheel drive

Trip Planning and Safety

Your checklist for getting started should include the choice of dependable companions and appropriate trails; choice and purchase of your equipment, maps, food, gear, and supplies; contacts with the forest or park headquarters for weather conditions and safety hazards, and permits (if required); and plans for daily or round-trip mileage, campsites, and vehicle parking or shuttles. Park and lock your vehicle at the trailhead. Descriptions of where to park at the trailheads are included in this book. Also, throughout the book I have indicated what areas require permits for camping and have explained how the permits can be acquired.

Ostensibly you wish the trail and the campsites to be natural and clean. You can help in keeping them desirable by avoiding impact. That means no-trace camping—removing all litter, trash, and garbage; erasing evidence of campfire; never digging trenches; refraining from using overused campsites, and avoiding shortcutting switchbacks.

In planning your trip you may wish to include other outdoor sports. For whitewater sports and mountain climbing, contact the Nantahala Outdoors Center, 133077 Highway 19W, Bryson City, NC 28713; 828-488-2175. For horseback-riding trails and camps, contact Horse Commodity Coordinator, Extension Horse Husbandry, Dept of Animal Science, NCSU, Box 7523, Raleigh, NC 27695; 919-737-2761. Bicycling information is available from the Division of Bicycle and Pedestrian (DOT), 1552 Mail Svc Center, Raleigh, NC 27699; 919-733-2804/05/07.

Concerning emergencies, the following numbers are in addition to a call to the local 911 operator: the NC Wildlife Resources Commission for boating accidents, missing persons, fishing and game laws, 800-662-7137; for toxic poisons, Carolina Medical Center, 800-848-6946, or 800-222-1222; Blueridge Parkway (BRP), for emergencies, 800-727-5928; or National Forests, 828-257-4264 for fires and 911 for emergencies. For weather and road conditions call 511.

Many describe hiking as a time to "hear myself think," or "get acquainted with my soul." Henry David Thoreau hiked "for absolute freedom and wildness." The American Hiking Society describes it as "brushing past a thousand life forms, beckoning,/ leading you onward to new sensations and discoveries around the bend./ In that moment when you are on a trail,/ your mind is free to roam,/ to observe, to daydream./ All extraneous concerns drop away . . . "

I hope you will become active also in preserving the natural resources by joining an organization whose mission is to protect and maintain the trails. And I hope that you enjoy hiking the trails as much as I have. Welcome to the trails of North Carolina.

Health and Safety

Accidents happen to even the most cautious hiker, and even a minor mishap can ruin an otherwise pleasant journey. To minimize risk and to maintain good health, some suggestions (more critical in the backpacking backcountry) are listed below. Although you may wish to hike alone, the park and forest officials (who must make plans for a rescue) encourage you to have one or more companions to reduce the danger of hypothermia, poisonous snake bites, injury from a fall, and being lost or sick. Someone in the group should carry a first-aid kit with water purifier, moleskin, assorted band-aids, antibiotics, disinfectant ointment, prescription pills for severe pain, simple painkiller, gauze pads, adhesive tape, tweezers, biodegradable soap, sunburn ointment, insect repellent, medicine for an upset stomach, and your personal medical prescriptions. A basic safety package would include waterproof matches, maps, compass, emergency freeze-dried food, a whistle, a 75-ft. rope, a knife (preferably Swiss), flashlight (preferably one with krypton bulbs), duct tape, and a windproof hooded jacket. Your guide or outdoor-store consultant may recommend more or less. You may wish to read *Medicine for the Outdoors* by Auerbach during your planning. Another book is *Practical Outdoor Survival* by McDougall.

Hypothermia, a major cause of death for outdoor recreationists, is caused by the lowering of body heat. It can be fatal even in the summertime. Sweaty and wet clothes lose about 90 percent of their dry insulating value, and wind-chill increases the danger. The best lines of defense are to stay dry; get out of the wind, rain, or snow to avoid exhaustion; and know the symptoms and treatment. The symptoms are uncontrollable shivering; vague, incoherent speech; frequent stumbling; and drowsiness. The victim may be unaware of all of these. Treatment for mild impairment is to place the victim in a dry place, in dry clothes, and in a warm sleeping bag, and give warm drinks (no alcohol). Try to keep semiconscious victims awake, warm the head and face, provide person-to-person warmth, and evacuate to an emergency hospital as quickly as possible.

If you become lost, use the universal distress signal of three of anything—shouts, whistles, light flashes, or smoke signals. Do not panic, stay in one place, make a fire and stay warm, conserve your food, drink plenty of water, and climb a tree if it will help determine your location. After a reasonable time without rescue, find a valley and follow its water sources downstream. Someone has said that to be safe in the forest "use your head first and if things go wrong remember to keep it." Some off-trail hikers are using global positioning system (GPS) equipment to rescue themselves, or cell phones for location or rescue assistance.

Lightning is another danger. Some precautions are to stay off sharp prominent peaks, avoid standing under a cliff or in a cave entrance, avoid seams or crevices on rocks, and avoid standing under prominent trees or other tall objects. Squat down and insulate yourself from the ground if possible. Also, do not stay on a beach or in a boat, or cross a stream or marsh. Anything metal, including your pack frame, should be removed from your body.

Some precautions to take when crossing a stream include unfastening your backpack bellyband, keeping your boots on (or using your spare pair), always facing upstream, keeping your balance with a steady pole, and avoiding rapids.

You should carry pure drinking water and use only water officially designated safe by the forest or park. My listing of springs and clear streams in this book does not mean the water has been tested. Properly boiling the water remains one of the best ways to be safe, or use a pump water purifier. For the health of you and others, particularly those downstream, camp at least 100 ft. away from streams. Human waste should be 300 ft. away from a campsite or stream and should be buried if vault toilets are not available. Another rule is to carry out all trash. A few other suggestions are not to hike at night, be sure your boots fit to avoid blisters, and use care with fires, knives, or firearms if hunting. Firearms are prohibited in national, state, and local parks, but are allowed for hunting in specific areas of national forests and wildlife refuges. If you have questions, contact the local sheriff's office and the state's Wildlife Resource Commission (license) at 919-662-4370. (In 1995 the NC legislature passed a law allowing concealed weapons. A permit is necessary; there are restrictions.)

Trail Courtesy

The majority of hikers say they choose trails to encounter the natural environment and to get away from people, particularly crowds. That desire may be realized on remote and infrequently used trails, but privacy is declining with an

xx   *North Carolina Hiking Trails*

increase in trail usage throughout North Carolina. Multiuse trails create the most immediate response because hikers may need to move aside to permit horse, bicycle, and motorized traffic to pass. Most hikers turn and stop to see what margins are required. On paved trails, the hiker confronts higher-speed bicycle traffic and in-line skaters. Equestrians should avoid any speed beyond the horse's walking stride, and bicyclists should slow down to prevent spooking the horses. Horses usually can be heard, but bicyclists are more silent and should sound a bell or a whistle to hikers. Both equestrians and bicyclists should dismount when crossing bridges.

For long-distance hikers the question of courtesy becomes more intense at shared campsites, shelters, and campgrounds. Tired and hungry, the main concerns are to have peace and quiet sans radios and television. (Cell phones offend some hikers; others consider them a lifesaver in an emergency.) At most campgrounds or shelters there is an unwritten code of early curfew for rest and sleep. Irritations flair easily when offending hikers leave toothpaste suds from dental care at the spring, or worse when body bathing is done at the spring. More offensive is the hiker who does not bury solid human waste. Another breach of courtesy is leaving trash and unburnable materials at the firesite or elsewhere. Strangers may be sensitive to random photography of them; gaining permission is advisable. Owners who insist on taking pets (almost always dogs) should respect the issues of leashing and control.

Hiking Gear

Where possible it is wise to purchase the best quality of hiking gear to ensure durability and comfort. Professional or experienced hikers can give you advice on this topic. The options for hiking equipment become more diverse each year. For the environmentally conscious hiker there are now choices in ecogear recycled fibers. Before you purchase, I recommend you examine *Backpacker* magazine's annual "Buyer's Guide," published in March. The guide covers packs, tents, sleeping bags and pads, boots, water filters, stoves, lighting, repairs, and more. The magazine also reviews such other essentials as food and clothing in other random months. Colin Fletcher's *The Complete Walker III* is an excellent guide on equipment and how to prepare for a "house on your back." Choose equipment stores nearest you in case you must make exchanges or need advice. If you order, there are a number of reliable companies, some of which are L. L. Bean, 800-221-4221; Campmor, catalog and order, 800-226-7667; Cabela's, 800-237-4444; and REI, 800-426-4840.

A Natural History of North Carolina's Trails

There comes a quiet in the woods,
As if it uttered solitude.
Demurely down the silent glade
Shimmers the reticence of shade . . .
—Archibald Rutledge "In a Forest"

Most of North Carolina's hiking trails are in forests, the type America's poet laureate Archibald Rutledge described as having musical sounds like an orchestra. To him and to the millions of hikers worldwide, we enter forests for their paths to glimmering streams, to clear waterfalls, to panoramic views on mountain tops, and to mystery. Rutledge wrote that forests were like a "veiled enchantress." Our state has four national forests with a total of 1,248,330 acres, 9,986 acres more than eight years ago. Additional land to forest acreage is difficult because residential and commercial development moves closer to the forest edges, and the United States Forest Service does not have the funding to buy the land. The situation is the same for the Blue Ridge Parkway in the National Park System. Since the third edition of this book, I have noticed major changes in the landscape. Where once private property on the mountain sides appeared to be much like the national forests, now it is dotted with large residences (many of them vacation homes) and roads. The change is not just in the mountains. In an article "It's man versus nature" by James Eli Shiffer in the News and Observer, December 3, 2001, he stated the lush forest in the Piedmont area of the state was bearing a greater loss. He reported that the Southern Forest Resource Assessment by the US Forest Service claimed "The Piedmont from Virginia to Georgia will experience the greatest loss of forest area among the ecological sections in the South." The assessment also indicated that the South has become "the largest agricultural-style timber producing region in the world," and that 70 percent of the forest land in the South has private or non-industrial owners. In another report from Gary B. Blank, a forest historian at North Carolina State University, the prediction was grim. He predicted the state's Piedmont would soon resemble "the heavily developed corridor between Baltimore and Washington." Is anything being done to slow the loss of forest land? The answer is yes and you will notice the state plans ahead under the topic of Conservation. You will also see the results of efforts to preserve the forests by private organizations such as the Triangle Land Conservancy and The Nature Conservancy in chapter 14.

I also noticed in my research for this book that hiking trails as we have known them for nearly a century are on a decline in relationship to the population. Taking their place are more multi-use systems and an increase in greenways. This is not a surprise as the population increases and additional citizens wish to have the pleasure of being in the forests by a variety of usage. Maintenance needs on all trails, particularly on natural soils, have increased. Even the Appalachian Trail Conference has distributed a warning that the famous route from Georgia to Maine must have continuous maintenance. The letter indicates the typical lifespan of a section of the AT is about thirty years. "It's a real challenge to maximize the Trail's lifespan," wrote Morgan Sommerville, the ATC regional representative for Georgia, North Carolina, and Tennessee. If history is an indication, the organizations such as the Carolina Mountain Club, Natahala Hiking Club, Smoky Mountains Hiking Club, and the Tennessee-Eastman Recreation Club (with maintenance along the state line) will continue their services of maintenance, repair, and funding. But away from the AT there is a great need for volunteers to assist the national forests and national parks in maintaining trail quality. In some of the national forest districts you will notice some heritage trails are no longer on inventory, and the few new trails may not be really new because they follow old or new timber roads.

The state park and natural area, and forest systems have fared better. More state parks are planned, and county and city parks are on the increase. The noticeable increase in trails, about 400 in the past eight years, are mainly on greenway systems, plus educational/recreational facilities. In this number is a major increase in bicycle and equestrian trails. For greenways this means the asphalt and concrete are replacing earthen paths. A new system of trails brings neighbors closer together on bicycles, tricycles, rollerskates, skate boards, and baby carriages. On hundreds of miles of pavement are landscaped designs with scenic beauty deep in the mountain coves. Farther east are outstanding plans for a network of trails on Triad Park in Forsyth and Guilford counties; a network of trails in the High Point–Greensboro area, and much larger greenway network to connect the triangle cities of Raleigh with Durham and Chapel Hill. In addition the state's largest city, Charlotte, and Mecklenburg County lead in the most expansive urban network of parks and trails.

This book provides a description in part or in more detail more than 1,350 trails covering more than 4,200 miles. The North Carolina landscape is immensely diverse and this book describes trails to suit every preference. There are long backcountry trails in the wilderness for mystery, "silence and whispers," "sudden radiances," and "idle aires," as Fiona MacLeod wrote in *Where the Forest Murmurs.* Or you can take short walks for magnificent views of sunsets over the Smokies on the Waterrock Knob Trail, or in the "land of waterfalls" follow the Whitewater Falls Trail, or listen to the "talking trees" on the Holmes State Forest trails, or walk an estuarian boardwalk on the Cedar Point Tidewater Trail, or appreciate the Wolf Creek Trail for the physically disabled in the Nantahala National Forest. Each of the state's trails is distinctive, unique, with its own ambiance, almost a personality. They all deserve superlatives, but I have restrained my descriptions so that you may have plenty of surprises. I have hiked all these trails at least once, some of them many times, and the Lake Trail more than once a week since 1963. Rehiking always brings a new experience. John Burroughs, a hiking friend of John Muir, said, "Follow the path you took yesterday to find new things" I have found many new things in observing the process of succession, in the changes of the seasons, and wildlife habitats. I found trails that were manicured, neatly blazed, frequently used, remote and wild, or clean but natural. In contrast some were eroded, neglected, mutilated by ATVs, or covered with US Forest Service (USFS) timbering slash. In addition to the natural forest duff, there are trails with soft grass, pea gravel, wood chips, clay, sand, sawdust, rocks, brick, asphalt, and concrete. Walking these trails again for the fourth edition of this book I learned more about their history, about the people who constructed them, their animal and plant life, and the cities and towns and countryside around them. For me it was an extraordinary field trip, a valuable natural history classroom. It was a long journey of reality, like the state's motto, *Esse quam videri* (to be rather than to seem).

Some of the trails have more distinctive features than others. For example, four of the longest singular trails are the Appalachian Trail (310 mi), the Bartram Trail (74.3 mi), the Cape Hatteras Beach Trail (75.8 mi), and the Lakeshore Trail (34.7 mi). The Mountains-to-Sea Trail, when completed, will be the state's longest. In contrast there are short trails such as Black Camp Gap Trail (66 yd.), on the Heintooga Rd, 3.6 mi off of the Blue Ridge Parkway at mp 458.2; Gwyn Memorial Trail (91 yd.) at mp 298.6 on the Blue Ridge Parkway; and Rob Taylor Trail (80 yd.) also on the parkway at mp 433.8. The highest trail is Balsam Nature Trail, and the highest changes in elevation are the Noland Divide Trail (4,155 ft.) and the Baxter Creek Trail (4,142 ft.), both in the Smokies. The lowest trail elevation is on the Cape Hatteras National Seashore.

The First Trails

Some archaeologists claim that American Indians were living in the area that is now North Carolina as long ago as 5000 BCE, during the Archaic period. They base their claim on excavations in Rowan, Stanly, Montgomery, and Orange counties. The Woodland period, the first 1500 years AD, shows the development of pottery, agriculture, and burial ceremonies. By the time of Spanish and English explorations, it is estimated the region had about 25 tribes in an aboriginal population of 30,000. The tribes constituted three major linguistic families: the Algonquin in the coastal area of the Albemarle and Pamlico Sounds (which included the Hatteras Indians); the Iroquoian, including tribes E of Raleigh to Beaufort County and all of the Cherokee in the mountains; and the Siouan tribes, including such groups as Catawba, Occaneechi, Keyauwee, and Waxhaw in the central area of the state.

The Indian trails developed from the paths made by animals to their food and water sources. As nomadic life changed to more permanent settlements with the advent of agriculture, the trails became major routes between communities for communication and trade. These trails were used also for warfare between the tribes and exploration by the Europeans, and later some trails became colonial roads. The 1928 trail map by W. E. Myer shows a remarkable similarity in trail location to some of the current superhighways. For example, I-85 follows part of the Lower Cherokee Trading Path in South Carolina and the Occaneechi Path from Charlotte to Petersburg. The Saponi Trail was a route much like the US-29 route from Greensboro to Charlottesville, and I-77, from Charlotte to Columbia on the Occaneechi Path. The Catawba Trail went NW from near Spartanburg, through Asheville, and on to Kentucky to join what became the Daniel Boone Trail (that was from the Yadkin River Trading Fort near Salisbury to Boonesborough, Kentucky). From an area near Lake Keowee in South Carolina, the Tuckalcechee Trail wove through the mountains to the Tennessee River and into Tennessee. A multiple-trail intersection was at Wilkesboro. The Occaneechi Path on its route from the Old Cherokee Path passed near Morganton to the Occaneechi Path near Hillsborough; the New River Trail went N into Virginia and West Virginia; the Northern Trail went S to join the Cherokee Trading Path near Spartanburg; and the trail that became the Daniel Boone Trail passed through from Salisbury on its route to the Cumberland Gap at the boundary of Tennessee, Virginia, and Kentucky. (Here it joined what was earlier called the Warrior's Path and later the Wilderness Trail).

The first known contact of Europeans with the Indians was in 1524 when Giovanni da Verrazzano, in the service of France, explored the coastline between areas now known as Wilmington and Kitty Hawk. In 1540 the daring Spanish explorer Hernando de Soto left Florida on his long march to the Mississippi. It was May 21 when he arrived in Xualla, a large village inhabited by the Saura tribe between the Saluda and Broad Rivers in what is now South Carolina. De Soto's route across the Appalachians has been disputed, but most studies indicate that he followed a trail across the Blue Ridge Mountains near present-day Highlands and Franklin and to Guasili (the mouth of Peachtree Creek at the Hiwassee River, 3 mi E of what is now Murphy). The Saura tribe must have had a trail from Xualla (in what is now Greenville County, South Carolina) to what is now the Asheville area, because the Cherokee name for Swannanoa means "trail of the Saura" or Suali (pronounced "Shualla" by the Spaniards). In 1566 another Spanish exploratory force, led by Juan Pardo, followed the trail that de Soto had traveled from Charleston to Xualla (called Joaro by Pardo), where they built a fort to make their excursions into the hills and mountains of the Appalachians.

English exploration on the Indian paths began in early July 1584 when Captains Philip Amandas and Arthur Barlowe went ashore in the Pamlico Sound (about 20 mi from an island called Roanoak). They stayed two months with friendly Indians who fed them fruits and white corn and "braces of fat bucks, conies, hares, fish, the best in the world." A year later, almost to the day, another English expedition of 108 arrived with Thomas Hariot, the first scientist-historian to visit the Indians. They stayed for nearly a year and in the process followed numerous trails and rivers. One trail led to a "great lake," Paquipe (Lake Mattamuskeet). But the year ended in warfare with the natives. The next expedition, July 22, 1587, became the historic "lost colony" of Roanoke Island. Following the English establishment of Jamestown in 1607, the trails into North Carolina began with John Pory in 1622. He made a 60-mi "fruitful and pleasant" overland journey to the Chowan River. In 1650 Edward Bland went to the Roanoke River, and in 1654, Nathaniel Batts established a permanent residence by the Chowan River (near present-day Winton).

Another explorer ("father of Piedmont explorers") was a German physician from Virginia, John Lederer, who in 1670 was sent by Sir William Berkeley into the heart of the Carolinas. Riding a horse, he and his Indian guide followed the "Trading Path" (Occaneechi Path) to Suala (mentioned by de

Soto). Lederer followed an eastern return route on his two-month excursion. He kept a detailed diary of his journey (much like current Appalachian Trail hikers, with the exception that it was written in Latin). In 1671 Thomas Batts followed a trail to the headwaters of the New River from the Occaneechi Path, and in May 1673 James Needham, Gabriel Arthur, and an Indian guide left Petersburg, followed the Occaneechi Path to the Catawba River, and journeyed west on a trail to Hickory Nut Gap by Chimney Rock. (Needham was slain by Indians on his second journey.)

In 1700, John Lawson, surveyor general for the North Carolina colony, began a 1,000-mi journey on the trails from Charleston, South Carolina, into the Piedmont and out to the coast of North Carolina. He kept a lengthy diary that was published in England as *Lawson's History of Carolina*. Understanding and generally sympathetic to the natives, he and his friend Baron Christoph von Graffenried (founder of New Bern) were captured upstream on the Neuse River by the Tuscarora in 1711. A few days after Lawson's torture and execution, the baron's ransom offer was accepted for his freedom. He was led "two hours" from the village (near Contentnea Creek, E of present-day Snow Hill) and sent home on foot (about 40 mi).

Other colonial trailblazers were pioneer explorer Daniel Boone, Methodist circuit rider Bishop Francis Asbury, and naturalist William Bartram. Boone, who lived near the Trading Fork of the Yadkin River (N of Salisbury), began an expedition with a party of six in 1767 to explore Kentucky. Twice captured and twice escaped, he returned in 1771, but started on another expedition in 1773. From 1771 to 1816 Bishop Asbury was the champion of equestrians. He covered 275,000 mi over the pioneer trails from New England to South Carolina, and his circuit included sixty trips across the Appalachians. On November 29, 1810, he wrote in his famous diary that "our troubles began at the foaming, roaring stream [Cataloochee Creek] and losing ourselves in the wood," but they arrived safely at their destination in present-day Clyde (see chapter 7, Asbury Trail). In 1775, when Bartram was on his 2,500-mi journey from Pennsylvania to Florida and back, he followed a "trading path" into the Cherokee territory on "serpentine paths of verdant swelling knolls . . . and fragrant strawberries, their rich juice dying my horse's feet" (see chapter 2, Bartram Trail).

Plants and Animals

North Carolina has 89 species of ferns and more than 3,674 species and varieties of other vascular plants. Flowering plants account for nearly 3,000 of these, with 487 species native only to the mountains, 183 species in the Piedmont, and 469 species in the coastal plains. Many others grow in two or more regions. Recommended botany-oriented guides are *Manual of the Vascular Flora of the Carolinas* by Radford, Ahles, and Bell and *Wild Flowers of North Carolina* by Justice and Bell.

Two pocket-size books on trees are *Common Forest Trees of North Carolina* by the North Carolina Department of Natural Resources, Division of Forest Resources, and *Important Trees of Eastern Forests* by the USFS. There are some exceptionally beautiful areas of gardenlike displays in all of the national forests and in the GSMNP. I have described their locations throughout this book, but I have avoided a description of areas with the most rare species. This information is provided for plants that are unusual to the locality or particularly prominent the area. Emphasis has been given some plants, with the botanical name in parentheses, because I rarely saw them or because they were exceptionally prominent. After the first mention of the botanical name, it is not used again. The most common rhododendron (one of nearly twenty species) is the *Rhododendron maximum,* called rosebay or great laurel, with light pink and whitish blossoms. It is the source of massive thickets or slicks in the mountains. *Rhododendron catawbiense,* called purple laurel, is less frequent. Craggy Gardens on the Blue Ridge Parkway and Roan Mountain have superb examples. Most of the other species are called azalea. My listing is according to what I saw at a particular time of the season.

Wildlife is likely to be seen on any day's hike, particularly in parks, refuges, and forests where wildlife is protected and hunting forbidden. Your best chance is to know the animals' watering and feeding places and look for them early or late in the day. Also, walk softly, talk at low decibels, and leave the dogs at home. In the Nantahala and Pisgah forests alone, there are about 400 vertebrate species. There are 138 species of reptiles and amphibians, 442 species of mollusks, and 418 species of fish. Your chance of hearing, or perhaps seeing, birds is good. A recommended book is *Birds of the Carolinas* by Potter, Parnell, and Teulings. Other books are *Amphibians and Reptiles in the Carolinas and Virginia* by Martof, Palmer, Bailey, Harrison, and Dermid; *Mammals of North Carolina* by Brimley; and the Golden Press pocket-size guideooks on butterflies and moths, spiders, and fishes.

Stewardship and Conservation

The state has a conservation program called On North Carolina Naturally (ONCN). Its three major groups are the NC Wildlife Resources Commission, the NC Department of Environment and Natural Resources (DENR), and the academic/nonprofit conservation sector. In the latter there are such powers as UNC–Chapel Hill, Duke University, The Nature Conservancy, Sierra Club, and Audubon Society. In the winter and spring of 2004, *Wildlife in North Carolina* magazine provided some of the major influences the three major groups could have on future conservation. In the first article the coverage was about clean water sources and the need for relicensing the 39 hydroelectric dams. The second article was about protecting the state's diminishing open spaces, and the third article was about Horizon 2100, a vision proffered by conservationists assembled by the Environmental Defense Fund.

In article two for the magazine in April 2004, Bill Ross, secretary for the DENR (in which is the Division of Parks and Recreation with its state trails programs) stated, "We are living beyond our means. There are limits to the natural resources that we depend on, and we have to pay attention to those limits. We've got to make our activities sustainable on a broad scale—statewise, nationwide, and worldwide. We need to write a new story." Lawrence S. Earley, who wrote the interview, explained how the old story has been our war against nature, abusing and wasting much of what we have considered unlimited resources. "We have to find a way to make our activities sustainable if North Carolina's people now and in the future are to have the quality of life that we want. To me, it's the most important issue of our time," Ross says.

To stress this issue as urgent, the state has lost 1 million acres of forest in the past 10 years and, combined with cropland, the figure is 2.8 million acres in the past 20 years, according to the NC Public Interest Research Group. Most of the loss of the state's forests is for residential and commercial development. During this time the population grew by 42 percent. The study shows that the state will lose another 2.4 million acres within the next 20 years. However, Secretary Ross thinks development within itself is not the problem, but in the haphazard methods of urban sprawl. Plans are to create eight state regions with input from local citizens using information from the Geographic Information System (GIS) to map and identify current protected lands and those needing protection in the future. (For more information, call 919-733-4984, or 919-715-4140/4131.)

What can hikers do to assist the cause of conservation? Some recommendations are to join a conservation organization to learn more about specific needs and how a group or individual can influence legislative issues on zoning for protection of natural resources. Read some of the more than 400 books on conservation and natural resources. A simple but important effort for hikers is to follow "Leave No Trace" rules, such as: (1) plan ahead and prepare; (2) camp and travel on durable surfaces and keep pollutants out of water sources; (3) pack it in, pack it out to leave no trace you have been there; (4) properly respect the natural environment; (5) minimize use and impact of fires to prevent scars to rocks or overhangs; (6) respect wildlife; and (7) respect other visitors. Additionally, join a local hiking club and be active with hiking organizations such as the American Hiking Society, 301-565-6704, or the Appalachian Mountain Club, www.outdoors.org.

Future Trails

In the pages ahead are descriptions of many trails, some constructed more than a century ago. Others are so new they are in the process of being constructed. In addition to this comprehensive list are future trails existing in dreams and on master-planning maps. Although the legendary masterwork is the Appalachian Trail, which passes 310 mi through the state, the Mountains-to-Sea Trail (MST) now surpasses the AT with more than 450 miles designated. It also rivals the AT in scenic value with its route from the GSMNP to a parallel of the BRP to Stone Mountain State Park. From there it crosses Linville Gorge before crossing central North Carolina for a beach route on the Atlantic seashore. If the MST East Plan, designed by Greenways, Inc. is implemented it will add another 180 mi from Raleigh to Cedar Island. Another 25 mi of the Falls Lake Trail will be added west of NC-50 to Durham if the memoranda of understanding between the Corps of Engineers, NC Wildlife, Raleigh and Durham city governments, and Wake and Durham counties are approved. Discussions are continuing on the MST Piedmont Plan for routing the MST from Eno River State Park to Greensboro and beyond to Hanging Rock State Park.

1   The Benton MacKaye Trail Association has plans for extending the Benton MacKaye Trail (BMI) from US-64 at Oconee River near the Tennessee/North Carolina state line to the current AT at Shuckstack Mtn. in the GSMNP. This connection will provide the 90 mi already developed from Springer Mtn. in Georgia to have one loop in the GSMPN and another on the AT back to Springer Mtn. for a total of 360 mi.

The Bicentennial Greenway from High Point north will connect with the Lake Brandt Greenway into north Greensboro. It has completed plans, and work is continuing to cross a bridge over I-40 and east of Piedmont Triad International Airport. In Durham its greenway plans are continuing north/south to connect with the 22-mi American Tobacco Trail (Greenway on old RR base) that passes south from City and County of Durham into Chatham and Wake Counties. Although deep into the piedmont and away from its coastal name, the East Coast Greenway Alliance, hopes to use the American Tobacco Trail as a piece of its 2,600-mi greenway/roadway on old RR grades, towpaths, esplanades, canal lanes, back roads, and sidewalks from Maine to Florida. On the drawing board and also under construction are parts of the expansive greenway network in the Triangle Area of Durham, Raleigh, Chapel Hill, Morrisville, Cary, and Apex. For Raleigh, its vision is eventually 200 mi; 85 mi have already been constructed.

In this book I have described some of the rail-trails. More in planning or **2-6** construction stages are the 8.0-mi Thermal Belt Rail-Trail from Spindale to Gilkey, made possible by a land trust and Bechtler Development Corp., and the Brevard to Pisgah Forest Greenway. A short section of the Sabina Gould Walkway in the Town of Littleton has been completed. The dream route of a 32-mi Waccamaw Cypress Trail would connect Fair Bluff to Whiteville Depot and to Lake Waccamaw near the coast. Another dream route would be the 30-mi Coastal Carolina Trail through Beaufort, Martin, and Pitt counties (a potential East Coast Greenway section). A mountain route in the development stage is Carolina Hearthland Rail-Trail for 12 mi from Wadesboro to McFarlan in Anson County. (For more information, contact NC Rail-Trails, 919-542-0022 [eastern NC]; 828-495-4472 [western NC].)

Connecting trails already exist and others are planned, such as a connection to the Palmetto Trail (South Carolina's mountains-to-sea trail) S of Bre- **7-8** vard. Others are the Northern Peaks Trail, N of Boone, to the Carolina Creeper Trail (rail-trail), which connects with the Virginia Creeper Trail (rail-trail) and the AT S of Damascus, Virginia. In the Pisgah ranger district of the Pisgah National Forest, the most visited of any district in the state's national forests and having the largest number of trails, more trails are planned for construction. (See chapter 3, section 3.) The MST and its alternate trail passes through this district. Two other potential long rail-trails are the Pender County Trail **9-11** and the Roanoke Valley Trail. Small town landmarks are being emphasized, such as the Wendell Historic Trail in Wendell.

The fastest growth in the number of trails in the past ten years has been in multi-use greenway systems. This effort will continue, probably at an increased rate. Examples of trails developed and on the drawing boards are Mecklenburg County (Charlotte area), Triad area of Winston-Salem/High Point/Jamestown/Greensboro; and Research Triangle area of Chapel Hill/Durham/Raleigh/Cary. Another city, Jacksonville, has nearly forty trails planned or under construction. With the passage of the Parks and Recreation Trust Fund by the 1995 state legislature that allocated 56.25 percent of the funds to improving the quality of state parks, a 15 percent allocation was made for local governments to apply for grants. This will increase the number of parks and potential trails in communities across the state. For more information on the development and progress of future trails in North Carolina, write or call the author at 3585 US-401 South, Louisburg, NC 27549; 919-496-4771.

Part I
Trails in the National Forests

Cypress knees on Neusiok Trail, Croatan National Forest.

Overview of Trails in the National Forests

The public's continued interest and help in maintaining and improving the USFS trail system is critical.
—Steve Hendricks, Research Planner
National Forests in North Carolina

There are four national forests in North Carolina with a total of 1,248,330 acres: Nantahala (531,341); Pisgah (506,920); Croatan (159,886); and Uwharrie (50,183). This is an increase of 9,986 acres since 1996. Land acquisition by the United States Forest Service (USFS) is determined by financial allocations and adjoining land availability. Current acquisitions are generally limited to exchanges of tracts more beneficial to the USFS. National forest lands are in 24 counties.

As one of the state's major natural resources, and as a recreational source for more than 20 million visitors annually, the forests continue to be of vital public interest. Public interest in additional recreational facilities has increased steadily in the past ten years. Within the forests are 191 developed recreational areas, an increase of 115 in 10 years (such as campgrounds, picnic areas, and boat ramps), and 51 special-interest areas (with 52,517 acres) where timber is not cut or vehicular traffic allowed (such as Joyce Kilmer Memorial Forest, Looking Glass Rock, and Linville Gorge). The forests have 502 trails with a total of 1,734 miles, including the AT and National Recreation Trails. Add the desirable gated forest roads, and hikers have more than the distance of the Appalachian Trail (2,171 mi) on which to hike, roam, and explore. Of inestimable value in the forests are the 1,885 identified plant species and 645 species of vertebrates, including the fish species.

The state is the birthplace of professional forestry management, initiated in 1892 when George Vanderbilt employed Gifford Pinchot (1865–1946) to manage the Vanderbilt Forest at Biltmore near Asheville. Pinchot (born in Simsbury, Connecticut) graduated from Yale University in 1889 and studied forestry at the Ecole Nationale Forestiere in France. His success at Biltmore

Forest prompted Vanderbilt to purchase an additional 120,000 acres, a section of which later became a nucleus of Pisgah National Forest, established in 1916. In 1895 Carl Schenck, a renowned German forester, succeeded Pinchot, and Pinchot was made a member of the National Forest Commission to work out the plans of the US Forest Reserve Act authorized by Congress in 1891. Pinchot headed the Department of Agriculture's Forestry Division from 1898 to 1910 (under three US presidents) while holding a professorship of forestry at Yale University. During this period he was influential in the establishment of the US Forest Service in 1905. By 1908 he had become chairman of the National Conservation Commission. Although his stay in North Carolina was only a few years, his pioneering philosophy of forestry laid the foundation not only for Dr. Schenk's first forestry school in America, but also for the shaping of USFS policy since. "National Forests exist today because the people want them. To make them accomplish the most good the people themselves must make clear how they want them run," Pinchot said in 1907. This statement has proven true many times both in Congress (25 acts) and in the nation's 133 national forests.

Among the congressional acts that affect North Carolina's national forests are the Weeks Law (1911), which authorized the purchase of lands for timber production; the Multiple-Use Sustained Yield Act (1960), which reemphasized the basic purpose of forests to protect natural resources and to serve the public's varied recreational interests; the Wilderness Act (1964), which established a system of preserving areas from all timber cutting and mining and development; the National Trails System Act (1968), which established a protective system of national recreational and scenic trails (such as the Appalachian Trail); the National Environmental Policy Act (1970), which required all federal agencies to prepare reports on the environmental impact of all planned programs and actions in formal Environmental Impact Statements (EIS); the Forest and Rangeland Renewable Resources Planning Act (RPA) (1974), which required the USFS to prepare long-range programs of forest administration, roads and trails, research, and cooperative programs; and the National Forest Management Act (NFMA) (1976), which required full public participation in the development and revision of land management plans and periodic proposal of a Land and Resource Management Plan (hereafter referred to as the Plan) by the national forests. Each new congressional act and each new national forest chief alters the directional policies of the USFS. That is the way Pinchot predicted it. Silviculturists who once read the public mind to emphasize timbering, mining, hunting, and fishing now find a public demanding additional parking space and campgrounds, trails for mountain biking, and less timber cutting and road building.

Land use planning itself is not a new exercise for the USFS. The agency has engaged in planning of national forest uses since its establishment in 1905. But the planning process has changed as the public's interest and expectations have changed. At present there are two levels of planning: the forestwide Land and Resource Management Plan, which is strategic in nature, and the project plans typically made at each ranger district prior to activities actually taking place in the forest. The forestwide plan is designed to make the following decisions: (1) establish forestwide multiple-use goals and objectives for all resources; (2) establish standards and guidelines for management activities; (3) establish management areas and management area objectives (somewhat similar to a county zoning ordinance); (4) designate lands suitable for timber production and establish an upper limit on the amount of harvest per decade; (5) make recommendations for wilderness; and (6) establish monitoring and evaluation requirements.

Now there is a focus on involving the public throughout the planning process. The public is involved in reviewing data, discussing issues and concerns, and reviewing draft plans. Members of the public may be included on field trips, invited to workshops and focus group meetings, or may participate by submitting written comments. The second level of planning takes place at the ranger district prior to an actual management project taking place. This provides another opportunity for public involvement. Involvement at the project level is just as important as it is at the forestwide level. For example, the forest-wide plan may give general directions about building trails, but the decision to actually build a specific trail at a specific place, or to maintain it, is the responsibility of the district. Likewise, while the forestwide plan decides which areas will allow timber harvest, the district makes a project decision to actually build a particular logging road and the method of harvesting. Public involvement can affect these decisions.

To learn more about the current goals and objectives and management philosophy for the four national forests in North Carolina, you can request a copy of the latest forestwide plans from the USFS supervisor's office in Asheville (address at the end of this introduction). To keep informed about the projects the ranger districts are planning, you may request to be put on the mailing list for the "Schedule of Proposed Actions" that is sent out periodically to interested parties. (These addresses are listed at the end of each introduction in chapters 1 through 4.) The USFS guidelines on trail maintenance are described in the forestwide plan.

There are 11 wilderness areas—six in the mountains, one in the Piedmont, and four in the coastal area—for a total of 103,226 acres. Trails in these areas are described in the next four chapters. Camping permits in the wilderness areas are not required except in the Linville Gorge Wilderness (see details in chapter 3, section 2). Legislation has been introduced in Congress for additional wilderness areas, but the bill has not made it past a Senate committee. For example, Lost Cove and Harper Creek areas in the Grandfather Ranger District were chosen for congressional approval more than 18 years ago.

Wilderness management takes its guidelines from the Wilderness Act of 1964, whose purpose is to preserve and protect natural environments, and to provide a wilderness experience for its users. As a result, a wilderness area is considerably different from other forestlands. Hikers need to be aware of the contrasts. Among the differences are that no timber is harvested in wilderness areas. Recreational usage is allowed but not promoted with blazes, signs (except at boundaries or trailheads), campsites, or shelters. Construction of reservoirs, electrical power projects, transmission lines or roads is prohibited. Any facility, however primitive, is there only to protect natural resources and user safety. All forest usage of wilderness is by nonmotorized means, and power tools are not used for maintenance (if any maintenance is done at all) of the trails. (Exceptions are allowed for the USFS to deal with health and safety issues, fire suppression, and insect or disease control.)

The USFS has prescribed a few set policies for hikers and other wilderness users. Basics include no-trace camping, and the regular rules of "pack it in, pack it out" apply. You should be familiar with the brochure "Leave No Trace Land Ethics" offered free by the USFS and National Park Service. The maximum group size is usually 10 (or may be restricted to six in some locations). Campsites should be at least 100 ft. from springs and other water sources, and wood for the fires should be from dead or down trees. The feeding of wildlife, particularly bears, is prohibited. Other suggestions are for you to plan and prepare well in advance to meet nature on its terms. (See "Health and Safety" in the introduction of this book). Avoid holidays or popular weekends. Walk quietly to prevent disturbing the wildlife. The USFS advises against cross-country or bushwhacking trips unless you are experienced or have wilderness survival skills. Careful planning with consideration of the above guidelines should prevent you from becoming lost or injured, and save the cost of search and rescue teams.

Hunting and fishing are allowed in the national forests, including the wilderness areas, but are restricted in recreational areas and some special areas. Licenses are required by the NC Wildlife Resources Commission, which determines and sets seasons, bag limits, and other regulations for wildlife and fish management. The commission also regulates private game lands that have been leased for public use. Some wilderness properties may be within or adjoining the national forests.

A lack of funding and staff within the USFS results in primitive conditions on many of the trails. Volunteer citizens' groups are helping in the maintenance of trails in the USFS. An example is work on the Appalachian Trail (USFS #1). (See chapter 5, appendix A, and appendix B, for organizational support groups on other trails in the USFS and other places in the state.)

Hikers may notice a difference in trail length and signage between the USFS descriptions and descriptions in this book. An explanation may result from USFS relocations, partial closures, extensions, distance estimation, and measuring methods. All the districts have or are in the planning stages of having each trail GPSed. The author's most recent measurements with a measuring wheel or by GPS were in 2003–04.

Some hikers find the unmaintained trails appealing and challenging. If you are interested in hiking such trails not described in this book or not clear on official maps, you may wish to contact the district ranger's office before traipsing on questionable routes.

Information: National Forests in North Carolina, 160A Zillicoa St., Asheville, NC 28801; 828-257-4200; www.cs.unca.edu/nfsnc (office hours: M–F, 8AM–4:30PM). To order maps, call 800-660-0671. For hunting and fishing information, call 919-662-4370, or go to www.wildlife.state.nc.us. For a free copy of *Carolina Connections,* a magazine-type guide with information on all four forests, call the main number above, or pick up a copy at any district headquarters. It provides information about new developments, camping, day-use, special day-use, trails, backcountry locations, hunting and fishing, a map showing all facility locations, and more.

Chapter 1

Croatan National Forest

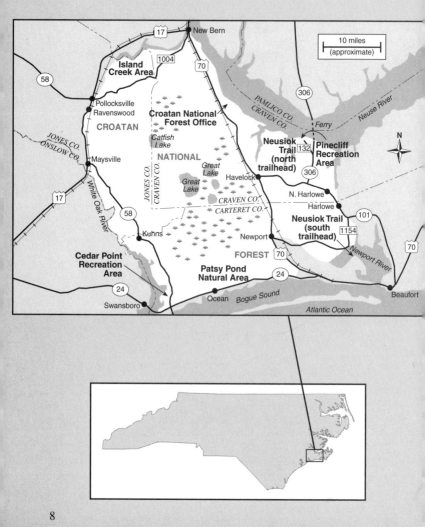

Introductions to Trail Areas

Except for the forest headquarters, trail locations are given counterclockwise. The longest trail is the Neusiok Trail, a part of the Mountains-to-Sea Trail, which passes through an outstanding example of coastal hardwoods, pocosin, swamp, and sand.

Croatan National Forest Office
The headquarters office for information, historic displays, books, and maps is on US-70, 8.0 mi E of New Bern's US-17 and US-70 bridge intersection over Neuse River.

Cedar Point Recreation Area *12*
Here is a wetland of wonder where salt and fresh water meet to make a nursery for seafood. A trail takes you over boardwalks for viewing birds in marshes and animals in the forest. Close by are places for canoeing, fishing, and camping.

Patsy Pond Natural Area *13*
Monitored by the North Carolina Coastal Federation, this priceless and diverse nature preserve has trails through resin-rich stumps for wildfires, chinquapins and avocado-related redbays, longleaf pines, plus flying squirrels and red-cockaded woodpeckers. And, of course, there is the mysterious Patsy Pond.

Pinecliff Recreation Area *13*
The north trailhead of the Mountains-to-Sea Trail, this quiet location has sandy banks of the mile-wide Neuse River, all in sight of the ferry to Minnescott Beach. River lapping had formed a natural sculpture with the wateroaks.

Neusiok Trail (South Trailhead) *14*
On the banks of Newport River you can feel a closeness to the salt bays of coastal North Carolina. To your R (SW) are the marshes of the river, and to your L (NE) is the end of Mill Creek. From this scenic point you can begin the 20.1 mi Neusiok Trail N to Pinecliff.

Neusiok Trail (North Trailhead) *14*
This long route through pocosin territory is a classic representation of soils and sands, marshes and swamps, evergreens and deciduous forests, diverse wildlife, carnivorous plants, peat bogs and ponds, estuaries, and beds of ferns and grasses to its terminus at the Newport River.

Island Creek Area *16*
Here is a picturesque and pristine place to view natural history in a climax forest, walk close to silent blackwater, and smell the scents of unique plant life.

Chapter 1

Croatan National Forest

The public needs to realize the value of the pocosin.
—Susan Marshall in *A Walk on the Wild Side*

The history of the Croatan National Forest, the most coastal of North Carolina's four national forests, and the most truly coastal E of the Mississippi River, began in 1933 when a purchase unit was established. In 1935, 77,000 acres were acquired. Today it encompasses 159,886 acres. The forest is almost totally surrounded by the Neuse, Trent, White Oak, and Newport Rivers. Bogue Sound and Bogue Banks separate its southern border from the Atlantic Ocean.

The name of Croatan comes from the Algonquin Indian word for "council town." Today, however, its coastal environment is used for year-round recreation. Within the forest are 95,000 acres of pocosin, which is a Native American word meaning, "swamp on a hill." Actually, pocosin is a layer of organic topsoil that has resulted from a series of physiographic and biological changes occurring within the last 9,000 years. A wet upland bog with black organic muck, pocosin varies in depth from inches at the edge to several feet in the central area. It has high acidity, dense vegetation, and no drainage pattern in low sections. In 1984, 31,221 acres of pocosin were designated by Congress as wilderness areas that represent a unique estuarian ecosystem. The largest of these is Pocosin (11,709 acres), a tract between NC-24 and Great Lake area. Others are Sheep Ridge (9,297 acres), bordered on the SE by beautiful Great Lake and Long Lake; Pond Pine (1,685 acres), between the Pocosin and Sheep Ridge areas; and Catfish Lake South (8,530 acres), between Maysville on NC-58 and Catfish Lake.

Adjoining this priceless forest is the US Marine Corps Air Station at Cherry Point US Naval Reservation. As a result of this proximity, the Corps has proposed twice, in 1986 and 1994, to establish a combat training air base in wetlands surrounded by wilderness. Both proposals failed when objections were filed by conservationists with the help of the Southern Environmental Law Center.

Hunting (both big and small game), fishing (both salt- and freshwater), boating, swimming, water-skiing, camping, picnicking, and hiking are popular in the Croatan. Catfish Lake and Great Lake are within the USFS boundaries. They have yellow bullheads, fliers, and black crappie. Brice Creek has catfish, bluegill, redbreast sunfish, largemouth bass, black crappie, yellow perch, bowfin, and gars. White Oak River and Hadnot Creek have striped mullet, chain pickerel, flounder, and croaker in addition to species found in Brice Creek. Although lake fishing is usually poor because of high acidity, the saltwater fishing is popular at the lower end of the Neuse River and in the saltwater marshes. Other activities include oystering, crabbing, and flounder gigging.

More than 90 species of reptiles and amphibians have been discovered in the forest. Among them are the spotted turtle *(Clemmys guttata);* Mabee's salamander *(Ambystoma mabeei)*; the more rare tiger salamander *(Ambystoma tigrinum)*; and the longest snake in the forest, the eastern coachwhip *(Masticophis flagellum)*. Poisonous reptiles are the cottonmouth, eastern diamondback rattlesnake, timber rattlesnake, Carolina pigmy rattlesnake *(Sistrurus miliarius)*, and copperhead. The bays, swamps, marshes, and creeks provide a haven for migratory ducks and geese. Such birds as egrets, including the snowy egret; flycatchers; woodpeckers; woodcocks; hawks, including the marsh hawk; osprey; and owls are plentiful, too. Among the threatened or endangered species are the red-cockaded woodpecker *(Picoides borealis)*, and the bald eagle *(Haliaeetus leucocephalis)*.

The forest is home to large stands of pines: pond, loblolly, and longleaf. Common hardwoods are oaks (including laurel *[Quercus laurifolia]*, bluejack, and blackjack), yellow poplar, sweet and tupelo gums, swamp cypress *(Taxodium distichum)*, American holly, and maple. Wildflowers—bright red pine lily *(Lilium catesbaei)*, orchids, gaillaria, and nine species of insectivorous plants—are profuse. Shrubs include titi, fetterbush, gallberry, wax myrtle, and honeycup.

The district has four major hiking trails, all described ahead. (Another unnamed forest trail is near the campground at Flanners Beach.) An 11.0-mi multi-use trail, Weetock Trail, is in the process of completion off NC-58, 2.5 **12** mi N of Kuhns community at Long Point Rd (FR-120). (Call the district office for updated information.) Other trail/road routes are mainly used by hunters, fishermen, and equestrians.

3

Address and Access: Maps and additional information are available from the District Ranger, Croatan National Forest, 141 E Fisher Ave, New Bern, NC 28560; 252-638-5628. Access is 7.3 mi SE of New Bern on US-70, at the jct with E Fisher Ave, L. From Havelock, drive NW on US-70 for 8.5 mi.

Support Facilities: There are facilities for camping and other activities in the Croatan National Forest at the Neuse River Recreation Area also known as Flanners Beach and Cedar Point campground (electrical hookups). (Call district office for open dates.) Access to the Neuse River Recreation Area from the ranger's office is 2.0 mi SE on US-70 and L on SR-1107 for camping and L on SR-1107 0.5 mi NW of the ranger's office on US-70 R on FR-141 to Fishers Landing. On the SW side of the NF is Cedar Point Campground near Swansboro. From the jct of NC-58/24, go N on NC-58 for 0.6 mi and L onto SR-1114 to FR-153-A. A nearby commercial campground is Waterway RV Park on NC-24 E at 850 Cedar Point Blvd, 1.0 mi W of the jct of NC-58 and NC-24; 252-393-8715. Another camping area is Whispering Pines Campground: From the jct of US-70 and NC-24, go W 8.5 mi on NC-24 (near the community of Ocean); full svc, rec fac; open year-round; address is 25 Whispering Pines, Newport, NC 28570; 252-726-4902.

Cedar Point Recreation Area (Carteret County)

The Cedar Point Recreation Area has facilities for boating, camping (hookups), drinking water, fishing, nature study trails, picnicking, flush toilets, and warm showers.

Access: From the jct of NC-58/24 E of Swansboro, go 0.6 mi N on NC-58 to the entrance to Cedar Point, L on SR-1114. Go 0.5 mi to a L on graveled FR-153-A. Parking area is located 0.8 mi on the road near White Oak River.

13   *Cedar Point Tideland Trail* (USFS #502) (F)

Length and Difficulty: 1.4 mi, easy

Trailhead and Description: From the parking area follow the trail signs and cross the first of six boardwalks at 0.1 mi. This beautiful natural area is where seawater mixes with the freshwater of White Oak River in a tidal estuary. Here are dark bronze cordgrass, marsh elder *(Iva frutescens)*, and succulents such as leafless glasswort *(Salicornia europaea)*. This species of glasswort has green stalks that turn red in late summer. Other plant species are star-shaped flowering sea purslane *(Sesuvium portulacastrum)*, sea oxeye *(Borrichia frutescens)*, and sweet bay magnolia. In this tranquil marsh, visitors may see osprey, great blue heron, and snowy egret. Cross fire road, the last boardwalk at 1.1 mi, and return on a loop trail to the parking lot at 1.4 mi. The trail is well graded through pine and hardwoods and includes 0.3 mi of cypress boardwalks in a marshland estuary. The trail is a national recreation trail, initially listed as the Chautauqua Trail. (USGS-FS Map: Swansboro)

Patsy Pond Natural Area (Carteret County)

Ecological succession is the process in which one or more species of plants gradually replace another in the same location over a period of time. Patsy Pond area is a good example of a number of such places in the Croatan National Forest. In addition to many species of botany, it also has an outstanding list of reptiles and amphibians. Black bear, deer, flying squirrel, and numerous birds are in the preserve. This natural area is a joint project of the national forest and NC Coastal Federation (NCCF). For information about the NCCF, contact 252-393-8185 or www.nccoastal.org.

Access and Address: From the jct of NC-58 and NC-24 at Cedar Point, drive E 6.7 mi on NC-24 to the entrance and parking area, L. Across the road, R, is the NCCFR headquarters at 3609 Hwy 24 (Ocean) with mailing address of Newport, NC 28570. From US-70 and NC-24 W of Morehead City, drive W 10 mi to entrance and parking, R.

Patsy Pond Nature Trail (USFS # None) (F)   **14**

Length and Difficulty: 1.7 mi, easy

Trailhead and Description: At the parking area, follow the blue (long loop) and white (short loop) signs among longleaf pine with an understory of oak, red bay, wax myrtle, and sweet bay. Insect repellent is recommended. Also, closely observe the signs to avoid being lost in a maze of criss-crossing sand paths and roads. Pass the first pond at 0.4 mi and other ponds at 0.7 mi. The resin-brown ponds receive their color from tannic acid in peat moss. Among the plants are sparkleberry, high blueberry, chinquapin, and carnivorous plants, such as bladderwort and sundew. There are three theories about the ponds' formation. One is that the New River once flowed here, while another is that the Atlantic Ocean was once here (the white sand is proof). A third theory suggests that an ancient layer of limestone collapsed here. (USGS-FS Map: Salter Path)

Pinecliff Recreation Area (Craven County)

The Pinecliff Recreation Area is on the S side of the Neuse River (within sight of the ferry to Minnesott Beach). Fishing, picnicking, and hiking are major activities. There are rest rooms, but no drinking water. It is the N trailhead for the Neusiok Trail that extends 20.9 mi S to the Newport River in Carteret County. If hiking the trail when the Pinecliff entrance gates are closed, park and walk either 1.6 mi or 0.2 mi to the picnic area. The district plans to create a loop off the Neusiok Trail from the Pinecliff Recreation Area S/SW for a day hike.

Access: From the jct of US-70 and NC-101 in Havelock, turn L on NC-101 and go 5.3 mi to the jct of NC-101 and NC-306. Turn L on NC-306, Neuse River Ferry Rd, and go 3.3 mi to FR-132. Turn L on an unpaved road and go 1.7 mi to Pinecliff Recreation Area.

15   *Neusiok Trail* (USFS #503) (F)

Length and Difficulty: 20.9 mi, moderate

Special Features: Neuse River beach, estuaries, pocosins

Trailhead and Description: The Neusiok Trail was designated part of the Mountains-to-Sea Trail system in May 1990. The best sections for backpacking and primitive camping on the Neusiok Trail are between the Neuse River and NC-306, where there is a small shelter between NC-101 and Billfinger Rd, where there is another small shelter, and S of Alligator Tram Rd. At the S end of the trail is a drive-in campsite with a restroom. Camping is impossible in the dense vegetation along Deep Creek Rd. Hiking is preferable in the winter months to avoid insects, heat, and snakes. Insect repellent is recommended. All water for drinking and cooking must be carried. Long trousers, high boots, watchful eyes, staying on the trail, and sleeping in tents are precautions against poisonous snakes. All trash must be packed out.

From the parking area at Pinecliff, enter the picnic area, turn L to pass the rest rooms into the woods, and follow white blazes to a boardwalk at 0.3 mi. If the boardwalk is underwater, go R to the beach and continue upriver or go L on an alternate route. Follow up the Neuse River beach among scenic swamp cypress groves and Spanish moss, or in the forest away from the beach and high banks. The Cherry Point US Marine Corps Air Station can be seen ahead. At 1.4 mi, leave the beach area, ascend the steps, and follow an erratic path through hardwoods and pine. Glimpses of Hancock Creek can be seen through the trees, R, at 2.0 mi. Pass L of a bog cove at 2.3 mi, cross a swamp at 2.7 mi on a boardwalk. (This and the next two boardwalks have been constructed by the Cherry Point and Carteret Wildlife Club.) Pass R of a USFS road at 2.9 mi. Cross a boardwalk through another swamp among palmetto *(Sabal minor)* at 3.1 mi. Make a sharp L at 3.6 mi to avoid a wide swamp, but cross a boardwalk over it and a tributary to Cahooque Creek at 4.4 mi. Turn

R on an old field road bordered with loblolly pine at 4.5 mi and enter a swamp with a boardwalk at 5.3 mi. Follow the edge of a hardwood timber cut and cross two boardwalks at 5.6 mi and 5.7 mi. At 6.0 mi is a grove of large beech and holly. For the remainder of this section follow an old road through pines and reach a gated road at NC-306 at 6.6 mi (NC-101 is 2.0 mi R; on NC-306 and FR-132, L, it is 2.7 mi for a return to the Pinecliff picnic area.) At the jct of the Neusiok Trail and NC-306 (E side) is a small parking area for hikers.

Cross the road and follow a footpath through dense undergrowth and tall pine. At 6.9 mi, cross a boardwalk and follow an old field road bordered with loblolly and pond pine. At 8.2 mi, turn sharply R onto an old forest road. Cross FR-136 (which goes 1.0 mi out to NC-101) and continue through the forest. At 8.6 mi, begin an 0.8-mi section of tall oak and pine and patches of sensitive fern (*Onoclea sensibilis*). After a boardwalk, reach NC-101 at 9.4 mi. (To the R, it is 6.8 mi back to the Pinecliff picnic area on NC-101 and NC-306. To the L, it is 2.1 mi to North Harlowe store with groceries, gasoline, and telephone.)

Cross NC-101 and enter a beautiful open forest of longleaf pine. Scattered undergrowth is yaupon, bracken, beard grass, blueberry, and Christmas fern. Cross a 300-ft. boardwalk at 10.2 mi to a hardwood forest. At a blue-blazed trail, R, is a two-man shelter. A 150-ft. boardwalk is at 10.7 mi. After a few yards the trail turns sharply L into a scenic pine forest. It has a dense undergrowth of red bay, inkberry, wax myrtle, and fetterbush, and scattered insect-eating plants. Exit at Billfinger Rd [FR-147] after 2.0 mi. Turn L and go 0.2 mi on Billfinger Rd to jct with Little Deep Creek Rd (FR-169) at 12.4 mi. (To the L on Little Deep Creek Rd, it is 1.1 mi N to NC-101 at North Harlowe. To the R, E, is a grocery store.)

Turn R on Little Deep Creek Rd (FR-169) and hike S on the road (the Neusiok Trail route) for 1.9 mi to where the trail turns abruptly L off the road at 14.3 mi. From the road cross a short footbridge to enter a dense forest of loblolly pine, wax myrtle, bays, maple, titi, sweet gum, greenbrier, and yellow jessamine. Trail blazes may be small metal tags nailed to trees. After 0.8 mi, begin to follow L of a small canal; pass a damp area, a drain into Money Island Swamp, at 15.6 mi. After another 0.2 mi, enter a more open area with small pines and switch cane. At 16.4 mi, turn E to parallel Alligator Tram Rd (FR-124) for 0.5 mi to the road crossing at 16.9 mi. (The road is gated to the R [W] where it accesses the Weyerhaeuser Paper Co., and to the L [E] the road is 1.8 mi to SR-1155. North from there it is 1.3 mi to a jct with NC-101; S from there it is 2.3 mi to the community of Mill Creek and jct with SR-1154.)

After crossing Alligator Tram Rd, cross a short canal footbridge to enter a dense area of undergrowth for 0.6 mi. Enter into an open longleaf pine forest at 17.5. Follow an old road, frequented by hunters, through sections of switch cane, pitcher plants, and bracken. Cross two small drains of Mill Creek at 18.5 mi and 18.9 mi. Leave the old road, and descend slightly to cross Mill Creek Rd (SR-1154) (also called Newport Rd or Orange St) at 19.3 mi.

Look for the trail sign and white blazes, and follow through hardwoods and pines for 1.6 mi; reach the Newport River parking area and S terminus of the trail at 20.9 mi. To the R is a restroom and space for a few campsites. It is 1.1 mi on FR-181 back to Mill Creek Rd (SR-1154) and 5.5 mi L (W) on Mill Creek Rd to Newport. It is 0.2 mi R (E) to the community of Mill Creek. From there it is 3.5 mi N to NC-101. (USGS-FS Maps: Cherry Point, Newport)

Island Creek Area (Jones County)

Access: In a separate N tract of the forest, this area can be reached from Pollocksville, jct of US-17 and Beauford Rd E that becomes Island Creek Rd. Drive E on Island Creek Rd for 5.5 mi to the Island Creek parking area, L. If coming S on US-17/NC-55 into New Bern, after crossing the New River bridge, turn L on US-70 Bypass, cross the Trent River bridge, and turn R onto SR-1004 to follow it 8.0 mi.

16 *Island Creek Trail* (USFS #509) (F)

Length and Difficulty: 0.6 mi or 2.8 mi, easy

Special Features: climax forest, limestone base, pristine

Trailhead and Description: From the parking area, enter the unusual natural history area of virgin forest that has progressed through plant succession stages to a beech climax forest. On a base of limestone the flora and fauna are unique to eastern North Carolina. Large beds of Christmas fern form a ground cover with tall oaks, hickories, pines, and cucumber trees. After 95 yd., the trail forks to make its 0.6-mi loop. Either route takes you to the blackwater Island Creek. For a longer loop, turn L at the creek and hike downstream among low-water vegetation. Cross small drains and follow the curve of the creek. (At 1.3 mi is a 0.2 mi shortcut in the loop.) Continue to a long L curve and pass a feeder stream to the creek. The forest becomes open and dry with hardwoods and scattered loblolly pines. (Pass the shortcut at 1.8 mi.) Arrive at Island Creek Rd at 2.5 mi. Turn L and walk on the road to trail origin and parking area at 2.8 mi. Its 146 acres have been registered as a natural area by the NC Natural Heritage Program. (USGS-FS Map: Pollocksville)

Chapter 2

Nantahala National Forest

Mountains are Earth's undying monuments.
—Nathaniel Hawthorne

The Nantahala National Forest, the state's largest (530,889 acres), is a vast area of mountain ranges, waterfalls, lakes, and rivers in the southwest corner of the state. In 1981 the Balsam–Bonas Defeat Land Purchase added 40,000 acres in Jackson County. Congress declared in Public Law 98–11 that the area would be designated the Roy Taylor Forest in recognition of Congressman Taylor's affection and respect for the mountains, forests, and streams of western North Carolina and for his "sustained efforts to protect areas especially suited to outdoor recreation and the enjoyment of nature and to assure public access thereto." While serving 16 years in Congress, Taylor was a member of the Committee on Interior and Insular Affairs and chairperson of the Subcommittee on National Parks and Recreation.

There are three wilderness areas in the Nantahala National Forest: Joyce Kilmer/Slickrock (13,562 acres) in the Cheoah District, Southern Nantahala (11,944 acres) in the Wayah District, and Ellicott Rock (3,394 acres) in the Highlands District. Within the Joyce Kilmer/Slickrock area is the Joyce Kilmer Memorial Forest, a 3,800-acre sanctuary of virgin timber and pristine wilderness splendor. No other forest can compare to its large groves of tulip trees (yellow poplar).

Established in 1920, the Nantahala National Forest received its name from a Cherokee word meaning "land of the noonday sun," an appropriate description for the many narrow gorges that receive the sun's direct rays only at midday. In the 8-mi-long Nantahala Gorge, mostly in Swain County, the precipitous gorge walls tower 2,000 ft. Other deep chasms are Tuskasegee, Wolf Creek, Cullasaja, Chattooga, and scores of deep north-side coves.

Nantahala is also a land of hundreds of waterfalls. Whitewater Falls, south of Sapphire, is considered to be the highest cascading river (411 ft.) in eastern America. Cullasaja Falls, west of Highlands, is similar to Whitewater Falls, with cascades thundering 250 ft. into the gorge. Other spectacular falls are Dry Falls, Bridal Veil Falls, and Glen Falls near Highlands; Rainbow Falls south of Sapphire; and Toxaway Falls near Sapphire. Ten major rivers flow through the forest. The turbulent Chattooga is a National Wild and Scenic River, with headwaters in the Highlands Ranger District, and a 4.5-mi section of the Horsepasture River near Sapphire has also become a part of the National Wild and Scenic Rivers system.

The Nantahala region is also a land of precious stones—ruby, sapphire, garnet, and amethyst. Wildlife roams its forest—deer, wild hog, fox, bear, mink, and raccoon. It is home for at least 38 species of birds, including grouse, turkey, hawk, and owl. First investigated by William Bartram in 1776, its plant life is a botanist's dream. All the hardwoods and conifers common to the southern Appalachians are found here. Rare and endangered species of flowering plants are hidden in countless vales and rock crevices or can be found blooming on fertile slopes.

Previous to the coming of Europeans, the forests of the Nantahala were the home of the Cherokee Indian Nation, whose domain was mainly from western Virginia to Alabama. Their famous Chief Junaluska, who lived nearly 100 years, was born near Dillard, Georgia, and lies buried in the town of Robbinsville, NC. (Near the gravesite is a Cherokee Museum and a 0.4-mi lower **17** and upper interpretive Medicine Trail. Access in the town is from US-129/NC-143 [Rodney Orr Bypass] on N Main St. A sign is here opposite the Phillips 66. Ascend on N Main St, which becomes Main St in front of the courthouse at 0.4 mi. Continue on Main St, descend, and after two curves, turn L at a sign on Junaluska St. After 0.1 mi, the museum is R [828-479-4727].) During different periods the Cherokee were both enemy and ally of the early settlers. For example, the Cherokees fought side by side with the troops of General Andrew Jackson against the Creek Indians at the Battle of Horseshoe Bend in 1814. Chief Junaluska later said, "If I had known that Jackson [US president, 1829–37] would drive us from our homes, I would have killed him that day at the Horseshoe." When the Supreme Court upheld the rights of the Indians after Georgia attempted to evict them, President Jackson is reported to have remarked, "John Marshall has made his decision; now let him enforce it." In 1838 President Jackson's successor, President Martin Van Buren, ordered General Winfield Scott to enforce the provision of a fraudulent 1836 government treaty the Cherokees signed for a move west of the Mississippi (now Oklahoma). The removal in the winter of 1838–39 of approximately 17,000 Cherokees was a shameful "Trail of Tears," and 25 percent died during the march. The Reverend Evan Jones of South Carolina described the exodus as "multitudes . . . allowed no time to take anything with them . . . their houses were left prey to plunder."

It is estimated that 1,000 Cherokees fled to the mountains, mainly in the area of Swain, Jackson, and Haywood Counties. One of those who fled was Tsali, who accidentally killed a soldier on the march. General Scott promised that all of the other Indians in the mountains would be permitted to remain if Tsali and two family escapees would surrender and be executed for the soldier's death. The military kept its promise and the Cherokee descendants today are part of the Qualla Reservation, the largest Indian reservation east of the Mississippi. (See Tsali Trail in this chapter, the Great Smoky Mtns National Park in chapter 7, and the Cherokee Arboretum and Lake Junaluska Trail in chapter 14.)

The history of the Cherokee is vividly portrayed in the summer outdoor drama "Unto These Hills" in the Mountainside Theatre in Cherokee, late June to late August. For information, contact Cherokee Tribal Travel and Welcome Center, P.O. Box 460, Cherokee, NC 28719; 828-497-9195 or www.cherokee-nc.com.

The four districts of the Nantahala National Forest are as follows:

- Cheoah Ranger District, USFS, 1133 Massey Branch Rd, Robbinsville, NC 28711; 828-479-6431. (From Robbinsville go 1.0 mi W on US-129/NC-143; turn L on NC-143.)
- Highlands Ranger District, USFS, 2010 Flat Mtn. Rd, Highlands, NC 28741; 828-526-3765. (From Highlands go 2.0 mi E on US-64 and turn L on Flat Mtn. Rd for 2.0 mi.)
- Tusquitee Ranger District, USFS, 123 Woodland Dr., Murphy, NC 28906; 828-837-5152. (Across the Hiwassee River at the first traffic light L from jct of US-19/219 and US-64. Go two blocks and turn L.)
- Wayah Ranger District, USFS, 90 Sloan Rd, Franklin, NC 28734; 828-524-6441. (Turn at first R off US-64 W from US-64 and US-441/23 S jct.)

Because the old and new Bartram Trail traverses three districts, it is described first.

Bartram Trail (74.3 mi; USFS #67) (F) (Sections 1 through 6 are in **18** Macon County and section 7 is in Swain County.)

Connecting Trails: (Hurrah Ridge Trail; USFS #004); (West Fork Trail; USFS #444); (Scaly Mountain Trail; USFS #67A); (Jones Knob Trail; USFS

#67B); (Whiterock Mountain Trail; USFS #67C); (Appalachian Trail; USFS #001); (Piercy Creek Trail; No USFS #); (Laurel Creek Trail; USFS #19F); (Mountains-to-Sea Bicycle Trail)

The Bartram Trail is named in honor of William Bartram (1739–1823), the first American-born naturalist to receive international fame for his botanical research. Born in Philadelphia, Bartram's expeditions in the southeastern states traversed at least 28 counties in North Carolina, 3 of which are Macon, Cherokee, and Graham. The exact route of his expedition is not known, but the North Carolina Bartram Trail Society and the Nantahala National Forest staff have jointly planned the trail to run as close to the original area he explored as is feasible in the Nantahala forest. Crossed in places by private property, the trail is continuous when using gravel and paved roads. Generally running SE to NW, it provides some remote areas where bear, deer, turkey, grouse, and numerous songbirds such as tanagers, towhees, and the Carolina junco may be seen.

From Oconee State Park in South Carolina, the yellow-blazed Bartram Trail traverses NW over Long Mtn., turning SW as it crosses the Chattooga River into Georgia's Chattahoochee National Forest near Earl's Ford for a 37.4-mi route to North Carolina. At Warwoman Dell near Clayton, Georgia, it goes N to Rabun Bald (4,696 ft.). From there it is 4.2 mi to FR-7, near the North Carolina state line and the southern entrance into the Nantahala National Forest. It is at this point that the description of the trail begins. Some suggested campsites and water sources are described along the trail, and support systems are listed at the end of each section. The North Carolina Bartram Trail Society has divided the trail route into seven sections, each with a detailed map and trail description. Map #1 includes a trailhead at Beegum Gap, near Rabun Bald, in Georgia. Former map #7 was once the Bartram Trail Western Extension to Porterfield Gap in the Snowbird Mountains, but there was not evidence that Bartram was in that area. (For descriptive purposes in this book, the distance has been divided into three major parts, with a description from the SE to NW.) In addition to the hiking trail, the society has included an 11.0-mi canoe trail in its trail system from Otto downriver to Franklin on the Little Tennessee River. For information about the trail maps, relocations, canoe trail, and available vehicle shuttle service, contact the North Carolina Bartram Trail Society, P.O. Box 144, Scaly Mountain, NC 28775; 828-293-3999 or www.ncbartramtrail.org. The society publishes a newsletter, has a membership, and holds regular and special meetings to which the public is invited. For information on the Bartram Trail in South Carolina, see *Hiking South Carolina Trails* by Allen de Hart, Globe Pequot Press, P.O. Box 833, Old Saybrook, CT 06475.

Bartram Trail Part I: Chattahoochee National Forest to Wallace Branch. Section 1 (9.8-mi); Section 2 (9.8 mi); Section 3 (14 mi)

Length and Difficulty: 33.6 mi, moderate to strenuous (elev change 3,023 ft.)

Special Features: vistas from Scaly Mtn., Jones Knob, Whiterock Mtn., Fishhawk Mtn., and Little Tennessee River Valley

Trailhead and Description: These sections are in the Highlands and Wayah Ranger Districts of the Nantahala National Forest. From the jct of NC-106 and US-64/NC-28 in Highlands, go S on NC-106 for 6.8 mi to Scaly Mtn. jct with Hale Ridge Rd (SR-1625) and turn L. Proceed for 2.6 mi and turn L on Chattahoochee FR-7. After 1.1 mi, park near the trailhead sign.

Section 1: Ascend N through hardwoods, buckberry, and rosebay rhododendron on a well-graded, yellow-blazed trail built by the YCC. Cross log bridges at 0.1 mi and 0.6 mi, and skirt a timbered area. Skirt E of Osage Mtn. at 0.9 mi, and cross a ridge at 1.1 mi. Ascend and descend on the graded trail between coves and streams that are tributaries of Overflow Creek, crossing footbridges at 1.5 mi, 1.7 mi, 2.1 mi, and 2.4 mi. (At 2.5 mi, pass jct with Hurrah Ridge Trail, R. It goes for 0.6 mi, leading to Blue Valley Rd, FR-79.) Continue under a heavy canopy of rosebay rhododendron, large oak, and white pine. (At 3.0 mi, pass a jct of West Fork Trail, R; it travels for 1.0 mi, leading to Blue Valley Rd, FR-79.) Begin ascent to NC-106 at 3.2 mi, and reach the scenic landscape of Osage Mtn., Blue Valley, and Little Scaly Mtn. from Osage Mtn. Overlook at 3.7 mi. Cross the highway, climb steeply at a power line and through open woods of oak and locust damaged by fire. At 4.1 mi, 35 yd. L, is a small waterfall, a natural shower. Rock-hop a cascading stream above the falls, pass through rhododendron thickets, ascend steeply, and turn R sharply onto a fire road at 4.5 mi. Continue the ascent for scenic views of Georgia, Osage Mtn., Blue Valley, and Little Scaly Mtn. At 5.2 mi is a jct with a blue-blazed spur trail, R (Scaly Mtn. Trail [USFS #67A] descends 0.8 mi to FR-52 that leads to a parking space at Hickory Knut Rd. Heading right [E] leads 1.0 mi to Turtle Pond Rd, R, and to NC-106. On NC-106 L [N] is 4.0 mi to Highlands.) Continuing on the Bartram Trail, scale Scaly Mtn. by ascending on switchbacks to the summit (4,804 ft.) at 5.6 mi. Descend on a ridge to Gall Tree Gap at 6.0 mi. Curve R in a descent to follow Lickskillet Ridge, then down to

Tessentee Creek and campsite at 8.1 mi. From here ascend gradually on the rocky W slope of Peggy Knob to reach Hickory Gap at 9.8 mi.

Section 2: From Hickory Gap, ascend steps to continue, then a steep climb to a ridge at 10.1 mi. Descend gently on an old forest road to Jones Gap at 10.8 mi to a trailhead and parking space. (To the R [N] is FR-4522, which switchbacks down the mountain 2.0 mi to Dendy Orchard Rd, where a R for 1.3 mi leads to Turtle Pond Rd. Make a R turn and travel 3.3 mi to access NC-106, 4.0 mi S of Highlands.) From Jones Gap, continue on the old seeded forest road to a turn R for passing N of Jones Knob. (To the L is 0.3 mi Jones Knob Trail [USFS #67B].) Along the way are some outcroppings, such as Whiterock Gap at 12.3 mi. (A water source is R on a 0.1 mi descent to Stephens Creek.) Continuing, make a horseshoe curve around the N slope of Whiterock Mtn. where 0.3 mi Whiterock Mtn Trail (USFS #67C) ascends L to the mountaintop. There are outstanding vistas of Tennessee Valley to the S and Nantahala range of mountains to the W. Cliffsides, three species of rhododendron, laurel, orchid, and other wildflowers, plus a combination of conifers and hardwoods make this mountain incredibly scenic. After crossing Little Fishhawk Mtn., the trail curves S of Fishhawk Mtn. at 13.8 mi. To the R is a 0.1-mi, blue-blazed spur to the mountaintop (4,748 ft.) where there is a bronze plaque memorializing William Bartram. Cross Wolf Rock, then descend by Cedar Cliff at 16.6 mi. After more switchbacks, descend to parallel Buckeye Creek. At 19.6 mi, arrive at a gravel parking lot. To access this section of the trail from Franklin, drive S on US-441 for 7.0 mi to Otto and turn L on Tessentee Rd (SR-1636). After 3.8 mi is a jct with Buckeye Creek Rd (SR-1640), L, and follow it 0.6 mi into USFS property.

Section 3: Whether hiking, bicycling, or driving the 14 mi of this section, the following description is the official route: Follow the 0.6 mi of Buckeye Creek Rd (SR-1640) and 2.2 mi of Tessentee Rd (SR-1636) to a R turn on Hickory Knoll Rd (SR-1643). After 2.0 mi is Riverside Rd, L, to the upstream public access for the Bartram Canoe route. Continuing on Hickory Knoll Rd another 0.6 mi, stay L at a jct with Clarks Chapel Rd (SR-1646). Follow it through the countryside for 2.0 mi to make a sharp L on Prentiss Bridge over the Little Tennessee River. After 0.3 mi, stay R to follow Wide Horizon Dr. (SR-1652) for 2.5 mi up and down low hills in forests and residential areas. Arrive at a jct with US-441/NC-23 and cross it to Belden Rd (SR-1152). (The Macon County Fairgrounds are on the E side of US-441.) After 0.3 mi, cross a bridge over Cartoogechaye Creek and turn L on Roller Mill Rd (SR-1154). For the next 0.8 mi ascend steeply, and afterwards pass Westage Plaza Shopping Center. Go under US-64 to follow Pressley Rd (SR-1315). After 1.0 mi, it becomes Ray

Cove Rd for 0.7 mi to a dead-end and parking lot at Wallace Branch, for a total of 14.0 mi (USGS-FS Maps: Scaly Mtn., Rabun Bald, Prentiss, Franklin.)

Support Facilities: There is lodging, restaurants, groceries, drug stores, spot supplies, and a hospital in Highlands. For detailed information (and due to seasonal services), contact Highlands Visitor Center, P.O. Box 404, Highlands, NC 28741; 828-526-2112 or www.highland-chamber.com. Franklin offers year-round services. Contact the Franklin Chamber of Commerce, 425 Porter St, Franklin, NC 28734; 828-524-3161, 800-336-7829, or www.franklin-chamber.com.

Bartram Trail Part II: Wallace Branch to Beechertown. Section 4 (10.7 mi); Section 5 (7.4 mi); Section 6 (15.8)

Length and Difficulty: 39.5 mi, moderate to strenuous (elev change 2,333 ft.)

Special Features: Wayah Bald, Nantahala Lake, surge chamber area

Trailhead and Description: These sections are in the Wayah District of the Nantahala National Forest and is a national recreation trail for the first 17.6 mi (dedicated May 18, 1985).

Section 4: Cross Wallace Branch on a footbridge and hike through a young forest with scattered mature poplar and oak. Cross a cascading stream R at 0.1 mi and cascades L on Wallace Branch at 0.3 mi. Enter a white-pine stand at 0.4 mi and cross an old road at 0.5 mi. Cross a small stream and ascend on the NE side of the ridge. Reach the ridge crest at 0.8 mi, and continue on the slope and follow the ridge W. At 1.6 mi, pass S of Bruce Knob, turn R sharply, and reach a gap at 1.8 mi. Begin a long ascent, steep in spots, along the ridge spine. Reach the crest at 2.4 mi, then descend to Locust Tree Gap #1 at 2.6 mi. Traverse a large black cohosh *(Cimicifuga racemosa)* garden. Ascend and skirt S of Wilkes Knob (3,800 ft.) at 3.2 mi. Descend and ascend over knobs for 3.3 mi, and reach a gravel road at 5.4 mi. There is an access here to US-441/64. From the US-441/64 jct in Franklin, go W on US-64 for 3.5 mi to Old Murphy Rd (SR-1442), R at Wayah Bald sign. After 0.2 mi, turn L on Wayah Rd (Sr-1310). After 2.0 mi, turn R on FR-713 and drive 4.1 mi to the trail. Continue on a ridge, skirt the N side of the knob, and descend and ascend over knobs for another 2.2 mi; reach a grazing road and Locust Tree Gap #2 at 7.6 mi. Follow the grazing road for 0.1 mi, then turn L and leave the old road at 7.8 mi; ascend at a sharp R. Along the ascent are trillium, doll's eyes *(Actaea pachypoda),* maidenhair fern *(Adiantum pedatum),* wild orchids, and bee balm *(Monarda didyma).* Hardwoods include hickory, locust, and oak. At 8.1 mi, skirt the S side of a knob in a horseshoe shape and ascend from a plateau at 8.6 mi. A deep and dangerous rock fissure is near the L of the trail at 9.2 mi and by a sharp switchback, R. (The fissure is 75-ft. deep. Respect the installed fence and do not go under or around it.) Ascend to a ridge at 9.4 mi, and curve R to make and easy descent into hardwoods and rhododendron. At 9.9 mi, cross a small stream in a dense rhododendron patch. There are a few dead but standing American chestnut trees about 20 ft. or more in height through this area among chestnut oak and flame azalea. The trail joins the AT at 10.0 mi. Turn L and ascend. There is a spring, R, at 10.1 mi. Continue ascending on a steep and rocky treadway through hemlock, maple, birch, fern, and more azalea. Cross a forest road at 10.3 mi, and arrive at Wayah Bald (5,340-ft., observation tower) at 10.6 mi. Views from the tower are outstanding, particularly E. At 10.7 mi, leave the paved access trail, R. (From the parking area ahead, it is 4.3 mi to Wayah Gap and Wayah Rd [SR-1310]).

Section 5: Follow the yellow and white blazes into the forest, R, and descend through yellow birch, conifers, and rhododendron, with Canadian violet and other wildflowers. At 12.4 mi, pass the old jct of the AT and Bartram Trail. A campsite area and spring are on the R at 12.5 mi. Turn R off the AT at 12.6 mi onto McDonald Ridge, W of Wine Spring Bald. Enter an open grazing field of orchard grass and clover at 12.9 mi. Blazes are infrequent. Follow a seeded road through two more grazing fields for 1.7 mi, and then reach Sawmill Gap and FR-711 at 14.6 mi. Turn L from the gaté, go 30 yd., turn R on a seeded road, and ascend. At 15.1 mi, turn L on a bank and follow to the crest of a rocky ridge. Follow the ridge up and down from cols for 1.8 mi, where there are partial views of Nantahala Lake. Descend; at 18.1 mi, near a small stream, R, reach Wayah Rd (SR-1310) at the lakeside (Heading L, it is 7.1 mi to Wayah Gap and the AT).

Section 6: Turn R on SR-1310; arrive at the Lake Side Camp Store at 0.6 mi. (The store has groceries, sporting goods, a snack shop, gasoline, telephone; open year-round.) Turn L, immediately past the store. Descend on a gravel driveway and cross Lee Branch into a young poplar forest. Reach an old woods road, fork R, and enter a white-pine grove at 1.1 mi. Leave the old road at 1.7 mi onto a foot trail among loosestrife *(Lysimachia lanceolata)* and white snakeroot *(Eupatorium rugosum)*. Cross a ridge, return to old road, and enter a stand of white pine at 1.9 mi. Leave old road on a footpath that curves around the ridge on a level contour; lake views, L, can be seen through the trees. At 2.7 mi, turn sharply L by tall poplar and descend on an old woods road. Pass through a rhododendron grove and through a patch of colicroot *(Aletris farinosa)*. Pass a view of the Nantahala Lake Dam at 3.1 mi and enter another old road for a view of a deep chasm, L. Bear L at a road fork, descend on three switchbacks, pass under a power line, and arrive at a gravel road at 3.6 mi (road to the R goes 0.9 mi to SR-1401). Ahead, follow an old road across the Nantahala River (low flow here), and turn R at a locked cable gate. Follow the private road downstream, pass cascading stream in Lambert Cove at 3.8 mi and a spring, L, at 4.8 mi. Pass under a large penstock from Whiteoak Dam at 5.7 mi, cross a wood bridge over Dicks Creek to SR-1401, and cross the road to the entrance of Apple Tree Group Camp at 5.8 mi. (To reach Beechertown by vehicle from this point, drive E on Wayah Rd (SR-1310) across the bridge and immediately turn L on FR-308. Go 3.2 mi to a jct with SR-1310; turn L and arrive at US-19 after another 4.1 mi.)

Continuing on the Bartram Trail, cross a split-rail fence near the Apple Tree Group Camp sign and go 0.2 mi to the old Piercy Creek Rd. Turn R, follow downstream, pass campsites C and D. At 7.8 mi, cross Walnut Creek, and Poplar Creek at 8.4 mi. (Heading R, it is 0.2 mi to the Nantahala River and FR-308). Ascend on a S slope, cross a ridge, and follow a N slope around Turkey Pen Cove at 9.6 mi. At 10.4 mi, turn R, downstream, and reach the confluence with Piercy Creek at 10.6 mi. Cross the stream and reach jct with the blue-blazed Piercy Creek Trail. (It descends 1.5 mi along the stream to the **24** creek's confluence with the Nantahala River. Rock-hopping or wading is usually necessary, but after a heavy rain the passage may be difficult or impossible. The best place to cross may be upriver for about 250 ft. After crossing to paved Wayah Rd (SR-1310), it is 1.6 mi L (N) to the Nantahala River BT parking lot in Beechertown.) Continue L on the Bartram Trail and follow an old road through a white-pine forest and good campsites. Reach a jct, L, with the blue-blazed Laurel Creek Trail at 10.9 mi. (Laurel Creek Trail goes 1.5 mi **25** to a jct with the blue-blazed Apple Tree Trail where a L turn provides a return to Apple Tree Group Camp after another 1.1 mi.) Continue upstream in a white-pine forest on a pleasant old road with switchbacks. At 11.2 mi, cross a small stream where trail is arbored with rhododendron. At 11.8 mi, turn sharply R on a footpath. (Ahead, the Nantahala Trail continues 0.5 mi to Sutherland Gap and a jct with the blue-blazed London Bald Trail, another loop option for a return to Apple Tree Group Camp.) On the footpath, follow along the slope and curve around spur ridges. Pass a spring at 12.2 mi, ascend, and curve around another spur ridge E of Rattlesnake Knob (4,052 ft.) at 12.6 mi. Slopes have hot-tempered yellow jackets and plenty of rattlesnake orchids. Other wildflowers on the banks of rich soil are meadow rue *(Thalictrum clavatum),* galax *(Galax aphlla),* flowering raspberry *(Rubus odoratus),* blue-bead *(Clintonia borealis),* sweet cicely *(Osmorhoza claytonii),* and Indian pipe *(Monotropa uniflora).*Trees include oak, birch, white pine, basswood, and butternut *(Juglans cinerea)* and shrubs, such as bladdernut *(Staghylea trifolia),* rhododendron, and laurel, are also found here. At 13.2 mi, follow an old woods road for 0.3 mi. At 13.8 mi, reach the crest of the ridge and the boundary of the Nantahala Power and Light Company (NPLC), where there are spectacular views of the Snowbird Mtns., the Nantahala Gorge, and N toward Cheoah Bald. Descend on 10 switchbacks to the NPLC surge chamber at 14.2 mi. Descend on the well-graded NPLC access road for 1.6 mi to a L turn down an embankment. Keep L on a gravel road and turn R, down steps to a parking lot (courtesy of NPLC) and 15.8 mi to end Section 6. It is 100 yds. down a gravel driveway to Wayah Rd (SR-1310) (also called Nantahala River Rd). (See Section 7 for its connections to Section 6.) Heading L on Wayah Rd, it is 0.2 mi to USFS Nantahala River Launch site. It offers drinking water, a comfort station, and a good location for vehicle shuttle, but camping is not allowed. Support facilities are described below. (USGS-FS Maps: Franklin, Wayah Bald, Topton, Hewitt)

Support Facilities: On US-19 L (SW), it is 1.5 mi to Brookside Campground with full service (including hot showers and laundry facilities), rec fac, open year-round, fully operational May 1 through October 1. For more information, contact the Nantahala River Launch Site, P.O. Box 93, Topton, NC 28781; 828-321-5209. On US-19 R (NE), it is 8.5 mi to Wesser and the Nantahala Outdoor Center for hiking and outdoor sporting goods, restaurant, groceries, and motel. For more information, contact The Outdoor Center 13077 US-19 W, Bryson City, NC 28713; 828-488-2175, 800-232-7238, or www.noc.com.

Bartram Trail Part III: Beechertown to Cheoah Bald. Section 7 (6.8 mi)
    Length and Difficulty: 6.8 mi, strenuous (elev change 3,043 ft.)
    Special Features: Nantahala River greenway, Ledbetter Creek Forge, Cheoah Bald
    Trailhead and Description: This section is in the Cheoah Ranger District of the Nantahala National Forest. From the parking lot described in Section 6, descend on a gravel road near the power-plant substation, cross Wayah Rd (SR 1310) at a R angle to cross a bridge over the Nantahala River. Turn L into a gravel parking area used for commercial rafting at 0.2 mi. At the parking area edge, cross a steel/cement bridge onto a wide asphalt greenway, the Mountains-to-Sea Bicycle Trail. Pass under a power line at 0.3 mi, and pass by a beaver dam at 0.8 mi. The scenic trail base is a former RR grade that parallels the

Nantahala River. At 1.4 mi is a jct with Winding Stairs Rd (FR-422), R and L. Turn L over the bridge to an island, then cross another bridge to a parking lot, trailhead, and information sign. Cross US-19/74, followed by crossing the Great Smoky Mountain Railroad tracks at 1.5 mi. Turn L and parallel the railroad tracks until crossing a stream, followed by crossing Ledbetter Creek at 1.9 mi. This is the first of seven crossings among rhododendron, conifers, and hardwoods. Ascend steeply on switchbacks to a ridge on the W side of the gorge and to an old logging road at 2.8 mi Follow the old road and at 3.6 mi, cross Ledbetter Creek. From here ascend near the stream with a number of scenic stream crossings among cascades, flumes, and waterfalls. At 6.1 mi, cross FR-259 for a steep climb out of the forge to Bellcolor Gap, and then ahead to a jct with the AT at 6.6 mi, R and L. (To the L on the AT it is 5.3 mi to Stecoah Gap parking/picnic area at NC-143.) Continue R and ascend to the panoramic summit of Cheoah Bald at 6.8 mi (5,062 ft.), the W terminus of the Bartram Trail. (USGS-FS Map: Hewitt) (Continuing E on the AT to US-19/74 at Wesser is 8.1 mi)

Support Facilities: (See Wesser in preceding section.)

Cheoah Ranger District

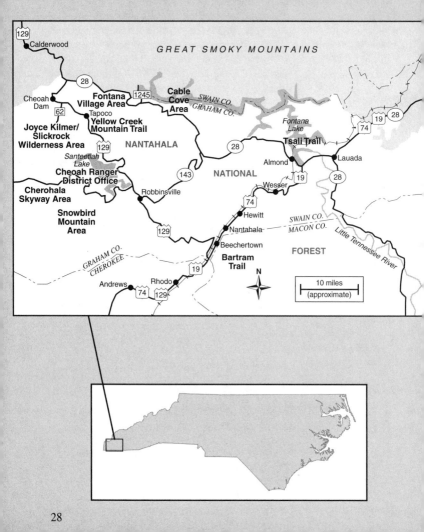

Introductions to Trail Areas

The trail areas in the Cheoah Ranger District are described counterclockwise. Because the Bartram Trail has its north terminus in this district, it is described first. Although it is in two other districts, its entire length of 74.3 mi in North Carolina is covered here for continuity.

Cheoah Ranger District Office
Near Santeelah Lake, check your physical fitness on the Massey Branch Fitness Trail, hike an educational trail, and check on the books and maps at the district office.

Bartram Trail
Ascend 6.6 mi of the 78-mi hiker's dream trail on switchbacks near a cascading stream. A gain of 3000 ft. in elevation awards you with panoramic views from Cheoah Bald (5,062 ft.) on the Appalachian Trail.

Tsali Recreation Area *32*
A popular oasis for equestrians and mountain bikers, there is a 40-mi network of four major trail loops on scenic peninsulas and scores of covers at Fontana Lake. Campground, hot shower, marina.

Cable Cove Area *33*
Campground, nature trail, excellent dock for boats and fishing in Fontana Lake.

Fontana Village Area *34*
Historic resort, a 15-mi network of trails, family oriented, Fontana Lake dock, and Fontana Dam, the highest in eastern North America.

Yellow Creek Mountain Trail *36*
Ruffed and scenic 9.0-mi former route of Appalachian Trail. It has connections with other trails to Fontana Village.

Joyce Kilmer/Slickrock Wilderness Area *39*
A large, 61-mi network of trails, a must-visit for the entire family. Here is the nation's largest grove of yellow poplar.

Cherohala Skyway Area *49*
Cheoah Ranger District's mile-high parkway with trails for the family and disabled. Magnificent views.

Snowbird Mountains Area *50*
From scenic Snowbird Creek here is a 36-mi network of hiking trails that leads to famous Hooper Bald and the Cherohala Skyway.

SECTION 1: CHEOAH RANGER DISTRICT

The Cheoah Ranger District has 120,524 acres with Lake Santeetlah in the center. On the N boundary is the Little Tennessee River, which is also the S boundary of Great Smoky Mtns National Park, but the river is dammed for the entire distance by Calderwood Lake, Lake Cheoah, and Fontana Lake. The S boundary is rimmed by the remote Snowbird Mtns., and its W border is more remote along the Tennessee line that fronts the Cherokee National Forest. Also in the W is the 13,562-acre Joyce Kilmer/Slickrock Wilderness Area, with its NW corner in Tennessee. Some of the most spectacular mountain views are in this district, particularly from the AT as it ascends to Cheoah Bald (5,062 ft.) from Wesser and crosses the Fontana Dam after 25.2 mi. Other panoramic views are from Wauchecha Bald (4,368 ft.), Johanna Bald (4,716 ft.), and Hangover Mtn. (4,170 ft.).

There are five recreational areas, all of which provide developed family campgrounds (except the Joyce Kilmer Memorial Forest, but Horse Cove has 17 camp units nearby). The Tsali area, with 42 camp units, is described under Tsali Trail, and Cheoah Point has 26 camp units. Horse Cove is described under the Kilmer/Slickrock Trails. Cable Cove, with 26 camp units, is near Fontana Lake, 4.5 mi. E on NC-28 from Fontana Village. Rattler Ford Group Campground (reservations required) has 4 sites for up to 50 people per site and is located near Santeetlah Creek by the entrance to the Kilmer Memorial Forest. (Call 828-479-6431 for reservations.) The national forest outside the campgrounds is also available for "primitive camping" unless the area is posted reserved (for activities such as boating, picnicking, trailheads, or administrative sites). The Kilmer/Slickrock Wilderness Area is protected by regulations and general etiquette as described in the introduction to this chapter.

The construction of the Cherohala Scenic Skyway, under the direction of the Federal Highway Administration, provides a 43-mi paved-road access from Santeetlah Gap jct with SR-1127 to Tellico Plains in Tennessee. The new road provides fast access to King Meadows Trail at Hooper Bald and to Big Snowbird Trail via Mitchell Lick Trail. There is an improved access route to Strawberry Knob and the Fodderstack Trail #94 (Tenn.) with completion of the highway. Construction of the Skyway (NC-143) took more than 30 years of planning and development (and more than $100 million). Of the 43 mi, 18 are in NC, from Santellah Gap W to Beech Gap at the state line and Cherokee National Forest. At the state line, it becomes TN-165 to Tellico Plains. As with the Blue Ridge Parkway, it is designed for slow traffic and for spectacular scenic overlooks. Its trails are described later. Conservationists tried for many years to prevent its construction.

There are two special-interest trails at the Cheoah Ranger Station. The Camp Santeetlah Historic Trail (USFS #152) begins at the parking area. Follow the signs on the paved trail that switchbacks up the hillside into a forest of hemlock, pitch pine, poplar, hickory, fern, laurel, and trailing arbutus. Along the way are history markers, one of which indicates that the trail was dedicated August 13, 1983, "in honor of the men who served the Civilian Conservation Corps (CCC) and their lasting contributions to our nation's national forests," specifically Camp NCF-24, Co 3447, that opened here in 1934 and closed in 1941. Reach an observation deck at 0.4 mi; backtrack. Another trail, the Massey Branch Fitness Trail, is 0.5 mi E of the ranger station on Massey Branch Rd (SR-1116). The loop trail is 0.55 mi with 14 exercise stations on a wood-chip treadway under white pine, oak, and maple. It has an excellent view of part of Santeetlah Lake after the 120-yd. climb to an easy route. **27**

28

Readers may notice the omission of some trails described in previous edition. Unfortunately, some trails are overgrown or not maintained and without blazed or signage, destroyed by ATV usage, or not being used according to USFS reports. (Some of the trails are still on National Geographic maps such as #784 or USGS-FS maps and inventory.) There was agreement between the author and the USFS district staff to omit the following trail descriptions: Bear Creek (3.2 mi; USFS #62); Cody Gap (0.4 mi; USFS #156); Fax Branch (1.4 mi; USFS #155); Funnel Top (2.5 mi; USFS #59); Indian Creek (0.7 mi; USFS #51); Locust Cove (1.6 mi; USFS #404); Panther Creek (4.0 mi; USFS # 68); Reid Branch (0.5 mi; USFS #69); Rock Creek (1.5 mi; USFS #405); Sand Creek (1.3 mi; USFS #51A); Santeetlah Lake (22.0 mi; USFS #156); Snowbird Loop Nature (0.5 mi; USFS #66); Valley River (9.3 mi; USFS #153) and Wauchecha Bald (8.3 mi; USFS #47), with the exception of 0.2 mi at its SW trailhead in Cheoah Point Campground from a telephone pole near the entrance of the campground to US-129. The campground is 6.0 mi W from NC-143 in Robbinsville to SR-1146 for 0.7 mi to Cheoah Point. (Perhaps volunteer groups will restore and use these trails in the future.)

Address and Access: District Ranger, Cheoah Ranger District, 1133 Massey Branch Rd, Robbinsville, NC 28711; 828-479-6431. From Robbinsville, go 1.0 mi W on US-129/NC-143 and turn L on Massey Branch Rd (NC-143) for 1.1 mi to the ranger station. District Ranger, Tellico Ranger District, Cherokee National Forest, 250 Ranger Station Rd, Tellico Plains, TN

37385; 423-253-2520. Graham County (NC) Travel and Tourism Authority; 828-479-3790 or 800-470-3790.

Tsali Recreation Area (Graham and Swain Counties)

The Tsali Campground and Lemmons Branch Boat Access (the latter located off Tsali Rd) provides a ramp for boating, fishing in Fontana Lake, water skiing, camping (with showers and flush toilets), horseback riding, mountain biking, picnicking, nature study, and hiking. The USFS and some recreation writers have described the Tsali Recreation Area as a "mecca for mountain bikers and horseback riders." The area is named in honor of the Cherokee Indian Tsali (Charlie), who escaped with his family from the "Trail of Tears" (see introduction to this chapter) to the Smoky Mtns. In the escape a US Army soldier was accidentally killed. General Winfield Scott asked Will Thomas, a Cherokee friend, to find Tsali and tell him that if he would surrender and pay the penalty of death, all the other Cherokee who had escaped the march to Oklahoma (approximately 1,000) would be permitted to remain. Tsali replied, "I will come. If I must die, let it be by our own people." Tsali, his oldest son, and his son-in-law were executed by a three-member Cherokee firing squad here at the old stockade.

    Access: From the jct of US-74/19/NC-28 (3.0 mi W of Lauada), go W on NC-28 3.5 mi to Tsali Campground sign, R, and on SR-1286 descend 1.6 mi to parking area.

29-32   *Tsali Right Loop Trail* (12.8 mi; USFS #38); *Tsali Left Loop Trail* (11.7 mi; USFS #38A); *Thompson Loop Trail* (4.4 mi; #152); *Mouse Branch Loop Trail* (6.5 mi; #153) (F, B, H).

    Length and Difficulty: 38.7 mi combined, easy to difficult

    Special Features: lake views, wildlife, wildflowers

    Trailhead and Description: Access to all trails begins at the parking-lot intersection. The Tsali right and left loops consist of a W loop and an E loop of the peninsula. A forest road cuts through the center with Graham County W and Swain County E. The E loop has two spur trails to provide connections for making choices of three loops with lesser distance. The large parking area at the main trailhead was constructed in 1994 to accommodate an increase in trail users. On two adjoining peninsulas are the color-coded Thompson Loop Trail and Mouse Branch Loop Trail, also multiple-use trails. Although hikers may use the trails at any time, there is a schedule for horses and mountain bikes. In 2004 the following list was on a sign between Thompson Loop Trail and the entrance road to the campground: Thompson Loop Trail and Mouse Branch Loop Trail for equestrians on Sunday, Monday, Wednesday, and Friday; for bikers on Tuesday, Thursday, and Saturday. On the Tsali right and left loops, bikers have Sunday, Monday, Wednesday, and Friday; equestrians have Tuesday, Thursday, and Saturday. Bikers must wear helmets and other appropriate safety gear. There is a $2 fee for all users.

The Tsali right and left loops have a well-graded treadway, connect to the campground, and have hitching racks and observation points along the peninsula. There are dips and curves in and out of more than 40 coves. Wildlife includes deer, raccoon, fox, squirrel, hawk, woodpecker, and songbirds. Vegetation is that of the lower-slope (less than 2,000-ft. elev) Appalachian hardwood forest. Most of the forest is open with light understory, but often there are small patches of berries, sumac, sourwood, and laurel. There are scattered hemlock, scrub and white pine, and yellow poplar. Wildflowers include sunflower, cone flower *(Rudbeckia hirta),* downy false foxglove *(Aureolaria virginica),* horsemint *(Collinsonia canadensis),* wild phlox, soapwort, gentian, orchid, henbit, and violet. Hikers and walkers interested in a slow pace to observe plant and wildlife will notice that there is less multiple usage on the trails on weekdays. Although the author measured all the trails in this area, the trails are subject to alteration. Therefore, consult the signboard at the parking-area shelter for distance options and select a brochure for current trail routings (USGS-FS Map: Noland Creek).

Support Facilities: Bryson City, with restaurants, motels, and shopping areas, is 12.0 mi E of Tsali Recreation Area on US-19.

Cable Cove Area (Graham County)

Cable Cove Nature Trail (USFS #58) (F)   33

Length and Difficulty: 1.1 mi round-trip, easy

Trailhead and Description: From the jct of NC-28 and SR-1245 near Fontana Dam, drive E for 3.8 mi on NC-28 to Cable Cove Campground Rd (FR-520), L. Follow the road 1.2 mi, and turn R. The campground has 26 camping units, 4 picnic units, and flush toilets (no showers). Nearby Fontana Lake is accessible for boating and fishing. To hike the trail, park near a kiosk and trail sign. Cross Powell Branch on a footbridge and ascend. At 0.1-mi is a jct with an old road R and L. (The old road L goes 0.5 mi to another stream with cascades and a grazing field.) Cross the old road and ascend. The historic nature trail once had many wooden signs with botanical information about the trees and wildflowers. (In 2004, some of the signs were decayed or missing, but the USFS staff has stated plans to restore the once-beautiful and educational trail.) At 0.5 mi, curve R and descend on route that parallels a stream with cascades at 0.9 mi. Complete the loop. (USGS-GS Maps: Tuskeegee, Fontana Dam)

Fontana Village Area (Graham County)

34-47

The historic Fontana Village Area has two trail systems, one within the village boundary of the Tennessee Valley Authority (TVA) and the other in the adjoining Cheoah Ranger District of the USFS. Some of the trails connect and most of the connecting USFS trails are maintained, monitored, or bear the cost of signage by administrative staff or volunteers at Fontana Village. The trail network within the village may begin or end near the resort cottages, or the service, or administrative buildings. Whether a guest or visitor, the hiker (or bicyclist or equestrian) is advised to contact or visit the Adventure Center, 800-849-2258 or www.fontanavillage.com to receive current information on the trails that are open, closed, or planned. A map is available for the following: Cafeteria Trail (0.7 mi); East Horse Trail (1.2 mi); Elmer Hollow Trail (1.6 mi); Great Smoky Mtn. Trail (1.1 mi); Hoor Hollow Trail (0.5 mi); Piney Ridge Trail (1.0 mi); Scenic Way Trail (0.2 mi); Squatter Trail (0.5 mi); Trout Pond Trail (0.2 mi); Turkey Chute Trail (0.8 mi); Welch Cove Trail (0.1 mi); West Horse Trail (0.5 mi); Whitting Rail Trail (1.9 mi). Lookout Rock Trail is partly in the Village and partly in the USFS property. The 2.2-mi round-trip trail has an elevation change of 640 ft. in a moderate to strenuous ascent on the N side of the Yellow Creek Mtns. There are views of the Village and Fontana Dam area. Access is from the Texaco station on NC-28 at the Village entrance. Follow the road through the Village, staying R all the way to cottage #1038 at 0.5 mi to drive steeply up a curve where on the L is a trail sign at 0.8 mi. Parking may be necessary farther around the curve to the Piney Ridge Trail trailhead. (See Yellow Creek Mountain Trail, ahead.)

The Village is the result of a community established by the TVA for the construction of nearby Fontana Dam and the 31-mi-long lake, which opened in 1947. Today the Village is considered a vacation place for families or ideal for scenic meeting and conference areas. Activities include fishing, boating, canoeing, scenic water cruises, and houseboat rentals. Some trails are for mountain bicycling and horseback riding. There is an administrative office, inn with conference rooms and restaurant, museum, general store, post office, laundromat, cottages, mini-golf course, basketball courts, softball field, tennis courts, horse stables, swim club, community church, fire station, service station, village café, game arcade, craft shop, archery field, and marina. The Village sponsors two five-day hiking programs: Spring Wildflowers in mid-April and Fall Colors in mid-October. Cabin and room rates are discounted for these programs. Access is on NC-28, 25 mi W from its jct with US-19/74, S of Bryson City. Contact the Fontana Village Area, P.O. Box 68, Fontana Dam, NC 28733.

Connecting trails in the adjoining Cheoah Ranger District are Lewellyn Cove Nature Trail, Fontana Loop Trail, Fold Branch Trail, Lookout Rock Trail, and Brooks Cove Trails, which are described below.

Lewellyn Cove Nature Trail (0.7 mi; USFS #50) (F); ***Fontana Loop*** **48-50**
Trail (2.2 mi; USFS #157 (F, B); ***Gold Branch Trail*** (2.5 mi) (USFS #421) (F, B)

Length and Difficulty: 5.4 mi round-trip and backtrack, easy to moderate
Connecting Trail: (Whitting Rail Trail)
Trailhead and Description: From the parking area at the Lewellyn Cove sign (1.4 mi W from Texaco station in Fontana Village), cross the road and ascend 116 yds. on the Lewellyn Cove Nature Trail to a fork. Turn L and reach another fork at 0.2 mi. If not following the Lewellyn Cove Nature Trail, turn L, where Fontana Loop Trail begins. Ascend on an old, rocky, and eroded road. The sound of Lewellyn Cove Creek is R. At 0.5 mi is a sign with Lewellyn Cove Loop Trail, but likely means Fontana Loop Trail. Turn L. (Although no sign here, the ascent is necessary to reach Gold Branch Trail. Arrive at Fontana Rd, R and L, at 0.7 mi. (This USFS road is in good condition, an excellent gated road for mountain biking or hiking.) Cross the road and ascend on the Gold Branch Trail (also listed by the USFS as Bee Cove Trail). Arrive at a gap at 0.7 mi and descend. There are two switchbacks near an access to Fontana Rd. Turn R on the road and complete the loop at 2.1 mi, but descend L to retrack access to the Fontana Loop Trail (Lewellyn Cove Loop Trail sign). Turn L.

On the Fontana Loop Trail, cross a culverted stream at 0.1 mi. Among the hardwoods are some hemlocks and banks of maidenhair fern. Cross another culverted stream at 1.0 mi, followed by a descent near a deep hollow. Pass under a powerline among yellow jewelweed and white snakeroot. Descend at 1.2 mi, arrive at NC-28 with the jct of Whitting Rail Trail, which is a popular mountain-bike trail that connects with the streets of Fontana Village. (On NC-28 it is 0.9 mi back, E, to the beginning of the nature trail.) Turn R on the Fontana Loop Trail and at 1.4 mi, cross a footbridge near a powerline. There are views of Fontana Dam at 1.8 mi. Among cascades cross a footbridge over Lewellyn Cove Branch and among a grove of fetterbush at 2.2 mi. Ahead is a reunion with the Lewellyn Cove Nature Trail. Along the way are signposts with vascular information. (Some of the signs have misinformation or the species is absent.) At 2.4 mi, return to the sign that indicated no bikers are allowed on the nature trail. Arrive at nature trail loop at 2.7 mi. After a descent of 0.1 mi, return to the parking area, E, on NC-28. (USGS-FS Map: Fontana Dam)

51 *Brooks Cove Trail* (USFS #422) (F, B, H)

Length and Difficulty: 3.1-mi loop, easy to strenuous
Connecting Trails: (Piney Ridge Trail); (Turkey Chute Trail)
Trailhead and Description: From the Texaco Station on NC-28 and entrance to Fontana Village, drive through the Village straight ahead on a road with a center yellow line and only one row of cottages on the R. At cottage #1038, turn R to steeply ascend to Fontana Heights on Rhymes Ferry Rd (SR-1246) at 0.5 mi. Drive past a trailhead of Piney Ridge Trail at 0.9 mi, and reach Brooks Cove Trail trailhead at a USFS gate, R, at 1.6 mi.

Follow the forest road 0.1 mi and suddenly leave the road, R, to descend on an old forest road. Pass through young forest growth from a timber cut at 0.3 mi. At 0.6 mi, follow an old RR grade and enter a rhododendron grove with tall hemlocks. Cross a footbridge at 0.8 mi and a footbridge over scenic Brooks Cove Branch at 0.9 mi. Ascend a steep section with switchbacks. At 1.2 mi, pass through mountain laurel on an ascent to a bridge and gap. Here is an attractive understory. At 1.7 mi, come to jct with Piney Ridge Trail. Turn R, follow a ridge with patches of galax. Continue ascending; there are trail signs at 1.9 mi, after which the trail curves R to other ridges. With some ascending and descending the trail makes a final climb and rapidly drops to the small parking area on Rhymes Ferry Rd. Here is also a signed access to Piney Ridge Trail and Turkey Chute Trail, both near the W edge of the Fontana Village Boundary. Turn R and walk the paved road through a residential area for an ascent to the USFS gate and completion of the loop at 3.1 mi. (USGS-FS Map: Fontana Dam)

52 Yellow Creek Mountain Area (Graham County)
Yellow Creek Mountain Trail (USFS #48) (F)

Length and Difficulty: 9.3 mi, strenuous (elev change 2,350 ft.)
Connecting Trails: (Lookout Rock Trail); (AT)
Trailhead and Description: In Tapoco (14.5 mi W from Robbinsville on US-129) at the jct of US-129 and Rhymers Ferry Rd (SR-1247) (which leads

8.5 mi to NC-28 in Fontana Village), park in a small area on US-129. Walk 30 yd. on SR-1247 and cross Meadow Branch on a footbridge. (This blue-blazed trail is beautiful, but, because it is infrequently hiked, it may need maintenance. One disadvantage is its lack of water sources. Until 1947 it was the circuitous route followed by the AT between the Smokies and the Cheoah Mtns. It was reopened in 1971 by the Boy Scouts of Tapoco, Troop 415.) Climb steeply up the switchbacks through rhododendron, scrub pine, white pine, dogwood, laurel, and witch hazel *(Hamamelis virginiana)*. Follow the ridge for 0.6 mi. and a burned S slope to reach Bearpen Gap at 1.4 mi under a power line. Along the route are splendid views of the Cheoah River Valley and Hangover Lead. Banks of wildflowers are profuse: trailing arbutus, coral bell, goldenrod, and Devil's shoestrings *(Tephrosia virginiana)* in clusters of pink wings and yellow standards (the latter plant contains rotenone, an insecticide ingredient). (At Bearpen Gap a loop trail can be made by following an unnamed trail L to Rhymers Ferry Rd, SR-1274, at Jenkins Grocery. Turn L and follow the road to the trailhead at 3.0 mi.) Continue on the Yellow Creek Mountain Trail up the mountain, using care to avoid other trails and woods roads, to Old Yellow Creek Rd (also called Oldfield Gap Rd, SR-1249) at 1.8 mi. Cross the road, L, and ascend an embankment to follow a ridge of oak, pine, sourwood, and laurel. Continue on the ridge, ascending and descending over knolls to a steep climb at 3.1 mi. Reach Kirkland Gap (2,800 ft.) at 5.6 mi and Green Gap (3,455 ft.) at 7.8 mi. Lookout Rock Trail is L of the gap. (It descends 1.0 mi to the SW corner of Fontana Village, connecting with SR-1246.) Arrive at Walker Gap (3,450 ft.) at 9.3 mi to join the current route of the AT. Backtrack or take the AT N for 2.7 mi to NC-28. Another route would be to take the AT S to Yellow Creek Gap at Tuskeegee Rd/ Yellow Creek Rd (SR-1242) for 3.7 mi. Vehicle switching is necessary. (USGS-FS Maps: Fontana Dam, Tapoco)

Belding Trail (USFS #52) (F)   53

   Length and Difficulty: 11.0 mi (13.2 to avoid backtracking), easy to strenuous

   Connecting Trails: (Hangover Lead Trail); (Yellow Hammer Creek Trail); Ike Branch Trail (1.5 mi of 2.2 mi; USFS #45)

   Special Features: Swinging Bridge, cascading streams, hemlock groves

   Trailhead and Description: The SE trailhead is on US-129, 6.0 mi SE of Tapoco and 9.5 mi NW from Robbinsville, at a small parking area between the highway and the Cheoah River. The NW trailhead is at Tapoco where a parking area is on the W side of US-129 and S end of bridge over Calderwood Lake (below Cheoah Dam). If hiking the historic trail from the SE trailhead, cross the pedestrian swinging bridge over the Cheoah River and turn R into a large grove of hemlock. You may see here, and at scattered places along trail, a light-green blaze on the trees. Follow the path to rock-hop Rock Creek at 0.1 mi, then curve L on the ridgeside. At 0.6 mi, cross an unnamed branch. There may be an old Laurel Branch sign here. Ascend a ridge and proceed to weave in and out of slight coves. Cross a small and mossy stream in a rhododendron patch at 0.9 mi. A rock formation is at 1.0 mi. After following an old forest road over a ridge, the trail descends to a wet area where two more small streams are crossed. Join another old road, but abruptly leave it, L, at 1.6 mi in a climb to where steps were once installed. At the top is a gentle ridge where the trail disappears in dense new growth from a timber cut. Until a clearing is made by the USFS for volunteers, ascend the ridge, L, by bushwhacking 0.2 mi to access a gravel and usable USFS road #2516, L and R. (Heading L, it is 2.0 mi to the road's gate at SR-1129, a paved road, at Gold Mine Branch.)

Turn R to continue on the Belding Trail. The well-graded road has two major coves in the next 2.0 mi; the first at culverted Laurel Creek and its cascades, and the second at culverted Persimmon Tree Branch. At 3.8 mi, the road has a three-way fork. On the approach bear slightly L around a curve to leave the roads and enter directly into the woods. (The author and Bruce Wisely tied orange and pink flagging at this entry point. Perhaps by the time readers reach this spot the USFS will have placed a sign or painted light-green blazes.) Descend easily and enter a potential and desirable campsite area. Among young white pines, followed by rhododendron, cross Falls Brook. At 4.0 mi, ascend to a ridge, then descend. A damp area is at 4.2 mi. Ascend to ridge saddle. After more descending, rock-hop Deep Creek at 4.8 mi. At 5.0 mi, cross Indian Grave Branch, a tributary to Deep Creek. Ascend gradually on switchbacks to arrive at Deep Creek Hunter Camp Rd (USFS #445) at 5.2 mi. (Hopefully, blazes and a sign have been placed here.) Turn R on the gravel road toward a space for parking. (It is 1.0 mi on the road to FR-62, where heading R, it is 0.3 mi to a bridge crossing of the Cheoah River and a jct with US-129.) Descend and walk on the road 0.3 mi to a curve and crossing of Frisby Branch. Turn L off the road (there may be an old sign) and ascend. There is a grove of large white pines at 5.8 mi. There is more descending and ascending, and a crossing of an old road before a casual descent on an old road exits to FR-62, L and R, at 6.8 mi. A sign may be here; the parking space is small. (Down the road, R, it is 1.6 mi to US-129.) Turn L and walk up the gravel road 0.4 mi to a small hollow, R. (Surprisingly, you may see some ancient wooden steps, or hopefully some new ones.) Ascend briefly, then gradually descend on the old trail to rock-hop or wade Bear Creek in dense rhododendron. At 7.5 mi, enter a wildlife field; stay R, and turn onto a forest road with new walnut trees. Cross a wooden vehicular bridge over Caney Branch at 7.8 mi. (The National Geographic map #784 and the USGS-FS map show the trail turning R here on an old FR to exit on private property at Tapoco. Avoid this routing.) At 7.9 mi, cross Little Black-gum Branch and ascend. At 8.4 mi, is a grassy field (elev 2,040 ft.). Curve L and remain on the FR. Bear R in a grassy field at 8.6 mi. (a green blaze may be seen at 8.7 mi). At 9.0 mi, leave the road and descend into the forest. Curve in and out of coves and pass through a handsome grove of hard-woods—beech, oak, cucumber tree, and yellow poplar—at 9.9 mi. After crossing a number of streamlets that become Yellowhammer Branch, reach jct with Hangover Lead Trail in Yellowhammer Gap at 11.0 mi, where trail signs are located. (Another sign forbids entry into the Yellowhammer water-shed, but a USFS spokesperson stated the Belding Trail did not violate the decree.) For an exit, descend 40 yds. to a jct with Ike Branch Trail, ahead and R, and Yellowhammer Creek Trail, L. Turn R on Ike Branch Trail, follow it 1.5 mi down the mountain and branch to Slickrock Creek Trail. Turn R and after another 0.7 mi, arrive at the parking area at the W end of the US-129 bridge over Calderwood Lake at 13.2 mi.

Joyce Kilmer/Slickrock Wilderness Area (Graham County, North Carolina; Monroe County, Tennessee)

The Joyce Kilmer Memorial Forest, of which 3,840 acres are in the Little San-teetlah Creek watershed, and the Slickrock Creek watershed, with 11,060 acres, together form two basins separated by a ridge between Stratton Bald and Haoe Lookout. The Smokies are N across the Little Tennessee River, and the Cherokee National Forest in Tennessee is to the W. Filled with virgin timber, the Kilmer Memorial was established by Congress in 1936 to honor the famous author of *Trees,* Alfred Joyce Kilmer, a soldier who was killed in World War I at the Battle of Ovreq. The Belton Lumber Company started cutting the virgin timber up the Little Santeetlah Creek in 1890, but before it reached the huge trees in what is now the Kilmer Memorial Forest, the company went bankrupt and the trees were spared. In 1936 the USFS also purchased the Slickrock Creek basin from the Babcock Lumber Company of Pennsylvania, which had cut more than 70 percent of the timber in the watershed.

This wilderness is rich in both flora and fauna. Hundreds of species of shrubs, wildflowers, vines, ferns, mosses, lichens, and herbaceous plants form the understory. Rhododendron, laurel, and flame azalea are also abundant. Trees include poplar, hemlock, sycamore, basswood, oak, maple, birch, and beech. Animal life includes wild hog, fox, bear, deer, raccoon, mink, and other smaller mammals. Two species of poisonous snakes—the copperhead and the timber rattler—are in the area. In addition to songbirds, the wilderness has grouse, wild turkey, owls, hawks, and raven. Under specific state laws, hunting and fishing are allowed in the wilderness by the NC Wildlife Resources Commission, Division of Game, as described in the introduction to this chapter.

Support Facilities: For the Slickrock Creek Wilderness Area, the closest USFS campground is Cheoah Point on Santeetlah Lake, 8.6 mi E on US-129 from the Cheoah Dam bridge and Slickrock Creek Trail parking area in Tapoco. Enter the campground on Old US-129 (SR-1146). Facilities include campsites, tables, grills, drinking water, comfort stations, and picnic area. (From the campground, it is 7.0 mi E on US-129 to Robbinsville.) From the Cheoah Dam bridge, it is 2.2 mi N on US-129 (near the jct with NC-28) to a motel, groceries, gasoline, and telephone. For more information, contact Slickrock Deals Gap, Tapoco, NC 704-498-2231. Also, from the Cheoah Dam bridge 0.4 mi E on US-129, turn L on Rhymers Ferry Rd (SR-1247) for 1.3 mi to Jenkins Grocery. A USFS campground for the Kilmer Wilderness Area is Horse Cove, 0.2 mi on FR-416 across Kilmer Rd (SR-1127) from the Kilmer Memorial Forest and picnic area entrance. Facilities at Horse Cove are the same as for Cheoah Point. Groceries, motel, and shopping centers are 13.4 mi E on Kilmer Rd (SR-1127) to Robbinsville.

Access: There are two road access points for the Slickrock Wilderness Area trails. One is at the S side of the US-129 bridge over Calderwood Lake, below Cheoah Dam, and the other is at Big Fat Gap, via FR-62, 2.2 mi SE from the Cheoah Dam bridge on US-129 and 7.0 mi W from the jct with US-19/74. FR-62 is closed to vehicles from late December to mid- or late March because of weather conditions.

54-55   *Slickrock Creek Trail* (13.0 mi; USFS #42); *Hangover Lead Trail* (5.4 mi [N 2.4, S 3.0 mi]; USFS #56) (F).

56-59   **Connecting Trails on Slickrock Creek Trail:** Ike Branch Trail (2.1 mi; USFS #45); Nichols Cove Trail (3.1 mi; USFS #44); Big Fat Trail (1.5 mi; USFS #41); Slickrock Creek Spur Trail (0.7 mi; USFS #42A); (Haoe Lead Trail)

Connecting Trails on Hangover Lead Trail: (Haoe Lead Trail); Deep   **60-63**
Creek Trail (3.9 mi; USFS #46); Locust Ridge Trail (0.8 mi; USFS #401); Big
Fat Trail (1.5 mi; USFS #41); Windy Gap Trail (1.3 mi; USFS #400); Yellow-
hammer Gap Trail (1.7 mi; USFS #49); Ike Branch Trail (2.1 mi; USFS #45)

Length and Difficulty: 26.5 mi combined, moderate to strenuous (elev
change 4,150 ft.)

Special Features: fishing, Lower Falls, Hangover outcroppings

Trailhead and Description: The greatly contrasting Slickrock Creek Trail
and the Hangover Lead Trail run N-S and can easily be connected with short
trails at either end to form a major loop into the Slickrock Wilderness Area
basin and E rim. Additional trail loops are possible into the Tennessee section
of the wilderness for the W rim to make a complete rim loop of approximately
26.6 mi. Sections of the wilderness are rugged and remote with minimum trail
signing and generally without blazes. Hikers are advised to take adequate food
and clothing, rain gear (there are thunderstorms almost daily in the summer),
tent, stove (frequently the wood is wet), topo maps, and compass. Although
there are plenty of water sources on all of the basin and mountainside trails,
water is absent or intermittent on the rim trails. (Drinking water from Slickrock
Creek should be boiled or treated.) Wilderness rules and regulations apply on
all the trails, and hikers are reminded to follow the "no-trace" policy of hiking
and camping. Slickrock Creek is an excellent brown trout stream.

From the parking area at the S side of the Cheoah Dam bridge follow the
Slickrock Creek Trail sign into the woods and parallel Calderwood Lake on a
wide scenic trail. At 0.7 mi reach jct with Ike Branch Trail, L (described on the
return route). Plant life in the vicinity includes poplar, birch, maple, hemlock,
fetterbush, jewelweed *(Impatiens capensis* and *pallida),* sweet cicely, and wild
hydrangea *(Hydrangea arborescens).* At 0.8 mi, cross a footbridge; at 1.0 and
1.4 mi cross boardwalks over a precipice. A pink rhododendron *(Rhododendron
minus)* grows here and frequently (with other species) in the entire Slickrock
basin. At 1.6 mi, cross another bridge over a precipice and turn L to the mouth
of Slickrock Creek. Pass the edge of the lake backwater and arrive beside the
pools and cascades of Slickrock Creek at 1.9 mi. Follow upstream on sections
of an old RR grade. (This was the access route of the Babcock Lumber Company of Pittsburgh, which cut 70 percent of the virgin forest in the gorge
between 1915 and 1922. It had to cease logging when Calderwood Lake was
constructed.) Rocky treadways, rock walls, wildflowers, and cascades make this
section of the trail scenic. Rock-hop or wade the creek at 2.7 mi into Tennessee
and reach the Lower Falls at 3.0 mi. Continue upstream and cross the creek

again at 3.5 mi to a jct with Ike Branch Trail at 3.7 mi. Good campsites are in this area. To complete this first loop turn L on Ike Branch Trail up Yellow-hammer Creek in a forest of poplar, sycamore, basswood, rhododendron, and ferns. Ascend; at 4.2 mi, reach jct with Yellowhammer Gap Trail, which leads to Nichols Cove Trail, R, at 4.3 mi. (The Hangover Lead Trail is described on the longer return loops.) Pass through an area of oak, pine, buckberry, flame azalea, and huckleberry on a dry ridge at 4.6 mi. Cross another ridge at 4.9 mi and descend into a deep hollow of hemlock, poplar, and rhododendron. Cross a stream four times and descend on an exceptionally steep slope by a ravine. Reach the N terminus of Ike Branch Trail and the jct with Slickrock Creek Trail at 5.8 mi; turn R and return to the parking area for a total of 6.5 mi.

For a second and longer loop, continue upstream on the Slickrock Creek Trail from the jct with the Ike Branch Trail at 3.7 mi. Cross a small tributary before fording Slickrock Creek into Tennessee at 4.0 mi. At 4.2 mi, reach the jct with Stiffknee Trail (USFS #106) at the state line. (Stiffknee Trail goes W up Little Slickrock Creek for 3.3 mi to Farr Gap and a jct with Fodderstack Trail [USFS #95]. The Stiffknee Trail could be a route to Fodderstack Trail for a complete hike of the rim by using Fodderstack, Stratton Bald, Haoe, and Hangover Lead Trails for approx. 26.6 mi. A major problem with such a loop is the lack of water on the basin's rim.) Continue upstream for 0.2 mi to a jct with Nichols Cove Trail, L, after fording Slickrock Creek in the process. Here the hiker has a choice of following Nichols Cove Trail to rejoin the Slickrock Creek Trail after 2.8 mi to Big Fat Trail, or follow Yellowhammer Trail off Nichols Cove Trail to Ike Branch Trail and return for a loop of lesser distance. If Nichols Cove Trail is chosen, ascend in a narrow scenic passage of water-falls and cascades, hemlock, fern, and rhododendron. Cross the stream six times and at 0.9 mi, reach jct with Yellowhammer Gap Trail, L. (The 1.7-mi Yellowhammer Trail ascends gently NW and crosses a number of small drains from the Hangover Lead. The trail weaves in and out of coves in a forest dom-inated by oak, poplar, birch, and rhododendron. At 1.8 mi, reach jct with Ike Branch Trail and the Hangover Lead Trail. A turn R on the Ike Branch Trail continues NW for a return to US-129 and a loop of 9.5 mi.) Continue ahead on the Nichols Cove Trail, pass signs of former human habitation at rock piles and terraces, tombstones, and once cleared fields at 1.3 mi. Begin a steep ascent at 1.8 mi to reach a ridge nose where a L curve goes to the ridge crest. At 2.3 mi, reach jct with Windy Gap Trail, L (E). (It descends 1.3 mi from Hangover Lead Trail.) Begin to descend at 2.4 mi. After 0.3 mi of a steep descent, reach a level area, cross Big Fat Branch, and reach jct with Big Fat Trail at 2.9 mi. There are good campsites here. Heading R, it is 150 yd. to Slickrock Creek Trail; to the L on Big Fat Trail, it is 1.5 mi up to Big Fat Gap. (The Big Fat Trail ascends to switchbacks at 0.2 mi and follows mainly on the S side of the stream, steeply in sections. Cross the stream at 0.9 mi, shift S to cross a tributary, and follow switchbacks to reach Big Fat Gap parking area and FR-62 at 1.5 mi. At the Fat Gap parking area, a L turn on the Hangover Lead Trail for 2.4 mi to a jct with Ike Branch Trail, R, will lead back to US-129 in Tapoco for a loop of 11.6 mi.

If choosing to hike the Slickrock Creek Trail instead of the Nichols Cove Trail, continue upstream on remnant sections of the old RR grade and cross the stream to the Tennessee side at 4.7 mi. Enter a rocky section at 5.2 mi, and pass through a narrow canyon at 5.4 mi. Cross Wildcat Branch, a tributary, curve around the nose of two spur ridges, and cross back into North Carolina at 6.2 mi. (For the next 0.2 mi, the area is good for camping.) Cross the creek again at 6.4 mi and at 6.6 mi (the last crossing from Tennessee) below Wildcat Falls. Cross Slickrock Creek and reach the confluence of Slickrock Creek and Big Stack Gap Branch and Big Stack Gap Trail (USFS #139), R, at 7.3 mi. (The Big Stack Gap Branch Trail goes 1.8 mi upstream to a cross-trail with Fodderstack Trail and Crowder Creek Trail #48 in Cherokee National Forest.) Cross a tributary at 7.5 mi and Slickrock Creek again to reach the jct with Nichols Cove Trail at 7.9 mi. A third loop option can be made here by returning to US-129 on either Nichols Cove, Yellowhammer, and Ike Branch Trails for a total of 13.8 mi or climbing the Big Fat Trail to a jct with Hangover Lead and Ike Branch Trails N for a total of 14.1 mi.

For the fourth and final loop option, continue upstream and ascend to the nose of a spur ridge to cross Buckeye Branch at 8.2 mi. Ascend gradually and cross two more drains before crossing Hangover Creek at 9.0 mi, the last generally level area for camping within the next 4.0 mi. At 9.6 mi the trail forks. (Ahead is a 0.7-mi dead-end trail to the cascading confluence of Slickrock Creek and Naked Ground Branch.) At the fork, turn sharply L on a W slope and curve around the ridge to cross a tributary that flows into Hangover Creek. For the next 2.9 mi, ascend on switchbacks (where some sections are overgrown) on a steep ridgeline, but cross a tributary four times before reaching the major ridge knoll. The forest in this area is mixed hardwoods, rhododendron, and scattered conifers. Reach a trail crossroads at 13.0 mi with Haoe Lead Trail and Naked Ground Trail (4,850 ft.). (With a vehicle shuttle, trail connections can be made to all trails described below in the Kilmer basin. The Haoe Lead Trail connects R, 0.5 mi, with the Stratton Bald Trail.) Follow the Haoe Lead Trail L for 0.8 mi along the ridgeline to a jct with a shortcut R of the Haoe Lead Trail and 0.1 mi farther for another jct of the Haoe Lead Trail, R, and the beginning of the Hangover Lead Trail, L, at Haoe Lookout (5,249 ft.) at 13.9 mi. (Here the Haoe Lead Trail goes down the mountain for 5.1 mi to Kilmer Rd.) The Hangover Lookout (the site of a former fire tower) has limited vistas. Proceed on the Hangover Lead Trail, descend easily to Saddle Tree Gap, and reach jct with the Deep Creek Trail, R, at 14.0 mi. (The Deep Creek Trail descends to join the Haoe Lead Trail described below.) Ahead at this point is a 0.3-mi dead-end spur to prominent rocks and cliffs for the most panoramic and spectacular viewing of the Slickrock Wilderness Area. Dense rhododendron landscapes the rocks. Back on the Hangover Lead Trail, descend in a forest of beech and birch to curve W of a knoll. Return to the ridge at 14.8 mi. Begin steep descent and enter a virgin hemlock forest at 15.2 mi. (Damp, often foggy, and dark serpentine-shaped roots in rhododendron thickets may offer the fantasy of a descent into the land of *The Hobbit.*) Begin a gradual descent at 15.4 mi, and follow the trail through oak, red- and green-striped maple, birch, sassafras, hemlock, and flame azalea to the edge of the ridge. At 15.8 mi is jct R with Locust Ridge Trail. It descends steeply 0.8 mi to FR-62, 0.9 mi E of Big Fat Gap. Descend steeply on six switchbacks at 16.6 mi and reach Big Fat Gap parking area at 16.8 mi. (The large public parking area is popular with both hikers and hunters.) To the L, the 1.5-mi. Big Fat Trail descends to connect with the Slickrock Creek Trail, and the 1.3-mi. Windy Gap Trail descends to the jct with Nichols Cove Trail. To the R, FR-62 winds down the mountain for 7.0 mi to US-129, 2.2 mi SE of Tapoco. Cross the parking area and ascend steeply on an old woods road into a hardwood forest with scattered conifers to the summit of Cold Spring Knob (3,480 ft.) at 17.2 mi. Follow the dry ridge on a moderate and gradual descent to the summit of Caney Ridge (2,800 ft.), which rises from the E, at 18.3 mi. Among hardwoods, huckleberry, and buckberry, descend to Yellowhammer Gap (2,520 ft.) and reach jct with Ike Branch Trail at 19.1 mi. Turn R, descend to the jct with Slickrock Creek Trail, turn R, and return to the parking area at US-129 at the Cheoah Dam bridge for a total loop of 21.4 mi. (USGS-FS Maps: Tapoco, Whiteoak Flats)

Kilmer Access: There are two road routes to the Kilmer section of the Kilmer/Slickrock Wilderness Area. One paved road entrance is from Robbinsville. Drive 1.0 mi W of Robbinsville on US-129, turn L on Massey Branch Rd (NC-143) toward the ranger station. At 4.3 mi, turn R on NC-143, pass the jct with the new Cherohala Skyway (also C-143) L at 12.2 mi, and descend to a crossroads with Santeetlah Rd (FR-416) at 13.4 mi. The Kilmer Memorial Forest and picnic area entrance road is L for 0.6 mi. The other route, 7.2 mi E of Tapoco on US-129, begins at the jct with Old US-129 (SR-1147). Drive 0.5

mi to Santeetlah Rd (SR-1134), which becomes FR-416 on a paved road, and reach the crossroads with SR-1127 at the entrance to the Kilmer picnic area after 6.0 mi.

Haoe Lead Trail (6.7 mi; USFS #53) (F)   **64-65**

Connecting Trails: Deep Creek Trail (3.9 mi; USFS #46); Jenkins Meadow Trail (3.3 mi; USFS #53A); (Hangover Lead Trail); (Slickrock Creek Trail); (Naked Ground Trail); (Stratton Bald Trail)

Length and Difficulty: 13.9 mi combined, moderate to strenuous

Special Features: Deep Creek cascades, Haoe Lookout area

Trailhead and Description: From the crossroads of Kilmer Rd and Santeetlah Rd, described above, drive up (W) Kilmer Rd (also called Wagon Train Rd, SR-1127) for 5.4 mi to a large parking area, R. Park here for entrance across the road to the Haoe Lead Trail. (Up the road it is 0.2 mi to the Maple   **66** Springs observation area and the cul-de-sac end of this previously controversial road that conservationists stopped from penetrating the Slickrock area. The Maple Springs Observation Trail (USFS #71) is a 220-yd. paved scenic loop [designed for wheelchair access] that provides N views of the Cheoah River Valley, Yellow Creek Mtn., and the Great Smoky Mtns.)

Ascend the graded Haoe Lead Trail (constructed by the YACC in 1979) in a forest of hardwoods and white pine. At 0.5 mi, reach a ridgeline and cross to the N slope in a rocky area. At 0.8 mi is water, L. Reach jct R at 1.1 mi with Deep Creek Trail.

Deep Creek Trail begins in a rocky area. Ferns are prominent with wildflowers that include umbrella-leaf *[Diphylleia cymosa]*, crested dwarf iris, black and blue cohosh, and twisted-stalk *[Streptopus roseus]*. Trees include basswood, hemlock, birch, and buckeye. Cross small streamlets, pass large rock formations at 0.7 and 1.1 mi. Pass a second-growth forest at 1.6 mi and reach cascading Deep Creek at 2.1 mi. Cross a footbridge to an old timber road and turn L. [To the R is the former entrance to the Deep Creek Trail, 2.5 mi downstream to FR-445, which forks from FR-62, the route to Big Fat Gap. Entrance remains possible on this route though sections are overgrown.] Ascend steadily into the Hudson Deaden Branch area through rhododendron, hemlock, and hardwoods, and more steeply on switchbacks to jct at 3.9 mi with the Hangover Lead Trail in Saddle Tree Gap [5,120 ft.], the boundary of the Kilmer/Slickrock Wilderness Area. (Heading R, it is 90 yd. to the fork where the Hangover Lead Trail goes L and a 0.2-mi spur route, R, ascends to panoramic views at Hangover Mtn. The L fork of Hangover Lead Trail ascends

0.2 mi to the Haoe Lookout [5,249 ft.] and the jct L with Haoe Lead Trail. A return can be made here on the Haoe Lead Trail for a total loop of 9.2 mi.)

To continue on the Haoe Lead Trail from the NE jct with the Deep Creek Trail, ascend steadily to Rock Creek Knob and follow W on the main ridgeline. Turn on a S slope, and at 3.3 mi, cross the Kilmer/Slickrock Wilderness boundary and reach jct with the N trailhead of Jenkins Meadow Trail at 3.6 mi.

(The Jenkins Meadow Trail, #54A, descends SE on a slope to join a ridgeline and wilderness boundary at 0.7 mi, and at 1.8 mi ends at a jct with Naked Ground Trail. It is another 0.9 mi L on the Naked Ground Trail to SR-1127.)

Continue on the Haoe Lead Trail up the slope and to the main ridgeline to a more level area known as Jenkins Meadow. Pass through dense groves of rhododendron and ascend steeply to Haoe Lookout at 5.1 mi and the jct with the Hangover Lead Trail, R. (From here a loop of 9.2 mi can be made by reversing the route described above for the Deep Creek Trail.) Continue L from the lookout, descend, follow narrow ridge crest at 5.6 mi, and at 6.0 mi arrive at the jct with Slickrock Creek Trail, R, and Naked Ground Trail, L. Ahead the Haoe Lead Trail ascends its final 0.5 mi to a jct with the Stratton Bald Trail and the boundary of the wilderness area at 6.5 mi. (To the R the Stratton Bald Trail goes 1.8 mi to the Fodderstack Trail, #95, in the Cherokee National Forest, and L it descends for 6.7 mi to SR-1127.) Backtrack, or use a connecting trail. (USGS-FS Maps: Big Junction, Santeetlah, Tapoco, or Joyce Kilmer/Slickrock Wilderness and Citico Creek Wilderness [Nantahala and Cherokee National Forests] trail map)

67-72 *Naked Ground Trail* (4.3 mi; USFS #55); *Naked Ground Alternate* (0.6 mi; USFS #55A); *Stratton Bald Trail* (8.2 mi; USFS #54) (F)

Connecting Trails: (Joyce Kilmer Loop Trail); (Jenkins Meadow Connector Trail); (Fodderstack Trail); (Haoe Lead Trail); (Slickrock Creek Trail); Wolf Laurel Trail (0.2 mi; USFS #57)

Length and Difficulty: 12.7 mi combined to include to and from Stratton Bald, strenuous (elev change 3,220 ft.)

Special Features: old growth forest, Stratton Bald, wildflowers

Trailhead and Description: These two trails can make a 13.5-mi loop that includes 0.8 mi of road walking. The Naked Ground Trail provides a study of the Little Santeetlah Creek drainage, and the second provides a major observation of Horse Cove Ridge high above the eastern flow of both the Little Santeetlah and Santeetlah Creeks. Park at either the space assigned at the Kilmer picnic area entrance on SR-1127 and Naked Ground Trail E trailhead or at the Rattler Ford Group Campground entrance across the bridge S of Stratton Bald Trail on SR-1127. It is 0.4 mi between the two parking options.

For the Naked Ground Trail trailhead, E, park at either the space assigned at the Kilmer picnic area on FR-416 (for day use), or at the entrance to the picnic area where SR-1127 and FR-416 intersect (for overnight use). This entrance is reached from Robbinsville at the jct of US-129 and W on NC-143 for 10 mi to Santeetlah Gap, where NC-143 goes L as the Cherohala Skyway and SR-1127 foes ahead and down the mountain 2.3 mi to the Kilmer entrance. If returning on the Stratton Bald Trail, the exit is 0.3 mi S on SR-1127 from the Kilmer entrance and is near a guardrail on the N side of the ridge over Santeetlah Creek at Rattler Ford Group Campground. Parking space is not available at the trailhead. (Day parking could be available in the nearby campground, but it is open for group reservations in-season only.)

The Naked Ground Trail enters the forest on a footbridge to jointly follow the Joyce Kilmer Loop Trail for a short section. After 0.3 mi there is a jct with the Jenkins Meadow Connector Trail, R. (It goes 0.9 mi NE to connect with the Jenkins Meadow Trail R and L). The forest has large yellow poplar, white pine, hemlock, red maple, and yellow buckeye with rhododendron, fern, and wildflowers in the understory. Ahead the Naked Ground Alternate Trail descends L to cross Little Santeetlah Creek, but it rejoins the main trial 0.6 mi upstream. Cross two streamlets and at 1.0 mi cross Indian Spring Branch. Cross Adamcamp Branch at 1.6 mi. Cross more streams in the deep hollow before beginning at 3.5 mi the final assent on 14 switchbacks, where yellow birch and flame azalea can be found. Arrive at Naked Ground Gap, the NW end of Naked Ground Trail at 4.3 mi and jct with Haoe Lead Trail, R and L. Across the gap is the S trailhead of Slickrock Creek Trail. This trail jct on the ridge is usually a popular campsite. A water source is nearby. (Heading R of the jct, NE, it is 1.4 mi to Hangover peak Hangover Lead Trail.)

To continue the loop, turn L and ascend 0.6 mi on the Haoe Lead Trail to its W end at the Stratton Bald Trail R and L. To the R, it is 0.7 mi to Bob Stratton Bald. The trail is rocky in sections and the hardwood tree growth is scrubby and gnarled among some conifers, grasses, and briars to an opening with outstanding views (elev 5,261 ft.). Beyond the bald, the trail passes through an open meadow after 0.6 mi; then another 0.4 mi to its W terminus at Fodderstack Trail. (The 12.6-mi Fodderstack Trail, for equestrian and hiker usage, flows a forest road mainly in the Citico Creek Wilderness of the Cherokee National Forest in Tennessee. Access to it is 2.9 mi from Beech Gap on NC-143 [Cherohaha Skyway], near the beginning of TN-165.)

For continuing the Stratton Bald Trail SE from end of Haoe Lead Trail, descend on Horse Cove Ridge with switchbacks. There is red oak, yellow birch, flame azalea, blue-beads, Indian cucumber-root *(Medeoa virginiana)*, and moosewood *(Viburnum alnifolium)*. At 1.2 mi is Wolf Laurel Trail, R. It descends 0.2 mi to an access at FR-81F. (To reach this access from the Kilmer entrance, drive 2.2 mi S on SR-1127 to the jct with NC-143 and FR-81 at Santeetlah Gap. Turn R on FR-81 [Santeetlah Creek Rd], a paved road, for part of the way, and after 6.7 mi turn R on FR-81F [Wolf Laurel Rd]. Ascend a steep gravel road [may need 4x4 wheel vehicle if road gravel is loose or erosion from bad weather] that later levels off for 4.8 mi to a parking area and gated dead-end.)

Continue to descend on the Horse Cove Ridge through sections of open oak forest where there is an understory of flame azalea, huckleberry, bloodroot, and mountain laurel in the 2.3-mi area. At 3.4 mi is a large rock overhang. Pass evidence of an old homestead at 5.2 mi, followed by a scenic forest slope at 5.4 mi. Cross a number of small streams at 6.0 mi and descend into a grove of hemlock, white pine, and smooth azalea *(Rhododendron arborescens)* and white honeysuckle to parallel Santeetlah Creek. Reach SR-1127 at 6.5 mi. To complete the loop, turn L and follow the road 0.3 mi to the parking area at Kilmer entrance, L. (USGS-FS Maps: Big junction, Santeetlah Creek, Tapoco)

73   *Joyce Kilmer Loop Trail (2.0 mi; USFS #43)*

Length and Difficulty: 2.0 mi combined, easy

Special Features: virgin forest, historic memorial

Trailhead and Description: From the parking area of the Joyce Kilmer Memorial Forest and picnic area at the end of FR-416 from SR-1127, follow the trail signs and ascend alongside cascading Little Santeetlah Creek to cross a footbridge. Log seats for rest and contemplation are along the national recreation trail in this primeval forest of mosses, rhododendron, hemlock, yellow poplar, fetterbush, trillium, cohosh, wood sorrel, and crested dwarf iris. At the jct with Poplar Cove Loop is a sign that indicates Alfred Joyce Kilmer was born in New Brunswick, New Jersey, December 6, 1886, and killed in action in France, July 30, 1918. The grove of yellow poplar is the most spectacular feature on the trails; many are 16-to-22 ft. in circumference and over 120-ft. tall. Cross another footbridge over Little Santeetlah Creek on the return loop to the parking lot. (USGS-FS Map: Santeetlah Creek)

Cherohala Skyway Area (Graham County)

Eighteen mi of the 43-mi Cherohala Skyway (NC-143) is in the Nantahala National Forest from Santeetlah Gap (10 mi W of Robbinsville) to Beech Gap, and the Cherokee National Forest in Tennessee at Tellico Plains. The state maintains the Skyway and the USFS maintains the picnic areas, trails, restrooms and other amenities. In North Carolina, the winding highway has at least 14 stops of which some have trailheads for short trails and others for access to longer trails. Some trails are constructed for disabled visitors.

Accesses and Addresses: From Robbinsville, drive N 1.0 mi to L on NC-143. Follow the signs for 9.0 mi to Santeetlah Gap and turn L. From Tellico Plains in Tennessee, drive E on TN-165 to enter NC at Beech Gap. For more information, contact Cherokee National Forest, Tellico Ranger Station, 250 Ranger Station Rd, Tellico Plains, TN 37385; 423-253-2521; Monroe county sheriff: 423-442-3911. (See chapter introduction for Cheoah Ranger Station in NC.)

Wright Trail (0.4 mi, easy) (F). From Skyway entrance at Santeetlah Gap, **74** drive W 5.6 mi to Wright Cove, R (elev 4,150 ft.). Easily descend on a professionally designed trail to a loop and go R or L. The forest has large hardwoods such as maple, undercover shrubs such as moosewood, a wide variety of ferns, and wildflowers such as white snake root.

Spirit Ridge Trail (0.7 mi round-trip, easy) (F). From Wright Cove, drive **75** W 2.8 mi to parking area, L (elev 4,950 ft.). This trail through hardwoods leads to outstanding views of the surrounding mountain ranges.

Huckleberry Trail (1.6 mi round-trip, moderate) (F). From Spirit Ridge **76** Trail, drive W 0.8 mi R (elev 5,300 ft.). Follow an old road through a grassy field of wildflowers and clover to a low knob at 0.4 mi. Continue into a slight descent, then ascend through a forest to panoramic Little Huckleberry Knob at 0.8 mi. Near the top is a white cross at the grave of Andy Sherman, one of two lumberjacks who became lost and froze to death near the mountain on December 11, 1899. Their remains were found nine months later by a deer hunter, Rorrest Denton. The skeleton of another lumberjack, Paul O'Neal, was presented by a jury to Dr. Robert Orr for a medical exhibit.

Hooper Bald Trail (1.0 mi round-trip, easy) (F) From Huckleberry Trail, **77** drive W 1.1 mi, L (elev 5,204 ft.). At signs follow a gravel trail through a forest, cross a private road at 0.1 mi, and arrive on a grassy bald at 0.5 mi to the R is a rock, the high point. Near this site George Moore had a hunting preserve of imported exotic animals at the turn of the twentieth century. At the parking area is a restroom, information kiosk, and the N trailhead of King

Meadows Trail. Connecting access is also here for Mitchell Lick Trail, Big Snowbird Trail, and Snowbird Mtn. Trail. (USGS-FS Maps: Santeetlah Creek, Big Junction)

Snowbird Mountain Area

78-83 *Big Snowbird Trail* (10.7 mi; USFS #64) (F)

Connecting Trails: Snowbird Mountain Trail (10.6 mi; USFS #415); Sassafras Creek Trail (2.5 mi; USFS #65); Middle Falls Trail (1.0 mi; USFS #64A); Burntrock Ridge Trail (1.7 mi; USFS #65A); Mitchell Lick Trail (1.5 mi; USFS #154)

Length and Difficulty: 26.3 mi combined, moderate to strenuous (elev change 2,739 ft.)

Special Features: RR history, remote, waterfalls

Trailhead and Description: Three major trails begin at Junction, the end of FR-75, deep in the enchanting backcountry of the Snowbird Mtns. The Big Snowbird Trail follows Snowbird Creek up and through the watershed for a gain of 2,600 ft. to Big Junction at the Tennessee state line. The Snowbird Mountain Trail rejoins the Big Snowbird Trail near the top of the basin but follows S on a high ridge route. King Meadows Trail also follows a high ridge route but is N of the basin; it ends near Hooper Bald after a 2,700-ft. elev gain and can be connected with the other two trails by the 1.5-mi Mitchell Lick Trail. These trails provide loop options, but scarce water sources on the ridges limit convenient campsites. A rugged and remote area, it was once the home of Cherokee who found security here from the "Trail of Tears." Early white pioneers prospected for minerals and set up scattered grazing farms, but it was the timbering of the virgin forests of chestnut, yellow poplar, and hemlock from 1928 to 1942 that severely altered the environment. Now healing from the scars of the Buffalo-Snowbird RR, hikers will see historic signs of both the old RR and pioneer life on the high plateaus.

Access: From the jct of US-129 and Kilmer Rd (SR-1127) in Robbinsville, go 3.3 mi to a jct with Massey Branch Rd (SR-1116), from which it is 2.3 mi R to Cheoah district office; bear L at the fork on SR-1127 for 2.2 mi to a jct with Little Snowbird Rd (SR-1115). Turn L on SR-1115 and go another 2.2 mi to jct with Hard Slate Rd (SR-1121). Turn a sharp L at the jct and continue for 1.0 mi to a bridge over Snowbird Creek. Look for Dead End sign and One Way sign on R at bridge over Little Snowbird Creek. This is Big Snowbird Rd (SR-1120), which becomes FR-75. Proceed on this gravel road for 6.0 mi to the Junction parking area, a total of 13.7 mi from Robbinsville and 12.7 mi from Cheoah district office.

Begin the trail on an old RR grade that crosses a number of earthen hummocks and goes under large yellow poplars and maples. At 0.2 mi, Snowbird Mountain Trail begins on the L. Continue on the Big Snowbird Trail on the old RR grade and L of cascading Snowbird Creek. The understory is composed of rhododendron, wild hydrangea, and sweet pepperbush; the forest trees are hemlock, birch, basswood, yellow poplar, and cucumber tree. At 2.8 mi, reach the jct of Sassafras Creek Trail, L, 250 yd. beyond Sassafras Creek. (This trail is an alternate to the Big Snowbird Trail. If you choose this one, ascend on an old RR grade for 0.7 mi to Sassafras Falls. After 0.1 mi beyond the falls, leave the old RR grade and turn R on Burntrock Ridge Trail. It goes 1.7 mi to a jct with Big Snowbird Trail. [An old trail continues upstream and forks after 0.1 mi, the L going up Fall Branch for 1.0 mi, the other, Sassafras Creek Trail, up Sassafras Creek for 2.2 mi, and both to a jct with the Snowbird Mountain Trail. Both may be abandoned and unmaintained.] Climb steeply on Burntrock Ridge Trail to Burnt Rock Ridge at 2.0 mi, descend to the mouth of Littleflat Branch, and rejoin Big Snowbird Trail at 2.5 mi.)

Continuing on Big Snowbird Trail and on an old RR grade, pass L of Big Falls at 3.9 mi. Reach an alternate trail, Middle Falls Trail, at 4.0 mi. (This trail, R, near Mouse Knob Branch, ascends steeply for 0.2 mi, and then descends gradually to the Big Snowbird Trail after 1.0 mi. It is an alternate that avoids 11 fordings of Snowbird Creek, which may be impossible to cross during high water.) If continuing on the Big Snowbird Trail, cross the creek frequently and arrive at beautiful Middle Falls and its large pool at 5.1 mi. At 5.3 mi, the Burntrock Ridge Trail jct is L, at the mouth of Littleflat Branch.

After a few yards, Middle Falls Trail rejoins Big Snowbird Trail, R. The Big Snowbird Trail continues to Upper Falls at 6.3 mi. Follow the trail past Meadow Branch, Rockbar Branch, a number of unnamed tributaries, Bearpen Branch, and two more tributaries before leaving the main stream, L, at 8.7 mi. Ascend steeply to a jct with Mitchell Lick Trail at 9.0 mi. (Mitchell Lick Trail is a 1.5-mi connector to King Meadows Trail described later.) Follow the Big Snowbird Trail L, and at 9.3 mi, reach jct with Snowbird Mountain Trail, L. (The Snowbird Mountain Trail is described later.) The final 1.4 mi of the Big Snowbird Trail to Big Junction may be overgrown. (Check with the district ranger's office about the trail's condition.) Continue the ascent along the Graham/Cherokee county line to the ridge top, the Tennessee–North Carolina boundary, and turn R at 9.8 mi. Follow the ridge NE, ascend to a knob and then to scenic Laurel

Top (5,317 ft.) at 10.3 mi. At 10.7 mi, reach the end of the trail at Big Junction at Cherohala Skyway. It is 11.5 mi NE to a jct with SR-1127 at Santeetlah Gap. A turn R (SE) on SR-1127 to SR-1115 and to FR-75 is about another 16.0 mi to the trail's origin as described. (See access as described previously.) Backtrack, return on one of the other two major trails, or arrange a vehicle switch to the Cherohala Skyway (NC-143) at Hooper Bald parking area.

To hike the green-blazed Snowbird Mountain Trail, begin at the Big Snowbird Trail, L, 0.2 mi from Junction (as described previously). On a graded trail cross two streams lined with birch, yellow poplar, sassafras, spicebush *(Linders benzoin),* hemlock, rhododendron, and violets. Pass Wildcat Branch Cove and reach Deep Gap (3,340 ft.) at 1.3 mi. Turn R, ascend to Wildcat Knob on Sassafras Ridge at 2.5 mi, and continue to descend and ascend over and around knolls. At 3.2 mi is a USGS benchmark on a knoll (3,830 ft.) and an old trail intersection (R to Snowbird Creek and L to Juanita Branch). At 5.0 mi, reach Bee Gap (4,040 ft.), where a faint trail, R, descends along Falls Branch to Sassafras Falls and the Sassafras Creek Trail. Continue traversing on gradual and sometimes steep grades through scattered grassy fields, hardwoods, laurel, flame azalea, and rhododendron. At 6.7 mi, pass an old trail (Sassafras Creek Trail, which may be abandoned) R that leads 2.2 mi down Sassafras Creek to Sassafras Creek Trail and Burntrock Ridge Trail at Sassafras Falls. Ascend to Pantherflat Top (4,680 ft.) at 8.5 mi and dip to a gap before ascending Dillard Top (4,680 ft.) at 9.0 mi. The trail's end and a jct with Big Snowbird Trail is at 10.6 mi. Return options include backtracking or descending on Big Snowbird Trail for 9.3 mi to make a 20-mi loop to Junction parking area or taking Mitchell Lick Trail to a jct with King Meadows Trail for 1.8 mi and a loop back to Junction for 18.4 mi. Another option is to turn L (N) on King Meadows Trail for 0.4 mi to Hooper Bald Trail and parking area at Cherohala Skyway NC-143. (See later.) (USGS-FS Maps: Big Junction, Marble, McDaniel Bald, Santeetlah Creek) (Snowbird Area Trail Map, from the district ranger's office, is recommended.)

84 *King Meadows Trail* (USFS #63) (F)

Length and Difficulty: 6.0 mi, strenuous (elev change 2,740 ft.)

Connecting Trail: (Mitchell Lick Trail)

Trailhead and Description: This yellow-blazed trail may be overgrown for the first 3.0 mi. (On some maps the entrance trailhead for King Meadows Trail and parts of its route from FR-75 in Junction may be different from the description later.) At the end of FR-75, at Junction, follow the Big Snowbird

Trail, pass the jct with the Snowbird Mountain Trail, L, at 0.2 mi, and go upstream for another 0.2 mi to a jct with the King Meadows Trail, R. (There may not be any signs here.) Cross Snowbird Creek and begin the ascent of Firescald Ridge (L of Owlcamp Branch). At 1.0 mi, reach the ridge of the Snowbird Creek Divide in a hardwood forest. Continue the ascent, and at 1.9 mi make a long curve around a high knoll to reach Deep Gap (also known as Twin Oaks Gap) at 2.8 mi. Intersect with an old sled road, R and ahead, that was used by early settlers of the mountain plateaus. Continue ahead, ascend steeply, curve around Bee Knob, and arrive at King Meadows at 3.7 mi at the E knob. Pass through a partially grassy area formerly cleared of trees by early settlers. Ascend for 1.1 mi, leave the ridge, and pass over a saddle in the main curve around Queen Ridge at 5.1 mi. Enter a small gap and ascend to a more level area and reach jct with Mitchell Lick Trail, L, at 6.1 mi. (The Mitchell Lick Trail, an old jeep road, connects to the Snowbird trails described above. It descends to cross Sarvis Branch at 0.4 mi, follows Flat Ridge before descending to cross Snowbird Creek in a forest of hemlock and hardwoods and reaches Big Snowbird Trail at 1.5 mi.) Ahead on the King Meadows Trail, it is 0.4 mi to Hooper Bald (5,429 ft.), the trail's end, and a jct with Hooper Bald Trail. Exit at the Cherohala Skyway (NC-143). Backtrack, or have a second vehicle. It is approximately 10.3 mi NE on the highway to SR-1127 at Santeetlah Gap. A turn R (SE) on SR-1127 to SR-1115 and to FR-75 is about another 16.0 mi to trail's origin. (See access above.) (USGS-FS Maps: Santeetlah Creek, Big Junction)

Support Facilities: The nearest USFS campground (no hookups) is Horse Cove, across from the entrance to the Joyce Kilmer Memorial Forest. It is 7.2 mi W on Kilmer Rd (SR-1127) from the jct with Little Snowbird Rd (SR-1115). Motels, shopping centers, restaurants, and other services are available in Robbinsville.

Highlands Ranger District

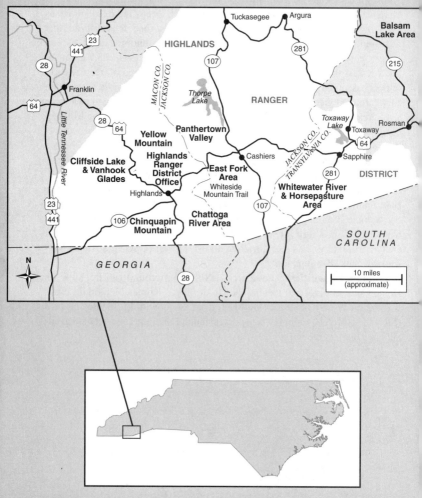

Introductions to Trail Areas

Trails in this district are first described west/southwest of Highlands, then southeast to Upper Whitewater Falls. The other trials are N/NE of Highlands all the way to the Blue Ridge Parkway. This is the land of waterfalls.

Highlands Ranger District Office
The office is 4 mi E of the town of Highlands, and it also has an information office in downtown Highlands. Here is a wealth of books, maps, souvenirs, and visitor assistance.

Mountains-to-Sea Trail
From the Blue Ridge Parkway, this 14.9 mi of the 967-mi state park dips into the district from Old Bald Knob (between mp 435–434) and Hayworth Gap (between mp 427–426).

Cliffside Lake and Vanhook Glade Recreation Area *58*
This area has picnicking, fishing, swimming, and hiking to waterfalls.

Chinquapin Mountain, Glen Falls, and West Blue Valley *59*
Here are scenic mountain peaks and more rock-hopping to waterfalls, plus a connector trail to the Bartram Trail that comes from South Carolina and Georgia to Cheoah Bald.

Chattoga River Area *61*
At this famous river are challenging and beautiful trails into the Ellicott Wilderness Area, where there are roaring waterfalls and black bears, all near the NC/SC boundary.

Whitewater River and Horsepasture River Areas *64*
North Carolina's highest waterfall and likely the most photographed is here. Spectacular scenery frames the gorge rim and steps to the river below. Nearby is access to the Foothills Trail, a spectacular trail in both of the Carolinas, where Turtlehead and Rainbow Falls are located.

Yellow Mountain Area *66*
Take in scenic views from multiple peaks to Yellow Mt. Summit (5,127 ft.), which reveals fantastic views.

East Fork Area *67*
A national recreation trail, this routing is near the precipitous edges of sheep cliffs (4,930 ft.) on a granite landmark.

Panthertown Valley and Bonas Defeat Areas *68*
In a labyrinth of unique trails, there are waterfalls, coves, cliffs, upland bogs, and river sculptured rocks.

Balsam Lake Area *73*
Here is a retreat for any age: A reclusive lodge with three scenic trails (easy for the physically disabled), fishing, and nature study.

SECTION 2: HIGHLANDS RANGER DISTRICT

The Highlands Ranger District almost doubled its size when the 40,000-acre Balsam–Bonas Defeat lands were acquired in 1981 and named the Roy Taylor Forest in 1982. A scenic observation overlook in his honor is at mp 433.8 on the BRP and another memorial on Charley Creek in Roy Taylor Forest. Congress appropriated $13.4 million for the purchase, identified by the USFS as probably the largest single holding suitable for the forest system in the eastern part of the nation. The new property, all in Jackson County, adjoins the Blue Ridge Parkway on the NE boundary of the district. Mead Lake and a small part of Wolf Creek Lake, 90 mi of streams, and eight waterfalls are in the tract. Headwaters of Tanasee Creek, Wolf Creek, Caney Fork, and Moses Creek drain into the scenic Tuckasegee River from high ridges such as Rich Mtn. and Coward Mtn. Among the peaks that are about a mile high are Coward Bald (5,187 ft.), Gage Bald (5,574 ft.), Charley Bald (5,473 ft.), and Rich Mtn. (5,583 ft.).

In 1988 the Panthertown Valley tract was purchased for $8 million. Its 6,295 acres extend SW of the Bonas Defeat Area to include the headwaters of the Tuckasegee River and to the rim of Blue Ridge, a high range of the Tennessee Valley Divide. Owned by Liberty Life Insurance Company, the tract was placed on sale in 1986 without a buyer until Duke Power Company purchased it in 1988. Duke Power sold it to The Nature Conservancy with the exclusion of a transmission power corridor from the NW to the SE. Negotiations followed with congressional approval of the addition to the Nantahala National Forest.

A wider range of the district's 116,435 acres is in the SE corner of Macon County. Its boundaries extend to the Georgia state line and the Chattahoochee National Forest, and the South Carolina state line and the Sumter National Forest. Its western border is with the Wayah district, but E of Franklin. The 3.394-acre Ellicott Rock Wilderness Area in NC covers a rugged and beautiful area of the Chattooga River in a tri-state tract. Some of the state's major waterfalls are in the district. They include the highest, 411-ft. Whitewater Falls; Dry Falls; Cullasaja Falls; Rainbow Falls; Glen Falls; and Flat Creek Falls. A major mountain attraction is Whiteside Mtn. (4,930 ft.), 5.0 mi E of Highlands. Its sheer rock face is considered to be among the highest in eastern America. Another scenic mountain is Yellow Mtn. (5,127 ft.) with abundant wildflowers and blueberries. The district's major trail is the Bartram, which enters from Georgia S of Osage Mtn. and ascends to the high country of Scaly Mtn., Whiterock Mtn., and Fishhawk Mtn. before descending to Hickory Knoll Creek. The district's major recreational areas are Cliffside Lake and Vanhook Glade Campground (open April 1–October 31, no hookups), 4.5 mi W of Highlands on US-64. Camping is prohibited at Whiteside, Cullasaja Gorge, Cliffside, Whitewater Falls, and Balsam Lodge.

The district has about 195 mi on at least 80 official trails to serve a wide range of users. The diversity includes 16 trails in an ORV compound, 47 for hikers only, 22 for bicyclists and equestrians (5 of which are multiple use), and three trails for those with physical disabilities, according to the 2002 National Geographic Trails Illustrated Map #785. As in other districts, some trails originate as social trails, those made by hunters, anglers, botanists, hikers, and visitors exploring the forest. If frequently used, they may become designated with an official number. One busy trail not listed with such a number is Horsepasture River Trail, but the USFS has made an effort to provide it with off-road parking and safer routing. Other examples of social trails are Chattooga Access Trail (USFS #434), a short descent at the E end of the Chattoga River bridge on Bull Pen Rd; Granite City Trail (USFS #475, a short steep climb up and into a labyrinth of rocks with caves and fissures harboring ghosts and goblins on Whiteside Cove Rd, L, 1.2 mi N from jct with Bull Pen Rd; and School House Falls Trail (USFS # 452), a double-side short crawl and scramble through rhododendron from Greenland Creek Trail in Panthertown Valley. (Parents are advised to accompany children on these trails.) A few trails are so popular that the district charges admission. A daily parking fee of $2 is required at Dry Falls, Whiteside Mtn., and Upper Whitewater River Falls. One ticket may be used for all three if used the same day.

Hunting and fishing are allowed in the district, except the fishing season is closed from March 1 to first Saturday in April for stocked waters. Panthertown Valley is a bear sanctuary. Mountain biking is allowed on specific trails in Panthertown Valley, Round Mtn., Little Yellow Mtn. Gap, Blue Valley, Stewart Cove, Moss Knob, and Brush Creek. Wilderness is off-limits to bikers, but all gated forest roads are available unless otherwise posted. Equestrians may contact the district office for both special trails and regular multi-use hiking trails. There is a specific location—Wayehutta ORV Section—NE of Cullowhee for ORVs and motorcycles. Special trails for the physically disabled are at Balsam Lake and Lodge, Whitewater Falls, and the fishing pier at Cliffside. The district's foot trail system does not have blazes except the Bartram, Mountains-to-Sea, and Foothills Trails. There are 14.8 mi of the Mountain-to-Sea Trail (MST) in the district. (See appendix A.)

There are not signs at all trailheads, but some trail networks have map display boards. The district has re-routed some trails, and at least 16 trails on its inventory are either overgrown or in a planning stage of maintenance. The district has 19.6 mi of the Bartram Trail (USFS #67) from FR-52 W to Buckeye Creek Rd. In addition, there are spur trails on Scaly Mountain Trail Rd (0.8 mi, USFS #67A) and Jones Knob Trail (0.3 mi, USFS #67B). (See Bartram Trail description at the beginning of this chapter.) It has 14.6 mi of the Mountains-to-Sea Trail (USFS #440) from Old Bald Ridge at the BRP boundary E to BRP boundary at Haywood Gap. It has an additional access by the Bearpen Gap Trail (0.7 mi; USFS #442) from the parking area of Bearpen Gap on the BRP. (See Mountains-to-Sea Trail in chapter 16.)

Address and Access: District Ranger, Highlands Ranger District, USFS, 2010 Flat Mtn. Rd, Highlands, NC 28741; 828-526-3765, 2.0 mi E from Highlands on US-64 and on Flat Mtn. Rd (N) 2.0 mi.

Cliffside Lake and Vanhook Glade Recreation Areas
(Macon County)

Cliffside Lake and Vanhook Glade recreation areas provide picnicking, fishing, swimming, nature study, and hiking on interconnecting trails. Vegetation in the area includes a mature forest of hemlock, white pine, oak, maple, rhododendron, buckberry, and numerous species of wildflowers. Fish are chiefly rainbow and brook trout. In 1995 a fishing pier opened for the physically disabled at Cliffside. (USGS-FS Map: Highlands)

Access: In Highlands at the jct of US-64 and NC-28, proceed NW on US-64/NC-28 for 4.4 mi to the Cliffside entrance. Go 1.4 mi on FR-57. The Vanhook Glade Campground is on the highway 0.2 mi before the Cliffside entrance.

87-89   *Clifftop Vista Trail* (1.5 mi; USFS #2A); *Potts Memorial Trail* (0.5 mi; USFS #2B); *Clifftop Nature Trail* (1.1 mi USFS #2F); *Vanhook Trail* (0.3 mi; USFS #2C) (F)

Length and Difficulty: 3.4 mi combined, easy to moderate

Trailhead and Description: From the parking area at Cliffside Lake, go W on the road across Skitty Creek for a few yards, where the Clifftop Vista Trail begins at a sign. Go either R or L to the summit of the ridge. If R, pass or take as a side trail the Potts Memorial Trail to a white-pine plantation. Continue in a circular direction and reach a gazebo at 1.8 mi, where views are provided of Flat Mtn. and the Cullasaja River basin (and the Highlands Sewage

Plant). Here is a jct with the Clifftop Nature Trail that goes R or L. To the R, the trail ends at FR-57, 0.4 mi from the Vanhook Glade Campground. To the L, it winds down the mountain on switchbacks to the point of origin at the parking area. The trail passes through trees and shrubs in a mixed hardwood forest with an understory of sourwood, buckberry, sweet pepperbush *(Clethra acuminata),* and dogwood. The Vanhook Trail is a connector trail from the Vanhook Glade Campground for 0.3 mi NW to FR-57 and another 0.6 mi on the road to Cliffside Lake.

Cliffside Loop Trail (0.8 mi; USFS #2); ***Homesite Road Trail*** (1.4 mi;   **90-92**
USFS #443); ***Skitty Creek Trail*** (0.3 mi; USFS #2E) (F)
    Length and Difficulty: 2.5 mi combined, easy
    Trailhead and Description: From the parking area at Cliffside Lake, walk to the loop on the road and circle the lake, or join the Homesite Road Trail for a longer hike. At the Cliffside Lake Dam, follow Skitty Creek for a few yards before turning E through a hardwood forest. At an old road on which there are private homes, turn R and reach a gate at 1.4 mi at US-64. Dry Falls is R, 0.4 mi on US-64, and Bridal Veil Falls is L, 0.4 mi on US-64. Backtrack, or follow US-64, R (NW) for 0.2 mi to Skitty Creek Trail, R, and return via FR-57 to the lake area.

Dry Falls Trail (USFS #9) (F)   **93**
    Length and Difficulty: 0.1 mi, easy
    Trailhead and Description: From the parking area on US-64/NC-28 (1.0 mi E of the Cliffside Lake entrance), follow the signs and descend to the 70-ft. waterfall with a trail running underneath. Rare plants are in the area, watered by a constant mist from the updraft in the Cullasaja Gorge (in Cherokee "cullasaja" means honey or sugar water). The surrounding stone is schist and gneiss, between 500 million and 800 million years old.

Chinquapin Mountain and Glen Falls Area (Macon County)
Chinquapin Mountain Trail (3.2-mi round-trip; USFS #3); ***Glen***   **94-95**
Falls Trail (2.8-mi round-trip; USFS #8) (F)
    Length and Difficulty: 6.0 mi combined, moderate to strenuous
    Trailhead and Description: From the jct of US-64 and NC-28/106 in Highlands, go SW on NC-106 for 1.7 mi to a sign for Glen Falls Scenic Area. Turn L and proceed on a gravel road for 1.0 mi to the parking area. Follow the Chinquapin Trail sign; bear R at the fork with Glen Falls Trail. Descend, cross

East Fork a number of times, and pass through hardwoods, conifers, and rhododendron. Rock-hopping is necessary at some of the stream crossings. At 0.5 mi, reach a jct with other access points from NC-106. Ascend gradually on switchbacks, pass a spur trail to views of Blue Valley, and reach the summit of Chinquapin Mtn. (4,160 ft.) at 1.6 mi. Backtrack. (Or continue along the top of the ridge and start to descend. At a T intersection and sign, turn R and make a short loop before intersecting with trail up Chinquapin Mtn. There are not any blazes but several signs directing hikers to scenic overlooks and the trail back to Glen Falls parking area.)

For the Glen Falls Trail, follow the same directions as above to the parking area. Enter the trail by following gray blazes and bear L. (To the R is the Chinquapin Mountain Trail.) Descend steeply through mixed hardwoods past three major cascades. Spur trails lead to impressive views from the main trail. Descend to FR-79C, Blue Valley Rd, at 1.4 mi. Return by the same route, or use a second vehicle placed on Blue Valley Rd, off NC-28, near the Georgia state line. (It is SR-1618 before it becomes FR-79C). (USGS-FS Map: Highlands)

West Blue Valley Area (Macon County)

96-97   *West Fork Trail* (0.9 mi; USFS #444); *Hurrah Ridge Trail* (0.6 mi; USFS #4) (F)

Length and Difficulty: 1.9-mi combined round-trip, moderate

Trailhead and Description: These two nonblazed spur trails form a loop with the yellow-blazed Bartram Trail (BT). From the US-64 and NC-28 jct in Highlands, take NC-28 S 6.0 mi to Blue Valley Rd (SR-1618), which becomes FR-79. Turn R on SR-1618 and go 6.0 mi to West Fork of Overflow Creek to park. Begin with the West Fork Trail on the R before crossing Overflow Creek; ascend on a rocky and frequently wet trail for 0.9 mi to the Bartram Trail. (On the Bartram Trail, R, it is 0.7 mi to Osage Mtn. Overlook at NC-106.) Turn L on the Bartram Trail and go 0.4 mi. Turn L again on Hurrah Ridge Trail. (The Bartram Trail continues on for 2.9 mi to Hale Ridge Rd, FR-7.) Descend on the Hurrah Ridge Trail through a dry area with mixed hardwoods and hemlock, and cross Overflow Creek to the parking area. Other vegetation on the trail is rhododendron, laurel, white pine, ferns, and wildflowers. (See introduction to Nantahala National Forest chapter 2, section 1.) (USGS-FS Maps: Highlands, Scaly Mtn.)

Chattooga River Area (Jackson and Macon Counties)

Bad Creek Trail (3.1 mi; USFS #6); ***Fork Mountain Trail*** (6.4 mi) (F) **98-99**

Length and Difficulty: 12.6-mi combined round-trip; easy to strenuous

Connecting Trails: (Ellicott Rock Trail); (Chattooga Trail); (East Fork Trail)

Special Features: Ellicott Wilderness Area, historic markers

Trailhead and Description: From the jct of US-64 and NC-28 in High-lands, drive SE on Main St, which becomes Horse Cove Rd (SR-1603) for 4.6 mi down the mountain to the end of the pavement and a jct with Bull Pen Rd (SR-1178). Turn R and go 3.0 mi to the bridge over the Chattooga River and continue for 2.7 mi to a small parking area and signboard for Bad Creek Trail, R. (The Ellicott Wilderness Area is now 100 ft. from Bull Pen Rd.) Follow the faded-brown-blazed trail through a forest of hemlock, white pine, and laurel on an old forest road. Cross a stream at 0.2 mi and enter a rhododendron grove. Turn R at 0.6 mi, reach a ridge crest at 0.8 mi, curve L on the ridge slope, but return to the ridge at 1.3 mi. Reach the former Ellicott Wilderness Area boundary at 1.4 mi. Turn R from an old road to a foot trail in beds of galax and huckleberry. At 1.8 mi, the Chattooga River is audible; reach jct with the Fork Mountain Trail at 1.9 mi, L. Continue ahead and descend on 10 switchbacks to a grove of large hemlock by the Chattooga River at 3.0 mi. (Here is a jct with the E terminus of Ellicott Rock Trail requiring a river ford-ing.) Proceed downstream for 0.1 mi to Ellicott Rock where a simple "NC" has been chiseled. Commissioner Rock is 10 ft. downstream, the true inter-section of NC, GA, and SC. Carved on this rock is "LAT 35 AD 1813 NC+SC." Both rocks are named for surveyors who first surveyed the state lines. Backtrack, or continue downstream in SC on the Chattooga Trail for 1.8 mi to a jct with East Fork Trail, which ends at the Walhalla Fish Hatchery after 2.4 mi.

The Fork Mountain Trail (also known as Sloan Bridge Trail) leaves the Bad Creek Trail in NC but after 265 yd. enters SC and follows a well-graded trail that weaves in and out of more than 20 coves and as many spur ridges. Blazed a rust color, it follows a S-side slope in hardwoods and laurel. Cross a small stream at 0.5 mi and at approx. 0.8 mi reenter NC. Pass a rock for-mation at 1.0 mi, and at 1.2 and 1.4 mi cross the dual forks of Bad Creek where the rocks are moss covered, the hemlocks tall, and the fetterbush thick. Pass a huge yellow poplar at 1.5 mi (near the reentry to SC) and another large poplar at 2.0 mi. Indian pipe and pink lady slippers are along the trail. Cross an old woods road at 2.5 mi and a ridge crest at 3.0 mi. Enter an arbor of laurel at 3.3 mi for 0.3 mi. Pass through a fern glen in an open forest and enter a grove of exceptionally large hemlocks and poplars to cross Indian Camp Branch at 3.9 mi. At 5.2 mi, cross a ridge into a beautiful open forest of hardwoods. Cross Slatten Branch at 5.7 mi near good campsites. Walk through an unforgettable virgin grove of rhododendron and laurel and cross more small streams. Arrive at SC-107 at 6.4 mi. It is 0.1 mi, R, across the East Fork of the Chattooga River bridge to the Sloan Bridge picnic area. (At the E corner of the picnic area is the Foothills Trail described below.) If using a second vehicle for the return to the Bad Creek Trail entrance in NC, drive N on SC-107 for 1.7 mi and turn L on Bull Pen Rd (SR-1100) for 2.6 mi. (It is 6.3 mi on SC/NC-107 N to Cashiers.) (USGS-FS Map: Cashiers)

100 *Slick Rock Trail* (USFS #11) (F)
     Length and Difficulty: 0.2-mi round-trip, easy
     Trailhead and Description: Follow the directions given above from Highlands, stay R on Bull Pen Rd (SR/FR-1178), go 0.7 mi, and park on a narrow road shoulder, R. An unmarked trail ascends for 0.1 mi to a large rock formation with scenic views W into the Chattooga River basin. A wide variety of mosses and lichens grow in the apertures. This scenic spot was the site for the filming of *The Mating Game*. (USGS-FS Map: Highlands)

101 *Ellicott Rock Trail* (USFS #431) (F)
     Length and Difficulty: 7.0-mi round-trip, moderate
     Special Feature: Ellicott Wilderness Area
     Trailhead and Description: From Highlands follow the directions given above, stay R on Bull Pen Rd (SR/FR-1178), and go 1.7 mi. (Pass primitive Ammons campsite on the R at 1.1 mi.) Turn R onto a parking spur with a trail sign. Hike an old road with an even grade for a gradual descent to Ellicott Rock Wilderness Area boundary at 2.0 mi. The trail begins as a set of steps to discourage ATVs because motorized vehicles and mountain biking in wilderness areas are prohibited. The forest is mainly hardwoods with mixed sections of hemlock. At 3.0 mi bear L off the old road, descend steeply, and reach the Chattooga River at 3.5 mi. (There are two descents into the gorge. The straight, longer trail is recommended. The shorter trail, L, has a number of large deadfalls.) To locate Ellicott Rock, pass a survey marker for the North Carolina–South Carolina–Georgia state boundaries, ford the river (wading is always necessary, and impossible during high water), and go downstream for approximately 0.1 mi. Exploratory trails in the area can be confusing and another rock, Commissioner Rock (10 ft. downstream from Ellicott Rock), is

the true boundary jct of the three states. Commissioner Rock bears the inscription "LAT 35 AD 1813 NC+SC." Both of these rocks were named for early surveyors of the state lines. (See Bad Creek Trail above.) The vegetation in this area is mixed hardwoods with scattered pine, hemlock, and thick rhododendron. Backtrack, or hike out on the 3.1-mi Bad Creek Trail described above. (USGS-FS Maps: Highlands, Cashiers)

Chattooga River Trail (3.5 mi; USFS #432); *Chattooga River Loop Trail* (1.0 mi; USFS #433)

102-103

Length and Difficulty: 1.7 mi (loop); 3.5 mi (linear); moderate

Trailhead and Description: None of these trails is the same as the Chattooga Trail in SC and GA downstream. To access the trails, follow the directions given above from Highlands, turn R on Bull Pen Rd (SR/FR-1178) at the paved end of Horse Cove Rd (and Whiteside Cove Rd (SR-1606), and drive 3.0 mi to park at the one-way Chattooga River bridge (also called Bull Pen Bridge and Iron Bridge). Enter the trail by an information board and sign honoring the YCC. To the R, the cascading river has huge boulders, large potholes, sandbars, and pools. Trees on the trail are oak, maple, white pine, beech, and hemlock. There are two species of rhododendron. Ascend among dense forest understory. Cross a small stream at 0.4 mi and reach a jct, L, with the Chattooga River Loop Trail at 0.7 mi.

Continue upriver, cross Holly Branch at 1.3 mi. Cross a bridge (lowered by helicopter) over Cane Creek at 1.7 mi and a spur access trail L. (The 1.2-mi access trail follows an old road for moderate walking among ferns and wildflowers to a ridge and saddle at Whiteside Cove Rd [SR-1606]. On the road, it is 0.8 mi L, SW, to the jct with Bull Pen Rd and Horse Cove Rd. On the R, NE, it is 2.7 mi to the Chattooga River Trail N trailhead at the Whiteside Cove Cemetery. The N trailhead is also accessible from NC-107 in Cashiers SW on Whiteside Cove Rd for about 3.9 mi. At 2.5 mi, cross a bridge (also lowered by helicopter) over Norton Mill Creek. Cascades on the creek and a rushing flumelike section of the Chattooga River make this one of the trail's highlights. At 2.8 mi, the trail crosses an old road and soon begins to ascend away from the Chattooga Cliffs. Near the trail's end it descends to a gap near the cemetery.)

To complete the Chattooga River Loop Trail, ascend and parallel the Chattooga River Trail for a return to Bull Pen Rd. At 0.3 mi, enter an old logging road and reach a large parking area above Bull Pen Rd at 0.8 mi. To the R is an access to Bull Pen Rd for vehicles, but to the L is a narrow trail that descends to the Chattooga River Trail and 90 yd. R to the bridge and completion of the loop. (USGS-FS Maps: Highlands, Cashiers)

Whitewater River Area (Transylvania and Jackson Counties)

104   *Whitewater Falls Trail* (USFS #437)

> **Length and Difficulty:** 1.4 mi round-trip, strenuous
>
> **Special Features:** Whitewater Falls, geology
>
> **Trailhead and Description:** From the jct of US-64 and NC-281 in Sapphire, take NC-281 (formerly SR-1171) for 8.6 mi S to the Whitewater Falls Scenic Area. Turn L for 0.3 mi to a parking area with views of Lake Jocassee. (Camping or use of alcoholic beverages is prohibited within the area surrounding the parking area, trails, and Whitewater Falls.) Hike for 0.2 mi on a paved trail to overlooks of the spectacular 411-ft. Upper Whitewater River Falls. (The trail is user-friendly for the physically disabled to the overlook.) To the R from the overlooks follow the trail's descent. After 100 steps there is an impressive view of the falls. In a series of 300 more steps, switchbacks, and steep treadway among rhododendron, arrive at a bridge to cross the Whitewater River at 0.7 mi. Backtrack, or hike 0.1 mi farther to see Corbin Creek bridge on the Foothills Trail. (See FT ahead.) (USGS-FS Map: Cashiers)

105   *Foothills Trail* (USFS #436) (F)

> **Length and Difficulty:** 7.8 mi, moderate to strenuous
>
> **Special Features:** Views of Lake Jocassee, Upper Whitewater Falls
>
> **Trailhead and Description:** This part of the 75.3-mi white-blazed Foothills Trail (FT) is Section A8 and part of A7. It is part of the 6.5-mi in the Highlands Ranger District. A second part goes through Duke Power Company property and a piece of Gorges State Park (see chapter 10, section 1), both in North Carolina. The trail's W trailhead is at Oconee State Park, and the E trailhead is Table Rock State Park, both in SC. This description begins W in Sumter National Forest at Sloan Bridge picnic area on SC-107, 8.0 mi S of Cashiers. Begin on the E side of the highway and ascend gently on the W slope of Chattooga Ridge. After 1.4 mi, leave Sumter National Forest and enter NC in the Nantahala National Forest. From switchbacks, ascend to a ridge crest for partial views of Lake Jocassee. At 2.1 mi, descend steeply to a gap between Grassy Knob and Round Mtn. at 2.5 mi. Stay R at the fork. (A spur trail, L, descends into a hollow where there are campsite and a spring at 0.3 mi. Beyond and downstream it is 1.1 mi to NC-281. On NC-281 L [N], it

is 7.8 mi to the town of Sapphire. Heading R (S) on NC-281, it is 0.8 mi to
the parking area of Whitewater Falls Scenic Area.)

Continue E on the FT and curve L on the Grassy Knob escarpment at
3.0 mi. Descend on switchbacks and parallel the state line to arrive at NC-281
at 4.7 mi. Cross the road to a small parking area, then descend to curve L. At
5.1 is a 0.1-mi spur, L, which ascends to a restroom at the Upper Whitewater
Falls visitor parking area. After another 0.4 mi, reach jct with Whitewater
River Trail, L and R. Descend R. (To the L is an access with steps to the overlooks of Whitewater Falls.) Descend rapidly on switchbacks and steps with
some views of the famous 411-ft. waterfalls, L. Cross a 60-ft. steel bridge,
lowered here by helicopter in 1993, at 6.1 mi. Then at 6.2 mi, cross Corbin
Creek on an elevated bridge into a damp but resplendent evergreen understory
of rhododendron and tall hemlock. More bridges and steps follow. At 6.6 mi,
cross the NC/SC state line at Duke Power Company sign. After more bridges,
rocks, and hemlocks, arrive at a jct of the Bad Creek Access at 7.8 mi. (Camping is prohibited in this area.) (The blue-blazed spur trail is 0.7-mi to the Bad
Creek parking area where a paved road goes to SC-130.) If turning L to continue on the FT, it is 0.5-mi to a connection with a spur trail L that goes 1.2 mi
to an overlook of the Lower Whitewater Falls. (The top areas of all waterfalls
are dangerous. Stay on the trails and overlooks. There have been fatalities here.)
(USGS-FS Map: Cashiers; See chapter 10.) (For a detailed description and map
of the Foothills Trail, see *Guide to the Foothills Trails* by Foothills Trails Conference, Box 3041, Greenville, SC 29602; 864-467-9537 and *Hiking South
Carolina Trails* (Globe Pequot Press, 2001) by Allen de Hart; 800-243-0495.)

Horsepaster River Area (Transylvania County)   106
Horsepasture River Trail (F)

Length and Difficulty: 2.8 mi round-trip, moderate to strenuous

Special Feature: outstanding series of waterfalls

Trailhead and Description: On October 27, 1986, this 435-acre tract
officially became part of the National Wild and Scenic River system. Earlier,
the area was threatened by an out-of-state power company that planned to
destroy the water flow of the magnificent falls. Local conservationists immediately began a grassroots campaign. With the help of legislators, state and
federal organizations and agencies saved the Horsepasture River Falls Area.

From the jct of US-64 and NC-281 in Sapphire (10.1 mi E of Cashiers
and 3.0 mi W on US-64 from Lake Toxaway bridge), turn S on NC-281 and

go 1.0 mi to the Gorges State Park, L, and enter to parking area. (Daylight parking here only.) Walk back to the entrance gate and turn L on gravel path for a few yards to a metal gate, L. Follow the signs to descend 1.5 mi to Horsepasture River. (Roadside parking on NC-281 in this area is prohibited.) At the river is Turtlehead Falls (also called Rooftop, Mushroom, or Umbrella) and pool. Continue downriver on rugged concourse among rhododendron. After 0.2 mi, Rainbow Falls thunders 150 ft. into a deep pool, spraying a mist against the canyon walls to form a rainbow when the sun is at the right angle. On the high side of the trail wildflowers grow in profusion. There are two observation decks here and a trail with a split-level fence to the base of the falls. (Caution: Never wade or walk on rocks at the top of this fall. Fatalities have occurred here.) If descending farther downriver, make an ascent of 240 yd. after 0.4 mi, then bear sharply R to descend another 0.4 mi, then bear sharply R to descend another 0.4 mi to Stairway Falls. Backtrack. (USGS-FS Map: Reid)

Yellow Mountain Area (Macon and Jackson Counties)

107 *Yellow Mountain Trail* (USFS #31) (F)

Length and Difficulty: 10 mi round-trip, strenuous (elev change 1,047 ft.)

Special Feature: vistas from Yellow Mtn. summit

Trailhead and Description: From the jct of US-64 and NC-28 in Highlands, proceed E on US-64 for 2.6 mi to Buck Creek Rd (SR-1538, also called Cole Mtn. Rd), and turn L. (From Cashiers W on US-64, it is 7.4 mi to Buck Creek Rd.) Go 2.2 mi to Cole Gap (4,200 ft.) and park on the L side of the road by FR-4535; trail sign is R. The nonblazed trail ascends gradually on an old woods road through hardwoods and abundant wildflowers. Orchids, trillium, false foxglove, Solomon's seal, hellebore, starry campion, and a number of rare species such as wolfsbane *(Aconitum reclinatum)* and grass-of-Parnassus *(Parnassia asarifolia)* line the trail. After 0.4 mi, narrow spur trails, L, extend a few yards to the Western Cliffs for scenic vistas of Round Mtn. and Panther Mtn. Reach Cole Mtn. (4,600 ft.) at 0.9 mi. Begin to ascend Shortoff Mtn. at 1.2 mi on 11 switchbacks among rhododendron and hardwoods. Level out at 1.4 mi among beds of trailing arbutus and scattered flame azalea, but undulate for the next 0.5 mi. At 1.9 mi, descend on the W side of the E ridge of Shortoff Mtn. Pass a trail distance sign and arrive at a gap at 2.5 mi. Veer L, descend on switchbacks, and cross a small stream with mossy rocks and a rhododendron cover at 2.9 mi. Follow an old road through a young forest from a recent timber cut and arrive at Yellow Mtn. Gap at 3.5 mi among hemlock and hardwoods. Old forest roads are R and L. (To the L [W] is Stewart Cove Trail [USFS #498], a bicycle route to FR-4593 and Cole Mtn. Rd for 3.5 mi.) Continue on the graded trail up switchbacks bordered by laurel, rhododendron, berries, and hardwoods to the summit of Yellow Mtn. (5,127 ft.) at 5.0 mi. Spectacular views from Yellow Mtn. are of Standing Indian, Whiterock Mtn., and Albert Mtn. The old fire tower was reconstructed in the 1990s and in 1992 was recognized as a national historic lookout. The rock formations are composed mainly of gneiss. Backtrack. (USGS-FS Maps: Highlands, Glenville)

Silver Run Trail (USFS #435) (F) 108
Length and Difficulty: 0.2 mi round-trip, easy
Trailhead and Description: From Cashiers at the jct of US-64 and NC-107, take NC-107 S for 4.0 mi and park on the L side of the highway. Descend on a graded trail into a damp forest of rhododendron, hemlock, and poplar. Cross a stream on a footbridge to beautiful 30-ft. Silver Run Falls, wading pool, and small beach. It is part of the headwaters of the famous Upper Falls of the Whitewater River described above. Backtrack. (USGS-FS Map: Cashiers)

East Fork Area (Jackson County)
Whiteside Mountain Trail (USFS #70) (F) 109
Length and Difficulty: 2.0 mi, moderate
Trailhead and Description: A national recreation trail, it was completed in 1974. From Cashiers, go W on US-64 to the Jackson and Macon county line and turn L on Wildcat Ridge Rd (SR-1600). Go 1.0 mi to the Whiteside Mtn. sign, L, into a parking area. (From Highlands jct of US-64/NC-28, go E on US-64 5.4 mi and turn R on SR-1600.) From the parking area begin the hike up steps. Ascend on a trail to the ridge at 0.2 mi and turn L. At 0.7 mi, reach Devils Point, the summit (4,930 ft.), for magnificent views of the Chattooga River Valley, Timber Ridge, Blackrock Mtn., Yellow Mtn., and Terrapin Mtn. Follow the precipitous edge of sheer cliffs, 400-to-600 ft. high, to an overlook at 1.1 mi. Begin the descent on an old road to the parking area to complete the loop. The granite landmark is composed of feldspar, quartz, and mica. Vegetation consists of oak, birch, maple, rhododendron, laurel, flame azalea, sweet pepperbush, abundant wildflowers, and scattered conifers. (USGS-FS Map: Highlands)

Panthertown Valley Area (Jackson County)

The Panthertown Valley area has a honeycomb of old RR grades and logging roads constructed in the past century. Some are completely filled with forest growth and not passable, others are partially filled with young trees and expansive ground covers of blueberry bushes and greenbriers. A few roads, more recently used but now closed to vehicular traffic, are the sources for trails described ahead. Hikers will discover a number of paths cut through the underbrush either to connect roads (trails) or to open potential loops. The paths have been made by volunteer citizens, who sometimes were not authorized to make these changes. It is recommended that hikers who plan to leave the old roads where evidence of usage is in question should have both topo maps and a compass. (Request current Big Ridge and Lake Toxaway USGS maps from the district office. Maps dated 1946 are not satisfactory.) Currently there are 24 named and officially numbered trails in the maze of both Panthertown and Bonas Defeat area. Thirteen trails are shown on the 2002 National Geographic map #785 for hiking, 2 for bicycling, 5 for equestrian usage, and 3 for motorized usage. The user problem is that this listing may not match what is found in the forest. In 2003, the USFS announced plans for a trail analysis to determine current status, future usage, and clarification of trail routings.

Purchased in 1988, the 6,295-acre Panthertown Valley tract is one of the most unique natural areas in North Carolina. There are upland bogs, outcroppings, grassy meadows, rare botanical sites, 20 mi of mountain trout streams, and elevations ranging from 3,000 to 4,777 ft. Because this valuable tract is now protected, thanks to congressional help and the wisdom of The Nature Conservancy, the property has been recommended as a national natural landmark. Users will find the valley and the rim of the ridges around it offer solace, challenge, education, and recreation. If the user has only one choice, walk down the road from Salt Rock Gap for 0.3 mi to the first ledge on the L and watch the sunrise over the valley or the sunset cast color and shadows on the fissures and crevices of Big and Little Green Mtns.

110-118   *Salt Rock Gap Trail* (0.8 mi; USFS #448) (F, B, H); *Deep Gap Trail* (1.1 mi; USFS #449) (F); *Panthertown Creek Trail* (1 mi; USFS #450) (F); *Granny Burrell Falls Trail* (0.4 mi; USFS #489) (F) *Sassafras Gap Trail* (5.5 mi; USFS #448A) (F, B); *Greenland Creek Trail* (2.2 mi; USFS #451) (F, B); *Schoolhouse Falls Trail* (0.1 mi; USFS #452) (F); *Hogback Mountain Trail* (2.9 mi; USFS #453) (F, H); *Big Green Mountain Trail* (1.2 mi; USFS #469) (F, H)

Special Features: scenic valley, cliffsides, waterfalls, plant life, geology, fishing

Trailhead and Description: From US-64 (1.9 mi E of Cashiers), turn N on Cedar Creek Rd (SR-1120) and ascend 2.2 mi to turn R on Breedlove Rd (SR-1121). Drive 3.5 mi to the end of the road at a USFS gate and information sign. (Cold Mtn. Rd access is described below.)

Salt Rock Gap Trail descends on a gravel road. At 0.3 mi is a cliffside with sweeping E views of Panthertown Valley. Particularly impressive are views of the Big Green Mtn. (nearest) and Little Green Mtn. (beyond) granite walls. Bristly locust, sweet-shrub, mosses, and wildflowers border the trail in a forest of hardwoods and pines. At 0.6 mi is a jct, R, with Deep Gap Trail.

Deep Gap Trail is an easy walk on the mountainside to follow upstream alongside Frolictown Creek. After 0.1 mi past pines is a grazing field bordered with autumn olive, an apple tree on the L, and pink lady slipper on the R side of the road. The road slightly descends to a jct with Panthertown Creek Trail, L, at 0.3 mi. Continue ahead 0.1 mi to rock-hop Frolictown Creek at the top of a waterfall. From here the trail gently ascends to the forest boundary. Within 80 yd. from the creek crossing, the trail passes through an incredible carpet of galax under tall hardwoods. After another 0.7 mi, the trail ends at a locked forest gate in Deep Gap. Backtrack to Panthertown Creek Trail, R. After 0.3 mi, rock-hop Panthertown Creek near the W wall of Big Green Mtn. (To the immediate L is 0.4-mi. Granny Burrell Falls Trail shortcut downstream to an extraordinary cascade with sloping rock formations in pastel colors, a wide pool, and white sandbars. The arbored trail connects with Hogback Mountain Trail, described below.) Continue upstream on the Panthertown Creek Trail. After 90 yd., R, is a grassy meadow for camping. Other campsites are upstream under tall pines toward the granite wall of Big Green Mtn. At 1.1 mi, the trail ends at the creekside. Backtrack. (An observant hiker may notice a blue-flagged, unnamed and unauthorized connector trail L, NE, which ascends a hollow for 0.5 mi to a jct with Big Green Mountain Trail, described below.)

If continuing on the Salt Rock Gap Trail and passing the Deep Creek Trail jct, descend 0.2 mi to a four-way trail intersection. Here is the end of Salt Rock Gap Trail. To the L is Sassafras Gap Trail, whose NE trailhead is on Rock Bridge Rd (SR-1140) outside Panthertown Valley; ahead is Greenland Creek Trail, whose E trailhead is at Cold Mtn. Rd (SR-1301); to the R is Hogback Mountain Trail, which descends at a boundary gate on Hogback Mtn.

To hike the Hogback Mountain Trail, turn R, descend through pines, pass flat and grassy sites for camping near the white sand pathway, and cross an old bridge over Panthertown Creek at 0.3 mi. (1.1 mi from the parking area at the Salt Rock Gap parking area). This area is sometimes flooded and debris may be washed against the birch, rhododendron, and bush honeysuckle. (Immediately to the R, after crossing the bridge, is the 0.4-mi shortcut trail, mentioned above, to a scenic spot on Panthertown Creek. Go upstream 0.1 mi among rhododendron to the waterfall and large pool.) Backtrack. To continue on the Hogback Mountain Trail, follow the grassy road ahead. After 0.1 mi, there is a wildlife clearing on the L, and the old road is darkened by dense white pine. Running cedar is part of the forest floor. Peaceful and serene, this section has only the soughing sound of the pines. At 0.9 mi on the trail, cross a small stream and begin to ascend. Pass a grassy road, L, and ascend steeply among yellow and black birch, maple, and oak. Reach a grassy four-way old road intersection at 1.7 mi. (To the L the old road goes 1.2 mi to the USFS boundary and a private road. It follows a generally even contour and passes the headwaters of Greenland Creek.)

(To the R of the intersection is Big Green Mountain Trail. It follows a grassy old road among hardwoods, passes an old road, R, and enters a clearing at 0.5 mi. It descends to a saddle at 0.7 mi [where on the L is the jct of the 0.4-mi. Granny Burrell Falls Trail shortcut up from Panthertown Creek Trail]. Follow straight ahead on the old road to a knoll, slightly descend, and reach a fork at 1.1 mi. [To the R the trail ends after 100 yd. in a cul-de-sac.] To the L from the fork is a 0.1-mi access to a breathtaking view from the W face of Big Green Mtn. Scrub pine, mountain laurel, heather, and mosses cling to the precipitous granite. Backtrack to Hogback Mountain Trail.)

To continue on the Hogback Mountain Trail, turn R at the four-way jct and begin to ascend. The forest is chiefly cherry, oak, birch, maple, and scattered pine. Blueberry is the dense understory, and a few pink shell azaleas are on the higher elevations. At 2.2 mi, turn W and ascend a knoll. Descend to cross a stream with a hollow log culvert in a rhododendron thicket. At 2.9 mi is a locked USFS gate at the E base of Little Hogback Mtn.; the current end of the trail is at a residential development. Backtrack to the Salt Rock Gap Trail intersection with Greenland Creek Trail. On the way back and after crossing the old bridge at Panthertown Creek, hikers may see a shortcut trail to the R. (It goes through a grove of white pine and grazing fields for 0.2 mi to Greenland Creek Trail.)

Follow the old road of Greenland Creek Trail past a small cascade, L, and into a boggy area at 0.2 mi. After passage through a white-pine grove, reach a scenic area on the R at 0.8 mi. Here is a low waterfall where white sheets of water flow into the valley's largest pool. An open-sided but roofed shed may be near the pool. At 0.9 mi, turn R to cross an old bridge over Panthertown Creek. Immediately to the L is a 30-yd. path to the confluence of Panthertown Creek and Greenland Creek, whose waters become the Tuckasegee River. Follow an eroded road upstream with Greenland Creek on the L, and cross an old bridge at 1.4 mi. To the R, on either side of the bridge, is the 0.1-mi. Schoolhouse Falls Trail. The waterfall and pool is one of the valley's most attractive and popular places to visit. To return to the Greenland Creek Trail, either backtrack or ascend 0.1 mi to the L for rejoining the road. (After 120 yd. from this access there is an unauthorized shortcut of 130 yd. up an embankment to avoid a switchback in the road.) Follow the well-designed road up two switchbacks to private property at a metal bridge and gate at 2.3 mi. Turn R, cross a footbridge over a small stream, and ascend to parking lot at 2.5 mi. (3.3 mi from Salt Rock Gap parking area). Vehicle access here from US-64 at Lake Toxaway is N on NC-281 for 0.8 mi to a turn L (W) on Cold Mtn. Rd (SR-1301) for 5.6 mi to entrance of private property. Turn L and go 0.1 mi to entrance R for another 0.1 mi to parking lot.

For hiking the Sassafras Gap Trail from the jct of Salt Rock Gap Trail, Hogback Mountain Trail, and Greenland Creek Trail, ascend slightly on an old road that is below the S wall of Blackrock Mtn. The road is parallel E with the Greenland Creek Trail but higher on the mountainside. Pass R of a cliffside at 0.4 mi, and at 1.6 mi begin a turn N and then W among coves filled with rhododendron and mountain laurel. Ascend gradually to the E base of Blackrock Mtn. at 2.5 mi. Turn E on the old road, slightly descend, and turn N again to cross Honeycamp Branch at 3.3 mi. From here, pass E of Sassafras Mtn. (4,430 ft.).

(Hikers may see exploratory trails that ascend to Blackrock Mtn. or Sassafras Mtn. These routes lead SW along the crest to access Salt Rock Gap and the parking area for a loop. An example is a narrow path beginning at the L side of the gate at the Salt Rock Gap parking area. It ascends to a ledge of Salt Rock and follows some old roads for 1.0 mi to Blackrock Mtn. Hardwoods, wildflowers, ferns, and pink shell azaleas are distinctive along the way. A topo map or advice from the district ranger's office is recommended.)

Reach Sassafras Gap at 3.9 mi. From here and beyond Rattlesnake Knob are views (particularly good in the wintertime) of Tuckasegee River basin, Cold Mtn. (S), and Shelton Pisgah Mtn. (E). Pass through saplings of birch and sassafras and blueberry bushes. At 4.8 mi, the trail follows former FR-4661, now grass seeded and constructed with Cowetta drains. Among hardwoods, rhododendron, and pine descend to tank traps at Rock Bridge Rd (SR-1140). (Parking space for one vehicle in 1996.) Vehicle access here from NC-381 is 0.8 mi, 9.5 mi S to US-64 at Lake Toxaway, and 1.5 mi N on NC-281 to Tanasee Creek Reservoir and Tanasee Creek Rd. (USGS-FS Maps: Big Ridge, Lake Toxaway)

(At the Sassafras Gap Trail trailhead on Rock Bridge Rd, described above, the road is an access to two other trails, both in a planning stage. To reach the first, drive 0.8 mi farther W on Rock Bridge Rd to the top of a ridge at a road jct. Here Rock Bridge Rd ends, but FR-4662 continues ahead. To the L is a private road, but between it and FR-4662 is Flat Creek Trail [USFS #447] [F, H]. The trail follows an old road. To reach the second trail, drive down the mountain on FR-4662 for 2.2 mi to a dead-end. Hike across logs of a former bridge over Flat Creek. [An old road to the R goes W 0.5 mi to private property at a saddle.] Inconspicuously, the Rocky Knob Trail [USFS #446] [F, H] enters slightly L into rhododendrons. Both trails are about 3.0-mi long and connect about 0.6 mi S of Rocky Knob. A loop could be formed of about 11.2 mi if using FR-4662 as a connector.) (USGS-FS Map: Big Ridge)

Bonas Defeat Area (Jackson County)

There are a few unofficial trails in the Bonas Defeat area of the Tuckasegee River Gorge, Wolf Creek Gorge, and the Tanasee Creek basin. The area is scenic, rugged, and remote. Because there are pockets of private property (particularly along NC-281), Lake Toxaway, Sam Knob, and Big Ridge USGS (modified for FS use) maps are recommended to determine boundary lines. (Also, contact the ranger's office at 828-526-3765 if you have questions.) Two exciting routes are described below.

Access to the Tuckasegee River Gorge from the W is by NC-281 from its jct with NC-107 in Tuckasegee (SE of Cullowhee) E 14.2 mi to Phillips Store, R, but park on the L near the old store. (From the E take NC-281 from US-64 [8.0 mi W of Rosman], and drive 11.2 mi to the Phillips Store.) If walking to **119** Tuckasegee Gorge Trail (USFS #438) (F) from the store, request permission from the store owner (or, if closed, the nearest neighbor) to walk over private property. (Or you may enter the gorge from a private driveway 0.2 mi W of the store on NC-281. Permission there should be requested from the landowner, whose house is off the curve, S. This road route is 2.0 mi W to the powerhouse for access to the gorge, L.) If going across the fence in front of the store, cross the pasture to the SW corner at 0.2 mi. Cross a barbed-wire fence and descend to a road. Pass a water gauging station, follow a pathway through the forest by Tanasee Lake, and reach another road. Follow the road, but take a sharp L to the lake at 0.5 mi. Climb down to the spillway and descend on rock layers below the dam. Descend with care by twisting around boulders, rock-hopping, and avoiding a fall into hundreds of water-carved potholes. (The area can be extremely dangerous. Nonslip shoe soles are a necessity. Avoid sections with red markings.) After passing Slickens Creek and Doe Branch mouths, L, the Bonas Defeat Cliffs loom upward, L. (The legend of Bonas Defeat is that a hunting dog named Boney chased a deer to the cliff edge; the deer jumped sideways, missing the cliff, but Boney dived over it, meeting his defeat.) Continue the descent to the powerhouse. Backtrack, or follow the gravel road (described above). At the first fork, take a R and return to the next fork near the dam. Bear L and return on the entrance route for a strenuous round-trip of 4.0 mi.

Less known than the Tuckasegee, the Wolf Creek Gorge also has soft spots in the rocks where the rapids have shaped the design. Access is to follow the directions as given above for the Tuckasegee River Gorge, except the Wolf Creek Gorge Trail (USFS #439) (F) is W, 1.5 mi from the old Phillips **120** Store, and 0.5 mi W of the Wolf Creek Dam. Park 0.2 mi S on NC-281 past Wolf Creek Baptist Church. Descend on a clear footpath. At 0.4 mi, reach Wolf Creek, whose fury has sculpted bowls and fissures, pools, and waterfalls. Huge hemlock, birch, white pine, and oak tower over rhododendron, laurel, ferns, and wildflowers. Return on the same route for a round-trip of 1.0 mi. (Wolf Creek flows SW for 1.4 mi to a confluence with the Tuckasegee River at the powerhouse. A descent to the river can also be made on Pioneer Lodge Rd [SR-1139] by going 0.3 mi W on NC-281 from the church. The Wolf Creek Gorge Trail is on USFS property, except the church lot and a section below the falls near the mouth of the creek at Tuckasegee River.)

Balsam Lake Area (Jackson County)

Robinson Trail (0.3 mi; USFS #477); *Wolf Creek Trail* (0.3 mi; USFS **121-** #478); *Malonee Trail* (0.6 mi; USFS #476) (F, W) **123**

Length and Difficulty: round-trip, easy

Special Features: scenic, wildlife, access for disabled

Trailhead and Description: These trails are part of Balsam Lake Recreation Area, acquired by the USFS in 1982. The Balsam Lake Lodge is rented to the public. Up to 16 overnight guests have accommodations. Lodge is open from March 1 to November 30. Call the district office for information. The Robinson Trail is a nature trail whose access can be either in front of the lodge at steps to the lake or to the S side by a wide gravel route for the disabled. A sheltered fishing and boat dock is at the Balsam Lake Dam. Part of the trail has wildflowers and overhanging rhododendron.

The other trails are at the N end of the lake in a recreational area that has sheltered picnic tables, restrooms, and a grassy playing field. The Wolf Creek Trail, constructed in 1992 with financial assistance from private organizations and volunteers, is an exceptional trail for the physically disabled. It is easy for wheelchairs to be positioned on spur trails to watch Wolf Creek splashing toward the lake. There are galax, painted trillium, white violet, and fern under birch, hemlock, and rhododendron. Nearby, and also from the parking area, is the Malonee Trail. It is flat, crosses Wolf Creek on a bridge, and winds through large trees at the lake's edge on the E side. Fishing is allowed from extended piers. Access is from NC-107 E on NC-281 for 9.2 mi to Little Canada. Turn L on Charlie's Creek Rd (SR-1756) for 4.0 mi to the lodge entrance, R. It is 0.6 mi farther to Balsam Lake Recreational Area. (If from NC-215, it is W 5.0 mi on Charlie's Creek Rd.) (USGS-FS Map: Sam Knob)

Tusquitee Ranger District

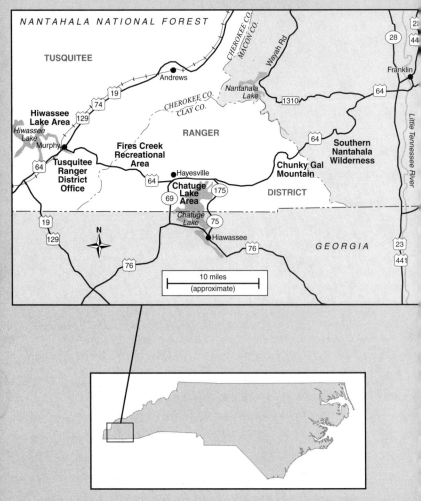

Introductions to Trail Areas

This district has 158,979 acres in Clay and Cherokee counties, the largest acreage of the four districts in the Nantahala National Forest. Descriptions of the trails begin a few miles W of Murphy, then E and SE near the Georgia state line.

Tusquitee Ranger District Office
The district office is in Murphy, a town at the eastern edge of the large Hiwassee Lake. Between the office and the Hiwassee River is a meadow with a greenway circle for a pleasant walk. The office has books, maps, and information for the public.

With 14 trails and 57 mi, this long basin between Valley River Mtns. and Tusquitee Mtn. offers a trail for a lone hiker to families and groups for hiking, horseback riding, mountain bicycling, camping, fishing, and nature study.

This nearly 1-mi high ridge received its name about a Native American girl who ran away with a banished brave. Part of an escarpment has quartz and olivine. Minimum distance, that includes approach trails, is 27.3 mi from Fires Creek basin to the Southern Nantahala Wilderness.

The Jack Rabbit Mountain Recreation has camping, picnicking, boating, fishing, swimming, nature study, and a scenic trail.

At Hanging Dog Recreation Area are campsites, picnic facilities, boat launching facilities for fishing and nature study. Among the trails is a rare one through a cemetery.

From Deep Gap and a crossing of the Appalachian Trail, a trio of trails are part of a drop into a gorge with waterfalls, cliffs, historic sites, wildlife, scenic overlooks, section of a climax forest, and isolation.

SECTION 3: TUSQUITEE RANGER DISTRICT

The Tusquitee (the Cherokee word for "where the water dogs laughed," based on a legend of thirsty, talking water dogs) Ranger District is the state's most western district and the largest—158,979 acres—in the Nantahala National Forest. Mainly in Cherokee County, its NW corner adjoins the Unicoi Mtns. and the Cherokee National Forest in Tennessee. Its N border is with the Cheoah Ranger District along the ridgeline of the Snowbird Mtns. On the E boundary is the Wayah district and a small connection with the Georgia state line in the SE where the district shared part of the Southern Nantahala Wilderness. Three major TVA lakes, the Hiwassee and Appalachia in Cherokee County and Chatuge in Clay County, provide large areas for fishing and other water sports. The largest of the lakes, Hiwassee has the Hiwassee River impounded from the dam at Hiwassee Village to Murphy. It was completed in 1940 at the cost of $23 million. In addition to the Unicoi Mtn. range, the Chunky Gal Mtn. range in the SE, and the Tusquitee Mtn. range in the center, there are outstanding areas for wildlife and natural beauty. The Fires Creek Wildlife Management Area with Fires Creek running through its basin and the Rim Trail circling its rim to Tusquitee Bald (5,240 ft.) is one of the most distinctive and eminent areas. Within the rim is a network of diverse hiking, bicycling, and horseback-riding trails. Its 14,000 acres are a bear sanctuary, but other game hunting and trout fishing are allowed. The district's other major trail is the Chunky Gal Trail, a NW-SE route from Tusquitee Bald to the AT in the Wayah Ranger District. The Tusquitee Ranger District has 40.0 mi of trails for motorbikes and ATV usage.

124-125   A couple of short and independent trails are North Shore Creek Falls Trail (0.4 mi round-trip; USFS #383) and Fires Creek Access Trail (0.4 mi round-trip; USFS #636). For access to the first from Hiwassee Village, cross the dam on Hiwassee Dam Access Rd and drive 4.9 mi to Morrow Rd (SR-1323), L. After 1.6 mi, turn L on Prospect Rd (SR-1324) and go 0.4 mi to small roadside parking. There are no signs or blazes here. Descend steeply on a severely eroded old road 0.2 mi to cove of Appalachia Lake. Turn R and squeeze through rhododendron to a scenic waterfall. Backtrack. The other trail is a misnomer because it does not access Fires Creek on private property. However, the trail is well designed and since it is open from a clear-cut, there are flora and fauna to see. Access on Fires Creek Rd (SR-1300) is to turn off at Fires Creek Baptist Church on Theron McCray St, and quickly turn L on Peaceful Patch driveway. Follow the single lane to a large parking lot cleared by the clear-cut. Descend on switchbacks to timber debris (and private property) to backtrack.

The Benton MacKaye Trail (BMT) (USFS #82) follows the Tennessee/   1
North Carolina state line on Unicoi Mtn. with the Cherokee National Forest
on the N side and the Nantahala National Forest on the S side for 5.6 mi. It
begins at Sixmile Gap in Tennessee and currently ends at Beaverdam Bald on
the state line. Ninety mi of the trail has been completed and plans by the Benton MacKaye Trail Association (organized in 1989) plans to make it 360 mi
for a double loop with the AT and the GSMNP. Its most southern trailhead is
a Springer Mtn. in Georgia. The association is working with the USFS to
honor MacKaye as "Father of the Appalachian Trail." For information, contact the association at P.O. Box 53271, Atlanta, GA 30355; contact@bmta.org
or www.bmta.org.

The district has two USFS-developed campgrounds: Jack Rabbit at Lake
Chatuge and Hanging Dog at Lake Hiwassee. Both places have camping, picnicking, day hiking, and fishing with boat-launching facilities. Other recreation areas are Cherokee Lake picnic area off NC-294, SW of Murphy, and
Bob Allison, a primitive camping and picnic area up Big Tuni Creek and NE
of the community of Tusquitee, which is NE of Hayesville. For more information, contact District Ranger, Tusquitee Ranger District, USFS, 123 Woodland Drive, Murphy, NC 28906; 828-837-5152. From the jct of US-19/129
and US-64 go S on all those highways, cross the bridge over the Hiwassee,
turn onto Hiwassee St at BB&T bank, then two blocks to L and entrance.

Fires Creek Recreation Area (Clay County)

The 16,000-acre Fires Creek watershed has three recreational sites, one of
which is a picnic area at Leatherwood Falls. The primitive campgrounds are
at Huskins Branch Hunter Camp near the Fires Creek entrance, and Bristol
Camp, 4.0 mi up Fires Creek Rd (FR-340) from the Leatherwood Falls
parking area. Other sites for camping are along the creeks and roads. No
camping is allowed in designated wildlife openings. Bristol Camp is divided
into two areas, one of which is a developed horse camp. The horse camp has
tables, fire rings, and corrals. (A fee is required.) The other camp has a vault
toilet and drinking water, shared by both camps. Fishing for rainbow, brook,
and brown trout is allowed according to NC Game Lands regulations. Bear
hunting and use of ORVs are prohibited. Hunting for wild turkey, deer, and
grouse is permitted in season. Both the copperhead and the timber rattler are
in the sanctuary. Among the bird species are woodpeckers, warblers, owls,
hawks, towhees, and doves. Vegetation includes all the Southern Appalachian

hardwood species and six species of pine. Rhododendron and laurel slicks are commonplace, and wildflower species number in the hundreds. The area is considered ideal for backpacking. The longest trail, the Rim Trail, traverses the boundary on a high, elongated rim for 25.0 mi with spur trails down to the basin. Some sections are restricted to hikers only, and other sections are used by both equestrians and hikers. Water is infrequent on the Rim Trail, but four springs are usually dependable. Signs and blazes sparse. All trails in the basin are used by both equestrians and hikers, except Leatherwood Falls Loop Trail, Shinbone Ridge Trail, Bristol Cabin Trail, and Omphus Ridge Trail, which are limited to hiking.

Access: At the jct of US-64/NC-69 in Hayesville go W on US-64 for 4.9 mi, and turn R at a store (gasoline/groceries) onto Fires Creek Rd (SR-1300). (From Murphy, go E 9.2 mi on US-64 from US-129/19.) Follow SR-1300 for 4.8 mi and turn L at Fires Creek sign. After 1.7 mi enter the gate and reach Leatherwood Falls parking area and picnic ground after 0.3 mi.

126-
137   *Rim Trail* (USFS #72) (F, partial H)

Length and Difficulty: 25.0 mi, easy to strenuous (elev change 3,390 ft.)

Connecting Trails: Cover Trail (0.3 mi; USFS #74, easy); Leatherwood Falls Loop Trail (0.7 mi; USFS #73, easy); Phillips Ridge Trail (3.3 mi; USFS #388, moderate; elev change 815 ft.); Rockhouse Creek Trail, (2.3 mi; USFS #387); Sassafras Trail (0.6 mi; USFS #62); Shinbone Ridge Trail (1.5 mi; USFS #80, strenuous; elev change 1,349 ft.); (Chunky Gal Trail); Far Bald Springs Trail (1.9 mi; USFS #389, strenuous; elev change 1,490 ft.); Bald Springs Trail (3.0 mi; USFS #78, strenuous; elev change 2,120 ft.); Little Fires Creek Trail (3.1 mi; USFS #386, strenuous; elev change 2,145 ft.); Bristol Cabin Trail (1.2 mi; USFS #76, moderate); Omphus Ridge Trail (1.3 mi; USFS #75, strenuous; elev change 1,000 ft.)

Special Features: Leatherwood Falls, heath balds, scenic

Trailhead and Description: The Rim Trail begins at the Fires Creek Picnic Area and Leatherwood Falls parking area and restroom. The Cover Trail and Leatherwood Falls Loop Trail also begins here. Cross an arched bridge to a paved trail area where the Cover Trail goes R to parallel Fires Creek. The trail is accessible for the physically disabled and makes a short loop on the return after 0.3 mi.

(The former 4.8 mi blue-blazed Cover Trail went upstream to Bristol Camp, but now has only access pieces used mainly for fishing. Wading to crisscross Fires Creek and its rapids can be dangerous. An 0.8 mi strip may be found if you use Bristol Cabin Trail and its footbridge to leave it and go downstream to Fires Creek Rd [FR-340] bridge.)

To continue to Leatherwood Falls Loop Trail, cross another bridge to Leatherwood Falls and jct with the Leatherwood Falls Loop Trail at 0.3 mi. (The Leatherwood Falls Loop Trail turns L and skirts the mountainside through rhododendron and hardwoods with occasional views of the falls. The trail descends to the FR at 0.6 mi for a L turn to cross Fires Creek Rd bridge, and a return to the parking area at 0.7 mi.) After the waterfall, the Rim Trail turns R to ascend and reach FR-6176 at 0.4 mi. Take a sharp turn R up the bank at 0.6 mi, and follow switchbacks. Join and rejoin old logging roads. At 1.6 mi there is a jct with the old trail on the ridge; bear R. Pass through an experimental forest section of hardwoods, and begin a steep rocky ascent at 1.8 mi. Reach a plateau at 2.0 mi, and an intermittent spring at 2.2 mi. Ascend on switchbacks constructed by the YACC in 1980 to another ridge crest on the Cherokee/Clay county line at 3.2 mi. A horse trail comes in from the L to join the Rim Trail. Keep R and follow the old road W of Shortoff Knob to a spring on the L at 3.3 mi and cross Big Peachtree Bald (4,186 ft.) with Peachtree Valley to the L at 4.4 mi. Follow the rim with Valley River on the SE and a precipitous edge on the NW to Will King Gap at 5.4 mi.

(To the R is 3.3-mi Phillips Ridge Trail, a horse/hiker trail, which descends gradually to the E before turning S after crossing the headwaters of Laurel Creek. It follows a logging road, first to enter coves on the W side of Phillips Ridge, but then crosses the ridge to descend for a crossing of Hickory Creek at 2.3 mi. After another mile it reaches a trailhead in a sharp curve at Laurel Creek. From here it is 0.5 mi downstream to a jct with Rockhouse Creek Trail, L, another horse/hiker trail that ascends NE for 2.3 mi to Rim Trail. At the confluence of Laurel Creek and Rockhouse Creek is FR-340A, an 0.8-mi access from Fires Creek Rd [FR-340], 1.7 mi from Leatherwood Falls parking area.) At 5.7 mi on the Rim Trail are occasional N views of the Chestnut Flats to the drainage. Follow a contour grade until an ascent to Big Stamp Lookout (4,437 ft.) is reached at 7.9 mi. The trail skirts the summit, but an access route of 0.2 mi to the top is on the S side. Views are limited because the fire tower has been dismantled.

(The access route, FR-427, R, descends 4.0 mi to Long Branch Rd. From there, R, it is 1.0 mi to Fires Creek Rd, and R 6.1 mi to Leatherwood Falls parking area. After 0.1 mi on the descent is Rockhouse Creek Trail, R, a horse/hiker route on an old forest road for 2.3 mi along Rockhouse Creek to FR-340A.)

Continue along the rim, with exceptionally steep drops on the N side. Ascend and descend over knobs—Whiteoak Knob, Defeat Knob, Beal Knob. (Soon after Beal Knob is Sassafras Trail, a horse/hiker trail, R, that descends S. It crosses the toe of Sassafras Ridge and Long Branch to access the terminus of FR-340 and the SW terminus of Shinbone Ridge Trail.) After Sassafras Knob, the Rim Trail is for hikers only to Tusquitee Bald. Ascend to Sassafras Knob (4,650 ft.) at 12.3 mi. Skirt S of Weatherman Bald (4,960 ft.) at 12.9 mi and reach the boundary of Cherokee, Macon, and Clay Counties at County Corner at 13.6 mi (5,149 ft.). A sign indicates the boundary, but the bears may have chewed all or parts of the sign. Here is a good open grassy spot for a campsite. (To the L [N] is the unmaintained Old Road Gap Trail that descends 1.6 mi to a FR, and L 1.1 mi to Junaluska Gap Rd [SR-1505]. Left on SR-1505, it is 3.5 mi to Andrews.) A spring is on the Shinbone Ridge Trail, 65 ft. SE from a small grassy area at Country Corner on the Rim Trail and 140 ft. R in a rhododendron grove. The spring is small but is usually dependable.

(From the spring the blue-blazed Shinbone Ridge Trail gradually descends on Shinbone Ridge in and out of grassy paths for 0.5 mi. In a scenic forest of white pine, hemlock, hardwoods, ferns, and flame azalea, there are views through the trees of Sassafras Ridge N and the Fires Creek watershed S. Descend steeply; a former clear-cut is L at 1.2 mi. At 1.5 mi, descend on steps to a timber road. There is space for three vehicles on a level area in the ridge grove. From here, L, it is 10.2 mi down the mountain on Fires Creek Rd to Leatherwood Falls parking area.)

Continue ahead on the Rim Trail to a spur trail, L, at 14.7 mi. (The spur leads 0.1 mi to views from Signal Bald, named for the Cherokee usage of smoke signals. From Signal Bald the spur extends another 0.1 mi to Tusquitee Bald [5,240 ft.] and makes a jct with the Chunky Gal Trail along the way. The Chunky Gal Trail is described ahead.) Descend from Tusquitee Bald and rejoin the Rim Trail. Another horse trail, 1.9-mi. Far Bald Springs Trail, goes R (W) to a jct with FR-340. The Rim Trail becomes a horse/hiker trail again for 2.3 mi. After 0.2 mi to rejoin the Rim Trail from Tusquitee Bald, there is a small saddle and a water source. Reach Potrock Bald (5,215 ft.) at 16.1 mi. Here is a good campsite with vistas of Chatuge Lake and beyond into Georgia. Potrock received its name from small and large "bowls" appearing to have been carved by the Indians or the weather. A good spring is on the R at 17.1 mi.

On a gentle grade reach Matlock Bald (4,949 ft.) at 17.2 mi. Ahead, the rim edge on the S drops steeply. (Just before Johnson Bald [4,949 ft.] a 3.0-mi horse/hiker trail, Bald Springs Trail, descends R. Its valley terminus is on

Fires Creek Rd [FR-340] W of Mule Flat Bend, and about 6.0 mi E of Leatherwood Falls parking area.) Continuing on the Rim Trail for about 0.7 mi, there is a jct with another horse/hiker trail, R. It is 3.1-mi. Little Fires Creek Trail. (It descends steeply partly on an old forest road to exit on FR-340, 0.3 mi NE of Bristol Camp.) From here to the end of the Rim Trail usage is for hikers only, but there is continuing evidence of horse traffic on this section to make a loop with Bristol Cabin Trail and Bristol Horse Camp.

Ascend Chestnut Stomp Knob (4,400 ft.) at 18.4 mi. From here continue the descent to Shearer Gap, Cold Spring Gap, and finally to Carver Gap (2,996 ft.) at 22.3 mi. (Bristol Cabin Trail jct is here; it descends R for 1.2 mi to Bristol Camp on Fires Creek Rd.) After 0.4 mi farther on Rim Trail is a jct with Omphus Ridge Trail R. (Both of these trails leave Fires Creek Rd 2.0 mi apart and connect with the Rim Trail 0.4 mi apart. They provide an excellent 4.9-mi loop trail combination from Bristol Camp if using Fires Creek Rd. From the Omphus Ridge Trail jct on Fires Creek Rd, it is 2.0 mi on the road SW to Leatherwood Falls parking area.)

From the Omphus Ridge Trail jct, continue on the ridge and enter a rhododendron arbor before crossing Graveyard High Knob at 23.6 mi. Descend and level off slightly at 23.9 mi, take an old road R, and follow the N side of the main ridge at 24.7 mi. Continue to descend to a small cove and leave the forest at a timber road at 24.8 mi. Follow the road L to Fires Creek Rd for 0.1 mi, turn L, and go another 0.1 mi to the Leatherwood Falls parking area at 25.0 mi. (USGS-FS Maps: Andrews, Hayesville, Topton)

Chunky Gal Mountain Area (Clay County)

Chunky Gal Mtn. is a high, remote, 8.0-mi ridge that averages 4,500 ft. in elev from the Tennessee Valley Divide of the Blue Ridge Mtns. NW to Shooting Creek Bald. It has three major gaps, the lowest of which is Glade Gap (3,679 ft.). Through it passes the celebrated US-64 from Manteo to Murphy, the state's longest highway (569.0 mi). The legend of Chunky Gal Mtn. is that a plump Indian maiden fell in love with an Indian youth of another tribe in another valley. To break up the romance her parents banished the young brave, but she deserted her family and followed him over the mountain that bears her sobriquet. Access to the mountain is described below under the Chunky Gal Trail.

Support Facilities: The nearest towns for supplies are E 17.4 mi on US-64 to Franklin and W 16.0 mi to Hayesville. The nearest campgrounds are the

Chatuge Lake Area (described ahead) or the Standing Indian Area, 7.5 mi E (described in detail in section 4 of this chapter).

138   *Chunky Gal Trail* (USFS #77) (F)

   Length and Difficulty: 21.7 mi, moderate to strenuous (elev change 2,160 ft.)

   Special Features: gemstones, isolated, wild herbs

   Trailhead and Description: This trail has exceptional potential for an extended backpacking trip. It is a connector trail between the AT at the Southern Nantahala Wilderness Area and the Rim Trail on the E rim of the Fires Creek basin. Access to either end is by foot: 2.9 mi using the AT, or 2.8 mi using the Shinbone Ridge Trail and the Rim Trail. Whichever route you choose, the minimum hiking distance is 27.3 mi. To extend the excursion, more than 10.0 mi of the Rim Trail can be used, or long distances on the AT.

   On US-64, 2.0 mi W of Rainbow Springs, or 0.3 mi W of the Macon/Clay county line, turn L on unmarked gravel FR-71. Follow the narrow, winding road for 5.4 mi to Park Gap and 1.4 mi farther to its jct with the AT in Deep Gap, where there is a parking and picnic area. From here begin the hike S on the graded AT section; ascend steeply, cross outcrops, and cross a footbridge at a water source at 1.2 mi. Circle the Yellow Mtn. ridge crest at 1.6 mi and descend to Wateroak Gap at 2.1 mi. Ascend to the ridge, skirt NW of Big Laurel Mtn. (5,100 ft.), descend, and reach a jct with the blue-blazed Chunky Gal Trail R at 2.9 mi (4,700 ft.).

   Follow the trail along Chunky Gal Mtn. ridge for 0.7 mi to a scenic escarpment L (W) with views of Ravenrock Ridge and the Muskrat Branch basin. Shooting Creek Knob can be seen NW beyond the valley. Follow a ridge spine in a forest of oak, birch, hemlock, rhododendron, laurel, and wildflowers. The escarpment contains quartz, garnet, and olivine. Descend steeply to Bear Gap at 1.5 mi. Ascend steeply to a high unnamed knob and descend to Grassy Gap at 2.3 mi. Deer are frequently seen here. For the next 1.3 mi, ascend and descend across four knobs and saddles and jct R with an old trail at 3.6 mi. Continue ahead to climb Riley Knob (4,480 ft.) at 4.4 mi. Descend and begin switchbacks at 5.0 mi. Cross a woods road and at 5.2 mi, exit to US-64 in Glade Gap. (It is 6.8 mi W to Shooting Creek and 16.0 mi to Hayesville. To Franklin, E, it is 17.4 mi.)

   Cross US-64, turn L on old US-64, and turn R on an old jeep road at 5.4 mi. Pass under the power line, cross Glade Branch on a footbridge, and on switchbacks pass under the power line again. (Avoid the shortcuts that have been made under the power line.) Reach jct with an old road at 5.6 mi. Turn R and ascend on Chunky Gal Mtn. with a combination of old roads and footpaths for 12 switchbacks before a more gradual contour at 6.4 mi. Enter a rhododendron tunnel at 7.1 mi, pass large boulders, and at 7.9 mi jct with a faint trail ahead. (The faint trail leads to Shooting Creek Bald [5,010 ft.], also called Boteler Peak.) The R turn makes a radical change in direction, but descend N on the ridge and pass through a natural garden of laurel, flame azalea, and ferns. At 8.7 mi, pass R of a clear-cut, reenter the forest, and exit at another clear-cut at 9.1 mi. Columbine *(Aquilegia canadensis),* sundrops *(Oenothers fruiticose),* spiderwort *(Tradescantia virginiana),* and flame azalea grow in profusion here, and in the forest are a variety of herbs collected by the mountain residents under permits from the USFS. After another section in the forest and another clear-cut, turn L on an old woods road at 9.3 mi. Skirt around the ridge and descend to a jct with a FR in Perry Gap at 10.3 mi. (It is 4.0 mi R [E] down the mountain to Buck Creek and US-64.) Continue ahead, N, on a gated FR through a former clear-cut to Tate Gap at 11.4 mi. Leave the road, follow on an old jeep road on the ridge with knobs for 1.9 mi where a sharp L (W) is made for a steep descent to Woods Rd (SR-1307), also called Tusquitee Rd, in Tusquitee Gap at 13.9 mi. (SR-1307 is an access S for 3.7 mi to a paved road and reach jct with the Tuni Gap Rd, described below.) Cross the road, ascend NW to a spur ridge of a peak at 14.3 mi. Curve around another spur and descend steeply to a gap at 15.0 mi. Pass old roads, ascend to the ridge crest, and skirt W of an unnamed knob. Leave the main ridge and descend to follow rippling spur ridges and coves with banks of galax, fire pink, and trailing arbutus to a trail jct at 17.3 mi. Here is a relocation: the Chunky Gal Trail turns sharply L. (Ahead the trail goes to Tuni Gap and ends.) Descend on a poorly designed and constructed trail to the Bob Allison Camp. At 17.5 mi, reach an old road; turn L, and leave, R, at 17.6 mi into a partial clearing. Reach an old RR grade at 17.7 mi, cross two streams on a rough RR grade, and rock-hop the Big Tuni Creek at 18.0 mi. Enter the edge of the campground and go upstream through a stand of hemlock and yellow poplar for a jct with FR-400 at 18.2 mi. The Bob Allison Camp has a vault toilet, drinking water, picnic tables, and a grassy area for camping. (The camp can be reached from Hayesville Town Square by following the Tusquitee Rd [SR-1307] NE for 8.7 mi to the end of the pavement. Continue L [N] for 4.3 mi on Mosteller Rd [SR-1311], which becomes FR-400, to the camp, 0.8 mi S of Tuni Gap.)

On FR-400, turn R and cross the cement bridge over Big Tuni Creek to enter L, a scenic area with cascades. Follow the blue blazes on a relocated trail that is rough, steep, and rocky. Part of the trail is not well graded and follows a wet treadway. Timber cuts affect its direction. After 1.2 mi, turn L and ascend steeply on switchbacks to Dead Line Ridge. Curve around a knoll to follow a narrow ridge that ends in a gentle saddle between Signal Bald R and Tusquitee Bald (5,240 ft.) L at 21.5 mi (elev change 2,160 ft.). Both peaks have outstanding scenery and Tusquitee provides views of Shooting Creek Bald SE, Wine Spring Bald E, Chatuge Lake S, and Nantahala Lake NE. Exit to the Rim Trail at 21.7 mi. Backtrack to Allison Camp or use the Rim Trail for egress. (USGS-FS Maps: Rainbow Springs, Shooting Creek, Topton)

Chatuge Lake Area (Clay County)

The Jackrabbit Mountain Recreation Area has 103 campsites, picnic facilities, boating, swimming, skiing, lake fishing, nature study, and hiking. Comfort stations and warm-water showers are available. Both the campgrounds and the swimming area are usually open from the first week of May to the end of October. (The nearest commercial campground is Ho Hum Campground on NC-175 near the entrance to Jackrabbit Mtn. Campground. It is open from March 15 to November 15. Full svc, rec fac; 828-386-6740.)

Access: Entry to Jackrabbit is from US-64 jct with NC-175 (4.7 mi E of NC-67 jct in Hayesville). Go S on NC-175 for 3.4 mi, turn R at Jackrabbit on Philadelphia Rd (SR-1155), and proceed 1.2 mi to the campground.

139 *Jackrabbit Mountain Scenic Trail* (USFS #384) (F)

Length and Difficulty: 2.4 mi, easy

Trailhead and Description: Follow the trail sign R of entry to a blue-blazed trail through generally open forest of white oak, sourwood, and pine. Cleared spots provide views of Chatuge Lake. Reach the crest of a ridge at 0.6 mi, cross wooden bridge near a spring at 1.3 mi, pass the edge of Chatuge Lake at 1.6 mi, and reach the boat ramp parking area at 2.1 mi. Return to the camping area and parking lot at 2.4 mi. (USGS-FS Map: Shooting Creek)

Hiwassee Lake Area (Cherokee County)

Located on Lake Hiwassee, Hanging Dog Recreation Area has 69 campsites, a picnic area with tables and grills, and boat launching facilities for fishing, boating, and skiing. Flush toilets are available, but there are not any showers. The area is usually open from April 1 to the end of October, but one camping area for tenting is open all year with a small fee. It is section D with a vault toilet and hand water pump. Other sections are A and C on the R, and B (with D) on the L when entering. There are six bicycle routes on ridges and peninsulas.

Access: From downtown Murphy, at the jct of Tennessee St and Valley River Ave (Business US-19), take Tennessee St W (it becomes Brown Rd, SR-1326) and drive 4.4 mi to the campground sign, L, and go 1.1 mi to the entrance.

Ramsey Bluff Trail (USFS #81) (F)   **140**

    Length and Difficulty: 2.1 mi combined, easy

    Trailhead and Description: The trail can be made into a loop by beginning at the end of the loop road in section B. There is an interpretive segment in between here and an exit to FR-652 in section D. To continue, turn L on FR-652 and walk to the upper boat ramp. Turn R near the corner of the parking area and go N through sections C and A to exit on FR-652 near the entrance to section B. On an even-grade terrain the forest has oak, pine, sourwood, dogwood, maple, birch, ferns, and wildflowers. A timber cut with new grassy roads may have altered this description. (USGS-FS Map: Murphy)

Southern Nantahala Wilderness Area (Macon and Clay Counties)

This scenic wilderness has 11,944 acres in NC and 11,770 acres in Georgia. Its highest peak in NC is legendary Standing Indian (5,499 ft.) from whose rocky edge provides breath-taking views of the multiple ridges, knobs, and coves of the upper Tullahah River Basin. Waterfalls and cliffs, narrow and deep gorges are part of the basin, which is rimmed by the Eastern Continental Divide. Federal and state endangered species of animals and plants are protected here. The basin is also a black bear sanctuary. Curving around the rim is 24 mi of the Appalachian Trail, plus that many more mi of connecting trails. The wilderness was severely logged in the early twentieth century, but a few sections such as on the rocky slopes of Big Scaly have never been timbered. The USFS purchased the land from a timber company in 1920, and it was designated a wilderness in 1984. (See "Overview of Trails in the National Forests" for USFS regulations for wilderness usage.)

Deep Gap Branch Trail (2.4 mi; USFS #377); *Beech Creek Trail* (6.6   **141-** mi; USFS #378); *Big Scaly Trail* (1.6 mi round-trip, USFS #638)   **143**

    Connecting Trails: (Appalachian Trail); (Kimsey Creek Trail)

Length and Difficulty: 13.7 mi round-trip, moderate to strenuous, water-falls, high cliff, gorges, flora, and fauna

Trailhead and Description: The main trailhead in NC is at Deep Gap, where FR-71 ends at a parking area and reach jct with the AT and Kimsey Creek Trail. Access from Franklin (US-441/64) is 14 mi W on US-64 to a Deep Gap sign, L. From the community of Shooting Creek on US-64, it is 10 mi E to the sign, R. From the sign follow old US-64 for 0.8 mi, then a sharp turn L on gravel FR-71. Drive 5.2 mi to the road's end and parking at Deep Gap. For Georgia access, drive 11 mi E on US-76/GA-2 onto Persimmon Rd (at a fire station). Drive 4.1 mi N and turn L on Tallulah River Rd. Follow this road through sections of Chattahooches National Forest and the community of Tate City for 7.7 mi to Beech Creek Trail parking area, L, and another 1.1 mi to the end of FR-56 and parking for Deep Gap Branch Trail. From Clayton, drive W on US-76 for 7.5 mi to Persimmon Rd and turn R at the fire station.

These trails can make a loop of 7.9 mi or 13.7 mi. If you have the time and interest for the mystique of the basin, plan to make your adventure more than a day hike. At Deep Gap (4,341 ft.) follow the carsonite sign and gently descend on an old road for 0.4 mi to faint blue blazes, L. Sharply leave the road, descend and follow another old road to curve downstream. Cross six small streams that form the headwaters of Deep Gap Branch from 0.6 mi to 1.0 mi in a hardwood forest. In the process descend steeply. Ascend an embankment in a rhododendron grove to avoid the treacherous cascading branch, then hold on to tree roots and limbs for a brief descent. Pass through a hemlock grove and good campsites at 1.8 mi. Cross Chimney Rock Branch at 2.0 mi. To the L (and easy to miss) is the unsigned and unblazed north trail-head of Beech Creek Trail. (Ahead and R, the Deep Gap Branch Trail follows the old road by a partial opening, the site of a former Girl Scouts Camp. On the R is the roaring stream, now the Tullulah River; and arrive at the parking area for the S end of Deep Gap Branch Trail).

On an old logging road ascend the Beech Creek Trail. It is moderate to strenuous through a hardwood forest. After five switchbacks and 1.2 mi, curve L at a ridge saddle. At 1.6 mi is a large rock, L, and on the R is a sign "Chim-ney Rock." (There is an unofficial 0.3-mi path up the slope of Big Scaly.) On the ascending old road are rocky sections and some damp areas with canopies of rhododendron or wildflower beds. Arrive at Case Knife Gap (4,720 ft.) at 2.6 mi. Here is a flat area and to the R of the curve (20 yd.) in the gap are two old and faded signs at the Big Scaly Trail. (The 0.8 mi trail ascends easily on the ridge through wind-swept red oak, chestnut sprouts, and [with astonishing frequency] flame azalea. After dense patches of rhododendron, escape to rock ledges for magnificent views. Backtrack.)

For the short loop from Case Knife Gap, you may have to search for a connector path that goes NE up the mountainside toward the AT. Ascend steeply on the path for 0.4 mi and with an increase of 460-ft. change in elevation. Exit in a dense grove of mountain laurel and rhododendron to the AT on a ridge. Turn L. After gradually ascending 0.5 mi, reach jct with a 0.1-mi ascent to the rock outcrop summit of Standing Indian, and R is the blue-blazed Lower Ridge Trail that descends 4.2 mi to Standing Indian Campground. From here continue on the AT in a 2.4-mi descent for a return to Deep Gap parking area at 7.9 mi.

If making a longer loop continue on Beech Creek Trail on the old logging road at Case Knife Gap, pass or hike the Big Scaly Trail, and easily descend among yellow birch and beech. After 280 yd., L, there is a rhododendron grove, a spring, and campsite. At 0.4 mi, the cascading sound of Beech Creek begins, a sound that will grow in intensity for the next 3.0 mi. On the old logging road, both on the ascent and now descending, there are many species of wildflowers. Among them are baneberry (doll's eyes) black cohosh, brook saxifrage, great blue lobelia *(Lobelia siphilitica),* fetterbush, fringed loosestrife, red turtlehead *(Chelone oblique),* and aster. At 1.0 mi is a rock wall, R, followed by a steep descent on seven switchbacks for the next 0.6 mi. At 1.4 mi is a sign to High Falls, L, where a 0.2 mi spur trail descends into the Beech Creek Gorge to view an exceptionally high waterfall. Descend deeper into the gorge on the old logging road, and notice scenic cascades with rock slides and pools near a rock cut in the road at 2.4 mi. Ford the creek at 2.8 mi, and step over a rusty gate at 2.9 mi. Before crossing Bull Cove Branch there is a path upstream, L, to a cliff and waterfall. The road levels out and at 3.4 mi the trail turns R to leave the road. Slightly descend into a tall hemlock grove with a carpet of partridge berries and Christmas ferns. Ford Beech Creek at 3.5 mi. Ascend on a graded trail to a saddle, then descend on switchbacks to the access road (FR-56) and parking area at 4.0 mi. Turn R on the forest road and walk 1.1 mi to the parking area for the S trailhead of Deep Gap Branch Trail. From here backtrack 2.4 mi on the Deep Gap Branch Trail for a loop of 13.7 mi. (USGS-FS Maps: Rainbow Springs, Hightower Bald)

Wayah Ranger District

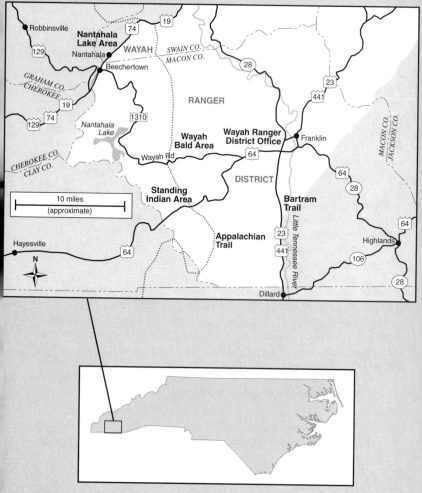

Introductions to Trail Areas

This district has 39 trails, all of which are hiking trails, though trails are used by hikers and equestrians. It has the longest sections of the AT and the Bartram Trail than any of the other three districts in the Nantahala National Forest. The AT is generally N/S and the Bartram Trail NW/SE, and one or the other have connections with all of the trails in the district except one.

Wayah Ranger District Office
The district office is located in the town of Franklin, a town with the major highway arteries of US-64 (E-W) (the state's longest highway) and US-23/441 S to Georgia and US-441 N to Tennessee. The office has books, maps, flyers, and other information on outdoor recreation.

Appalachian Trail
From the south the trail almost makes a circle of Standing Indian Recreation Area, crosses the famous Wayah and Wesser Balds with panoramic views from observation towers, and leaves the district at Wesser Falls in the Nantahala Gorge.

Bartram Trail
If counting the backcountry roads from Riverside N to Wallace Branch, this scenic trail has 44.7 mi in the district. For a super loop with the AT (of which 13.5 mi would be in the Cheoah Ranger District) the distance is 60.3 mi, the longest loop in the Nantahala Forest.

In a marvelous location, Apple Tree Group Camp (all services except electricity) has wild-trout waters, a network of trails, and a climb to London Bald (4,450 ft.).

Here is popular and impressive Standing Indian Campground (all services except electricity) with 15 trails branching out to the AT, Backcountry Information Center, the second largest yellow poplar in the nation, and Albert Mtn. Tower.

Wesser Creek Trail is a former route of the AT with access to panoramic Wesser Bald.

This special trail to a waterfall honors the late Rev. Rufus Morgan, affectionately called a modern Moses, who founded the Nantahala Hiking Club in 1950.

SECTION 4: WAYAH RANGER DISTRICT

The Wayah Ranger District has 134,894 acres of which 5,750 are in the Southern Nantahala Wilderness Area. The W side of the district is within the Macon County line where it borders the Tusquitee and Cheoah districts. Its NW boundary extends into Swain County to Fontana Lake and includes an isolated section of the Cowee Mtns. at the jct of Swain, Macon, and Jackson Counties. The Highland District is E and the Georgia state line and the Chattahoochee National Forest is the S boundary. The AT goes NW for 51.7 mi on the Nantahala Mtn. range from Deep Gap to Wesser at the Nantahala River. Some of the magnificent peaks on the AT are Standing Indian Mtn. (5,490 ft.), Albert Mtn. (5,280 ft.), Siler Bald (5,216 ft.), Cooper Bald (5,249 ft.), Rocky Bald (5,180 ft.), and Wayah Bald (5,336 ft.). In addition to the AT, another long trail, the Bartram Trail, passes through the district for 44.7 mi. The wilderness boundary surrounds the AT in the Standing Indian Area and at the headwaters of the Nantahala River. Adjoining the wilderness boundary in the NE is Coweeta Experimental Forest.

The district has nine recreational areas: Standing Indian with a campground, picnic, and fishing areas; Wayah Crest picnic area; Nantahala Gorge with fishing and water-sports facilities; the Apple Tree Group Campground (requires reservation); Wayah Bald and Arrowwood Glade picnic areas; and Almond Point, Alarka, Greasy Branch, and Wilderness Marina serving as boating sites at Fontana Lake.

The district's 39 trails are color blazed except the ones not maintained and **144** used mainly by hunters. Examples are Wildcat Trail (2.5 mi; USFS #14) (F), accessible from US-441/23 (between Otto and Norton communities) on Norton Rd (W) to FR-751, L (W), and to the trailhead at the end of the road. **145** Another hunters' trail is Cullowhee Trail (7 mi; USFS #370) (F). The W trailhead is at private property, but the NE access is from NC-107 and Speedwell Rd (SR-1001) 1.3 mi SE on NC-107 from the main entrance of Western Carolina University for a turn R on SR-1001; go 6.4 mi to park in a small area on the L of the highway. Cross the road into a stand of white pine. Kirby Knob is reached at 1.5 mi, and Sheep Knob is at 2.8 mi. Timbering may have blocked some of its passage. Other hunters' trails are described near Wayah Bald near the end of this section. Hiking trails are blazed blue, the AT white, and the Bartram Trail yellow. At the time this edition went to press there were not any designated mountain bike trails.

All horse trails in the district are blazed orange. Big Indian Loop Trail is **146-** described ahead. It and three other horse trails are on the same road, FR-67, **150** for easy access. Access to Blackwell Gap Loop Horse Trail (4.2 mi; USFS #366) (F, H) is at FR-67B near the Backcountry Information Center at Standing Indian Campground. Its other access is 1.8 mi farther upriver on FR-67 to FR-7282, L. This also is the trailhead access for Hurricane Creek Loop Horse Trail (4.3 mi; USFS #36) (F, H), which circles Hurricane Creek to the end of FR-67 in the shadow of Albert Mtn. Another equestrian trail is Thomas Branch Loop Horse Trail (3.8 mi; USFS #375) (F, H) 0.4 mi farther upriver on FR-67, L, at a horse camp. Camp Shortcut Trail (0.5 mi; USFS #36B) (F, H), is a connector between the horse camp and Blackwell Gap and Hurricane Gap horse trails to avoid using FR-67.

Address and Access: District Ranger, Wayah Ranger District, USFS, 90 Sloan Rd, Franklin, NC 28734; 828-524-6441. From the jct of US-441/23 and US-64 in Franklin, go W on US-64 for 1.0 mi and turn R on SR-1153 at the sign and go 0.3 mi.

Nantahala Lake Area (Macon County)

Access to all the trails in this area can begin at the Apple Tree Group Camp. The camp received its name from the fruit trees that once grew near Apple Tree Branch, the route of the Cherokee Indians between areas that are now Franklin and Robbinsville. At least two distinguished travelers passed this way. It is likely that Atakullakulla, "Little Carpenter," a Cherokee peace chief known to British royalty, met the famous botanist William Bartram in this location. (See the Bartram Trail description in the beginning of this chapter.) The camp is designed for group tent camping at four campsites, two of which serve 25 people and two of which serve 50 people; they are signed A through D. Water, sanitary facilities, and hot showers are provided. Reservations are necessary from the ranger's office. (USGS-FS Map: Topton)

Access: From Wesser on US-19 go SW to Beechertown Power Station. Turn L on SR-1310, follow up the river for 4.4 mi to FR-308, R, at a horseshoe curve. Go 3.1 mi on FR-308 to a jct with Dicks Creek Rd (SR-1401). Turn R, cross the bridge, and turn R to the camp entrance. From Franklin on US-64, go W 3.8 mi to Wayah Gap sign R and follow SR-1310 W 18.6 mi to Andrews Rd (SR-1400), which becomes SR-1401, L. Go 2.4 mi to the camp entrance, R. From Andrews take the Junaluska Rd (SR-1505) and go 12.5 mi E to the camp entrance, L.

151-   *Apple Tree Trail* (USFS #19B) (F)
154   **Length and Difficulty:** 2.2 mi, strenuous (elev change 1,640 ft.)
        Connecting Trails: Junaluska Gap Trail (4.3 mi; USFS #19, moderate)
(F); Diamond Valley Trail (0.9 mi; USFS #19D, easy) (F); Laurel Creek Trail
(1.5 mi; USFS #19F, easy) (F); (London Bald Trail)

        Trailhead and Description: Park across the road from Apple Tree
Branch and follow the blue blazes R of the branch on an old road. Cross the
branch and pass a jct with the blue-blazed Junaluska Gap Trail L at 0.3 mi.

        (On the Junaluska Gap Trail skirt E of the mountain, curve SW with SR-
1401 on the L to jct with the white-blazed Diamond Valley Trail at 1.6 mi.
Continue on an even grade through mixed hardwoods, hemlock, and rhododendron, occasionally going in and out of small coves to a jct with Hickory
Branch Trail at 3.0 mi. [Hickory Branch Trail is a 1.3-mi connector trail
between this point and the London Bald Trail.] Cross Matherson Branch at 3.5
mi, and jct with the London Bald Trail at 4.2 mi. Turn L to the highway, SR-
1401, in Junaluska Gap at 4.3 mi. Backtrack, or make a loop with the London
Bald Trail, or use a vehicle shuttle.)

        Continue on the Apple Tree Trail, cross the stream again at 0.7 mi, and
then pass a faint road jct. Proceed on a gradual grade through a forest of oak,
elm, white pine, beech, sassafras, silver bell *(Halesia carolina),* laurel, rhododendron, and numerous wildflowers. At 1.1 mi pass a jct with the blue-blazed
Laurel Creek Trail, R.

        (Laurel Creek Trail is similar to Diamond Valley Trail in that access and
exit are dependent on other trails. On the Laurel Creek Trail descend, first on
a slight ridge in hardwoods, and then into a deep dense grove of rhododendron
along Piercy Creek and to the mouth of a tributary, L, at 1.5 mi. A loop trail
at the jct with the Bartram Trail [formerly the Nantahala Trail], R, requires
another 5.5 mi of hiking to the campground. A turn L for 1.5 mi connects with
the London Bald Trail to form a loop back to the camp for 5.9 mi.)

        Continue ahead on the Apple Tree Trail to the white-blazed Diamond Val-
ley Trail jct at 1.4 mi, L.

        (Descend on the Diamond Valley Trail for 0.9 mi, following Diamond
Valley Creek to a jct with the Junaluska Gap Trail in a clearing at SR-1401
and Dicks Creek. Backtrack, or return L on the Junaluska Gap Trail for a loop
total of 4.2 mi.)

        On the Apple Tree Trail reach the summit of a knob at 1.7 mi. Climb
steeply on a second knob, reach the summit of a third peak SE of London Bald,
and reach a jct with the blue-blazed London Bald Trail at 2.2 mi. Backtrack, or

turn L to follow the London Bald Trail for 6.2 mi out to Junaluska Gap and SR-1401, or turn R and follow the London Bald Trail for 2.8 mi to its NE terminus at Sutherland Gap and jct with the Nantahala Trail. A return loop to the campground can be made from here on the London Bald Trail R and the Nantahala/Bartram Trail for a total of 9.3 mi. (See Nantahala Trail below.)

Nantahala Trail (USFS #19E) (F) 155
Length and Difficulty: 6.5 mi, moderate
Connecting Trails: (London Bald Trail); (Laurel Creek Trail); (Bartram Trail)
Trailhead and Description: Except for the last 0.5 mi W on this trail, it is now the Bartram Trail. It requires either backtracking for a total of 13.0 mi, connecting with other trails such as the N trailhead of London Bald in Sutherland Gap, or Laurel Creek Trail (1.5 mi E from Sutherland Gap) on the Bartram Trail as described above. (See the beginning of chapter 2 for details of the Nantahala/Bartram Trail from Apple Tree Group Camp.)

London Bald Trail (9.0 mi; USFS #19C) (F); *Hickory Branch Trail* (1.3 mi; USFS #19A) (F) 156-157
Length and Difficulty: 10.3 mi combined, strenuous (elev change 1,360 ft.)
Connecting Trails: (Junaluska Gap Trail); (Apple Tree Trail); (Nantahala Trail)
Trailhead and Description: This trail requires either backtracking for a total of 18.0 mi, or hiking a lesser distance by using a connecting trail to a second vehicle. Ascend on switchbacks of a timber road to a L turn on the S slope of a ridge to reach the crest at 0.8 mi. Slope L off the ridge, parallel the Macon/Cherokee county line, and turn NE at the headwaters of Pine Branch at 1.5 mi among oak, pine, maple, laurel, and hemlock. From here the trail weaves in and out of fern-covered coves on a generally level contour of about 4,000-ft. elev. Pass through a saddle on a spur ridge at 3.1 mi. At 3.7 mi, jct L with a spur trail to the ridge crest and NE end of FR-6166A. Continue from a cove and jct R at 3.9 mi with Hickory Branch Trail on a ridge.

(The Hickory Branch Trail follows the ridge crest but soon curves E to descend and cross the headwaters of Hickory Branch. From there it ascends to a knob before descending to cross Hickory Branch again. After another crossing of the branch among rhododendron and tall trees, it reaches a jct with Junaluska Gap Trail at 1.3 mi.)

Continuing on the London Bald Trail, slightly ascend to the S shoulder of Hickory Knob at 4.4 mi. Begin a long curve in a cove before turning L on a ridge. Switchbacks follow in the ascent to the E side of London Bald at 6.2 mi. Here is a jct R with Apple Tree Trail. (It descends 2.2 mi to the campground.) The trail continues on a moderate contour until Piercy Bald, where it descends rapidly on the main ridge to switchbacks. At 7.4 mi, jct R with FR-7082. It descends to jct with Apple Tree Trail, Branch Trail, and Diamond Valley Trail.) The London Bald Trail continues to descend, crosses small knobs, and drops to Sutherland Gap at 8.9 mi. It turns R and after 0.3 mi, is a jct with the Nantahala Trail. Backtrack, or take the Nantahala Trail and the Bartram Trail for another 6.5 mi to the campground. (USGS-FS Map: Topton)

Standing Indian Area (Macon County)

The Standing Indian Campground, a FS facility, has camping and picnic sites that are open all year. Reservations are not required except at the adjoining Kimsey Creek Group Camp. Water and sanitary facilities are provided, but there are not any electrical or sewage hookups. A special parking area for hikers and backpackers has been constructed at the Backcountry Information Center on FR-67/2 (0.2 mi L of the campground and picnic entrance gate). The Nantahala River, which flows through the campground, is a popular trout stream. The campground is exceptionally well landscaped in an area where the Ritter Lumber Company had its main logging camp for the Upper Nantahala basin. Downstream, at Rainbow Springs, the company had a double-head rig band saw mill to process huge trees. Although timber harvesting has continued in the area since it was first purchased in the 1920s, the upper headwaters are now protected by the Southern Nantahala Wilderness Area. The AT wraps around the S and E ridge of the basin and provides a master connecting route for the ascending trails. Forest vegetation in the area includes all the Southern Appalachian hardwoods, with groves of pine and hemlock. Bear, deer, turkey, grouse, fox, squirrel, raccoon, hawks, and owls are part of the wildlife.

The Cherokee Indian legend of Standing Indian Mtn. is that a Cherokee warrior was posted on the mountaintop to warn the tribe of impending danger from an evil winged monster that had carried off a village child. Beseeching the Great Spirit to destroy the monster, the tribe was rewarded with a thunderstorm of awesome fury that destroyed the beast, shattered the mountaintop to bald rubble, and turned the warrior into a stone effigy, the "standing Indian," in the process.

Access: From the jct of US-64 and Old US-64 (0.4 mi E of the Nantahala River bridge in Rainbow Springs and 12.0 mi W from Franklin), take Old US-64 for 1.8 mi to Wallace Gap and turn R on FR-67/1.

Support Facilities: A commercial campground, The Pines RV Park, is 5.0 mi W from Franklin on US-64. Full svc, open year-round. For more information, contact 490 Hayesville Hwy, Franklin, NC 28734; 828-524-4490.

Pickens Nose Trail (USFS #13) (F) 158

Length and Difficulty: 1.4 mi round-trip, easy

Special Features: rock-climbing area, nature study

Trailhead and Description: From the Backcountry Information Center drive 8.7 mi on FR-67 up the mountain to a parking area, L (0.7 mi beyond the AT crossing in Mooney Gap). Hike across the road and ascend before leveling on a rocky ridge. The first vistas, E-S, are at 0.3 mi, but the vistas W-S at 0.7 mi at Pickens Nose (5,000 ft.) are exceptionally scenic. The Chattahoochee National Forest is S and the Betty Creek basin is down 2,000 ft. from the top sheer cliffs. A beautiful area any season with all the evergreens, June is particularly colorful with laurel, rhododendron, azalea, black locust, and Bowman's root *(Gillenia trifoliata).* (USGS-FS Map: Prentiss)

Bearpen Gap Trail (USFS #22) (F) 159

Length and Difficulty: 4.8 mi round-trip, strenuous (elev change 1,200 ft.)

Trailhead and Description: From the Backcountry Information Center, drive 3.2 mi on FR-67 to the trail sign and parking area. (Parts of this trail have been relocated because of a timber sale.) Enter the forest L of a locked gate, hike 0.2 mi to a logging road, and take the R fork. Follow the road, and at 1.0 mi take the R fork to curve around a ridge. At 1.9 mi, cross the last stream near a large quartz rock in a hemlock grove. Galax, blue-bead, and wood betony are along the trail. Ascend steeply in a mixed forest; at 2.4 mi, reach the AT on gated FR-83 (Ball Creek Rd) in Bearpen Gap. (Across the road it is 0.3 mi up a steep and rocky path to Albert Mtn. [5,280 ft.] fire tower for the most panoramic views in the Standing Indian Area. Backtrack to the Bearpen Gap Trail or take the AT N 3.1 mi to Long Branch Trail and 1.9 mi down to the information center, or S on the AT for 6.3 mi to Timber Ridge Trail, R, which descends 2.5 mi to FR-67, and another 1.6 mi on the road to the W trailhead of Bearpen Gap Trail and parking area for a loop of 12.8 mi.) (USGS-FS Maps: Prentiss, Rainbow Springs)

160 *Kimsey Creek Trail* (USFS #23) (F)

Length and Difficulty: 7.4 mi round-trip, moderate

Trailhead and Description: From the Backcountry Information Center follow the blue-blazed trail to the picnic area, cross the Nantahala River bridge, follow Park Creek Trail N for 0.1 mi, and turn L at Kimsey Creek Trail sign. Skirt E of the mountain and follow a gradually ascending grade up Kimsey Creek. Three wildlife-grazing fields are on this route. At 2.6 mi, pass the confluence with Little Kimsey Creek; reach Deep Gap and the AT at 3.7 mi. Backtrack, or go L on the AT for 2.5 mi to Standing Indian (5,499 ft.) and return L on the Lower Ridge Trail to the campground and picnic area for a total circuit of 9.7 mi. (USGS-FS Map: Rainbow Springs)

161 *Lower Ridge Trail* (USFS #28) (F)

Length and Difficulty: 7.8 mi round-trip, strenuous (elev change 2,105 ft.)

Special Feature: views from Standing Indian

Trailhead and Description: This is a frequently used and exceptionally steep trail to the top of Standing Indian. There are views of the Nantahala basin on its ascent. Begin at the Backcountry Information Center parking area, follow the blue-blazed trail to the campground road, cross the bridge over the Nantahala River, and turn L to begin the trail. Go up the riverside and cross a road and footbridge over Kimsey Creek at 0.2 mi. Cross another stream at 0.5 mi. At 1.0 mi, begin a series of switchbacks in a forest of hardwoods, hemlock, and colorful patches of trillium and hepatica. At 1.5 mi, reach the ridge crest and follow the ridge L to arrive on top of a knob at 1.8 mi. Descend to John Gap at 2.1 mi. Skirt W of a knob, reach another gap, skirt W of Frog Mtn., and reach Frank Gap at 3.1 mi. Continue a steep ascent and reach jct with the AT at 3.9 mi for a spur climb of 0.2 mi to Standing Indian (5,499 ft.). Here from rock outcroppings are magnificent views of the Blue Ridge Mtns. and the Tallulah River Gorge running into Georgia. Backtrack, loop back to camp on the Kimsey Creek Trail, going R on the AT for 2.5 mi at Deep Gap for a return at 10.3 mi, or go L on the AT for 3.5 mi to Beech Gap Trail, turn L, and descend for 2.8 mi to FR-67 at a parking area (4.0 mi from the Backcountry Information Center parking area, the point of origin). (USGS-FS Map: Rainbow Springs)

162- *Big Laurel Falls Trail* (0.6 mi; USFS #29) (F); ***Timber Ridge Trail***
163 (2.5 mi; USFS #20) (F)

Length and Difficulty: 6.2 mi combined round-trip, easy to moderate

Special Features: scenic area at Big Laurel Falls

Trailhead and Description: From the Backcountry Information Center parking area drive 4.7 mi on FR-67 to joint trailheads of Big Laurel Falls Trail and Timber Ridge Trail. The blue-blazed Big Laurel Falls Trail goes R and crosses a footbridge over Mooney Creek in a forest of hemlock, yellow birch, and rhododendron. Follow an old RR grade arbored with rhododendron, curve L around Scream Ridge, and follow to the base of Big Laurel Falls at the confluence of Kilby Creek, Gulf Fork, and Big Laurel Branch at 0.6 mi. Backtrack. For the Timber Ridge Trail follow the blue blazes L from FR-67, ascend steeply on switchbacks, and skirt L of Scream Ridge in an area of rhododendron, birch, ferns, and cohosh. Cross an old forest road on the ridge at 0.7 mi and begin a descent through large beds of galax. Rock-hop Big Laurel Branch at 1.0 mi. Ascend to Timber Ridge and go through fern beds with a canopy of oaks. Reach the AT at 2.5 mi, 0.5 mi W of the AT Carter Gap Shelter. Backtrack. (USGS-FS Maps: Prentiss, Rainbow Springs)

Mooney Falls Trail (USFS #31) (F)   **164**

Length and Difficulty: 0.2 mi round-trip, easy

Trailhead and Description: From the Backcountry Information Center go up FR-67 for 5.5 mi to roadside parking for Mooney Falls. Hike 0.1 mi through a tunnel of rhododendron and laurel to a cascading fall on Mooney Creek. Remains of a fallen American chestnut tree are at the falls and on the ground are prominent wildflowers. Backtrack. (USGS-FS Map: Prentiss)

Park Ridge Trail (3.2 mi; USFS #32) (F); *Park Creek Trail* (4.8 mi;   **165-**
USFS #33) (F)   **166**

Length and Difficulty: 8.0 mi combined round-trip, moderate to strenuous (elev change 880 ft.)

Connecting Trails: (Lower Ridge Trail); (Kimsey Creek Trail)

Trailhead and Description: These trails connect at both the N and S trailheads to form a loop. From the Backcountry Information Center parking area follow signs and blue blazes through rhododendron and hemlock to cross a footbridge over Wyant Branch at 0.1 mi. On the paved campground road, turn L, cross the Nantahala River bridge, and reach a jct L with the Lower Ridge Trail. (The 3.9-mi. Lower Ridge Trail is a scenic route to the AT and Standing Indian Mtn.) Turn R and follow an old RR grade. At 0.3 mi, jct with the Kimsey Creek Trail, L. (The 3.7-mi Kimsey Creek Trail goes upstream to Deep Gap and a jct with the AT.) At 0.4 mi, is a jct with the Park Ridge Trail, L. Ahead on the old RR grade is the Park Creek Trail. If choosing the Park Ridge Trail, ascend, cross a small stream, and skirt E of Bee Tree Knob from a cove. At 1.0 mi arrive at a gap and ascend Middle Ridge in a hardwood forest. Leave the ridge at Penland Gap at 2.9 mi and reach FR-71/1 at Park Gap picnic and parking area at 3.2 mi. To the R is a jct with Park Creek Trail. (FR-71/1 goes L for 1.4 mi to Deep Gap and the AT, and R for 5.4 mi to US-64, 2.4 mi W of US-64/Old US-64 jct at Rainbow Springs.)

To follow the Park Creek Trail from N to S continue downstream of the Nantahala River after leaving the Park Ridge Trail. After 0.2 mi a narrow footpath leaves the old RR grade, L, and parallels the old RR grade for 0.9 mi. Either route can be hiked, but the footpath appears to be in need of more use by hikers; it is also a high-water route. The small dam on the river at 1.2 mi is constructed to permit upstream migration for spawning trout. Reach Park Creek at 1.6 mi and cross on a footbridge. Follow up the cascading Park Creek where the trail is flanked by mixed hardwoods, hemlock, rhododendron, ferns, mossy rocks, and profuse wildflowers. At 2.6 mi cross a small stream and ascend gradually on the E side of the slope to cross two more streams before beginning switchbacks at 4.5 mi. Reach FR-71/1 and the Park Gap picnic and parking area at 4.8 mi. Backtrack or return on the Park Ridge Trail. (USGS-FS Map: Rainbow Springs)

167-   *Big Indian Loop Trail* (8.0 mi; USFS #34) (F, H); *Beech Gap Trail*
168   (2.8 mi; USFS #35) (F)

Length and Difficulty: 10.8 mi combined, moderate to strenuous (elev change 910 ft.)

Trailhead and Description: From the Backcountry Information Center, drive 2.8 mi on FR-67 to the parking area and signs for Big Indian Loop Trail and Big Indian Rd (FR-67/A). The trail is designated a horse trail, but it is used by hikers, bikers, fishermen, and hunters. Begin at the footbridge across the Nantahala River. Turn R and then curve L around a knoll for 0.5 mi to a fork near a tributary to Big Indian Creek. Choose the L fork if taking the shortest route to Beech Gap Trail. On a generally level contour proceed through a forest of oak, maple, poplar, hemlock, and rhododendron to cross Big Shoal Branch, followed by a L turn to cross Big Indian Creek at 1.1 mi. Parallel the river in an ascent, then move away from the river in a steep approach at 1.8 mi (where a spur trail descends L 0.6 mi to FR-67). Reach a knoll on Indian Ridge at 2.1 mi, and after 0.3 mi farther arrive at Kilby Gap. Ascend steeply before leveling off at the jct with Beech Gap Trail at 2.8 mi. It goes ahead, S; the Big Indian Loop Trail turns sharply R, NW.

(The Beech Gap Trail weaves around the base of Blue Ridge through a forest of hardwoods, laurel, and flame azalea to cross a streamlet flowing to Kilby Creek in a deep cove at 0.6 mi. Then it makes a longer curve around a toe of Blue Ridge to jct with the AT at Beech Gap at 1.1 mi. Backtrack, or follow the AT L (N) for 2.5 mi to a jct with the Timber Ridge Trail. It begins L and descends 2.5 mi to the parking area at Mooney Creek and FR-67. From here it is 1.9 mi down FR-67 to the Big Indian Loop Trail parking lot.)

If continuing on the Big Indian Loop Trail from the Beech Gap Trail jct, the trail at first ascends on the NE slope of Blue Ridge to a curve at 3.1 mi. For the next 2.0 mi through hardwoods, laurel, and rhododendron slicks, the elev stays slightly above the 4,600-ft. contour. At the greater change it is 4,800 ft. NW and above Deadening Knob. After approaching the S slope of Upper Trail Ridge, the trail begins to descend rapidly at 5.4 mi to the headwaters of Nichols Branch. After a switchback and crossing of Nichols Branch, the trail turns E, then S, on a return to the fork for a completion of the loop. Turn L for a return to the parking lot at FR-67 at 8.0 mi. (USGS-FS Map: Rainbow Springs)

Long Branch Trail (USFS #86) (F)   169

Length and Difficulty: 3.8 mi round-trip, moderate

Trailhead and Description: From the parking area at the Backcountry Information Center go E across the road and climb gradually to a partial lookout of the Nantahala basin at 0.6 mi. Pass through a forest of hemlock, yellow birch, maple, and wildflowers, and cross a horse trail and grazing field with strawberries at 1.5 mi. At 1.7 mi, cross Long Branch, which has remnants of an old RR grade. Cross a seeded road, begin a steep climb at 1.8 mi, and at 1.9 mi reach the AT on the main ridge line. Backtrack, or make a loop by hiking R on the AT for 3.4 mi to Albert Mtn., described above, and reach jct with the Bearpen Gap Trail for a descent to FR-67 for 2.4 mi. Hike downstream on FR-67 for 3.2 mi to the point of origin for a total of 10.9 mi. (USGS-FS Map: Rainbow Springs)

John Wasilik Memorial Poplar Trail (USFS #30) (F)   170

Length and Difficulty: 1.4 mi round-trip, easy

Trailhead and Description: From Wallace Gap on Old US-64 go 0.4 mi on the Standing Indian Campground road, FR-67, to Rock Gap. Follow the trail sign to a graded trail through an impressive and significant stand of yellow poplar and cherry to the second largest yellow poplar in the US (26.1 ft.

in circumference and 9.0 ft. in diameter). An early Wayah district ranger, John Wasilik, has been remembered by naming the poplar in his honor. (USGS-FS Map: Rainbow Springs)

Wesser Area (Swain and Macon Counties)

171   *Wesser Creek Trail* (USFS #26) (F)

Length and Difficulty: 3.5 mi, strenuous (elev change 2,227 ft.)

Trailhead and Description: This blue-blazed trail is part of the former white-blazed AT, which was relocated in 1980 to avoid highway traffic and a residential district. At the jct of US-19 and Wesser Creek Rd (SR-1107), drive up SR-1107 for 1.7 mi and turn L to a parking area. Hike 0.4 mi to cross Wesser Creek in a grassy meadow near the old shelter. Ascend on switchbacks and join the roadway in sections to cross a small stream at 1.5 mi. At 1.7 mi, cross another small stream and leave the road to a graded trail with switchbacks. In a forest of hardwoods ascend steeply in sections and at 3.5 mi, reach a jct with the new route of the AT. A spring is to the L. Backtrack, or take the AT for an extended hike. To the L, it is 0.7 mi to Wesser Bald (4,627 ft.) for panoramic vistas of the Nantahala Mtn. range from the newly constructed Wesser Bald platform. Beyond the peak it is 1.4 mi to Tellico Gap and Tellico Rd (SR-1365). If taking the AT N, it is 4.8 mi of undulating trail to the A. Rufus Morgan Shelter and another 0.8 mi to US-19 and the Nantahala Outdoor Center by the Nantahala River. (USGS-FS Map: Wesser)

Wayah Bald Area (Macon County)

172   *A. Rufus Morgan Trail* (USFS #27) (F)

Length and Difficulty: 1.0 mi round-trip, moderate

Trailhead and Description: From US-64 and US-441/23 jct S of Franklin, go W on US-64 for 3.8 mi. Turn R at sign for Wayah Bald, and go 0.2 mi to sign for Lyndon B. Johnson Conservation Center at jct of Old US-64 and SR-1310. Turn L and go 4.1 mi to FR-388 and turn L. Proceed for 2.0 mi on a gravel road and park at the trail sign, R. Ascend on switchbacks through open woods of tall poplar, cucumber tree, maple, oak, and birch, with ferns and wildflowers banking the trail. Deer may be seen on the trail. Cross a stream at 0.2 mi and reach the lower cascades of Left Prong of Rough Fork at 0.4 mi. Continue on the trail to the base of the upper falls at 0.5 mi. Backtrack.

(The trail is named in honor of the Rev. Albert Rufus Morgan, 97 years old when he died in Asheville, February 14, 1983. Affectionately called the

"Modern Moses" and "Uncle Rufus," no one has ever loved the mountains, and the AT in particular, more than he. He was founder of the Nantahala Hiking Club in 1950. One of his favorite peaks was Mt LeConte in the Smokies; he climbed it 172 times, the last on his 92d birthday. "He was a poet, a priest, and a great friend of the Appalachian Trail," wrote Judy Jenner in a tribute to him in the *Appalachian Trailway News (ATN)*, May/June 1983. She also wrote a feature story on him in the Nov/Dec edition of ATN, 1979.) (USGS-FS Map: Wayah Bald)

Wilson Lick Trail (0.2 mi; USFS #369) (F); *Wayah Bald Trail* (0.3 mi; USFS #374) (F, W)   **173-174**

Length and Difficulty: 1.0 mi round-trip, easy

Trailheads and Description: From the jct of Boardtree Rd (FR-380) and Ball Rd (SR-1310) continue up the mountain on SR-1310 to Wayah Gap. Turn R (N) on gravel FR-69. In addition to two short trails from the road, there are two longer unblazed hunters' trails. At 0.5 mi, R, at a parking area is 1.5-mi Shot Pouch Trail (USFS #17). An unmaintained hunters' trail, it crosses the AT and goes L on the slope of a ridge to cross Shot Pouch Creek before continuing to a dead-end. Farther up the road after 0.8 mi is the blue-blazed Wilson Lick Trail on the R. It ascends to the AT. Continuing up the road for 0.3 mi is FR-69B on the L. Turn or walk from here to a hairpin curve, the S trailhead for 3.5-mi Rocky Bald Trail (USFS #18). An unmarked and unmaintained hunters' trail, it crosses the AT and follows a ridge before descending to the E side of Rocky Bald. It exits at FR-711 at a hairpin curve on a ridge. (Vehicle access to this exit from the community of Kyle is to turn off Whiteoak Rd onto FR-711 and ascend 3.9 mi to the ridge.) Beyond the jct with FR-69B, continue to a parking area at Wayah Bald (5,342 ft.). Follow paved Wayah Bald Trail to a tower for spectacular views of Trimont Ridge E and Nantahala Mtns. S. (USGS-FS Map: Wayah Bald)

Chapter 3

Pisgah National Forest

The mountain cannot frighten one who was born on it.
—Johann Friedrich von Schiller

In the 1994 Land and Resource Management Plan of the Nantahala and Pisgah National Forests, 17 special-interest areas (18,458 acres of the forest's total 495,979 acres) are described in the Pisgah National Forest. Such designated areas are set apart from land for "timber production and not available for use by vehicles." Although not classified as wilderness under the Wilderness Act of 1964, the protection has some of the same characteristics for protecting the natural environment. These areas may consist of unusual geological formations, botanical and wildlife concentrations, bog locations, heath balds, and old-growth forests. Because of the selections, the public is better served. Some of these special-interest places are described in this chapter.

There are three wilderness areas: Middle Prong (7,460 acres) and Shining Rock (18,483 acres) in the Pisgah Ranger District and Linville Gorge (12,002 acres) in the Grandfather Ranger District. Two others in the Grandfather district, Lost Cove and Harper Creek, were proposed by the mid-1980s, but Congress has not acted. The wilderness areas, watershed, and streams provide protection for the many species of wildlife common to the Appalachian region. More than 200 species of plants have been found in the Roan Mtn. area alone, and 39 of 55 species of wild orchids in the state are found in the Pisgah. Dominant trees are oak, birch, maple, and yellow poplar (also called tulip tree). Conifers range from shortleaf pines to red spruce and fragrant fir. Primary among the fish is the brook trout, often stocked in the cascading tributaries. Deer among the big game and squirrel among the small game are the most plentiful.

Pisgah National Forest is the oldest of the state's four national forests. Its irregular boundaries encircle three districts—Pisgah in Buncombe, Haywood, Henderson, and Transylvania Counties; Grandfather in Avery, Burke, Caldwell,

McDowell, and Watauga Counties; Appalachian (former Toecane) in Avery, Buncombe, Madison, Mitchell, and Yancey Counties; and the former French Broad in Haywood and Madison Counties.

The Pisgah is a natural world unto itself with the Blue Ridge Parkway dividing it, the AT on its border with TN, and such extraordinary natural attractions as Looking Glass Rock and Falls, Mt. Pisgah, Bald Mtn., Roan Mtn. Gardens, Table Rock, Hawksbill Mtn., Harper Creek Falls, Sliding Rock, Shortoff Mtn., Upper Creek Falls, Black Mtns., and Big Lost Cove Cliffs. It is also the site of a number of historic firsts. Gifford Pinchot, hired by George Vanderbilt to manage his vast Biltmore Estate, initiated the first forest management program here in 1892, and six years later Carl A. Schenck opened here the first school of forestry in America, the Biltmore Forest School. (Reconstructed and named the Cradle of Forestry, it is located in the Pisgah Ranger District on US-276.) After Vanderbilt's death in 1914, the area was sold to the US government and in the process became one of the first tracts of the Pisgah National Forest. The first property purchased under the federal Weeks Act of 1911 was 8,100 acres on Curtis Creek in the Grandfather Ranger District.

Pisgah has 40 recreational areas for fishing, picnicking, nature study, hiking, and camping. Some of the areas are designed for primitive camping and have limited facilities to protect the ecology. A directory of these facilities may be requested from one of the addresses below. The Mountains-to-Sea Trail (MST), planned and under construction from Clingmans Dome to Nags Head since the early 1980s, incorporates a number of trails already on the NF inventory plus new trails through the Pisgah National Forest from the Haywood Gap in Middle Prong Wilderness to the Beacon Heights area (see appendix A).

The three districts of the Pisgah National Forest are as follows:

- Appalachian Ranger District, USFS, P.O. Box 128, Hot Springs, NC 28743. French Broad Station 828-622-3202. (On Bridge St, US-25/70, in Hot Springs.) Toecane Station 704-682-6146. (On US-19E Bypass in Burnsville.)
- Grandfather Ranger District, USFS, 109 East Lawing Dr, Nebo, NC 28761; 828-652-2144. (At NE corner of I-40, Nebo Exit 90, and Harmony Grove Rd.)
- Pisgah Ranger District, USFS, 1001 Pisgah Highway, Pisgah Forest, NC 28768; 828-877-3265. (From jct of US-276/64 and NC-280, N of Brevard, 2.0 mi W on US-276.)

Appalachian Ranger District
French Broad Station

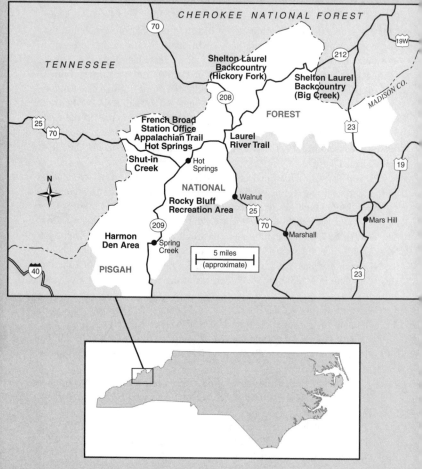

Introductions to Trail Areas

The trail descriptions begin with trails NE to SW along the Tennessee/North Carolina state line, then emphasize the trails central to the Hot Springs area, before returning to the state line area farther SW for Harmon Den.

French Broad Station Office of Appalachian Ranger District
This office was formerly the district office of the French Broad district. It is in the heart of the historic town of Hot Springs. Books, maps, and flyers are available to the public in the station office. In addition there are free maps and flyers with AT and other trail information at a bulletin board outside the office entrance to serve visitors when the office is not open.

Appalachian Trail
About 88 mi of the AT passes through this station's area, including passing by the front door of the station's headquarters. (See chapter 5 for points of interest information.)

Shelton Laurel Backcountry Area (Big Creek) *109*
The wilderness-like trails in this area ascend by cascading streams, undergrown streams, wildlife flats, and scenic cliffs.

Shelton Laurel Backcountry Area (Hickey Fork) *111*
These trails are also wilderness-like with waterfalls and flumes, ferns and wildflowers, plus lookouts to the vastness of two national forests in two states. The Laurel River Trail boasts splashing cascades in its final miles to join the wide French Broad River, this historic trail is a floral garden unequaled in this station.

Hot Springs Area *114*
Home to much of the AT, examples of some the trails are a ledge of the French Broad River and a panoramic view from Rich Mountain.

Rocky Bluff Recreation Area *116*
Here is a campground with rocky bluffs and scenic trails near the mesmerizing sound of Spring Creek and the summer signing of cicadas. Shut-in Creek has streams, meadows, wildlife, butterflies, and the mystery of Betty.

Harmon Den Area *118*
This place has trails for hikers, an outstanding horse camp, and the magic of all bald knobs, the unquestionable scenic quality of Max Patch Mountain.

SECTION 1: APPALACHIAN RANGER DISTRICT
A. FRENCH BROAD STATION

The district was formerly two districts, the French Broad and Toecane. Now
the names are retained as ranger stations. The French Broad Station has
80,373 acres, some of which are the most rugged and isolated terrain in the
Appalachians. Its boundaries are almost exclusively in Madison County, with
the NE corner of Haywood County adjoining. Its W boundary is flanked by
the Cherokee National Forest in Tennessee. Along most of this border is 66.0
mi of the AT on high, scenic, and remote ridges and peaks such as Big Butt
(4,838 ft.); Camp Creek Bald (4,844 ft.), the district's highest; Rich Mtn.
(3,643 ft.); Bluff Mtn. (4,686 ft.); Walnut Mtn. (4,280 ft.); Max Patch Mtn.
(4,629 ft.); and Snowbird Mtn. (4,263 ft.). Sparse population in Madison
County allows this beautiful area to remain a tranquil and natural place to love
and visit. Hunting, fishing, and running the white water of the French Broad
River are popular sports in the district. The varied flora is an enticement to any
botanist. An example is described below in the Laurel River Trail section.

The recreation areas and points of interest in the district are Rocky Bluff
(campground and picnic area, described below); Silver Mine (group campground and picnic area, see Pump Gap Trail below); Murray Branch Picnic
and Canoe Launch Site (see River Ridge Trail below); and in Harmon Den
area is dispersed use, picnic facility, and Harmon Den Horse Camp. A desig-
175   nated bicycle loop trail is 5.4-mi Mill Ridge Bike Trail (also open to hikers).
To access this trail, drive 3.4 mi E of Hot Springs on US-27/70 to Tanyard Gap
(under the AT bridge), turn L on first road, and turn L again to cross the highway on the bridge. Follow the road to its end at a parking area. The trail has
scenic views, particularly of the Laurel River Forge. A more recent bicycle
176   loop trail has been designated. It is 7.5-mi Golden Ridge Bike Trail (also open
to hikers) that begins on FR-3577 off FR-467. To access the trailhead from
Tanyard Gap and the AT bridge, go R on the paved road. At the end of the
pavement turn L on FR-467. After 4.5 mi is the jct with FR-3577. The
unblazed trail follows forest roads and you may need a map with instructions.
If so, contact the station office (828-622-3202) for information. The Laurel
River Trail, described ahead is also used by hikers and bicyclists. The station
office has some free single-page maps of individual or group trails with
accesses and statistics. For information on a rafting and canoeing outfitter in
Hot Springs, contact French Broad Rafting Co at 800-842-3189, or the Madison County Chamber of Commerce at 828-689-9351 for other outfitters and

other recreational activities; for warm, natural mineral baths at Hot Springs, call 828-622-7676.

Address and Access: French Broad Station of the Appalachian Ranger District, USFS, P.O. Box 128, Hot Springs, NC 28743; 828-622-3202. (On Bridge St, US-25/70, in Hot Springs.)

Support Facilities: Because Rocky Bluff Campground (5.0 mi S of Hot Springs) does not have hookups or showers, a nearby commercial facility is Hot Springs Spa and Campground, 828-622-7676, 800-462-0933, or www.hotspringsspa-nc.com. It is located between the French Broad River and the RR in Hot Springs. It has hot showers (arrangements can be made for natural mineral baths), massage therapy, primitive campsites, and sites with hookups. The campground is open year-round. The AT goes through the heart of the city where the forest office, motel, post office, grocery store, service station, and restaurants are within two blocks of one another. Two restaurants are Smoky Mountain Diner (828-622-7571) and Paddler's Pub and Grill (800-303-7238).

Shelton Laurel Backcountry Area (Big Creek) (Madison County)

Jerry Miller Trail (USFS #290) (F) 177

Length and Difficulty: 9.2 mi round-trip, moderate to strenuous (elev change 2,020 ft.)

Connecting Trails: (AT)

Special Features: Big Creek footbridge, white oak flats, Baxter cliff

Trailhead and Description: From the jct of US-25/70 and N-208, take NC-208 N 3.5 mi to jct with NC-212 in the community of Belva. Turn R on NC-212 and drive 10.7 mi to Big Creek Rd (SR 1313) that forks L at Carmen Church of God. (A USFA sign here may have Big Creek Backcountry Area.) Follow SR-1313 1.2 mi to end of paved road and at a sawmill, R. Stay ahead on a narrow road that fords a small stream into the national forest (FR-111). After 0.3 mi is a small sign (may be an arrow), L. After a few yards is a dispersed campsite with a picnic table. The trailhead is L at a stone monument that honors Jerry W. Miller, whose maternal family name was Shelton, settlers in this valley in 1790. Miller was an assistant US attorney and advocate of laws to protect national forest resources.

Follow a yellow blaze across a handcrafted footbridge over Big Creek. Enter a flat area filled with wildflowers, then up seven switchbacks to a ridge crest at 0.3 mi. Follow the ridge's S flank among patches of teaberry, galax, and trailing arbutus. To the L and below is White Oak Flats Branch with slender flumes and cascades. The trail joins a former RR timber track and gradually ascends to 1.4 mi at historic white oak flats, a fertile plateau used as a grazing field (bear, deer, and squirrel may be seen here.) Turn R (there may be a yellow blaze on a post here) on an old road and pass through the field. Through the middle of the field is a line of Chinese chestnuts, planted by the USFS for wildlife. Reenter the forest at 1.6 mi and follow and old forest road that curves and switchbacks in backcountry coves to 4.2 mi. On the ascent the hardwood forests provide outstanding autumn colors, particularly the understory of golden yellow striped maple. At 2.9 mi is a rhododendron canopy, and at 4.0 mi is Huckleberry Gap. (Here is a short side trail, L, to Baxter Cliff.) After the road ends in a L curve, ascend a rocky and narrow trail through rhododendron, laurel, and azalea. Connect with the AT, R and L, in Bearwallow Gap at 4.6 mi. Backtrack. (To the L on the AT it is 0.2 mi to scenic views from Blackstock Cliff, R, and another 0.2 to White Rock Cliff, L.) If not backtracking, a loop can be made by hiking R on the AT 3.0 to jct R with Fork Ridge Trail (also called Big Creek Trail). (See description ahead.) Follow it down into the hollow for 2.0 mi and to a parking space on FR-111. Follow the road downstream 0.7 mi to where you parked for the Jerry Miller Trail at 10.3 mi. (USGS-FS Map: Greystone TN/NC)

178   *Fork Ridge Trail* (USFS #285) (F)

Length and Difficulty: 4.0 mi round-trip, strenuous (elev change 1,610 ft.)

Trailhead and Description: This yellow-blazed trail is also known as Big Creek Trail. From the jct of US-25/70 and NC-208, follow NC-208 up Big Laurel Creek for 3.5 mi to a jct with NC-212 at Belva. Turn R on NC-212 and proceed for 10.7 mi to Big Creek Rd (SR-1312), which forks L at Carmen Church of God. Follow SR-1312 for 0.7 mi where the pavement ends at a fire warden station. Continue for another 0.6 mi on a gravel road and enter Pisgah National Forest where the road becomes FR-111. After 1.0 mi farther reach parking space, L, at Wildcat Hollow Creek's confluence with Big Creek.

From the R side of the parking area ascend gradually on a well-graded slope that runs E of Fork Ridge. Reach the ridge crest at 0.7 mi. Forest flora consists of hardwoods, with the lower elevation having rhododendron and buckeye, and the higher elevation having laurel, flame azalea, and copious patches of large, sweet, highbush blueberries. Spots of wintergreen, dwarf iris, and galax furnish a ground cover. The wildlife includes bear, deer, turkey, grouse, and chipmunk. After reaching a ridge sag at 0.9 mi, ascend steadily, sometimes steeply, on switchbacks to jct with the AT at 2.0 mi (It is 0.2 mi R on the AT to the Jerry Cabin Shelter.) Backtrack, or make a 9.2-mi loop with a R (E) on the AT for 4.3 mi to a jct with the 3.9-mi Green Ridge Trail and a return on FR-111 (see below). (USGS-FS Maps: Greystone, Flagpond)

Green Ridge Trail (USFS #287) (F)   179

   Length and Difficulty: 3.9 mi, strenuous (elev change 2,420 ft.)
   Special Features: underground creek, remote, wildflowers
   Trailhead and Description: From the jct of NC-208 and NC-212 at Belva, turn on NC-212 and proceed 10.7 mi to the Carmen Church of God. Turn L at the fork of Big Creek Rd (SR-1312) and go 1.3 mi to the Shelton Sawmill, R. Cross Dry Creek at the FR-111 sign and park in a small area, or turn R if FR-3509 is not gated. Cross the creek and after 1.0 mi leave the gravel road onto an old forest road. Cross the creek repeatedly on a yellow-blazed trail. Forest vegetation is ironwood, poplar, white pine, hemlock, oak, and birch. Both spring and summer wildflowers are exceptionally profuse; they include starry campion, bee balm, trillium, orchids, twisted-stalk, helle-bore, meadow rue, Indian-physic, and phlox. Among the forest animals are bear, bobcat, turkey, grouse, owls, chipmunk, and the timber rattlesnake. The creek goes underground in places, appearing dry; thus its name. (Some of the mountain residents have a number of ghost stories about this hollow.) At 1.4 mi, the old road ends and the trail begins across the creek. Cross small cove streams in switchbacks at 1.7 and 1.8 mi. Waterfalls are R at 1.9 mi. Curve L and continue to ascend on a well-graded trail that may have borders of nettles. After ascending the slope of Green Ridge, reach the top in a flat area and jct with the AT at 3.9 mi. Backtrack. The jct may not be signed, but it is 4.4 mi R to Devil Fork Gap on the AT to NC-212, and L on the AT for 4.3 mi to the jct with Fork Ridge Trail (see Fork Ridge Trail above). (USGS-FS Maps: Greystone, Flagpond)

Shelton Laurel Backcountry Area (Hickey Fork)

Hickey Fork Trail (2.3 mi; USFS #292); *Pounding Mill Trail* (2.4 mi,   180-
USFS #297); *White Oak Trail* (2.3 mi; USFS #293) (F)   182

   Length and Difficulty: 7.0 mi combined one-way; 6.6 mi shortest loop with FR-465, moderate to strenuous
   Connecting Trails: (AT)
   Special Features: flumes and waterfalls, lookout tower, wildlife

Trailhead and Description: From the jct of US-25/70 and NC-208, take NC-208 N 3.5 mi to a jct with NC-212 in the community of Belva. Turn R on NC-212 and drive 6.9 mi to a USFS sign: Shelton Laurel Backcountry Area. Turn L on Hickey Fork Rd (SR-1310). (Farther NE on NC-212 for 3.8 mi is entrance L to Big Creek Backcountry Area.) After 1.1 mi on SR-1310 and FR-465 is a small parking area and USFS gate. From the gate go upstream 75 yd. and descend on steps to cross a bridge over the East Prong of Hickey Fork. Follow and old RR grade and ascend to a ridge top, then descend. Turn R to rock-hop a creek at 0.5 mi. For the next 0.8 mi, ascend, sometimes steeply, to cross small tributaries with flumes in a gorge of hemlock, yellow poplar, and rhododendron. At 1.4 mi in the West Prong of Hickey Fork is a spectacular flume and waterfall. Continue to ascend and reach Weng Gap at 2.3 mi. Here is a jct with Pounding Mill Trail, R and L. (To the L the trail is closed because of private property boundaries.)

Turn R on Pounding Mill Trail and ascend and descend on two knobs. At the nose of Seng Ridge, reach a jct with White Oak Trail, R, at 0.7 mi. There is a natural spring at 0.9 mi but it may be seasonal. Ascend steeply on Seng Ridge, then level some at 1.1 mi. The last water source is at 1.3 mi and 1.6 mi. At 2.4 mi, reach a jct with the AT, R and L in a rhododendron grove. (To the L the AT is 6.2 mi SW to Allen Gap at NC-208, and 13.9 mi NE to Devil Fork Gap at NC-212. Also going NE it is 2.2 mi on the AT to Jerry Miller Trail, described on a preceding page.) (Ahead a 0.2 mi spur trail steeply ascends to the top of Camp Creek Bald [4,844 ft.] at the Tennessee state line. From a lookout tower are fantastic views W of the Cherokee National Forest and into the Tennessee Valley, N and E is the chain of Bald Mtns., and SW are views of the Great Smoky Mtns.)

In backtracking, there are two options. One is to use the Hickey Fork Trail; the other is to hike the White Oak Trail and follow the Hickey Fork Road 1.3 mi downstream to where you parked. The White Oak Trail descends to cross the headwaters of Hickey Fork at 0.1 mi, then drops deeply into a damp and dark hollow at 0.4 mi. In a rocky hardwood forest with groves of rhododendron and tall hemlock, the trail approaches a waterfall, R, at 0.6 mi. Descend steeply and proceed around a ridge (scenic views in the wintertime) to switchbacks. At 1.5 mi is a jct with a forest road, R, but turn L among laurel. There is jct with a logging road at 2.0 mi; keep R; a new growth forest is L. Descend and arrive at FR-465 at 2.3, the trailhead. Here is a cul-de-sac among rhododendron, roadside patches of coltsfoot, and tall yellow poplar.

From here it is 1.3 mi R, with scenic East Prong of Hickey Fork by the roadside, to the parking space at Hickey Fork Trail described above. (FR-465 may be closed because of flooding. The USFS staff has requested that until the road is repaired and officially open, do not attempt to hike the road.) (USGS-FS Maps: Greystone, White Rock)

Betty's Place Trail (No USFS #) (F)   183
Length and Difficulty: 1.1 mi round-trip, easy
Trailhead and Description: From the parking space of Shut-in Creek Trail, drive 1.9 mi farther upstream on Upper Shut-in Creek Rd to Betty's Place, a nature preserve, L in a curve. (There should be a sign here.) After 0.1 mi, park in a designated parking lot. Hikers will find trail information at kiosks. Follow blazes into the forest and cross a footbridge over a cascading stream, a tributary to the West Fork of Shut-in Creek. Pass through an extraordinary natural garden of ferns, mosses, wildflowers, flowering shrubs, evergreens, and hardwoods on a curve and gradual ascent. After 0.5 mi is a flat cove with rich soil and between two small streams, the vanished home site of Betty. Briefly ascend on the loop, then descend partially on an old road to the parking lot. (USGS-FS Map: Lemon Gap)

Laurel River Trail (USFS #310) (F, B)   184
Length and Difficulty: 6 mi round-trip, easy
Special Features: RR history, exceptional diversity of plant life
Trailhead and Description: Park at the jct of US-25/70 and NC-208 in the parking area, near dumpsters, on the E side of Big Laurel Creek (1,600 ft.). Enter on a private gravel road, descend slightly, and bear R to a fork at 0.1 mi. Arrive at a private dwelling and a gate at 0.2 mi. Follow an old RR grade with vertical cliffs L and white-water rapids R. Pass a spring at 0.4 mi L and a burley tobacco barn L at 0.7 mi. Cross the Pisgah National Forest boundary at 0.9 mi. On a yellow-blazed trail unsurpassed for riverside beauty, pass a series of rapids at 1.2 mi. Turn L at 2.9 mi to a logging and mining settlement of the past. Reach the Southern RR tracks and the French Broad River at 3.0 mi. Backtrack.

In the spring and summer of 1977 and 1978, the NC Natural Heritage Program of the Department of Natural Resources and Community Development made a botanical study of this 3.0-mi trail. The discovery of more than 250 species of vascular plants was an overwhelming surprise. Five species listed as threatened or endangered were found. Among them are alumroot *(Heuchera longiflora)*, wild rye grass *(Elymus riparius),* saxifrage *(Saxifraga caroliniana),* and a species each of phacelia and corydalis. Bluebell, Dutchman's pipe, orchid, and soapwort *(Saponaria officinalis)* were among the common wildflowers. (USGS-FS Map: Hot Springs)

Hot Springs Area (Madison County)

185   *Roundtop Ridge Trail* (USFS #295) (F)

Length and Difficulty: 3.1 mi (or 3.7 mi if using S access road); backtrack 7.4 mi, moderate to strenuous (elev change 1,400 ft.)

Connecting Trails: (AT)

Special Features: wildflowers and mature forest, side trail to Rich Mtn. Lookout

Trailhead and Description: This trail is historic but awkward for access at both ends because the S trailhead is on private property, and the N trailhead can only be accessed by using the AT. (Many years ago the AT routing from Hot Springs N followed the private road off River Rd on the private property, but after about 0.2 mi switchbacked L (W) away from the private homes. It then went up a ridge to Locust Gap, and N to the Tennessee/North Carolina state line. There it turned R to Ramsey Gap, crossed Rich Mtn., and connected with the current AT routing.) If starting from the top (N) at Hurricane Gap, the access is as follows: From Hot Springs by vehicle, drive 3.5 mi E on US-25/70 to Tanyard Gap. Drive under the AT overpass to the first road, L. At the overpass road jct, turn R and follow the paved road. At the end of the pavement, turn L on FR-467. Drive 4.3 mi to Hurricane Gap where the AT crosses FR-467. Park on the roadside.

Ascend and then descend S on the AT for 1.3 mi. In the process swing around the ridge to a spring and campsite in a ravine at 1.0 mi (Nearby is a spur trail, R, that leads up to the Rich Mtn. firetower [3,364 ft.] for superb panoramic views.) Descend and at 1.3 mi, take the R fork in a curve, the N trailhead of Roundtop Ridge Trail. (At this point the AT continues L to descend 2.1 mi to the bridge over US-25/70 at Tanyard Gap.) After a slight ascent on the yellow-blazed trail descend on a professionally designed trail constructed by the CCC. The trail curves in and out of small ridges on the E side of Roundtop Ridge. Tall hardwoods partially shade a continuing display of galax, pipsissewa, and trailing arbutus. Also on the side and top of the ridge are dense stretches of Lily of the Valley whose roots are poisonous (a disturbing revelation to those who mistakenly harvest it as ramp). One of the largest beds of the lily is at 1.4 mi. At 0.6 mi, 1.1 mi, and 1.9 mi are steep, deep, and scenic coves of tall hardwoods with minor understory. Cross over the ridge at 2.1 mi and descend into a cove to approach another ridge with young white pines on an old road. At 2.6 mi, leave the ridge to the R and curve L toward the trail's end at the Hot Springs water tower at 3.1 mi. Backtrack, or descend on a gated road to a private home on the L. Stay R on a gravel access road, cross Cascade Branch, and descend on the private road to River Rd, R and L, at 3.7 mi. No parking space here. A turn L is 0.3 mi to US-25/70 and a reconnection with the AT at the French Broad River bridge and Hot Springs. (USGS-FS Map: Hot Springs)

Jack Branch Trail (2.4 mi; USFS #299) (F); *River Ridge Loop Trail* (1.3 mi; USFS #281) (F) 186-187

Length and Difficulty: 6.1 mi combined round-trip, easy to strenuous (elev change 1,400 ft.)

Trailhead and Description: From US-25/70 at the end of the French Broad River bridge in Hot Springs, turn on Paint Rock Rd (SR-1304). Follow downriver for 4.1 mi to end of pavement, and continue another 0.3 mi on a gravel road. Park L by the river, across from Bartley Island. Enter the trail near a sign and follow a blue-blazed trail on an old road in a deep ravine up the E slope, away from Jack Branch, for 0.1 mi. The forest flora includes mixed hardwoods with hemlock, rhododendron, fetterbush, and buffalo nut *(Pyrularia pubera)* in the lower elev, and chestnut oak, laurel, and pines in the upper elev. At 0.4 mi leave the damp area and reach a ridge crest at 0.5 mi (Plans by the district are to construct a short connector trail, L, on the ridge to River Ridge Loop Trail.) Follow the ridge in a generally xeric environment with patches of wintergreen, trailing arbutus, blueberries, and azalea. At 0.9 mi, turn NW, follow an upgrade in and out of tributary coves of Murray Branch to 1.9 mi, and begin a NE ascent through old fields with views of French Broad River Valley. Reach the Tennessee state line and Cherokee NF in a gentle gap at FR-422 at 2.5 mi. Backtrack. (Primitive trails lead L for 1.9 mi to Bearpen Gap and Ricker Branch Trail into Tennessee and R for 3.5 mi to Rich Mtn. Lookout Tower and the AT.)

For the River Ridge Loop Trail trailhead continue downriver 0.7 mi from Jack Branch Trail on SR-1304 to Murray Branch Rec Area (mainly for picnicking near the French Broad River). Park on the L. Walk across the road to the R side of a small stream at the trailhead. Ascend 0.2 mi to a fork in the loop. Turn R through white pines, and arrive at the ridge rim for a beautiful view of the river, R. (Before turning L to return, a connector trail may have been constructed R to connect with Jack Branch Trail.) Turn L at 0.7 mi to follow an old road for a return to Murray Branch Rec Area. (USGS-FS Map: Hot Springs)

188-   *Pump Gap Trail* (5.5 mi; USFS #309) (F); *Lover's Leap Trail* (0.6 mi;
189   USFS #308) (F)

> **Length and Difficulty:** 7.1 mi combined round-trip, moderate to strenuous
>
> **Trailhead and Description:** From the N side of the French Broad River bridge on US-25/70 in Hot Springs, curl under the bridge on Lover's Leap Rd for 0.3 mi to the FS boundary gate and parking area at Silver Mine Creek. Begin Pump Gap Trail (loop) whether on the road upstream to the campground, or jointly with the orange-blazed Lover's Leap Trail, which ascends on the R near the gate. After 0.2 mi the Pump Gap Trail descends L to the campground area and the Lover's Leap Trail turns sharply R. (It climbs 0.4 mi to a jct with the AT and a remarkable vista of the French Broad River, the town of Hot Springs, and Spring Creek Mtns. beyond. From this rocky precipice is a drop of 500 ft. and part of a Cherokee Indian romance legend. Backtrack, or descend on the AT to the river and return to the parking area for a loop of 1.6 mi. If following the AT L [N] from Lover's Leap it is 1.9 mi to Pump Gap, where a return on the Pump Gap Trail makes a loop of 4.0 mi to the parking area.)
>
> On the yellow-blazed Pump Gap Trail pass the Silver Mine Campground and follow upstream among hemlock, tulip tree, rhododendron, and fetter-bush. Pass two former explosive storage bunkers, R. Cross tributaries of Silver Mine Creek five times and at 1.0 mi, reach jct with the return trailhead of the loop, L. Ascend through evergreens and at 1.5 mi, intersect with the AT in Pump Gap, an area with tall hardwoods and hemlock. Cross the AT, gradually descend, make a sharp L away from Pump Branch at 2.1 mi. Ascend two switchbacks around a dry mountain side where banks of wintergreen and trailing arbutus grow. Turn L on a ridgeline at 2.3 mi. Cross, or briefly follow, a few old logging roads before an ascent to cross the AT again at 3.1 mi. After 100 yd., R, is the grave site of Lucinda Daniel. Start a descent into a beautiful cove of hemlock, rhododendron, and cascades at 4.3 mi. Complete the loop at 4.5 mi, turn R, and return to the parking lot at 5.5 mi. (USGS-FS Map: Hot Springs)

Rocky Bluff Recreation Area (Madison County)

The Rocky Bluff Recreation Area provides camping, picnicking, hiking, nature study, and fishing in Spring Creek. The area is open usually from mid-

April to mid-December. It has flush toilets, lavatories, and water fountains but
no showers. The campground is on a high ridge under tall white pines and
oaks and has cement tables, a grill, and graveled tent sites. The area was formerly a residential settlement with farms and a school.

Access: From Hot Springs, go S on NC-209 for 3.3 mi.

Spring Creek Nature Trail (1.6 mi; USFS #312) (F); *Van Cliff Trail* (2.7 mi; USFS #313) (F)   190-191

Length and Difficulty: 4.3 mi combined, easy to strenuous

Trailhead and Description: From the S edge of the center of the Rocky
Bluff Recreation Area (3.3 mi S of Hot Springs on NC-209), follow the trail
sign and descend gradually on the yellow-blazed Spring Creek Nature Trail.
At 0.5 mi, arrive at a vista of Spring Creek near a large rock formation. Turn
L for 65 yd. and then turn R to follow a well-graded and scenic trail around
the mountain on the L side of the cascading stream. At 1.2 mi turn L and
begin an ascent on an old road to the campground and picnic area. Flora
includes white pine, hemlock, fetterbush, basswood, oak, liverwort, and
abundant wildflowers.

For the more strenuous Van Cliff Trail, follow the yellow blazes SW from
the S edge of the center of the picnic area on a grassy road. At 0.1 mi, turn R
over a rocky treadway (with poison ivy) and climb to NC-209 at 0.3 mi. Turn
L on the highway for fifty yd. and go R on an old road. Ascend, sometimes
steeply, R of cascading Long Mtn. Branch. At 0.7 mi, turn sharply L over the
branch and follow another old road; hike the N side of the ridge. Forest trees
consist of white pine, hemlock, basswood, oak, and hickory. Parts of the trail
have running cedar, cancer root *(Conopholis americana),* and Indian pipe
(Monotropa uniflora). Make a sharp L over a stream in a cove at 0.9 mi. Reach
the top of a ridge at 1.3 mi, and begin a descent into a rocky ravine at 1.6 mi.
Follow an old road and switchbacks to NC-209 at 2.2 mi. Cross the highway
and descend steeply, turn sharply R among boulders at 2.4 mi, cross Long
Mtn. Branch at 2.5 mi, and return to the campground at 2.7 mi. (This trail is
also known as the Long Mountain Branch Trail.) (USGS-FS Map: Spring
Creek)

Shut-in Creek Trail (USFS #296) (F)   192

Length and Difficulty: 4.0 mi round-trip, easy

Trailhead and Description: From Hot Springs, drive W on US-25/70 for
2.7 mi to Upper Shut-in Creek Rd (SR-1183) and turn L at a store. Go 2.3 mi

to a small parking area on the N side of the Shut-in Creek bridge. Follow an old jeep road, SE, and upstream of the East Fork of Shut-in Creek, in a hollow. Frequently rock-hop the stream and its small tributaries. Other sections of the trail are wet from mountain seepage. Liverwort covers some of the rocks. At 1.0 mi, pass through a beautiful meadow of clovers, asters, daisies, and other wildflowers. Deer have been seen here. Enter a white-pine stand and at 1.7 mi a hemlock stand. Ascend to ruins of a pioneer homestead at 1.8 mi. Reach a jct with the AT and FR-3543 at 2.0 mi in Garenflo Gap. Backtrack. (To the L, it is 6.6 mi on the AT to Hot Springs, and to the R, it is 3.5 mi to Bluff Mtn. [4,686 ft.].) (USGS-FS Maps: Lemon Gap, Paint Rock)

Harmon Den Area (Haywood and Madison Counties)

This area is in the western corner of the French Broad Station of the Appalachian Ranger District. On its south border is I-40 and Pigeon River, and its north border is Cherokee National Forest in TN. Near Brown Gap and the AT is Harmon Den Mtn., a legendary name for an early settler who resided under a rock overhang. During the nineteenth century, the lands were habitually timbered. In 1936 the USFS purchased a large section of the Harmon Den property from a timber company, and a CCC camp was established. Many of the white pines now in the forest were planted by the CCC teams in the 1940s. Near and on the border of the state is 24.4 mi of the AT with Groundhog Creek and Roaring Fork shelters. Generally remote with dispersed usage, the Harmon Den area has numerous scenic gaps, knobs, branches, and springs. Recreational usage includes hiking, horseback riding, hunting, fishing, picnicking, and camping (primitive and Harmon Den Horse Camp facilities). (There are not any designated bicycle trails, but mountain bikers may use open and gated roads signed with a bicycle symbol.) The most awesome and panoramic viewing site is from Max Patch Mtn., a massive grassy bald 4,629-ft. high. If you are in this area, do not leave until you experience the spectacular views; a sunset or sunrise in unforgettable. On clear days you can see the Smokies to the SW and Mt. Mitchell to the E. In spring and summer, the bald has many species of flowers and clovers. By August there are patches of yarrow and butter-and-eggs (*Linaria vulgaris*). The AT crosses the bald as part of a 5.0-mi relocation of the AT in 1983. The change was the result of 14 years of work and negotiation by the late Arch Nichols and the Carolina Mountain Club, USFS, and others. Initially, in the early 1880s the mountain top was cleared for cattle and sheep pastureland. To keep the landscape grassy, the USFS must now use a prescribed management of fire and mowing. In the mid-1990s there was an archaeological discovery of a Midland Indian dwelling site (c. 300 BC) near the base of the mountain. The Harmon Den Area distinctly has three locations of activities. One is in the Max Patch Mtn., the scenic showpiece of the area, NE of the Harmon Den Horse Camp; another is Cold Springs Creek basin of FR-148 with the Harmon Den Horse Camp the center of activity; and another is W of Harmon Den Horse Camp with Brown Gap being the access to a cluster of hiking trails. They are described in that order.

Max Patch Upper Loop Trail (1.5 mi) (F); *Max Patch Lower Loop Trail* (2.6 mi) (F); *AT* (part of Max Patch loops; USFS #1) (F) *Buckeye Ridge Trail* (3.8 mi or 4.9 mi; USFS #304) (F, H) **193-195**

Length and Difficulty: 1.5 mi to 4.9 mi loops, easy to moderate

Special Features: expansive and scenic bald, wildflowers, photography options

Trailhead and Description: The main access route to the parking lot for Max Patch Mtn. is Exit 7 on I-40 N on Cold Springs RD (FR-148) (7.0 mi E of Tennessee state line). Follow FR-148 to a jct with Max Patch Rd (SR-1182) at 6.2 mi and stay L. Follow SR-1182 for another 1.8 mi to the Max Patch parking lot R. If arriving from Hot Springs at a jct of US-25/70 and NC-209, drive S 8.0 mi on NC-209 and turn R on Meadow Fork Rd (SR-1175). (A sign indicates 10 mi to Max Patch.) After 5.0 mi is a sign to turn R on Little Creek Rd (SR-1181). Pavement ends after 0.3 mi. After 3.3 mi is a sign for Max Patch, R. (To the L, it is 0.2 mi to Robert Gap Horse Trail.) If arriving from Del Rio, TN (E of Newport) at US-25/70 and TN-107, and after 6.0 mi (end of TN-107), turn L on Round Mtn. Rd. Follow it 6.0 mi to Round Mtn. Campground high in the Cherokee National Forest. Continue 1.8 mi to Lemon Gap and the AT, and another 3.5 mi to Max Match Mtn. parking lot, L.

There are two access loops (hiking only) from the parking lot on SR-1182. The 1.5 mi Max Patch Upper Loop Trail, clockwise, is from the gate, L. (To avoid erosion, a sign forbids a direct climb, and other regulations do not allow camping or fires on any part of the grassy areas.) After an ascent of 0.5 mi, reach a jct with the AT, R and L. Turn R and at 0.6 mi, reach the summit, where there is a 1933 benchmark. To complete the loop, continue on the AT ridgeline route S to a steep descent with steps. At 1.1 mi, leave the AT at an old gravel road and turn R on a grassy road for a return to the parking lot at 1.5 mi. For the 2.6 mi Max Patch Lower Loop Trail, leave the parking area L and follow the same routing to the summit at 0.6 mi, except backtrack 0.1 mi on the AT and descend into the woods. At a level area is a campsite under a grove of maples at 1.3 mi. After 0.1 mi farther is a trail-distance sign where the AT turns L. Leave the AT by turning R on an old road. Along the way are blueberry and blackberry patches and outstanding views of the E side of Max Patch Mtn. At 1.7 mi, join the Buckeye Ridge Trail (USFS # 304) (F, H) and follow it 0.3 mi (where it abruptly turns L into the woods to its S trailhead at Max Patch Rd after 0.7 mi). Continue on the old road for 0.2 mi to cross the AT at a sign. Turn R and follow a grassy road near the SW base of the mountain for 0.4 mi to the parking lot at 2.6 mi.

(For an unofficial third and fourth loop, you could go farther on the AT and the Buckeye Ridge Trail. [The following distances include the 0.5 mi up the mountain from the parking lot to the AT and the 0.1 mi to the summit with a 0.1 mi backtrack as described in the Max Patch Lower Loop Trail.] At the trail-distance sign [the one mentioned above, 0.1 mi from the maple grove] stay on the AT, L, and go NE. Pass through a rhododendron tunnel and at 1.6 mi connect with the Buckeye Ridge Trail, R. Your choice here is to continue on the AT for 0.2 mi to connect with the Buckeye Ridge Trail [now on FR-3535] for a L turn. After 1.3 mi on the Buckeye Ridge Trail, exit at Max Patch Rd [SR-1182], turn L by Max Patch fishing pond and return to the parking lot at 3.4 mi. Alternatively, follow the Buckeye Ridge Trail NE after the rhododendron tunnel, up a grassy hill. On this route you can look back toward Max Patch for astonishing views of its E side. At 2.1 mi, turn R at the edge of the woods, then L into the woods. After connecting with FR-3535, turn L at 2.5 mi. Cross the AT at 2.7 mi and follow the Buckeye Ridge Trail, as described above, to SR-1182 at 4.0 mi. Turn L and pass the Max Patch fishing pond for a return to the parking lot at 4.4 mi. The fields and forest roads of the Buckeye Ridge Trail have many wildflowers in the spring and summer. On FR-3535, for example in the summer, are red monarda, filmy angelica *(Angelica triquinata),* and yellow and orange jewelweed. The road is in good condition and shows very little indication that it is both a hiking and equestrian trail. However, the first 0.7 mi of the Buckeye Ridge Trail from its south origin at SR-1182 is not recommended for hiking. The grade may have muddy multiple trail cavities and erosion. The trail is 3.8 mi between its two trailheads on SR-1182, or 4.9 mi if using SR-1182 for a loop.)

Harmon Den Horse Camp Trails

The Harmon Den Horse Camp is located in an upstream plateau between Cold Springs Creek and Fall Branch. The general area there and nearby Little Fall Branch is the widest flat section in all of the Harmon Den Area. The campground has 10 sites with horse stalls. Each site has a picnic table, tent pad, grill, lantern post, and manger. In addition there is a hand water pump, vault restroom, garbage receptacle, horse water trough, and manure dump. Although designed for horseback riders, the campsites are open to other forest users. There is a campground-site fee of $15 per night, and a maximum of four horses and eight people per site. The campground is open from March 1 to the end of October. Reservations are required. For more information, contact Hot Springs Station (828-622-3202) Mon through Fri from 8 AM to 4:30 PM. It is from this camp that equestrians (or hikers or mountain bikers) could use 5 designated trails and a network of more than 20 gated or open forest roads. A USFS map shows the equestrian trail symbols on the roads, and the USFS also provides a guide list on trail and camp usage by horseback riders.

Trail access: Beginning with the Harmon Den Horse Camp location, the easiest entrance is from I-40, Exit 7 (7.0 mi E of Tennessee state line) onto Cold Springs RD (FR-148). After 3.6 mi, turn R on FR-3526. To the immediate L is a grassy picnic area. Drive 0.3 mi to a L gated camp entrance (FR-3570 curves R and is one of a network of other roads S of the camp). The following five designated horse trails are all accessible from FR-148. Although hikers may also use the trails, hikers rarely do, with the exception of parts of Buckeye Ridge Trail. Also, with exception of the Buckeye Ridge Trail, the four trail lengths may have changed because of rerouting. Near the jct of FR-148 and FR-3526, pass the picnic area on FR-3526, cross the bridge over Cold Springs Creek, and immediately turn L to enter the Cold Springs **196** Trail (3.6 mi; USFS #302). Follow the trail upstream (NE). In parallel with FR-148, it crosses the stream occasionally and a number of tributaries. It crosses the creek for the last time and turns S to a jct with FR-3562, the road that can be followed S to enter the Harmon Den Horse Camp.

Continuing up the mtn of FR-148, it is 0.8 mi to the S entrance of Cherry **197** Creek Trail (1.6 mi; USFS #300), L, in a curve. It ascends along Cherry Creek, crosses a number of tributaries, crosses a forest road, and ends at Max Patch Rd (SR-1182), S of the AT and N of the Buckeye Ridge Trail. Continuing up the mountain another 1.0 mi on FR-148 from the Cherry Creek Trail

198   is the S entrance of Cherry Ridge Trail (1.1 mi; USFS #301). (This trail may
be overgrown and out of service.) Continuing up the mtn of FR-148, it is 0.8
199   mi to Robert Gap Trail (2.5 mi; USFS #303), R. FR-148 ends here and SR-
1182 begins. At the trail entrance is space for loading and unloading horses,
and there are bridle hitching posts. The trail follows on an old timber road S on
the W side of a mountain to exit on SR-1182 near Whiteoak Spring. Now leaving FR-148 and continuing 0.2 mi up the mountain toward Max Patch on SR-
1182, pass a jct with Little Creek Rd (SR-1181), R. (Little Creek Rd is 3.3 mi
E to SR-1175 [Meadow Fork Rd], L, and another 5 mi NE to NC-209, where
a L is N to Hot Springs and a R is S to I-40.) Remaining on Max Patch Rd (SR-
1182) up the mountain is 0.4 mi to the N trailhead of Cherry Ridge Trail with
hitching posts, L. (This trail may be overgrown.) After another 0.5 mi is Buckeye Ridge Trail S entrance, R. Continue ascending 0.3 mi on SR-1182 the
parking lot for Max Patch Mtn. and signboard is R. From here on SR-1182 the
road descends 0.4 mi to the NW exit of Buckeye Ridge Trail. (See description
of Buckeye Ridge Trail and Max Patch loop trails above.) Below is a description of the third location of activity in the Harmon Den Area.

200-   *Rube Rock Trail* (4.3 mi; USFS #314) (F); *Groundhog Creek Trail*
201   (2.0 mi; USFS #315) (F); *Appalachian Trail* (2.9 mi; USFS #1) (F)
   Length and Difficulty: 9.8 mi combined round-trip, strenuous (elev
change 1,840 ft.)
   Trailhead and Description: From I-40, Exit 7, described above for
Cherry Creek Trail, drive up FR-148 to FR-148A, L, just before the Harmon
Den parking lot. Drive up FR-148A 1.3 mi to Browns Gap and intersect the
AT. Park here. Follow the AT S 0.6 mi to a jct with the Rube Rock Trail, L. (It
is 2.3 mi on the AT to Deep Gap, from which a return on the loop is made.)
The trail descends on the E side of the ridgeline of Harmon Den Mtn. for 0.5
mi before easing out on the crest. After a knob, it descends to a jct with FR-
357A (which is also a horse trail) at 0.9 mi. Turn R, follow it 0.5 mi, turn L
off the road, and continue the descent to a tributary of the Rube Rock Branch
at 1.4 mi. Crisscross the stream and at 2.2 mi, cross the main branch among
tulip tree, hemlock, and rhododendron. Cross the branch twice more to the
slopes of a side ridge of Harmon Den Mtn. Descend steeply in hardwoods and
laurel to Tom Hall Branch, where the traffic sounds of I-40 can be heard at 3.3
mi. Turn W around a toe of the ridge to enter the hollow of Rube Rock
Branch. Cross the branch again, curve around the toe of Hickory Ridge to
more I-40 sounds, and go N to jct with Groundhog Creek Trail. (To the L, it

is 0.5 mi out to a field, FR-3522, and a gate at a dead-end I-40 ramp, 5.9 mi W from the welcome center and rest area. No parking is allowed at the ramp or forest gate.)

Ascend the hollow of Groundhog Creek Trail through tulip tree, maple, hemlock, and birch. At 0.9 mi, cross Chestnut Orchard Branch, followed by Ephraim Branch. At 1.8 mi, reach Groundhog Creek Shelter, a stone shelter with five bunks. A spring is nearby. Continue ahead for 0.2 mi to reach the AT at Deep Gap (also called Groundhog Creek Gap). A loop can be made R to join the Rube Rock Trail after 2.3 mi on the AT for a return loop of 9.7 mi. (On the AT at Deep Gap it is 5.6 mi NE to Max Patch Rd [SR-1182], and 7.8 mi SW to Pigeon River and I-40.) (USGS-FS Map: Waterville)

Appalachian Ranger District
Toecane Station

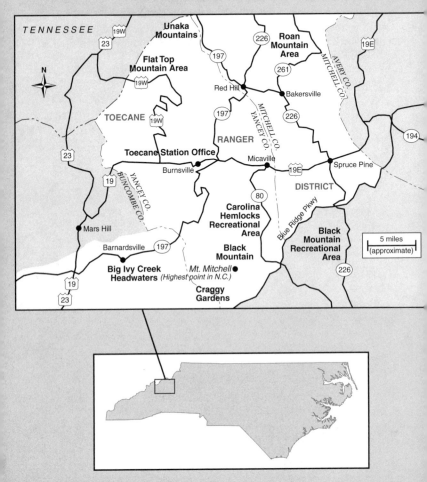

Introductions to Trail Areas

The order of these trail descriptions are from SW to NE near the Blue Ridge Parkway, on or near the AT.

Toecane Station Office of Appalachian Ranger District
Toecane Station was formerly Toecane District; it is now part of Appalachian Ranger District in Burnsville. The office has books, maps, flyers, and other material available to the public.

Appalachian Trail
The station trails connect with about 50 mi of the AT, which allows for a number of circuit arrangements to be made. (See chapter 5 for AT points of interest.)

Mountains-to-Sea Trail
It connects with other trails for 40 mi in this district, touches Blue Ridge Parkway outcrops, and climbs to rocky mountainsides.

Craggy Mountains Area 128
Among purple rhododendrons and moss covered rocks are trails, one of which is Snowball Mountain Trail. Access is at BRP milepost 367.6 at Beetree Gap.

Big Ivy Creek Headwaters 129
A dozen trails are here among tributaries, waterfalls, cliffs, wildlife, and wildflowers. At the end of FR-74 is access to classic Douglas Falls pristine grove of hemlock.

Black Mountain Recreation Area 132
A campground, waterfalls, cascades, picnic area, and trails beside the South Toe River.

Black Mountains 135
Leading north from Mt. Mitchell State Park is the rugged Black Mountain Crest Trail up and over scenic peaks such as Cattail (6,583 ft.) and Celo Knob (6,427 ft.).

Carolina Hemlock Recreation Area 136
Beside the rapids and pools of South Toe River is a campground, picnic area, and a scenic nature trail.

Flat Top Mountain Area 138
Historic and remote, the high and scenic trails are on the N flank of Flattop Mt. and above the Nolichucky River.

Unaka Mountains 139
On a forest road, this marvelous loop trail takes you to the high cliffs over the Nolichucky River for stunning views.

Roan Mountain Area 140
In groves of purple rhododendron and flame azalea the trails take you through an alpine wonderland of evergreen forests and rock formations.

B. TOECANE STATION

The Toecane Station (formerly the Toecane Ranger District) received its name from the Toe and Cane Rivers. According to legend, the white settlers shortened the name of an Indian princess, Estatoe, who wished to marry a brave from another tribe, whom her tribe rejected and killed. In her grief she drowned herself in the South Fork of the Toe River. The station's 78,009 acres are in four major segments: two in the N that border the Tennessee state line and the Cherokee NF, and two in the S that border the BRP and a portion of the Grandfather Ranger District. The most SW segment covers the Craggy Mtn. Scenic Area and Big Ivy Creek drainage in the NE corner of Buncombe County. The most E section is the Black Mtn. range, an area with 18 peaks over 6,300 ft. in elev, and the South Toe River drainage area in Yancey County. Mt. Mitchell State Park, the state's oldest and highest, adjoins the W side of this section. The largest NW segment in Yancey and Mitchell Counties is a remote area through which flows the Nolichucky River in a canyon inaccessible except by whitewater and the Clinchfield RR. Farther E in the N segment of the station is the majestic Roan Mtn. Area and its famous gardens in Mitchell County.

The station's first 25,000 acres were purchased in 1913 to protect the South Fork of the Toe River's watershed and for its great supply of timber. Because the major timbering and railroad building were abandoned in 1915, large groves (some of the largest in the US) of red spruce and Fraser fir have remained.

The AT follows the ridgeline in and out of North Carolina and Tennessee except in an area near Erwin where it crosses a highway bridge over the Nolichucky River. Another famous trail, the Overmountain Victory Trail (OVT) (USFS #308), a national historic trail, enters this district from Tennessee at the Yellow Mtn. Gap intersection with the AT (see Yellow Mtn Gap Area ahead). It was near the state line that the frontier patriots camped September 27, 1780, on their march S. The route of the OVT is approximately 315.0 mi, beginning in Craig's Meadow in Abingdon, Virginia, and ending at Kings Mtn. National Park battlefield in South Carolina where the defeat of the British Col Patrick Ferguson's forces was a turning point in the Revolutionary War.

Recreational facilities include two family campgrounds, one at Black Mtn. on FR-472 and Carolina Hemlock on NC-80, both along the South Fork of the Toe River. One group campground is at Briar Bottom, adjoining Black Mtn. Picnic areas are Corner Rock on FR-74 E of Barnardsville, Lost Cove on FR-472 near Black Mtn., Roan Mtn. off NC-261, Spivey Gap (also called Bald Mtn.) on US-19W near the Tennessee border, and Carolina Hemlock Pavilion on NC-80 at the Carolina Hemlock Campground. Some of the special-interest areas are Roan Mtn., North Fork Ivey Creek, Walker Cove, Big Bald Mtn., Black Mtn., and Craggy Mtn. (all described in the 1994 Plan, Amendment 5, of the Nantahala and Pisgah NFS).

The district has three major waterfalls, one at Black Mtn. Campground; one on FR-471, an entrance road to the campground; and one isolated near Elk Park. Access to Roaring Fork Creek Falls Trail (not related to the Roaring Creek above) is off NC-80 (2.0 mi W of BRP on FR-471, L, at Black Mtn. **202** Campground sign. After crossing the first bridge, turn L at entrance to USFS maintenance center. Park near a gate R, and ascend on the grassy road 0.5 mi, where at a curve enter a rocky path through rhododendron to a large multiple-level waterfall. Backtrack. For Big Falls Trail (USFS #172) access is from **203** Main St in Elk Park, US-19E, and proceed N on Elk River Rd (SR-1305), which becomes FR-190 for 5.0 mi to Elk Falls parking area. Begin the hike on a timber road to Elk River, and descend to the bottom of the 50 ft. amphitheater-like falls for a round-trip of 0.5 mi. Camping is not allowed here.

As in other districts the list of trails in use varies. Some trails are overgrown and unsigned and without name or maintenance, but useful for game hunters. The USFS staff continues to maintain and repair trails according to funding and work force (including volunteers) available. A few trails are tentatively slated to be taken off the official trail system list. They are Straight Creek Trail (USFS #160); Hensley Fields Trail (USFS #168); Camp Alice Shelter Trail (USFS #181); Locust Ridge Trail (USFS #193); Shope Creek Trail (USFS #169); and Annie's Cove Trail (USFS #185). Woody Ridge Trail **204** (2.2 mi one-way, USFS #177, is being restored with grant funds. Access is 1.7 mi N on NC-80 from Carolina Hemlock Recreation Area to a L turn on Whiteoak Rd. After 0.6 mi turn R, drive 0.9 mi to a curve, and stay L on another road. Parking is 0.6 mi ahead. Another trail needing restoration is Big **205** Hump Trail (2.0 mi one-way, USFS # 163) from US-19E near Elk Park to the AT. (If you know about these trails and wish to assist in restoring and maintaining them, perhaps you could offer volunteer service by calling the station office [828-682-6146].)

Address and Access: Appalachian Ranger District, USFS, P.O. Box 128, Burnsville, NC 28714; 828-682-6146. Access is on the US-19 E bypass, in Burnsville.

Craggy Mountains Area (Buncombe County)

206   *Big Butt Trail* (USFS #161) (F)

> **Length and Difficulty:** 6.0 mi, moderate to strenuous
>
> **Special Features:** remote, scenic views
>
> **Trailhead and Description:** From Burnsville on NC-197, go SW 16.0 mi to the top of Cane River Gap, or from Barnardsville on NC-197, go NE 10.0 mi. Begin at a parking area and ascend on a white-blazed trail along the Yancey/Buncombe county line. Reach Mahogany Knob, after 20 switchbacks, at 1.7 mi, Flat Spring Knob at 2.4 mi, and Flat Spring Gap at 2.6 mi. Primitive campsite and water are available here. Ramps, a long-lasting, garlicky wild onion, is found in sections along the trail area. Curve around the W side of Flat Spring Knob, dip to a saddle, and then slope to the E side of Big Butt (5,960 ft.). Switchback to the S side of the peak and follow a narrow ridge at 3.4 mi where the views of Black Mtn. range, Mt. Mitchell, and Cane River Valley are magnificent. Reach Little Butt at 3.7 mi for more great views. Descend on steep rocky switchbacks among rhododendron to a long saddle before climbing 10 switchbacks to Point Misery (5,715 ft.) at 4.4 mi. Descend to Brush Fence Ridge, climb a knob, and descend again before the last ascent to the BRP Balsam Gap parking lot, mp 358.8 (5,320 ft.) at 6.0 mi. Here is a jct with the Mountains-to-Sea Trail, which crosses the highway. Backtrack or have a second vehicle. (USGS-FS Maps: Mt. Mitchell, Montreat)

207   *Douglas Falls Trail* (USGS #162) (F)

> **Length and Difficulty:** 5.6 mi round-trip, strenuous
>
> **Special Features:** waterfalls, wildflowers, wildlife, old-growth hemlocks
>
> **Trailhead and Description:** At the end of FR-74 parking lot, enter the white-blazed trail. (See Big Ivy Creek Headwaters ahead.) Descend easily 0.5 mi to the base of beautiful 70-ft. Douglas Falls. Tall hemlock, maple, and oak rise from the misty gorge. Wild hydrangea and witch hazel are on the trail bank. Follow the trail L, steeply, among huge old-growth hemlock among large boulders to 0.7 mi. From here to the trail's end at the MST, the steep, rough, wet climb is through a botanical display of ferns, mosses, mushrooms, beds of partridgeberry, patches of moosewood and yellow root, merrybell, and umbrella leaf *(Diphylleia cymosa)*. The treadway is rocky with snags, tree roots, and logs in a treacherous but scenic passage. On wet rocks the tenacious and mucky clay makes shoes as slippery as soap. Cross a cascading stream at 1.2 mi and arrive at spectacular Cascades Falls R and L at 1.8 mi. Carefully cross the falls. (Power of the cascades has bent the steel posts holding the

cable.) Cross another tributary of Waterfall Creek at 2.0 mi. Ascend on switchbacks up Sprucepine Ridge in a forest of yellow birch, beech, and oak. Reach a jct with the MST at 2.8 mi R and L. Backtrack. (To the L is 1.5 mi on the MST to Graybeard Mtn Overlook on the BRP, mp 363.4, and R is 1.7 mi to Craggy Gardens Picnic Area parking lot, mp 367.7.) (USGS-FS Maps: Craggy Pinnacle, Montreat, Mt. Mitchell, Barnardsville)

Snowball Trail (USFS #170) (F)   **208**
   Length and Difficulty: 6.0 mi round-trip, moderate
   Trailhead and Description: An old trail, which once had about 30 switchbacks in its final descent and was abandoned, is now open sans switchbacks. Access is off the BRP, mp 367.7, to the Craggy Gardens Picnic Area. At the second curve, Beartree Gap, Barnardsville Rd (FR-63) begins L at a gate. The road to the picnic area turns R and the MST crosses the entrance road here. Park off the intersection and ascend S on the MST. Immediately is Snowball Trail, R. Ascend the slope of Snowball Mtn in a growth of mountain ash, maple, hawthorne, and locust to the ridge at 0.7 mi. Descend and continue NW on the main ridge through birch and chestnut oak, and rich displays of wildflowers. Avoid all trails on old roads L or R from the ridgeline. The trail undulates, passes over Hawkbill Rock, drops to Snowball Gap at 2.1 mi, curves E of Little Snowball Mtn, and ascends to the site of former Little Snowball Lookout Tower at 3.0 mi, the trail's end. (The trail formerly descended on multiple switchbacks to follow Hawkbill Creek to FR-63.) Backtrack. (USGS-FS Map: Craggy Pinnacle)

Big Ivy Creek Headwaters (Buncombe County)

This remote area is a land of waterfalls and cascades, ridges and coves with handsome trees, a rock wall for mountain climbing, a natural drinking fountain, a long and high grassy road that meanders above the scenic hollows, and nearly a dozen shorter trails in a labyrinth of connecting and interconnecting passages for multiple usage. Garnishing the steep pathways are scores of wildflower species and mossy seeps. On this 8.8-mi mountainside road is Little Andy Creek, Big Andy Ridge, Walker Falls, Walker Cove Natural Area, Staire Branch, Bullhead Ridge, and classic Douglas Falls as a climax.

Elk Pen Trail (1.5 mi, USFS #116) (F, H) (elev change 740 ft.) mod-   **209-**
erate; *Upper Corner Rock Trail* (1.0 mi, USFS #173) (F, H, B) (elev   **216**
change 650 ft.) moderate; *Little Andy Trail* (0.6 mi, USFS #174) (F, H, B) (elev change 455 ft.) strenuous; *Perkins Road Trail* (1.2 mi,

USFS #175) (F, H, B) (elev change 670 ft.) strenuous; *Walker Creek Trail* (1.8 mi, USFS #165) (F, H, B) (elev change 1,055 ft.) strenuous; *Bear Pen Trail* (1.5 mi, USFS # 176) (F, H, B) (elev change 680 ft.) strenuous; *Staire Creek Trail* (1.2 mi, USFS #183) (F, H, B) (elev change 1,010 ft.) strenuous; *Laurel Gap Trail* (0.7 mi [backtrack 14.0 mi] USFS #184) (F, H, B) (elev change 250 ft.) easy to moderate; *Douglas Falls Trail* (see separately, in Craggy Mountains Area)

Length and Difficulty: (see above)

Special Features: history, waterfalls, remoteness, biology

Trailheads and Description: Access from Asheville is 14 mi N on expressway US-19/23 to Flat Creek interchange. Take NC 197 NE 6.0 mi to Barnardsville for a R, off NC-197, on Dillingham Rd (SR-2731). Drive 5.0 mi to where the paved road ends and gravel FR-74 begins. In from Burnsville, a route can be S on NC 197 for about 25 mi to Barnardsville.

(Along the Dillingham Rd, after 3.7 mi to the community of Dillingham, is paved Stony Creek Rd, R, by a Presbyterian church. On Stony Creek Rd [may also be called Craggy Garden Rd] and after 1.7 mi the pavement ends and the gravel FR 63 begins. It ascends steeply up Mineral Creek hollow for 5.0 mi to Craggy Gardens Picnic Area and MST at BRP mp 367.6).

Trailheads for all of the above trails are on FR-74 and described in order of access with milepoints on the gravel road from the forest entrance. The road ends at a parking area for Douglas Falls Trail. Carsonite signs are at most trailheads and scattered blazes are orange. At milepoint 0.4 mi is an access road R and over a bridge to Corner Rock Picnic Area where there are only picnic tables by the creek and parking lot.

At 0.6 mi on FR-74 is the S access of Elk Pen Trail. The trail follows upstream among large stands of rhododendron and fern ground cover. In the process of switchbacks it ascends more to a ridgeside before its NE exit at FR-74 in a curve (FR milepoint 2.3 mi); at FR milepoint 2.1 were cascades). The historic trail was used in the movie *Last of the Mohicans.* Across the road from the trail is the W access for Upper Corner Rock Trail. The trail is steep, passes a large boulder and has some switchbacks. It ends at Laurel Gap Trail after a 1.0 mi climb. On Laurel Gap Trail the hike can continue S to make a loop with other trails described ahead.

Little Andy Trail is a FR milepoint 2.7. The trail is L and goes steeply up the mountain for 0.6 mi to end at Laurel Gap Trail, either for a backtrack or a turn R or L to form a loop, The trail is similar to Elk Pen Trail with the types of hardwoods and rhododendron. On FR-74 there is a wide place in the road for a turnaround at FR milepoint 3.4. At milepoint 3.7 is a high rock wall, L, for rock climbing. There are cascades, L, at FR milepoint 4.0. Then at FR milepoint 4.1 is Walker Falls, high, tumbling and splashing in a descent from the coves of Brush Fence Ridge. Here is a short space for parking. At FR milepoint 4.2 are more cascades R and L. Following this point is Walker Cove Natural Area on the N side of Walker Ridge. At FR milepoint 4.4 is Perkins Road Trail. There is parking space here for two or three vehicles. The trail follows an old forest road over berms. After crossing a ridge and streams it nears a rock overhang at 0.7 mi. Along the way are Bowman's root, cohosh, Turk's cap lily, and rattlesnake orchids. There is a cascading stream at 1.0 mi, and after a switchback, R, the trail ends at Laurel Gap Trail at 1.2 mi. Backtrack, or go R or L for making a loop back to FR-74.

Across FR-74 from Perkins Road Trail is Walker Creek Trail. This longest (1.8 mi) and highest elevation change (1,055 ft.) among the mountainside trails has a sign that states it is for hiking only. Although you do not see much use, if any, by equestrians here, the trail does have horse traffic farther down the mountain. In the descent on the N side of Walker Ridge is a rocky drain area with beds of bee-balm and ferns at 0.2 mi, followed by curves and switchbacks with scenic views in coves with tall oak, yellow poplar, and hemlock at 0.7 mi. At 1.4 mi is a jct with Staire Creek Trail from the L. As the trail levels on an old road it crosses Walker Creek at 1.6 mi. Here deer and raccoon may be seen. Exit at the Corner Rock Picnic Area road R at 1.8. (The road L passes over a bridge to private property.)

At FR milepoint 5.3 is Bear Pen Trail L, and Staire Creek Trail R. There is a parking space here on the R side. From it the Staire Creek Trail enters a grove of vines to make a descent into the forest on a ridge. It has a number of switchbacks and passes through sections of large granite boulders. It makes a jct with Walker Creek Trail at 1.2 mi, where the hiker can make a loop up the mountain for 1.4 mi. After crossing some seepage and streams, one of which is Staire Branch, and a few switchbacks, it exits at Laurel Gap Trail at 1.5 mi. Here a loop can be made L for shorter distances to Perkins Road Trail or a longer distance R to Laurel Gap Trail (FR-5548) entrance gate for about 2.0 miles and a return R on FR-74 for 2.3 mi.

Continuing on FR-74 to milepoint 5.5 is a waterfall/cascade, L, and another waterfall, L, at milepoint 6.3. At milepoint 6.8, L, is a natural spring; at milepoint 7.0 are some primitive campsites, R and L; at milepoint 7.1 is a USFS gate, L; and at milepoint 7.6 is gated Laurel Gap Trail (FR 5548), L. There is a waterfall/cascade at FR milepoint 7.9, then at 8.8 mi is the road's end where there is a turnaround and parking area. From here there is an access trail to Douglas Falls. (See description above.) (USGS-FS Maps: Craggy Pinnacle, Barnardsville)

Black Mountain Recreation Area (Yancey County)

The Black Mtn Rec Area has facilities for tent and RV camping (no hookups, but water and comfort sta), fishing, picnicking, and hiking. The Briar Bottom Group Campground (reservation required) adjoins upstream on the South Toe River.

Access: From the BRP mp 347.6 at Big Laurel Gap descend 2.5 mi on FR-2074 to jct with FR-472. Turn L, go 0.7 mi, and cross South Toe River, R. Or, from BRP mp 351.9, descend 4.9 mi on FR-472 and turn L at the campground entrance. The N access is from the jct of NC-80 and FR-472 near the Mt Mitchell Golf Course, followed by a 3.0-mi drive upstream. Support facilities are the same as for the Carolina Hemlock Rec Area (see ahead).

217-
220
River Loop Trail (3.8 mi; USFS #200) (F) moderate; *Briar Bottom Bicycle Trail* (1.2 mi; USFS #1006) (F, B) easy; *Setrock Creek Falls Trail* (0.2 mi; USFS #197) (F) easy; *Devil's Den Nature Trail* (0.7 mi; USFS #192) (F) easy

Length and Difficulty: (See above)

Special Features: scenic, river rapids and waterfall, botany

Connecting Trails: (Lost Cove Ridge [Green Knob] Trail); (Mt. Mitchell Trail/MST); Lower River Loop Trail (2.7 mi; easy to moderate) (F)

Trailheads and Description: (See access above.)

The River Loop Trail is almost always in sight or sound of either S Toe River Rd or the rapids of S Toe River. The trail is a combination of new construction, old roads, and trails in Black Mtn Rec Area. Begin at the parking area opposite the bridge entrance to Black Mtn Rec Area Campground. The trailhead sign is behind the information kiosk. Ascend white-blazed Lost Cove Ridge (Green Knob) Trail and yellow-blazed River Loop Trail through a grove of hemlock on the W flank of Lost Cove Ridge. At 0.3 mi River Loop Trail forks R. At 0.9 mi are views of towering Black Mtn NE side. There are other views at 1.5 mi, followed by sections of rhododendron, mountain laurel, galax, wildflowers, grassy patches, and briars. Arrive at FR-472 at 1.9 mi, turn L, and cross the bridge over S Toe River ascend R on an embankment (where to the L is a primitive campsite) to make a brief ascent to an old roadbed. Turn R for the scenic descent that parallels the white water river. Pass through groves of hemlock, large maples, and patches of mountain laurel. Cross small streams in rhododendron groves at 2.3 mi and 2.6 mi. At 2.8 mi is a stone restroom and picnic shelters with such names as "Laurel" and "Poplar" in Briar Bottom Group Campground. The Briar Bottom Bicycle Trail's upstream trailhead is here and the River Loop Trail follows all or parts of it downstream through a large hemlock grove, and over two locust trestles (which are wheelchair accessible). The routing connects with Setrock Creek Falls Trail, L, at 3.2 mi. (The frequently used Setrock Creek Falls Trail ascends 0.2 mi to a rocky area where the splashing waterfall makes it last display of beauty from its other falls, including one on the Higgins Bald Trail.) Meet the blue-blazed Mt. Mitchell Trail and white-blazed MST at 3.5 mi. At 3.7 mi is a water spigot, L; turn R at campsite #45. Nearby is campground office. Stay R to cross the campground entrance bridge for a return to the parking lot and completed loop.

(Access to Devil's Den Nature Trail from the campground office is L of the building, then the first R on the one-way upper campground loop road. Follow the road to the first bathroom, R, (near campsites #24/25) and notice the trail sign adjacent to the amphitheater. Turn L on the white-blazed trail among large hemlocks, the R on an old forest road. After 0.1 mi the road ends and a footbridge crosses a gully. The trail makes a horseshoe curve. At 0.2 mi is rocky area among mountain laurel and hemlock, followed by large yellow poplar, oak, and hickory. There is a large boulder, L, at 0.4 mi. Complete loop at 0.7 mi.)

(On the Devil's Den Nature Trail there is a jct with an unofficial Lower **221** River Loop Trail. [The trail was initially created as a route of the MST. Currently the MST passes E across the campground entrance bridge, follows L on FR-472 for 0.7 mi to make a R on another FR that crosses Big Lost Cove Creek.] You may see a yellow blaze or an MST white dot. If following it downstream the trail is narrow on a steep slope. It passes through groves of mountain laurel, rhododendron, fetterbush and patches of galax. At 0.3 mi descend to a scenic riverside floodplain. At 0.7 mi cross an old road, and 0.9 mi are MST blazes. At 1.0 mi turn R to cross the river on a log bridge. Turn upstream with a L slant through a rocky floodplain, and arrive at FR-472 at 1.2 mi. Here is parking space. Turn R and follow the road. At 2.0 mi fork R and follow the white-blazed MST on the road. Complete the loop at the parking lot opposite the entrance to Black Mtn. Campground at 2.7 mi.) (USGS-FS Maps: Old Fort, Celo)

222   *Lost Cove Ridge Trail* (USFS #182) (F)

   Length and Difficulty: 3.3 mi, moderate to strenuous (elev change 2,070 ft.)

   Trailhead and Description: This trail is also called the Green Knob Trail. From BRP mp 350.4 at Flinty Gap (4,782 ft.), stop at the parking lot and cross the road to climb switchbacks to Green Knob Lookout Tower (5,070 ft.). The 360-degree views are outstanding, particularly of the Black Mtn. range. Turn R a few yd before reaching the tower and descend on a white-blazed trail between FR-472 and Big Lost Cove Creek. Trees are hardwoods and scattered conifers. At 2.7 mi the trail descends steeply to FR-472. Cross the road, the South Toe River, and enter the Black Mtn. Rec Area at 3.3 mi. (USGS-FS Maps: Old Fort, Celo)

223   *Bald Knob Ridge Trail* (USFS #186) (F)

   Length and Difficulty: 2.8 mi, easy to moderate (elev change 1,300 ft.)

   Special Features: virgin spruce and fir groves

   Trailhead and Description: From the parking area at BRP mp 355 (5,200 ft.), descend 0.1 mi on the white-blazed trail to the FS boundary, and follow Bald Knob Ridge N of the Left Prong of South Toe River. At 1.0 mi begin switchbacks. The trail passes through magnificent stands of virgin red spruce and Fraser fir. Reach FR-472 at 2.8 mi. Return by the same route or have a vehicle at FR-472, 1.0 mi down the mountain from BRP mp 351.9 in Deep Gap.

224- *Mount Mitchell Trail* (USFS #190) (F)

225   **Length and Difficulty:** 5.6 mi, strenuous (elev change 3,684 ft.)

   Connecting Trails: (Briar Bottom Bicycle Trail); Higgins Bald Trail (1.5 mi; USFS #190A, moderate) (F); (Buncombe Horse Range Trail); (MST)

   Special Features: rugged, highest point E of the Mississippi River

   Trailhead and Description: (Also see Mount Mitchell Trail description in Mt. Mitchell State Park, chapter 10.) Begin the hike near the bridge in the Black Mtn Rec Area. Walk across a meadow and pass the amphitheater at the upper level near the campground host's residence. Follow a blue-blazed, well-graded trail past Devil's Den Nature Trail at 0.1 mi. Ascend on switchbacks in a virgin hardwood forest. Large banks of meadow rue are passed at 0.9 mi. Come to a jct with Higgins Bald Trail at 1.5 mi, L. (The Higgins Bald Trail is a 1.5-mi alternate route from Long Arm Ridge to Flynn Ridge where it rejoins the Mt. Mitchell Trail. At its crossing of Setrock Creek is an outstanding cascade and waterfall.) A forest of conifers predominates for the next 0.4 mi. Come to a jct with the old Old Ridge Trail, R, at 1.7 mi. Cross Setrock Creek at 2.6 mi, and reach a jct with the Higgins Bald Trail, L, at 2.7 mi. Junction with Buncombe Horse Range Trail (described ahead), formerly the Maple Camp Trail, at 3.9 mi. Turn L and at 4.0 mi turn R into the forest. (A spring is nearby.) Ascend steeply over a rough and eroded treadway for 1.6 mi to the summit of Mt. Mitchell and the picnic area at the parking lot. Backtrack or use a vehicle shuttle. (USGS-FS Maps: Celo, Mt. Mitchell)

Black Mountains (Yancey County)

Black Mountain Crest Trail (USFS #179) (F)   226-
    Length and Difficulty: 12.0 mi, strenuous (elev change 3,550 ft.)   227
    Connecting Trails: Big Tom Gap Trail (0.4 mi; USFS #191A, strenuous) (F); (Colbert Ridge Trail)
    Special Features: rugged, high altitude, solitude
    Trailhead and Description: (Sections of this trail were formerly called Deep Gap Trail and Celo Knob Trail. A former 3.5-mi access route, Woody Ridge Trail [USFS #177] [F] SW from the community of Celo is planned for repair.) The S trailhead is in Mt. Mitchell State Park, and vehicles must be registered with the park ranger if left overnight. The N trailhead is on FR-5578 off Bowlens Creek Rd (SR-1109), 3.0 mi S of Burnsville.

    Leave the Mt. Mitchell picnic area and parking lot to hike N on what is considered to be the most rugged trail in the district. It is also the highest with a traverse of a dozen peaks over 6,000 ft. within 6.0 mi. Follow the orange-blazed trail over rocky terrain and through dense vegetation. Sections of spruce/fir groves are dying from acid rain and woolly aphids. At 1.0 mi ascend to Mt. Craig (6,645 ft.), the park's second highest peak. It was named in honor of Governor Locke Craig (see Mt. Mitchell State Park in chapter 10). Reach Big Tom Mtn. after another 0.1 mi (6,593 ft.); it was named in honor of Thomas Wilson. There is a jct at 1.6 mi with the primitive Big Tom Gap Trail, R. (The Big Tom Gap Trail is a 0.4-mi steep connector to the Buncombe Horse Range Trail described ahead.) Continue on the crest among ferns, thornless blackberry, Clinton's lily, moosewood, spruce, and fir to the summit of Balsam Cone (6,611 ft.) at 1.9 mi. Ascend to Cattail Peak (6,583 ft.) at 2.5 mi. Leave the state park boundary and enter the NF boundary to ascend Potato Hill at 3.0 mi. Reach Deep Gap at 3.9 mi (Tent camping sites are at the gap, and water is 300 yd down the mountain to the E.) Reach a jct with the Colbert Ridge Trail, R, at 4.0 mi. (The Colbert Ridge Trail is a 3.6-mi access route from near (N) Carolina Hemlock Rec Area.) Reach the summit of Deer Mtn

(6,200 ft.) at 4.5 mi. Reach a jct with an old road L at 6.2 mi. Continue ahead on an old road, skirting W of Gibbs Mtn. and Horse Rock. Leave the old road at 7.2 mi, and reach the summit of Celo Knob (6,427 ft.) at 7.4 mi. Turn L and begin the descent into Bowlens Creek watershed on an old logging road at 7.6 mi. Pass a spring on the R. Cross a small stream at 8.8 mi, pass a dangerous open mine shaft L at 9.5 mi, and go past a gate at 10.3 mi. From 11.0 mi, follow the cascading Bowlens Creek to gated FR-5578, the N trailhead, and a small parking space. Follow the road through an area of private property and reach Bowlens Creek Rd (SR-1109, also called Low Gap Rd) at 12.0 mi (It is 2.4 mi N to NC-197 and 0.7 mi to a jct of US-19E in Burnsville.) (USGS-FS Maps: Mt. Mitchell, Celo, Burnsville)

Carolina Hemlock Recreation Area (Yancey County)

The Carolina Hemlock Rec Area has facilities for tent and RV camping (no hookups, but water and comfort sta), picnicking (a shelter pavilion can be
228   rented for groups), fishing, swimming, and hiking. The Carolina Hemlock Trail (USFS #1003) (F, I) makes a 1.0-mi loop and begins and ends from the campground amphitheater. It passes a scenic part of the cascading South Toe River, crosses NC-80 and has switchbacks to clockwise enter the campground. Two other trails, Colbert Ridge Trail and Buncombe Horse Range Trail, have trailheads nearby. Season of operation is usually from the middle of April to the end of October.

Access: From Micaville, reach jct of NC-80 and US-19E, drive 8.6 mi S on NC-80 to the Carolina Hemlock Rec Area. From BRP mp 351.9 in Buck Creek Gap, drive 5.3 mi N on NC-80.

229   *Colbert Ridge Trail* (USFS #178) (F)

Length and Difficulty: 3.6 mi, strenuous (elev change 2,950 ft.)

Trailhead and Description: From the Carolina Hemlock Rec Area go N 0.4 mi on NC-80, turn L on Colbert Creek Rd (SR-1158), and after 0.5 mi park at the trailhead, R. Follow the white-blazed trail, ascending gently at first. Rock outcroppings provide scenic views of South Toe River Valley, Black Mtn range, Roan Mtn, and Grandfather Mtn. At 2.7 mi ascend switchbacks on the E side of Winter Star Mtn. Reach a spring, L, at 3.3 mi, and jct with the Black Mountain Crest Trail at 3.6 mi (A turn L extends 0.1 mi to Deep Gap [5,700 ft.]. Space for tent camping is nearby. A return loop can be made from here by going S on the Black Mountain Crest Trail for 2.3 mi, turn L for 0.5 mi on the Big Tom Gap Trail, turn L on the Buncombe Horse Range

Trail for 6.0 mi, and go another 0.5 mi to the point of origin on Colbert Creek Rd for a loop of 13.0 mi) (USGS-FS Maps: Mt. Mitchell, Celo)

Buncombe Horse Range Trail (USFS #191) (F, B, H)   **230**

Length and Difficulty: 16.5 mi or 17.0 mi, moderate to strenuous (elev change 2,860 ft.)

Connecting Trails: (Big Tom Gap Trail); (Mt. Mitchell Trail); (MST)

Special Features: RR history, Camp Alice, spruce/fir groves

Trailhead and Description: (This trail is rugged and unless recently repaired is not completely suitable for horse traffic. Hikers may also find passage difficult from damage by ATVs NE from Thee Creek. Original mileage was 17.0 mi or more. Plans are to restore the trail and blazes. Call the district office for an update on conditions. Access is described from the NE trailhead.) From the Carolina Hemlock Rec Area go N 0.4 mi on NC-80, turn L on Colbert Creek Rd (SR-1158), and proceed 0.8 mi to jct with Aunt Julie Rd (SR-1159). Turn R, go 0.2 mi, and park L near a private home. Follow the white blazes on an old jeep road. Take the L fork at 0.6 mi. Cross rocky Middle Fork at 1.3 mi. At 1.8 mi bear R at the jct to begin steep switchbacks up Maple Camp Ridge in a hardwood forest. Cross Maple Camp Creek at 3.4 mi, and reach a heath bald with good views at 4.8 mi. Arrive at Maple Camp Bald (5,613 ft.), R, at 5.3 mi. At 6.0 mi cross Thee Creek and reach jct with primitive Big Tom Gap Trail, R, which ascends steeply for 0.4 mi to the jct with Black Mountain Crest Trail. Reach jct with the blue-blazed Mt. Mitchell Trail/MST, R and L, at 7.8 mi near a spring. Reach the former Camp Alice Shelter on Commissary Hill (5,782 ft.) at 8.0 mi. (A spring is nearby.) Continue ahead on the old RR grade to Commissary Rd and the site of Camp Alice at 8.5 mi, R. (Camp Alice was a thriving logging camp in the 1920s. It later served as a lodge for Mt. Mitchell visitors. Only remnants of the stone foundations remain.) Cross Lower Creek at 8.7 mi and a number of small streams that drain into Middle Fork and South Fork before approaching the base of Potato Knob at 11.7 mi. (Here is an access route, R, to NC-128, the road from the BRP to the top of Mt. Mitchell.) Turn L and pass through a beautiful spruce/fir grove at 12.6 mi. At 14.0 mi enter a large wildlife habitat clearing with fine views and soon begin to follow an old logging road on long, level switchbacks that descend to the Right Prong of the South Toe River. At 16.5 mi reach FR-472 (3,560 ft.), the SW trailhead. (To the R it is 2.0 mi to the BRP on FR-472, and L it is 2.9 mi to Black Mtn. Rec Area on FR-472.) (USGS-FS Maps: Mt. Mitchell, Celo, Montreat, Old Fort)

Flat Top Mountain Area

231-   *Devils Creek Trail* (3.6 mi) (USFS #188) (F) (elev change 810 ft.);
232   *Lost Cove Trail* (1.8 or 2.5 mi) (USFS #196) (F) (elev change 940 ft.)

    Length and Difficulty: 5.4 mi one way combined; 12.2 mi backtrack separately

    Special Features: remote, scenic, wildlife

    Trailheads and Description: To access the W end of Devil's Creek Trail take US-19W at its jct with US-19E (6 mi W of Burnsville). Follow the curvey US-19W for about 25 mi, mainly N and along Cane Creek until a bridge crossing S on the community of Sioux. After Sioux US-19W runs more to the W in its ascent to Spivey Gap. Watch for a small blue sign—Flat Top Rd W, NFS 278—R, 0.1 mi before reaching Spivey Gap. Ascend on the FR road 1.4 mi to a flat area (Devil's Creek Gap). Park here, but avoid blocking gated FRs on either side or the AT, which crosses here.

    Begin the hike on gated Bear Woods Road (FR 5506), L. (The AT briefly parallels the road.) (The trail sign has been far ahead, but it may change with the Forest Service placing a sign here near the gate.) Follow the grassy road in a gradual descent. At 0.7 mi stay R at a wildlife field. At 1.6 mi is a gate and beyond a large wildlife field on a hillside. Hike 36 yd. R and close to the woods for a white-blazed trail. (A carsonite trail sign may be here.) The trail stays close to contour lines of 3,400 to 3,000 ft. for the remainder of the journey. Because the trail is on the N flank of Flat Top Mtn., sunshine never reaches parts of the trail. In some damp almost boreal coves the emerald green mosses are dense and artistic. Once an easy route with consistent white blazes, the trail is now very rocky and overgrown. At 2.4 mi is the large standing remains of what may be an American chestnut. This special site is followed by a carpet of ground pine. After a section of dense rhododendron you will enter an opening among tall oak and hemlock trees to a ridge at 3.5 mi. Here is a lone tree, likely a sourwood, near a large oak with evidence of a white blaze, one of other former blazes slanted R for a descent of 0.1 mi to connect with Lost Cove Trail. Backtrack or ascend the Lost Cove Trail for 1.8 mi to use a vehicle shuttle system from FR-278. (See directions below.)

    To access S trailhead of Lost Cove Trail follow US-19W from US-19E as described above, but when you pass the community sign of Sioux, go about 1.0 mi farther to turn R on gravel SR-1415 (close to a private home and where US-19W curves L). Ascend 1.0 mi to jct with other gravel roads. Stay L. After 2.5 mi watch for a gated FR-5505 up the bank, R. Drive ahead 40 yd. to a small parking area R.

Walk back to the gated road (FR-5505 number may be missing). Ascend, pass a small field at 0.3 mi and stay L to pass into a profuse cove of ferns. At 0.5 mi there may be a Lost Cove Trail carsonite sign near an aged apple tree. Turn R up the grassy knob (elev 3,800 ft.) where rare vehicle traffic has left some tracks at 0.5 mi. The grassy area is called Joe Lewis Fields (named for a former settler's homesite). The knob is part of Flat Top Mtn. and has panoramic views, one of which is the Unaka Mt. range NE across the Nolichucky River and where the Shinbone Trail is located. Curve W, descend and in a shallow gap be alert to find the Lost Cove Trail R. On a well designed trail (formerly with baby blue blazes) you will have six switchbacks before a rockbed at 1.0 mi. After a steep decline at 1.2 mi, you may see one or more of the faded blazes. At 1.8 mi is an access L to the E end of Devil's Creek Trail. (It moderately ascends 0.1 mi to a ridge and with the remnants of its white blaze near a large oak tree and other white blazes along the way.) From this point the Lost Cove Trail varies in its direction—from part of its original to a plummeting new tracking. One route to match the USFS listing of 2.5 mi is to descend on the most used path to where two switchbacks are within 100 yd. of each other at 1.9 mi. From 2 mi to 2.5 mi are plunges into rhododendron patches, and a variety of potential passages where you could be more lost than the cove. Backtrack, unless you are familiar with the area, or have consulted with the district's office for a map to define the private property line of the abandoned and ghostly Lost Cove community. (Lost Cove's name came from a community of workers for the construction of the Clinchfield RR in the early 1900s. A few homes were constructed, followed by a church, school, and gristmill. After the RR was completed some residents remained and used the RR for access.) (USGS-FS Maps: Chestoa, Huntsdale NC-TN)

Unaka Mountains (Mitchell County)

Shinbone Trail (USFS #187) (F, H, B)   233

Length and Difficulty: 10.4 mi round-trip, moderate to strenuous (elev change 1,140 ft.)

Special Features: wildflowers, wildlife, cliffs at Nolichucky gorge

Trailhead and Description: In E Burnsville jct of US 19E and NC-197, drive N on NC-197 for 19.4 mi to near the Tennessee-North Carolina state line in the Unaka Mountain. Turn L off NC-197 on FR-5583. After 0.9 mi stop and park on the roadside at a fork in the road. Begin the hike at the gated USFS road, L. (There may not be any trail signs or blazes here.)

On a well maintained former timber road curve in and out of coves where tributaries begin the descent E to Shinbone Creek. At 1.8 mi the road forks. Go R on the older road. At 2.0 mi in a horseshoe curve is a small pool frequented by deer. Go through a wildlife field at 2.4 mi to re-enter the forest at a large oak. Descend. Curve R at 3.0 mi and notice a deep hollow, L, at 3.3 mi. On a ridge at 3.4 mi is a sunny opening with a surprise natural garden of wildflowers among mountain laurel, sumac, blueberry, and dogwood. Continue descending around a horseshoe curve, L. At 3.5 mi, L, is a rocky mountainside, and on the R the sound of whitewater rapids can be heard from the Nolichucky River. On the S side of the river is the north flank of Flat Top Mtn., where at this base in the gorge is a winding RR. Farther up on the flank, SE, is the Lost Cove Trail. In the summer you may see and faintly hear canoeists and rafters on the river rapids. Such a majestic view is worth this long hike in any season of the year.

The return trail from here is on a more recent timber road, carefully designed for a moderate serpentine ascent. Bordering the grassy roadside are wildflowers and rhododendron. Small streams are at 5.9 mi, 6.2 mi, and 7.5 mi. Complete the loop at 8.6 mi and return to gate and parking space at 10.4 mi. (USGS-FS Maps: Chestoa, Huntsdale)

Roan Mountain Area (Mitchell County)

234-235   *Cloudland Trail* (3.0 mi round-trip; USFS #171) (F); *Roan Mountain Gardens Trail* (2.0 mi; USFS #290) (F, W)

Length and Difficulty: 5.0 mi combined round-trip, easy

Trailheads and Description: Take the Roan Mtn. Rd (SR-1348) for 1.8 mi at jct with NC-261 in Carvers Gap on the Tennessee–North Carolina state line (13.0 mi N of Bakersville). For the Cloudland Trail turn R to parking lot #1. Follow the trail sign W on the crest of Roan Mtn. through spruce, fir, mountain avens *(Geum radiatum),* rhododendron, and sections of heavy moss on the trees and the ground. Pass parking lots #2 and #3 and climb to Roan High Bluff (6,267 ft.) at 1.5 mi for superb views of Bald and Unaka Mtns. from a wood platform. Backtrack. For the Roan Mountain Gardens Trail begin at parking lot #2, pass an information display board, and follow a triple-loop trail (partially paved) through an extraordinary display of purple rhododendron *(catawbiense)* and flame azalea. One of the trails has 16 interpretive signs, and another loop passes through a large grassy bald with rhododendron —usually at their flowering peak the last two weeks of June. The trail has easy access for the handicapped. (Contact the ranger station for information on the date and events of the Rhododendron Festival.) (USGS-FS Map: Bakersville)

Support Facilities: Roan Mtn State Resort Park. From jct of US-19E and TN-143 go 5.0 mi S from the town of Roan Mtn. on TN-143 (which becomes NC-261 in N.C. at Carvers Gap). Call 615-772-4178. Full svc, rec fac, open all year.

Yellow Mountain Gap Area (Avery County)

Overmountain Victory Trail (also called Historic Bright's Trace)   **236**
(USGS #308) (F)

    Length and Difficulty: 1.5 mi round-trip, easy

    Connecting Trail: Appalachian Trail

    Trailheads and Description: From turn-around parking space go around gate of old road that gradually ascends by a stream. After 0.1 mi turn L and follow an old road through a scenic hayfield. Enter a forest where during the second week of May are carpets of mayapple, patches of wood betony, and showy masses of white fringed phacelia. The latter also has dense displays on the open slopes. On the approach to gap there is a sign, L, for an AT access path, 0.3 mi, to the red barn Overmountain Shelter for AT hikers. At 0.75 mi the OVT crosses the AT on its descent into Tennessee. Backtrack. (S on the AT it is 4.7 mi to NC-261 in Carvers Gap; to the N on the AT it is 8.7 mi to US-19E.)

    Access: On US-19E and NC-206 jct in Spruce Pine take US-19E to Plumtree for 12.4 mi and another 3.3 mi to Roaring Creek Rd, L. Here is an OVT state marker and welcome sign to Roaring Creek community. After 3.7 mi is end of pavement, then 0.5 mi further is OVT plaque, L, at former turn-around. Another 0.7 mi is parking space turn-around for trailhead.

Grandfather Ranger District

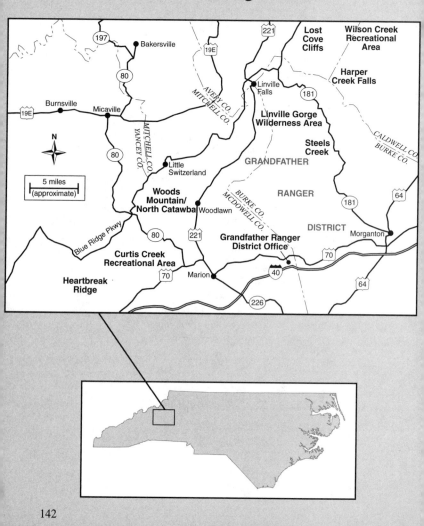

Introductions to Trail Areas

This district covers the most counties, has the most acreage, adjoins the longest section of the BRP, and has the longest section of the MST than any other USFS district in the state. The trails are described from SE to NE.

Grandfather Ranger District Office
The location is visible from I-40, Exit 90 (Lake James); turn R. The office has a large supply of books, maps, flyers, and brochures, plus a nature display.

Mountains-to-Sea Trail
Hikers report this section of the MST as the most scenic and challenging of any in its mountain journey. Route includes North Fork of Catawba River, Bald Knob, Pinnacle, Linville Gorge, Shortoff, Chimneys, and Table Rock.

SECTION 2: GRANDFATHER RANGER DISTRICT

The Grandfather Ranger District with 189,033 acres is partially in McDowell, Burke, Caldwell, Watagua, and Avery Counties. The Linville Gorge Wilderness Area, in the center of the district, is in Burke County and has 92,002 acres that protect the natural environment of the Linville River and its divides. Two other wilderness-study areas, Lost Cove and Harper Creek, are located in the Harper Creek Area of Caldwell and Avery Counties. The district's W boundary is the Blue Ridge Parkway, and a section of the Toecane Station of Appalachian Ranger District adjoins in the SW near Mt. Mitchell. Among the outstanding localities for scenic beauty are Table Rock, Hawksbill Mtn., Shortoff Mtn., the three cliffs of Lost Cove, the major waterfalls of Harper and North Harper Creeks, and Wiseman's View. In 2000, Wilson Creek was designated as a Wild and Scenic River. There are five picnic areas: Barkhouse on NC-181; Mulberry NW of Lenoir; Old Fort W of Old Fork; Table Rock NW of Morganton; and Woodlawn on US-221 (see below). There are two picnic and camping areas (without hookups) at Curtis Creek, N of Old Fork and off US-70 NW, and Mortimer, SE of Edgemont and off NC-90.

The district has 65 trails on inventory, some of which have been abandoned because of overgrowth and lack of use. (The district management staff is continuing to determine trail needs for maintenance, signage, blazing, and user options.) Trails are not blazed (with the exception of the MST); thus, hikers should have a map of the district (two specific ones are Linville Gorge Wilderness Area and Wilson Creek Area). One of the shortest and most popular trails is Wiseman's View Trail (0.2 mi; USFS #224) (F, W). It is the only paved trail suitable for wheelchair use and is accessible on Kistler Memorial Highway, 3.8 mi from NC-183 in the community of Linville. There are two short access trails for anglers: Jarrett Creek in McDowell County and Boone Fork Pond in Caldwell County. The longest trail, Wilson Ridge Trail (14.7 mi; USFS #269) (F, B), is primarily used by bikers. A number of backcountry forest roads are used by equestrians. Combining a number of established trails, for a total of 70 mi, is the MST. It goes through the district from the W end of Woods Mountain Trail to Beacon Heights near Grandfather Mtn. (see MST in appendix A). There is an exercise trail, the 14-station loop Woodlawn Trail (0.5 mi; USFS #220), at the Woodlawn Picnic Area, 5.5 mi N of Marion, where the MST crosses US-221. The Brown Mtn. OHV Trail System has 10 trails and 34 mi. Access is off NC-181 on Brown Mtn. Beach Rd, L on FR-299 to a fee station.

Address and Access: District Ranger, Grandfather Ranger District, USFS, 109 E Lawing Dr, Nebo, NC 28761; 828-652-2144; Exit 90 (Nebo–Lake James) on I-40.

Old Fort Picnic Area (McDowell County)

Young's Ridge/Kitsuma Peak Trail (USFS #205) (F, B)   **238**

    Length and Difficulty: 4.2 mi, moderate to strenuous (elev change 1,565 ft.)

    Trailhead and Description: (This trail includes the former Kitsuma Peak Trail and the Young's Ridge Trail and is also used by mountain bikers who use this trail with old US-70 to make a loop.) In Old Fork on US-70 at the jct with Catawba Ave, go W 0.3 mi on US-70 and turn R on Mill Creek Rd (SR-1407). Drive N 3.0 mi and turn L into the Old Fort Picnic Area. Park and follow the trail upstream on the L through a ravine dark with heavy hemlock shade. (To the R, there is a 0.5-mi loop trail near Swannanoa Creek.) Goats beard *(Aruncus dioicus)* grows on the damp banks. Follow the switchbacks to the ridge top at 0.9 mi. Turn R and continue W up and down knobs to Kitsuma Peak (3,195 ft.) at 3.6 mi. Views of Greybeard Mtn. and Mt. Mitchell Wildlife Management Area are impressive. Descend on switchbacks to an open path by a fence on the N side at I-40 at 4.0 mi. Turn R and at 4.2 mi, reach a parking overlook at Ridgecrest. (Access from I-40 is Ridgecrest, Exit 66.) (Overlook gate usually closed at 8:00 PM. Check with the Blue Ridge Baptist Conference Center across the street from the gate for permission to park daily or overnight.) (USGS-FS Maps: Black Mtn., Old Fort)

Heartbreak Ridge Area (McDowell County)

Heartbreak Ridge Trail (4.5 mi; USFS #208) (F); *Star Gap Trail* (1.5   **239-**
mi; USFS #209) (F)   **240**

    Length and Difficulty: 6.0 mi combined, strenuous (elev change 2,928 ft.)

    Special Features: Glass Rock and Licklog Knobs, scenic, remote

    Trailhead and Description: The N trailhead access is at BRP milepost 354.7, and the S trailhead is at Brookside Baptist Church on Graphite Rd (SR-1408). Access to the church from Old Fort is W on Old US-70 to Mill Creek Rd (SR-1400), R. After 2.2 mi, it turns R on Graphite Rd. The church is 0.2 mi farther, R. There are no signs or blazes.

    If hiking from the N trailhead, park on a grassy flat shoulder of the BRP (but do not leave vehicles here overnight). Cross the road and enter an inconspicuous opening in dense rhododendron. After 0.1 mi is Hemphill Spring,

40 ft. L from skeletal roots of an American chestnut. At 0.2 mi, reach a jct with a pioneer road at a beech tree in a flat area. (Across the road is the abandoned Glass Rock Knob Trail [6.0 mi; USGS #226]. It drops precipitously on switchbacks with scattered quartz and mica into a gorge with cascades and multiple tributaries to Mill Creek. Its S trailhead is closed at private property NW of Graphite community.)

On the pioneer road turn L, ascend to 4,840 ft., then descend to a wildlife clearing with remnants of a farm at 0.5 mi. Keep L at the trail fork, and go 0.1 mi to another trail fork. Heartbreak Ridge Trail goes R at an Adopt-A-Trail, Camp Woodson sign. (The pioneer road to the L becomes an overgrown trail for an isolated exploratory route to Iron Mtn., a ridge that parallels Heartbreak Ridge. The route skirts Rocky Mtn., crosses Star Gap Trail after about 3.5 mi, and then follows FR-4030 about 6.5 mi to exit at Curtis Creek Rd [SR-1227] 1.5 mi NW of US-70 and 1.8 mi E from RR tracks in Old Fort. Modified USGS topo maps Montreat and Old Fort should be used for this exploratory route.)

After a few yards from the Heartbreak Ridge Trail adoption sign, there is an overlook, R, into Mill Creek Gorge and the Pinnacle (5,665 ft.) to the NW. Descend on a well-maintained trail through chestnut, oak, maple, laurel, and scattered patches of witch hazel and galax. At 1.2 mi, turn sharply L (avoid ATV route ahead). Continue descending to a twin knob at 2.1 mi. From a saddle, ascend to Licklog Knob (3,225 ft.) at 4.1 mi. Descend to a saddle at 4.5 mi to jct with Star Gap Trail. (Ahead is an abandoned section of Star Gap Trail that drops to Jarrett Creek, ascends to Star Gap, and descends to private property at Newberry Creek.)

Turn R on Star Gap Trail and descend on 20 switchbacks for 1.0 mi to a campsite. In the descent are oaks, black gum, laurel, two species of rhododendron, and banks of meadow rue, bloodroot, and yellow violets. Follow an old forest road downstream to rock-hop Pritchard Creek at 1.1 mi, cross Southern RR at 1.3 mi, and after 100 yd. turn L off the old road for a descent to a meadow at Brookside Baptist Church at 1.5 mi, the end of the trail. (See access description above.) (USGS-FS Maps: Montreat, Old Fort)

Curtis Creek Recreation Area (McDowell County)
Recreation activities here are camping (with vault toilets and hand water pump), picnicking, fishing, and hiking. Snooks Nose trailhead offers a natural spring. The area is historic because it is part of the first 8,100-acre

tract purchased under the 1911 Weeks Act. The tract is dedicated to Dr. Chase P. Ambler (1865–1932) of Asheville for his efforts to establish the national forests.

Access: From I-40 Exits 72 and 73 at Old Fort, go 0.2 mi into town, turn R on US-70, and go 1.0 mi to jct, L, on Curtis Creek Rd (SR-1227), which becomes FR-482. After 5.1 mi from US-70, reach the campground.

Support Facilities: Triple C Campground is open April 1 through October; it is 6.0 mi N on NC-80 from its jct with US-70, NW of Marion. Full svc, swimming pool. Address: 6621 Buck Creek Rd, Marion, NC 28752; 828-724-4099. Service stores in Old Fort; motels and shopping centers are in Marion.

Snooks Nose Trail (USFS #211) (F)   241

Length and Difficulty: 4.0 mi, strenuous (elev change 2,800 ft.)

Special Feature: views of Iron Mtn. range and Newberry Creek watershed

Trailhead and Description: At the S entrance to the campground (near old rock post of former CCC camp), enter on the old road (a natural spring is R in the hemlocks); curve in a cove; rock-hop a stream at 0.3 mi in a forest of hemlock, poplar, birch, and beech; and ascend steeply. At 0.7 mi reach a spur ridge, level off, then ascend steeply again, R, off the old road (trail direction is vague here). Reach a ridge crest, turn L at 1.2 mi. Pass R of a large cliff at 1.3 mi and reach an outcropping with vistas at 2.0 mi, after a number of switchbacks. A religious testimony about the mountains is lettered on the rocks. Continue along the ridge crest, ascend to Laurel Knob (4,325 ft.) without views at 3.0 mi. In a forest of galax, laurel, and rhododendron, reach a gap at 3.4 mi. Ascend steeply to the Green Knob Overlook and a sign about the USFS on the Blue Ridge Parkway (mp 350.4) at 4.0 mi. Backtrack or use second vehicle up to the BRP from the campground on FR-482. (USGS-FS Map: Old Fort)

Hickory Branch Trail (USFS #213) (F)   242

Length and Difficulty: 4.0 mi round-trip, moderate to strenuous (elev change 1,100 ft.)

Special Features: primitive, waterfalls, wildlife

Trailhead and Description: There are two campground trailheads. One ascends the hillside by the hand water pump, the other from the lower end of the campground on a FR. They join 0.6 mi up Hickory Branch. From the pump ascend to the ridge, descend, and follow an old woods road upstream to a ravine wash and reach jct with the other route. If using the FR route, rock-hop Curtis Creek on the FR but leave the road at the end of the meadow at a holly tree and a beech tree. Go upstream, cross the branch, and join the other route near cascades and pools in the ravine. Hemlock and rhododendron are prominent. At 0.8 mi, reach the confluence of streams, cross the L fork, and ascend L of scenic cascades. After 11 switchbacks through laurel, blueberry, and turkey grass, reach the ridge top in a saddle at 2.0 mi. Backtrack. (The Leadmine Gap Trail [USFS #212] goes L but is obstructed with forest growth. The old open trail R leads down to Mackey Creek.) (USGS-FS Map: Old Fort)

243   *Mackey Mountain Trail* (USFS #216) (F)

Length and Difficulty: 8.0 mi, moderate to strenuous (elev change 2,115 ft.)

Special Features: bear sanctuary, remote

Trailhead and Description: The NW access to this trail is at the jct of Curtis Creek Rd (FR-482) and Sugar Cove Rd (FR-1188), 4.4 mi up from the Curtis Creek Campground on FR-482 and 1.8 mi down the mtn on FR-482 from BRP mp 333. The trail is not blazed, but the orange bear sanctuary markers make good directions for the first 5.0 mi. Water is infrequent or nonexistent on the ridgeline. Begin at the road jct and ascend an embankment or follow the old road R through rhododendron and oak to the W slope of the ridge. In addition to the bear, grouse, and turkey habitat, yellow-jacket nests are commonplace on the trail banks. At 1.0 mi, switch to the E side of the ridge, but soon return to follow across a long knob and to a narrow ridge before ascending Narrow Knob (3,440 ft.) at 2.8 mi. Follow a narrow rim, then a level area to skirt W of Mackey Mtn. (4,035 ft.) at 4.0 mi and reach a jct with an old trail, R. Continue ahead along the ridge, ascend to a knob

244   (3,960 ft.), and descend to a trail jct at 6.2 mi, R. Greenlee Mountain Trail (USFS #222) descends 2.0 mi to Maple Hill Rd (SR-1414). Turn L on the Mackey Mountain Trail and descend, partially on steep woods roads among virgin yellow poplar. Follow switchbacks (difficult to follow in places) and cross a dry streambed at 6.7 mi. Bear R at an old road jct at 7.5 mi. Leave the forest boundary at 7.6 mi, cross Deep Cove Creek, go 160 yd., turn a sharp L, cross the creek again, go 35 yd., and turn R on an old road at 7.8 mi. Exit from the trees in the center of two private driveways. Go across the bridge over Clear Creek to a small parking area on public Clear Creek Rd. (If parking here, use caution not to block the gated road upstream or to drive across the private bridge to park.) A second vehicle is advisable. It is 2.6 mi downstream on Clear Creek Rd (SR-1422) to US-70, and R 5.4 mi on US-70 to Curtis Creek Rd, R. (USGS-FS Maps: Old Fort, Marion W)

Woods Mountain Area (McDowell County)

Woods Mountain Trail (USFS #218) (F)   **245-**
Length and Difficulty: 10.6 mi round-trip, moderate   **247**
Connecting Trail: (Woods Mountain Access Trail, moderate); Armstrong
Creek Trail (2.5 mi; USFS #223, strenuous, elev change 1,420 ft.)
Special Features: chinquapin patches, remote, vistas
Trailhead and Description: (This trail is also the MST, which has a
white circle blaze.) Park at the Buck Creek Gap jct of NC-80 and BRP mp
344.1, on the E side. Follow a sign up the BRP svc road (Woods Mountain
Access Trail) that parallels the BRP for 0.7 mi to Hazelwood Gap, the beginning of the Woods Mountain Trail. Turn R on the trail, opposite a large white
oak, and skirt S of the knob. After 0.2 mi, jct with Armstrong Creek Trail, L
in a small gap.

(The Armstrong Creek Trail is primitive and may be passable in its steep
descent on switchbacks to the headwaters of Armstrong Creek at 0.7 mi. In a
forest of oak, birch, poplar, hemlock, and rhododendron, it parallels the creek
generally, but crosses it eight times and crosses some small drains. Reach a
cul-de-sac in the road at the Armstrong Fish Hatchery at 3.0 mi. Ingress here
is up Armstrong Creek Rd [SR-1443] for 4.5 mi from NC-226A, 7.4 mi SE of
Little Switzerland.)

On the Woods Mountain Trail the ridge becomes a narrow spine covered
with blueberries, turkey grass, laurel, and chinquapin. Dominant trees on the
trail at this point are oak and pitch pine. Scenic views of Table Rock, Hawksbill, Mt. Mitchell, Green Knob, and Armstrong Valley are found. Other views
along the ridge include Mackey Mtn. and Lake Tahoma. Descend to a saddle
of oak, hemlock, and laurel at 1.0 mi. At 1.7 mi, the trail slopes on the N side
of the ridge in an arbor of rhododendron and galax. There are more views L
(N) from an outcrop at 3.2 mi. Particularly attractive is a stand of tall hemlock
after a saddle at 3.8 mi. Ascend steeply on a rocky ridge at 4.2 mi where for
the next 0.2 mi are impressive views L (N) of Grandfather Mtn., Hawksbill,
and Table Rock. At 5.1 mi, reach a jct with an old road, R and L. Turn R. Follow the trail on a long descent, using care to follow the MST white (circle)
blaze. At the base of the mountain, cross a low cement bridge at 10.3 mi. At
12.2 mi, reach a wider road and turn L into yellow poplar, and white and Virginia pine. At 12.0 mi, connect with Woodlawn Trail (a physical-fitness trail)
and descend to a parking lot at 13.1 mi. Across the road is Woodlawn Work
Center for the USFS. To the R of the parking lot are picnic tables and a

restroom on US-221. (See Chapter 16.) (USGS-FS Maps: Celo, Little Switzerland)

Support Facilities: (See Curtis Creek Rec Area.) Motels and restaurants are 5.5 mi S on US-221.

Linville Gorge Wilderness Area (Burke County)

The Linville Gorge Wilderness Area has 12,002 acres of wild, rugged, and scenic terrain. It is a distinct challenge to the climber, hiker, camper, and naturalist. Its boundaries are on the canyon rims. Its W side is near the Kistler Memorial Highway (SR-1238), a gravel road on Linville Mtn. The E boundary extends from Jonas Ridge to the S base of Shortoff Mtn. The wilderness does not include the famous Linville Falls, 0.3 mi upstream from the N boundary. (The Falls are part of the BRP described in chapter 6.) For 14.0 mi through the wilderness, the Linville River's white water cascades in a descent of 2,000 ft. Major escarpments rise on the river's walls. The wilderness is rich in both plant and animal life. There are five species of rare plants, four species of rhododendron, and virgin forests in the deep coves. Among the flowering plants are sand myrtle *(Leiophyllum prostratum),* red chokeberry *(Sorbus arbutifolia),* azalea, turkey beard, bristly locust, yellow root, silverbell, orchids, ninebark, and wild indigo *(Baptisia tinctoria).* The major species of animals are deer, bear, squirrel, raccoon, grouse, turkey vulture, hawk, owl, and brown and rainbow trout. The poisonous snakes are the timber rattler and the copperhead. Free permits from the USFS are required for camping in the gorge only on weekends and holidays from May 1 through October 31. Time limit in the gorge is three consecutive days and two nights, one weekend permit per month per visitor, and group size not to exceed 10. No-trace camping is the rule. Permits may be obtained at the ranger's office in Nebo M–F, 8:00–4:30, or by mail (see address in the introduction). Also, permits are available in person at the Linville Visitor Information Cabin, open April 15 to November 1, 9:00–5:00. Access to the cabin is 0.5 mi S on Kistler Memorial Highway (SR-1238) from NC-183, 0.7 mi E from its jct with US-221 in Linville Falls.

The Linville Gorge Trail is the major trail; its traverse is in the gorge, paralleling the river on the W side. Seven short but steep access trails descend from Kistler Memorial Highway (SR-1238) along the W rim. **248** (Another trail, the 0.2-mi Wiseman's View Trail, is only an overlook into the gorge. It is 3.8 mi from NC-183.) The E rim has two short access trails from

FR-210, but other trails on the E rim connect with each other. There are some trail signs at access points to the gorge, and at trail junctions within. The district staff continues to emphasize trail maintenance work on existing trails and close illegal trail routes in the wilderness. The use of a recent topo map or the Linville Gorge Wilderness Map is recommended. (USGS-FS Maps: Linville Falls, Ashford)

Support Facilities: Campgrounds, motels, restaurants, svc sta, and small grocery stores are at Linville Falls on US-221 and NC-183 jct.

Linville Gorge Trail (USFS #231) (F)

249-256

Length and Difficulty: 11.5 mi, strenuous (elev change 2,025 ft.)

Connecting Trails: West Rim: Pine Gap Trail (0.7 mi, easy) (F); Bynum Bluff Trail (1.0 mi, moderate; USFS #241,) (F); Cabin Trail (0.8 mi, strenuous; USFS #246, elev change 900 ft.) (F); Babel Tower Trail (1.2 mi, strenuous; USFS #240, elev change 920 ft.) (F); Sandy Flats Trail (1.0 mi, strenuous; USFS #230, elev change 900 ft.) (F); Conley Cove Trail (1.4 mi, strenuous; USFS #229, elev change 930 ft.) (F); Pitch-In Trail (1.4 mi, strenuous; USFS #228, elev change 1,760 ft.) (F)

Connecting Trails: East Rim: (Devil's Hole Trail); (Spence Ridge Trail)

Special Features: rugged, geology, scenic

Trailhead and Description: All the trails on the W rim can be used as loops with SR-1238 as a connector. A vehicle switch is another option. The nearest and easiest access to the Linville Gorge is on the Pine Gap Trail on SR-1238, 0.9 mi from the jct of NC-183 and SR-1238 (0.7 mi from the US-221/NC-183 jct in Linville Falls). From the parking area descend easily into the gorge and at 0.7 mi is a jct with the Bynum Bluff Trail, R. To the L is a short spur to views of the canyon, and the Linville Gorge Trail begins ahead. (The Bynum Bluff Trail ascends 1.0 mi, steeply at first, to a parking area on SR-1238, 1.5 mi from NC-183). Descend in a forest of hardwoods, hemlock, and dense rhododendron. At 1.2 mi, reach a jct with the Cabin Trail, R. (The 0.8-mi Cabin Trail is a primitive spur that is extremely steep and rough to SR-1238, 1.9 mi from NC-183.) At 2.0 mi on the Linville Gorge Trail, reach jct R with the Babel Tower Trail at a cliffside for overlooks of a horseshoe bend and river rapids. (The Babel Tower Trail ascends 1.2 mi to a parking area on SR-1238, 2.7 mi R to NC-183. It is a popular route with switchbacks, but generally a scenic ridge route. It is 1.1 mi S on SR-1238 to Wiseman's View.)

Continue the descent on a slope near the river for excellent views of the gorge at 2.5 mi. At 3.4 mi, pass the jct L with the Devil's Hole Trail. (The 1.5-

mi Devil's Hole Trail may be difficult to locate, but it crosses the river at a less steep area than usual and follows up Devil's Hole Branch to a ridge between Sitting Bear Mtn. and Hawksbill Mtn. to exit at FR-210.) At 3.7 mi are scenic views of Hawksbill Mtn. At 3.8 mi is a spring, a campground, and a jct R with Sandy Flats Trail. (The Sandy Flats Trail, primitive and steep, ascends 1.0 mi to SR-1238, 3.7 mi S of NC-183.) Reach Spence Ridge Trail, L, at 4.6 mi (Spence Ridge Trail fords the river and ascends for 1.7 mi on switchbacks to a level area and then the rim's parking area on FR-210, described below.) Continue downriver and at 5.5 mi, reach jct with Conley Cove Trail, R. (The Conley Cove Trail ascends on a well-graded route through a forest of oak, pine, cucumber tree, silverbell, and wildflowers. At 1.0 mi is a water source and a few yards farther is a primitive trail jct, L. [The unmaintained route is Rock Jock Trail, USFS #247, which follows above the escarpment for 2.8 mi] Pass a cave and on switchbacks reach SR-1238 at 1.4 mi, 5.3 mi from NC-183.) The Linville Gorge Trail continues 100 yd. downriver to a swimming hole and a large open outcropping with views of the Chimneys and Table Rock on the E rim. Other views follow. Cross a small branch at 6.8 mi. The next 2.0 mi of the trail and the river have a mild decline. Come to a jct with the Pitch-In Trail, R, at 9.1 mi. (The Pitch-In Trail ascends 1.4 mi with excellent views of the gorge, particularly of Shortoff Mtn., to SR-1238, 7.3 mi R to Pine Gap Trail. To the L on SR-1238, it is 2.3 mi to the MST and the Pinnacle 0.2 mi off the road E, and 0.8 mi farther to the trailhead and parking area R (W) of the Overmountain Victory Trail. Down the mountain on SR-1238 it is 4.1 mi to NC-126, from where it is 16.0 mi E to Morganton and 10.2 mi W to I-40 at the Nebo exit.)

The Linville Gorge Trail follows an old jeep road and passes through grassy glades under tall poplar and elm. At 10.9 mi is a good swimming hole. In a few yards, wade the river in a flat area and reach the wilderness boundary at private property at 11.5 mi. Backtrack.

257-
265   ***Devil's Hole Trail*** (1.5 mi; USFS #244) (F); ***Jonas Ridge Trail*** (4.4 mi round-trip; USFS #245) (F); ***Hawksbill Mountain Trail*** (1.4 mi round-trip; USFS #217) (F); ***Spence Ridge Trail*** (1.7 mi; USFS #233) (F); ***Table Rock Gap Trail*** (1.6 mi; USFS #243) (F); ***Little Table Rock Trail*** (1.2 mi; USFS #236) (F); ***Table Rock Summit Trail*** (1.4 mi round-trip; USFS #242) (F)

Length and Difficulty: 13.2 mi combined round-trip, moderate to strenuous (elev change from 520 ft. to 1,340 ft.)

Special Feature: exceptional vistas

Trailhead and Description: These short trails are grouped because they have an access from FR-210 on the E rim; two of them descend to connect with the Linville Gorge Trail. A longer trail that follows the rim, Shortoff Mountain Trail, is described below separately. From the jct of NC-183/181 at Jonas Ridge, go S on NC-181 for 3.0 mi to the Old Gingercake Rd (SR-1264) and turn R. At 0.3 mi turn L, at the first fork, on Gingercake Acres Rd (SR-1265), which becomes FR-210. At 2.6 mi, reach a small parking space, R, for access to the Jonas Ridge Trail and Devil's Hole Trail. Ascend for 240 yd. on a path that may be divided to approach the same ridge crest to Jonas Ridge Trail. (A turn L is 0.6 mi on a primitive path up the ridge to Hawksbill Mtn. and jct with Hawksbill Mountain Trail.) Turn R and after 280 yd., is a jct with the primitive Devil's Hole Trail, L. (Ahead up the ridge Jonas Ridge Trail dead-ends on Gingercake Mtn. at 1.6 mi, but not before a steep climb on Sitting Bear Mtn. and past huge rock formations.) Descend steeply (elev change 1,160 ft.) on Devil's Hole Trail among rhododendron, large hemlock, and chestnut oak in the cove. Cross rocky sections of the streambed and arrive at a cliff top at 1.4 mi. Climb down to the river at 1.5 mi. If planning to connect with the Linville Gorge Trail on the mountainside across the river, cautiously look for the safest rock formation on which to rock-hop or be prepared to wade the river. Otherwise, backtrack.

Drive down FR-210 another 1.3 mi and park L for the Hawksbill Mountain Trail, R (W). Ascend steeply on Lettered Rock Ridge through laurel and rhododendron arbors to a trail jct at 0.5 mi. Turn L. (The R trail follows the ridge for an access L to rock climbing and N for 0.7 mi to SR-210 at Devil's Hole access.) Reach the rocky summit (4,020 ft.) of Hawksbill Mtn. at 0.7 mi at the E boundary of the wilderness. Vistas are superior. Mountain ash and blueberry bushes are colorful in autumn. Backtrack.

The rim access to Spence Ridge Trail is another 1.0 mi on FR-210 to the parking area, R and L. A frequently used route, the first 0.2 mi is level and arbored with rhododendron. At 0.4 mi, curve R at jct and descend. (Ahead on the old road is a primitive trail, Little Table Rock Trail, which descends to a curve L and crosses a small stream at 0.3 mi. It ascends on a spur ridge, descends to a small drain, and ascends a very steep grade through white pine and hemlock. At 1.1 mi, it reaches the top of Little Table Rock. A campsite and vistas are R. To the L is another primitive route, Little Table Rock Trail, to a water source at 160 yd. Ahead is a jct with Table Rock Summit Trail at 1.2 mi and an access to Table Rock Gap Trail, L.) Continue on the Spence

Ridge Trail. Descend on switchbacks to a jct across the river with the Linville Gorge Trail at 1.7 mi.

At the parking area for the Spence Ridge Trail, the Table Rock Gap Trail follows an old road S for 0.4 mi to a cul-de-sac and a jct with the MST. Turn R, ascend steeply, and after two switchbacks in a rhododendron slick reach a jct with the Table Rock Summit Trail. Backtrack, or use the Table Rock Summit Trail, L, for a 0.4-mi ascent to the top, or take a R 100 yd. for an option to descend on the Little Table Rock Trail described above, or continue on the Table Rock Summit Trail for 0.3 mi to the Table Rock Picnic Area and parking lot.

For vehicle access to the Table Rock Picnic Area, drive ahead on FR-210 for 1.1 mi to FR-210B. Turn R and go 2.9 mi to the picnic area (passing an entrance to the Outward Bound School and climbing steeply the last mile). The picnic area has a vault toilet but no water source. Camping is prohibited here. Follow the Table Rock Summit Trail N on white-blazed MST. Come to a jct with the Little Table Rock Trail, L, at 0.3 mi. Pass the Table Rock Gap Trail 100 yd. ahead, and ascend on six rocky switchbacks to the summit (3,909 ft.) at 0.7 mi with magnificent views and a 360-degree panorama.

264 *Shortoff Mountain Trail* (USFS #235) (F)

Length and Difficulty: 11.2 mi round-trip, strenuous (elev change 1,048 ft.)
Special Features: The Chimneys, vistas of Linville Gorge
Trailhead and Description: This trail is also the MST, and it skirts the E rim of the wilderness except at the Shortoff Mtn. area, which is in the wilderness. From the S edge of the Table Rock Picnic Area (described above), follow the trail on a gentle path to an open ridge of chinquapin, blueberry, and bracken at 0.4 mi. Pass W of the Chimneys (3,557 ft.), an area of fissures, irregular spires, and overhangs, to the ridge return at 0.8 mi. Descend steeply to a cliff with a view of Table Rock and a deep watershed at 1.3 mi. Descend to Chimney Gap (2,509 ft.) at 1.8 mi. At 2.1 mi in a saddle, R, is the obscure
265-266 and primitive 1.3-mi Cambric Ridge Trail, which dead-ends at the river). At 2.3 mi is Spring Trail an intermittent spring, L (60 yd. from the trail) in a grove of galax and rhododendron. Ascend and descend, reach a knob at 2.7 mi, turn R at 3.0 mi at an old trail jct, and soon follow an old jeep road. At 5.0 mi, pass a natural wildlife water hole. Turn R at an old road jct at 5.4 mi to reach the precipitous edge of Shortoff Mtn. (3,000 ft.) at 5.6 mi. Here are exceptionally scenic views of the gorge and both rims. Vegetation includes hemlock, spruce, blueberry, oak, and bristly locust. South 0.1 mi on the trail

is a usually dependable spring in a gulch. Backtrack or continue ahead on the MST. (The MST descends to an old road R. After a steep descent on the old road the MST crosses Linville River by wading. It then steeply ascends W to the Pinnacle for a jct with Kisler Memorial Rd [SR-1238]. Before crossing the river there is Linville River Access Trail, L. Under construction at press time **267** of this book, the trail has an access at NC-126, E of the Linville River bridge and parking near Lake James.)

Brushy Ridge Trail (USFS #232) (F)   **268**

Length and Difficulty: 4.0 mi round-trip, moderate

Trailhead and Description: This is an isolated trail in the wilderness that does not connect with any of the other trails. Access is on a private residential road and parking space is limited to two cars. (The private area should be respected by not parking off the road space anywhere else, or blocking any driveway.) To access, follow the Old Gingercake Rd (SR-1264) (as described above) 0.3 mi from NC-181 and turn R. After 0.9 mi on the L are two driveways close together; take the second one and after 0.2 mi in a curve, park on the small space to the R. An old forest road slightly descends SW of the curve to follow an easy treadway for 1.2 mi, where it becomes a footpath. Begin a descent and at 1.3 mi are spectacular views of the gorge, R. In a rocky descent to 1.6 mi are equal views downriver of Hawksbill, Table Rock, and the Babel Tower. On an overgrown rocky route are both Canadian and American hemlock. Reach a knob with stereophonic sounds of the river at 2.0 mi. Backtrack. (USGS-FS Map: Linville Falls)

North Catawba Area (McDowell County)

Overmountain Victory Trail (USFS #308) (F)   **236**

Length and Difficulty: 3.5 mi, moderate

Trailhead and Description: In celebration of the bicentennial (1780–1980) of the "Overmountain Men," this yellow-blazed trail was planned, constructed, and designated a national historic trail in 1980. During the American Revolution, when Col. Patrick Ferguson of the Loyalist Army sent word to the frontier mountain men that he would destroy them, the men responded by mustering a troop of 1,000 from VA, TN, and NC to seek out Col Ferguson, who was killed at the Kings Mountain battle in SC. Marching for 12 days from Sycamore Shoals in Tennessee, the men passed along this route on September 30, 1780. East access is on the Kistler Memorial Highway (SR-1238), 0.8 mi S from the Pinnacle and 4.1 mi N from NC-126. From the parking lot follow an old wagon road through a forest of white pine, laurel, and hardwoods. Cross a small stream at 0.3 mi and the Yellow Fork at 1.0 mi in thick rhododendron. At 1.5 mi, cross a FR (accessible by vehicle 1.9 mi N from the trailhead on SR-1238). Descend gradually on a grassy road through hardwoods. Pass two grazing fields, L, and reach a flat ridge at 3.1 mi. A water source is R. Reach the W terminus at a FS gate, trail sign, and paved Old Linville Rd (SR-1560), L and R, at 3.5 mi. Bridge Branch is R in a residential area. (About 0.1 mi of this exit is private property. It is 2.5 mi, R (N), on SR-1560 to a jct with US-221 in Ashford. (USGS-FS Map: Ashford)

Wilson Creek Area (Avery, Burke, and Caldwell Counties)

This large area has a network of more than 25 trails. They are concentrated in the deep valleys and gorges from the foldings of metamorphic rock that runs NW to SE from the Blue Ridge Mtn. crest to the hill country W of Lenoir. From S to N the drains that flow E are Steels Creek; Upper Creek; Harper Creek; North Harper Creek; Lost Cove Creek; and the major basin, Wilson Creek. In the center of the area is Mortimer Recreation Area, the only family campground (no hookups), but commercial full-svc campgrounds are near the NF boundary. Mortimer has facilities for picnicking, camping, fishing, and hiking. The 4.5-mi double-loop Thorps Creek Trail (USFS #279) (F) at the edge of the campground, which is the location of a former CCC camp. The area also has two other picnic sites: Barkhouse on NC-181 and Mulberry N of Lenoir. Mortimer is now a ghost area; once, nearly 1,000 residents worked here at the Riddle Lumber Company or other plants. Major forest fires devastated the mountains in 1916 and 1925, and floods washed away the town in 1916 and 1940. The rough but scenic state road that provides access to the community was constructed on an old RR grade in 1950. Streams are stocked with trout; the forests have bear, turkey, deer, grouse, raccoon, skunk, and squirrel. Rattlesnake and copperhead are also in the area. The forests are chiefly birch, oak, hickory, poplar, hemlock, white pine, laurel, and rhododendron. The area is well known for its Brown Mtn. Lights, a mysterious flickering light that according to legend is the spirit of a Civil War slave with a lantern looking for his master.

269

Access: To reach Mortimer Recreation Area from Morganton go 10.5 mi N on NC-181 to a jct R on Brown Mtn. Beach Rd (SR-1405, also called Collettsville Rd) at Smyrna Baptist Church. Go 5.0 mi on SR-1405 to SR-1328, L at the Mortimer sign. Go 4.5 mi to cross the Wilson Creek bridge. After another 1.0 mi, L, is Wilson Creek Visitor Center. Beyond the center is 3.4 mi to reach the campground. From Collettsville, go SW on Adako Rd (SR-1337) for 2.2 mi and turn R at the Mortimer sign to follow the directions above.

Support Facilities: Three commercial campgrounds in the area. Steels Creek Park, 828-433-5660, is 1.2 mi N on NC-181 from Smyrna Baptist Church, and Daniel Boone Family Campground, 828-433-1200, is 1.7 mi N on NC-181 from Smyrna Baptist Church, approx. 13.5 mi N of Morganton. A third commercial campground is 1.0 mi, L, after turning off SR-1405 (at Mortimer Rec Area sign) to SR-1328. Call the campgrounds for schedules. Morganton and Lenoir have shopping centers, restaurants, motels, and hospitals. The Wilson Creek Visitor Center (mentioned above) is owned and operated by Caldwell County. For more information, contact 828-759-0005.

Lower Steels Creek Trail (2.9 mi; USFS #238) (F); *Upper Steels Creek Trail* (2.9 mi; USFS #237) (F)

270-271

   Length and Difficulty: 5.8 mi combined, moderate
   Special Features: waterfalls, fishing, wildlife
   Trailhead and Description: These trails can be connected with 1.8 mi on FR-2128 for a total of 7.6 mi. To reach the upstream trailhead of the Lower Steels Creek Trail, turn off NC-181 on FR-2128 (9.6 mi S of NC-181/183 jct in Jonas Ridge and 4.4 mi up the mountain from SR-1405 at Smyrna Baptist Church), and drive 2.1 mi to a jct with an old forest road, L. Park and walk on the road for 0.2 mi to a gate and descend to Steels Creek at 0.5 mi Rock-hop, pass a fish barrier, L, and at 0.8 mi leave the road L into a grazing field. Re-enter the forest at 0.9 mi and rock-hop the creek. Immediately rock-hop again and follow a path through white pine, birch, and ironwood. At 1.2 mi, rock-hop the creek, L (watch for a NC Wildlife Commission trout sign on a white pine facing the stream, otherwise you may miss the crossing). Rock-hop again at 1.4 mi and pass through a clear-cut. (Passage may be difficult here because of timber slash and overgrowth to the next stream crossing.) Cross the stream at 1.6 mi (either on a log bridge or by wading). Enter a rhododendron canal with orange-fringed orchids *(Habenaria ciliaris)* in sunny spots. At 2.0 mi, turn L at remnants of an old log cabin and ascend gently on an old road to NC-181 at 2.9 mi. Descend the embankment. (There are no trailhead signs here, but watch for the end of a guardrail across the road from the trailhead, 0.3 mi up the mountain from the National Forest sign and 0.2 mi down the mountain from FR-4095.) Backtrack or use a second vehicle 1.7 mi up the mountain to FR-2128, L.

For the Upper Steels Creek Trail, follow the same route to FR-2128, but pass the parking area for the Lower Steels Creek Trail and drive 1.8 mi farther to a parking area at the road terminus. Hike upstream on a jeep road to creek cascades at 0.2 mi. Rock-hop the creek and reach jct with the white-blazed MST after 75 yd. Turn R, ascend through a rhododendron thicket with rapids and pools, R. Pass a waterfall at 0.6 mi. At 0.9 mi, turn sharply L, ascend steeply to an old RR grade, and at 1.3 mi pass through an ideal camping area of tall trees and grassy grounds. Enter a grazing field and reach a FR, R. Cross Gingercake Creek and Steels Creek to follow under tall poplar and white pine. At 1.9 mi, rock-hop the creek and again at 2.0 mi. Follow a well-graded FR to a ridge top at 2.8 mi and at 2.9 mi, leave the MST (which goes R). Continue ahead for 120 yd. to a locked FR gate and jct with FR-496. Backtrack or take FR-496, R, for 1.3 mi to NC-181, then R to FR-2128. (USGS-FS Map: Chestnut Mtn.)

272 **Upper Creek Falls Trail** (USFS #268B) (F)

> **Length and Difficulty:** 1.6 mi, strenuous
>
> **Trailhead and Description:** From the Barkhouse Picnic Area on NC-181, drive N 0.8 mi to the parking lot, R. (From the jct of NC-181/183, drive S, down the mountain, 4.1 mi to the parking lot, L.) This popular loop and scenic trail begins at the side of the parking lot. Follow it through hardwoods, laurel, and rhododendron; descend on switchbacks; and arrive at the top of Upper Creek Falls at 0.4 mi. There are huge boulders and pools upstream. Rock-hop the creek into more rhododendron and descend steeply among rocks, mosses, and ferns to cross the creek again at 0.7 mi. Ascend, pass under a large overhanging rock, and climb switchbacks to the side of the parking lot at 1.6 mi. (USGS-FS Map: Chestnut Mtn.)

273- **Greentown Trail** (5.7 mi; USFS #268) (F); **Greentown Short-cut**
274 **Trail** (1.2 mi; USFS #268A) (F)

> **Length and Difficulty:** 6.9 mi combined, strenuous (elev change 1,268 ft.)
>
> **Connecting Trails:** (MST); (Raider Camp Trail)
>
> **Trailhead and Description:** The trailhead is on the E side of NC-181 (across the road from FR-496), 0.4 mi S of Barkhouse Picnic Area. Follow an old logging road (white-blazed MST) and descend into a cove. At 1.0 mi, reach Upper Creek, but go upstream to cross at 1.2 mi; turn R. At 1.8 mi reach jct with Greentown Short-cut Trail, R, near the mouth of Burnthouse Branch. (Greentown Short-cut Trail descends in a gorge on the E side of Upper Creek

to the scenic Lower Upper Creek Falls at 0.7 mi. Exit at a parking area to FR-197 at 1.2 mi FR-197 descends to FR-982, R to NC-181, 4.0 mi S from the Greentown Trail entrance.) Continue on an old eroded road; reach an old parking and primitive campsite at a jct, R, with FR-198 at 3.8 mi. Bear L, make a long curve to a saddle with forks at 4.5 mi. Avoid the forks, go straight (from Burke County to Avery County), and descend. At 4.9 mi, take the L fork; reach Raider Camp Trail at 5.7 mi. (Raider Camp Trail, described ahead, goes L for 0.2 mi to South Harper Creek Falls and Harper Creek Trail, and R for 2.6 mi to jct with the E trailhead of Harper Creek Trail.) (USGS-FS Map: Chestnut Mtn.)

Harper Creek Trail (USFS #260) (F)   275-
    Length and Difficulty: 6.3 mi, strenuous (elev change 1,000 ft.)   282
    Connecting Trails: Yellow Buck Trail (2.1 mi; USFS #265, moderate) (F); Raider Camp Trail (2.8 mi; USFS #277, moderate) (F); (MST); (Simmons Ridge Trail); North Harper Creek Trail (4.5 mi; USFS #266, strenuous, elev change 1,320 ft.) (F); Persimmon Ridge Trail (2.7 mi; USFS #270, moderate) (F); North Harper Creek Access Trail (1.0 mi; USFS #266A, easy) (F); North Harper Creek Falls Trail (1.3 mi; USFS #239, moderate) (F)
    Special Features: waterfalls, fishing
    Trailhead and Description: If using the E trailhead at Wilson Creek, the combination of Harper Creek and North Harper Creek trails is shaped like a crooked Y with North Harper forking R. An advantage for using one or both of these trails is to create options for eight loop routes from modest to more challenging lengths. All but Simmons Ridge Trail are in the Harper Creek Wilderness Study Area. The clear rushing streams have sculpted the metamorphic rocks in falls, flumes, and pools. Trout are stocked and the NCWRC requires artificial lures. The two main trails follow the stream banks and cross the creeks frequently. Under normal weather conditions all fording can be rock-hopping. Water snakes and copperheads are seen sunning in the summer, and brilliant cardinal flowers *(Lobelia cardinalis)* bloom on wet grassy islands in late summer. Trail access routes connect from SR-1328 (E), FR-464 (N), and FR-85 (W).
    Begin the Harper Creek Trail at a narrow parking area on Wilson Creek Rd (SR-1328), 1.4 mi S of the Mortimer Rec Area. (The district staff is working with local landowners to create a larger parking area for this busy access to Harper Creek Trail system.) Ascend gradually on a well-graded trail to a ridge crest and jct, R, with Yellow Buck Trail at 0.4 mi. (The Yellow Buck Trail

ascends steeply on an old skid road for 0.7 mi to slope W of Yellow Buck Mtn. [2,470 ft.] and continues on a gentle route with white pine and bristly locust *[Robina hispida]* to a jct with the Persimmon Trail, L, at 1.8 mi. Ahead it is 0.3 mi to FR-464, the trail's end, and 4.0 mi E on FR-464 to Mortimer.) Continue on the Harper Creek Trail on a wide clear woods road to a jct, L, with Raider Camp Trail at 1.3 mi. The Harper Creek Trail turns R.

(The Raider Camp Trail, also the white-blazed MST, goes 135 yd. to cross Harper Creek, turn L. The trail follows up Raider Creek through good campsite areas 0.7 mi before ascending on an eroded old road to a ridge crest and crossroads at 2.0 mi. It goes straight to follow a level and scenic woods road in an open forest to jct with Greentown Trail, L, at 2.6 mi. Turn R at the jct and descend to a cliff for views of the spectacular 200-ft. waterfall and cascades known as South Harper Creek Falls. Continue on switchbacks to cross Harper Creek and intersect with Harper Creek Trail at the top of the falls at 2.8 mi. Harper Creek Trail goes L for 1.1 mi to its terminus on FR-58 and R downstream [also part of alternate MST] for 3.9 mi to its first encounter with Raider Camp Trail and back to SR-1328 for a loop of 9.3 mi.)

To continue on Harper Creek Trail from the first encounter, turn R, ascend gently for 0.1 mi to a spur route, and go another 0.2 mi to views of the scenic Harper Creek Falls and pool. Continue on the main trail, also the white-blazed MST, and pass the falls on a precipitous slope. Rock-hop the creek three times before a jct at the mouth of North Harper Creek, R, at 3.4 mi North Harper Creek Trail ascends 4.5 mi to FR-58 and is described in more detail below. Continue on the Harper Creek Trail where the treadway becomes rough in some sections. At 4.1 mi, cross a tributary in a forest of hemlock, hardwoods, and rhododendron. At 5.2 mi, arrive at the spectacular 200-ft. falls and cascades known as South Harper Creek Falls. A few yards beyond the top of the falls is a jct L with Raider Camp Trail, described above, for a reverse loop. Curve R at the nose of a ridge and ascend for 0.1 mi to an easy grade through oak, maple, and laurel and reach FR-58 at 6.3 mi, the W trailhead. Across the road is the S trailhead of Simmons Ridge Trail, described below. On FR-58, L, it is 0.5 mi to private property (the early settlement of Kawana), and R on FR-58 it is 0.5 mi to the W trailhead of Persimmon Ridge Trail. Here is another potential loop route, using North Harper Creek Trail, for a return total of 12.8 mi to SR-1328.

At the confluence of Harper and North Harper Creeks the North Harper Creek Trail starts upstream, R, and at 0.5 mi it intersects with Persimmon Ridge Trail, L and R.

(Persimmon Ridge Trail, L, is a steep ascent W for 0.1 mi to a ridgeline. Ascend gradually to a knob [2,785 ft.] at 1.7 mi and drop to FR-58 on a woods road at 2.1 mi. It is 0.5 mi L on FR-58 to the W trailhead of Harper Creek Trail and 3.0 mi R on FR-58 to the N trailhead of Simmons Ridge Trail. The E section of Persimmon Ridge Trail leaves North Harper Creek and ascends 0.6 mi to a jct with Yellow Buck Trail. To the L is 0.3 mi to FR-464; to the R on Yellow Buck Trail would provide a loop of 8.1 mi back to SR-1328.)

Continue on the North Harper Creek Trail; rock-hop the creek three times while passing through a flat area for campsites at 0.6 mi and by a deep pool, flumes, and ferns at 1.4 mi. At 1.8 mi, reach a jct with North Harper Creek Access Trail (also called Clearcut Trail), R. (Clearcut Trail is a well-graded, scenic, open-woods access route of 1.0 mi from FR-464, 5.4 mi from Mortimer.) Cross the creek a number of times and reach another campsite at 3.1 mi. At 3.3 mi, L, is Chestnut Cove Branch Falls, and at 3.4 mi is jct, R, with a dubious trailhead of North Harper Creek Falls Trail. An ax mark on a tulip poplar, L, is a simple sign.

(The North Harper Creek Falls Trail ascends 0.3 mi on an erratic manway to a logging road. Follow the road through dense blackberry patches and saplings, and bear L at another old road to reach FR-464 at 1.3 mi. It is 1.3 mi R to North Harper Creek Access Trail and L on FR-464 1.9 mi to FR-58.)

Continue up North Harper Creek Trail, ascend steeply through rhododendron to a large, high rock formation, L. Cross the creek and arrive at the base of an exceptionally beautiful North Harper Creek Falls at 3.6 mi. Ascend on switchbacks to the top of the falls for another scenic area of cascades and pools. Cross the creek to campsites, turn L, ascend, cross the creek three more times, the last at 4.4 mi. Reach the W terminus of the trail at 4.5 mi Left. on FR-58, it is 0.4 mi to Simmons Ridge Trail, and R on FR-58 it is 0.2 mi to FR-464. It is 8.6 mi R on FR-464 and NC-90 to Mortimer Rec Area, and L it is 4.5 mi to the jct of NC-181/183 in Jonas Ridge. For the NC-181 access route, go 2.5 mi L on FR-464 to Long Ridge Baptist Church, turn L on SR-1518, and go 0.5 mi. Turn R on SR-1471, go 0.8 mi to a jct with NC-181 and BRP, and turn L on NC-181 for 0.7 mi to the jct of NC-181/183. (USGS-FS Maps: Chestnut Mtn., Grandfather Mtn.)

Simmons Ridge Trail (USFS #267) (F)   283
Length and Difficulty: 5.2 mi, moderate
Special Features: RR grade, wildlife

Trailhead and Description: Access is described above from NC-181 to the W trailhead of North Harper Creek Trail. From that trailhead on FR-58, go 0.4 mi to a small parking space, L, but the trailhead is R at a large cucumber tree. (Passage may be difficult on the trail for a section because of timber slash and overgrowth.) Ascend 90 yd. to a ridge and follow an old logging road in a hardwood forest to the top of Headquarters Mtn. (3,970 ft.) at 1.4 mi. Descend to a gated dirt FR (R, 0.4 mi to old Jonas Ridge Rd [SR-1518, also called Mortimer Rd]. To the L, SR-1518 becomes SR-1401 in Burke County and leads 2.1 mi to NC-181 in Jonas Ridge. To the R, SR-1501 is 0.7 mi to Long Ridge Baptist Church and R to FR-464.) Cross the dirt road and descend to join an old RR grade at 2.8 mi. Follow it for the remainder of the trail through a forest of oak, locust, maple, laurel, and rhododendron. Exit at FR-58 at 5.2 mi. Ahead is the W trailhead of Harper Creek Trail described above. To the R it is 0.5 mi to private property and the South Fork of Harper Creek. It is 3.5 mi L to the N trailhead of Simmons Ridge Trail. (USGS-FS Maps: Chestnut Mtn., Grandfather Mtn.)

284-286   *Big Lost Cove Cliffs Trail* (1.2 mi; USFS #271) (F); *Little Lost Cove Cliffs Trail* (1.3 mi; USFS #271A) (F); *Darkside Cliffs Trail* (0.5 mi; USFS #272) (F)

Length and Difficulty: 5.7 mi combined round-trip, moderate

Special Features: geology, spectacular vistas

Trailheads and Description: These three trails do not connect but are grouped because of proximity and similarity. The easiest access is from NC-181, 0.7 mi N of jct with NC-183. Turn R on SR-1471 and go 0.8 mi, turn L on SR-1518 and go 0.5 mi, and turn R at Long Ridge Baptist Church on FR-464. Descend 2.0 mi to a narrow parking edge in a sharp L curve. The trail ascends 0.4 mi in laurel and rhododendron with ground cover of wintergreen *(Gaultheria procumbens)* to an old jeep road. Descend to the cliffs at 1.2 mi for a grand 180-degree view of Lost Cove, Grandfather and Grandmother Mtns., and the BRP. Drive down FR-464 for 1.1 mi to W trailhead of Little Lost Cove Cliffs Trail. Park R, and ascend on an old jeep road. At 0.6 mi is the first of a number of spurs for a 360-degree view of Grandfather Mtn., Timber Ridge, Wilson Creek basin, Harper Creek basin, Hawksbill Mtn., and Blowing Rock area. Descend to FR-464 on a gated jeep road at 1.3 mi. Drive down FR-464 another 0.6 mi to Darkside Cliffs Trail, L, but park R of road. Walk this easy 0.5-mi route first through hardwoods and then rhododendron and pitch pine for superb views of the Wilson Creek basin, Blowing Rock area, and Grandfather

Mtn. range. Backtrack. On FR-464 it is 6.1 mi down the mountain to NC-90 and to Mortimer Rec Area. (USGS-FS Map: Grandfather Mtn.)

Timber Ridge Trail (1.5 mi; USFS #261) (F); ***Lost Cove Trail*** (7.5 mi; USFS #262) (F); ***Hunt-Fish Falls Trail*** (0.8 mi; USFS #263) (F)   **287-289**

    Length and Difficulty: 9.8 mi combined, moderate to strenuous
    Special Features: wildlife, waterfalls, vistas
    Trailhead and Description: These trails connect as a group and are within the Lost Cove Wilderness Study Area. The N access (described first) is on FR-981 and the S access is on FR-464. From the Mortimer Rec Area, go 2.0 mi W on NC-90 to the S edge of Edgemont and turn L on FR-981. Drive 4.0 mi to a parking space, L, before crossing the bridge of Gragg Prong, opposite FR-192. (Ahead on FR-981 it is 0.4 mi to Roseborough and Roseborough Rd, SR-1511. It goes 4.5 mi up the mountain to the BRP and Linville.) Hike across the bridge, turn L on a short jeep road, and begin the Lost Cove Trail (also the white-blazed MST route) at the downstream corner of a small meadow. Rock-hop Gragg Prong four times in the first 2.0 mi. At 1.0 mi, reach jct with a spur trail, R, that ascends gradually to Timber Ridge Trail for 0.4 mi. At 1.2 mi are falls, sunbathing rocks, pools, and campsites in a forest of white pine, oak, laurel, hemlock, and rhododendron. Pass a high falls at 1.5 mi to reach a jct with Timber Ridge Trail, R, at 2.3 mi near convergence with Lost Cove Creek. Rock-hop Lost Cove Creek and reach the high cascades L and three-tiered Hunt-Fish Falls, R, at 3.0 mi, an excellent fishing and sunning area. (The Hunt-Fish Falls Trail ascends L steeply, 0.8 mi on switchbacks to FR-464 for a S access. This access is 1.7 mi W from Mortimer Rec Area on NC-90 to FR-464, L, and 3.1 mi farther up the mountain to the trailhead parking area, R.) Cross Lost Cove Creek above the falls and turn L, upstream. (A number of side trails to campsites are confusing with a spur trail that goes R to Timber Ridge Trail. If using the spur trail as a shortcut, look for the spur with the most usage. After 0.6 mi, steeply, it comes to a jct with the Timber Ridge Trail. A turn R will connect with the E trailhead at Cragg Prong; a L turn is 0.4 mi to its original W jct with Lost Cove Trail.)

    Continue upstream on the Lost Cove Trail, but the trail may be overgrown enough to make it difficult to follow for the next 1.7 mi in its crisscross passage of the stream. At 4.3 mi, L, is Little Lost Cove Creek and falls. Turn R, cross the creek, and ascend on switchbacks to jct with an old trail, L, at 5.4 mi. Turn R (SE), curve around Bee Mtn., and follow the ridge to the W trailhead of Timber Ridge Trail at 6.4 mi. It goes ahead; Lost Cove Trail makes a sharp turn L. At 6.5 mi, descend into a huge natural amphitheater landscaped by nature with ferns, rocks, wildflowers, and a spring. At 7.5 mi return to the parking area. (USGS-FS Map: Grandfather Mtn.)

290- *Wilson Creek Trail* (6.6 mi; USFS #258) (F); *Wilson Creek Access*
292 *Trail* (1.4 mi; USFS #258A) (F); *White Rocks Trail* (0.8 mi; USFS #264) (F)

>   **Length and Difficulty:** 8.8 mi combined, moderate to strenuous
>   **Special Features:** remote, fishing, wildlife, rugged
>   **Trailhead and Description:** These primitive trails combine to provide two accesses NW and two SE. Signs and blazes are absent except unofficial markings by hikers or fishermen. Wading is necessary at some of the fordings, particularly downstream. For the SE trailheads, from Mortimer Rec Area, drive N on NC-90 through Edgemont, cross Wilson Creek Trail trailhead, L, at 4.0 mi. Parking area is small. Another 1.5 mi up the mountain on FR-45 is the White Rocks Trail trailhead, L (it is an 0.8-mi shortcut down Bark Camp Ridge to jct with the Wilson Creek Trail at the mouth of Laurel Mtn. Branch). Begin the Wilson Creek Trail by ascending Bark Camp Ridge in a forest of oak, white pine, and laurel. Curve L of a knob, descend, and in a cove cross Crusher Branch at 0.8 mi. Ford the creek twice and reach jct with White Rocks Trail at 1.8 mi. Cross Laurel Mtn. Branch and ford the creek frequently in the next 3.0 mi. Campsites are good at Turkey Branch and Flat Land Branch. At 4.8 mi, reach the confluence of Andrews and Wilson Creeks. Between them, in a fork, Wilson Creek Trail turns R at red paint marks and the Wilson Creek Access Trail proceeds ahead. (If following the Wilson Creek Access Trail, rock-hop Andrews Creek a number of times and reach the convergence with Stackrock Creek, R, at 0.8 mi. In a rhododendron thicket are scenic cascades and pools. Arrive at a grazing field at 1.2 mi, turn R, and follow a gated old road to FR-192 at 1.4 mi [6.2 mi from FR-45]. It is 1.0 mi L to Old House Gap and 2.6 mi R to Edgemont Rd [SR-1514].) The main Wilson Creek Trail is overgrown, but you may follow the red markers up Wilson Creek to its jct with an alternate route. Cross Wilson Creek immediately after forking R from Wilson Creek Access Trail, pass two huge rock overhangs, cross the creek twice more, and at 0.5 mi, reach a frequently used campsite. Two signs are on trees in memory of Mike Borders and J.C. Bryant, both killed in a vehicular accident. There are two routes out from here. The roughest is to go 390 ft. upstream in a mainway to a rocky island and a paint marker. Cross the creek at a cucumber tree and the mouth of Bee Branch. Turn sharply

R and follow red "B.B." initials on a poplar to an old RR grade. Follow the "B.B." and white markers to the convergence of Wilson Creek and Little Wilson Creek, R. Ascend an old RR grade between the creeks but leave the grade at 0.4 mi. Pass through a rhododendron grove and exit by a campsite at FR-192 at 0.6 mi (5.9 mi from FR-45 entrance). The other option is to follow the jeep road at the memorial campsite. After 0.8 mi, come to jct with an old logging road. Turn L and follow to FR-192 at 1.3 mi. From here it is 0.3 mi L to the Little Wilson Creek Access, and 1.9 mi farther to Wilson Creek Access Trail. To the R, it is 0.6 mi to the Edgemont Rd (SR-1514). From this jct, it is 4.1 mi L to US-221 (0.5 mi E of the BRP); R on SR-1514 it is 5.8 mi down the mountain to FR-45 and the SE trailhead of Wilson Creek Trail. Along FR-45 are two other isolated trails described below.

Woodruff Branch Trail (2.4 mi; USFS #256) (F, B); ***Bill Crump Trail*** (1.2 mi; USFS #257) (F)

293-294

Length and Difficulty: 4.8 mi round-trip, easy

Trailhead and Description: These trails do not connect, but both have trailheads on FR-45 within 1.6 mi of each other and are old roads closed to vehicular use. (The Woodruff Branch Trail is designated for mountain bicycle use.) For access go N from Edgemont on SR NC-90, which becomes FR-45 for 4.7 mi (pass Wilson Creek Trail access at 2.0 mi) to Woodruff Branch Trail, R. Cross hummock (also called "tank trap") and follow pleasant seeded road across Barn Ridge, and descend to a parking area near the mouth of Woodruff Branch at Anthony Creek to Anthony Creek Rd (SR-1362) at 2.4 mi. Backtrack, or use a second vehicle 2.1 mi NW to Gragg on FR-45, R, for 4.5 mi (SE) on Globe Rd (SR-1516), which becomes SR-1362. The Bill Crump Trail is 1.6 mi up FR-45 from the Woodruff Branch Trail. A rarely used trail, it descends S and crosses Cary Flat Branch in a young forest of laurel, hemlock, and oak. It drops to the nose of a hill and dead-ends at a private road. Backtrack. (USGS-FS Maps: Grandfather Mtn., Globe)

Thunderhole Creek Area (Caldwell and Watauga Counties)

China Creek Trail (2.6 mi; USGS #250) (F, B); ***Thunderhole Falls Trail*** (0.1 mi; USGS #253) (F)

295-296

Length and Difficulty: 5.4 mi round-trip, moderate

Special Features: Thunderhole Falls, cascading stream, wildlife

Trailhead and Description: Access is on gravel Globe Rd (SR-1367) 3.4 mi S of Blowing Rock from S Main St (also US-321B). Parking space is R

(W) at FR-4071. (If approaching from Collettsville, it is 15.6 mi on NC-90 to Anthony Creek Rd [SR-1632]. Turn R and go 1.0 mi to turn R on Globe Rd; ascend for 4.4 mi to access L [W].) There are not any signs or blazes at the parking area or on the trail or forest road.

From the parking space follow FR-4071 over tank traps (where a forest gate has been removed). Descend and at 0.4 mi, turn L off the road to a pioneer road and reach a flat area among walnut, poplar, and wildflowers. Wildlife includes deer and raccoon. Rock-hop or wade Thunderhole Creek at 0.8 mi, cross the creek another three times, and at 1.5 mi, cross China Creek to a fork in the old road. A turn L is on the Thunderhole Falls Trail. It ascends 0.1 mi among rhododendron to a combination flume and waterfall. Backtrack to the fork and proceed upstream by China Creek. At 1.8 mi, cross FR-4071 (a low-water concrete bridge is R on the road). Cross the creek twice and at 2.2 mi, cross a small tributary, Long Branch. After three more creek crossings, reach a tributary to the R, the ending of the trail at 2.6 mi. (There is a trackable route to the L, which follows up China Creek to the Moses H. Cone Memorial Park of the BRP, but the route's N passage may be on private property. The USFS lists the N terminus at Mayview Park in Blowing Rock.) Backtrack. If using FR-4071 for a return to the Globe Rd, it is 2.5 mi from the low-water concrete bridge to Globe Rd. (USGS-FS Maps: Globe, Boone)

SECTION 3: PISGAH RANGER DISTRICT

This district of 155,881 acres and historic distinction is the flagship of the state's NF districts. It is the most popular, attracting approximately 5 million visitors annually. The district is a hiker's mecca with more than 390 mi of trails, most of which are blazed in white, red, orange, blue, or yellow (except in the two wilderness areas, where blazes or maintenance are not provided). At each trailhead and connection there is likely a sign with the trail's name, its color, and logos for its usage (foot trail, bike, or horse), difficulty, and direction. Hikers have an exceptionally wide choice of trails—for ecological study and forest history; on steep rocky balds, dry ridges, and in remote forested canyons and coves; into the backcountry for solitude; and by creek-sides and waterfalls.

In the preceding districts the order of trail description has followed the order of USFS trail inventory numbers (as seen on USGS maps) from lowest to highest. This district is treated differently because of its exceptionally long list of trails. I have divided the trails into 12 groups according to trail proximity, disregarding both the USFS numerical order in its TIS and the additional trail numbers printed on the district's alphabetized map. However, it is important for the user to acquire the district trail map for not only knowing the topographical trail outline, but by looking closely, for seeing the USGS quad map numbers reproduced alongside the trail in a parallelogram.

All trails that loop or that can be connected are described together. Isolated or singular trails are described in the introduction of the area. One trail is particularly different. It is Mount Pisgah Trail (1.3 mi; USFS #355) (F), whose access is from Mt. Pisgah parking lot at mp 407.6 of the BRP (see chapter 6). The trail begins at a sign, soon enters the national forest, and begins a strenuous climb at 0.4 mi. After a rocky ascent on switchbacks, it reaches the summit (5,721 ft.) at an observation deck. The panoramic views include Pigeon River Gorge and Shining Rock Wilderness.

The district's longest trail, Art Loeb Trail (30.0 mi), is described as a single area. The MST follows many original trails and is frequently described with them. It passes through the district as a mainline from Haywood Gap, BRP mp 426.5 to NC-191 at BRP mp 393.8 for 46.2 mi, but 21.3 mi is new construction. The alternate MST (MST-A) is 13.2 mi longer and follows original trails all the way.

Since the printing of the third edition of this book, a few trails have been removed from the system by the USFS because of disuse, erosion, or danger to users. Examples are Fire Scald Ridge Trail (USFS #111); Beetree Trail (USFS #612); Cedar Rock Trail (USFS #124); and Grassy Knob Trail (USFS #338).

Descriptive grouping in this district is generally from W to E, first covering the two wilderness areas and a pocket of trails around the Black Balsam Knob between the wildernesses—all on the N side of the BRP. On the S side of the BRP the descriptions begin with Courthouse Creek Area, followed by Upper Davidson River, Lower Davidson River, Avery Creek, Pink Beds, South Mills River, Laurel Mtn., North Mills River, and Bent Creek, the latter the most eastern on the NW side of the BRP.

The district has exceptionally strong public relations with volunteer groups in trail maintenance and recommendations. The largest and most historical is the Carolina Mountain Club for foot trails. An active bike group is the Blue Ridge Bicycle Club and an active equestrian group is the Pisgah Trailblazers. (For more information, contact the district office [828-877-3265] about other task forces and how you may assist as a volunteer.)

Recreational facilities provide four family campgrounds: Davidson River, the largest, (161 sites with one section open year-round and limited services) across the Davidson River from the ranger station; Lake Powhatan in the Bent Creek Experimental Forest near the French Broad River (98 sites open April-Oct), off NC-191 near the BRP; North Mills River (31 sites and open year-round, but no water in winter), W of North Mills; and Sunburst (10 sites open April-Oct) on NC-215, N of the BRP at Sunburst. There are three group camps that require reservations: Upper and Lower Cove Creek, near the US Fish Hatchery; North and South White Pines, on FR-477 near the ranger station; and Kuykendall, off US-64 between Rosman and Brevard. Picnic areas are Coontree, Pink Beds, and Sycamore Flats, all on US-276 between the BRP and Brevard; North Mills on Mills River Rd (SR-1345); Sunburst, as above; and Lake Powhatan, as above. Primitive and roadside camping and picnicking are indicated at appropriate signs throughout the district. Among the major natural attractions are Looking Glass Falls, Looking Glass Rock, and Sliding Rock, all on US-276 W of the ranger station; Courthouse Creek Falls off NC-215 NW of Rosman; and Mt. Pisgah off the BRP. Other attractions are the US Fish Hatchery off US-276 NW of the ranger station and the Cradle of Forestry in America N of Sliding Rock on US-276. The district has two wilderness areas—Middle Prong (7,460 acres) and Shining Rock (18,483 acres), both NW in the district; and Bent Creek Experimental Forest (where a number of state champion trees may be observed) at the N edge of the district. The district has numerous streams for fishing, game animals for hunting, old roads and trails for equestrians and mountain bikers, routes for cross-country skiing, and domes for rock climbers. (Inquire at the ranger station for information on native trout fishing.) Swimming is at Lake Powhatan off NC-191, and observation/water play areas are at Sliding Rock (there is a $1 parking fee from Memorial Day through Labor Day) and Looking Glass Falls, both on US-276 W of the ranger station. There is a 79.0-mi scenic byway, Forest Heritage Scenic Byway, auto loop in the district and vicinity. (Request a free brochure for its route.)

The district boundaries are N at the French Broad River near and S of Asheville, W with the Highlands District of the Nantahala National Forest, S by the Toxaway River area, and E by US-64 and NC-280. Sections are in Buncombe, Henderson, Transylvania, and Haywood Counties, and through the district runs the BRP. The district is named after Mt. Pisgah (5,721 ft.). According to legend the peak was named after the Biblical mountain, Pisgah, where Moses saw the "promised land," by the Rev. James Hall, an Indian-fighting Presbyterian chaplain who was in the area in 1776 with Gen. Griffith Rutherford's expedition against the Cherokee. Another legend is that George Newton, a Presbyterian teacher-minister, gave it the name. The district originated when George W. Vanderbilt acquired more than 125,000 acres upon which was constructed Biltmore Estate, a reproduction of a sixteenth-century large French chateau. (Biltmore is not part of the current Pisgah National Forest.) His vast forests, which included Mt. Pisgah (earlier owned by Thomas Clingman, for whom Clingmans Dome is named), were first managed by conservationist Gifford Pinchot and later by Carl A. Schenck, the famous German forester. It was Schenck who established the Biltmore Forest School in 1898, the birthplace of scientific forestry in America (see Pink Beds Area in this section). After Vanderbilt's death in 1914, his heirs sold tracts of the forest in 1917 to the US government for forest preservation.

Address and Access: District Ranger, Pisgah Ranger District, USFS, 1001 Pisgah Highway, Pisgah Forest, NC 28768; 828-877-3265. Access is 1.6 mi W on US-276 from the jct of US-276/64 and NC-280, N of Brevard.

Pisgah Ranger District
Western Area

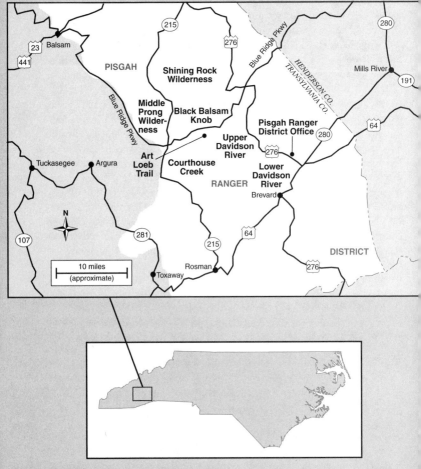

Introductions to Trail Areas

This district has the remarkable honor of having more trails (142) and mileage (395) than any district in any national forest in the state. Visitors have multiple choices and frequently return to some of their favorite trails. The trail descriptions and map information are counterclockwise.

Pisgah Ranger District Office
The district is on US-276 near Brevard. It has a nature trail from the parking area and inside are nature displays, books, maps, flyers, and a wide range of information.

Mountains-to-Sea Trail
The MST (mainline) passes through this district for 21.4 mi and its MST (alternate) for 37.8 mi.

Art Loeb Trail 172
A national recreation trail, this historic 30-mi scenic route undulates between cols, peaks, and grassy and rocky balds with priceless views and connects with the MST (elev change 4,084 ft.).

Middle Prong Wilderness 175
This area is home to remote, rugged, lush coves, fir/spruce groves, bears, red and gray squirrels, turkey and grouse, splashing tributaries, and historic trails.

Shining Rock Wilderness 177
The Art Loeb Trail goes through part of this wilderness on peaks more than a mile-high with white shining rocks, wildflowers, and heath groves.

Black Balsam Knob Area 180
An exceptionally popular and elegant grassy bald (6,214 ft.), this area has an access trail and is on the route of the Art Loeb Trail. Trails on the Blue Ridge Parkway are nearby.

Courthouse Creek Area 184
Part of the French Broad River Headwaters, the creek descends on mossy rocks with flumes and cascades, all in the shadow of Devil's Courthouse walls.

Upper Davidson River Area 185
Along with the Art Loeb Trail, other trails drop from the sky in this sensational locality. A granite massif is home to lady bugs. Down the mountain are trout streams and cascades for sliding into a pool. Looking Glass Dome is a challenge to rock climbers.

Lower Davidson River 190
From a fish hatchery and parking area, trails fan up the ridges and hollows. There is a large campground (all services except electricity) and tubing down the Davidson River. Black Mountain Trail ascends to hug a ridge with outcroppings and a campsite shelter.

A. WESTERN AREA OF PISGAH RANGER DISTRICT

297   *Art Loeb Trail* (30.0 mi; USFS #146) (F)

Length and Difficulty: Section I, 12.2 mi, strenuous; Section II, 7.0 mi, strenuous; Section III, 7.0 mi, moderate; Section IV, 3.8 mi, moderate to strenuous (elev change 4,084 ft.); 33.0 mi total if Cold Mountain Trail is included

Connecting Trails: (MST Alternate); (North Slope Ridge Loop Trail
298   Connector); (Cat Gap Trail); Art Loeb Bypass Trail (0.7 mi, easy) (F, B);
299   (Butter Gap Trail); (Farlow Gap Trail); Art Loeb/Black Balsam Trail (0.6 mi,
300   easy; USFS #108) (F); Ivestor Gap Trail (4.3 mi, easy; USFS #101) (F);
301   (Graveyard Ridge Trail); (Shining Creek Trail); (Old Butt Knob Trail); Cold
Mountain Trail (1.5 mi, strenuous; USFS #141, elev change 1,025 ft.) (F)

Special Features: Pilot Mtn., Black Balsam Knob, Shining Rock Wilderness, geology, vistas, wildlife, wildflowers

Trailhead and Description: The Art Loeb Trail, designated a national recreation trail in 1979, is named in honor of the late Arthur J. Loeb, a hiking enthusiast and dedicated leader of the Carolina Mountain Club. The trail is the district's longest and most challenging. Its elev gain from the Davidson River to Black Balsam Knob is 4,084 ft., or 2,926 ft. if ascended from the Daniel Boone Boy Scouts Camp. It undulates between cols and peaks with rapturous vistas. Although the full trail can require much exertion if backpacked S to N, it is divided into four sections with connecting or loop trails to allow for modest excursions and easier vehicle shuttle. For the first 18.0 mi the blue-blaze is for the MST, jointly followed by a white rectangular blaze for the Art Loeb Trail. It is rarely marked in its passage through the Shining Rock Wilderness. The trail passes through an exceptional variety of hardwoods and conifers, heath gardens, wildflowers, and shrubs. Mammals common to the area are bear, deer, gray fox, red and gray squirrels, rabbit, chipmunk, and woodchuck. Among the songbirds are Carolina junco, winter wren, nuthatch, scarlet tanager, warblers, and vireos. Snow bunting are seen in the winter. Other birds in the area are hawk, owl, turkey, grouse, raven, and woodpecker.

Section 1: From the Pisgah Ranger Station, go E 0.3 mi to the Davidson River Campground sign (1.3 mi W from US-276/64, NC-280 jct). Turn, and before the bridge, turn L into the Art Loeb Trail parking lot. Walk downstream 0.2 mi to the swinging bridge. Cross the swinging bridge over the Davidson River, turn L, and follow white blazes on a river plain through bee balm, coneflowers, and virgin oak and poplar. Cross a footbridge at 0.5 mi. Turn R on a grassy road for 50 ft. before turning L up steps. Begin an ascent W on the Shut-In Ridge. Ascend through rosebay rhododendron and reach the crest at

2.9 mi. Descend to Neil Gap at 3.3 mi. At 3.7 mi, reach jct R with the yellow-blazed 1.3-mi North Slope Ridge Loop Trail Connector, which descends for 2.0 mi to the Davidson River Campground parking lot; it is described above in the Davidson Rec Area. Climb to Chestnut Knob (3,840 ft.), and descend to Cat Gap and a double trail jct at 6.3 mi (The Cat Gap Trail goes R [NE] for 2.2 mi to the Fish Hatchery on FR-475 [a section formerly called Horse Cove Trail], and the Cat Gap Trail goes L [NW] for 2.5 mi for a loop to the same exit.) At 6.9 mi is Sand Gap. Cross a stream at 7.0 mi, circle S of Cedar Rock, and reach an A-frame shelter at 8.6 mi. Two streams are nearby. Ascend to Butter Gap at 8.8 mi, a jct of seven roads and trails. (Butter Gap Trail descends R [N] for 2.7 mi to join Cat Gap Trail for 0.8 mi for an exit to the Fish Hatchery on FR-475. Continue ahead, L, on the ridge through open woods of hickory, oak, maple, locust, and sourwood with an understory of buckberry. Reach the summit of Chestnut Mtn., cross FR-471 at 11.6 mi, reach the summit of Rich Mtn. at 11.8 mi, and descend to Gloucester Gap (3,250 ft.) and Davidson River Rd (FR-475) at 12.2 mi (To the R, FR-475 descends 6.7 mi to a jct with US-276, and L for 2.7 mi to a jct with NC-215 via SR-1321. Also at Gloucester Gap is FR-471, which goes SE for 8.2 mi on Cathey Creek Rd to US-64 at Selica. Another road here is FR-229, which ascends NW from Gloucester Gap for 2.5 mi to a parking area near Deep Gap.) (USGS-FS Maps: Pisgah Forest, Shining Rock)

Section 2: Cross FR-475, ascend, cross FR-229 at 12.8 mi and again at 13.8 mi. Begin strenuous multiple switchbacks on Pilot Mtn. and reach the summit (5,020 ft.) at 14.4 mi. Vegetation is chinquapin, bush honeysuckle *(Diervilla sessilifolia),* laurel, blueberry, and chestnut oak. Hundreds of ladybird beetles have been seen here. Views are outstanding. Descend on switchbacks through yellow birch and other hardwoods to Deep Gap, follow FR-229 for 0.1 mi, and reach an A-frame shelter at 15.2 mi. A spring is 75 yd. NW of the shelter. Climb Sassafras Knob with a ground cover of galax and wood betony and an understory of laurel, mountain ash, and azalea. Descend to Farlow Gap at 16.1 mi and jct with Farlow Gap Trail. (The blue-blazed Farlow Gap Trail, described above, goes 3.1 mi to Daniel Ridge Trail, which goes down the mountain to Davidson River Rd [FR-475].) Ascend to Shuck Ridge through oak, beech, and spruce. Reach BRP mp 421.2 at 17.6 mi. Turn L on the road and go 90 yd. to trail steps up an embankment. Ascend on an exceptionally steep treadway with steps to the crest and jct with the MST, L and R, at 18.0 mi. The MST leaves the Art Loeb Trail L and goes 3.2 mi to NC-215 and beyond. To the R of the MST, go 1.1 mi on the Art Loeb Trail before turning off, R, on a new 11.9-mi route to Buck Spring Trail. (See appendix A.) On a narrow trail through fir and spruce pass Silvermine Bald and reach FR-816, the end of Section II, at 19.1 mi. To the R, it is 0.8 mi to the BRP. To the L, it is 0.3 mi to a water source and at 0.5 mi the Black Balsam parking area, a popular base for hikes to a variety of surrounding trails.

(From the parking area, Ivestor Trail goes W on a broad old RR grade for 4.3 mi to a jct with the Art Loeb Trail at Ivestor Gap and again at Shining Rock Gap. It is used more than any other access trail by hikers and backpackers to the Shining Rock Wilderness. It is also used by blueberry pickers, birders, equestrians, and hunters who use the wilderness boundary at Ivestor Gap from August 15 to January 2. Springs are at 0.9 mi and 1.6 mi. In the wilderness, campfires are banned and campsite groups are limited to 10. Blazes are not used.) (USGS-FS Maps: Shining Rock, Sam Knob)

Section 3: From FR-816 and the MST (which goes NE for 11.9 mi to join the Buck Spring Trail and MST Alternate), ascend through a heath bald area to jct L at 19.5 mi with the Art Loeb/Black Balsam Trail. Reach the grassy scenic summit of Black Balsam Knob (6,214 ft.), the highest peak in the district, at 19.6 mi. Continue N on the ridge to Tennent Mtn. (6,046 ft.) at 20.8 mi (The mountain is named in honor of Dr. G. S. Tennent, an early leader in the Carolina Mountain Club.) Descend and follow an old road entry to Ivestor Gap and the E boundary of the (18,483-acre) Shining Rock Wilderness at 21.5 mi (R is Graveyard Ridge Trail, which connects after 0.2 mi with Greasy Cove Trail before the Graveyard Ridge Trail goes 3.2 mi farther E to the BRP, mp 418.8.) Contact here is with the Ivestor Trail, which continues to parallel the W side of the ridge toward Shining Rock Gap. The Art Loeb Trail skirts the E shoulder of Grassy Cove Top. At 22.7 mi, reach Flower Gap and skirt E of Flower Knob on an old RR bed through an arbor of beech with bush honeysuckle, purple Habenaria orchids, and sundrops in sunny places. A spring is R at 23.1 mi. Proceed to Shining Rock Gap at 23.3 mi, an overused camping area and trail terminal. (The Ivestor Trail ends here after collecting the traffic from Fork Mtn. Trail and Little East Fork Trail from the W. This is the W terminus for the Shining Creek Trail and the Old Butt Knob Trail, both separately but steeply ascending from Big East Fork at US-276.) Ahead are the white quartz outcrops (less pretentious than some visitors expect, but geologically venerable) that have given the area its name. It is easily reached in 0.2 mi partially by the Old Butt Knob Trail. (Overuse camping has damaged the thick stands of laurel, bristly locust, fetterbush, blueberry, and fly poison).

(Hikers are requested to protect the environment and read the material on "No-Trace Use" on the back of the Pisgah District Trail Map and signboards.) Continue the Art Loeb Trail on an old RR bed N of Shining Rock Gap to a spur trail R at 23.8 mi (which leads 0.5 mi to Old Butt Knob Trail). Reach Crawford Creek Gap at 23.9 mi, leave the old RR grade, and ascend to Stairs Mtn. (5,869 ft.) at 24.1 mi. Enter a red spruce grove at 24.9 mi, and pass through the scenic Narrows where painted trillium and a number of rhododendron species create color and fragrance at 25.2 mi. At 25.6 mi and 25.7 mi are two magnificent views of the W Fork of the Pigeon River Valley, Lickstone Ridge, and Great Balsam Mtn. Descend to Deep Gap, an open grassy area with scattered locust at 26.2 mi. (Ahead is the 1.5-mi Cold Mountain Trail, which ascends to a dead-end on the summit of Cold Mtn. [6,030 ft.]. Halfway up the ascent is a spring. Backtracking is required.) (USGS-FS Maps: Cruso, Shining Rock, Sam Knob)

Section 4: The Art Loeb Trail makes a 90-degree turn L for its descent into the lush headwaters of Sorrell Creek. The first seepage is at 26.9 mi, and at 28.0 mi are cascades, campsites, and part of a copious display in a mixed hardwood forest of such wildflowers as saxifrage, umbrella leaf, lady slipper, golden Alexander, and trillium. At 28.9 mi, leave the ridge crest of laurel and descend on switchbacks to the trail's N terminus and parking area at the S edge of the Daniel Boone Boy Scouts Camp at 30.0 mi. If leaving vehicles here, it is necessary to inform the Boy Scouts Camp director. Access here is on Little East Fork Rd (SR-1129), which goes 3.8 mi downstream to NC-215 (13.0 mi L [S] to the BRP and 5.3 mi R [N] to US-276). (USGS-FS Maps: Cruso, Waynesville)

Middle Prong Wilderness (Haywood County)

In 1984, a wild, remote, and rugged 7,460-acre section of the district officially became the Middle Prong Wilderness. Its boundary is NC-215 (E), the BRP (S and W), and near the toe of Big Beartrail Ridge (N). In the center of the wilderness is long Fork Ridge, whose waters drain E into the W Fork of the Pigeon River and W into the Middle Prong of the W Fork at Sunburst. Sunburst was a lumber town for the Champion Paper Company in the early 1900s. It had more than 10 camps harvesting the huge hemlock, chestnut, and poplar. Although the forest is recovering, parts of old RR and skid grades and logging equipment remain scattered in the Middle Prong area. Wildlife includes bear, deer, red and gray squirrel, turkey, and grouse, and Middle Prong has native brook trout.

Rich, lush coves are full of wildflowers, and large sweet blueberries are prominent on the grassy meadows of Fork Ridge and its E escarpment. Old roads and old trails provide numerous manway options, but none of them is blazed, marked, or signed. Two of the longer and better-known trails are described below. Access to them is easy, but once in the wilderness it is advisable to have a topo map and compass or hike with experienced companions familiar with the similar ridges and coves. A developed base camp can be Sunburst Rec Area. It has campsites with water, toilets and a picnic area.

Access: Sunburst Rec Area is on NC-215, 8.6 mi W from the BRP, and 9.6 mi S from US-276 near Woodrow. Access on the BRP is described below.

Support Facilities: The nearest groceries and services are in Woodrow, with full provisions and services 5.0 mi W from Woodrow to Waynesville.

302-303   *Haywood Gap Trail* (5.8 mi; USFS #142) (F); *Buckeye Gap Trail* (4.0 mi; USFS #126) (F)

Length and Difficulty: 13.8 mi combined round-trip, strenuous (elev change 2,468 ft.)

Trailhead and Description: From the S end of Sunburst Campground, hike 1.6 mi upstream W of Middle Prong on FR-97 and ascend two switchbacks. On the third major curve leave FR-97, L, and follow a primitive route across Little Beartrap Branch. Enter the wilderness boundary to campsites near the mouth of Big Beartrap Branch, R, at 2.7 mi. Rock-hop the Middle Prong at an area once called the "cattle crossing." Cross Camp Two Branch and at 3.4 mi, come to jct with the Buckeye Gap Trail. At this point either trail can be ascended to a jct with the MST, which can be used for a connector to return here after 8.0 mi. If taking Haywood Gap Trail, cross the Grassy Ridge Branch and follow the main stream for 2.2 mi to Sweetwater Spring (W side of trail). From here it is 0.2 mi to Haywood Gap (5,225 ft.) and BRP mp 426.5. Turn L on the MST, which has routed wood signs, and go 1.8 mi on a graded footpath to jct with the Buckeye Gap Trail on an old RR grade. (The Buckeye Gap Trail access here is out 0.2 mi across a small stream to Rough Butt Bald Overlook [mp 425.4], elev 5,300 ft. If vehicle is left on the BRP overnight, contact the BRP ranger [704-456-9530, weekdays 9:00–4:30.]) Turn L on the Buckeye Gap Trail and follow jointly with the MST for 1.0 mi where Buckeye Creek is crossed in a rhododendron grove. The forest also has birch, beech, cherry, maple, and scattered fir and spruce. After 75 yd. ahead, the MST turns sharply R up the slope, but the Buckeye Gap Trail continues on the old RR grade with numerous seeps. Descend gradually and after 1.5 mi from the MST, turn abruptly L off the old RR grade. (For exploratory hikers who wish to follow part of the old and obscure 7.0-mi Green Mountain Trail [USFS #113], bushwhack R [E] approx. 0.4 mi up to scenic Fork Ridge anywhere along the 1.5-mi stretch after leaving the MST.) Descend steeply to cross Grassy Ridge Branch and rejoin the Haywood Gap Trail at 4.0 mi. Turn R downstream and return to the Sunburst Rec Area. (USGS-FS Map: Sam Knob)

Shining Rock Wilderness (Haywood County)

To emphasize connecting trail options from the East Fork (parallels US-276) and West Fork (parallels NC-215) of the Pigeon River and from the BRP (S) into the Shining Rock Wilderness (N), the following 18 trails are grouped under the title of Shining Rock Wilderness. Because the longest section of the Art Loeb Trail is in the Davidson River area, it and three other connecting trails have been described earlier in this chapter. Also, the MST is described in chapter 16. All the trails connect directly with or have trail access to the Art Loeb Trail, the area trail most impacted by visitors. Among the least used trails are Little East Fork, Fork Mountain, Fire Scald Ridge, Old Butt Knob, and Cold Mountain. All trails are for hikers only. The highest concentration of visitors is at the Black Balsam parking area at the end of FR-816 (1.2 mi from BRP mp 420.2). Four official trails (and one created by hikers) fan out from the parking area. Camping permits are not required in the Shining Rock Wilderness, and in 1982 the FS established a "volunteer ranger program" to educate and monitor the public on "wilderness ethics." Group size is limited to 10, and fires are prohibited. Nevertheless, high-impact camping remains a problem. (See "Wilderness Experience" in the introduction to part I.) Five trails are found exclusively in the Shining Rock Wilderness: Big East Fork, Cold Mountain, Greasy Cove, Old Butt Knob, Shining Creek, and almost all of Little East Fork.

Little East Fork Trail (USFS #107) (F, H)   304
Length and Difficulty: 5.0 mi, strenuous (elev change 2,312 ft.)
Trailhead and Description: From the jct of NC-215 and the BRP, go N 13.0 mi on NC-215 to Little East Fork Rd (SR-1129) and turn R (5.3 mi S from US-276 and turn L). Proceed 3.8 mi to the parking area past the Daniel Boone Boy Scouts Camp, R. Hike up the road a few yards cross the Little East Fork of the Pigeon River bridge, and turn L through Boy Scout camps named for a variety of Indian tribes. Follow an old RR grade, rough in sections, for the entire distance. (There may be overgrowth.) The river has numerous

cascades and pools. The forest is mainly hardwood with groves of hemlock and rhododendron in the lower elevations and spruce with birch near the top. Enter the NF at 0.3 mi, and cross Cathey Cove Creek. At 1.0 mi, enter the Shining Rock Wilderness. Cross Hemlock Branch at 1.3 mi and at 2.8 mi, cross the Little East Fork. The gradient increases, but follow switchbacks for the remainder of the route to a jct at 5.0 mi with Ivestor Gap Trail. To the L, it is 0.4 mi to Shining Rock Gap and connection with the Art Loeb Trail, and to the R, it is 3.9 mi to the Black Balsam parking area. (Using the Art Loeb Trail, N, a loop of 12.1 mi can be made for a return to Camp Daniel Boone.) (USGS-FS Maps: Sam Knob, Shining Rock, Waynesville)

305   *Fork Mountain Trail* (6.2 mi; USFS #109) (F)
   Length and Difficulty: 6.2 mi combined, strenuous (elev change 2,620 ft.)
   Trailheads and Description: From the BRP/NC-215 jct in Beech Gap, descend N on NC-215 8.4 mi to parking space, R, beside the river (0.2 mi before the Sunburst Rec Area). Because the footbridge has been washed away, rock-hop or wade (river may be impassable with high water) the West Fork of the Pigeon River. After crossing, immediately turn R, go upstream for 0.4 mi, cross and turn L at the mouth of Turnpike Creek, and turn sharply R to leave the stream at 0.8 mi. Ascend on switchbacks to a narrow gap on the Fork Mtn. ridgeline at 2.0 mi (The old timber road L is 0.4 mi to High Top [5,263 ft.].) Turn R and follow an old road (except in a few relocations), undulate on knobs but leave the ridge to skirt E of Birdstand Mtn. at 3.2 mi. The forest is chiefly hardwoods with laurel, rhododendron, blueberry, and fern. At 4.7 mi is a shallow gap.

   Continue ahead on the Fork Mountain Trail and skirt E of the ridge for the final mile to reach Ivestor Gap Trail at 6.2 mi. (It is 1.7 mi R to the Black Balsam parking area, and 0.5 mi L to Ivestor Gap and connections with the Art Loeb Trail.) (USGS-FS Maps: Sam Knob, Shining Rock, Waynesville)

306-   *Big East Fork Trail* (3.6 mi; USFS #357) (F); *Greasy Cove Trail* (3.2
308   mi; USFS #362) (F); *Bridges Camp Trail* (1.0 mi; USFS #607) (F)
   Length and Difficulty: 7.8 mi combined, moderate to strenuous (elev change 2,256 ft.)
   Special Features: scenic river, fishing
   Trailhead and Description: At the BRP/US-276 jct in Wagon Rd Gap, descend W on US-276 2.9 mi to the Big East Fork of Pigeon River parking area, L. Hike up US-276 (across the Big East Fork bridge) 0.1 mi and turn R at the Big East Fork Trail access. Follow an old road that becomes an old RR grade.

At 0.4 mi is a jct R with a 0.2-mi spur connector to Shining Creek Trail (on the other side of the river). Ahead the trail forks L at 0.5 mi. (The R fork is a dead-end side trail to a waterfall and pool.) At 1.1 mi, pass a rocky area with rapids, white azalea, and cinnamon ferns. At 1.3 mi, leave the river and ascend on the slope, rock-hop Bennett Branch, and return to the riverside at 1.8 mi. For the next 1.8 mi, follow the scenic riverside where the loud rattle of kingfishers can be heard over the roar of the rapids. Excellent camping and fishing locations are along the way, and scenic flumes and clear pools are frequent. The forest is mostly birch, hemlock, rhododendron, maple, yellow poplar, buckeye, and wildflowers. At 3.6 mi, reach the end of the Big East Fork Trail at Bridges Camp, a frequently used campsite at the confluence of Greasy Cove Prong. Here is a connection with Bridges Camp Trail that goes upstream along the E side of the river. After 0.6 mi it curves L away from the river to ascend in a cove. At 1.0 mi, it reaches the MST at Bridges Camp Gap of the BRP, mp 416.8. (On the MST it is 9.9 mi W to NC-215 and 0.3 mi E to Looking Glass Overlook on the BRP, mp 417.0.) To hike the Greasy Cove Trail, rock-hop or wade the East Fork of the Pigeon River to begin the Greasy Cove Trail. (A USGS-FS topo map [Shining Rock] may be necessary for hikers to locate and follow this trail.) (There are no signs or blazes for the Greasy Cove Trail.)

Across the river, follow Greasy Cove Trail steeply upstream on the N side of Greasy Cove Prong, a splashing stream with moss-covered rocks. At 0.9 mi, leave the stream and veer R up a steep hollow of birch, hemlock, and yellow poplar to a level area on Greasy Cove Ridge at 1.7 mi. Continue the ascent and end the trail at the jct with the Graveyard Ridge Trail at 3.0 mi. (The Graveyard Ridge Trail goes L 3.2 mi to its S end and jct with the Graveyard Fields Trail at the BRP. Ahead, the trail gently ascends 0.2 mi to its N end at a jct with the Art Loeb Trail and Ivestor Gap Trail in Ivestor Gap. It is 1.7 mi N on the Art Loeb Trail for a return loop on either the Shining Creek Trail or the Old Butt Knob Trail described below.) (USGS-FS Map: Shining Rock)

Shining Creek Trail (4.1 mi; USFS #363) (F); ***Old Butt Knob Trail*** (3.6 mi; USFS #332) (F)   309-310

  Length and Difficulty: 7.7 mi combined, strenuous (elev change 2,556 ft.)
  Connecting Trails: (Art Loeb Trail); (Ivestor Gap Trail)
  Special Features: vistas from outcroppings
  Trailhead and Description: At the BRP/US-276 jct in Wagon Rd Gap, descend W on US-276 2.9 mi to the Big East Fork parking area, L. At the end

of the parking area follow the unblazed Shining Creek Trail through a clearing, and at 0.3 mi turn R at a fork. (The L fork is a spur trail that goes to the East Fork of the Pigeon River, where wading or rock-hopping is necessary to reach jct with the Big East Fork Trail. The best approach to this trail is to follow the directions described above under Big East Fork Trail.) Ascend on switchbacks to a small saddle, Shining Creek Gap, at 0.7 mi, and reach jct R with unblazed Old Butt Knob Trail in a rhododendron thicket.

(The Old Butt Knob Trail ascends on the extremely steep Chestnut Ridge in sections of dense rhododendron, laurel, oak, and chestnut saplings to a knob at 1.5 mi. Follow an easier grade for the next 0.5 mi to Old Butt Knob and pass outcroppings along the way for scenic views of Shining Rock Wilderness. Descend to Spanish Oak Gap in a forest of oak, birch, and maple. Ascend to Dog Loser Knob and more off-trail vista points at 2.8 mi. Descend gradually to Beech Spring Gap and a spring, L, at 3.0 mi. Ascend on switch-backs to Shining Rock [5,940 ft.], the highest point of the trail, and curve L [S] to Shining Rock Gap at 3.6 mi. Here is a jct with the Art Loeb Trail, Ivestor Gap Trail, and Shining Creek Trail.) There are not likely to be any signs here. Hikers may need a USGS-FS topo map (Shining Rock).

To continue on the Shining Creek Trail, descend from Shining Creek Gap to the bank of Shining Creek in a forest of hemlock and mixed hardwoods at 1.0 mi. Follow large boulders upstream on the steep R and flumes, cascades, and pools, L, in the creek. Among abundant wildflowers, cross Daniels Cove Creek at 2.0 mi, and at the confluence of the N and S prongs of Shining Creek, stay R. Follow the streamside in a forest of tall hickory, oak, and birch, and at 3.1 mi, cross at a stream fork to begin a steep climb on a ridge slope. On switchbacks, enter sections of rhododendron, beech, spruce, and moss beds to reach Shining Rock Gap at 4.1 mi. Reach a jct here with Art Loeb Trail, Ivestor Gap Trail, and Old Butt Knob Trail. A return loop on the Old Butt Knob Trail totals 8.4 mi to the parking area. (USGS-FS Map: Shining Rock)

Black Balsam Knob Area (Haywood County)

At a SE corner between the Middle Prong Wilderness (W side of NC-215) and Shining Rock Wilderness (E side of NC-215) and the BRP on the S side is a triangular section of the district that is distinctly different. It is a plateau with fields of wildflowers, knobs, and balds with Black Balsam Knob (6,214 ft.) the highest in the district. From grassy slopes and rocky coves is drainage into the headwaters of both forks of Pigeon River. Both the Art Loeb Trail and the

Mountains-to-Sea Trail intersect here. In this place of scenic beauty among windswept rocks, grasses, and spruce is also a fragile environment. There are endangered species of wildlife and plants and it deserves protective usage. Those who use the Black Balsam parking lot for access into the Shining Rock Wilderness will need not only to know how to use and be safe in the backcountry, but to have a district map for planning any long-range journeys on unmaintained trails described above.

Sam Knob Trail (USFS #617)   311

Length and Difficulty: 2.7 mi round-trip, easy to moderate

Trailhead and Description: From BRP mp 420.2, take FR-816 for 1.3 mi to parking area. Here is the S trailhead of Ivestor Gap Trail, the NE trailhead of Flat Laurel Creek Trail, the W trailhead of Art Loeb/Black Balsam Trail, and the E trailhead of Sam Knob Trail. Near a sign board and restroom, follow the blue-blazed trail on a gated old road 0.2 mi in a partial forest that opens to a sweeping grassy meadow ahead. Pass through the field of flowers and grasses to a sign at a forest edge at 0.5 mi. (To the L, the Sam Knob Trail descends 0.4 mi to end at the Flat Laurel Creek Trail [itself formerly a part of the Sam Knob Trail].) To the R, the Sam Knob Trail also goes 150 ft. to quickly enter a grove of rhododendron for the ascent to the knob. The scramble up the E side hosts switchbacks and steps. Near the top, after 0.6 mi, curve around the S moss and heath-clad edge where surreal views demand your attention. Reach a fork after 0.1 mi; the L climb of 0.1 mi is closest to the summit. Clinging tightly to the gray and white rocks are mountain ash, aster, blueberry, mountain laurel, and tough grasses. Visit the other outcropping from the fork. To the W and below is the deep valley of West Fork of Pigeon River and beyond is the long Fork Ridge in Middle Prong Wilderness. In the center of it is Green Knob. To the SW is Little Sam Knob, and to the east is the mammoth Black Balsam Knob. (For a number of years Sam Knob was closed to the public because of the knob being home to falcons.) Backtrack.

A loop could be made by taking the Sam Knob Trail to Flat Laurel Creek Trail, turn L and follow it through additional scenic and rolling grasslands to the parking area at 3.5 mi. A longer loop could follow the same route except after 0.4 mi on the Flat Laurel Creek Trail, turn R (S) on the Little Sam Knob Trail. Follow it 1.3 mi to a jct with and L on the MST that unites with and follows E the Art Loeb Trail 0.4 mi to grassy Black Balsam Knob, then down the west side on a 0.6 mi spur to the parking area at 7.5 mi, give or take a few tenths for the appealing sideshows. (USGS-FS Maps: Sam Knob, Shining Rock)

312-   *Flat Laurel Creek Trail* (3.7 mi; USFS #346) (F, B, H); *Little Sam*
313   *Knob Trail* (1.3 mi; USFS #347) (F)

        Length and Difficulty: 5.2 mi combined, easy

        Connecting Trails: (MST); (Ivestor Trail); Art Loeb Spur/Black Balsam Trail (0.6 mi, easy; USFS #108) (F)

        Special Features: Scenic views of Sam Knob and Fork Ridge

        Trailhead and Description: At the BRP/NC-215 jct in Beech Gap, descend N on NC-215 0.8 mi to parking area, R, to begin the orange-blazed Flat Laurel Creek Trail (formerly called Sam Knob Trail), which can be used for cross-country skiing. Rock-hop Bubbling Spring Branch and follow an old RR grade with borders of bush honeysuckle, rhododendron, cherry, maple, blackberry, blueberry, and gentian. Cross a cement bridge at 0.7 mi where a 125-ft. cascade is R. At 1.6 mi are scenic views of Mt. Hardy, Fork Ridge, and the gorge of the West Fork of the Pigeon Valley. Spectacular views of Sam Knob (6,130 ft.) begin at 1.8 mi, and at 2.0 mi, L, near a landslide are scenic views of Flat Laurel Creek cascades and pools. Campsites are 0.3 mi farther in a flat area near Flat Laurel Creek, as are three routes to the Black Balsam parking area. Two routes are across the creek and the other route follows the old RR grade. (The routes across the creek are described first.) To continue on the Flat Laurel Creek Trail, rock-hop the creek in a rhododendron grove and reach a trail fork in a flat area. Turn L and cross a streamlet, follow any of a number of camp trails up to a large wildlife field with scenic views, L, of Sam Knob. Bear R, and ascend easily in the field to an old logging road at 2.7 mi. Follow the road to a gate and pass the rest rooms to the Black Balsam parking lot.

        The second route is from the fork, mentioned above. Veer R on an open field path that ascends casually 0.8 mi to the SW corner of the Black Balsam parking lot. (Some hikers call the path the Goldenrod Trail for the magnificent exhibition of Solidago species that bloom in late September. It is a time when the fall colors come early to these gentle hillsides, mile-high meadows, and heath balds, all covered with the xanthous and ochre of goldenrod, purples of asters, and crimson of the blueberry bushes.)

        The third route is the original Flat Laurel Creek Trail, which begins on the old RR grade where the Sam Knob Trail turned L. Follow the wide trail 180 yd. to rock-hop a tributary and reach jct, R, with the Little Sam Knob Trail at 0.4 mi. At 0.8 mi, rock-hop Flat Laurel Creek in an area of scattered spruce, mountain ash, and blackberries. Cross culverts for other small streams in an easy scenic approach to Black Balsam parking area at 1.4 mi (The Ivestor Gap Trail begins here, N, on an old RR grade, and the Art Loeb/Black Balsam Trail ascends E to a jct with the Art Loeb Trail. On FR-816, S, it is 1.3 mi to BRP mp 420.2.)

The yellow-blazed Little Sam Knob Trail, mentioned above, follows an old RR grade through a forest of spruce, birch, and rhododendron and open spots with thornless blackberry *(Rubus canadensis)* SE of Little Sam Knob (5,862 ft.). Rock-hop a tributary at 0.4 mi, ascend to a jct with an unnamed trail, L, turn sharply R, and follow an old RR grade on the W slope of Chestnut Bald Ridge. At 0.8 mi is a scenic view of Mt. Hardy; enter a ravine from a former RR trestle; and reach jct with the MST at 1.3 mi. (It is 1.0 mi L to jct with the Art Loeb Trail and 2.2 mi R to NC-215. The latter could form a 7.0-mi loop to the beginning of the Sam Knob Trail on NC-215.) (USGS-FS Map: Sam Knob)

Graveyard Fields Trail (3.2 mi; USFS #358) (F); *Graveyard Ridge Trail* (3.4 mi; USFS #356) (F, B, H)   **314-315**

Length and Difficulty: 6.6 mi combined, easy to moderate

Special Features: Yellowstone Prong waterfalls

Trailhead and Description: (The Graveyard Fields Trail is also called Yellowstone Falls Trail.) On the BRP at the Graveyard Fields Overlook mp 418.8 (5,120 ft.), begin on a paved trail through dense rhododendron. Descend to a rocky area and bridge over the Yellowstone Prong of the East Fork of the Pigeon River at 0.2 mi. Cross and turn R for a trail to the Second Falls at 0.3 mi. Backtrack to the bridge, but stay on the N side of the stream for a jct with Graveyard Ridge Trail. (There may be a relocation of the Graveyard Ridge Trail farther upstream because of erosion.)

(The Graveyard Ridge Trail follows an old logging road that ascends gently 0.4 mi to Graveyard Ridge, but quickly curves to follow the S slope. [This route may be relocated.] At 1.5 mi, hiking N, cross Dark Prong Gap and intersect the MST [E of Black Balsam Knob]. Cross the headwaters of Dark Prong, curve E at the base of Tennent Mtn. in a forest of birch, rhododendron, and spruce, and come to a jct with Greasy Cove Trail, R, at 3.2 mi. Turn sharply L and reach Ivestor Gap at 3.4 mi to jct with the Art Loeb Trail.)

Continuing on the Graveyard Fields Trail, after another 0.6 mi, come to a jct L with a return loop but continue ahead for 0.5 mi to the scenic Upper Falls. Return for a complete loop at 3.2 mi. (Yellowstone is named from the yellow mosses, lichens, and minerals on the rocks. The area received its name from moss-covered fallen spruce trunks and stumps that resembled a grave-yard. The trunks were destroyed by a fire in November 1925 that burned 25,000 acres of prime timber.) (USGS-FS Map: Shining Rock)

Courthouse Creek Area (Transylvania County)

316   *Courthouse Creek Trail* (USFS #128) (F)

Length and Difficulty: 1.8 mi, strenuous (elev change 1,880 ft.)

Trailhead and Description: There are three access points to FR-140: (1) From the jct of the BRP in Beech Gap (mp 423.2) and NC-215 descend SE 6.6 mi on NC-215 to Courthouse Creek Rd (FR-140); turn L. (2) From US-64 and NC-215 jct in Rosman, drive N 10.2 mi on NC-215; turn R. (3) From US-276 (3.5 mi NW of the ranger station) turn L on Davidson Creek Rd (FR-475), which becomes McColl Rd (SR-1327), for 8.0 mi to NC-215. Turn R on NC-215 and drive 2.6 mi to FR-140; turn R. Follow gravel FR-140 for 0.9 mi, veer L, and continue 3.0 mi to a parking area at the road's end. The creek is part of the headwaters of the French Broad River. The trail may be blazed blue, but unmaintained. Ascend steeply upstream, L, by cascades and flumes. Cross the scenic stream at least twice, depending on stream erosion. There are remnants of an old RR grade at 0.5 mi. At 0.6 mi, bear R at creek's fork, and at 0.8 mi ascend steeply L of a large cascade. Through a rocky and rough gorge, climb steeply to the jct of an unmarked trail at 1.7 mi (used by mountain climbers to the Devil's Courthouse wall), turn L, and ascend to the Devil's Courthouse parking overlook at BRP mp 422.4. Vegetation on the trail includes dense fetterbush and rhododendron, black cohosh, birch, buckeye, white snakeroot, oak, and red spruce. (USGS-FS Map: Sam Knob)

317-   *Summey Cove Trail* (USFS #129) (F, B); *Courthouse Falls Trail*
318   (USFS #130) (F)

Length and Difficulty: 2.3 mi combined, moderate

Special Features: Courthouse Falls, wildflowers

Trailhead and Description: Follow the same directions described for access to Courthouse Creek Trail, except follow FR-140 for 3.1 mi (0.8 mi before road's end) and park on the R. The trail is unsigned and unblazed. The first trail, which is the orange-blazed Courthouse Falls Trail, begins at the bridge and follows an old road downstream. At 0.2 mi, L, is a narrow path (with sections of steps) that descends 0.1 mi to a pool at the scenic Courthouse Falls. Continue on the old road to campsites at Mill Station

Creek at 0.5 mi; turn L, cross the creek. Ascend in a forest of poplar, basswood, hemlock, and buffalo nut. Curve R at the ridgeline at 1.0 mi and descend gently to good campsites in Summey Cove at 1.3 mi. Cross the stream and ascend Big Fork Ridge; descend in a hardwood cove with numerous wildflowers, including orange fringe orchids that bloom in mid-August. Arrive at NC-215, the S trailhead, at 2.1 mi. (It is 5.4 mi R to Beech Gap at the BRP and 1.2 mi L to FR-140.)

Upper Davidson River Area (Transylvania County)

Across Pilot Mtn. and Sassafras Knob, E from Courthouse Creek, are Laurel, Shuck, Daniel Ridge, Cove, and Caney Bottom tributaries, which form Davidson River. Along the spine of Pilot Mtn. and other peaks, weaves the N-S flow of the Art Loeb Trail in ascents and descents. Three trails in this area rise to make connections with it. On its high warm rocks are ladybugs and gnarled windblown chestnut oaks hovering over tight patches of buckberry. To the N of the large cove is the mile-high BRP on the Eastern Continental Divide. In addition to wild trout, the streams below this ridge are stocked with brook, brown, and rainbow trout for catch and release. Within 3.0 mi of the river's forming, the crystalline clear rushing river flows between Looking Glass Rock on the N side and John Rock on the S side. Both are granite massifs whose trails to the top bear their names. Here in this sunny, but easily flooded, valley are waterfalls, fish hatchery, timber history, group campgrounds, and seven trails looping skyward. Access to the area is on FR-475, which begins W off US-276, 3.5 mi W of the ranger station.

There are three rock-climbing access trails to Looking Glass Rock. After turning off US-276 on FR-475, drive 1.6 mi to a gravel road, FR-475B, R (opposite side of the road from the Fish Hatchery entrance). Ascend the serpentine mountain road 1.1 mi to a narrow parking space, R, for Slick Rock **319** Falls Trail (USFS #117) (F). It ascends upstream 0.7 mi to the W wall. Continue up the mountain on FR-475B for another 1.8 mi to Sunwall Trail (USFS **320** #601) (F), R at a sign. Enter rhododendron on steps and ascend 0.4 mi to NW wall. For the third access slightly descend on FR-475B 0.2 mi to parking space for two vehicles, R. Descend and follow a well-graded 0.8 mi North **321** Face Trail (USFS #132) (F) to a rocky base. (Part of the wall may be closed for falcon protection.) It is 3.3 mi ahead on FR-475B to US-276. 0.9 mi S of Forestry Discovery Center.

322- ***Daniel Ridge Loop Trail*** (4.0 mi; USFS #105) (F, B); ***Farlow Gap***
323 ***Trail*** (3.2 mi; USFS #106) (F)

    Length and Difficulty: 10.2 mi combined round-trip, moderate to strenuous (elev change 1,924 ft.)

    Special Features: cascades for sliding, Shuck Ridge Creek waterfalls, geology

    Trailhead and Description: From the ranger station, go 3.5 mi W on US-276, turn L on Davidson River Rd (FR-475), and go 4.1 mi to FR-137, R, and park. Cross the cement bridge at the pool and sunbathing rocks. At 0.1 mi, turn L off the main road. Follow upstream to the site of a former fish hatchery and fork in the trail. The L route is near the river with campsites, pools, and sliding rocks. The R route follows an old RR grade and rejoins the other trail at 1.2 mi at a pool and campsite. Turn R to another RR grade; reach jct with the blue-blazed Farlow Gap Trail at 1.8 mi.

    (The Farlow Gap Trail goes upstream 250 ft. to cross the Right Fork of the Davidson River. Ascend gradually on an old road and cross Fork River Ridge Creek at 1.4 mi. Curve around Daniel Ridge and ascend to the top of scenic Shuck Ridge Creek waterfall at 2.2 mi. Ascend steeply to pass an old mica mine at 2.7 mi and reach Farlow Gap and a jct with the Art Loeb Trail at 3.2 mi. [To the L, the Art Loeb Trail ascends Sassafras Mtn., dips to a saddle, and ascends mile-high Pilot Mtn. for exceptionally scenic views.] Vegetation at the gap is mainly maple, oak, and birch. Backtrack to Daniel Ridge Loop Trail.)

    Continuing on the Daniel Ridge Loop Trail, follow the red blazes through a young forest and on an old road to wildlife grazing fields. After 0.5 mi, the trail curves around a knob before descending on switchbacks to FR-5046 at 3.1 mi. Cross the road and descend the NE side of the ridge to close proximity with a stream and a jct with FR-5046 at 3.6 mi. Turn R and follow the road to the point of origin at 4.0 mi. (USGS-FS Map: Shining Rock)

324- ***Caney Bottom Loop Trail*** (4.6 mi; USFS #361) (F, B on the W side);
325 ***Caney Bottom Extension Trail*** (0.7 mi; USFS #340) (F, B)

    Length and Difficulty: 6.0 mi combined round-trip, easy to moderate

    Trailhead and Description: At the jct of US-276 and Davidson River Rd (FR-475), follow FR-475 upstream (past the state fish hatchery) for 3.5 mi to a parking area, L. Cross the road to the gated entrance road of Cove Creek Group Camp. Cross a footbridge over Cove Creek at 0.1 mi. At 0.3 mi is a waterfall, R, and at 0.4 mi is a trail sign, L. Leave the road, ascend, and bypass the group camp area on a trail heavily used by bikers. In a hemlock grove at 0.8 mi are good campsites. Other vegetation along the trail includes oak, poplar, locust, maple, and laurel. Cross a footbridge over Cove Creek to jct with the loop portion of the trail. If going R, pass a rock formation at 1.2 mi, L, and a waterfall, R, at Caney Bottom Creek. Follow an old RR grade that parallels Caney Bottom Creek and pass a high cascading waterfall at 1.5 mi. At 2.1 mi, reach a jct with the blue-blazed Caney Bottom Extension Trail, R. (The extension goes easily up the ridge for 0.7 mi to jct with FR-225, a dead-end road to Cove Creek, L, but R is an access road to FR-475B near Looking Glass Rock.) Continue on the Caney Bottom Loop Trail by turning L to cross a footbridge. At 2.4 mi the trail is on an old RR grade that it follows on a gradual descent for nearly 1.8 mi. Along the way, in a mixed hardwood forest, the trail passes high above a waterfall, L, at 3.8 mi. Return to the loop jct at 4.2 mi for an exit to the point of origin. (USGS-FS Map: Shining Rock)

Long Branch Trail (2.5 mi; USFS #116) (F, B); *Cemetery Loop Trail* (1.2 mi; USFS #341) (F, B)

326-327

Length and Difficulty: 3.7 mi combined, easy to moderate

Trailhead and Description: At the jct of US-276 and FR-475 (3.5 mi W from the ranger station), drive 5.4 mi on FR-475 to a small parking area for Long Branch Trail, L. (It is 0.1 mi beyond the trailhead for Cemetery Loop Trail.) Follow the orange-blazed trail in a slight descent to parallel Long Branch. At 0.4 mi, reach a jct with yellow-blazed Cemetery Trail, L, which leads to a former pioneer settlement and the McCall Cemetery. (It slopes around a low hill to follow at 0.8 mi an old wagon road to FR-475. A turn L up the road makes the 1.2-mi loop.)

Continuing on the Long Branch Trail, cross Long Branch and weave in and out of cove hardwoods and rhododendron to ascend a short ridge. Descend to cross FR-5095 at 1.8 mi. After another easy walk, descend steeply to cross Searcy Creek. Ascend and come to a jct with Butter Gap Trail at 2.5 mi (described ahead). Backtrack, or with a second vehicle go L another 1.5 mi on Butter Gap Trail and Cat Gap Loop Trail to exit at the fish hatchery for a total of 4.0 mi. (The use of Butter Gap Trail, R, for 2.0 mi to Butter Gap at the Art Loeb Trail, R, and 3.4 mi on the Art Loeb Trail to Gloucester Gap returns you to FR-475. A turn R with a descent of 0.7 mi on FR-475 to the entrance of Long Branch is a loop of 8.6 mi.) (USGS-FS Map: Shining Rock)

328   *Cat Gap Loop Trail* (USFS #120) (F, B partial)
          Length and Difficulty: 4.7 mi, strenuous
329-   **Connecting Trails:** Butter Gap Trail (2.7 mi; USFS #123, moderate) (F,
331   B); Cat Gap Bypass Trail (0.6 mi; USFS #120A, moderate) (F); (Art Loeb
          Trail); John Rock Trail (1.8 mi; USFS #365, moderate) (F)
          Special Features: wildlife, wildflowers, scenic John Rock
          Trailhead and Description: (Usage of the Cat Gap Loop Trail provides
          access to four loop options.) At jct of US-276 and FR-475, go 1.5 mi on FR-
          475 to the state fish hatchery, L, and to the parking area. (Visitors are welcome
          at the hatchery where 60,000 trout are raised annually.) To access Cat Gap
          Loop Trail from the parking area, pass between the bulletin board and educa-
          tion center building to cross a gated vehicle bridge over Cedar Rock Creek.
          Bear R on this frequently used orange-blazed trail in a forest of cove hard-
          woods, hemlock, and running cedar. Cross a footbridge at 0.3 mi. Ascend,
          pass R of cascades and pools. Reach a jct with the blue-blazed Butter Gap
          Trail, R, at 0.8 mi in Picklesimer Fields.

          (The Butter Gap Trail is an optional loop. It follows an old RR grade,
          crosses Grogan Creek at 0.4 mi, and follows upstream on the W side through
          a forest of mixed hardwoods, hemlock, and rhododendron. At 0.7 mi, it
          reaches a jct with orange-blazed Long Branch Trail (which goes W for 2.5 mi
          to FR-475). The Butter Gap Trail passes cascades, and at 1.1 mi a waterfall.
          At 2.1 mi, the trail becomes steep at the headwaters of the creek, and at 2.7
          mi, it reaches the trail terminus and reaches jct with the Art Loeb Trail in But-
          ter Gap. Here are multiple trails and roads. [The spur trail, L, ascends 0.5 mi
          to Cedar Rock Mtn. with outstanding views. Ahead the Art Loeb Trail
          descends 0.2 mi to an A-frame shelter, and 2.3 mi farther on the Art Loeb Trail
          is a jct with Cat Gap Loop Trail in Cat Gap to make a loop back to the fish
          hatchery for 8.5 mi.])

          Continue upstream on the Cat Gap Loop Trail among blueberries, yellow
          root, spicebush, white pine, and oak. At 1.9 mi, reach a jct L with orange-
          blazed Cat Gap Bypass Trail to Horse Cove Gap. (This beautiful 0.6-mi trail
          follows a wide old RR grade through tall hardwoods, scattered hemlock, and
          fern beds. Songbirds are prominent. If using this route the loop back to the
          parking area is 4.3 mi) Continue an ascent on the Cat Gap Loop Trail among
          dense laurel to Cat Gap (3,350 ft.) at 2.5 mi and reach jct with the Art Loeb
          Trail. Here are two white oaks with unique knobs on their trunks. Turn L on
          the Cat Gap Trail, first to descend on a slope, then down the ridge to a jct in

Horse Cove Gap with Cat Gap Bypass Trail, L, the yellow-blazed John Rock Trail ahead, and the continuance of Cat Gap Loop Trail, R.

(The scenic John Rock Trail ascends steeply to a knoll among hardwoods, laurel, indigo bush, and buckberry, descends to a saddle, and up to John Rock at 0.7 mi [The monolith is part of 435 acres protected as a special interest area.] Descend and to the L is exposure to the granite dome where views are of the fish hatchery, Davidson Valley, Looking Glass Rock, and the range of BRP mountains. [Because of water oozing from the edges of mosses and laurel, the rock can be slippery.] Continue descending to a level wet area among rhododendron before descending on the E slope of John Rock. Rejoin Cat Gap Loop Trail after 1.8 mi.)

If continuing R on the Cat Gap Loop Trail from Horse Cove Gap, descend steeply on rocky treadway. Reach a jct with the John Rock Trail, L, at 3.4 mi. Descend, pass sections of wild geraniums, mayapple, blue and black cohosh, and maidenhair ferns. Rock-hop Horse Cove Creek and follow an old flat RR grade. Cross small streams and a major footbridge over Cedar Rock Creek for a return to a field at 4.6 mi and parking area at the fish hatchery at 4.7 mi. (USGS-FS Map: Shining Rock)

Looking Glass Rock Trail (USFS #114) (F)   332

Length and Difficulty: 6.2 mi round-trip, strenuous (elev change 1,369 ft.)

Special Features: scenic granite dome, rock climbing

Trailhead and Description: From the jct of US-276 and FR-475, go 0.4 mi on FR-475 to a parking area, R. Ascend steadily on the yellow-blazed trail that has numerous switchbacks for the first 1.8 mi. A frequently used trail, it is eroded in sections on the steep E slope. Pass through a mixed hardwood forest with scattered Carolina hemlock *(Tsuga caroliniana)* and an understory of mountain laurel. At 2.7 mi, arrive at the edge of the N face; ascend to the highest point and trail terminus (3,969 ft.) at 3.1 mi. Here is the NW face with magnificent views of the Pisgah National Forest and the BRP areas. (Caution: the dome is not protected with guardrails and is dangerous when wet, icy, or dry. Lives have been lost here.) Backtrack. (USGS-FS Map: Shining Rock)

Case Camp Ridge Trail (USFS #119) (F)   333

Length and Difficulty: 3.4 mi round-trip, strenuous (elev change 1,100 ft.)

Trailhead and Description: From the ranger station, go W on US-276 8.6 mi, turn L on Headwaters Rd (FR-475B), and proceed 0.8 mi to Case Ridge Gap for parking. Ascend R on the blue-blazed Case Camp Ridge Trail through a forest of oak, laurel, hemlock, locust, buckberry, and blueberry to a gap at 0.2 mi. (To the L a new trail is being constructed; it will ascend W to gated FR-5045 and S trailhead of 1.3-mi blue-blazed Seniard Ridge Trail [USFS #609] [F]. It ascends steeply on switchbacks to the BRP between mp 417 and 418. Access to FR-5045 is off FR-225, which is off FR-475B farther S from the Case Camp Ridge Trail trailhead.) At 0.5 mi, reach the ridgeline where there are excellent views of Looking Glass Rock when the leaves are off the trees. Ascend on switchbacks, pass ruins of an old house at 1.3 mi, and arrive at BRP mp 415.9. Backtrack. (USGS-FS Map: Shining Rock)

Lower Davidson River Area (Transylvania County)

Hardly more than 1.0 mi E from the US Fish Hatchery in Upper Davidson River Area is the mouth of Looking Glass Creek and an intersection with US-276. With the creek's sparkling wild trout waters it widens the Davidson River in its 5.0-mi passage to the forest boundary at the intersection of US-276/64 and NC-280 in the unincorporated town of Pisgah Forest. When entering the district from this intersection on US-276 you are on a Forest Heritage national scenic byway. After the first 0.4 mi is Sycamore Flats Picnic Area, L, followed by a parking area on the riverbank, L, for the Sycamore Cove Trail, R. At 1.2 mi is the entrance, L, to Davidson River Recreation Area, the district's largest and most popular campground. It has 161 sites (mainly shaded by the forest) for tents, RVs, and motor homes. There are grills, tables, group water sources, flush toilets, and hot showers (no hookups). Activities are mainly hiking and fishing, and tubing in the summer. A fee campground, it is usually open year-round on a first-come basis. (Reservations can be made by a seven-day advance call to 800-280-2267.) E of the campground is the Schenck Civilian Conservation Center.

Farther W 0.4 mi on US-276 is the entrance, R, to the Pisgah Ranger Station and Visitor Center (adjoined R by a maintenance work center). Farther upriver are the English Chapel, L (across the river bridge), and on US-276 the Coontree Picnic Area, L. After 3.5 mi from the visitor center on US-276 begin an ascent to Looking Glass Falls, R, and beyond to Sliding Rock Recreation Area, L. In this grand entrance to the district's busy headquarters hub are two long-distance trails and eight loop trails from diminutive to lengthy multiloops.

334   Two loop trails begin at the visitor center parking area. The Andy Cove Nature Trail (USFS #288) (F), a national recreation trail constructed by the YCC, is a 0.6-mi loop that has interpretive stations, some on an elevated walkway. At

0.2 mi is a swinging bridge over a deep ravine. After crossing Andy Cove Branch and more boardwalks among hemlock and rhododendron, it makes a jct with the 1.5-mi Exercise Trail (USFS #344) (F) in a grove of tall white pine. If going R, **335** cross US-276 and the bridge over Davidson River at 0.2 mi, turn L of the English Chapel, and exit at Davidson River campground bridge. Turn L, cross the bridge, turn L on a fishing road, and go 230 ft. before leaving the road. Cross US-276 again and return to the visitor center parking lot.

At the campground, a good base for day hikes, is the 3.7-mi North Slope **336** Loop Trail (USFS #359) (F, B partial) entrance. It begins at a parking lot 0.1 mi L, after the main campground entrance. Orange-blazed, the trail passes the amphitheater to an old timber road. It curves in and out of coves on the N side of North Slope Ridge. Cove hardwoods, ferns, and wildflowers are dominant. At 2.1 mi, cross a small stream and come to a jct with yellow-blazed North **337** Slope Connector Trail (USFS #149) (F). (It ascends steeply on switchbacks for 1.3 mi to connect with the Art Loeb Trail on the N side of Stony Knob. Backtrack, or use the Art Loeb Trail L for a return to its trailhead at the swinging bridge over Davidson River near the campground for a loop of 7.5 mi.) Continuing on the North Slope Loop Trail turn R, and at 2.5 mi, turn R to pass S of the English Chapel. Switchback on an old road to bypass a section of the campground before returning to point of origin. (USGS-FS Maps: Pisgah Forest, Shining Rock)

An isolated short linear trail is Moore Cove Trail (USFS #318) (F). **338** Access is 1.0 mi W of Looking Glass Falls on US-276. Park near a bridge, R (between the highway and the creek). The yellow-blazed trail may begin down steps across the bridge and up the stream bank. Follow an old RR grade; cross Moore Branch three times on footbridges among rhododendron. Reach 45-ft. Moore Branch cascades at 0.7 mi. Camping is prohibited at the waterfall. Backtrack. (USGS-FS Map: Shining Rock)

Coontree Loop Trail (USFS #144) (F, B) **339**

Length and Difficulty: 3.7 mi, strenuous (elev change 1,160 ft.)

Connecting Trails: (Bennett Gap Trail)

Trailhead and Description: From the ranger station go W on US-276 for 3.0 mi to park at the Coontree Picnic Area parking lot, L. Cross the road to the blue-blazed Coontree Loop Trail entrance. Follow upstream through ironwood, poplar, birch, and oak. At 0.2 mi is the loop fork. If taking the R prong, follow an old road by a stream through ferns, wildflowers, and rhododendron. Ascend to Coontree Gap (2,960 ft.) at 1.2 mi and come to a jct with the red-blazed Bennett Gap Trail, R and L. (The Bennett Gap Trail goes 0.9 mi R through a forest of hardwoods and hemlock on a N slope for a descent to Avery Creek Rd [FR-477] at a low bridge.) Turn L and follow both trails for 0.5 mi; turn L on Coontree Loop Trail and descend steeply on switchbacks to Coontree Creek. Follow it downstream, crossing it at least twice (depending on erosion) in a gradual descent. Rejoin the loop at 3.5 mi. (USGS-FS Map: Shining Rock)

340   *Sycamore Cove Trail* (USFS #143) (F, B)

   Length and Difficulty: 3.2 mi, moderate

   Connecting Trails: (Art Loeb Trail); (MST); Grassy Road Trail (1.1 mi; USFS #364, easy) (F, B)

   Trailhead and Description: Although a loop, there are two trailheads. Because of the popularity of this trail and the heavy traffic on the highway, the district prefers parking at the Art Loeb Trail parking lot. It is accessible off US-276 immediately L (before crossing the bridge) after entrance to Davidson River Campground (0.2 mi E of the ranger station). Walk downriver to the Art Loeb Trail trailhead and swinging bridge, R (and the MST, R and L). Turn L, cross a small stream and US-276 to enter the trail (whose other exit is 0.2 mi R on US-276). Pass under tall poplar, sycamore, and hemlock where spicebush and ferns provide a fresh forest smell. At 0.5 mi, cross a stream on a log bridge and reach a jct where the MST forks L at 0.6 mi. Ascend R on the

341   Sycamore Cove Trail among white pine to a jct with Grassy Road Trail, L, at 0.7 mi. (The orange-blazed 1.1-mi Grassy Road Trail is a former logging road. It has sunshine and wildflowers and is a connector to Thrift Cove Trail, MST, and Black Mountain Trail.)

   Curve R and ascend among white pine, later under rhododendron arbors. At 1.5 mi, reach the highest area of the trail, turn S, and follow an old road on the slope of the ridge. Laurel and rhododendron are prominent. Descend gradually to a stream and turn R at 2.8 mi. Under hemlock, beech, and poplar pass spicebush, fetterbush, mandrake, club moss, and ferns. Descend steeply; cross the stream six times before an exit at US-276. It is 0.3 mi L (E) to Sycamore Flats Picnic Area, and 150 ft. R (W) to roadside parking. Another 0.2 mi upriver is back to the other trailhead. (USGS-FS Map: Pisgah Forest)

342   *Black Mountain Trail* (USFS #127) (F, B)

   Length and Difficulty: 7.8 mi, strenuous (elev change 2,086 ft.)

   Connecting Trails: Thrift Cove Trail (3.8 mi; USFS #603) (F, B); MST (Alternate); Pressley Cove Trail (1.2 mi; USFS #112) (F); (Turkey Pen Gap

Trail); Buckhorn Gap Trail (N) (1.7 mi, S 2.9 mi; USFS #103) (F, B, H); (Club Gap Trail); (Avery Creek Trail); (Buckwheat Knob Trail)

Special Features: wildlife, wildflowers, views from Clawhammer Mtn.

Trailhead and Description: On US-276, 0.2 mi E of the ranger station, park outside the fence of the district work center in a paved parking lot or grassy area. Follow the trail sign upstream on an old timber road. At 0.2 mi is a jct R with the red-blazed Thrift Cove Trail, another timber road. (The Thrift **343** Cove Trail, used mainly by bikers, crosses Thrift Creek and ascends a ridge for 0.2 mi to an open area and jct with the MST, R. For the next 230 ft. the MST follows the road to a turn, L, down in the gorge. Ahead, up the ridge, continues Thrift Cove Trail, and to the R is easy orange-blazed 1.1-mi Grassy Road Trail [USFS #364] [H, B], appropriately named. [Its NE terminus is with Sycamore Cove Loop Trail.] The Thrift Cove Trail follows a ridge or its shoulder to the headwaters of Thrift Creek where the trail crosses at 2.4 mi. Here it turns S to a jct and follows the Black Mountain Trail to Thrift Cove Trail's origin.)

Continuing on the Black Mountain Trail there is a jct at 0.5 mi with the MST, R. (The MST goes R on a separate trail to join part of Sycamore Cove Loop Trail to a crossing of US-276. From there it jointly runs with the Art Loeb Trail to the BRP area, but from here it follows jointly on the Black Mountain Trail before leaving it on the N side of Rich Mtn. ridge. See appendix A.) Continue ascending steeply in Thrift Cove on the old road, cross the creek four times, and at 1.4 mi, pass an old road R, which is the Thrift Cove Trail. At 1.8 mi, the road becomes more of a path. Ascend steeply to Hickory Knob at 2.4 mi, and descend to Pressley Gap at 2.9 mi. Here is FR-5099, R and L. Access to Pressley Cove Trail is L, 0.2 mi down the road.

(The orange-blazed Pressley Cove Trail descends in an arbor of laurel. **344** Cross a small stream at 0.4 mi, descend steeply on a S slope with scenic views of the cove, L. Pass through hemlock and beech. Reach a grazing field at Avery Creek Rd [FR-477] at 1.2 mi. It is 126 yd., L, to the bridge over Avery Creek (and reach jct with E trailhead of Bennett Gap Trail described below), 1.4 mi to US-276, and 0.5 mi, L, on US-276 to the ranger station. Right on FR-477 it is 0.3 mi to a parking area at Clawhammer Rd [FR-5058], R. The road can be used as an access to Buckhorn Gap and Black Mountain Trail.)

From Pressley Gap on the Black Mountain Trail follow the ridge on sections of old logging roads, and at 3.9 mi, reach jct with Turkey Pen Gap Trail, R. Here is a small spring in a forest of large oak and hickory with beds of hay-scented and cinnamon ferns. (The Turkey Pen Gap Trail follows a ridgeline E for 5.5 mi to Turkey Pen Gap and FR-297 off NC-280.) To continue on the Black Mountain Trail, ascend to skirt W of Black Mtn. peak in arbors of rhododendron and laurel to rejoin the ridge at 4.2 mi. Descend steeply and follow a narrow ridge to reach a rock overhang at 4.4 mi. Ascend to Clawhammer Mtn. (4,140 ft.) at 4.6 mi. From the outcroppings are superb views of Pilot Mtn., Looking Glass Rock, and NW to Pisgah Ridge. Blueberries, rhododendron, and galax are prominent. Descend steeply to Buckhorn Gap **345** (3,520 ft.) at 5.7 mi to cross the orange-blazed Buckhorn Gap Trail in an old RR grade cut. The cut is now a gravel and improved forest road. To the R (N) it is 0.6 mi on the road before the Buckhorn Gap Trail leaves the road R. It descends on switchbacks to a jct at 1.7 mi with South Mills River Trail on Grassy Ridge. On the S side of the gap the gravel road descends 1.0 mi to a 0.1-mi spur off the R, but the trailhead for Buckhorn Gap Trail is farther down the mountain, S, and to the R. The Buckhorn Gap Trail ends at Avery Creek Trail (see Avery Creek Area below).

Continue on Black Mountain Trail up log steps from Buckhorn Gap. After 0.3 mi, R, is the Buckhorn Gap Shelter with bunk beds. A spring is nearby. Ascend on the ridge. Pass coves with cinnamon ferns and ascend on switchbacks to SW slope of Soapstone Ridge. At 6.6 mi, reach the crest of Rich Mtn. in an oak-hickory forest. At 6.8 mi, L, is a rock outcrop with views of the Avery Creek drainage. The MST leaves the trail at 7.0 mi, R, near a large oak, and descends on an old forest road to the Pink Beds (see appendix A). Continue on the Black Mountain Trail, which is an old woods road with woodland sunflowers, mountain mint, and wood betony. Descend to Club Gap at 7.8 mi, the end of Black Mountain Trail. Here is an intersection with Buckwheat Knob Trail ahead; Club Gap Trail, R; and Avery Creek Trail, L (see Avery Creek Area below). (Access to US-276 is on Club Gap Trail for 0.8 mi. Descend on an old woods road with switchbacks to FR-477, 0.3 mi R to US-276 near the entrance to the Cradle of Forestry.) (USGS-FS Maps: Pisgah Forest, Shining Rock)

Pisgah Ranger District
Eastern Area

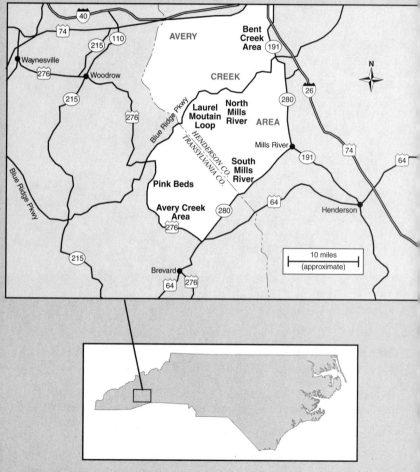

Introductions to Trail Areas

This narrow valley has tent camping. There are waterfalls, creek pools, native trout, tall trees, owls and cicada, floral fragrances, and other connecting trails for loops.

There is more than upland bogs dense with the pink rosebay rhododendron, pink phlox, and pink rose. The more is in the prominence of the Cradle of Forestry historic tours.

This circuitous river flows through a gorge-like valley with many tributaries. More than 40 mi of trails follow, connect, or cross its banks on swinging bridges or fording. There are deer, chipmunk, and raccoon. Some trails are equestrian delights.

Loop and linear trails on upstream and ridgelines lead to the Blue Ridge Parkway, Pisgah Inn and Campground. On the way is Pilot Rock monolith and (on some trails) dry wind-blown ledges, as well as others with cascades in rhododendron thickets.

In a wide cove, this beautiful river has 30 tributaries; a campground; roadside primitive camping; horse, bike, and hiking trails; and a road/trail access to the BRP.

Here is impressive Lake Powhatan Recreation Area with a large campground (all services except electricity). Nearby is the renowned Western NC Arboretum with a visitor center. There are roadside primitive campsites. Bicycle and equestrian trails are prominent with a variety of loops.

Mountains-to-Sea Trail
The MST will be more than 900 mi when completed. Currently almost half of the trail is finished in sporadic sections and the other half follows official bicycle backcountry roadways. In this district, it weaves in and out from the BRP for hiking only and follows some older trails such as the Shut-In Trail. The mainline MST is 46.2 mi and the alternate route through the Davidson River Valley is 13.2 mi longer. (See appendix A.)

B. EASTERN AREA OF PISGAH RANGER DISTRICT

Only 0.6 mi W upstream on US-276 from the ranger station is the mouth of Avery Creek at Davidson River. Here is the S entrance of FR-477, which parallels the creek NW before ascending on a crooked journey to a high ridge where it crosses Bennett Gap. It then descends to exit near the Cradle of Forestry in America (also called Forest Discovery Center). Up this narrow road in a narrow valley are North and South White Pine Group Horse Camps (tents only, no vehicles except horse trailers with sleepers are allowed). Avery Creek drops 1,186 ft. from its headwaters to the Davidson River, thus creating many cascades and waterfalls. Native trout are in the creek's pools. To the valley's NE is Black Mtn.; FR-5088 winds N from Avery Creek Rd to Buckhorn Gap and Buckhorn Shelter at Black Mountain Trail; and off Buckhorn Gap Trail is Twin Falls. Coves have dense gardens of ferns, wild geranium, white snakeroot, and tall tulip trees. Hikers will find many loop options by using multiple-use trails and/or forest roads.

Avery Creek Area

346- *Avery Creek Trail* (USFS #327) (F, B)
350   **Length and Difficulty:** 3.2 mi, strenuous (elev change 1,340 ft.)
        Connecting Trails: Club Gap Trail (0.8 mi; USFS #343, moderate) (F, B); (Black Mountain Trail); Buckwheat Knob Trail (1.5 mi, moderate; USFS #122) (F, B); Buckhorn Gap Trail (S) (2.4 mi, moderate; USFS #103) (F, B, H); Clawhammer Cove Trail (1.1 mi, moderate; USFS #342) (F)
        Special Features: waterfalls, wildlife, wildflowers
        Trailhead and Description: Access to the NW trailhead of Avery Creek Trail is on yellow-blazed Club Gap Trail, whose trailhead is 0.3 mi L on Avery Creek Rd (FR-477) after it leaves US-276 at the S edge of Cradle of Forestry. Club Gap Trail ascends 0.8 mi on an old road with switchbacks to Club Gap. On the L is the NW trailhead of Black Mountain Trail; ahead is Avery Creek Trail; and to the R is Buckwheat Knob Trail.

        The blue-blazed Avery Creek Trail descends steeply on a W slope of the rim among upland hardwoods. It passes under a power line at 0.4 mi and 0.9 mi; it follows switchbacks to an old RR grade near Avery Creek at 1.1 mi. In a forest mix of hemlock, yellow poplar, and rhododendron the trail passes excellent campsites. Wildflowers are profuse at openings under the power line. At 2.2 mi, reach jct with Buckhorn Gap Trail, L.

        (The orange-blazed Buckhorn Gap Trail [S] begins on the N side of Avery

Creek under a power line opening with a grassy meadow and sparse saplings. The trail enters a deep, damp, and dense forest on the E side of Henry Branch, but crosses it twice. Tall cove hardwoods give depth to the gorge. At 0.7 mi, reach jct with yellow-blazed Twin Falls Trail [USFS #604] [F], a 0.4-mi spur to a scenic waterfall. From this area the Buckhorn Gap Trail leaves its N direction and turns E to the option of two exits at Clawhammer Cove Rd [FR-5058]. The first forks L to meet the road at 1.4 mi [1.0 mi L and up the road to Buckhorn Gap]; the second forks R, turns S, and meets the road at 2.0 mi [1.6 mi L and up the road to Buckhorn Gap].)

The Avery Creek Trail continues down Avery Creek, hugging its banks, but after 0.3 mi it divides with Avery Creek Trail (multiple-use) following R a wide and easy forest road 0.7 mi to exit at a small parking area on FR-477, and Avery Creek Trail (hiker/biker) going L to cross a footbridge over the creek. If going L, continue downstream on an old RR grade among hemlock, rhododendron, and fetterbush. At 0.3 mi are cascades on the creek, R, and a small waterfall on a tributary, L. At 0.4 mi are more cascades and a flume, R. At 0.6 mi, reach jct with orange-blazed Clawhammer Cove Trail, L.

(The Clawhammer Cove Trail (hikers only) moves away from Avery Creek and turns N on an old RR grade to parallel Clawhammer Cove Creek. The beauty of the cove is in the open forest of high yellow poplars and acres of dense ferns spreading throughout the stream area and up the mountainside. At 0.7 mi, rock-hop the stream and ascend. To the L, for 100 yd. is a waterfall. Turn SE, ascend on an old woods road, and reach FR-5085 at 1.1 mi among clusters of yellow poplar and maple. Backtrack.)

On the return to Avery Creek Trail (hiker/biker), turn L and follow it on a footbridge to an old roadbed for 0.2 mi where it ends at FR-477. On FR-477, R, it is 0.3 mi up the road to the parking area for Avery Creek Trail (multiple-use), and 4.6 mi farther to US-276 near Cradle of Forestry. To the L, down the mountain, it is 0.3 mi to a horse camp and stable and FR-5085, L. After another 2.0 mi, FR-477 exits at US-276 0.5 mi W from the ranger station.

(The yellow-blazed Buckwheat Knob Trail begins at Club Gap, ascends, and passes under a power line. It reaches Buckwheat Knob at 0.5 mi. It then descends to a shallow gap, crosses another knob, and descends partially on a jeep road to the trail's end in Bennett Gap at Avery Creek Rd [FR-477]. Across the road begins red-blazed Bennett Gap Trail, described below. To the R on FR-477 it is 2.3 mi to US-276 near the Cradle of Forestry, and L it is 2.3 mi to the SE end of Avery Creek Trail.) (USGS-FS Maps: Shining Rock, Pisgah Forest)

351   *Bennett Gap Trail* (USFS #138) (F, B)

Length and Difficulty: 2.9 mi, strenuous (elev change 1,191 ft.)

Connecting Trails: (Buckwheat Knob Trail); Perry Cove Trail (1.2 mi, strenuous; USFS #151) (F, B); (Coontree Gap Trail); (Pressley Cove Trail)

Trailhead and Description: Access to the NW trailhead of Bennett Gap Trail is on Avery Creek Rd (FR-477) 2.3 mi from US-276 at the Cradle of Forestry (8.0 mi NW on US-276 from the ranger station). The trail begins on the S side of the road in Bennett Gap (3,516 ft.). (Across the road, N, is the S trailhead of Buckwheat Knob Trail.) Ascend E on a ridgeline of hardwoods and turn SE. Ahead are occasional views of Avery Valley, L, and Looking Glass Rock and Pilot Mtn., R. At 0.8 mi begin a descent to Saddle Gap where a jct with Perry Cove Trail is L.

352   (The red-blazed Perry Cove Trail descends rapidly from upland hardwoods to cove hardwoods. At 0.5 mi, it begins to follow Perry Cove Branch to its confluence with Avery Creek. It exits at FR-477 near a horse stable and FR-5058, 0.5 mi NW on FR-477 from the E exit of Bennett Gap Trail.)

To continue on the Bennett Gap Trail, ascend on the NE slope of Coontree Mtn. for a jct with Coontree Loop Trail at 1.1 mi. Coontree Loop Trail goes R to US-276, but at this point jointly follows Bennett Gap Trail for 0.6 mi in a descent to Coontree Gap. (Here Coontree Loop Trail turns R to exit at Coontree Picnic Area on US-276.) Bennett Gap Trail forks L (E) and starts descending on the dark shoulder of the ridge to FR-477 at 2.9 mi. Spring wildflowers are prominent among the coves, and rosebay rhododendron are among poplar, oak, and hemlock. At FR-477 it is 126 yd. L (over the low bridge) to Pressley Gap Trail trailhead, R. The trail enters a patch of wildflowers and autumn olive. Downstream on FR-477 it is 1.4 mi to US-276, 0.5 mi W of the ranger station. (USGS-FS Maps: Shining Rock, Pisgah Forest)

Pink Beds Area (Transylvania County)

The Pink Beds is an unusual forested upland bog with an average altitude of 3,250 ft. It extends more than 5.0 mi between the E slopes of the Pisgah Ridge and the W slopes of Soapstone Ridge and Dividing Ridge. The headwaters of the South Fork of Mills River converge here. Its name most likely has come from the dense pink rosebay rhododendron and laurel common throughout the area. Other sources may be the pink rock formerly quarried in the region or the masses of wild pink phlox and pink roses among the fern meadows. A gravel forest road and trails give access into its floral displays and near its numerous serpentine streams. On US-276 is the Cradle of Forestry Discovery Center and nearby is Pink Beds Picnic Area. Yellow Gap Road (FR-206) from US-276 to North Mills River Rec Area goes through the Pink Beds.

Two loop trails originate at the Forest Discovery Center's main building. The Biltmore Forest Campus Trail (USFS #006) (F, W) is a 0.9-mi easy, **353** paved, national-recreation loop trail that provides a historic tour of the buildings of the Biltmore Forest School. It was founded by Carl A. Schenck, a German forester employed by George Vanderbilt to manage his vast forest empire. Schenck became the father of American forestry management because of his work here from 1897 to 1909. The school opened in 1898, and had 367 alumni before closing in 1914. In 1968, Congress passed the Cradle of Forestry in America Act, which established 6,400 acres commemorating a natural national historic site. The Forest Festival Trail (USFS #319) (F, W) is **354** also a paved, easy, 1.0-mi interpretive loop trail that features exhibits of forestry management and logging equipment, based on Dr. Schenck's Biltmore Forest Fair of 1908. From the parking area there is an access to the N trailhead of Club Gap Trail, which makes a S jct with Black Mountain Trail, described in the Davidson River Area. The Forest Discovery Center is open from mid-April to early November, daily, 10:00 AM to 6:00 PM. A small fee is charged for entrance. (For more information, contact the Forest Discovery Center [828-877-3130].)

Access: From BRP mp 412, descend E on US-276 for 3.8 mi, or from Brevard jct of US-64/276 follow US-276 W for 12.0 mi.

Pink Beds Loop Trail (USFS #118) (F, B) 355

Length and Difficulty: 5.0 mi, easy

Connecting Trails: (MST); (South Mills River Trail)

Trailhead and Description: On US-276 (0.2 mi W of the Cradle of Forestry entrance) enter the Pink Beds Picnic Area and parking lot. At the NE end follow the trail sign, descend to cross Pigeon Branch and to a meadow where the trail begins its loop at 0.1 mi. Turn R, follow the orange blaze into a hemlock grove with soft duff, and cross a number of tributaries of the South Fork of the Mills River on footbridges. Most of the treadway is on an old RR grade and can easily accumulate standing water in rainy seasons. At 1.6 mi, reach a jct with the white-blazed MST (L on the MST it is 0.3 mi to the N side of the Pink Beds Loop Trail). After 75 yd., the MST veers R on its route to join the Black Mountain Trail. Continue ahead downstream in a natural garden of tall ferns, white azaleas, fox grapes, and pink wild roses at 1.9 mi. Turn sharply L at 2.7 mi at a jct with a Pink Beds connector trail to the South Mills River Trail, R. (It is 0.9 mi downstream to the gauging sta and FR-476 described in the South Mills River Area.) Follow an old RR grade in sections of open forest of oak, yellow poplar, birch, and pine, and cross Barnett Branch on footbridge 120 yd. before a jct with the MST at 3.8 mi (R it is 0.5 mi to FR-1026, and L it is 0.3 mi to the S side of the trail loop.) Continue ahead and return to the meadow and point of origin at 5.0 mi. (USGS-FS Maps: Pisgah Forest, Shining Rock)

356   *Buck Spring Trail* (S) (USFS #104) (F)

Length and Difficulty: 6.2 mi, moderate (elev change 1,200 ft.)

Trailhead and Description: On US-276 (2.3 mi E from the BRP and 1.3 mi W from the Pink Beds Picnic Area) park on the N side of the highway. Follow the trail sign on a gently graded footpath. Cross Bearwallow Branch at 0.3 mi, the first of 13 streams on this scenic trail that winds in and out of coves and around 10 ridges on a gradual ascent to the Pisgah Inn. At 0.9 mi is a jct with MST, L, and at 1.1 mi, reach a jct with the blue-blazed MST (Alternate), R. (The 119-mi MST goes SW to connect with the Art Loeb Trail at FR-816.) At 4.3 mi, begin a steeper ascent to where two long switchbacks reach an old RR grade at 5.9 mi. On a level area with superb vistas of the Pink Beds and Black Mtn., arrive at the Pisgah Inn at 6.2 mi. The MST continues (see chapter 6 and appendix A). (USGS-FS Maps: Shining Rock, Cruso)

South Mills River Area (Henderson and Transylvania Counties)

South Mills River forms in the Pink Beds, and on its circuitous route it flows through a rugged, remote, gorge-like valley between two long ridges out to join the North Fork near the town of Mills River. On the N side are peaks and ridges such as Funneltop, Rich, Grindstone, and Buttermilk. On the S side are Soapstone, Clawhammer, Black, and Sharpy. From them flow numerous tributaries that, like the river, have native trout. Wildlife in the forest includes bear, deer, grouse, turkey, raccoon, fox, owls, hawks, and many species of songbirds. The area is considered one of the best for equestrian traffic—more than 40.0 mi of trails, plus another 10.0 mi on gated forest roads. At least eight loops can be formed for trail users. There are four access routes to the interior of this challenging area: One from NC-280 on Turkey Pen Rd (FR-297), described first; South Mills River Rd (FR-476) off Yellow Gap Rd (FR-1206) from US-276; Bradley Creek Trail off FR-1206, 4.5 mi W from North Mills River Rec Area; and Clawhammer Cove Rd (FR-5058) off Avery Creek Rd (FR-477), whose access is from US-276.

South Mills River Trail (USFS #133) (F, B, H)   357-
   Length and Difficulty: 12.0 mi, easy to moderate   361
   Connecting Trails: (Turkey Pen Gap Trail); (Vineyard Gap Trail);
(Bradley Creek Trail); Mullinax Trail (1.2 mi, easy; USFS #326) (F, B, H);
Poundingmill Trail (1.5 mi, easy; USFS #349) (F); Wagon Road Gap Trail
(0.7 mi, moderate; USFS #134) (F); Cantrell Creek Trail (1.9 mi, moderate;
USFS #148) (F, B, H); (Squirrel Gap Trail); (Buckhorn Gap Trail); (Pink Beds
Loop Trail)
   Special Features: fishing, forestry history, wildlife
   Trailhead and Description: From the jct of US-276/64 and NC-280 near
Brevard, proceed NE on NC-280 5.0 mi to Henderson/Transylvania county
line. Turn L between private homes on Turkey Pen Rd (FR-297) and drive 1.2
mi on a narrow gravel road to a parking area in Turkey Pen Gap, a source of
multiple trailheads for both hikers and equestrians. To the L begins the Turkey
Pen Gap Trail; to the R begins Vineyard Gap Trail. Ahead (on a continuation
of the FR) is the Bradley Creek Trail beginning at a gate, and on a footpath (L
of the gate) is the E trailhead of the South Mills River Trail. This remarkable
trail stays almost exclusively in sight and sound of the fast-moving South Fork
of Mills River, whose headwaters are in the Pink Beds and the E slope of the
BRP Pisgah range. Although high peaks, such as Black Mtn. (4,286 ft.) on the
S and Funneltop Mtn. (4,266 ft.) on the N, rise from the gorge, they are never
seen from the trail's forested route. The trail crosses the river 13 times, 9 of
which must be forded. Because crossing the river can be difficult or impossible after heavy rains, alternate routes or plans are advised. The route basically
follows an old RR grade that evokes historical fantasies of the way it was a
century ago. A hiker has written "visitation is only by ghosts" on a sign at the
chimney of the former Cantrell Creek Lodge. It is a multiple-use trail for
horses, bikers, hikers, and trophy trout anglers, and short sections are used by
ATV riders. In addition to some of the less used connecting trails, there are
numerous old logging roads that may offer hikers solitude.
   Begin the South Mills River Trail by descending on a heavily used footpath to the river at 0.4 mi, cross the swinging footbridge, and ascend to an old
road (R and L) at 0.6 mi. Turn L and follow a S slope of maple, yellow poplar,
birch, and rhododendron. At 0.7 mi, reach jct with Mullinax Trail, R. (The
Mullinax Trail follows an old seeded road that is rough in places and is used
both by hikers and equestrians to the jct with Squirrel Gap Trail at 1.2 mi. A
5.0-mi loop can be made from this point by going L on the Squirrel Gap Trail

0.7 mi to turn R on the 1.8-mi Laurel Creek Trail, another R on the Bradley Creek Trail, and a final R at the E-end jct with the Squirrel Gap Trail.)

At 2.0 mi, reach a jct, R, with the Poundingmill Trail (hiking only). (The Poundingmill Trail follows the Poundingmill Branch upstream and follows sections of old logging roads. At 1.5 mi, reach a jct with the Squirrel Gap Trail on Poundingstone Mtn. after a steep ascent from the branch. It is 0.8 mi R on Squirrel Gap Trail to jct R with Mullinax Trail.)

Continue on the South Mills River Trail, pass a wildlife field, R, at 2.7 mi, and cross the South Mills River on a swinging footbridge at 2.2 mi. At 3.1 mi, reach a jct with the Wagon Road Gap Trail. (The Wagon Road Gap Trail is an orange-blazed foot trail that ascends 0.7 mi on a steep and sometimes rocky treadway in Big Cove to jct with the Turkey Pen Gap Trail in Wagon Road Gap. It is 2.5 mi L on the Turkey Pen Gap Trail to Turkey Pen Gap parking area.)

At 3.7 mi, cross the South Mills River on a swinging footbridge. Enter a large grassy meadow with tall yellow poplar and oak. Rock-hop Cantrell Creek at 3.9 mi and arrive at the remnants of Cantrell Creek Lodge in a meadow at 4.0 mi. Only a chimney with a double fireplace remains; the lodge was moved in 1978 to the Cradle of Forestry on US-276. A few yards N, at the edge of the forest, is the S terminus of the Cantrell Creek Trail. (This is the trail route to follow for avoiding the eight fordings of the South Mills River in the next 4.7 mi. It ascends gradually upstream 1.9 mi to a jct with Squirrel Gap Trail, but along the way at 1.0 mi, L, is the Horse Cove Gap Trail, a 0.8-mi connector that shortens the route from 5.4 mi to 3.8 mi to the South Mills River Trail at Wolf Ford.)

To continue on the South Mills River Trail, cross the meadow of wild-flowers at Cantrell Creek Lodge site, ascend a low hill, and return to the river-side. Follow the old RR grade and wade the river eight times before a jct with the blue-blazed Squirrel Gap Trail, R, at 8.7 mi at a swinging footbridge over the South Mills River. To the R is the former South Mills River Rd (Wolf Rock Rd) (FR-476), now unmaintained but an alternate route (USFS #133A). To the L the South Mills River Trail begins its ascent on switchbacks to go in and out of coves on the NE slope of Clawhammer Mtn. (At its jct with Buckhorn Gap Trail, there is an access to FR-5058, which connects with Avery Creek Rd [FR-477] and out to US-276, 0.5 mi W of the ranger station.) After leaving the jct with the Buckhorn Gap Trail it descends on switchbacks to rejoin the former FR-476.

If hiking the alternate route, and after 0.1 mi, leave the old road R, in a curve, and follow a footpath across Clawhammer Creek. Pass scenic High

Falls, cascades, and pools in a forest of hemlock, rhododendron, and fetter-bush. Rock-hop or wade the river at 9.4 mi. Cross West Ridge Branch at 9.7 mi. At 10.2 mi is a jct with the main South Mills River Trail, which crosses N of a large horseshoe curve in the river. Arrive at the parking area of Wolf Fork Rd (FR-476) at 11.1 mi. Here is a water-level gauging sta, built in 1935. (It is 1.3 mi N on FR-476 to Yellow Gap Rd [FR-1206] and another 3.3 mi L to US-276 near the Pink Beds Picnic Area.) The trail continues upstream on a beau-tiful footpath among laurel, ferns, fetterbush, and white azalea. Cross the river on a log bridge (which may be washed away) at 11.8 mi and a small log bridge into a flat area of ferns in the approach to a jct with the orange-blazed Pink Beds Loop Trail at 12.0 mi. (USGS-FS Map: Pisgah Forest)

Bradley Creek Trail (5.1 mi; USFS #351) (F, B, H); ***Squirrel Gap*** **362-**
Trail (7.5 mi; USFS #147) (F, B, H partial)   **366**

   Length and Difficulty: 12. 6 mi combined, one-way; moderate to strenuous

   Connecting Trails: (South Mills River Trail); Riverside Trail (3.1 mi, moderate; USFS #115) (F, B, H); (Mullinax Trail); (Vineyard Gap Trail); Lau-rel Creek Trail (1.8 mi, moderate; USFS #348) (F, B, H); (Poundingmill Trail); (Cantrell Creek Trail); Horse Cove Gap Trail (0.8 mi, moderate; USFS #325) (F, B, H)

   Trailhead and Description: From Turkey Pen Gap parking area (see access to South Mills River Trail above) enter the gate and descend 0.4 mi to the river where the South Mills River Trail goes upstream. Fork R on the Bradley Creek Trail and ford the river at 0.8 mi (the county line). Continue downstream to where the old road forks L and the other, Riverside Trail, fords the river. (The yellow-blazed Riverside Trail goes 3.1 mi downstream. It is used mainly by equestrians who must ford the river at five crossings and often on muddy treadway. The trail ends at a jct with the Vineyard Gap Trail near an old homestead site in a grassy flat area.)

   The Bradley Creek Trail takes the L fork at the river and ascends gradu-ally to Pea Gap. It descends to and crosses Pea Branch for a jct L with the E terminus of Squirrel Gap Trail at 1.7 mi. Continue R and follow Pea Branch downstream to Bradley Creek where the trail crosses Case Branch at 2.2 mi and reaches jct with Vineyard Gap Trail, R. Hike upstream parallel with Bradley Creek, but cross it a number of times. In wet weather there is fre-quent seepage from the mountainsides and the tributaries. At 3.4 mi is a jct L with yellow-blazed Laurel Creek Trail. (It serves as a 1.8-mi connector up Laurel Creek to Squirrel Gap Trail near Poundingstone Mtn.) Pass a jct with

FR-5051, which winds up the W side of Queen Creek Mtn. to Yellow Gap on the Yellow Gap Rd (FR-1206). Ahead on the Bradley Creek Trail is Bradley Creek Reservoir. From here the trail continues another 1.5 mi to its N terminus in a hollow at Yellow Gap Rd (FR-1206), 4.5 mi W of North Mills River Rec Area. Backtrack or have a second vehicle.

To access the Squirrel Gap Trail, follow the Bradley Creek Trail from Turkey Pen Gap parking area for 1.7 mi before leaving it, L. Begin the blue-blazed Squirrel Gap Trail up Pea Branch; after 0.7 mi, reach jct with Mullinax Trail, L. (The Mullinax Trail is an easy 1.2-mi yellow-blazed route to South Mills River Trail.) The Squirrel Gap Trail turns R and passes through Mullinax Gap for a jct, R, with Laurel Creek Trail at 1.4 mi on the N side of Poundingstone Mtn. After 260 yd., reach jct L with the Poundingmill Trail. (The orange-blazed 1.5-mi. Poundingmill Trail is for hiker traffic only to the South Mills River Trail.) Continue ahead, first on the ridge of Laurel Mtn. and then on the N slope through a forest of hardwood, laurel, and rhododendron. Pass through Laurel Gap (3,480 ft.), the trail's highest point, and where, if you do not see a squirrel, you may hear a chipmunk. Follow the S slope of Rich Mtn. in and out of coves. Reach jct L with red-blazed Cantrell Creek Trail and Cantrell Creek crossing at 4.0 mi. In a forest of oak, maple, hemlock, and hickory, reach the jct L with the orange-blazed Horse Cove Gap Trail (an 0.8-mi connector to the Cantrell Creek Trail) at 5.4 mi. Cross the headwaters of Laurel Brook and pass through Squirrel Gap (3,320 ft.) at 6.7 mi. Descend gradually to Glady Branch waterfalls, L, at 7.3 mi. Reach the trail's terminus at 7.5 mi at a jct with the South Mills River Trail. Backtrack, or exit upriver on the South Mills River Trail for 2.4 mi to the parking area for FR-476 if a second vehicle is used. (USGS-FS Map: Pisgah Forest)

367   *Turkey Pen Gap Trail* (USFS #322) (F, B)
   Length and Difficulty: 5.5 mi, strenuous
   Connecting Trails: (Wagon Road Gap Trail); (Black Mountain Trail)
   Trailhead and Description: From Turkey Pen Gap parking area at the end of FR-297, ascend L on steps (W) to a dry ridge with blue blazes. Reach Simpson Gap at 0.7 mi. At 1.1 mi, begin a 0.4-mi climb on switchbacks to Sharpy Mtn. Descend moderately in an oak forest with an understory of laurel, rhododendron, blueberry, and ground patches of galax. Arrive at Wagon Rd Gap and Wagon Road Gap Trail, R, at 2.5 mi (The orange-blazed Wagon Road Gap Trail descends rapidly 0.7 mi to jct with the white-blazed South Mills River Trail.) Ascend to McCall Mtn. Descend to Deep Gap at 4.0 mi.

Continue on the ridge and enter Muleshoe Gap at 4.7 mi (N of Horse Knob). Begin a 0.8-mile ascent to a jct with the Black Mountain Trail (S of Black Mtn. peak, 4,286 ft.) at 5.5 mi. (It is 1.8 mi N on the Black Mountain Trail to Buckhorn Gap Trail, where a R turn offers a potential 18.8-mi loop by using the South Mills River Trail. It is 3.9 mi L on the Black Mountain Trail to the ranger station on US-276.) (USGS-FS Map: Pisgah Forest)

Vineyard Gap Trail (USFS #324) (F, B)   368
   Length and Difficulty: 3.3 mi, moderate
   Trailhead and Description: From Turkey Pen Gap parking area at the end of FR-297, ascend on steps R (E) on a dry ridge, and at 0.2 mi bear R on the ridge. Follow the ridgeline, but descend to a damp hollow before ascending to another ridge. Descend to Vineyard Gap and turn L. (The trail ahead follows Forge Mtn. ridge to private property.) Descend on a spur ridge and ford South Fork of Mills River at 2.3 mi. Pass the mouth of Bradley Creek and follow Bradley Creek upstream. Twice wade or rock-hop the stream in a forest of hardwoods, hemlock, and rhododendron. Arrive at campsites and a crossing of Bradley Creek to Bradley Creek Trail at 3.3 mi. Backtrack or follow Bradley Creek Trail for 2.2 mi to Turkey Pen Gap parking area. (USGS-FS Map: Pisgah Forest)

Laurel Mountain Area (Transylvania and Henderson Counties)

Separating the South Mills River Area from the Laurel Mtn. Area is gravel FR-1206 running from US-276 near the Cradle of Forestry E for nearly 12.0 mi to North Mills River Rec Area, and 5.2 mi beyond on paved North Mills River Rd (SR-1345) to NC-191. Five trails ascend N from FR-1206, three of which can connect with the Buck Spring Trail at Pisgah Inn and Campground on the BRP. From the W slopes of Pilot Rock and Forked Ridge are unforgettable views into the Pink Beds and Funneltop Mtn. (4,226 ft.). Parking space is small at all the trailheads on FR-1206.

Thompson Creek Trail (2.4 mi; USFS #602) (F); *Pilot Rock Trail*   369-
(3.6 mi; USFS #321) (F, B); *Laurel Mountain Trail* (7.4 mi; USFS   372
#121) (F, B, no biking at BRP); *Laurel Mountain Connector Trail*
(0.3 mi; USFS #110) (F, B)
   Length and Difficulty: 13.7 mi combined one-way, strenuous (elev change 2,078 ft.)
   Special Features: Pilot Rock monolith, rock outcrops, wildlife, wildflowers

Trailhead and Description: The trails connect near the BRP, but the first three all have different trailheads on Yellow Gap Rd (FR-1206). One desirable loop can be made at Little Bald Mtn., but all other attempts require road walks on FR-1206. Access to Thompson Creek Trail on FR-1206 is 3.1 mi from US-276 (0.4 mi W of the Pink Beds Picnic Area) to the W side of the creek, L. Ascend gradually 0.5 mi to cross a tributary among rhododendron, hemlock, and poplar. Here the trail begins a steady ascent on a ridge with the tributary and Thompson Creek, R. After 1.0 mi on the ridge curve R to a descent and crossing of the creek's headwaters at 1.6 mi. Here are ferns, mosses, rhododendron, and hardwoods. Ascend to the spine of Dividing Ridge where on the E side is a jct with Pilot Rock Trail at 2.4 mi.

To the L Pilot Rock Trail ascends to the top of Little Bald Mtn. (5,280 ft.) in the BRP property at 0.5 mi. It descends to jct with Buck Spring Trail where, if turning L, you reach Pisgah Inn parking lot at mp 408.6 at 1.2 mi. If ascending Pilot Rock Trail from FR-1206, 0.9 mi E from the Thompson Creek trailhead, park in a cove at Greasy Lot Gap. Ascend the orange-blazed trail on the N side of the road into a forest of yellow poplar, beech, locust, and oak. Cross small Bradley Creek after 100 yd., pass through a young forest, and begin switchbacks on a well-graded trail at 0.4 mi. At 0.9 mi are exceptionally scenic views of the Pink Beds, South Mills River Valley, and Funneltop Mtn. (4,266 ft.) from Pilot Rock. Ascend a ridge on switchbacks among beds of galax and trailing arbutus and groves of laurel and chestnut oak. At 2.3 mi, reach jct with a 0.3-mi side trail (Laurel Mountain Connector Trail), R, that connects with Laurel Mountain Trail. After 0.2 mi ahead on Pilot Rock Trail, reach jct with the Thompson Creek Trail, L.

Blue-blazed Laurel Mountain Trail forms a dry crescent on the S shoulder of Laurel Mtn. It begins on FR-1206 and ends also on the Buck Spring Trail near the BRP terminus of Pilot Rock Trail. From the jct of US-276 and Yellow Gap Rd (FR-1206) (0.4 mi W of the Pink Beds Picnic Area), drive 8.5 mi to the trailhead L, but park on the R side of the road. (It is 0.2 mi ahead to Yellow Gap, and a descent of 3.1 mi to North Mills Rec Area. Beyond on North Mills River Rd [SR-1345] it is 5.2 mi to NC-191, 0.9 W of the community of Mills River.) Ascend over hummocks on an old roadbed and follow through a former clear-cut of young oak, yellow poplar, locust, and hemlock. Ascend gradually around a round knob at 0.8 mi. At 1.3 mi is a wide cove on a level contour. After another two coves the trail follows the contour line on the S slope of Black Mtn., a knobby triangular ridge top unseen from the trail.

Reach Rich Gap at 2.7 mi with views in the wintertime of North Mills River Valley. Continue to a sharp curve on a steep ridge, return to coves S of Rich Gap Mtn., and reach Johnson Gap at 4.4 mi. Winding in and out of coves the trail curves in Sassafras Gap at 5.2 mi and straight through Good Enough Gap at 5.6 mi. The trail ascends on switchbacks on the ridge crest to Turkey Spring Gap at 6.4 mi and reaches jct with Laurel Mountain Connector Trail, L. (The 0.3-mi connector allows for a good hiking or biking loop of 2.5 mi with Pilot Rock Trail, Laurel Mountain Trail, and Buck Spring Trail.) Continue ahead on the E slope of Little Bald Mtn. in oak, birch, laurel, and rhododendron on switchbacks into the BRP boundary. Reach jct with the Buck Spring Trail, R and L, at 7.4 mi (see chapter 6). It is 0.3 mi R to the BRP Buck Spring Overlook parking area, mp 407.7, or L 0.8 mi to Pisgah Inn. Backtrack or use a second vehicle. (USGS-FS Map: Dunsmore Mtn.)

Pilot Cove/Slate Rock Creek Trail (4.3 mi; USFS #320) (F, B) *Pilot Cove Loop Trail* (2.1 mi) (F, B)

373-374

Length and Difficulty: 6.4 mi combined, moderate

Special Features: rock outcrops, wildlife, wildflowers

Trailhead and Description: South of Laurel Mtn. is a pair of trails that rise and fall from wet coves to dry windblown ledges. Access to them from US-276 (0.4 mi W of the Pink Beds Picnic Area) is 5.2 mi on Yellow Gap Rd (FR-1206) (1.2 mi E of Pilot Rock Trail trailhead on FR-1206). Enter the trail on the R side of the stream in Pilot Cove. After 0.2 mi is a jct with yellow-blazed Pilot Cove Loop Trail, R. Continue on the blue-blazed Pilot Cove/Slate Rock Creek Trail, cross a log footbridge in a laurel thicket, and enter an open flat area. At 0.5 mi, cross the stream on a log bridge where fern beds are expansive. Ascend, pass through a growth of saplings, cross an old overgrown logging road at 1.0 mi, and ascend steeply. Trailing arbutus and gold star are among the wildflowers. Grouse may be heard on the ridges. Arrive at the top of Slate Rock Ridge and reach jct with the N end of Pilot Cove Loop Trail at 1.3 mi.

(If following the Pilot Cove Loop Trail ascend to a higher ridge among laurel and descend on switchbacks to a saddle at 0.8 mi. After another 0.1 mi, come to a rock dome with weather-sculpted bowls. Here are outstanding views SW of the Pink Beds, S to Funneltop Mtn., and NW to the BRP range. Laurel, mosses, wildflowers, and table mountain pine *[Pinus pungens]* cling to the rock crevices. Ascend to another knoll among chestnut oak at 1.3 mi, after which begin a descent on switchbacks. Return to the main trail at 2.1 mi.)

Continuing on the Pilot Cove/Slate Rock Creek Trail descend 85 yd. to cross a trickling stream. At 1.6 mi, cross Slate Rock Creek at a tributary confluence (where for the trail's remaining 2.7 mi follows an old RR grade). Cross small tributaries and pass frequent cascades among rhododendron patches. At 2.4 mi, enter a more open forest with tall poplar, maple, oak, and scattered hemlock. Ferns and wildflowers are profuse. Cross two more tributaries near each other, followed by a crossing of the creek at 3.6 mi. Cross the creek again at 3.9 mi, and exit at FR-1206 (near a concrete bridge) at 4.3 mi. It is 1.6 mi R (W) on FR-1206 to Pilot Cove, the other trailhead. (USGS-FS Map: Dunsmore Mtn.)

North Mills River Area (Henderson County)

In a huge cove, much like the headwaters of Davidson River, the North Fork of Mills River receives its drainage from more than 30 tributaries, all funneled into an outlet between Seniard Mtn. in the N and Little Rich Mtn. in the S. At the pass is North Mills River Rec Area with a campground, and it is where FR-1206 ends and North Mills River Rd (SR-1345) begins. The river and paved SR-1345 parallel E to SR-191 and the town of Mills River. Along the way the South Fork of the river and North Fork converge. Separating these forks in the W are high mountains such as Funneltop, Rich, Grindstone, and Queen Creek. On the W and N side of the valley is the BRP from Little Pisgah Mtn. N to Truckwheel Mtn. In this area are turkey, bear, deer, grouse, squirrel, quail, and many species of cove and ridgeline hardwoods and wildflowers. Wild trout waters are upper Big Creek, Middle Fork, and Fletcher Creek. Trail and road users will notice scattered wildlife fields in the area. The fields are maintained by the North Carolina Wildlife Resources Commission. One forest road, Wash Creek Rd (FR-5000) runs through the area. It begins at the campground off FR-1206 and winds up the E side of Wash Creek to Bent Creek Gap at the BRP (mp 404), where it becomes Bent Creek Gap Rd (FR-479), which descends to Lake Powhatan.

All the trails in the system are linear, but with the use of forest roads there can be at least nine loops. The hub for the options is at the Trace Ridge Trail parking lot. Also here are gated Hendersonville Reservoir Rd (FR-124) and FR-5097, both essential for loop plans. One trail, for hikers only, is on the E side of Wash Creek Rd. It is Bad Fork Trail (USFS #323), a strenuous 1.8-mi orange-blazed path whose S trailhead is 0.5 mi up FR-5000 from the jct with FR-124. The N trailhead is on the BRP exit to FR-5000. Because of its steepness a second vehicle may be a good choice for hiking down the trail. If so, descend gradually at first on a woods road, then drop 650 ft. in elevation to a damp cove with rhododendron. Cross Bad Fork at 1.2 mi. On an old road the decline decreases in a beautiful forest of tall yellow poplar, hickory, maple, ferns, rock formations, and cascades.

Bear Branch Trail (1.3 mi; USFS #328) (F, B, H); ***Wash Creek Trail*** (0.8 mi; USFS #606) (F, B, H); ***Trace Ridge Trail*** (3.1 mi; USFS #354) (F, B, H); ***Spencer Gap Trail*** (1.6 mi; USFS #600) (F, B); ***North Mills River Trail*** (1.6 mi; USFS #353) (F, B, H); ***Fletcher Creek Trail*** (2.4 mi; USFS #350) (F, B, H); ***Spencer Branch Trail*** (2.3 mi; USFS #140) (F, B, H); ***Middle Fork Trail*** (1.8 mi; USFS #352) (F, B, H); ***Big Creek Trail*** (4.9 mi; USFS #102) (F, B, H)

375-383

Length and Difficulty: 20.0 mi combined one-way (additional distances on the roads), easy to strenuous (elev change 2,581 ft.)

Trailhead and Description: From the jct of NC-191/280 in the community of Mills River, drive N 0.9 mi to North Mills River Rd (SR-1345), L (W) at the North Mills River Rec Area (Campground) sign. Drive 5.0 mi on SR-1345 to the edge of the campground and turn R on Wash Creek Rd (FR-5000). Drive 2.0 mi, turn L on Hendersonville Reservoir Rd (FR-142), cross a cement low-water bridge, and at 0.5 mi reach a parking area and gated roads. All of the above trails can be accessed from this point.

To use Bear Branch Trail go back to FR-5000, cross the road, and climb the hummock and follow the easy blue-blazed route to near the branch's headwaters. Reach jct with FR-5001; either backtrack or return on FR-5001 to FR-5000 and turn L to point of origin.

For yellow-blazed Wash Creek Trail, go 0.4 mi back toward FR-5000 and turn R. It parallels Wash Creek on a flat and easy old timber road for 0.8 mi to a gap. Turn on a S extension of Trace Ridge Trail and return to the parking lot after 0.5 mi. Or, from the gap descend 0.4 mi to jct with North Mills River Trail in a wildlife field.

The scenic blue-blazed North Mills River Trail goes upriver, sometimes fording it. Mainly a horse trail, hikers have to wade the river, which is likely over the knees. The trail's NW terminus is at FR-142 in a grassy meadow. It is 0.6 mi R on FR-142 to the parking lot.

Orange-blazed Trace Ridge Trail begins N (R of the gated FR-5097) from the parking lot on an old forest road. Follow a dry ridgeline after first skirting W of the first knob, but ascend and descend on all the other knobs. Along the way are oak, maple, white pine, dogwood, locust, laurel, and azalea. Descend to a gap at 2.7 mi and jct with Spencer Branch Trail, L. Ascend steeply and at 3.0 mi, reach jct with Spencer Gap Trail, R. Ascend another 0.1 mi to the BRP (mp 401.8, 0.1 mi W of Beaverdam Gap Overlook). Backtrack to Spencer Gap Trail.

The blue-blazed Spencer Gap Trail for hikers and bikers goes E on generally level treadway on the S side of Ferrin Knob and below the BRP. At 0.7 mi, it crosses a small tributary of the headwaters of Wash Creek, then descends on switchbacks to an old logging road at 1.3 mi. Here it turns L and reaches FR-5000 in a sharp curve, 1.6 mi down the mountain from Bent Creek Gap of the BRP. Backtrack, or descend on FR-5000 for 2.0 mi to the entrance for Trace Ridge Trail parking lot. If not backtracking on the Trace Ridge Trail or the Spencer Gap Trail, the Spencer Gap Trail can be chosen as an option for 4.0 mi (2.5 mi on the Spencer Branch Trail and 1.5 mi on FR-142) back to Trace Ridge parking lot.

Access to the Fletcher Creek Trail and the Spencer Branch Trail is on gated FR-142 (L of the gated FR-5097 at the parking lot). Descend to the N edge of the North Fork of Mills River at 1.0 mi, pass cascades of Long Branch, R. At 1.2 mi is the Fletcher Creek Trail trailhead, R. (Ahead on FR-142 it is 0.3 mi to the trailheads of Spencer Branch Trail and Big Creek Trail at the Hendersonville Reservoir.) Turn R off FR-142 on blue-blazed Fletcher Creek Trail (an old road) and ascend. Achieve a minor crest on the slopes of Coffee Pot Mtn. after 0.6 mi. Begin a slight descent and reach the confluence of Middle Fork and Fletcher Creek and good campsites at 1.1 mi. Reach jct with Spencer Branch Trail, R and L. (To access Middle Fork Trail cross Fletcher Creek, bear L a few yards on Spencer Branch Trail, before turning R up Middle Fork Trail as well as by the stream itself. See Middle Fork Trail below.) Turn R and follow jointly 0.2 mi with Spencer Branch Trail and Fletcher Creek Trail to a trail fork. If taking Fletcher Creek Trail, cross the creek and follow an old RR grade in a forest of hardwoods, hemlock, and rhododendron. Pass two wildlife clearings and end at FR-5097. Backtrack or follow FR-5097, L, to Middle Fork Trail for a return to Spencer Branch Trail or R on FR-5097 to Spencer Branch Trail.

After leaving the fork with Fletcher Creek Trail, the Spencer Branch Trail continues upstream, E of Fletcher Creek, until the stream's confluence with Spencer Branch. Ahead the trail crosses Spencer Branch three times before crossing FR-5097 at 0.6 mi. After another 0.5 mi upstream, veer R and ascend for 0.3 mi to jct with the Trace Ridge Trail described above. When going downstream from its jct with Fletcher Creek Trail, the Spencer Branch Trail crosses Fletcher Creek at 0.6 mi, passes a large rock overhang, L, at 0.7 mi, and ends at a jct with Big Creek Trail at the reservoir at 0.9 mi. It is 1.5 mi L on FR-142 to the parking lot.

The orange-blazed Middle Fork Trail is moderate in its ascent and is accessed from the Fletcher Creek Trail. A popular trail for bikers and equestrians, it follows an old RR grade from side to side of Middle Fork. When the Fletcher Creek Trail makes its jct with the Spencer Branch Trail, cross Fletcher Creek, bear L a few yards on Spencer Branch Trail, then turn R up Middle Fork. (There may be a bridge for hikers and bikers across Fletcher Creek. If so, follow that route to jct with the Middle Fork Trail.) After 0.5 mi, cross Middle Fork; enter wildlife clearings at 0.6 mi and 1.0 mi to reach FR-5097 at 1.8 mi. Backtrack, or turn R (N) on FR-5097 to follow Fletcher Creek Trail or Spencer Branch Trail or all the way to the parking lot on FR-5097.

To reach yellow-blazed Big Creek Trail, follow FR-142 1.5 mi to the Hendersonville Reservoir from the Trace Ridge Trail parking lot. Reach jct with the Spencer Branch Trail and after a few yards turn L. Follow around the back side of the reservoir and go upstream (SW and W) on an old RR grade. A number of good campsites are along the route in a cove hardwood area of birch, poplar, oak, and rhododendron. Big Creek will be crossed a number of times; wading or rock-hopping is necessary. A strenuous trail, the climb is 2,400 ft. in elev. At 2.5 mi, cross Bee Branch and begin an ascent on an old timber road with switchbacks on a S slope. At 3.5 mi, follow a footpath, steep in sections, among oak, maple, laurel, and locust along Little Pisgah Ridge. Reach the trail's terminus at BRP mp 406.9 at the S end of Little Pisgah Ridge Tunnel and service road. There is not a parking area here. Backtrack, or arrange to be picked up. (The trailhead may be difficult to locate from the BRP, but cues are to cross a rock landfill E for 0.1 mi to steps and a more obvious trail route.) (USGS-FS Map: Dunsmore Mtn.)

Support Facilities: The North Mills River Rec Area (operated by private concessionaire) has a campground with tent/trailer sites (no hookups), flush restrooms, picnic tables, and sewage disposal. Facilities are fully open all year. A fee is charged. Groceries, restaurant, svc sta, and other services are at Mills River, 6.0 mi E from the campground.

Bent Creek Area (Buncombe County)

Northeast and across the BRP from the North Mills River Area is the Bent Creek drainage. It flows NE to empty into the French Broad River close to the BRP jct with NC-191 about 8.0 mi S of Asheville. The area is known for its beautiful Lake Powhatan Rec Area (operated by private concessionaire) with a system of connecting trails and a campground with 96 sites (no hookups), flush toilets, sewage disposal, picnic tables with grills, central water sources, and hot showers. The season is usually April through November. Swimming is allowed and lifeguard is on duty during open hours; boats and canoes are not allowed on the lake; and a parking fee is required of noncampers.

There are at least six loop options for hikers. Only hiking (and some biking) are allowed between the BRP and through the recreation area to FR-479. In the Stradley Mtn. area NW of Lake Powhatan, some are forest roads, used mainly by equestrians. An example is North Boundary Trail (3.8 mi, USFS **384-** #485) (F, B, H). Other trails may be Sidehill Trail (2.1 mi, USFS #145) (F, B, **388** H); and Lower Sidehill Trail (3.2 mi, USFS #137); Little Hickory Top Trail (1.8 mi, USFS #136) (F, B, H); and Ingles Fields Gap Trail (1.5 mi, USFS #150) (F, B, H). All these trails may be accessed from gated forest roads 479C, -F, and -E, reaching out like tentacles NW up Stradley Mtn. from FR-479 near Lake Powhatan. As you drive from NC-191, past the entrance to the Western North Carolina Arboretum, there is a sheltered signboard, R. It pro- **389** vides information on the Ledford Branch Demonstration Trail, which has interpretive signs to guide visitors on a 4.6-mi tour into the Bent Creek Demonstration Forest. The emphasis is on forest regeneration methods and Southern Appalachian hardwoods. The former Southeastern Forest Experiment Station, now known as Southern Forest Experiment Station, has moved to Asheville from its location on NC-191 near the entrance to Lake Powhatan. The Bent Creek Area has long been significant in forest history and research. An example is the Bent Creek Experimental Forest, where 10 state champion big trees are located (white walnut; northern white and Port Orford cedars; sweet cherry; ponderosa, red, and Scotch pines; spicebush; and white and Norway spruce). The arboretum, fenced and gated, but open daily, is planning botanical trails and special trails for people with disabilities (PWD).

Access: From the jct of I-40/26 in SW Asheville, take I-26 1.5 mi to jct with NC-191, turn L, and follow NC-191 2.1 mi to the Lake Powhatan sign, R. Go 0.3 mi on SR-3480, turn L on Wesley Branch Rd (SR-3484, which becomes FR-479), and go 3.0 mi (From BRP mp 393.6, turn at the French Broad River bridge and drive 0.3 mi to NC-191; turn L and go 0.3 mi to entrance road, L. Another access is off the BRP on FR-479 (under the BRP bridge) at Bent Creek Gap Rd, mp 404. There are not any access signs on the BRP.

390- *Homestead Trail* (1.1. mi; USFS #333) (F, B); *Small Creek Trail* (0.4 **395** mi, USFS #334) (F, B); *Deerfield Loop Trail* (0.6 mi; USFS #335) (F, B); *Pine Tree Loop Trail* (1.8 mi; USFS #336) (F, B); *Explorer Loop*

Trail (3.0 mi; USFS #337) (F, B); *Sleepy Gap Trail* (1.0 mi; USFS #339) (F, B)

Length and Difficulty: 7.9 mi combined, easy to moderate

Trailhead and Description: The trails are marked and color-coded, but a map from the campground office may clarify the original trails and the spur trails made by hikers, bikers, and campers. From the beach parking area at Lake Powhatan follow E on the orange-blazed Homestead Trail at a hiking sign, and go around the lake through a hardwood and white pine forest. Pass an area where Carl A. Schenck (see Biltmore Forest Campus Trail in this section) had a lodge from where he managed the Biltmore Forest. Cross Bent Creek at FR-480 and return around the lake at 1.1 mi. The red-blazed Small Creek Trail is a 0.4-mi connector from the yellow-blazed Deerfield Loop Trail and the Homestead Trail.

For the Deerfield Loop Trail, leave the beach parking area, follow E (but S of the Homestead Trail), and meander through a mixed forest and a wildlife field to a jct with the blue-blazed Pine Tree Loop Trail at 0.6 mi. After another 0.6 mi, reach jct with the yellow-blazed Explorer Loop Trail, but follow a new trail, R, on the S side of Bent Creek in a return to the campground beach area at 2.4 mi.

From the trail sign on Bent Creek Gap Rd (FR-479) parking area (between FR-479F and FR-479C jcts), follow the Explorer Loop Trail sign across Bent Creek, and at the fork, turn L. Cross Beaten Branch, reach jct L with the Pine Tree Loop Trail, cross Beaten Branch again, and reach jct L with the red-blazed Sleepy Gap Trail at 0.5 mi (The Sleepy Gap Trail ascends an E slope, crosses South Ridge Rd [FR-479M], and ascends in a forest of hardwoods and rhododendron for 1.0 mi to Sleepy Gap at BRP mp 397.3 to jct with the Shut-in Trail/MST.) Continue on the Explorer Loop Trail to a jct with Cold Knob Rd (FR-479H) at 1.7 mi. Turn R on FR-479H, and after 0.4 mi (before the gate at Bent Creek Gap Rd [FR-479]), leave the road and parallel Bent Creek to the point of origin after a loop of 3.0 mi. (USGS-FS Maps: Dunsmore Mtn., Skyland)

Chapter 4

Uwharrie National Forest

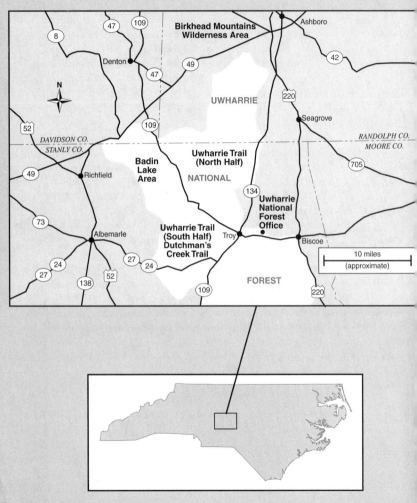

Introductions to Trail Areas

Some archaeologists have reported that the Uwharrie National Forest is North America's oldest known mountain range. The descriptions are in the N from W to E, then central from S to N.

Uwharrie National Forest Office
There are maps, books, and reservations for facilities. There are also two trails here for physical fitness and nature study of milky quartz and vegetation.

Badin Lake Area *220*
Bordering a scenic shoreline trail, the loop trails rise and fall on hills and valleys to camp, swim, and even fish on a floating pier.

Birkhead Mountains Wilderness Area *222*
In a hardwood forest with brilliant cardinal flowers and snowy white quinine, hikers can scale scenic peaks, such as Coolers Knob. For a trail on history, pause at the remnants of Birkhead Plantation.

Uwharrie Trail Area (South Half) *223*
Ascend Dennis Mtn. for views of Morrow Mtn. State Park and Lake Tillery.

Uwharrie Trail Area (North Half) *223*
After crossing NC-109, complete the north half of the 20.5-mi trail by ascending the rocky peak of Dark Mtn.

Dutchmans Creek Trail (South Half) *225*
Shaped like an S, it makes a double loop by crossing the Uwharrie Trail on its south section. Its scenery is among multiple streams and sections of reforestation.

Dutchmans Creek Trail (North Half) *225*
This loop follows Dutchman's Creek in a scenic area of gentle cascades, clear pools, and dense beds of wildflowers and ferns.

Canebrake Horse Camp
Open year-round, this outstanding horse camp has 29 sites with good facilities and 25 trails.

Chapter 4

Uwharrie National Forest

White rocks on a trail are more
Scenic than a yellow brick road . . .
—Matt Crenshaw in *Rocky My Sole*

In the center of the state, the 50,189-acre Uwharrie National Forest spreads into a patchwork of private and public tracts in three counties—mainly Montgomery, but more than 8,000 acres in Randolph and another 1,000 acres in Davidson. Nearly 300 mi of county, state, and private roads form part of that patchwork, and another 185 mi of forest roads give easy access to its streams, recreational areas, and trails. With its mountainous range rarely over 900 ft. in elev, it disguises its 400-million-year history. Archaeologists have reported that the composite geography has been eroded by the Yankin, Pee Dee, and Uwharrie Rivers to expose parts of the hard basalt and rhyolite deposits in the oldest known mountain range in North America. Its rocky and worn ridges have been mined for gold, silver, copper, and lead, and the early settlers impoverished an already poor soil with inadequate timber and farm management. In 1931 much of the acreage was identified as the Uwharrie Purchase Unit, and in 1935 it was transferred to the USFS for administration. Finally, in 1961 it became a national forest, the state's youngest. During the 1930s the CCC and subsequently the USFS reforested hundreds of acres with pines and allowed groves of hardwoods to mature in the coves and by the stream banks. Slopes with mountain laurel, dogwood, and sourwood became natural understory gardens with 700 species of plants and abundant wildflowers and ferns. A further preservation was made in 1984 when federal Public Law 98-324 created the 5,160-acre Birkhead Mountains Wilderness Area. The Final Environmental Impact Statement of the 1986 Land and Resource Management Plan reported 255 historic sites as "recommended for further testing or preservation." The origin of Uwharrie's name is unclear; perhaps it came from the Suala Indians. As early as 1701 it was spelled Heighwaree, an early map of 1733 lists it as Uharie, and it is listed as Voharee on a 1770 map.

Recreational facilities include four family campgrounds: Arrowhead Campground has 50 tent or trailer sites of which 35 have individual electrical hookups, picnic tables, drinking water, bathhouse, flush toilets, and waste disposal system (access is on FR-576 off SR-1153 for 2.9 mi to FR-597, turn R, then the first L on FR-597A); and Badin Lake Campground has tent sites, picnic tables, drinking water, and toilet facilities (access is the same as for Arrowhead Campground, except farther on FR-597 to FR-597B, L). Another campground, Badin Lake Group Camp, has a large field for tent camping, drinking water, and toilet facilities. (Reservations are required to use the group camp.) Access is on the same road to Badin Lake Campground, but turns R near the campground entrance. There is a fee for all the campgrounds; all of these campgrounds are open year-round. Each of these camping areas has access to boat launching to Badin Lake at Cove Boat Ramp, accessible at the end of FR-597B, described above. The lake has largemouth bass, white bass, bream, yellow perch, sunfish, and catfish.

There are three primitive camps: West Morris Mtn. Camp with picnic tables and vault toilets (access is at Uwharrie, 0.3 mi N on NC-109 from its jct with SR-1150, to a R turn on Ophir Rd [SR-1303], then 1.2 mi, R); Uwharrie Hunt Camp has tent sites with picnic tables and sanitary facilities (access from Uwharrie intersection of NC-109 and SR-1150 is 1.5 mi N on NC-109 to a sharp L on SR-1153 for 0.4 mi, R); and Yates Place Camp at the end of a 0.5-mi spur trail E off the Uwharrie Trail (0.1 mi S of Dusty Level Rd [SR-1146] and FR-6746 jct.)

The district has horse trails in the Badin area with access from Canebrake Campground, foot trails (the longest of which is 20.5-mi Uwharrie Trail), and 16 mi of ORV trails. The latter is confined to an area between Badin Lake W and Uwharrie River E, and accessible S off FR-576. Some of the trails are Dutch John Trail (2.1 mi; USFS #90); Rocky Mountain Loop Trail (2.8 mi; USFS #92); and Dickey Bell Trail (3.4 mi; USFS #96A). (A map is available from the district office.) **396-397**

The fourth family campground is the Canebrake Horse Camp, which opened to the public in the spring of 2002. It features 28 campsites designed especially for equestrians. Facilities offer drinking water, showers, flush toilets, and a sewage-disposal station. Access from Uwharrie jct of NC-109 and SR-1150 is 1.5 mi N on NC-109 to a sharp L on SR-1153 for 0.4 mi, then R on FR-576 for 0.5 mi, then R on FR-544 for 1.0 mi, then L (still on FR-544) for 0.2 mi to the campground. There is a fee for each site per night. For reservations, contact 877-444-6777 (toll free) or www.reserveUSA.com. For maps,

398-
422
contact the forest office at 910-576-6391. Also open to hikers, the network of trails are as follows: easy routes are Greg's Loop Trail (1.3 mi); Blackburn Trail (1.9 mi); Josh Trail (2.0 mi); Lake Trail (0.6 mi); Indian Trail (1.0 mi); Megan's Trail (1.4 mi); Home Trail (1.4 mi); Larry's Trail (1.2 mi).; Helen's Loop (1.8 mi); Wren Trail (0.3 mi); Tanager Trail (0.6 mi); Randolph Trail (0.3 mi); Burl Tree Way (1.3 mi); Morgan Trail (1.4 mi); Berner Trail (0.5 mi); Robbins Trail (1.3 mi); moderate ratings are Leslie Trail (1.3 mi); Big Rock Trail (0.9 mi); Tony Trail (0.8 mi); Todd Trail (1.8 mi); River Trail (3.0 mi); Buttermilk Trail (1.0 mi); Bates Trail (1.7 mi); and most difficult ratings are Hang Glider Trail (1.0 mi); and Fraley Trail (1.9 mi).

423
An interpretive double-loop white-blazed trail, Densons Creek Nature Trail (0.9 mi or 2.2 mi; USFS #97) (F) begins from the ranger station parking lot. Numbered posts describe flora, fauna, history, and geology. Scattered pines are among the hardwoods, and the predominant rock formations are
424
milky quartz. The Uwharrie Fitness Trail (0.4 mi; USFS #397) (F) connects with the Densons Creek Nature Trail, but its parking lot is accessed on the first turn R, Page Rd, off NC-24/27, a few yards W of the ranger station. Maps and brochures are available from the ranger's office.

In season, hunting and fishing in the forest are allowed in accordance with state laws and licenses. Forest game animals are deer, turkey, raccoon, squirrel, fox, rabbit, and quail. Numerous species of songbirds, owls, and hawks are here also. Among the species of reptiles are box turtles, lizards, and snakes (including the infrequently seen rattlesnake and copperhead).

Address and Access: District Ranger, Uwharrie National Forest, USFS, 789 Hwy 24/27 East, Troy, NC 27371; 910-576-6391. Access is on NC-24/27, 1.8 mi E of Troy.

Support Facilities: Motels, restaurants, and shopping centers are in Troy, Asheboro, and Albemarle, and hospitals are in the latter two. Stores for groceries and sporting goods are at Uwharrie, jct of NC-109 and SR-1303/1150, and on Hwy 109N, just beyond its intersection with SR-1153.

Badin Lake Area (Montgomery County)

This is a concentrated recreational area with facilities for boating, fishing, camping, picnicking, and hiking as described above. At the Arrowhead Campground (completed in 1996), plans are for a 1.0-mi paved bike trail to encircle the campground, with an access trail to the lake. (This new route is used to connect with the Badin Lake Trail, described below, so campers would have a long loop trail to connect with the other campgrounds.) Cove Boat Ramp has been refurbished.

Access: From the jct of NC-109 and Reservation Rd (SR-1153) (1.5 mi NW from the community of Uwharrie), go 0.4 mi on SR-1153 and turn R on FR-576 (at Uwharrie Hunting Camp/Picnic Area). Drive 2.9 mi and turn R on FR-597. The first L (on FR-597B) goes to Cove Boat Ramp and Arrowhead Campground. The second L (on FR-597A) goes to Badin Lake Campground and Badin Lake Group Camp.

Badin Lake Trail (USFS #94) (F)   **425**
Length and Difficulty: 6.5 mi, moderate

Trailhead and Description: This trail has a white painted blaze, a well defined tread, and offers great views of Badin Lake. Begin the trail at the Cove Boat Ramp parking area (described above) and follow N along the Badin Lake shoreline. Curve around a knoll (on whose top is the Arrowhead Campground) and reach a jct with the return loop route, R, at 0.4 mi. Continue ahead by the lake and at 0.5 mi arrive in a rocky cove with ferns and wildflowers. Enter another cove at 1.0 mi with white alder, oaks, and pines where the Badin Lake Campground is up the hill. Stay close to the waterfront and continue around the campground to a cove at 1.8 mi. From here there is less evidence of the campground spur trails. At 2.3 mi, enter a cove where the trail leaves the shore and slightly ascends to an old road, R and L, at 2.5 mi. (To the R the old road goes to the Badin Lake Group Camp and FR-597A. To the L the road extends 0.5 mi to the tip of the peninsula.) Ahead is a beautiful open forest and the other side of the peninsula.

Descend slightly to the lake's edge and pass R of a floating fishing pier. Follow the shoreline to a cove at 2.8 mi, ascend, and curve L to cross a long ravine at 3.2 mi. At 3.3 mi, reach a large sloping rock on the hillside into the lake. Here are lichens, mosses, wildflowers, scrub pine, and laurel. From here the trail soon ascends on the hillside, then drops to the lake before entering a long and dense cove, a favorite place for spring peepers and bullfrogs. At 4.2 mi, reach a jct with a sign that indicates an access to the Badin Lake Group Camp. Turn R steeply to the hilltop at 4.3 mi at the NE corner of the Badin Lake Group Camp field.

If continuing on the Badin Lake Trail from the sign, descend to the stream and rocky area. Then ascend a ridge, descend, cross a hollow, ascend, and cross FR-597A at 0.7 mi. Arrive at a wildlife field at 0.8 mi and curve R. Cross a woods road at 1.0 mi, pass through a damp area among saplings at 1.1 mi to cross an old road with patches of wild quinine and rabbit's pea. Cross another road; descend into more saplings. Before a wildlife field, the trail forks at 1.5 mi. To the L is a faint 0.1-mi trail to FR-597, a few yards N of its jct with FR-597B. To the R the trail goes around the wildlife field and exits at FR-597B at 1.6 mi. To the R is the Arrowhead Campground where the trail connects to the paved trail surrounding campsite. Follow the paved trail back to Cove Boat Landing. (USGS-FS Map: Badin)

Birkhead Mountains Wilderness Area (Randolph County)

Access: From the Asheboro jct of US-220 and NC-49, go W on NC-49 for 5.5 mi and turn R on Science Hill Rd (SR-1163). After 0.4 mi, turn L (S) on Lassiter Mill Rd (SR-1107), and go 5.2 mi to a wilderness sign at FR-6532. Turn L and drive 0.5 mi to the parking area at the end of the road. (If arriving from the SW on NC-49 [11.0 mi NE of NC-109 jct], turn R on Mechanic Rd [SR-1170]. After 0.7 mi reach a jct with Lassiter Mill Rd, turn R, and go 4.3 mi to the wilderness.) If from the S, Uwharrie for example, take SR-1303 for 5.3 mi N to Ophir, SR-1134 and SR-1105 for 2.7 mi N to Eleazer, and SR-1107 5.1 mi N to FR-6532, R.

426-   *Robbins Branch Trail* (3.2 mi) (F); *Birkhead Trail* (5.6 mi; USFS
428   #100) (F); *Hannahs Creek Trail* (1.4 mi) (F)

Length and Difficulty: 10.2 mi combined, easy to moderate

Special Features: pioneer history

Trailhead and Description: (These trails do not receive maintenance; some old white blazes remain.) Follow the trail sign and at 0.4 mi, reach a fork where the Robbins Branch Trail goes L and the Hannahs Creek Trail goes R. If following the Robbins Branch Trail proceed through a young forest; ascend gently. At 1.2 mi pass through an open area of sumac and wildflowers with a vista of the Uwharrie Mtns. Descend gradually, enter an older forest at 1.5 mi, and at 1.7 mi pass R of rock erosion barriers left by pioneer farmers. Turn sharply L on a footpath at 1.9 mi. After 92 yd. cross Robbins Branch, bordered with Christmas ferns, and continue upstream to cross the branch three times and a tributary once. (In late August cardinal flowers are brilliant near the branch.) Leave the branch headwaters and reach a jct with the Birkhead Trail at 3.2 mi.

To the L, the Birkhead Trail goes 2.6 mi to Tot Hill Farm Rd (SR-1142), its N terminus. To the R it runs 2.0 mi to a jct with Hannahs Creek Trail and another 1.0 mi to its S terminus at the forest boundary. If taking the N route, curve R at 0.2 mi to a shallow saddle for a traverse on the Coolers Knob Mtn.

crest. Pass Camp #1-B, L, at 0.7 mi. Reach Coolers Knob with a scenic view E on a 50-yd. spur at 1.4 mi Cedar Rock Mtn. and peaks from 900 to 1,050 ft. are visible from here. Descend, and at 1.5 mi leave the Birkhead Mtn. Wilderness Area and cross private land for 0.2 mi before reentering the NF. Cross Talbotts Creek at 2.4 mi and reach SR-1142 at 7.2 mi. (It is 2.0 mi L to NC-49 and 5.1 mi R on NC-49 to Asheboro.) If taking the Birkhead Trail R (S), pass patches of wild quinine *(Parthenium integrifolium)* and Camp #5 with a grill at 0.4 mi. Descend gradually in a hardwood forest. Reach the remnants of the Birkhead Plantation at 1.0 mi. (Boy Scout Troop 570 has erected a sign about John W. Birkhead [1858–1933] and his wife, Lois Kerns [1868–1943], and their 10 children. The family later moved to Asheboro where Mr. Birkhead was clerk of court and county sheriff.) At 1.7 mi, pass Camp #4, R, with a spur. At 2.0 mi is the site of the Christopher Bingham Plantation (ca. 1780) and reach a jct, R, with the Hannahs Creek Trail. Ahead the Birkhead Trail goes another 0.4 mi to cross the North Prong of Hannahs Creek and to a campsite at 0.9 mi. At 1.0 mi arrive at the S boundary of the Birkhead Mtn. Wilderness Area and the trail's S terminus. (Ahead it is 1.0 mi on a private jeep road to a crossing of the South Prong of Hannahs Creek and entry to SR-1109 at Strieby Church. From here it is 0.6 mi on the road to jct with SR-1143. To the R [W], it is 2.1 mi to Lassiter Mill crossroads with SR-1107, and L [E] 10.8 mi to Ulah and US-200.)

On the Hannahs Creek Trail follow the old woods road, cross a streamlet, and pass a chimney and foundation L at 0.2 mi. Cross another streamlet at 0.5 mi, pass a man-made rock wall, and cross Robbins Branch at 0.9 mi. Ascend to the jct with the Robbins Branch Trail at 1.4 mi. Veer L and return to the parking area. (USGS-FS Maps: Eleazer, Farmer)

Uwharrie Trail Area (Montgomery County)

Uwharrie Trail (USFS #276) (F)

Length and Difficulty: 20.5 mi, moderate

Connecting Trails: West Morris Mtn. Trail (2.2 mi; USFS #95, moderate) (F); (Dutchmans Creek Trail)

Special Features: Dennis Mtn., Island Creek

Trailhead and Description: The Uwharrie Trail (a national recreation trail since 1980) is a N-S route, which at the S end forms a reversed S crosses the middle of Dutchmans Creek Trail and forms an irregular figure eight. Access to the S trailhead is at a parking lot on NC-24/27, 2.0 mi E of the Pee

429-
430

Dee River bridge and 10.0 mi W from the center of Troy. From the NW corner of the parking space, enter a footpath through small oaks and descend on the white-blazed trail into a more mature forest of hardwoods, pine, and laurel. Pass under a power line at 0.3 mi. At 1.0 mi cross Wood Run Creek in a laurel grove, and at 2.0 mi reach jct with a 0.3-mi spur, R, to Wood Run primitive campsite. At 2.4 mi, pass a spur a few yards R to FR-517. Follow the trail downstream, cross it six times, observe crested dwarf iris, and pass the remnants of an old automobile at 2.5 mi. Cross a timber road at 3.5 mi, ascend steeply to the top of Dennis Mtn. (732 ft.) at 3.7 mi for views W of Morrow Mtn. State Park and Lake Tillery. Descend, join an old woods road R, rock-hop Island Creek at 4.6 mi, turn R on a footpath, and go upstream in a scenic forest with galax and royal ferns. After crossing the creek four times, ascend to and cross the terminus of FR-517 at 5.6 mi. At 5.7 mi arrive at a cross-trail with the yellow-blazed Dutchmans Creek Trail. (Dutchmans Creek Trail goes 5.3 mi L to rejoin the Uwharrie Trail N, and 5.9 mi R [S] to the NC-24/27 parking area. A loop can be formed here for either trail.) For the next 2.2 mi, the trail ascends and descends three hilltops, crosses three old forest roads and four streamlets, and reaches Dutchmans Creek at 7.0 mi. Deer and turkey may be seen in this area. The forest is open in a number of places, but laurel is dense near some of the stream areas. At 8.2 mi, ascend from a young forest to jct with the Dutchmans Creek Trail, L, at 8.4 mi. At 8.9 mi,reach a jct R with a spur trail of 0.5 mi to primitive Yates Place Camp. At 9.0 mi, arrive at Mtn. Road (SR-1146) where the trail crosses. (Heading L, it is 2.1 mi to SR-1150; R, it is 0.5 mi to Yates Place Camp and then 5.0 mi on Correl Rd [SR-1147] and NC-109 to Troy.)

Continue ahead on the Uwharrie Trail, and cross a tributary of Cedar Creek at 9.3 mi and Watery Branch at 10.0 mi. Follow downstream, R, for 0.5 mi. Begin a steep rocky climb and reach the hill summit at 10.8 mi. At 11.3 mi make a sharp turn off a logging road and reach NC-109 at 11.9 mi. Cross the road to a parking space. (It is 1.8 mi L on NC-109 to jct with SR-1150 and Uwharrie for groceries, telephone, gasoline, and supplies; R, it is 5.0 mi to Troy.)

At 12.4 mi is a spring, L. Cross Cattail Creek at 12.8 mi and cross Spencer Creek hiking bridge at 14.0 mi. Ascend and pass a bed of running cedar at 14.1 mi and intersect with the yellow-blazed West Morris Mtn. Trail, L at 14.3 mi. (The West Morris Mtn. Trail descends 1.0 mi to the West Morris Campground, a primitive camp with tables, grills, and two vault toilets on Ophir Rd [SR-1303], 1.2 mi N of Uwharrie.) On the Uwharrie Trail ascend and reach the mountain summit at 14.6 mi. Cross an old forest road at 15.0 mi, and at 17.0 mi cross two streams on bridges a few feet apart at Panther Branch. Cross SR-1134 at 18.1 mi. Reach a high ridge at 19.2 mi and continue to a rocky peak of Dark Mtn. (953 ft.) at 19.4 mi, where there is an excellent W view. After a rocky descent, reach a parking area on Flint Hill Rd (SR-1306) at 20.5 mi. Ophir is 1.8 mi L, Flint Hill is 2.8 mi R, and it is 7.0 mi to NC-134. (A former 5.4-mi Uwharrie Trail Extension [USFS #99] from here to SR-1143 has been discontinued because of its traverse on private property.) (USGS-FS Maps: Lovejoy, Morrow Mtn., Troy)

Dutchmans Creek Trail (USFS #98) (F)   **431**

Length and Difficulty: 11.1 mi, moderate to strenuous
Connecting Trail: (Uwharrie Trail)
Special Features: reforestation, old mines, remote, Dutchmans Creek
Trailhead and Description: The S-shaped Dutchmans Creek Trail begins, ends, and crosses the middle of the S section of the Uwharrie Trail to jointly form the shape of an erratic figure eight. The trailheads are at a parking lot on NC-24/27, 2.0 mi E of the Pee Dee River bridge and 10.0 mi W from the center of Troy. The yellow-blazed trail begins at the NE corner of the parking lot, across FR-517. Cross a natural-gas line at 0.3 mi, then enter a clear-cut at 0.4 mi and leave it at 1.0 mi. Cross a small branch at 1.1 mi and Dumas Creek at 2.2 mi. Ascend steeply to an open area for S views, and at 2.5 mi turn sharply L (N) at a 1978 reforestation project. Leave the clear-cut, dip into a ravine, and at 3.0 mi, cross a road in use to the private Piedmont Sportsmen Club. Pass under a power line at 3.1 mi. Ascend gently to the top of a long flat ridge at 4.4 mi and descend to cross FR-517 at 4.9 mi. Cross Island Creek twice; ascend. Cross FR-517 again at 5.5 mi to ascend a rocky ridge. Reach a level area and a cross-trail jct with the Uwharrie Trail at 5.9 mi. (On the Uwharrie Trail it is 5.7 mi L to NC-24/27 and 3.3 mi R to NC-1146; see description below.) Follow the Dutchmans Creek Trail R of a clear-cut, and reach a rocky hill at 6.3 mi. Descend into a grove of laurel and follow Little Island Creek for four crossings before ascending steeply on a rocky scenic mountain of hardwoods, Virginia pine, and wildflowers at 7.3 mi. (In the winter you can see Badin Dam [W] through the trees.) Reach the mountain summit at 7.6 mi. Descend for the next 0.4 mi and notice disturbed earth from old mines. Cross a streamlet three times before climbing another steep mountain to reach the top at 8.6 mi. (Badin Lake area can be seen through the trees in the winter, and Lick Mtn. can be seen to the E.) At 9.1 mi, descend to a

gardenlike area of laurel, galax, trailing arbutus, and wild ginger *(Hexastylis shuttleworthii).* At 9.5 mi, rock-hop Dutchmans Creek and go upstream in a scenic area of gentle cascades and clear pools. Pass through a mature forest of tall oak, beech, and poplar with scattered holly. Rock-hop the creek three times before reaching a road at 10.8 mi. Continue straight ahead to reach a jct with the Uwharrie Trail at 11.1 mi. It is 0.6 mi L on the Uwharrie Trail to SR-1146, and 2.7 mi R to rejoin the Dutchmans Creek Trail. (Volunteer assistance for trail maintenance in both the Uwharrie Trail and Dutchmans Creek Trail is provided by the Central Piedmont Group of the Sierra Club from Charlotte and the Uwharrie Trail Club from Asheboro.) (USGS-FS Map: Morrow Mtn.)

Part II

Trails in the National Park System

Bluff Mountain Trail.

Appalachian National Scenic Trail

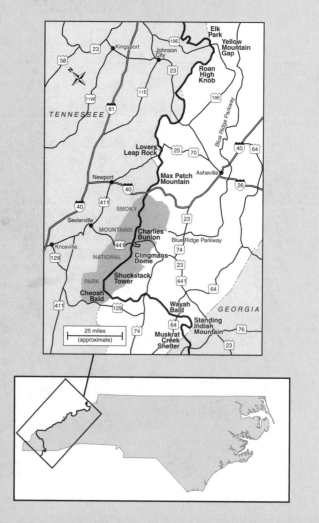

Introductions to Trail Areas

The Appalachian National Scenic Trail, the most famous walking trail of the modern world, has 310 mi in NC. Among the many shelters, mountain tops, gaps, and historic sites, a dozen points of interest are listed below from Georgia to Tennessee. In addition to the AT headquarters in WV, there is a regional AT office with the USFS office in Asheville.

Chapter 5

Appalachian National Scenic Trail

For the love of nature is healing,
If we will only give it a try
And our reward will be forthcoming,
If we go deeper than what meets the eye.
—Emma "Grandma" Gatewood
from *The Reward of Nature*

432   Hikers do not need an explanation for why they hike the Appalachian Trail, other than because it is there. But on the menus of reasons are the trail's challenge and magnetic and kinetic appeal. Thousands walk sections of the sacred 2,157-mi path in the sky. A continuous scenic corridor through 14 eastern states from Maine to Georgia, it crosses eight national forests, six national parks, more than 60 state parks, memorial sites, and game lands. It is a living, changing masterpiece of incredible dreams, design, and dedication. To hike from end to end, the average number of footsteps is 5,240,000 and the average time is between four and five months.

By 2003 a few more than 7,500 hikers are known to have walked the entire distance since an unbroken route was completed August 14, 1937. Of those who start with the intent to finish, more than 90 percent drop out. Most run out of will. One hiker in particular almost dropped out when she first started in Maine without map or guidebook and got lost. When found by park rangers, they told her to go home due to her condition. It is reported that she told them if she could not hike in Maine, then she would go to Georgia. And she did. Again, without maps or guidebooks, she packed her meager trail gear in a denim sack, tied up her high top Keds and headed north. *Sports Illustrated* later named her "Pioneer Grandmother." When she was nearing Mt. Katahdin, the rangers welcomed her like their own grandmother. She has stated that she was inspired by a story in *National Geographic* in 1949 about Earl Shaffer completing the AT the year before as the first known solo hiker of the mystery route. By now readers who have hiked the AT know about this legendary example of stamina. A verse of one of her poems graces the heading of this chapter, and there is more to come about her. In stories and books by AT hikers,

230

there is a theme about stamina, mind-set, and independence. Earl Shaffer, 29, and the first through-hiker in 1949, had these qualities, as did the second solo through-hiker, Gene Espry, 24, from Cordele, Georgia, who hiked the trail in 1951. A U.S. Navy veteran of WW II, he traveled light, used ATC guidebooks, and, like Shaffer, did not have caches or anyone to meet him along the way. It took him 123 days, one day less than Shaffer. In some of the shelters, Espry read notes and poems left by Shaffer. One poem had the lines "And though it be sun or rain / I walk the mountaintops with spring." Espry told news reporters that he enjoyed the trail in spite of bad weather and being lost on occasion. Maine's *Daily Sun* praised him as a conqueror of the nation's "most exacting thoroughfare."

Four years later, Emma Gatewood (Grandma Gatewood) of Thurmond, Ohio, and mother of 11 grown children, started hiking the AT in Georgia on May 3, 1955 and finished in Maine on September 25. She followed the same route again in 1957, and by 1964, at the age of 77, completed her third trip in sections. In 1959, she hiked the Oregon Trail. She was dearly loved by the trail world for many reasons. She inspired hikers with her simplicity (no backpack or fancy gear, no sleeping bag, and no hiking boots—only sneakers), her stamina, her love for people, and her great sense of humor. An example of the latter is an occasion in Maine (before her serious through-hikes) when she became lost. When found by a forest official and reminded of it, she replied, "Not lost, just misplaced." In 1973 at the age of 85, Grandma died of natural causes.

In 1957 another solo through-hiker, Dorothy Laker, a teenager from Tampa, Florida, began the AT in Georgia and finished in Maine. An observant account of her journey is in *Hiking the Appalachian Trail.* She hiked the AT again in 1964 and a third time in sections by 1972. "Any memory of worry, frustration, and misery of the 1957 hike flew out of my mind . . . all I could remember were magic days and friendly campfires."

Solo through-hiking carries with it the risk of loneliness, particularly in members of a close family. Two examples are teenagers who hiked the AT in the 1960s. Jeffrey Hancock, 16, from Wenham, Massachusetts, hiked the AT in 1969. During the month before leaving he, his father, and his brother buried 28 caches of food along the AT's route from Georgia to Maine. In his diary he wrote of his blistered feet, losing the trail, and severe loneliness. Like hikers before him, he had stamina. "A yearning for the outdoors was born in me," he wrote in *A Long Way Home.* During July of that summer his path crossed with Eric Ryback, 17, from Belleville, Michigan, who was hiking solo from Maine to Georgia. "He was really moving, averaging 25 miles a day," said Hancock.

Ryback finished the trail in 80 days because he wished to be back before school started. He wrote about his loneliness and being lost. "Fear crept through me . . . I was confused." The lonely feeling was painful; "formed into one huge lump," he wrote in his story for *Hiking the Appalachian Trail*. The next summer he hiked the Pacific Crest Trail, and two years later he pioneered a hike of the Continental Divide Trail, the first hiker to complete such a transnational adventure. "After this, I hung up my boots," he said. In a 1995 interview with Peter Olive of *Backpacker* magazine, Ryback discussed mental strength as an ingredient in his success as president of a multi-million-dollar mutual-fund company in St. Louis, Missouri: "You have to have a focused mind-set and stay on course, just as you would on a long trail."

Early hikers to complete the AT in sections were Myron H. Avery, of Lubec, Maine, from 1920 to 1936; the second was George W. Outerbridge of Philadelphia (usually with hiking companions) from 1932 to 1939. In his writings about trail conditions, Outerbridge emphasized that if the AT was made too easy, it "would not be so much fun." Mary Kilpatrick, also from Philadelphia, completed the AT in sections by 1939.

Unknown to the AT Conference founders, leaders, and experienced hikers until 1993 was a remarkable hike in 1936 from Maine to Georgia by six Boy Scouts, ages 15 to 17, from the Bronx in New York City. Harry (Pop) O'Grady, a Scout leader, and a group of WW I veterans organized and shaped the hike with a support truck that took food to the boys at regular intervals. "At the time, we really didn't know what a feat this had been," said one of the group, Max Gordon, who now lives in Beverly Hills, Florida. The US Army veterans and the truck were their lifeline. "We were poor kids. We couldn't have done it without them," he said to Judy Jenner, editor of *Appalachian Trailway News*, the newsletter of the AT Conference. Some of the boys were ready to quit after the snow and drifts in Maine, but they stayed together, determined to finish.

The highly publicized father and son team of Chuck Ebersole (a retired US Navy chief) and his 17-year-old son Johnny hiked the AT in 1964 with Snuffy, their beagle. Their diaries are heartwarming adventure stories to be appreciated by all families. Only once, in a dangerous storm near Standing Indian Mtn., in their Georgia-to-Maine journey did the question of continuing arise. "We came within a snap of the fingers of quitting today," Johnny said. Chuck hiked the AT again in 1966 with his youngest son, Mike.

Some of the outstanding hikers of the AT whose journeys have received considerable national recognition since the 1970s are Edward Garvey (1970), an ATC leader and author of *Appalachian Hiker: Adventure of a Lifetime and Hiking Trails in the Mid-Atlantic States;* Warren Doyle (from his first time in 1973 to his 10th time in 1995) who with a group of other AT hikers founded the Appalachian Long Distance Hikers Association (ALDHA), which holds an annual gathering of experienced hikers and others interested in long-distance hiking; and Dan (Wingfoot) Bruce, who has hiked the AT seven times (1985, and 1987 through 1992). In his 1987 Golden Anniversary Expedition hike, the 50th year since the AT had become one continuous link, his leadership brought unparalleled public attention to the AT and the ATC. He is author of *The Thru-Hiker's Planning Guide* and annually *The Thru-Hiker's Handbook.* He plans a network project to survey and publish information on all the common wildflowers seen along the AT. Bill Erwin from Burlington, North Carolina, with help from his friends and Seeing Eye dog, Orient, completed the AT in 1990. Among his current interests are the Irwin Ministries, founded in 1994, and hostels for AT hikers in remote locations of the trail. He is author of *Blind Courage* and a children's book, *Orient.*

The first known hikers from North Carolina to complete the AT were Joseph Marion, from Winston-Salem, in 1972 and Marjorie Fowler, from Pittsboro, in 1974. Between 1974 and 2003, 415 North Carolinians made the journey. They represent 108 different cities and towns in a wide cross section of the state.

The name and the concept of this supertrail belong solely to Benton MacKaye, a forester and author from Shirley Center, Massachusetts. He has said that he thought of it in the early 1900s, before the Long Trail was begun in Vermont in 1910. It was in that year that James P. Taylor, a Vermont schoolmaster, established the Green Mountain Club and the concept of the Long Trail from Canada to Massachusetts. Others who had long-trail and connecting-trail concepts were Philip W. Ayers, a New Hampshire forester, and Allen Chamberlain, a Boston newspaper columnist and early president of the Appalachian Mountain Club (founded in 1876). They formed the New England Trail Conference in 1916. One of the conference's goals was to connect the New England trails, a linkage that remarkably resembles the later path of the AT.

Two other founding fathers were US forester William Hall, who envisioned a link with the southern Appalachians, and Will S. Monroe, professor and seer of the Green Mountain Club. Monroe's concept was to connect the New England trails to trails in New York and New Jersey. In December 1921, Monroe's friend, J. Ashton Allis, proposed connecting the trails as far as the

Pennsylvania state line. Two months before Allis's proposal the *Journal of the American Institute of Architects* carried MacKaye's article "An Appalachian Trail: A Project in Regional Planning." The response to a singular name for the trails was immediate, and within a year the Palisades Trail Conference (which later became part of the New York–New Jersey Trail Conference) began construction of a 6.0-mi section between Lake Tiorati Circle and Arden to connect with another trail in Palisades Interstate Park. The trail opened on Sunday, October 7, 1923, the first and original section of the AT. (The entire AT design was initially completed on August 15, 1937, but considerable relocation was to follow.)

In 1926 the leadership of Arthur Perkins of Hartford, Connecticut, began to translate MacKaye's dream and proposal into reality, but it was Myron H. Avery of Lubec, Maine, who probably more than any other leader was instrumental in implementing MacKaye's proposals. He worked and coordinated agreements with government agencies, including the important CCC, and thousands of volunteers to complete the AT. He was the first president of the Potomac Appalachian Trail Club, formed in November 1927 in Washington, DC, and served as chairman of the Appalachian Trail Conference from 1930 to 1952. In his final conference report he gave what has since become a classic definition of the AT: "Remote for detachment, narrow for chosen company, winding for leisure, lonely for contemplation, it beckons not merely north and south but upward to the body, mind, and soul of man."

Congress created the National Trails System Act in 1968 and gave further protection to the AT with the Appalachian Trail Act in 1978. In 2004 less than 10.7 mi of the AT remain unprotected. Affected are about 10,596 acres, of which 4,918 (48 tracts) are in Tennessee/North Carolina for 1.5 mi. Congressional appropriations to the NPS for this purpose will determine additional protective purchases.

AT mileage in North Carolina is 310 mi, most of which (209.5 mi) frequently weaves back and forth on the Tennessee border between Doe Knob in the Smokies and Elk Park NE of Roan Mtn. The AT is jointly maintained by private clubs of the ATC, USFS, and NPS. The Nantahala Hiking Club maintains 58.7 mi from the Georgia–North Carolina state line to the Nantahala River at Wesser on US-19. From there the Smoky Mountains Hiking Club maintains 100.4 mi to Davenport Gap at NC-284/TN-32. For the next 92.5 mi, the Carolina Mountain Club maintains the AT to Spivey Gap, US-19W. At that point the Tennessee Eastman Hiking Club maintains 60.2 mi to Elk Park (and

66.7 mi exclusively in Tennessee, which takes the AT to the Virginia state line 3.5 mi S of Damascus).

Hikers on the AT should acquire the latest edition of the *AT Guide to Tennessee–North Carolina* and *AT Guide to North Carolina–Georgia*. If not available in the local bookstore, the guidebooks can be ordered from the ATC, P.O. Box 807, Harpers Ferry, WV 25425; 304-535-6331.

Access: To reach the AT at the Georgia–North Carolina state line at Bly Gap (3,840 ft.), begin in GA at US-76, Dicks Creek Gap (2,675 ft.), 11.0 mi E from Hiawassee and 18.0 mi W from Clayton. After 4.3 mi arrive at Plumorchard Gap Shelter, and at 8.6 mi arrive at the state line at a cleared crest. If beginning at the N end of the AT in the state, follow US-19E 1.6 mi W from Elk Park NC, or 16.0 mi E from Hampton TN.

The following information is a condensed listing of the major locations and prominent features of the AT through NC. Water is at all shelters except No Business Knob and Apple House shelters, and the letter *w* follows other places with water listed. Milepoints are listed north to south and south to north. Features include shelters, post offices, highway crossings, support services, and other trail connections. Bold type numbers (the first is 362 for Betty Creek Gap Trail) are for the purpose of matching trails in the book to the pocket maps. Beginning with Russell Field Trail, 363, they run W into TN and are not described in this book. The other connecting trails (that are not numbered here) run E into NC. They are described and numbered under GSMNP, chapter 7.

Appalachian National Scenic Trail

Milepoints		*Location and Prominent Features*
N to S	*S to N*	
		The first 75.6 mi of the AT are in GA, beginning at Springer Mtn.
310.0	0.0	Bly Gap, NC-GA state line (3,840 ft.); nearest all-weather road is 8.6 mi S on US-76 in GA (w)
308.5	1.5	Court House Bald (4,650 ft.)
307.0	3.0	Muskrat Creek Shelter
306.3	3.7	Whiteoak Stamp, spring E (w)
306.0	4.0	Jct W with Chunky Gal Trail, 5.2 mi to US-64
303.0	7.0	Deep Gap (4,330 ft.); FR-71 leads 6.0 mi W to US-64 (w)

Milepoints		Location and Prominent Features
N to S	*S to N*	
203.1	7.9	Standing Indian Shelter
300.6	9.4	Standing Indian Mtn. (5,490 ft.); a rocky heath bald with excellent views of GA and the Tullulah River gorge (w); Lower Trail Ridge Trail, 4.1 mi N
397.7	12.3	Beech Gap (4,508 ft) (w)
294.9	15.1	Timber Ridge Trail, 2.3 mi N
294.5	15.5	Carter-Gap Shelter (4,550 ft.)
290.8	19.2	Betty Creek Trail (USFS #367), 0.3 mi to FR-67 (w)
289.9	20.1	Mooney Gap, FR-67-2, 8.0 mi W to Standing Indian Campground
288.6	21.4	Bear Pen Trail, 2.5 mi N to FR-67
288.3	21.7	Albert Mtn. (5,280 ft.) (named for the grandfather of A. Rufus Morgan); fire tower and outstanding views of Coweeta Experimental Forest
287.7	22.3	Big Spring Gap Shelter
282.4	27.6	Rock Gap Shelter (3,750 ft.)
282.3	27.7	Rock Gap/Standing Indian Campground, FR-67 access, 1.5 mi W
281.7	28.3	Wallace Gap (3,738 ft.); Old US-64; town of Franklin: lodging, groceries, campground, 15.0 mi E
278.6	31.4	Winding Stair Gap, US-64; town of Franklin: lodging, groceries, restaurant, PO, 10.0 mi E
277.7	32.3	Campsites (w)
274.9	35.1	Siler Bald Shelter, 0.5 mi E and Siler Bald Mtn. (5,216 ft.) (named in honor of William Siler, great-grandfather of Rufus Morgan)
272.7	37.3	Wayah Gap (4,180 ft.); cross SR-1310
270.4	39.6	Jct W with yellow-blazed Bartram Trail and Wine Spring
268.5	41.5	Wayah Bald Observation Tower (5,342 ft.) and John B. Byrne Memorial
267.9	42.1	E jct with Bartram Trail
266.3	43.7	Licklog Gap (4,408 ft.) (w)
264.0	46.0	Burningtown Gap (4,250 ft.), SR-1397
262.8	47.2	Cold Springs Shelter

433

Milepoints		*Location and Prominent Features*
N to S	*S to N*	
262.1	47.9	Copper Bald (5,249 ft.); scenic view of Nantahala River Valley
261.7	48.3	Tellico Bald (5,130 ft.), laurel
261.5	48.5	Black Bald (5,000 ft.), rhododendron
260.9	49.1	Rocky Bald (5,180 ft.), heath bald of rhododendron and azaleas
259.2	50.8	Tellico Gap (3,850 ft.), FR-Otter Creek, leads E to SR-1310
257.8	52.2	Wesser Bald Fire Tower (4,627 ft.)
257.0	53.0	Wesser Bald Shelter; Wesser Creek Trail, E, 3.5 mi to SR-1107
255.4	54.6	Jumpup Lookout (4,000 ft.)
252.1	57.9	A. Rufus Morgan Shelter
251.3	58.7	US-19, Wesser, NC (1,650 ft.), lodging, groceries, and restaurant
251.2	58.8	Cross Nantahala River bridge
250.1	60.9	Tyre Top (3,760 ft.)
248.2	61.8	Grassy Gap (3,050 ft.) (w)
244.4	65.6	Sassafras Gap Lean-to
243.2	66.8	Cheoah Bald (5,062 ft.), magnificent panoramas
242.9	67.1	Bellcollar Gap; W terminus of Bartram Trail
240.8	69.2	Locust Cove Gap
237.7	72.3	Stekoah Gap (3,165 ft.); jct with Sweetwater Creek Rd (NC-143)
235.3	74.7	Brown Fork Gap Shelter
233.3	76.7	Jct W with Wauchecha Bald Trail, 1.2 mi to Wauchecha Bald (4,385 ft.)
230.1	79.9	Yellow Creek Gap; Tuskeegee Rd (SR-1242) E to NC-28
229.2	80.8	Cable Gap Shelter
228.2	81.8	High Top (3,786 ft.), highest in Yellow Creek range, no vistas
226.4	83.6	Walker Gap (3,450 ft.); jct with Yellow Creek Mountain Trail, W

	Milepoints		*Location and Prominent Features*
	N to S	*S to N*	
	223.7	86.3	NC-28, Fontana Dam, NC, lodging, groceries, restaurant, recreational facilities, PO (Permit required for camping in the Smokies)
	222.6	87.4	Fontana Dam Shelter
	222.3	87.7	Fontana Dam Visitor Center
	221.9	88.1	Cross Fontana Dam; (Little Tennessee River) S boundary of Great Smoky Mountains NP
	217.9	92.1	Shuckstack Mtn. (4,020 ft.); Shuckstack Tower for scenic views
	216.7	93.3	Birch Spring Shelter (3,830 ft.)
	214.4	95.6	Doe Knob (4,520 ft.); jct with Gregory Bald Trail into TN
	211.3	98.7	Mollies Ridge Shelter (4,600 ft.) 0.1 mi ahead to Devils Tater Patch
434	208.8	101.2	Russell Field Shelter (4,400 ft.); Russell Field Trail descends W 3.5 mi toward Cades Cove Campground, TN
	205.9	104.1	Spence Field Shelter (4,890 ft.); Eagle Creek Trail descends E leading to Fontana Lake; Bote Mtn. Rd leads W 6.6 mi to Cades Cove Rd in TN
	105.5	104.5	Side Trail E, Jenkins Ridge Trail leading S in NC
	204.7	105.3	Rocky Top (5,440 ft.)
	204.1	105.9	East Peak of Thunderhead (5,530 ft.)
	203.8	106.2	Beechnut Gap (4,840 ft.) (w)
	202.0	108.0	Starky Gap (4,530 ft.)
	199.6	110.4	Derrick Knob Shelter (4,880 ft.)
435	199.4	110.6	Sams Gap (4,840 ft.); AT goes E, Greenbrier Ridge Trail descends W 5.1 mi to Tremont Rd, TN (w)
	197.4	112.6	Cold Spring Knob (5,240 ft.)
436	197.3	112.9	Miry Ridge Trail exits W to Elkmont Campground, TN
	196.8	113.2	Buckeye Gap (4,820 ft.) (w)
	194.1	115.9	Silers Bald Shelter (5,440 ft.) (named after Jesse Siler, great-great uncle of A. Rufus Morgan); Two shelters; scenic view of Mt. LeConte NE
	193.7	116.3	Welch Ridge Trail descends E to High Rocks and connects with Hazel Creek trails in NC

Milepoints		*Location and Prominent Features*
N to S	*S to N*	
192.4	117.6	Double Springs Gap Shelter (5,590 ft.); Goshen Prong **437** Trail exits W to Little River Rd in TN
190.1	119.9	Mt. Buckley (6,580 ft.)
189.5	120.5	Clingmans Dome (6,643 ft.), highest elevation on the entire AT; Tower provides panoramic views, 0.5 mi to parking area and Clingmans Dome Rd (named for Thomas L. Clingman, US Senator, explorer) (w); W terminus of MST
186.1	123.9	Mt. Collins (6,190 ft.) and Mt. Collins Shelter; Sugarloaf Mountain Trail exits W in TN Fork **438** Ridge Trail/MST exits E in NC
183.3	126.7	Indian Gap; Road Prong Trail exits W 3.3 mi to **439** Chimney Tops parking area in TN
181.6	128.4	Newfound Gap (5,040 ft.) and highway (formerly US-441); GSMNP headquarters W and Gatlinburg; Cherokee E (w)
179.9	129.1	Sweat Heifer Trail exits E 3.6 mi to Kephart Prong Shelter (5,830 ft.)
178.9	131.1	Boulevard Trail (6,030 ft.) exits W to Mt. LeConte **440** and the Jumpoff, outstanding vistas
178.6	131.4	Ice Water Spring Shelter (5,900 ft.)
177.7	132.2	Charlies Bunion (5,400 ft.) Outstanding view of the Smokies and Mt. LeConte; crowded by visitors, dangerous in icy weather
177.4	132.3	Dry Sluice Gap (5,380 ft); Dry Sluice Gap Trail exits E to connect with Bradley Fork and Kephart Prong Trails in NC
172.5	137.5	Bradleys View (5,800 ft.) provides excellent vistas into Bradley Fork gorge
171.2	138.8	Pecks Corner Shelter (5,850 ft.), 0.4 mi E, Hughes Ridge Trail exits E, 11.8 mi to Smokemont Campground in NC
168.5	141.5	Mt. Sequoyah (5,980 ft.)
167.0	143.0	Mt. Chapman (6,220 ft.), forests of balsam and spruce
166.0	144.0	Tri-Corner Knob Shelter (5,920 ft.) Balsam Mountain Trail exits E 5.8 mi to Laurel Gap Shelter in NC

Milepoints		*Location and Prominent Features*
N to S	*S to N*	
164.2	145.8	Guyot Spring (6,200 ft.)
164.1	145.9	Mt. Guyot Spur (6,180 ft.) leads to summit of Mt. Guyot (6,621 ft.)
162.2	147.8	Maddron Bald Trail exits W to Snake Den Mountain and Indian Camp Creek Trails in TN
160.8	149.2	Camel Gap (4,700 ft.); Yellow Creek Trail goes E 5.2 mi to Walnut Bottoms in NC
158.3	151.7	Cosby Knob Shelter (4,800 ft.)
156.0	154.0	Low Gap (4,240 ft.) Low Gap Trail exits E 2.3 mi to Walnut Bottoms in NC; Cosby Creek Trail exits W 2.5 mi to Cosby Campground in TN
155.5	154.5	Mt. Cammerer side trail goes W 0.6 mi to summit (5,025 ft.), spectacular 360-degree panorama
152.2	157.8	Chestnut Branch Trail, E 2.0 mi to Big Creek ranger sta and campground
151.2	158.8	Davenport Gap Shelter (2,200 ft.)
150.3	159.7	Davenport Gap, TN-32, NC-284 (1,975 ft.), groceries E 2.0 mi, camping another 0.5 mi
148.7	161.3	Big Pigeon River bridge (1,400 ft.)
148.5	161.5	I-40, 15.0 mi W to Newport, TN
147.9	162.1	Waterville School Rd, W, 0.2 mi to groceries, camping, lodging
145.6	164.4	Painter Branch, camping (w)
143.2	166.8	Snowbird Mtn. (4,263 ft.), excellent scenic views
140.7	169.3	Deep Gap, 0.2 mi E to Groundhog Creek Shelter; Ground Hog Creek Trail leads E 2.3 mi to I-40
138.4	171.6	Harmon Den Mtn. (3,840 ft.), Rube Rock Trail E, 4.0 mi to I-40
137.8	172.2	Brown Gap, campsites; jct with FR-148A, 1.3 mi SE to FR-148 and S to I-40, exit 7, 4.4 mi (w)
135.1	174.9	Max Patch Rd (SR-1182), 1.6 mi E to FR-148
134.3	175.7	Max Patch Mtn. (4,629 ft.) Panoramic views of the Smokies, TN Valley, Mt. Mitchell
129.4	180.6	Roaring Fork Shelter
128.9	181.1	Lemon Gap, SR-1182 and TN-107 (3,550 ft.)
128.0	181.1	Walnut Mtn. Shelter

441

Milepoints		*Location and Prominent Features*
N to S	*S to N*	
125.2	184.8	Bluff Mtn. (4,686 ft.)
123.1	186.9	Big Rock Spring
121.1	188.9	Garenflo Gap (2,500 ft.) FR, E; Shut-in Trail, NW, 2.0 mi to SR-1183
117.7	192.3	Deer Park Mtn. Shelter
114.5	195.5	Hot Springs, NC (1,326 ft.); Lodging, groceries, PO, restaurant, laundromat; roads US-25/70 and NC-209
113.1	196.9	Lovers Leap Rock; scenic view of the French Broad River
111.2	198.8	Pump Gap; Pump Gap Trail leads W as alternate AT route to French Broad River
109.6	200.4	Campsites
108.6	201.4	Tanyard Gap (2,278 ft.) cross US-25/70
106.2	203.8	Rich Mtn. Fire Tower (3,643 ft.); panoramic views of Black Mtn. range and the Smokies (w)
103.5	206.5	Spring Mtn. Shelter (3,300 ft.)
99.8	210.2	Allen Gap (2,234 ft.); roads NC-208 and TN-70, groceries
94.9	215.1	Little Laurel Shelter
93.1	216.9	Camp Creek Bald (4,844 ft.); jct with Pounding Mill Trail, S 6.4 mi to NC-208, 0.2 mi NW to fire tower, scenic
91.9	218.4	Blackstack Cliffs, superb views of N and W TN
90.7	219.3	Spring (w)
88.4	221.6	Jct Fork Ridge Trail, S, 2.0 mi to FR-111
88.2	221.8	Jerry Cabin Shelter
86.3	223.7	Big Butt (4,838 ft.); campsites (w)
85.8	224.2	Shelton gravestones; great-great nephew and other relatives live S of here in Big Creek and Laurel Creek valleys
82.3	227.7	Flint Mountain Shelter (3,550 ft.)
79.6	230.4	Devil's Fork Gap (3,107 ft.), NC-212, N to US-23
73.6	236.4	Hogback Ridge Shelter
72.9	237.1	High Rock (4,460 ft.)
71.1	238.9	Sams Gap (3,800 ft.); road US-23, groceries, restaurant 3.0 mi E

Milepoints		Location and Prominent Features
N to S	*S to N*	
64.6	245.4	Big Bald (5,516 ft.); grassy bald with spectacular views
64.4	245.6	Big Stamp, campsites (w) 0.3 mi W
64.4	246.5	Bald Mtn. Shelter
62.1	247.9	Little Bald (5,185 ft.)
59.4	250.6	Trail to High Rocks (4,100 ft.)
58.3	251.7	Campsites (w)
57.8	252.1	Spivey Gap (3,200 ft.); road US-19W (w)
52.9	257.1	No Business Knob Shelter (no water)
50.5	259.5	Temple Hill Gap (2,850 ft)
46.6	263.4	Nolichucky River (1,700 ft.); Erwin TN; lodging, groceries, restaurant, PO, 1.8 mi W
45.3	264.7	Nolichucky Whitewater Exp., lodging, groceries, restaurant, campsites
42.4	267.6	Curley Maple Gap Shelter (3,080 ft.)
38.3	271.7	Indian Grave Gap (3,360 ft.); 3.0 mi W to USFS Rock Creek Rec Area
37.2	272.8	FR-230, N; 50 yd. to spring (w)
36.0	274.0	Beauty Spot (4,337 ft.); grassy scenic bald (w)
33.9	276.1	FR-230, W
32.9	277.1	Unaka Mtn. (5,180 ft.); summit of conifers
30.2	279.8	Cherry Gap Shelter
27.5	282.5	Iron Mtn. Gap; TN-107/NC-226 roads (3,723 ft.); groceries 0.5 mi E
23.4	286.6	Greasy Creek Gap, campsites (w)
21.5	288.5	Clyde Smith Shelter
18.4	291.6	Hughes Gap (4,040 ft.); accommodations 2.0 mi E; town of Buladean E on NC-26, 5.3 mi; town of Burbank W, 3.2 mi
15.7	294.3	Spur trail to Roan High Bluff
15.1	294.3	Roan High Knob (6,285 ft.); Cloudland Rhododendron Gardens; summit forested with evergreens
15.1	294.9	Roan High Knob Shelter
13.7	296.3	Carvers Gap (5,512 ft.); TN-143/NC-261 roads (w)
10.4	299.6	Stan Murray Shelter in Low Gap (5,050 ft.)

Milepoints		Location and Prominent Features
N to S	*S to N*	
8.7	301.3	Yellow Mtn. Gap (4,682 ft.); site of John Sevier's "Overmountain Men," historic Bright's Trace, and Overmountain Victory Trail; Overmountain Shelter 0.3 mi E
6.9	303.1	Little Hump Mtn. (Big Yellow Mtn.) (5,459 ft.); grassy balds with extraordinary views
5.4	304.6	Hump Mtn. (5,587 ft.); superb panorama of Doe River Valley NW, Whitetop and Mt. Rogers in VA, Beech Mtn. to NE, and Grandfather Mtn. to E
0.5	309.5	Apple House Shelter (no water)
0.0	310.0	US-19E, Elk Park, NC; lodging, groceries, restaurant, PO, 2.3 mi E (AT continues 69.0 mi NW through TN to Damascus, VA)

Blue Ridge Parkway

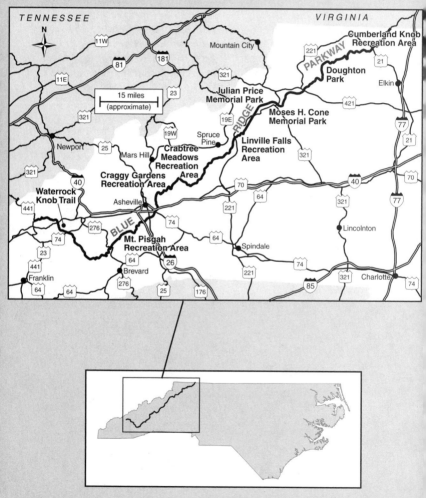

Introductions to Trail Areas

The nation's longest and most scenic skyway is 469 mi of which 241 mi are in NC. There are more than 60 trails in between and in eight memorial parks or recreational areas. The rec/park areas are listed below in order of mileposts N to S, plus the parkway's highest trail. The MST (completed, planned, or under construction) is on BRP property for 196 mi. Full service at the rec centers is closed in the winter, but trails are open. Some trails may not be accessible due to weather conditions. The BRP headquarters is in Asheville.

245

Chapter 6

Blue Ridge Parkway

*The Parkway is American history, past, present,
and future waiting to be enjoyed.*
—Harley B. Jolley

The Blue Ridge Parkway (BRP), a two-lane 469-mi highway described as the most scenic in America, averages 3,000 ft. in elev and runs along the majestic crest of the Blue Ridge Mtns. In the beginning it was a trail made by surveyors, landscape architects, and naturalists. "They stamped out a trail with their hobnailed boots / Cutting blazes on trees as they went / Over ridges and hollows they marked the way / For the men and machine that would follow," wrote Albert Clarke Haygard Jr., in his 1959 *The Skyline Saga.* It is a link between Shenandoah National Park at Rockfish Gap in Virginia and Cherokee at the edge of Great Smoky Mtns. National Park in North Carolina. It is a "road of unlimited horizons, a grand balcony," wrote Harley E. Jolley in 1969 in The Blue Ridge Parkway. It is also a classic piece of engineering that has preserved the physical and cultural aspects of the Blue Ridge.

Although the NPS archives have not identified a single originator of the BRP idea, a number of historians give the credit to Harry F. Byrd, a U.S. senator from Virginia. (Another claim for the credit is from Theodore E. Straus of Maryland, a member of the Public Works Administration [PWA], who said in 1962, "I am the originator of the mountain road connecting the Skyline Drive to the Smokies." Fred L. Weede, from Asheville and one of the leaders in the routing of the BRP through Asheville, said in 1954 that he recognized Straus as "the father of the idea.") Senator Byrd accompanied President Franklin D. Roosevelt on an inspection tour of the CCC camps in the Shenandoah National Park in August 1933. When the president expressed his enjoyment of such natural beauty, Byrd suggested an extension of the mountaintop route to the Smokies. President Roosevelt liked the suggestion, even stated that it should begin in New England. Senator Byrd later stated that the president said, "You and Ickes (Harold L. Ickes, Roosevelt's secretary of the interior, who was with them on the CCC tour) get together for the right of way." It was not that simple. Not only did a political controversy arise over the routing through North Carolina and Tennessee, but a final right of way was not deeded until October 22, 1968. (The original construction route was long opposed by the owners of Grandfather Mtn.) Initially the plan called for the BRP to be a toll road, something North Carolina governor J. C. B. Ehringhaus opposed. After considerable political debate, Secretary Ickes decided in 1934 to eliminate any Tennessee routing, probably due to the strong influence of Ambassador Josephus Daniels, a North Carolinian and close friend of President Roosevelt and Secretary Ickes.

On September 11, 1935, the first rocks were blasted on the BRP near the Cumberland Knob area, and 52 years later the missing link (6.5 mi that included the engineering wonder of the Linn Cove Viaduct on the E slope of Grandfather Mtn.) was completed and dedicated September 11, 1987. The day of dedication was one of great pride for those who had spent a lifetime as part of this innovative dream. Many had not been aware of the political perils in its construction. Once begun, Virginia and North Carolina were determined to complete it with or without federal assistance. Congress debated the management of the parkway as much as or more than its financing. In July 1934, Secretary Ickes notified the NPS that he desired that agency to maintain and administer the parkway. But Congress had to approve this idea, and on April 24, 1936, North Carolina congressman Robert Lee Doughton introduced the bill. "I think that this is the most ridiculous undertaking that has ever been presented to Congress . . . a colossal steal," argued Jesse P. Wolcott, a congressman from Michigan. The bill barely passed on June 20, 1936 (145 for, 131 against, and 147 abstaining). It was approved quickly by the Senate, and President Roosevelt signed the bill into public law (#848) on June 22, 1936.

The BRP is a popular tourist attraction (nearly 20 million visitors annually) with a wide range of cultural and recreational facilities. There are more visitors in July than other months, and October is second. Its 241.0 mi through North Carolina begin at milepost 217 in Cumberland Knob Park. Along the way are facilities for camping, fishing, bicycling, picnicking, horseback riding (Cone Park), hiking, and cross-country skiing. In addition there are lodges, historic exhibits, museums, parks, and mountain-culture preserves. Campgrounds are at Doughton Park, Price Park, Linville Falls, Crabtree Meadows, and Mt. Pisgah. There are more than 60 trails: some are graded, manicured, and short; some are simple pathways for views of valleys below; others are rugged and natural into deep coves or high jagged rocks. Long segments of the MST follow its narrow corridor, some of which follow older trails, and others constructed only for the MST. For example, the Tanawha Trail is a crown jewel of design and natural beauty of the E slopes of Grandfather Mtn. A number of BRP trails join a network of trails in the adjoining national forests.

Bicyclists are allowed to travel the entire distance of the parkway if adhering to the BRP and Department of Transportation regulations. For long journeys, planning is essential. Bikers should contact the BRP office in Asheville (828-298-0398) for information on regulations, safety, emergencies, camping, and services. Horse traffic is prohibited on the parkway or its shoulders. (Crossings are allowed at the Roanoke Trail in Virginia, Moses Cone Memorial Park, and at Basin Creek Fire Road in North Carolina.) All trails are foot trails only, unless otherwise indicated.

Because of the density of visitors and user damage to the natural environment, the NPS has a number of regulations for the benefit of all. Some of them are listed here to assist hikers in their planning. Camping is not allowed on any BRP trail—only in the campgrounds or in primitive camps with a permit. No alcohol or open containers of alcohol are allowed in passenger compartments of vehicles. Pets must be kept on leashes. Quiet hours in the campgrounds are 10:00PM to 6:00AM. Weapons are unlawful (including bows, air guns, and slingshots). Fires are allowed only at designated campgrounds. All plants and animals are protected—only berries, nuts, and edible fruits may be gathered for personal consumption. Maximum speed is 45 mph. No vehicles may be parked overnight on the BRP without advance notice to and permission from a ranger (see district telephone numbers below). No swimming in lakes or ponds and no rock climbing unless permission is obtained from a ranger of the NPS. Emergency dispatch telephone number is 800-PARKWATCH (800-727-5928) for emergencies, accidents, fires and criminal activity.

Address: For general BRP information call 828-298-0398; for district ranger offices (may be weekdays only): Highlands District Ranger (336-372-8568) (between mp 216.7 and 303.0) at Bluffs near Laurel Springs; address is 49800, Blue Ridge Parkway, Laurel Springs, NC 28644. Pisgah District Ranger (between mp 304 and 469) (828-298-0281) at Oteen in Ashville; address is Oteen Maintenance, 51 Ranger Drive, Asheville, NC 28805. For road conditions: www.nps.gov/blri.

For written information ask for, or pick up at visitor centers, the "Strip Map" or Blue Ridge Parkway Directory. In addition, the Blue Ridge Parkway Association provides an "Info Pack," also free, by writing BRPA, 199 Hemphill Knob Rd, Asheville, NC 28803.

The most detailed description of trails on the BRP, available at bookstores and BRP visitor centers, is in *Walking the Blue Ridge* by Leonard M. Adkins and *Hiking the Blue Ridge Parkway* by Randy Johnson.

Cumberland Knob Recreation Area (mp 217.5)

The Cumberland Knob Recreation Area is a 1,000-acre forest and park, 1.0 mi from the Virginia state line. It is the first recreation area constructed as part of the first 12.7 mi of the BRP in 1935–36. It is probably named for William Augustus, Scottish Duke of Cumberland (1721–65). Picnic areas and a visitor information center are open May 1 to October 31. Camping is not available. Elev 2,740 ft. Galax VA, is 8.0 mi N on NC/VA-89. (USGS Map: Cumberland Knob)

Cumberland Knob Trail (0.6 mi); *Gully Creek Trail* (2.5 mi)   **442-**
   Length and Difficulty: 3.1 mi combined, easy to strenuous   **443**
   Trailheads and Description: Follow the signs to the information center, turn R, and reach the summit (2,855 ft.) at 0.3 mi. Circle the knob and return through picnic areas, or descend on the Gully Creek Trail. Follow the Gully Creek Trail L of the visitor center, descending on a well-graded trail with switchbacks to Gully Creek at 0.8 mi. Trail crisscrosses the stream and begins ascent on switchbacks at 1.3 mi. A scenic knob is at 1.9 mi. Return by the Cumberland Knob, or take a shorter trail, R, to the parking lot.

Fox Hunters Paradise Trail (mp 218.6)   **444**
The trail is an easy 0.2-mi path that provides a scenic view of forests in western Surry County where fox hunters once listened to their hounds from High Piney Knoll.

Little Glade Pond Trail (mp 230)   **445**
The trail is an easy 0.3-mi loop around the site of a turbine-type mill operated about 1895 to 1915.

Doughton Park (mp 238.5–244.7)

Doughton Park is named in honor of Robert Lee "Muley Bob" Doughton, an enduring congressman (1911–53) from NC's 9th district, and a leader and advocate for establishing and developing the BRP. The 6,000-acre park has Bluff Lodge (open May through October), svc sta, camp store, campground, backcountry camping, picnic area, nature studies, special exhibits, fishing and

446   more than 30 mi of trails. Its most frequently used trail is the scenic Fodder Stack Trail. It goes 0.7 mi NE from the parking lot at the lodge to Wildcat Rock and to Fodder Stack outcropping. From here are impressive views of the Basin Creek watershed and the pioneer cabin of Martin and Janie Caudill seen deep in the valley. Along the trail are Fraser magnolia, hemlock, rhododendron, minnie-bush, white moss, and, for this far S, a rare grove of bigtooth aspen. All other trails are interconnecting; they form loops that converge as a funnel into Basin Cove. Backpack camping is allowed near the confluence of Basin and Cove Creeks, but a permit is required from the ranger's office. There is a trail system signboard at Alligator Back Overlook, mp 242.2. (USGS Map: Whitehead)

Address: District Ranger, Rte 1, Box 263, Laurel Springs, NC 28644; 910-372-8568.

447-   *Bluff Mountain Trail*
452   **Length and Difficulty:** 7.5 mi, easy to moderate

      Connecting Trails: Cedar Ridge Trail (4.3 mi; strenuous, elev change 2,265 ft); Bluff Ridge Trail (2.8 mi; strenuous, elev change 2,229 ft.); Basin Cove Trail (3.3 mi, moderate); Grassy Gap Trail (6.5 mi, strenuous, elev change 1,805 ft.); Flat Rock Ridge Trail (5 mi, strenuous, elev change 1,880 ft.)

      Special Features: Brinegar and Caudill cabins, Bluff Mtn.

      Trailhead and Description: Park at the Brinegar Cabin parking lot, mp 238.5 (3,508 ft.). The Brinegar Cabin has a handicraft exhibit. The cabin was the home (begun in 1885) of Martin Brinegar (1856–1925), his wife, the former Caroline Jones (1863–1943), and their children. From the parking lot follow the trail sign 0.2 mi to the trailheads of Bluff Mtn. Trail, R, and the Cedar Ridge Trail, L. A long loop of 16.5 mi can be made by going in either direction to include the Flat Rock Ridge Trail, or a shorter loop of 12.9 mi if using the primitive Bluff Ridge Trail. The description below follows these trails in a counterclockwise route. (The MST follows the Bluff Mtn. Trail S to Basin Cove Overlook, mp 244.7, but it will go N on a separate route before leaving the BRP on its E route. See appendix A.)

      Begin the yellow-blazed Bluff Mountain Trail on an easy grade of grassy fields, wildflowers, and groves of white pine, and after 1.0 mi enter the campground for long RVs. Cross the BRP and briefly parallel the tent and small RV section of the campground. Cross the BRP at Low Notch (mp 239.9) at 1.7 mi and ascend slightly to open and more level areas. Cross the BRP again to arrive at the restaurant and svc sta at 2.6 mi. From here go past the souvenir shop into the forest, come out to the BRP, and cross. Immediately cross the picnic road and follow the trail through the heath and grassy meadows of Bluff Mtn. (3,792 ft.) to the picnic parking area at 3.9 mi. Continue ahead to the jct of primitive Bluff Ridge Trail, L at 4.2 mi.

(The primitive Bluff Ridge Trail passes a picnic shelter after 240 ft. and follows the ridge of the Alligator Back escarpment. There are views of the Cove Creek drainage and Flat Rock Ridge. Descend on the red-blazed trail to a gap after 0.5 mi, ascend to Brooks Knob at 0.7 mi, and consistently descend for 1.2 mi to the trail terminus and jct with the Grassy Gap Trail [fire road] R and ahead, and the Basin Creek Trail, L. The Grassy Gap Trail goes 4.7 mi up Cove Creek to the Bluff Mtn. Trail and the BRP at mp 243.9 near Grassy Gap. The Grassy Gap Trail also goes downstream from the jct with Basin Creek Trail for 1.8 mi to jct with Cedar Ridge Trail, Flat Rock Ridge Trail, and a parking area at Long Bottom Rd [SR-1728]. If hiking the Basin Creek Trail, follow the dark-blue blazed old wagon road 3.3 mi up Basin Creek. Rock-hop the creek frequently in a lush valley of poplar, oak, maple, and rhododendron. Pass L of the mouth of Caudill Branch at 1.5 mi. Reach Wildcat Branch, which flows from the L at 3.2 mi. Turn R from here and ascend 0.1 mi to an open area and the one-room cabin of Martin and Janie Caudill. Although the Caudill family had 16 children, only a few were born here. In 1916 a flood washed away most of the houses downstream and drowned some of the residents. The Caudill cabin was not damaged. Backtrack.)

Continuing on the Bluff Mtn. Trail, descend from the jct with the Bluff Ridge Trail, in the picnic area, on switchbacks to Alligator Back Overlook (mp 242.2) at 4.7 mi. Bear L and parallel the BRP to reach Bluff Mtn. Overlook (mp 243.4) at 5.8 mi. Here are views of the rock wall and cliffs of Bluff Mtn. Join the Grassy Gap Trail (fire road) and follow it 0.1 mi before leaving it R, at 6.3 mi.

(The Grassy Gap Trail descends on a green-blazed winding road to jct with Bluff Ridge Trail and Basin Creek Trail at 4.7 mi. Thirty yd. L of the jct is the grave site of Alice Caudill, a child bride, who was drowned in the 1916 flood. Downstream after 0.1 mi is the primitive campsite, and beyond the trail crosses Basin Creek to end at Long Bottom Rd at 6.5 mi.)

Proceed on the Bluff Mtn. Trail and pass through white and table mountain pine. At 7.4 mi come to jct with light-blue-blazed Flat Rock Ridge Trail, L. Continue R to a grassy area, go through a stile, and ascend to the Basin Cove Overlook at 7.5 mi (mp 244.7).

The Flat Rock Ridge Trail descends on a scenic ridge in a hardwood forest with scattered pines, two species of rhododendron, and a number of open rocky outcroppings. At 1.6 mi and 1.7 mi are some of the best views of Bluff Mtn. and the Cove Creek drainage area. At 5.0 mi reach the end of the trail at Long Bottom Rd and come to jct with the Cedar Ridge Trail and the Grassy Gap Trail. Vehicle access to this point is from the jct of the BRP and NC-18, 7.0 mi SW on the BRP from Doughton Park. Turn S on NC-18, go 5.9 mi to McGrady, turn L on Long Bottom Rd (SR-1728), and drive 7.1 mi to the parking area and gated road L. (Long Bottom Rd becomes SR-1730 en route.) (Absher is 2.5 mi ahead on Long Bottom Rd, and 3.0 mi farther is the W entrance to Stone Mtn. State Park.)

To complete the loop begin the orange-blazed Cedar Ridge Trail (90 yd. inside the gated Grassy Gap Trail gate) on a series of switchbacks for 0.6 mi. Ascend gradually along the ridgeline and park boundary in a forest of hardwoods, conifers, and laurel. At 3.5 mi begin another series of switchbacks, and at 4.3 mi return to the Bluff Mtn. Trail jct and Brinegar Cabin parking lot.

453 *Jumpinoff Rocks Trail* (mp 260.3)
Follow the easy trail 0.5 mi through a forest with beds of galax and tufts of arbutus to rocky cliffs (3,165 ft) for scenic views. Backtrack to complete 1.0 mi.

454 *The Lump Trail* (mp 264.4)
The trail leads 0.3 mi to a grassy bald with 360-degree scenic views, particularly of the Yadkin Valley.

E. B. Jeffress Park (mp 271.9)

The park has rest rooms, drinking water, and picnic tables. It is named in honor of the 1934 state highway commission chairman who crusaded for the
455 BRP. The moderate Cascades Nature Trail loops through a forest of hardwoods, laurel, and hemlock to cascades on Falls Creek. Complete the loop after 1.0 mi.

456 *Tompkins Knob Trail* (mp 272.5)
The trail is an easy 0.6-mi loop from the parking lot around the historic (log) Cool Spring Baptist Church and the Jesse Brown Cabin.

Moses H. Cone Memorial Park (mp 292.7–295)

The 3,517-acre mountain estate of Moses H. Cone (1857–1908), textile "denim king," was donated to the NPS in 1950 as a "pleasuring ground" for the public. The Southern Highlands Handicraft Guild occupies part of Cone Manor. A stable is nearby and down the mountain in front of the mansion is the 22-acre Bass Lake. To the L (W) of the manor is the Craftsman's Trail (F), **457** a 0.6-mi figure-eight self-guiding trail with medicinal herbs. There are more than 22 mi of old carriage trails that provide one-way trips, loops, and cross-trail connections for hikers, equestrians, and cross-country skiers. High pastureland, deep and damp coves, and a forest with plenty of wildlife make this area ideal for an all-day hike. Access to the network of trails (carriage roads) is from the parking area to the paved road in front of the manor and E to the gravel road at the stable. Three of the trails are N of the BRP; all others are S. The MST follows two of the trails—Rich Mountain Trail and Watkins Trail— (see appendix A). The shorter trails that connect S of the manor are the 2.5-mi Duncan Trail (F, H), the 0.5-mi Black Bottom Trail (F, H), the 1.7-mi Bass **458-** Lake Trail (F, H), the 2.3-mi Maze Trail (F, H), and the 1.7-mi Rock Creek **462** Bridge Trail (F, H). The three longest trails are described below. For the most detailed description of the carriage/horse trails at the park see *Walking the Blue Ridge* by Leonard M. Adkins. (USGS Map: Boone)

Rich Mountain Trail (4.3 mi) (F, H); *Flat Top Mountain Trail* (3.0 **463-** mi) (F, H); *Watkins Trail* (4.0 mi) (F, H) **465**

Length and Difficulty: 11.3 mi combined, moderate
Special Features: Cone Manor and cemetery
Trailheads and Description: From the parking area, walk E to the gravel road behind the stable. To the L follow the road and enter the BRP underpass to a fork at 0.1 mi. To the L is the Rich Mountain Trail, to the R is the Flat Top Mountain Trail. If hiking L, descend to a crossing of Flannery Fork Rd (SR-1541, also called Payne Branch Rd) at 0.7 mi. Follow E of Trout Lake (may be drained) to the dam, turn L, and follow switchbacks up a stream under tall hemlocks. Pass a gate at 2.2 mi. After ascending to a scenic open pasture, turn R at the curve at 2.6 mi. Reenter the forest. At 3.2 mi the MST turns sharply L off the road. (The MST descends W on its route to Price Park. See chapter 16.) Continuing on the road reach a scenic circle and advance to the top of Rich Mtn. (4,370 ft) at 4.3 mi. Backtrack to the BRP underpass.

On the Flat Top Mountain Trail ascend in a pasture. At 0.8 mi take a spur trail L and enter an avenue of Fraser fir to the Cone family cemetery. Continue on the ascent with switchbacks and reach the scenic summit of Flat Top Mtn. (4,558 ft.) at 3.0 mi. Backtrack to the stable. Begin the Watkins Trail here. From the stable go S, but turn sharply L in front of the manor (at 0.2 mi from the BRP). Descend into a forest of hemlock and white pine; go straight at a curve at 0.7 mi. Follow the well-graded switchbacks through large rhododendron slicks and groves of hemlock. At 2.8 mi keep L in a curve. (The road R is Black Bottom Trail, which leads to the Maze Trail and the Bass Lake Trail.) Pass L of a lake and spillway, and at 3.8 mi cross Penley Branch in a forest of exceptionally tall maple, oak, and hemlock. Turn R at a road used by residents and arrive at US-221 at 4.0 mi. Across the highway is the New River Inn. (It is 1.0 mi R on US-221 to Blowing Rock, 0.2 mi L to the BRP, and 2.3 mi L on the BRP to Cone Manor.)

Julian Price Memorial Park (mp 295.5–300)

Julian Price purchased this land in the early 1940s to develop it into a resort for the employees of Jefferson Standard Life Insurance Company. Because of his unexpected death in 1946, the company gave the property to the NPS with an agreement that a lake and park would bear his name. Although the area had been logged in the early part of the century, few settlers ever lived here. One early settler, probably between 1810 and 1817, was Jesse Boone, nephew of Daniel. Boone Fork, which flows N from the lake, bears his name. The 4,344-acre plateau has a developed campground with 134 tent sites (some open all year) and 60 sites for trailers (no hookups). The park is usually fully open from May 1 through October; 704-963-5911. There is also a large scenic picnic area, trout fishing, boat rentals, and hiking. The MST follows part of the Boone Fork Trail. (USGS Maps: Boone, Valle Crucis, Grandfather Mtn)

466 *Green Knob Trail*

Length and Difficulty: 2.3 mi, moderate

Trailhead and Description: From the Sims Lake parking lot (E of the picnic area on the BRP) descend to the lake, cross the bridge, and circle L. Follow up the side of Sims Creek and cross under the BRP bridge at 0.7 mi. Cross the stream in a forest of hemlock, poplar, birch, and oak to ascend Green Knob. Reach the top (3,930 ft) at 1.5 mi, and descend to the BRP parking lot.

467 *Price Lake Loop Trail*

Length and Difficulty: 2.4 mi, easy

Trailhead and Description: Follow the signs counterclockwise around the lake from any beginning point in the lakeside camping area. Cross Cold Prong stream at 0.7 mi, Boone Fork stream at 0.9 mi, and Laurel Creek at 1.6 mi. The trail is well graded and wet only in a few spots near the upstream marshes. Parts of the trail are arbored with rhododendron. Return at the dam and the parking lot to reenter the campground at 2.4 mi. At the S end of Boone Fork Overlook is access to a special 0.5-mi part of the loop that includes access to a fishing dock. It meets the guidelines of Americans with Disabilities Act.

Boone Fork Trail 468

Length and Difficulty: 4.9 mi, moderate

Trailhead and Description: From the picnic area parking lot, cross Boone Fork on a bridge to the trail system sign and enter the woods ahead for a clockwise loop. Ascend gently to the campground and pass through Section B (between campsites) at 0.6 mi to enter a low area. Ascend through a rhododendron grove and reach jct, R and L, with the Tanawha Trail (described below) at 0.7 mi. Turn R and jointly follow the Tanawha Trail to a stile and pasture at 1.1 mi. After 35 yd. the Tanawha Trail turns L, but the Boone Fork Trail picks up the MST that has come up from the S on the Tanawha Trail. Continue on the Boone Fork Trail, jointly with the MST, on an old farm road through the pasture. Keep straight at a road fork at 1.3 mi, ascend slightly in a patch of woods, and at 1.4 mi turn abruptly R at a signpost. Descend 40 yd. to a stile and enter a dense forest to the headwaters of Bee Tree Creek. Cross it 16 times, sometimes on a footbridge. At 2.6 mi turn sharply R off the old RR grade, cross Bee Tree Creek for the final time, and reach Boone Fork at 2.7 mi. Stay on the high N side of the mountain in dense rhododendron, birch, and hemlock. Ascend in a large rocky area at 3.2 mi, elevated from the cascades. Reach an old dam site, L, at 3.6 mi. Pass a large scenic rock slope to immediately leave the MST at 3.8 mi. (The MST requires rock-hopping Boone Fork on its journey upward to Rich Mtn. See appendix A.) Continue upstream on an old RR grade and exit into a partial field that has copious patches of blackberries and wild pink roses at 4.6 mi. (This is a good area for birders.) Pass a fence and return to the picnic area at 4.9 mi.

Tanawha Trail 469-472

Length and Difficulty: 13.4 mi, moderate

Connecting Trails: (Boone Fork Trail); (MST); Cold Prong Pond Trail; Upper Boone Fork Trail; (Grandfather Trail); Grandfather Mountain Access Trail; (Daniel Boone Scout Trail); (Beacon Heights Trail)

Special Features: trail design, Rough Ridge boardwalk, Linn Cove

Trailhead and Description: This exceptional trail has been designed, constructed, and supervised at the cost of $700,000. There is not a similar trail elsewhere in the state. The Cherokee Indian name means "fabulous hawk," the name they gave the mountain now called Grandfather. Markers with a feather logo are placed at strategic points on the trail. The trail parallels the BRP from the Price Lake parking area (mp 297.3) to the Beacon Heights parking area (mp 305.3). In the process it passes through pastureland and deep forest coves, ascends to rocky outlooks, crosses cascading streams, and goes under the engineering marvel of the Linn Cove Viaduct. It is a trail for day hikes; no camping is allowed. Camping options are either in Price Park or outside the BRP boundary with fee permits for designated campsites from Grandfather Mtn., Inc. (see chapter 14). The trail is described N to S, beginning at the Price Lake parking area. Except for the first 0.7 mi, the trail is also the MST route (see appendix A). (USGS Maps: Grandfather Mtn., Valle Crucis, Boone)

Follow the trail sign and cross the BRP to Section B of the park's campground. Bear L of the campsites and enter a rhododendron grove. At 0.3 mi reach jct R with Boone Fork Trail (described above). Arrive at a pasture and stile at 0.7 mi. Go 35 yd. and turn sharply L into the woods. (The Boone Fork Trail continues ahead.) Cross two small footbridges and exit from the woods into the pasture at 0.9 mi. Ascend gently to enter the woods again, and pass through three more stiles before crossing Holloway Mountain Rd (SR-1559) at 1.7 mi (It is 1.0 mi L on the road to BRP mp 298.6.) Enter another stile across the road to ascend a scenic pasture. Views of the Grandfather Mtn. range can be seen ahead. Enter another forest and another pasture before passing the last stile at 2.8 mi. Descend gently into a low area of poplar, ash, and white snakeroot at 3.0 mi. Pass through a forest of tall hardwoods and groves of rhododendron to reach at 3.7 mi a jct with Cold Prong Pond Trail, L. (It goes 0.2 mi to the Cold Prong parking area and Cold Prong Pond at mp 299.2. Backtrack.) For the next 1.0 mi cross small streams and pass through a mature forest deep into Price Park. Upon coming out around a ridge, leave the Price Park boundary (but the trail continues unchanged within the BRP corridor). Pass a rich display of rosebay rhododendron, witch hazel, and at 5.5 mi a patch of flame azalea. Follow an old RR grade a short distance before arriving at an access to Boone Fork parking at 5.6 mi. (A sharp L goes 135 yd. to Boone Fork parking, mp 299.9. Along the way, the 0.5-mi Upper Boone Fork Trail forks R and follows the Boone Fork under the BRP to scenic Calloway Peak Overlook at mp 299.7.) Immediately after the jct cross a high footbridge over cascades and pools of Boone Fork. Within 100 yd, L is the 0.4-mi Grandfather Mountain Access Trail, which is also the Daniel Boone Scout Trail access. (It descends on an old road under the BRP bridge to a parking area on

US-221. This route is recommended for hikers with required fee permits to the trails of Grandfather Mtn., Inc.) At 5.9 mi jct R with the Nuwati Trail, and at 6.0 mi the Daniel Boone Scout Trail, R. (Both trails require fee permits and are described in chapter 14.) Descend to a stream crossing at 6.2 mi, curve around a ridge, and descend to a footbridge over Dixon Creek at 7.1 mi. Pass through a lush cove of tall hardwoods, jewelweed, and black cohosh at 7.4 mi. At 8.6 mi reach jct L with the 0.1-mi access route to Raven Rocks Overlook, mp 302.3 on the BRP. Cross a footbridge over a fork of cascading Little Wilson Creek at 9.0 mi. A 60-yd. access trail to Rough Ridge parking on the BRP, mp 302.9, is at 9.3 mi. Immediately cross a footbridge over a fork of Little Wilson Creek. Curve around and up the ridge to the spectacular views from the Rough Ridge boardwalk at 9.5 mi. In late September and early October the rocky mountainside turns multiple hues of red from the blueberry bushes. Other plants here are turkey grass, Allegheny sand myrtle, red spruce, and mountain ash. This scenic area is environmentally fragile; trail users are urged to stay on the trail and boardwalks. Descend into a scenic area of rocky overhangs at 10.4 mi, and after 0.2 mi cross a footbridge over the cascading Wilson Creek. To the L is a 70-yd. access trail under the BRP to the Wilson Creek Overlook at mp 303.7. Reach a pedestrian overlook at 11.4 mi, descend to cross Linn Cove Branch, and pass under the Linn Cove Viaduct to an observation deck at 11.6 mi. After 200 yd. arrive at the Linn Cove parking area, mp 304.4. Reenter the forest to a section of huge boulders, descend to cross a footbridge over cascading Stack Rock Creek, and reach Stack Rock, L, at 13.2 mi. Reach the BRP Stack Rock parking area, R, mp 304.8, at 12.5 mi. Cross small Andrews Creek, follow a boardwalk alongside the BRP, and cross US-221 at 13.1 mi. (US-221 is a serpentine route of asphalt between Blowing Rock and Linville. It follows the route the Cherokee called the Yonahlossee Trail. There is an overlook on the BRP, mp 303.9, which gives a view of part of the route.) At 13.4 mi reach jct R and L with the Beacon Heights Trail and the end of the Tanawha Trail. (A turn L goes 0.2 mi to Beacon Heights [described below], and the MST goes with it nearly to the top before forking R to descend to Old House Gap in the Pisgah National Forest. See appendix A.) Turn R and after 130 yd. arrive at the Beacon Heights parking area, mp 305.3.

Gwyn Memorial Trail (mp 298.6)   **473**

This 91-yd. garden trail honors Rufus Lenoir Gwyn (1877–1963), whose efforts were influential in the location of the BRP through the Blue Ridge. The trail is at a jct with Holloway Mountain Rd 1.0 mi from US-221.

474   *Beacon Heights Trail* (mp 305.3)
An easy 0.3-mi graded trail ascends to a bare quartzite summit (4,205 ft.) for spectacular views of the Pisgah National Forest, Hawksbill and Table Rock Mtns., and Grandfather and Grandmother Mtns. Along the way the trail reaches jct with the Tanawha Trail, L, and the MST running jointly L and R. The summit was named by A. M. Huger, poet and trailblazer at the turn of the century.

475   *Grandmother Mountain Trail* (mp 307.4)
From the Grandmother Mtn. parking lot ascend 0.2 mi on a moderate trail arbored with rhododendron to the NP boundary.

476   *Flat Rock Trail* (mp 308.2)
The easy 0.7-mi trail is a well-graded, self-guiding loop. Signs provide geological and biological information. The summit supplies outstanding views of Grandfather Mtn., Linville Valley, Black Mtn., and Roan Mtn. The quartzite outcropping is weather sculpted.

477   *Camp Creek Trail* (mp 315.5)
An easy leg stretcher, this short walk through rhododendron is to the cool banks of Camp Creek for a round-trip of 0.1 mi from the parking lot.

Linville Falls Recreation Area (mp 315.5–316.5)

The 440-acre Linville Falls Rec Area was acquired by the NPS from the philanthropy of John D. Rockefeller Jr, in 1952. It is named for explorer William Linville and his son, who, according to a legend, were killed by Indians in 1766 while they slept near the headwaters of Linville or Watauga River. Sixteen-year-old John Williams, left for dead, survived. At the major falls the Linville River cuts through quartzite to plunge dramatically into a hidden drop before it thunders from a lower open level. The area has 100 picnic sites, two campgrounds (190 sites), trout fishing, and an information shelter. There are four nature trails, but other trails, such as the Linville Gorge Trail, are in the Linville Gorge Wilderness Area under the jurisdiction of the Pisgah National Forest and do not make a connection (see chapter 3, section 2). The 0.2-mi round-trip
478 Linville River Bridge Trail is separate from the parking area of the four trails described below. It is at mp 316.4, 0.1 mi farther S on the BRP than the entrance road to the falls. However, the trail connects with the picnic area from the entrance in its descent to the riverbank for viewing the architecturally significant stone bridge. (USGS Map: Linville Falls)

Linville Falls Trail (2.0 mi, round-trip); *Plunge Basin Overlook Trail* (0.5 mi, round-trip); *Linville Gorge Trail* (1.4 mi, round-trip); *Duggers Creek Trail* (0.3 mi)   **479-** **482**

Length and Difficulty: 4.2 combined round-trip, easy to moderate

Trailheads and Description: To hike the Linville Falls Trail, begin at the parking lot and cross the Linville River bridge to follow a wide and heavily used trail to Upper Falls. Ascend from the Upper Falls through hemlock and rhododendron to a choice of three lookouts for outstanding views of the 90-ft. (total) Linville Falls. (This trail is also known as Erwins Trail and goes to Erwins Lookout at 1.0 mi.) Backtrack. For the Plunge Basin Overlook Trail and the Linville Gorge Trail, leave the parking lot, L. Ascend through rhododendron to a jct with Plunge Basin Overlook Trail, R. Turn R and descend to the overlook for a superb view of the Lower Falls. Carolina, catawba, and rosebay rhododendron bloom on the weather-sculpted walls of the gorge. Return to the jct with the Linville Gorge Trail and turn at the sign to descend steeply on a rocky slope to the basin of the Lower Falls at 0.9 mi. Backtrack. For the Duggers Creek Trail, follow the signs E of the parking lot for an interpretive loop trail over a rocky area with thick mosses and fern patches. Return to the parking lot.

Chestoa View Trail (mp 320.8)   **483**

This scenic, short, and easy 0.8-mi route to Chestoa View was named by A. M. Huger. (Chestoa is the Cherokee Indian word for "rabbit.") From the parking lot enter a paved trail and follow the loop through mature hardwoods and numerous wildflowers, including large clusters of Bowman's root. Take the gravel trail to return and pass scenic views of the Linville Gorge Wilderness Area and Grandfather Mtn.

Crabtree Meadows Recreation Area (mp 339.5–340.3)

The 253-acre Crabtree Meadows has a restaurant that is open from May through October and a gift shop, camp store, and svc sta. Adjoining are an amphitheater and campground with tent and trailer sites (no hookups). The picnic area is on the S edge of the park on the BRP. Crabtree Falls is the central feature of the campground, but the more than 40 species of wildflowers and 35 species of songbirds are significant also. (USGS Map: Celo)

484   *Crabtree Falls Trail*

>   **Length and Difficulty:** 2.5 mi, moderate

>   **Trailhead and Description:** From the campground parking lot follow the posted directions N to 0.4 mi and begin at the steps. Reach the waterfalls at 0.8 mi and cross the bridge to begin a return climb. At 1.4 mi cross the stream and walk through spreads of trillium and wild orchids at 1.7 mi. Follow L at all trail jcts until the jct with the original trail.

Woods Mountain Access Trail (mp 344.1)

This is a moderate walk on an old dirt road from mp 342 to mp 344.1. It passes a few other dirt roads from the L and passes a cemetery at 0.5 mi. In a hardwood forest with a rhododendron understory, it descends to Hazelnut Gap at 1.3 mi. To the L is the W end of Woods Mountain Trail (USFS #218) opposite a large white oak tree. (The Woods Mountain Trail, now part of the MST, follows a ridgeline for 5.3 mi to a former fire tower, but the MST continues for 7.9 mi to US-221 N of Marion at Woodlawn Picnic Area.) Continue on the old dirt road and descend to Buck Creek Gap parking lot at NC-80 (mp 344.1) at 2.0 mi (See chapter 3, section 2.)

485   *Green Knob Trail* (mp 350.4)

From the Green Knob Overlook (4,761 ft.) follow the trail N and across the parkway and up switchbacks to reach the fire tower at 0.6 mi for outstanding views of the Black Mtn. range. (The trail R at the ridgeline is Lost Cove Ridge Trail [USFS #182], Pisgah NF; it descends 3.3 mi to Black Mtn. Recreation Area. See chapter 3, section B, Toecane Station Area.)

486   *Deep Gap Trail* (mp 351.9)

The BRP has 0.1 mi on this unmaintained trail (USFS #210) (listed as Newberry Creek Trail by Pisgah NF of the USFS). It descends S on switchbacks in a hardwood forest with rhododendron and laurel for 1.9 mi to the headwaters of Newberry Creek and a jct with FR-482A. (The road may be gated farther downsteam before its jct with FR-482.) Backtrack.

487   *Bald Knob Ridge Trail* (mp 355)

This is a terminus point (0.1 mi) of the Bald Knob Ridge Trail (USFS #186), Pisgah NF, which descends 2.8 mi toward Black Mtn. Rec Area on a white-blazed trail to FR-472.

Big Butt Trail (mp 359.8)

The BRP claims only the first 0.2 mi of this 6.0 mi Pisgah NF trail (USFS #161). Here at Balsam Gap (5,676 ft.), the highest point on the BRP N of Asheville, is a crossing of the MST. Its N route ascends on switchbacks to curve around scenic Potato Knob and to NC-128 (entrance road to Mt. Mitchell SP). Its S route is seen again at mp 361.2 in Cotton Tree Gap (Glass-mine Falls Overlook). The white-blazed Big Butt Trail goes W to descend and ascend on a ridgeline of wildflowers and ramp for magnificent views of the Black Mtn. range. The trail drops on numerous switchbacks to NC-197W (see chapter 3, section B, Toecane Station Area).

Craggy Gardens Recreation Area (mp 364–367)

The 700-acre Craggy Gardens (5,220 ft.) has a grassy picnic ground in Bear Pen Gap with tables, grills, water, and comfort sta. The visitor center has exhibits and BRP information. Although this area is colorful during all seasons with wildflowers, mountain ash, and wild crab apple, the highlight of color is in mid-June when the Craggy summits turn purple with catawba rhododendron. The Craggy Gardens visitor center and picnic area are usually open from April 1 through October.

To hike the Craggy Pinnacle Trail (1.2 mi round-trip), follow the signs **488-** from the parking lot at Craggy Dome Overlook up switchbacks to the summit **490** (5,840 ft.) with 360-degree scenic views. For the Craggy Gardens Trail, follow signs from the parking lot of the visitor center to the picnic area, a one-way distance of 1.0 mi. The Bear Pen Gap Trail is 0.2 mi long and runs through the picnic area. (The MST route follows the E side of the parking lot.) (USGS Map: Craggy Pinnacle)

Rattlesnake Lodge Trail (mp 374.4)   **491**

The strenuous 0.4-mi Rattlesnake Lodge Trail is accessed from a parking area at the S end of the Tanbark Tunnel. Ascend steeply on an orange-blazed trail to connect with the MST and the ruins of the summer home of Dr. Chase P. Ambler, an Asheville physician who built the lodge in 1900. To the R of the jct is a spring and the N route of the MST. To the L it is 10.0 mi on the MST to the Folk Art Center (mp 382). (See appendix A.)

492   *Shut-In Trail* (mp 393.6–407.7)

   Length and Difficulty: 16.4 mi, strenuous (elev change 3,611 ft)

   Trailhead and Description: A national rec trail and the MST route, it follows mainly a former horse trail named and constructed in the 1890s by George Vanderbilt as an access route from Biltmore to his Buck Spring Hunting Lodge. It was originally 20.0 mi long and included a fording of the French Broad River. With the creation of the BRP, parts of the trail were obliterated and the remainder became overgrown. But in the 1970s Pop Hollandsworth of the Asheville School, Jack Davis and Arch Nichols of the CMC, and others cleared sections of the old trail and relocated others. It is listed on the inventories of both the BRP and the Pisgah NF because it weaves in and out of the boundaries. Water is infrequent. Tree species are diverse because of the high altitude changes. Among them are beech, red oak, cucumber tree, hemlock, yellow poplar, maple, locust, chestnut oak, and birch. Wildflowers include trillium, mandrake, wild orchids, wild geranium, gold star, galax, and trailing arbutus. Cancer root, a parasitic leafless yellow brown stalk, is commonplace in the springtime. Game animals likely seen or heard are turkey, grouse, deer, and squirrel (no hunting is allowed on the BRP).

   For the NE access, turn off the BRP ramp at the NC-191 jct (sign for I-26), and immediately turn L to park at gated entrance of FR-479M. Access the MST by walking back and up the BRP access road to the R at an embankment. It follows a tunnel of rhododendron, passes through a gated fence of the NC Arboretum, and at 0.5 mi curves L. Here is a former parking area access, R, 125 ft. to FR-479M. (An access to this point can be made by walking 0.3 mi on FR-479M from where you parked your car to a L turn to cross Bent Creek bridge for 0.1 mi.) Starting at the former access, ascend on switchbacks through rhododendron thickets and reach an old road at 0.4 mi. Reach jct with a gravel road at 1.7 mi; turn L. Leave the road and begin an ascent at 1.8 mi. Reach a crest at 2.4 mi and the W side of the BRP at 3.1 mi. Walnut Cove Overlook (2,915 ft.) (mp 396.4) is on the E side of the BRP.

   Ascend and skirt NW of Grassy Knob, but at 4.4 mi intersect with Grassy Knob Trail (USFS #338), Pisgah NF, which goes L 0.3 mi in an ascent to the top of the knob (3,318 ft.) and R for 0.2 mi to FR-479M in the Bent Creek Experimental Forest. Pass through tall hardwoods and dense sections of rhododendron to reach Sleepy Gap and Overlook (mp 397.3) at 4.7 mi. To the R (SW) is 1.8-mi Sleepy Gap Trail (USFS #339). It descends to a network of trails in the Bent Creek Experimental Forest (see chapter 3, section A).

Continue to ascend through hardwoods and laurel to the ridge top of Truckwheel Mtn. and then descend to Chestnut Cove Gap and Overlook (mp 398.3) (3,035 ft.) at 5.8 mi. From here begin a long descent that takes the trail away from the BRP. Cross a small stream at 6.3 mi and make a L turn on an old road at 6.8 mi. Cross Chestnut Creek at 7.1 mi. Ascend through dark passages of rhododendron and laurel to swing around the ridge of Cold Knob. In an ascent from a hollow reach FR-479 in Bent Creek Gap (mp 400.4) at 8.6 mi. (To the R, down the mountain, FR-479 goes to Lake Powhatan Rec Area [and campground], and a network of trails in the Pisgah NF. To the L [under the BRP bridge] the road becomes FR-5000 and descends to the North Mills River Rec Area [and campground] also in the Pisgah NF. A few yards up the access ramp from the BRP, on the R, is the trailhead for 1.8-mi Bad Fork Trail [USFS #323].) (See chapter 3, section A, Eastern Area.)

Cross FR-479 and curve away W from the BRP to ascend. At 8.5 mi are excellent views of the city of Asheville and Craggy Mtn. (Views are easier to notice if hiking N rather than S.) Reach the summit of Ferrin Knob after a long switchback, to the site of an old fire tower (4,064 ft.) at 9.7 mi. Descend on a ridge through oak and locust to reach Beaver Dam Gap Overlook (3,570 ft.) (mp 401.7) at 10.2 mi. Ascend and descend knobs among chestnut oak, maple, and wildflowers to reach Stoney Bald Overlook (3,750 ft.) (mp 402.6) at 11.0 mi. Cross the BRP to Big Ridge Overlook (3,815 ft.) (mp 403.6). Continuing to ascend among hardwoods, blueberry patches, mosses, and gold star, reach River Valley Overlook (4,085 ft.) (mp 404.5) at 13.4 mi. Cross the BRP at Elk Pasture (also called Cutthroat Gap) (4,235 ft.) (mp 405.5) at 14.6 mi for a jct with NC-151 (known as Pisgah Highway), R. (It descends to Candler for a jct with US-19/23/74.)

Climb to a plateau through large oaks with a dense understory. Reach the crest of Little Pisgah Mtn. at 16.1 mi. (A side trail is R for 1.2 mi to Mt. Pisgah [see below].) Continuing on the Shut-in Trail descend slightly to Buck Spring Gap parking area at 16.4 mi (4,980 ft.). Across the parking space the MST continues with the Buck Spring Trail for 1.1 mi at arrive to Pisgah Inn. (USGS-FS Maps: Asheville, Dunsmore Mtn.)

Mount Pisgah Receation Area (mp 407–409)

The mile-high Mt. Pisgah complex has a modern motel and dining hall at the 52-room Pisgah Inn. It is open by May 1 through October. There are sweeping views over the Pisgah NF that melt away toward SC. Writer William G.

Lord has said that "sleep is quiet as a moth's wing" at the inn. The area is part of the original 100,000-acre estate owned by the late George W. Vanderbilt. (George Weston, who was Vanderbilt's farm superintendent, built and opened the first inn in 1920. In the 1940s it fell into disrepair but was reopened in 1952 by Leslie and Leda Kirschner of New York. The current inn was opened in 1967 and operates under a concession contract with the NPS.) There is a svc sta, a picnic area, and a large (140 sites) campground for trailers and tents (no hookups), with water and flush toilets. Information: Pisgah Inn, PO Box 749, Waynesville, NC 28786; 704-235-8228 (usually open from April 1 to November 1). (USGS-FS Maps: Cruso, Asheville, Skyland, Dunsmore Mtn.)

493- 496 ***Buck Spring Trail*** (1.1 mi); ***Mount Pisgah Trail*** (1.2 mi); ***Mount Pisgah Campground Trail*** (1.0 mi); ***Frying Pan Mountain Trail*** (2.0 mi)

Length and Difficulty: 6.5 mi combined round-trip, easy to strenuous

Special Features: Mt. Pisgah and Frying Pan Mtn. vistas

Trailheads and Description: To hike the Buck Spring Trail, a national recreation trail, begin at a signboard at the NE corner of the Pisgah Inn parking lot. (There is a connection here for the Buck Spring Trail in the Pisgah NF [6.2 mi, USFS #104] and Pilot Rock Trail [3.6 mi, USFS #321]. Follow the easy trail through a natural garden of laurel banks and bluets [Houstonia caerules] and weather-formed chestnut oaks. At 0.7 mi reach jct R with the Laurel Mountain Trail [7.4 mi, USFS #121], which descends into the Pisgah NF.) At 1.0 mi visit the historic site of Vanderbilt's Buck Spring Hunting Lodge. Reach the Buck Spring Gap parking overlook at 1.1 mi. (The Shut-in Trail begins on the N side of the parking area, and the MST follows both of these trails.)

To hike the Mt. Pisgah Trail follow the paved access road N 0.2 mi to the Mt. Pisgah parking area. Enter at the trail sign and into the Pisgah NF to begin a strenuous climb at 0.4 mi. After a rocky route to the summit (5,721 ft) reach an observation deck for panoramic views of the Pigeon River and the Blue Ridge range. Backtrack. An easy return to the Pisgah Inn is on the Mt. Pisgah Campground Trail from the Mt. Pisgah parking area. Descend, parallel W of the BRP, pass through the picnic area, and reach the campground at 1.0 mi. From the campground entrance gate there is a sign for the Frying Pan Mountain Trail. Ascend to Big Bald where azaleas, filbert, mountain ash, and leatherflowers *(Clematis viorna)* thrive. Reach Frying Pan Gap (4,931 ft., mp 409.6) at 1.3 mi. (The gap was named by pioneer livestock herders.) Follow FR-450 to the fire tower at 2.0 mi for panoramic views. Backtrack.

Graveyard Fields Overlook (mp 418.8)

Length and Difficulty: 3.2 mi, easy

Trailhead and Description: From the parking overlook examine the Graveyard Fields Trail design board. Enter a paved trail in the Pisgah NF and through a dense section of rhododendron to the Yellowstone Prong of the East Fork of the Pigeon River at 0.2 mi. Cross a bridge, turn R to view Second Falls, and return to the bridge, but keep R. (A section of the trail is planned for relocation.) Immediately come to jct R with the Graveyard Ridge Trail (USFS #356) that ascends 3.4 mi to Ivestor Gap (see chapter 3, section A). Continue upstream among open places, near pools, and through grasses; come to jct at 0.6 mi with a return loop, but continue ahead another 0.5 mi to the scenic Upper Falls. Backtrack for a loop of 3.2 mi (including the round-trip distance to the Upper Falls). (The area received its name from moss-covered fallen spruce trunks and stumps that resembled a graveyard. The trunks were destroyed by a fire in November 1925 that burned 25,000 acres of prime timber.) (USGS-FS Map: Shining Rock)

Devil's Courthouse Trail (mp 422.4)   497

From the parking lot and signs (5,462 ft.) follow the paved trail 0.1 mi toward the BRP tunnel and ascend on a steep but moderately difficult trail. At 0.3 mi come to jct L with a 0.1-mi spur to the MST. Turn R and reach the summit (5,720 ft.) at a stone observation deck and disk directors at 0.4 mi. (According to the Cherokee Indian legend, Judaculla, a slant-eyed giant devil, had his legal chambers inside this mountain.) Views from this point are spectacular; on clear days you can see NC, GA, and TN. The SE side of the rock face is used by rock climbers. Backtrack. (USGS-FS Map: Sam Knob)

Tanasee Bald/Herrin Knob Trail (mp 423.5)   498

From the jct of the BRP and NC-215 go S on the BRP for 0.3 mi to the Courthouse Valley parking overlook (5,362 ft.), L, and park at the second parking area. The trail begins at the SW corner behind a picnic table. Follow an unmarked, narrow (perhaps overgrown) trail under beech, fir, hawthorne, arrowwood, and birch. The ground cover is ferns, galax, and wood sorrel. Pass R of Tanasee Bald at 0.4 mi and turn R at a fork at 0.5 mi. After a few yards enter a natural summertime garden of fragrant wildflowers, birds, butterflies, and blueberries. At 0.7 mi climb steeply to the SW slope of Herrin Knob (5,720 ft.), named for James P. Herren (correct spelling), a prominent timberman. This rocky bluff is naturally landscaped with laurel, orchids, and multiple moss species. Descend to BRP, mp 424.2, at 1.2 mi. Backtrack, or hike the BRP for 0.8 mi as a loop. (USGS-FS Map: Sam Knob)

499   *Grassy Ridge Trail* (mp 424.2)

The Grassy Ridge Trail (across the BRP from the Tanasee Bald/Herrin Knob Trail) begins on the R (N) side of the BRP at Mt. Hardy Gap. (There is no designated parking place here.) Enter the forest in a dense stand of beech and yellow birch to climb rocky switchbacks on the N side of Mt. Hardy. At 0.6 mi reach a faint trail, R, on open Fork Ridge. (Fork Ridge is in the Middle Prong Wilderness Area of the Pisgah NF with a number of bald areas.) Turn L up the ridge to a partially bald summit of Mt. Hardy (6,110 ft) at 0.8 mi. (Formerly called Black Mtn., it was named in honor of Dr. James F. E. Hardy, Asheville Civil War physician, by the United Daughters of the Confederacy [UDC] in 1942.) Backtrack. (An old unmarked trail follows the ridgeline W through a fir/spruce forest with plush carpets of moss and wood sorrel for 1.1 mi to a jct with an access trail to the MST. A left turn leads a few yards to Rough Butt Bald Overlook, mp 425.4. A turn R on the access trail leads 100 yd. to the Buckeye Gap Trail [USFS #126].) (USGS-FS Map: Sam Knob)

500   *Bear Pen Gap Trail* (mp 427.6)

The trailhead is at the SE corner of the parking lot (5,560 ft.). It is only 0.1 mi within the BRP boundary, but it is an excellent access route to the MST and to an open grassy plateau with wildflowers at 1.3 mi in the Wet Camp Gap of the Nantahala NF (see appendix A).

501   *Richland Balsam Trail* (mp 431.4)

At the Richland Balsam Overlook the BRP attains its highest point (6,053 ft.). To hike the 1.4-mi round-trip trail, begin at the NW corner of the parking area and follow an interpretive sign. The trail runs through a damp Canadian-zone type of forest, chiefly of fir and spruce. (The Fraser fir has been devastated by the balsam woolly aphid in this area.) Other vegetation includes mountain ash, rowan, birch, pin cherry, witherod, wood sorrel, golden moss, and blueberry. Reach the summit (6,292 ft.) at 0.6 mi and return on the loop. (An old trail, Lickstone Ridge Trail, is heavily overgrown from the summit.) (USGS-FS Map: Sam Knob)

502   *Roy Taylor Forest Trail* (mp 433.8)

This overlook (5,580 ft.) has a 75-yd. asphalt walk to an observation deck in honor of Congressman Taylor, a conservationist who said "Next to preservation of liberty and security, government's greatest responsibility is the stewardship of natural resources." (See chapter 2, sec. 2.)

Waterrock Knob Trail (mp 451.2)   503
A plaque here honors H. Getty Browning (1881–1966), a leader in the location of the NC BRP route. From the parking area's E side, enter the paved trail (which becomes a rocky path) for a moderate climb to the summit (6,400 ft.) at 0.6 mi. Here are superb views of the Smokies and Pisgah and Nantahala NFs. (A faint trail L of the summit follows the ridge for 2.5 mi to private Mt. Lyn Lowery, and NE on the high Plott Balsams to Oldfield Top after another mi) Some of the vegetation is fir, birch, gooseberry, bush honeysuckle, turtlehead *(Chelone lyonii),* meadow parsnip, and mountain lettuce *(Saxifraga micranthidifolia).* Views from the summit are panoramic. Backtrack. (USGS-FS Map: Sylva North)

Black Camp Gap Trail (mp 458.2)   504
On the Heintooga Rd (a spur from Wolf Laurel Gap) drive 3.6 mi to the 66-yd. trail R. It approaches a Masonic plaque, but its name is from the black ashes of a long-ago forest fire.

Chapter 7

Great Smoky Mountains National Park

Introductions to Trail Areas

Big Creek is known for its rainbow trout. It has a ranger station, tent camping, waterfalls, springs, and historic sites (7 trails, 29.8 mi moderate to strenuous). For a challenge: Baxter Creek Trail leads to Mt. Sterling, a 4,142 ft. elev change.

In Cherokee, Cataloochee means "waves of mountains." There are historic settlements, where descendants return each summer for dinner on the ground (13 trails, 58.6 mi, moderate to strenuous; 10.8 mi, hiking only.). This campground is family oriented.

A special hiking only trail in this area—a 1.2-mi climb on Spruce Mountain Trail to tent site (elev 5,657 ft.) (4 trails, 16.7 mi, easy to strenuous). Access on one-way Balsam Mtn. Rd, open May through October.

A network of 60 mi of trails, all open to equestrians and hikers except 14 mi for hikers only. Main access at Smokemont Campground, near Oconaluftee Visitor Center (18 trails, 51.2 mi, moderate to strenuous). This campground is family oriented.

Some of the highest, longest, and most scenic in the Smokies. The Noland Divide Trail has an elevation change of 4,155 ft. Campground with 108 sites; ranger station, waterfalls. The first 26 mi of the Mountains-to-Sea Trail is E for Clingmans Dome (12 trails, 70.1 mi, moderate to strenuous).

This area is the grandfather of rugged hiking trails. They are from the lapping lake shores into the dark and wet hollows to the grassy domes of the AT (16 trails, 148.6 mi, easy to strenuous; 20 mi hiking only). A classic loop of 80 mi is possible. The 34.7-mi Lakeshore Trail is the showpiece and is accessible by boat from the Fontana Village Marina.

A network of trails touches the AT for magnificent views from Shuckstack fire tower. Other trails ascend to a dazzling display of flame azaleas on grassy fields and heath knobs, such as Gregory Knob (elev 4,948 ft.) in mid-to-late June (Five trails, 26 mi, moderate to strenuous; 2.9 mi hiking only).

Chapter 7

Great Smoky Mountains National Park

Air pollution . . . 50 years ago at Newfound Gap you
could see 113 miles, today only 25. In Summer only 14 miles.
—Smokies Guide, Summer 2003

One of the oldest uplands on Earth, the magnificent Smokies cover 520,004 acres, of which 275,895 are in North Carolina (the remainder in Tennessee). Authorized by Congress in 1926 and dedicated in 1940 by President Franklin D. Roosevelt, the Great Smoky Mtns. National Park (GSMNP) receives more than 10 million visitors annually and is the nation's most heavily used national park. The property was not acquired easily. Initially, Congress did not appropriate federal funds for land purchase, and 85 percent of the proposed land was owned by timber industries, most of which were initially unwilling to sell. Although state legislatures appropriated funds and local fund-raising campaigns were widespread, it was not enough. The turning point came in 1928 when John D. Rockefeller Jr. donated $5 million. By the early 1930s Congress had appropriated another $3.5 million. Finally, after 14 years of negotiations (and some litigation) with 18 timber companies and the purchase of more than 6,000 separate tracts, the park became a reality; a former domain of the Eastern Cherokee would be preserved forever.

More than 70 percent of the luxuriant virgin forest had been cut by the timber companies prior to the land sales. Today, the second-growth forests are maturing and blending in natural succession. Since 1966, with the beginning of wilderness hearings about the Smokies, there has been growing public demand to protect the wilderness character. With this trend, it is likely that the 35-mi North Shore road between Fontana Dam and Bryson City, promised by the NPS in 1943, will never be completed. (The road is also called Lakeview Drive and the Road to Nowhere.) Six miles have been constructed from Bryson City to Forney Ridge (also called Tunnel Ridge because the road dead-ends after passing through a tunnel). The road was halted because of insufficient funding and questions regarding environmental damage. Public hearings about the road's future are being held. See www.northshoreroad.info, or contact 865-436-1200 or www.nps.gov/grsm.)

For the naturalist, the park is a paradise with more than 1,400 varieties of flowering plants, 130 species of trees, 205 mosses, and more than 2,000 fungi. There are more than 200 species of birds, 65 species of mammals, 38 species of reptiles, and 58 different kinds of fish. This was the listing in 1997, but in 1998 a search began by scientists from around the world to identify other species in the park. The project, to last perhaps 17 years, is called Taxa Biodiversity Inventory (ATBI). By 2004, more than 3,100 new species had been discovered, of which 400 were new to biologists. Scientists now estimate there may be more than 100,000 different species of flora and fauna in the park. For more information, contact 865-430-4752 or www. discoverlifeamerica.org. Because the park is a wildlife sanctuary, it is forbidden to disturb any of the plants or animals. The park has 10 developed campgrounds, 5 of which are in North Carolina. In addition to camping as a recreational activity, the park has 600 miles of streams for fishing. The park is famous for its hundreds of miles of trails for hiking, horseback riding, and cross-country skiing. There are waterfalls on both the Tennessee and North Carolina sides of the park. At least 25 waterfalls are accessible by a combination of motor vehicle roads and trails. One of the most unique in Tennessee is Place of a Thousand Drips at stop #15 on the Roaring Fork Motor Nature Trail. Access begins at traffic light #8 in Gatlinburg on Cherokee Orchard Rd. Among the waterfalls in North Carolina are two examples—Juney Whank and Indian Creek—near Deep Creek Campground, accessible on Deep Creek Rd N from Bryson City. (For more information or to request a waterfall map/guide, contact 865-436-0120 or www.SmokiesStor.org. A solitary loop trail is 0.4 mi Spruce/Fir Nature Trail **505** 2.5 mi SW on Clingmans Dome Rd from Newfound Gap and US-441.

The highest mountain in the park is Clingmans Dome (6,643 ft.), accessible within 0.5 mi by auto road or by hiking the AT. There are 16 other peaks that tower over 6,000 ft. Geologists estimate that the original peaks in the Smokies were over 15,000 ft. in elev when formed 250 million years ago. It is to these high peaks and ridges and into the lower coves that more than 800 mi of hiking and horse trails (of which approximately 510 mi are in North Carolina) form a vast network of highly visible backcountry routes. The longest trail is the 71.6-mi AT from Fontana Dam to Davenport Gap, which follows the Tennessee/North Carolina state line from Doe Knob in the west to near the park boundary at NC-32. The second longest is the combined routes of the 34.7-mi Lakeshore Trail on the N shore of Fontana Dam. Only the trails on the North Carolina side of the park are described in this book.

During the 1930s the CCC operated 16 camps in the Smokies. As a result, numerous trails were regraded from old RR grades or roads, and others were rerouted. Trail usage declined during the WW II years, but hiker and horse traffic has continuously increased since the 1960s. The increase has made permits and reservations necessary for those who stay overnight in the backcountry.

There are a number of rules and regulations for hiking the backcountry; they are designed to protect both the quality of the natural environment and the quality of the backpacking experience. "It is our attempt to enable you and others to love this wild place without loving it to death," say park officials. Overnight trips require a free permit. (For more information, contact 865-436-1297.) Self-registration permits are allowed at ranger stations, campgrounds, and visitor centers by following posted instructions. Some campsites require reservations because of heavy trail traffic. The numbered sites on the North Carolina side of the park (form NE to SW) are Upper Walnut Bottom #36 and Lower Walnut Creek Area); Enloe #47 on Enloe Creek Trail and Lower Chaseen Creek #50 on Chasteen Creek Trail (Oconaluftee Area); Pole Road #55 and Bryson Place #57 on Deep Creek Trail (Deep Creek Area); CCC #71 on Forney Creek Tail (Forney Creek Area); Bone Valley #83 on Hazel Creek Trail (Hazel Creek Area); and Birch Spring Gap #113 on the AT (Twentymile Area). All shelters on the AT also require reservations. Reservations are recommended up to a month in advance. (For backcountry reserved campsite information, contact 865-436-1231; for campground reservations, contact 800-365-2267; for ordering maps or books, contact 865-436-0120.) The following rules listed by the park are backcountry ethics: Maximum size of party is eight; only one consecutive night at a shelter and three at a campsite; campers must stay in designated sites of the itinerary; do not reserve more space than you intend to occupy; do not damage animal or plant life; carry out all food and trash; use toilet at least 100 ft. from campsite (bury all human waste 6 in. deep); do not wash dishes or bathe with soap in a stream; use only wood that is dead and on the ground (the use of backpacker stoves and candle lanterns are encouraged instead of campfires); practice minimum impact on campsites; no pets, motorized vehicles, or bicycles; no firearms or hunting of animals; and feeding of wildlife is prohibited. Maximum fine for each violation is $5,000 and /or six months in jail. Bears are more prominent in the park than anywhere else in the state. Remain watchful for them and report all bear incidents to the ranger. The most dangerous bears in the park are the solitary males, but that does not mean a female (with or without her cubs) will not be aggressive. Because the bears are generally shy and secretive and have a keen sense of detecting people, the average hiker will probably not see them. The best way to avoid any bear problems is to avoid attracting them with food. Proper food storage is a necessity, so do not keep food in tents or sleeping bags and do store it in an odor-proof bag tied with a rope at least 4 ft. from the nearest limb and 10 ft. above the ground. Also, refrain from throwing any food to a bear or leaving food for the bear to eat. Bears are more likely to visit campsites and shelters from May to October.

For the purpose of grouping trail network areas, the descriptions in this book begin in the NE with Big Creek and follow west to Cataloochee, Balsam Mtn., Smokemont, Deep Creek, North Shore, and Twentymile Creek.

Address and Access: The park has three visitor centers: Oconaluftee, 2.0 mi N of Cherokee on the Newfound Gap Rd (designated US-441 outside the park); Sugarlands, 2.0 mi SW of Gatlinburg; and Cades Cove, 12.0 mi SW of Townsend, TN. (The centers are open daily except December 25. The office hours are December–February: 8:00AM–4:30PM; March–May: 8–5; June–August 8–7; September–October: 8AM–6PM. Schedule is subject to change. Oconaluftee Visitor Center, 1194 Newfound Gap Highway, Cherokee, NC 28719, 828-497-1904, fax: 828-497-1910.) For more information, contact GSMNP, 107 Park Hqs Rd, Gatlinburg, TN 37738; 856-436-1200; District Ranger Office, P.O. Box 4, Park Circle, Cherokee, NC 28719; 828-497-1902. Other addresses for the ranger stations are listed at the end of each park-area introduction.

Big Creek Area (Haywood County)

The Big Creek Area is the most northern corner of the park. The area comprises the Big Creek drainage from Balsam Mtn. (SW), Mt. Sterling (SE), Mt. Cammerer Ridge (N), and Mt. Guyot (W) along the state line. The area was logged in the early 1900s, and a logging town was established at Crestmont, the site of a CCC camp in the 1930s. The site is now Big Creek Campground, a developed fee camp of 12 campsites for tents only. It has flush toilets, grills, and tables. A pay telephone is nearby at the ranger station. A connecting trail to the AT, 2.0 mi Chestnut Branch Trail, ascends from the Chestnut Branch **506** bridge here near the parking area. Big Creek, which flows on the E side of the camp, is a good rainbow trout stream. Bear, rattlesnake, deer, raccoon, grouse, and squirrel are in the area. Spring wildflowers are prominent.

Address and Access: From I-40 at the state line at Waterville, take exit #451, cross the Pigeon River bridge; turn L on Waterville Rd (SR-1332), pass the Waterville Power Plant, and at 2.0 mi, intersect with Old NC-284 Rd (SR-1397, also called Mt. Sterling Rd). (Heading R, it is 1.0 mi to Davenport Gap and the AT at the state line; L, the road passes through the Mt. Sterling Village and ascends to Mt. Sterling Gap for a descent to the Cataloochee area after 16.0 mi.) Cross the road to the ranger station. For more information, contact Big Creek Ranger Station, GSMNP, Star Route, Newport, TN 37821; 828-486-5910.

Support Facilities: There is a general store on Waterville Rd, 0.5 mi from the ranger station. Shopping centers, motels, and restaurants are in Newport, TN, 15.0 mi W on I-40.

507   *Big Creek Trail* (F, H)

Length and Difficulty: 5.3 mi, moderate (elev change 1,375 ft.)

508-   **Connecting Trails:** Swallow Fork Trail (4.0 mi, strenuous; elev change
511   2,180 ft.) (F, H); Low Gap Trail (2.5 mi, strenuous; elev change 1,240 ft.) (F, H); Gunter Fork Trail (4.1 mi, strenuous; elev change 2,430 ft.) (F); Camel Gap Trail (4.9 mi, moderate; elev change 1,611 ft.) (F, H)

Special Features: historic, waterfall

Trailhead and Description: From the ranger station, follow the road 0.5 mi to the picnic/parking area. Big Creek Trail goes to Walnut Bottom where the other four trail connections begin. Pass Mouse Creek Falls (on the far L of the river) at 2.0 mi, and at 2.9 mi pass Brakeshoe Spring. Forest vegetation includes maple, oak, hemlock, butternut, rhododendron, phacelia, and ramps. Cross Flint Rock Cove Branch at 4.5 mi and come to jct with Swallow Fork Trail, L, at 5.0 mi, at the lower edge of Walnut Bottom. It is a former logging camp and now backcountry campsite #37. (Big Creek Trail ends at 5.3 mi upstream at Upper Walnut Bottom campsite #36, but the Camel Gap Trail begins here.)

The Swallow Fork Trail leaves Walnut Bottom and ascends dramatically to Pretty Hollow Gap. At 0.4 mi, pass a spring, R. Ascend and follow an old RR grade for a short distance. At 0.9 mi, cross Swallow Fork. Cross a number of small tributaries, the last of which is at 2.5 mi on the ascent. After another 0.5 mi, make a switchback and ascend to Pretty Hollow Gap at 4.0 mi to a jct with the Mt. Sterling Ridge Trail and the Pretty Hollow Gap Trail.

(The Mount Sterling Ridge Trail, L, goes 1.4 mi to the jct with the Mount Sterling Trail and the Mount Sterling fire tower. To the R it goes 4.0 mi to Laurel Gap to a jct with the Balsam Mountain Trail.)

The Camel Gap Trail joins the Gunter Fork Trail 0.8 mi from its origin at the end of the Big Creek Trail in Walnut Bottom (near Upper Walnut Bottom campsite #36). Follow the Camel Gap Trail straight ahead on an old RR grade along the N side of Big Creek. Turn sharply R from the creek at 3.2 mi (near the confluence with Yellow Creek). Ascend steeply and at 4.3 mi, begin scenic views of the valley. Reach Camel Gap at the state line to a jct with the AT at 4.9 mi. A loop can be made here, R, on the AT for 2.4 mi to Low Gap Trail, which is described below.

The Gunter Fork Trail forks L from the Camel Gap Trail, crosses Big Creek, and ascends by cascades of Gunter Fork. At 2.3 mi, cross the base of a major cascade that drops nearly 200 ft. At 2.5 mi, leave the stream and ascend steeply on a ridge with mountain laurel, rhododendron, oak, and hemlock where there are scenic views of the Big Creek Valley. Continue ascent in an evergreen forest and thick mossy duff. Arrive at the crest of the Balsam Mtn. range and a jct R and L with the Balsam Mountain Trail. (From here, R, it is 5.6 mi to the AT and Tricorner Knob. To the L, it is 0.9 mi to Laurel Gap and a jct with the Mount Sterling Ridge Trail.)

The Low Gap Trail leaves Big Creek at the lower end of the Walnut Bottom campsite (0.2 mi before the upstream end of Big Creek Trail). On the W side of Big Creek turn R and parallel downstream with Big Creek. Pass R of an old cemetery at 0.4 mi, and at 0.8 mi leave the Big Creek area at the mouth of Low Gap Branch. Turn L upstream and cross the branch at 1.8 mi, the last water on the ascent to Low Gap and the AT. To the R it is 7.3 mi on the AT to Davenport Gap. Left it is 0.8 mi to the Cosby Shelter and another 1.6 mi to Camel Gap Trail in Camel Gap. (A loop of 12.0 mi back to Walnut Bottom is possible using Camel Gap Trail.) (USGS Maps: Cove Creek Gap, Luftee Knob, Waterville)

Baxter Creek Trail (F)

Length and Difficulty: 6.2 mi, strenuous (elev change 4,142 ft.)

Connecting Trail: Mt. Sterling Trail (2.8 mi, strenuous; elev change 1,952 ft.) (F, H)

Special Features: Mt. Sterling (5,842 ft.), scenic views

Trailhead and Description: From the Big Creek picnic area, cross the steel bridge near the lower end of the picnic area, turn R upstream, and follow

512-
513

through a former area of old fields and home sites. With a cliff on the L and through rhododendron, veer away from Big Creek and ascend on the E side of Baxter Creek by 0.7 mi. Cross tributaries and after a final crossing of the streams turn W on a rocky slope. There are views of Big Creek and Pigeon River valleys, R, and Mt. Cammerer ahead. Through a rocky section and among oak, maple, hemlock, and rhododendron, ascend steeply on switchbacks. At 4.0 mi, reach Mt. Sterling Ridge and ascend. By 4.5 mi, spruce and fir become dominant. There is a spring at 5.8 mi. At 6.2 mi, reach the summit of Mt. Sterling to a grassy spot at rationed backcountry campsite #38. Here is a fire tower from which there are spectacular views of Mt. Cammerer (NW), Clingmans Dome (SW), Snowbird Mtn. range and Max Patch (NE), and Mt. Pisgah (SE). Backtrack or use Mt. Sterling Trail.

The NW trailhead of Mt. Sterling Trail is here. It descends steeply and after 0.5 mi, reach jct with Mt. Sterling Ridge Trail, R. Continue to descend on an old road also used by equestrians. There are switchbacks at 1.5 mi, after which there are fewer conifers and more oaks and maple. At 2.3 mi, reach jct with Long Bunk Trail, R. (It descends 3.7 mi to Little Cataloochee Trail.) Arrive at Mt. Sterling Gap at Old NC-284 to a small parking area at 2.8 mi. Across the road is Asbury Trail (see Cataloochee Divide Trail ahead). It is 6.7 mi L (N) on Old NC-284 to the community of Mt. Sterling and access to the Big Creek picnic area, L.

A loop can be made by taking the Mt. Sterling Ridge Trail for 1.4 mi to Pretty Hollow Gap Trail. Turn R (N) on Swallow Fork Trail, follow it 4.0 mi to Big Creek Trail, R (described above) for a return descent to the point of origin for a loop of 17.1 mi. (USGS Maps: Cove Creek Gap, Waterville)

Cataloochee Area (Haywood County)

In Cherokee, Cataloochee means "waves of mountains or ridges." This area has ridges, a picturesque valley, and a history of the model pioneering spirit of endurance and resilience. Descendants of the early settlers lived in the basin into the 1960s. Since then, they return each summer to special homecomings and dinner on the grounds at the chapel. A number of the original buildings are preserved by the NPS. An example is the Palmer Chapel, built in 1898. The drainage, like the Big Creek drainage, flows N into the Pigeon River, and except for the Cataloochee Creek that flows into Waterville Lake, the basin is surrounded by mountain ridges. The Balsam Mtn. range is on the W edge, Mt. Sterling Ridge on the N, and the Cataloochee Divide on the S and E. Only two roads, one over Cove Creek Gap (SR-1395) and the other over Mt. Sterling Gap (SR-1397), connect with the outside world. Plans by the NPS in the 1960s to construct a fast route from I-40 to the heart of the basin were only partially completed, and conservationists stopped a recreational development that would have destroyed the valley's peaceful character. The valley has a developed campground with flush toilets for tenting, and a ranger station is nearby. All trails in the area are horse/hiker trails except the Asbury Trail and Boogerman Trail, which are for hikers only. Fishing is popular in Cataloochee Creek. Flora and fauna are similar to the Big Creek Area.

Address and Access: On US-276 (on the W side of the bridge) before its jct with I-40 (exit 20) in Cove Creek, turn N on Little Cove Rd (SR-1331). (There may be a Cataloochee sign here.) Drive 1.3 mi and turn R on Old NC-284 Rd (SR-1395, also called the Cataloochee Rd). After 4.5 mi, reach Cove Creek Gap, the park boundary. Descend 1.8 mi to a paved road, turn L, and after 2.7 mi bear L across the Cataloochee Creek bridge and reach jct with the Cataloochee Rd, R. (It is 7.0 mi to Mt. Sterling Gap and another 7.0 mi to the Big Creek Ranger Station described above.) From the jct, it is 0.7 mi on the paved road to the Cataloochee ranger station, R. Address: Cataloochee Ranger Station, GSMNP, Rte 2, Box 555, Waynesville, NC 28786.

Support Facilities: Shopping centers, motels, restaurants, and commercial campgrounds (some open year-round) are in Maggie Valley, 6.5 mi S from Cove Creek on US-276 and W on US-19.

Mount Sterling Ridge Trail (F, H)

514-515

Length and Difficulty: 5.4 mi, strenuous (elev change 1,950 ft.)

Connecting Trails: (Mount Sterling Trail); (Asbury Trail); (Baxter Creek Trail); Long Bunk Trail (3.7 mi, moderate) (F, H); (Swallow Fork Trail); (Pretty Hollow Gap Trail); (Balsam Mountain Trail)

Special Features: Mt. Sterling, spruce/fir forest

Trailhead and Description: The trail can be accessed from two directions. In the Cataloochee basin at the jct of the paved road and the graveled Cataloochee Rd (0.7 mi N of the ranger station), drive 7.0 mi N on the Cataloochee Rd to Mt. Sterling Gap. The other access is 7.0 mi S on the same road (usually called Old NC-284 Rd) from the Big Creek ranger station to Mt. Sterling Gap. In the gap, the trailhead of the Asbury Trail is SE and the Mt. Sterling Trail goes W. On an old road, ascend on the Mt. Sterling Trail 0.4 mi to a jct L with the rarely used Long Bunk Trail. At 0.7 mi, begin switchbacks. Enter a spruce/fir forest, and reach the ridge top to the Mt. Sterling Ridge Trail at 2.3 mi. (To the R is a 0.5-mi spur to connect with Baxter Creek Trail, back-country campsite #38, and panoramic views from the Mt. Sterling fire tower.) Continue along the ridge. Reach Pretty Hollow Gap and cross trails at 3.7 mi. Pretty Hollow Gap Trail goes 5.3 mi L, down the mountain to Cataloochee Rd, and the Swallow Fork Trail goes R 4.0 mi to join the Big Creek Trail. Continue on the ridge and pass Big Cataloochee Mtn. (6,122 ft.) on the S slope. Cross streamlets at 6.0 mi and 7.0 mi. At 5.4 mi, the trail ends at a jct with the Balsam Mountain Trail, R and L. (Left, it is 0.1 mi to the Laurel Gap Shelter, and R, it is 4.9 mi to the AT.) Backtrack, or make a 21.5-mi loop by using the Balsam Mountain Trail, R, to the AT, followed by Gunter Fork Trail and the Swallow Fork Trail. If turning L, a 23.9-mi loop can be made by using the Balsam Mountain Trail, the Palmer Creek Trail, and the Pretty Hollow Gap Trail. (USGS Maps: Cove Creek Gap, Luftee Knob)

516- *Pretty Hollow Gap Trail* (F, H)
518   **Length and Difficulty:** 5.3 mi, strenuous (elev change 2,190 ft.)
       Connecting Trails: Little Cataloochee Trail (5.2 mi, moderate) (F, H); Palmer Creek Trail (3.3 mi, strenuous) (F, H); (Mt. Sterling Ridge Trail); (Swallow Fork Trail)
       Special Features: pioneer history, wildlife
       Trailhead and Description: On the Cataloochee Rd, 1.1 mi upstream from the ranger sta, park near the trail sign at Palmer Creek. Hike up the road that parallels the scenic stream. At 0.8 mi, reach jct R with the Little Cataloochee Trail.

       (The Little Cataloochee Trail follows an old road alongside a creek 1.2 mi and reaches Davidson Gap at 1.8 mi. Pass through Noland Gap at 2.2 mi, cross Coggin Branch, and pass the foundations of what was once the Daniel Cook house [1856]. [Cook Cabin was rebuilt on this site in 1999 through a grant from Craft Food—"Log Cabin Pancake Syrup Co."] Cross Coggin Branch again and at 3.0 mi, pass L of the Little Cataloochee Baptist Church [1889] with its tall belfry. Cross Little Cataloochee Creek and a bridge at 3.5 mi. At 4.2 mi, pass R of the John Hannah cabin [1862] built of logs hewn on location. Ascend and come to jct with the rarely used Long Bunk Trail, L at 4.0 mi. [The Long Bunk Trail ascends 3.2 mi as a connector to the Mt. Sterling Ridge Trail.] Continue on the dirt road and cross Dude Branch to terminate at Cataloochee Rd at 5.0 mi. It is 5.2 mi R on Cataloochee Rd to the ranger station.)

To continue on the Pretty Hollow Gap Trail, enter a partially cleared area at 1.3 mi and reach jct with the Palmer Creek Trail L. (The Palmer Creek Trail crosses Pretty Hollow Creek on a footbridge and begins an ascent. Named after pioneer settler and bear hunter Turkey George Palmer, the trail parallels the cascading trout stream. Poplar, maple, and hemlock tower over rhododendron, ferns, and trillium among rock formations. Cross Lost Bottom Creek at 1.1 mi and Beech Creek at 1.7 mi. Ascend through an oak-hickory forest with rhododendron to reach Balsam Mtn. Rd at 3.3 mi. One-way vehicle passage only is allowed from Heintooga campground-picnic area to Round Bottom, where it becomes two-way. To the L on the road, it is 1.8 mi to N terminus of Spruce Mountain Trail and 0.7 mi R on the road to the S trailhead of Balsam Mountain Trail. Either trail can be used for connections with other trails to form long loops in rejoining the Palmer Creek Trail and Pretty Hollow Gap Trail.)

The Pretty Hollow Gap Trail goes ahead on the E side of Pretty Hollow Creek after its jct with Palmer Creek Trail. It passes heavily used Turkey George campsite #39 at 1.5 mi. Cross the stream three times and at 4.3 mi, cross Onion Creek. Ascend through the narrow valley among hardwoods, but in the climb the forest becomes partly hemlock, then spruce-fir near the end of the trail. Arrive at the N terminus at 5.3 mi to a cross-trail jct with Mount Sterling Ridge Trail, R and L, and Swallow Fork Trail down the other side of Mt. Sterling Ridge. Backtrack, or use Mount Sterling Ridge Trail R to other trails for a loop of 11.1 mi. If going L on Mount Sterling Ridge Trail, a loop of 12.3 mi can be made with 0.7 mi of the route on Balsam Mtn. Rd. (USGS-Maps: Cove Creek Gap, Luftee Knob)

Cataloochee Divide Trail (F, H)

519-
520

Length and Difficulty: 11.5 mi, moderate

Connecting Trails: (Rough Fork Trail); (Hemphill Bald Tail); (McKee Branch Trail); Asbury Trail (7.0 mi, strenuous; elev change 1,810 ft.) (F)

Special Features: scenic, historic

Trailhead and Description: The Cataloochee Divide Trail follows the Cataloochee Divide and is a ridge trail with a road access at either end. If beginning in the N, park at Cove Creek Gap on the Old NC-284 Rd (SR-1395) at the park boundary (see access directions in the introduction). Follow the sign and reach Panther Spring Gap and a spring at 2.0 mi. Reach jct R with the McKee Branch Trail at 4.6 mi. (To the L, on private property, is a short trail to Purchase Knob, 5,086 ft.) At 6.4 mi, reach jct R with Hemphill Bald

Trail where a water source is a few yards downhill. Ascend along the ridge and at 7.0 mi reach scenic Hemphill Bald (5,540 ft.) with vistas of the Plott Balsam range, the highest point of the trail. Descend the Pine Tree Gap at 7.5 mi, ascend to the N side of Sheepback Knob, and reach Maggot Spring Gap at 9.0 mi. At Garrett Gap follow an old RR grade to reach Polls Gap at 11.9 mi and a jct with the Rough Fork Trail, R. Here also is a connection with the BRP Heintooga Ridge Rd (2.4 mi S of the Balsam Mtn. Campground).

The Asbury Trail begins R (N) at Cove Creek Gap. A foot trail, it is usually not maintained except by Boy Scout troops. Follow the trail 1.0 mi through a forest of white pine and hardwoods to Hogan Gap (where the incomplete new highway to I-40 ends), and after another 1.2 mi on the ridgeline of Whiteoak Mtn., turn L on a spur ridge. Descend and ford Cataloochee Creek (2,474 ft.), or go upstream 0.2 mi to cross the Cataloochee Rd bridge at 3.6 mi. Go R 0.2 mi, leave the road, R, after a horseshoe curve, and ascend to Scottish Mtn. (4,287 ft.) at 5.4 mi. Follow the park boundary to Mt. Sterling Gap at 7.0 mi. From here the trail/road follows SR-1395 to Davenport Gap. (USGS Maps: Bunches Bald, Cove Creek Gap, Dellwood)

521- 526   *Caldwell Fork Trail* (F, H)

    Length and Difficulty: 6.5 mi, moderate

    Connecting Trails: Boogerman Trail (3.8 mi, moderate) (F); Big Fork Ridge Trail (3.1 mi, moderate) (F, H); McKee Branch Trail (2.3 mi, strenuous; elev change 1,710 ft.) (F, H); Hemphill Bald Tail (8.5 mi, strenuous; elev change 1,800 ft.) (F, H); Rough Fork Trail (6.5 mi, strenuous; elev change 2,380 ft.) (F, H)

    Special Features: historic, fishing, "Big Poplars"

    Trailhead and Description: The Caldwell Fork Trail, named after the valley's Caldwell families, begins 0.1 mi SW of the Cataloochee Campground, a good base camp. (The trail is also a horse trail; the route has wet and muddy sections.) Cross a footbridge and go upstream in a forest of hemlock, beech, birch, and rhododendron. At 0.8 mi, reach jct L with the Boogerman Trail near Den Branch. (The Boogerman Trail follows an old rough road built by Robert Palmer, who built his cottage on the mountainside, a clearing at 2.0 mi on the trail. Huge oak and poplar seen on this trail are there because Palmer never allowed logging. At 2.9 mi, descend near Smoke Branch to return to the Caldwell Fork Trail at 3.8 mi.)

    Continue on the Caldwell Fork Trail; cross the creek a number of times. At 2.8 mi, reach jct with the returning Boogerman Trail, L, and after another

0.5 mi, reach jct R with the Big Fork Ridge Trail. (The Big Fork Ridge Trail descends to the Caldwell Fork to cross on a footbridge and ascend on an old jeep road to the site of a former Caldwell Fork schoolhouse at 0.3 mi. It reaches the crest of the Big Fork Ridge at 1.2 mi and descends gradually to cross Rough Fork on a footbridge to a jct with the Rough Fork Trail at 3.1 mi. Here is the gated Cataloochee Rd and parking area for the Rough Fork Trail N trailhead. [It is 2.4 mi R on the road to the N trailhead of the Caldwell Fork Trail for a loop of 8.2 mi.])

On the Caldwell Fork Trail it is 0.1 mi from Big Fork Ridge Trail to a jct with the McKee Branch Trail, L. (The McKee Branch Trail ascends 2.3 mi, steeply, to Purchase Gap on the Cataloochee Divide to the Cataloochee Divide Trail and the park boundary. This grassy horse trail route was used by the early settlers to get over the mountain to Maggie Valley.)

At 4.4 mi on the Caldwell Fork Trail, reach jct with the Hemphill Bald Tail, L. (The Hemphill Bald Trail ascends for 0.4 mi before crossing a stream. At 1.9 mi, R, is a huge black cherry tree. Continue to ascend steeply to reach the Cataloochee Divide Trail at 3.0 mi.)

Ahead on the Caldwell Fork Trail cross Double Creek to Caldwell Fork backcountry campsite #41. Ahead enter a forest of tall hardwoods and exceptionally large "Big Poplars" to the R (similar in size to some seen in Joyce Kilmer Memorial Forest). Ascend gradually to the trail terminus at 6.5 mi and the jct with Rough Fork Trail, L and R. (If turning R on the Rough Fork Trail, descend 1.5 mi to Big Hemlock backcountry campsite #40. Pass through a grove of large trees and at 2.0 mi, arrive at a well-preserved log house (now a larger frame building), which was the original home of Jonathan Woody and his family in the 1860s. From here follow the NPS road downstream in a forest of rhododendron, birch, and white pine to the road gate and parking area. Another 2.4 mi on the road to the N trailhead of Caldwell Fork Trail is a loop of 11.1 mi. If taking the Rough Fork Trail L from the jct with the Caldwell Fork Trail, ascend steeply for the first 0.7 mi before joining an old RR grade that leads another 2.8 mi to a jct with the Hemphill Bald Trail in Polls Gap. Here is a connection with the BRP Heintooga Ridge Rd (2.4 mi S of the Balsam Mtn. Campground and 6.2 mi N of the BRP.) (USGS Maps: Bunches Bald, Cove Creek Gap, Dellwood)

Balsam Mountain Area (Swain County)

The Balsam Mtn. Ridge is the only ridge that connects the Smokies with the Blue Ridge Mtns. Much of the Heintooga Ridge area with its dark green forest of fir (balsam) and spruce can be seen from the BRP, but a special paved spur road, Balsam Mtn. Rd, takes the visitor 9.0 mi into a section of the ridge. Wildlife is frequently seen, and wildflower species are numerous. The Balsam Mtn. developed campground has 46 campsites, usually open from late May to late September. There are flush toilets and water but no hookups and no showers. (This is black-bear habitat, and food storage regulations are strictly enforced.) The 0.5-mi Balsam Mountain Nature Trail begins R, soon after entrance. It descends into a forest of fir, birch, white snakeroot, and rhododendron. The Heintooga Picnic Area, 0.6 mi beyond the campground, has 41 picnic sites and a loop parking area. From here the easy Flat Creek Trail begins at a gated access. Follow a sign to the Heintooga Overlook (5,335 ft.) for exceptional vistas of the ridges and the Raven Fork drainage. Follow the trail through spruce, birch, and rhododendron for 2.6 mi to the Heintooga Ridge Rd. Along the way (at 1.8 mi) is a side trail, R, 0.2 mi to Flat Creek Falls. At the road it is 3.7 mi back (L) to the picnic area.

527
528

Access: From BRP mp 458.2, turn onto Heintooga Rd (closed in winter) and go 8.4 mi to the Balsam Mtn. Campground. From there it is 0.6 mi to the Heintooga Picnic Area. (A one-way, 14.0-mi gravel road continues N to Round Bottom where the road becomes open for two-way traffic at Straight Fork Rd. No trucks, buses, or trailers; gates are closed at night.)

Support Facilities: All provisions and other camping needs are 20.0 mi in either direction of the BRP to Cherokee or Maggie Valley.

529- **Spruce Mountain Trail** (1.2 mi) (F); **Balsam Mountain Trail** (10.1
530 mi) (F, H)

Length and Difficulty: 11.3 mi, moderate to strenuous (elev change 1,650 ft.)

Connecting Trails: (Rough Fork Trail); (Hemphill Bald Tail); (Palmer Creek Trail); (Beech Gap Trail); (Mt. Sterling Ridge Trail); (Gunter Fork Trail); (AT)

Special Features: spruce/fir forest groves, geology

Trailhead and Description: Although separated by 2.5 mi of road, the descriptions of these two trails are combined because they cover the same major ridgeline and have similar terrain and vegetation. To reach the Balsam Mountain Trail, follow Balsam Mtn. Rd N for 2.5 mi to Pin Oak Gap (8.3 mi from Heintooga Picnic Area). Reach jct with Palmer Creek Trail along the way at 1.8 mi. Ascend to Ledge Bald (5,184 ft.), descend to Beech Gap at 2.3 mi, and come to jct L with the Beech Gap Trail, a 3.0-mi steep and rough access trail from Balsam Mtn. Rd in Round Bottom. Ascend in a spruce/fir forest to Balsam High Top (5,640 ft.) at 3.6 mi; descend to Laurel Gap at 4.1 mi. A shelter (space for 14) and a spring are here. At 4.3 mi, reach jct R with the Mt. Sterling Ridge Trail. At 5.2 mi, reach jct R with the Gunter Fork Trail. Continue on a generally level trail in a mixed forest with ferns, mosses, and moosewood. Pass L of Luftee Knob (6,200 ft.) and reach Mt. Yonaguska at 9.5 mi. Turn R and reach the AT and Tricorner Knob Shelter at 10.1 mi. (See chapter 5 for other trails connecting with the AT.) (USGS Maps: Luftee Knob, Mt Guyot)

Smokemont Area (Swain County)

The developed Smokemont Campground is on the NE side of the Oconaluftee River and at the confluence of the Bradley Fork in the Oconaluftee Valley. Oconaluftee in Cherokee means "by the riverside." The watershed for this area begins from the high elevation near Newfound Gap (N), Mt. Kephart (N), Hughes Ridge (NE), Richland Mtn. (N), and Thomas Divide (NW). The campground has 150 sites (no hookups or showers) and three group camps. (This is black-bear country, and food storage regulations are strictly enforced.) Fully operational from mid-April to the first of November, 35 sites are open year-round. There are flush toilets, water, and sewage disposal. Its crowded condition during the summer and fall months is not suitable for a hiker who loves solitude and remoteness, but it is a good base camp for hikers with such multiple interests as hiking, fishing, and horseback riding. Reservations for the campground are made through National Park Reservation System (May 15 to October 31). For more information or reservations, contact 800-365-CAMP. Hitchhiking is forbidden on Newfound Gap Rd.

Access: From Cherokee drive N, 5.7 mi on US-441 (becomes Newfound Gap Rd at the park boundary) to entrance, R.

Support Facilities: Cherokee has shopping and service centers, motels, commercial campgrounds, restaurants, and a hospital.

Hyatt Ridge Trail (F, H)
531-534

Length and Difficulty: 4.5 mi, strenuous (elev change 2,065 ft.)

Connecting Trails: Enloe Creek Trail (3.6 mi, moderate) (F, H); Beech Gap Trail II (2.9 mi, strenuous; elev change 1,860 ft.) (F, H); Beech Gap Trail I (2.5 mi, strenuous; 2,010 ft.) (F, H)

Special Features: wildlife, old-growth forest

Trailhead and Description: From the Smokemont Campground, drive 3.0 mi S on Newfound Gap Rd and turn L on a 0.6-mi connector road (across the Oconaluftee River) to Big Cove Rd. Turn L and follow Big Cove Rd (which becomes Straight Fork Rd) 11.0 mi to the trailhead, L. Follow an old trail beside Hyatt Creek and begin a steep ascent at 1.0 mi. Reach Low Gap at 1.9 mi and a jct L with the Enloe Creek Trail, L.

(The Enloe Creek Trail descends on an old trail into a beautiful forest of tall hardwoods and hemlock. At 1.0 mi, reach Raven Fork, a stream of rapids that would be impossible to cross after heavy rains. Enloe Creek rationed backcountry campsite #47 is near the creek. Continue ahead and after 0.4 mi, the treadway is rocky and sometimes muddy from horse traffic. Pass a number of small waterfalls and arrive at Enloe Creek at 2.0 mi. Cross the creek on a footlog bridge [difficult after heavy rains] and at 2.7 mi, ascend on switchbacks to a jct with Hughes Ridge Trail at 3.6 mi [To the R it is 4.7 mi to the AT, and L it is 7.9 mi to Smokemont Campground.])

Continue on the Hyatt Ridge Trail, ascend steeply on the ridge, and the jct at 3.6 mi with Beech Gap Trail II, R. (Beech Gap Trail II descends, steeply in sections, on an E slope of a hardwood forest. After 2.9 mi, it emerges at Straight Fork Rd and parking area in Round Bottom. Turn L, wade a cement autoford, and turn L off the road to ascend Beech Gap Trail I. It ascends through a hardwood forest, crosses Thumber Branch at 1.1 mi, and a jct with Balsam Mountain Trail in Beech Gap at 2.5 mi. [It is 2.3 mi R to Balsam Mtn. Rd, and 2.0 mi L to a jct with Sterling Rigde Trail.])

The Hyatt Ridge Trail continues to ascend and ends at the McGhee Spring backcountry campsite #44 at 4.5 mi. Backtrack. (The continuation of Hyatt Ridge Trail and the adjoining Raven Fork Trail at McGhee Spring have been deleted from the park's trail inventory.) (USGS Maps: Bunches Bald, Luftee Knob, Smokemont)

**535-
540**   *Bradley Fork Trail* (F, H)

Length and Difficulty: 7.3 mi, strenuous (elev 2,840 ft.)

Connecting Trails: Chasteen Creek Trail (4.4 mi, strenuous; elev change 2,300 ft.) ; Smokemont Loop Trail (3.9 mi, moderate; elev change 1,240 ft.); Cabin Flats Trail (1.1 mi, easy; dead-end); Hughes Ridge Trail (4.7 mi, moderate; elev change 1050 ft.); Dry Sluice Gap Trail (4.1 mi, strenuous; elev change 2,540 ft.); (Grassy Branch Trail); (AT)

Special Features: wildlife, wildflowers, historic

Trailhead and Description: On entry to the campground, turn L and go to a gate at the end of the campground. Bradley Fork Trail makes connections to provide two circuits from the campground (5.7 mi and 15.4 mi). Pass a hemlock grove at 1.0 mi; at 1.2 mi, jct with Chasteen Creek Trail, R.

(The Chasteen Creek Trail begins as a gated jeep and horse road-trail. After 0.1 mi, reach Lower Chasteen Creek rationed backcountry campsite #50, and at 0.8 mi is a waterfall in a forest of poplar, oak, and maple. Parallel the creek and leave the road at 2.3 mi. Pass backcountry campsite #48, and ascend steeply on switchbacks to a jct with Enloe Creek Trail and Hughes Ridge Trail at 4.4 mi (The Hughes Ridge Trail ascends on a wide treadway mainly on the W side of the ridge in an oak/hickory forest with sections of galax and wintergreen ground cover. At 2.5 mi, it makes a jct with the N trail-head of Bradley Fork Trail (which descends 7.3 mi to Smokemont Camp-ground). Ascend and descend into a number of low gaps and reach Pecks Corner Shelter and spring at 4.5 mi [reservations required]. Ascend another 0.2 mi to the AT and the state line with Tennessee at 4.7 mi.)

Continue upstream on the Bradley Fork Trail. At 1.6 mi, reach jct with Smokemont Loop Trail, L. (It returns to the campground. Ascend Bradley Fork on a footbridge, on the lower slopes of Richland Mtn. in a hardwood for-est mixed with pine, hemlock, and laurel. At 1.7 mi, reach the ridge crest, then descend on a long switchback before lesser curves. Return to the stream area, and pass L of the Bradley cemetery at 3.4 mi. Enter a white grove to join a svc road, cross Bradley Fork on an old concrete bridge to the campground. Bradley Fork Trail is 0.3 mi L for a loop of 5.7 mi.)

On the Bradley Fork Trail pass a waterfall at 2.5 mi, and cross the creek twice on road bridges before a turnaround at 4.0 mi. Ahead (N) begins Cabin Flats Trail. Bradley Fork Trail turns R and ascends on Long Ridge to a num-ber of outcroppings with scenic views. Cross Taywa Creek twice, at 5.0 mi and 5.6 mi. Ascend steeply on switchbacks to reach Hughes Ridge Trail at 7.3 mi (It is 2.2 mi L on Hughes Ridge Trail to the AT, and 2.5 mi R to Chasteen Creek Trail (15.4 mi to Smokemont Campground) for a loop.

(On the Cabin Flats Trail, go upstream, cross Bradley Fork and Tennessee Branch before a jct with the Dry Sluice Gap Trail [formerly Richland Moun-tain Trail] at 0.5 mi. Ahead, 0.6 mi farther, the trail ends at Cabin Flats back-country campsite #49. Backtrack.)

(Dry Sluice Gap Trail ascends and crosses a bridge over Tennessee Branch at 0.1 mi. It crosses the branch three more times and a number of drains to 0.9 mi. Ascend steeply and reach jct L with Grassy Branch Trail at 2.8 mi. Begin an easier gradient and pass views of Thomas Divide L [W]. At 4.1 mi, reach jct with the AT near Dry Sluice Gap. [It is 0.4 mi L to the spectacular views of the AT's Charlies Bunion and L 4.4 mi farther to Newfound Gap Rd.]) (USGS Maps: Mt Guyot, Smokemont)

541-
543
Kephart Prong Trail (F, H)

Length and Difficulty: 2.0 mi, easy

Connecting Trails: Grassy Branch Trail (2.5 mi, strenuous; elev change 1,740 ft.) (F, H); Sweat Heifer Creek Trail (3.7 mi, strenuous; elev change 2,270 ft.) (F)

Special Features: historic, wildflowers, fish hatchery

Trailhead and Description: From the Smokemont Campground, drive up Newfound Gap Rd for 3.7 mi to the parking area, R. Cross the Oconaluftee River on a road bridge and pass the remains of an old CCC camp. Cross Kephart Prong on a footbridge and pass the site of an old fish hatchery. Cross Kephart Prong three more times and reach the overused Kephart Prong Shelter (accommodates 14) at 2.0 mi. (The stream is named for Horace Kephart [1862–1931], authority on mountain lore and author of *Our Southern Highlanders*. Mt. Kephart, NW of the shelter, was named in his honor October 3, 1928.) Go R from the shelter to follow the Grassy Branch Trail, which parallels Kephart Prong. At 0.8 mi, it crosses Lower Grassy Branch near a cascade and crosses the stream again at 2.1 mi. Here are views of the valley and Thomas Divide beyond. Reach jct with the Dry Sluice Gap Trail at 2.5 mi (On the Dry Sluice Gap Trail, it is 1.3 mi L to the AT; R, it descends 3.3 mi to the Bradley Fork Trail.)

Left of the shelter is the infrequently used Sweat Heifer Creek Trail. Cross a small stream, ascend, and reach an old RR grade at 0.7 mi. Ascend and cross a cascading stream at 1.8 mi and leave the old RR grade at 2.1 mi. Wildflowers are prominent in a hardwood forest. Reach the AT at 3.7 mi. It is 1.7 mi L to Newfound Gap Rd. (The trail's name may derive from the practice of driving livestock over the mountain on the Oconaluftee Turnpike, a wagon road constructed in 1931.) (USGS Maps: Clingmans Dome, Mt Guyot, Smokemont)

544
Kanati Fork Trail (F)

Length and Difficulty: 2.9 mi, strenuous (elev change 2,110 ft.)
Connecting Trail: (Thomas Divide Trail)

Trailhead and Description: From Smokemont, drive 3.9 mi NW to the trailhead parking area, L (0.2 mi beyond the Kephart Prong Trail, described above). Follow the graded trail, parallel to Kanati Fork, in a cove of oak, poplar, maple, and birch. At 1.0 mi, leave the cove and ascend on switchbacks in a section of hemlock. Cross a small branch at 1.6 mi and ascend in a forest with rhododendron and laurel to a jct with the Thomas Divide Trail at 2.9 mi. (To the R it is 1.8 mi to the Newfound Gap Rd, and L it is 10.9 mi to the Thomas Divide Trail access in Deep Gap. See the Deep Gap Area descriptions below.) (USGS Maps: Clingmans Dome, Smokemont)

Newton Bald Trail (F, H)

545-546

Length and Difficulty: 5.4 mi, strenuous (elev change 2,900 ft.)
Connecting Trails: Mingus Creek Trail (5.8 mi, moderate) (F, H); (Thomas Divide Trail)
Special Features: wildlife, wildflowers
Trailhead and Description: Park across the road from the Smokemont Campground entrance. Hike up the Newfound Gap Rd (NW) for 0.1 mi, and turn L on an old woods road. At 0.3 mi, join a horse trail, turn R, but leave it, R, at 0.5 mi on a well-graded trail. Ascend steadily on a N slope. Cross a small stream in an area of hemlock and rhododendron at 2.7 mi and another water source at 3.0 mi. Reach jct L with the Mingus Creek Trail at 4.7 mi on the ridge crest of Newton Bald (5,142 ft.). Descend slightly and reach jct with the Thomas Divide Trail at 5.4 mi. (The Thomas Divide Trail goes R 5.2 mi to Newfound Gap Rd, and L for 9.7 mi to Deep Creek Campground. The Mingus Mill Trail is part of the MST. From Newton Bald Trail it descends on a ridge, then turns L to follow Mingus Creek to Mingus Mill. The mill is a heritage water-powered grist mill, open from 9:00AM to 5:00PM daily from mid-April to the end of October. From here there is a parking lot, then to US-441 and the Ocanaluftee Visitor Center. (USGS Map: Smokemont)

Deep Creek Area (Swain County)

Some of the longest and most scenic trails on the E side of the Smokies are on the ridges and valleys that run N-S in or near the Deep Creek basin. The historic area was home to the Cherokee, who were visited by William Bartram in the early part of the nineteenth century; a Civil War battle; sites of CCC camps; and one of the park's first trails in the 1930s. The Thomas Divide Trail is on a high E border, the central Deep Creek Trail weaves through a lush valley to its watershed near Newfound Gap, and the Noland Divide Trail is a lofty

W-side route to Clingmans Dome. The famous conservationist Horace Kephart had a permanent camp, Bryson Place, on Deep Creek, and the stream remains a popular route (eight separate backcountry campsites) for hikers, equestrians, and fishermen. With the exception of the Noland Divide Trail, all access routes to the trails begin at the Deep Creek Trail parking area N of the Deep Creek Campground. The developed campground has 108 sites for tents or RVs (no hookups or showers), flush toilets, water, and a large picnic area. The campground opens in mid-May and closes in early November. The ranger station is R after the entrance gate. Waterfalls, cascading streams, outcroppings, and virgin forests provide an area of natural beauty. Unfortunately, the wild hogs wallow in the springs and destroy plant life and the food chain for the native animals. The Mountains-to-Sea Trail (MST) passes through this area for 26 mi from Clingmans Dome to Oconaluftee Visitor Center on the following trails: the AT, 3.5 mi; Fork Ridge Trail, 5.1 mi; part of Deep Creek Trail, 4.2 mi; Martins Gap Trail, 1.5 mi; Sunkota Ridge Trail, 4.8 mi; part of Thomas Divide Trail, 0.4 mi; part of Newton Ball Trail, 0.7 mi; and Mingus Creek Trail, 5.8 mi. (See MST, appendix A.)

Address and Access: From downtown Bryson City on US-19, turn N at the Swain County Courthouse, turn R after crossing the bridge, and follow the signs for 3.0 mi. Address: Deep Creek Ranger Station, GSMNP, 1912 E Deep Creek Rd, Bryson City, NC 28713; 828-488-2493. All inquiries about the trails in the areas of Noland Creek, Forney Creek, Chambers Creek, or the campground office, should also be directed to the Deep Creek ranger (828-488-3184).

Support Facilities: Bryson City has motels, restaurants, shopping centers, commercial campgrounds, and a hospital. For more information, contact the Chamber of Commerce: 800-867-9246.

547-
552   *Deep Creek Trail* (F, H)

Length and Difficulty: 14.3 mi, strenuous (elev change 2,820 ft.)

Connecting Trails: Indian Creek Trail (3.9 mi, moderate to strenuous; elev change 1,555 ft.) (F, H); Loop Trail (1.0 mi, easy) (F, H); Martins Gap Trail (2.7 mi, moderate) (F, H); Pole Road Creek Trail (3.2 mi, strenuous; elev change 1,800 ft.) (F, H); Fork Ridge Trail (5.1 mi, strenuous; elev change 2,880 ft.) (F)

Special Features: Bryson Place, virgin hemlock, fishing

Trailhead and Description: From the Deep Creek Campground and ranger station, upstream is a jct L with the Noland Divide Trail, and a few yards farther N is the 0.3-mi Juney Whank Falls Trail. After the parking area begins the Deep Creek Trail. Hike upstream on the gated Deep Creek Trail. Pass Tom Branch Falls, R, at 0.4 mi, and pass at 0.7 mi the jct R with the S trailhead of Indian Creek Trail and Thomas Divide Trail. At 1.7 mi, pass Jenkins Place, a former home site, and a jct R with the 1.0-mi Loop Trail (which connects with the Sunkota Ridge Trail, described below). At 2.2 mi, reach the end of the road and continue on the Deep Creek Trail upstream. Follow the sign to an old jeep road that will follow the E side of the creek up and down spur ridges of Sunkota Ridge for 3.9 mi. Pass the first backcountry campsite, Bumgardner Branch #60, at 3.0 mi. At 3.5 mi is a view of the valley from the highest spur on the route. A spring is 0.2 mi ahead. At 4.3 mi, pass McCracken Branch backcountry campsite #59, and Nicks Nest Branch backcountry campsite #58 at 5.8 mi. Emerge at Bryson Place backcountry campsite #57 at 6.0 mi. It is a large grassy area with tables, a horse-hitching rack, and a clear stream at the campsite entrance. Before crossing the stream, L, at 200 ft., is a memorial plaque on a millstone honoring Horace Kephart, the "dean of American campers." On the R (E) of the campsite is jct with the Martins Gap Trail.

(The well-graded Martins Gap Trail ascends through a beautiful forest of hardwood, white pine, rhododendron, and fern beds for 1.5 mi to Martins Gap [3,430 ft.] on the Sunkota Ridge and a cross-trail jct with the Sunkota Ridge Trail. [To the L the Sunkota Ridge Trail goes 4.8 mi to a jct with the Thomas Divide Trail, and 4.3 mi R to a jct with the Deep Creek Trail.] Descend rapidly on the E side of the ridge on switchbacks to cross Indian Creek for a sharp R turn downstream at 2.4 mi. Arrive at the end of a road at 2.7 mi and follow it to its entrance gate at Deep Creek Rd at 7.3 mi. Along the way at 5.8 mi, pass a 1.0-mi spur trail [Indian Creek Loop Trail] R that leads to Sunkota Ridge Trail and to the Deep Creek Trail at Jenkins Place. At 6.1 mi, pass R of the Stone Pile Gap Trail S terminus, and at 6.6 mi, pass the 50-ft. Indian Creek Falls. Reach jct at Deep Creek Rd at 6.6 mi for a loop distance of 13.3 mi back to the parking area.)

From Bryson Place slightly descend to the riverbank and proceed upstream to pass Burnt Spruce backcountry campsite #56 at 6.3 mi. Reach jct with Pole Road Creek Trail, L, at 6.7 mi. (The Pole Road Creek Trail crosses a high scenic footbridge over Deep Creek and serves chiefly as a wide connecting trail between Deep Creek and Noland Divide. It crosses Pole Road Creek a number of times, but after 2.0 mi ascends steeply in a forest of tall hardwood and hemlock to reach Upper Sassafras Gap. Here it reaches jct with the Noland Divide Trail at 3.3 mi. It is 3.7 mi N to Clingmans Dome Rd and 7.9 mi S to the Deep Gap Campground.)

Continuing upstream, the Deep Creek Trail passes Pole Road backcountry campsite #55 at 6.8 mi and Nettle Creek backcountry campsite #54 at 7.7 mi. Pass banks of Fraser sedge *(Cymophyllus fraseriana)* at 8.1 mi, and ascend R of a precipice at 9.3 mi. At 10.3 mi, reach jct L with Fork Ridge Trail. Poke Patch backcountry campsite #53 is here.

(The Fork Ridge Trail crosses Deep Creek and ascends steeply but soon more gradually. At 0.9 mi is a scenic view of Clingmans Dome Rd area and Bearpen Ridge. Enter a dense laurel grove at 1.5 mi, one of a number of groves on the route through a forest of maple, birch, cucumber tree, and flame azalea. At 2.6 mi are huge hemlocks. After the final switchback on the ridge at 3.8 mi, the trail turns R on a more moderate grade, passes seeps and springs [the last one at 5.0 mi], and exits at a small parking area on Clingmans Dome Rd at 5.1 mi. [To the L, it is 3.5 mi to Clingmans Dome parking area, and R, it is 3.5 mi to Newfound Gap Rd.] Across the road it is 125 ft. to the AT.)

On the Deep Creek Trail ascend upstream on a bank and parallel the creek until veering R at 10.5 mi. Ascend steeply in a forest dominated by hemlock before a final ascent on switchbacks that leads to the N terminus at the Newfound Gap Rd and parking area at 14.3 mi. (From here, on the road, it is 1.6 mi L [N] to Newfound Gap and 1.6 mi R [S] to the Thomas Divide Trail.) (USGS Maps: Bryson City, Clingmans Dome)

553-   ## *Thomas Divide Trail* (F, partly H)
556   **Length and Difficulty:** 13.8 mi, strenuous (elev change 3,310 ft.)
         Connecting Trails: Stone Pile Gap Trail (0.9 mi, easy) (F, H); Deeplow Gap Trail (6.0 mi, moderate) (F, H); Sunkota Ridge Trail (8.6 mi, strenuous; elev change 2,640 ft.) (F, H); (Indian Creek Trail); (Newton Bald Trail); (Kanati Fork Trail)
         Special Features: wildlife, wildflowers, historic
         Trailhead and Description: From the N side of the Deep Creek Campground, take Deep Creek Trail and after 0.7 mi turn R at the Indian Creek Trail, cross Indian Creek on a bridge, and at 0.5 mi. Turn R at Stone Pile Gap Trail. Cross Indian Creek again and begin ascending on a gradual grade to Stone Pile Gap at 0.9 mi and the intersection with Thomas Divide Trail. At 3.4 mi, turn sharply R. In a forest of hardwood, laurel, and flame azalea, reach a knob at 5.0 mi. Descend to a spring at 5.2 mi and to a jct with the Deeplow Gap Trail, R and L, in Deeplow Gap at 5.8 mi.

(The Deeplow Gap Trail descends R [E] on the S slope of Thomas Divide and enters a cove to cross Little Creek at 0.5 mi. At 0.8 mi it reaches the base of 75-ft. Little Creek Falls. It crosses the creek, follows a series of switch-backs down to a road, and reaches jct with the 0.6-mi. Cooper Creek Trail at 1.7 mi. Use the Thomas Divide Trail to the Newton Bald Trail for an alternate route. The Deeplow Gap Trail goes L [W] from the Thomas Divide Trail and descends on switchbacks to a hemlock grove where it joins an old road at 1.8 mi. It crosses Georges Branch at 2.1 mi and Indian Creek on a bridge to a jct with Indian Creek Trail, R and L. A 12.0-mi loop could be made L on the Indian Creek Trail to the parking area at the Deep Creek Campground.)

Continue ahead on the Thomas Divide Trail to a jct R with the W end of the Newton Bald Trail at 8.9 mi. (The Newton Bald Trail goes E 5.4 mi to Newfound Gap Rd at Smokemont.) At 9.4 mi reach jct with the N terminus of the Sunkota Ridge Trail, L.

(The Sunkota Ridge Trail descends moderately and in some places gently for 4.8 mi to Martins Gap where it intersects with Martins Gap Trail. Along the way it is on the E slope for almost the entire distance. It has trail banks of trailing arbutus, gentian, ferns, and wood betony. Sassafras, flame azalea, and striped maple make up part of the understory. Intermittent springs are at 3.5 mi and 4.3 mi [In Martins Gap the Martins Gap Trail goes R 1.5 mi to a jct with the Deep Creek Trail, and L 5.8 mi to a jct with Deep Creek Rd.] From Martins Gap the trail begins on the E slope among rhododendron and laurel and follows the slope and the ridgeline for another 3.8 mi before beginning a steep descent of 1.2 mi to reach its S terminus and the jct with a connector trail, the Indian Creek Loop Trail at 9.8 mi L, it is 0.5 mi to the Indian Creek Trail; R, it is 0.5 mi to the Deep Creek Trail at Jenkins Place. From here it is 1.7 mi back to the parking area at the Deep Creek Campground, a total loop of 21.1 mi using part of the Thomas Divide Trail and all of the Sunkota Ridge Trail.)

Continue on the Thomas Divide Trail. (Although not known just where on this historic ridge, the Cherokee Tsali hid his family from the infamous "Trail of Tears" in 1838 somewhere "on the far side of this ridge." It was William Thomas (1805–93) who located him and requested he turn himself in to the US Army for accidentally killing a soldier. Thomas had been adopted by the Cherokee chief Yonaguska as his son, Little Will, near the age of 12. After the death of Yonaguska in 1839, Thomas became the Cherokee chief. Because Thomas was a white citizen, he was able to represent the Cherokee in their land claims. His strong leadership before Congress had a permanent influence on the US government establishment of the Qualla Reservation that adjoins part of the park. Thomas Divide is named in his honor. See introduction and Tsali Trail in chapter 2.) Descend to Tuskee Gap and ascend to Nettle Creek Bald at

11.8 mi. At 12.2 mi, reach jct R with the Kanati Fork Trail (which descends 2.9 mi to Newfound Gap Rd). At 13.0 mi, arrive at Turkey Flyway (5,160 ft.) for general views of Mt. Kephart and Richland Mtn. Follow a narrow ridge to Beetree Ridge before descending to a gap at 13.6 mi. Ascend to Newfound Gap Rd and trail terminus at 13.8 mi. (On the highway it is 0.3 mi R to an overlook and parking area, and 1.7 mi N to a jct L with the N trailhead of the Deep Creek Trail.) (USGS Maps: Bryson City, Clingmans Dome, Smokemont)

557   *Noland Divide Trail* (F, H)

Length and Difficulty: 11.6 mi, strenuous (elev change 4,155 ft.)

Connecting Trails: (Noland Creek Trail); (Pole Road Creek Trail)

Special Features: vistas and botanical variation

Trailhead and Description: This hiker/horse trail has the highest elev change of any trail on the E side of the Smokies. (Other high elev changes are Baxter Creek Trail and Forney Creek Trail.) An outstanding display of flora is on the trail, ranging from the tulip tree of the valley to the pine, laurel, and blueberries of the dry ridges and spruce/fir near the trail's highest point. Trillium, galax, asters, ferns, orchids, berries, and lichens are present in great variation. Begin at the sign to the L (W) of the Deep Creek Campground. (To **558** the R of the trailhead and near the parking area is 0.3-mi Juney Whank Falls Trail, a scenic 90-ft. cascade.) Follow an easy route for 0.4 mi. Ascend to a ridge, but leave it at 1.2 mi to follow an exceptionally steep slope to the headwaters of Juney Whank Branch at a long switchback. Reach Beaugard Ridge at 3.5 mi with vistas of Bryson City and the Alarka Mtns, S, in the Nantahala National Forest. Curve R and ascend steeply on the crest to springs at 4.9 mi, the last water source up the trail. Slope R of Coburn Knob and arrive at the ridgeline of Noland Divide. Reach Lower Sassafras Gap at 7.2 mi and Upper Sassafras Gap at 7.9 mi at cross-trails. (The N end of Noland Creek Trail is L; it leads S 9.0 mi to North Shore Rd. On the R the W end of Pole Road Creek Trail descends E 3.2 mi to a jct with the Deep Creek Trail.) Continue the ascent on Noland Divide and at 11.0 mi, turn R on a road that emerges at Clingmans Dome Rd at 11.6 mi. (To the L on the paved road, it is 1.5 mi to Clingmans Dome parking; to the R, it is 2.0 mi to Fork Ridge Trail, described above.) (USGS Maps: Bryson City, Clingmans Dome)

North Shore Area (Swain County)

This large area covers the rugged drainage pattern of Noland, Forney, Hazel, and Eagle Creeks, which flow S and SW into Fontana Lake from the crest of the Smokies. Hiking trails ring its borders and provide an interconnecting web within the loop. The spectacular outer loop of 79.5 mi includes 32.4 mi of the AT from Clingmans Dome to the Lakeshore Trail near Fontana Dam, 34.7 mi of the Lakeshore Trail to 10.3-mi Forney Creek Trail, and a final mi of Forney Ridge Trail to the Forney Ridge parking area at Clingmans Dome. Such a loop is one of the most scenic, adventuresome, and unforgettable in the Smokies backcountry. Many of the trails in this area were built by the CCC in the 1930s, and others are old roads used by generations past. A historic area, its lush coves were once populated, predominantly by employees of mining and lumber companies. There are many memories about this vast and beautiful forest and its people. The famous writer of mountain lore, Horace Kephart, author of *Our Southern Highlanders* (published in 1913), lived in a mining cabin in the remote hollow of Little Fork for three years in the early part of the century. Uninhabited since 1943, when the Little Tennessee River was impounded by the Fontana Dam TVA project, the area still has more than 20 cemeteries. They have such family names as Proctor, Bradshaw, Mitchell, Posey, and Welch, and such locations as Fairview and Bone Valley. Of the nearly 600 families removed from the project, more than half were from this area. Descendants are provided regular, free boat access (the easiest route) by the NPS. But the bitter controversy of a North Shore road and a designated wilderness area continues. "The public value of that park for wilderness preservation is more important than a road for those cemetery people," said Ronald J. Tipton of the Wilderness Society in Atlanta. "We won't give up," said Fred Chandler of the North Shore Cemetery Association. "We got children and grandchildren, they won't give up." (See the introduction to this chapter.)

Access: From downtown Bryson City at the Swain County Courthouse, drive N on Everette St, cross the bridge, and go straight on what becomes Fontana Rd (SR-1364) to the park gate after 3.0 mi. Continue ahead on what is also called Lakeview Dr, 5.0 mi to Noland Creek Trail access, L, and another 0.7 mi to an access parking area at the tunnel for all North Shore trails. The W access is at the Fontana Dam parking area where a hike of 1.1 mi on the AT (across the dam) connects with the Lakeshore Trail for an access to all other trails. Another vehicle access is at Forney Ridge parking area at Clingmans Dome. (Clingmans Dome Rd is closed in winter.) (See chapter 5 for AT access points.) Contact information for Noland, Forney, and Chamber Creeks area is the same as for Deep Creek.

Support Facilities: Bryson City has motels, restaurants, shopping centers, commercial campgrounds, and a hospital. For more information, contact the Chamber of Commerce (800-867-9246). Fontana Village has limited seasonal services; for more information, contact 828-498-2211. A TVA campground with hot showers is at the base of Fontana Dam, open April 15 to October 1. Boat access, rentals, and shuttle service are available. For more information contact the Fontana Marina (828-498-2211, ext 277) off NC-28, 1.6 mi E of Fontana Village.

559   *Noland Creek Trail* (F, H)

Length and Difficulty: 10.0 mi, strenuous (elev change 2,440 ft.)

560   Connecting Trails: Springhouse Branch Trail (8.3 mi, moderate) (F, H); (Noland Divide Trail); (Pole Road Creek Trail)

Special Features: fishing, wildlife, wildflowers

Trailhead and Description: Follow the access description above, from Bryson City. At the trail sign, ascend a few feet to the gate and then descend 0.2 mi to where the trail divides. Left, it is 1.0 mi to the edge of Fontana Lake and Lower Noland Creek backcountry campsite #66. Backtrack, and pass under the highway bridge. Cross Noland Creek on a bridge, and follow upstream in a forest of hardwood, hemlock, and rhododendron. At 1.7 mi, reach the mouth of Bearpen Branch and the Bearpen Branch backcountry campsite #65, L. Cross Noland Creek on a bridge at 3.0 mi and follow the R bank. Arrive in Solola Valley, an area once inhabited, at 4.0 mi. At 4.2 mi, reach the mouth of Springhouse Branch and the Mill Creek backcountry campsite #64.

(The Springhouse Branch Trail begins L and ascends gradually up Mill Creek. Evidence of old farms [rock piles] is noticeable at 0.5 mi.) Cross Mill Creek at 0.6 mi. Pass a spring at 2.4 mi and reach the crest of Forney Ridge in Board Camp Gap at 2.8 mi. Reach jct here with the Forney Ridge Trail, R. It is 5.4 mi R to Clingmans Dome Rd. Springhouse Branch Trail continues another 5.5 mi to Forney Creek.)

After leaving Solola Valley, pass a waterfall and cross Noland Creek at 5.0 mi. Ford the stream twice more and ascend. At 5.4 mi is Jerry Flats backcountry campsite #63, and at 6.5 mi is Upper Ripshin backcountry campsite #62. Cross Upper Ripshin Branch at 7.2 mi and immediately cross Noland Creek again. Ascend to and cross Sassafras Branch at 8.6 mi. From Bald Creek backcountry campsite #61, ascend 0.5 mi to approach Sassafras Gap, the trail's terminus at 9.6 mi and a cross-trail jct. (It is 3.4 mi L on the Noland Divide Trail to Clingmans Dome Rd and 1.5 mi L on the road to Forney Ridge

Trail. At Sassafras Gap the Pole Road Creek Trail descends 3.2 mi to the Deep Creek Trail.) (USGS Maps: Bryson City, Clingmans Dome, Noland Creek, Silers Bald)

Lakeshore Trail (F, H)   561

Length and Difficulty: 34.7 mi, easy to strenuous

Connecting Trails: Tunnel Bypass Trail (1.6 mi, easy) (F, H); Goldmine   562-
Loop Trail (2.0 mi, moderate) (F, H); Whiteoak Branch Trail (1.9 mi, easy) (F,   566
H); (Forney Creek Trail); (Hazel Creek Trail); Jenkins Ridge Trail (8.9 mi,
strenuous) (F, H); (Eagle Creek Trail); Lost Cove Trail (3.1 mi, strenuous) (F,
H); (AT)

Special Features: former home sites, secluded, fishing

Trailhead and Description: Access is described above in the North Shore Area. Boat access is possible at Chambers Creek, Pilkey Creek, Hazel Creek, and Eagle Creek at normal lake level. (For more information, contact the Fontana Village Marina (828-498-2211, ext 277.) The trail follows a contour generally between 1,800 and 2,500 ft. Infrequent trail signs help guide the hiker in and out of scores of ridge spines, coves, and cross-trails. The forest is predominantly hardwood with a mixture of pine, hemlock, rhododendron, mountain laurel, and azalea. Leucothoe and ferns are commonplace near the many streams. Wildflowers are profuse and include orchids, cohosh, arbutus, cardinal flower, turtlehead, and dwarf iris. In some of the former residential settlements are vines, shrubs, and domestic flowers. Bear, wild hog, deer, fox, beaver, grouse, and turkey are among the wild animals. Songbirds are prominent.

At the tunnel parking area, the "Portals to the Wilderness," there is a choice of trail directions. The direct route is through the tunnel. A longer route is the 1.6-mi. Tunnel Bypass Trail. It is accessed across the road from the parking area. (It ascends among evergreens and after 0.5 mi, reach jct with the 2.1-mi Goldmine Loop Trail, L. The Tunnel Bypass Trail continues R, crosses Tunnel Ridge, and descends to partially follow Hyatt Creek headwaters before rejoining Lakeshore Trail.) (The Goldmine Loop Trail descends S to Tunnel Branch and mainly in a hardwood forest. After curving W, pass an old home site at 1.1 mi. It crosses Hyatt Branch, and after 0.3 mi follows Goldmine Branch before ascending to a ridge. At 1.9 mi is Goldmine Branch backcountry campsite #67, and at 2.0 mi, the trail makes a jct with Lakeshore Trail. [It is 1.0 mi E to Lakeshore Trail parking area.])

After passing through the tunnel on the Lakeshore Trail, pass the W jct with the Tunnel Bypass Trail, L, and the Goldmine Loop Trail at 1.0 mi, also on the L. Follow a graded treadway and stay L of an unnamed path. Pass L of Whiteoak Branch Trail at 2.2 mi (The 1.9-mi Whiteoak Branch Trail is a shortcut, from this point, to Forney Creek Trail. The trail ascends, crosses Gray Wolf Creek, and ascends to cross a ridge saddle among conifers. It descends, crosses Whiteoak Branch, and reaches jct with Forney Creek Trail.)

Continue on the Lakeshore Trail through former home site areas with former cleared forests. Cross a bridge over Gray Wolf Creek, pass a cemetery, and at 3.0 mi, reach jct with Forney Creek Trail (which follows an old RR grade for most of its 10.3 mi to Forney Ridge Trail, 1.0 mi from Clingmans Dome Rd). Here the Lakeshore Trail turns L and runs jointly with a former section of Forney Creek Trail. After less than 0.2 mi, cross an old bridge over Forney Creek to Lower Forney backcountry campsite #74, a popular campsite with both hikers and fishermen. Under a forest cover of white pine and hemlock, the campsite has picnic tables and a pit toilet.

Follow a gradual and graded ascent to curve the multiple ridge spines of Pilot Knob. At 5.2 mi is a minor gap and a jct with old trails; go straight. Descend slightly, cross small Jenny Branch at 6.1 mi and Gunter Branch at 6.7 mi. At 7.2 mi, cross a small branch in a small glade by old walls made by early settlers. For the next 2.0 mi, pass through a former settlement with evidence of old home sites. There are some switchbacks among open and mixed hardwood forests. Cross Welch Branch at 8.8 mi. (The McClure cemetery is on a gentle knoll, R, on a 0.1-mi side trail at 8.9 mi.)

Chambers Creek is crossed on a footbridge at 9.6 mi and to the right is backcountry campsite #98. Nearby is a chimney from an old home site. From this area Fontana Lake is visible for the next 5.0 mi, the best views for the entire route. At 11.7 mi, pass an old home site chimney and arrive at Kirkland Branch backcountry campsite #76. A bridge over the creek is at 11.9 mi. Pass an old rusty antique car at 13.1 mi, one of a number of similar relics seen on trails in the North Shore Area. Where side trails come to jct at 15.0 mi, go straight on an old road. Cross a park bridge over Pilkey Creek at 16.0 mi and follow the creek briefly. From here the trail ascends a ridge for a descent to Clark Branch and backcountry campsite #77, near an old home site at 16.6 mi. Pines and hardwoods shade the area, and S of the campsite it is only 0.2 mi to the edge of Fontana Lake.

From here the trail continues around ridge spines, rocky sections, and crosses cascading Chesquaw Branch at 18.6 mi. The next backcountry campsite, #81, is at Mill Creek, near an old home site with a chimney at 21.4 mi.

Ascend a ridge, dip to a cove, and reach a gap on Welch Ridge at 22.6 mi. Begin a descent to Hazel Creek Valley. At the mouth of Hazel Creek is a long cove of Fontana Lake, and a svc road from the lake's edge upstream by Hazel Creek. Here are trial signs. To the L is Proctor backcountry campsite #86 and an access to boat docking. (At this campsite was the former Proctor School ball field before Fontana Dam was constructed during 1942–45.) Cross the bridge over Hazel Creek at 24.3 mi into an area that was formerly the community of Proctor. At more signs, Hazel Creek Trail begins R (and its jct with Jenkins Ridge Trail). (See description ahead.) The Lakeshore Trail curves L between the creek and the Calhoun House, constructed in 1928. Follow an old road (the new Lakeshore Trail routing) and pass by a grove of sycamore at 24.8 mi. At 25 mi are steps up an embankment, R, to 198 gravesites of the Proctor cemetery. There is a stream on the L, the product of two tributaries, Hickory Bottom Branch and Shehan Branch. At 25.3 mi, the road narrows in the approach to Ramp Cove and to the L is relocated backcountry campsite #88 (a number from a former backcountry campsite on Pinnacle Creek where the former routing of Lakeshore Trail is no longer maintained).

Continue up the cove on a well-designed trail with frequent waterbars. After passing through a grove of hemlock, cross a ridge at 26.7 mi. Descend in a continuing hardwood forest. After three more ridges, including Pinnacle Ridge, descend to a switchback, L. At 28.7 mi, descend among rhododendron to a jct with Eagle Creek Trail, R. (See description ahead.)

Turn L on the Lakeshore Trail and after 75 yd. cross a steel and wood bridge over Eagle Creek. Pass Lost Cove backcountry campsite #90 at 29.2 mi. This popular camping area has large shade trees, the cascades of Lost Cove Creek, and a beach (depending on the Fontana Dam water level). Access is also available here for boat docking. Cross a footbridge and briefly parallel Lost Cove Creek, then at 29.6 mi, leave the creek on a switchback, L, in a canopy of rhododendron and mountain laurel. The E terminus of Lost Cove Trail is here.

(The Lost Cove Trail is the only trail connecting directly from North Shore Area to the Twentymile Creek Area. It gradually ascends along Lost Cove Creek, crossing it at least a dozen times. At 1.4 mi is Upper Lost cove backcountry campsite #91, L. The trail ascends on switchbacks after leaving the stream and ends at Sassafras Gap on the AT at 3.1 mi. Ahead on an old road begins 4.7-mi Twentymile Creek Trail (see description ahead). Left on the AT it is 0.3 mi to a 0.1-mi spur for Shuckstack fire tower and fantastic views. Farther down the mountain on the AT, it is 4.5 mi to the S side parking lot across Fontana Dam. On the AT, R, it is 0.9 mi to Birch Spring Gap Shelter (which, as with other AT shelters, requires a reservation for usage).

After two more switchbacks on the Lakeshore Trail, level off at 29.7 mi. A level route does not last long. The trail trend is to rise and fall on at least seven finger ridges that are part of Snakeden and Shuckstack main ridges. Maple, oak, sourwood, and some yellow poplar and dogwood on the slopes provide rainbow colors for autumn. In contrast, the coves and many streamlets offer greens with hemlock, rhododendron, and ferns. At 30.1 mi is a horseshoe curve with sporadic views of Fontana Lake and scenic Birchfield Branch is crossed at 31.6 mi. An example of what old NC-288 was like as the only access road before the dam was built is at 32.3 mi. Near here and beyond to 32.8 mi are scattered overlook views of the lake. At 33 mi are remnants of old cars, and at 33.4 mi is an open home site. This area has (as nearby areas have) a history of timber cutting and mining. Some of the mining was for gold, silver, and copper. Cross cascading Payne Branch at 33.9 mi in a dark cove of tall and handsome hardwoods with thickets of rhododendron. After an ascending switchback on old road construction, the trail levels out on a road to arrive at a gate, the W end of Lakeshore Trail at 34.7 mi. Here is a small parking area and on the road and to the R is the AT. From here it is 1.1 mi on the paved road to cross Fontana Dam and arrive at its visitor center. (USGS Maps: Noland Creek, Tuskeegee, Fontana Dam, Thunderhead Mtn., Cades Cove.)

567   *Forney Creek Trail* (F, partly H)

   Length and Difficulty: 10.3 mi, strenuous (elev change 4,030 ft.)

568-   **Connecting Trails:** (Lakeshore Trail); Bear Creek Trail (5.8 mi, strenu-
571   ous; elev change 3,100 ft.) (F, H); Springhouse Branch Trail (8.3 mi, strenuous; elev change 1,640 ft.) (F, H); Jonas Creek Trail (3.5 mi strenuous; elev change 3,200 ft.) (F, H); Forney Ridge Trail (5.7 mi, strenuous; elev change 2,500 ft.) (F)

   Trailhead and Description: Follow the Lakeshore Dr and the Lakeshore Trail descriptions above. (Another access is 1.1 mi on the Forney Ridge Trail from Clingmans Dome Rd.) After 4.0 mi (2.9 mi if using the tunnel route) on the Lakeshore Trail, reach jct with Forney Creek Trail, R. (To the L the Forney Creek Trail crosses a bridge to Lower Forney backcountry campsite #74 and the lake after 0.2 mi. The Lakeshore Trail continues from the campsite W to Fontana Dam.) Go upstream on the Forney Creek Trail on an old RR grade for the first 9.0 mi. It crosses the creek at least 15 times; wading or rock-hopping is necessary. At 0.6 mi, reach jct L with the Bear Creek Trail (formerly Jumpup Ridge Trail).

(The Bear Creek Trail follows an old RR grade near Bear Creek. At 2.8 mi is backcountry campsite #75 at Poplar Flats. From here the trail ascends on curves and switchbacks to the top of Jumpup Ridge at 5.0 mi. The trail terminates on Welch Ridge [4,890 ft.] at a jct with Welch Ridge Trail. [To the R, it is 6.5 mi on the Welch Ridge Trail to Silers Bald and the AT. To the L, it runs 0.8 mi to a jct with Cold Spring Branch Trail and scenic High Rocks.])

Reach the site of an old CCC camp with scattered old farm artifacts at 2.8 mi. Here is CCC backcountry campsite #71. After crossing the creek, reach jct with the Springhouse Branch Trail (formerly the Bee Gum Branch Trail), R. (The Springhouse Branch Trail ascends by Bee Gum Branch to leave it at 2.3 mi in a cove. Reach the S end of Forney Ridge Trail at 5.5 mi. From here the Forney Ridge Trail is 5.7 mi to Clingmans Dome Rd, described below.)

Continue on the Forney Creek Trail through cove hardwood and a mixture of rhododendron, hemlock, and white pine. At 4.0 mi arrive at the Jonas Creek Trail, L, and Jonas Creek backcountry campsite #70. (The Jonas Creek Trail fords Forney Creek and follows an old RR grade up Jonas Creek for 1.5 mi where it becomes a path. After crossing Jonas Creek and Yanu Branch, begin switchbacks that end at 2.6 mi. Reach jct with the Welch Ridge Trail on Welch Ridge at 4.2 mi. To the L, it is 4.8 mi on the Welch Ridge Trail to its S terminus at Cold Spring Gap Trail. To the R, it is 2.5 mi to Silers Bald and the AT.)

Continue on the Forney Creek Trail, crossing Forney Creek frequently, and reach the mouth of Huggins Creek and Huggins backcountry campsite #69, L, at 5.3 mi. From here the old RR grade gradually ascends on switchbacks to cross other streams such as Buckhorn Branch and Little Steeltrap Creek. After the old RR grade ends at 9.0 mi, follow an old timber road for 0.5 mi to cross Forney Creek for the last time. Ascend on a footpath with a number of seeps in a damp forest of hemlock, fir, and beech. Terminate the trail at 10.0 mi to reach jct with the Forney Ridge Trail, R and L.

(To the L the Forney Ridge Trail ascends 1.0 mi on a rough and rocky footpath in a spruce/fir forest to the parking area on Clingmans Dome Rd. A 0.5-mi spur trail, Clingmans Dome Bypass Trail, to the AT goes L 0.1 mi before **572** reaching the parking area. To the R the Forney Ridge Trail descends 4.6 mi to a jct with the Springhouse Branch Trail described above. At 0.7 mi, it reaches Andrews Bald, which received its name from mountain-born Andres (not Andrews) Thompson, who built a hand-hewn cabin here in the 1850s. Owning

1,280 acres here and elsewhere in the vicinity, he became a prosperous cattle raiser. A scenic area with views of the Little Tennessee River Valley and beyond, the bald's grassy beauty is enhanced in late June when a concentration of flame azalea and catawba rhododendron is in bloom. Ferns, wildflowers, spruce, and fir assist in the display. Descend to gaps and lower knobs to reach Springhouse Branch Trail at 4.6 mi. (The Springhouse Branch Trail runs 2.8 mi to the Noland Creek Trail, described above.) Reach a scenic area at 6.5 mi and slope R of the knob to jct with Springhouse Branch Trail, also described above. From here it is 5.5 mi to the Forney Creek Trail, a potential loop of 17.3 mi (USGS Maps: Clingmans Dome, Noland Creek, Silers Bald)

573   *Hazel Creek Trail* (F, H)

> **Length and Difficulty:** 14.7 mi, strenuous (elev change 3,580 ft.)

**574-
577**

> **Connecting Trails:** (Lakeshore Trail); (Jenkins Ridge Trail 8.9 mi, strenuous; elev change 2,899 ft.) (F,H); Bone Valley Trail (1.8 mi, easy; dead-end) (F, H); Cold Spring Gap Trail (3.5 mi, strenuous; elev change 2,450 ft.) (F, H); Welch Ridge Trail (7.3 mi, moderate) (F, H); High Rocks Trail (0.4 mi, moderate) (F), dead-end

> **Special Features:** trout fishing, sites of former communities, High Rocks, Hall Cabin

> **Trailhead and Description:** The Hazel Creek Trail, widely known for its trout fishing, is in the heart of the North Shore Area. It is accessed by other trails or by boat on Fontana Lake. The latter provides the quickest route (approx 6.0 mi) from the Fontana Boat Dock; the AT route from Clingmans Dome Rd is the shortest trail route (4.7 mi, including 0.5 mi from Clingmans Dome parking area and the 1.7 mi on Welch Ridge Trail). From the lake trailhead, follow the narrow park road, reach Proctor backcountry campsite #86 at 0.5 mi and a jct R with the Lakeshore Trail, described above. (It is 24.3 mi E and 10.4 mi W on Lakeshore Trail.) Hazel Creek Trail (formerly part of the routing of the Lakeshore Trail) begins on the W side of Proctor bridge and the Lakeshore Trail (there are signs). Follow an old road, once called Calico St during the period Proctor was a thriving community, which was estimated to have a population of more than 1,000. The community received its name from Moses Proctor, who with his wife and son, built a log cabin here in 1830. At 0.3 mi are examples of building foundations, one of which was the Proctor Baptist Church. Ahead, the trail and creek make a long horseshoe curve. At 3.3 mi is Sawdust Pile backcountry campsite #85. (The campsite received its name from a sawmill operator who was not part of the huge Ritter

Lumber Company that cut more than 201 million board feet of lumber from 1902 to 128 in the Hazel Creek watershed.) At 4.5 mi is a fork where Jenkins Ridge Trail begins. To the R, across Haw Gap Branch bridge, is Sugar Fork backcountry campsite #84 (hikers use only). This is the former community known as Medlin.

(The Jenkins Ridge trail parallels the S side of Haw Gap Branch, the Sugar Fork Creek to nearly Pickens Gap. Along the way is a second growth forest of white pine, hemlock, and rhododendron closer to the stream and mainly oak, maple, and sourwood on the ridge sides. Some of the outcroppings are slate and schist. At 1.7 mi, the trail passes the confluence of Little Fork where up the hollow, Horace Kephart [1862–1931] lived in a cabin near a copper mine. An outstanding scholar, he arrived here in 1904 and stayed nearly three years collecting information on the folklore of the Great Smoky Mountains. [See introduction to North Shore Area and Kephart Trail elsewhere in this chapter.] At 2.4 mi, Jenkins Ridge Trail turns R, N, from Pickens Gap to ascend ridges to the AT. [To the L in the gap the former Pinnacle Creek Trail descended SE for 4.0 mi to Eagle Creek Trail. The route is lush, difficult, and wet. There are not any bridges, and hikers, if making an effort to use it must ford the rushing cold water in 15 places. The wet trail is no longer maintained.] The Jenkins Ridge Trail ascends steeply and is extremely difficult on the climb to Woodward Knob. At 4.6 mi, it ascends Cherry Knob. After Haw Gap, the trail is not as strenuous. At 5.0 mi is a stream crossing in a gap. From here the ascent is more moderate; there is an increase of beech and birch trees. Near the N terminus with the AT and Spence Field at 8.9 mi, the vegetation in partly grassy with rhododendron, flame azalea, and blueberry.)

Continuing on Hazel Creek Trail up the old road, reach Bone Valley backcountry campsite #83 at 5.3 mi. (Reservations are required for this campsite.) To the L is Bone Valley Trail. (The Bone Valley Trail begins across the bridge and gently ascends by the Bone Valley Creek. Ford the stream four times en route to the Crate Hall Cabin, a national historic site, at 1.7 mi. The Hall cemetery is N of the cabin. Ruins of other buildings are nearby. Backtrack.) On the Hazel Creek Trail continue to follow the road upstream and reach jct R with the Cold Spring Gap Trail at 6.6 mi.

(The Cold Spring Gap Trail is rough, wet, and without bridges; it is eroded and exceptionally steep. It should not be hiked in winter or when there is flooding or high water. From the Hazel Creek Trail it descends 0.2 mi to Hazel Creek, where wading is necessary. It then begins its ascent in following old RR grades and passes evidence of former home sites, particularly at 0.5

mi and 1.0 mi. The old RR grades end about 3.0 mi where trail steepness is increased. It reaches Cold Spring Gap at 3.5 mi, the trail's E terminus, and the S terminus of 7.2 mi Welch Ridge Trail. [After ascending 0.5 mi on the Welch Ridge Trail there is High Rocks Trail, 0.4-mi spur trail, L, to scenic rocks described below. The Welch Ridge Trail ascends to a jct with Bear Creek Trail, Jonas Creek Trail, and Hazel Creek Trail before its N terminus at the AT, 0.2 mi E of Silers Bald.])

On the Hazel Creek Trail at 8.1 mi, reach Calhoun Place backcountry campsite #82 (named in honor of Josh Calhoun, former homesteader). AT 8.6 mi, wade or rock-hop Walkers Creek and into a place called Walder Fields, a site of a former residential community and school. Wade or rock-hop Proctor Creek a number of times. Pass the former Hazel Creek Cascades campsite, and begin an ascension to Welch Ridge at 12.9 mi. Although the trail follows switchbacks, the elevation change is about 1000 ft. At 14.7 mi, the trail ends at a jct with Welch Ridge Trail, R and L. If turning L, it is 1.7 mi to the meadows of Silers Bald at a jct with the AT. (On the AT, R, it is 4.5 mi to the Clingmans Dome Rd parking area. If turning R on the Welch Ridge Trail, notice the description from the AT below.)

(If hiking the Welch Ridge Trail from the AT, pass through meadows, rhododendron groves, and mixes of hardwoods and conifers. At 1.0 mi from the AT it descends among slate rocks on switchbacks to Mule Gap. The jct with Hazel Creek Trail is R at 1.7 mi. At 2.5 mi, it meets Jonas Creek Trail, L. [The Jonas Creek Trail descends 4.2 mi to Forney Creek Trail.] At 3.8 mi, it passes a rock outcrop and descends to a gap at 4.4 mi. It then ascends steeply to Mt. Glory at 4.7 mi. It passes R of Hawk Knob at 5.0 mi, spring at 5.2 mi, and a beautiful open area at Bearwallow Bald before a jct L with Bear Creek Trail at 6.5 mi. The Bear Creek Trail descends 5.8 mi to Forney Creek Trail. At 6.8 mi on the Welch Ridge Trail there is a 0.4-mi spur trail, R, to High Rocks (5,188 ft.), a scenic sandstone and quartz knob. An old fire tower has been dismantled. Views may be North Shore mountain ranges, the Little Tennessee River Valley, S, and the Stecoah Mtn range, S. At 7.3 mi, Welch Ridge Trail ends at a jct with Cold Spring Branch Trail, described above.) (USGS Maps: Fontana Dam, Noland Creek, Thunderhead Mtn., Tuskeegee, Silers Bald)

578   *Eagle Creek Trail* (F)
>   **Length and Difficulty:** 8.2 mi, strenuous (elev change 3,170 ft.)
>   **Connecting Trails:** (Lakeshore Trail); (AT)
>   **Special Features:** trout fishing, historic, geology, scenic

Trailhead and Description: The easiest and shortest trail access is on Lakeshore Trail for 6.0 mi from the S side parking lot of Fontana Dam. A popular trail with frequent traffic, its disadvantage is having to wade the creek 16 times; some crossings can be swift and risky. Former human inhabitants included Cherokee Indians, loggers, miners, and moonshiners.

Begin the trail N on the E side of Eagle Creek, pass through a hemlock grove, and after 0.2 mi, wade Eagle Creek for the first time. At 0.8 mi, arrive at Lower Ekaneetlee Creek backcountry campsite #89, then cross Ekaneetlee Creek. Moderately ascend the hollow and reach Eagle Creek Island backcountry campsite #96 at 2.2 mi. At 4.2 mi is Big Walnut backcountry campsite #97. Ascend, follow L of cascading Gunna Creek at 4.7 mi, then cross it at 5.4 mi. At 5.7 mi, ascend steeply, cross the creek again, begin switchbacks among rock formations, and go through open woods of maple, oak, beech, and buckeye. Arrive at Spence Field Shelter (reservations required for usage) at 8.0 mi. Ascend to the AT at 8.2 mi in a grassy bald with scenic views. To the R, it is 0.4 mi to a jct R with Jenkins Ridge Trail. (Using Jenkins Ridge Trail for 6.5 mi, the Hazel Creek Trail for 4.5 mi, and the Lakeshore Trail for 4.4 mi can make a loop of 17.8 mi.) (USGS Maps: Cades Cove, Fontana Dam, Thunderhead Mtn.)

Twentymile Creek Area (Swain County)

In the W corner of the park, in NC, the Twentymile Creek Area is bordered by the state line N and W, the Twentymile Ridge E, and NC-28 and Cheoah Lake (Little Tennessee River) S. The area received its name from being 20.0 mi downstream from the confluence of the Little Tennessee River and the Tuckasegee River. (Farther W, into Tennessee, the park extends to Chilhowee.) The AT formerly followed the state line from Doe Knob over Gregory Bald, Parson Bald, Sheep Wallow Knob, and down to Deals Gap. Here it crossed US-219 and descended to Cheoah Dam where it crossed the bridge to ascend Yellow Creek Mtn. (see Yellow Creek Mountain Trail, chapter 2, section 1). High on the mountain balds were the grazing fields for cattle and sheep before the 1930s. It is on these balds that spectacular displays of flame azalea are seen in mid-June.

Address and Access: From Fontana Village, drive W on NC-28 for 6.0 mi to Twentymile Ranger Station, R. Access to the trails is here. Address: Twentymile Ranger Station, GSMNP, Fontana, NC 28733, but call Deep Gap Ranger Station for information: 828-488-2493.

Support Facilities: The nearest developed campground is Fontana Dam Campground at the base of Fontana Dam, 5.0 mi E from the ranger station. It has hot showers (no hookups) and is usually open from April 15 to early October. Groceries, gas, telephone, motel, and restaurant are W on NC-28, 2.8 mi from the ranger station.

579   *Twentymile Trail* (F, H)

Length and Difficulty: 5.0 mi, strenuous (elev change 2,355 ft.)

580-   **Connecting Trails:** Wolf Ridge Trail (6.4 mi, strenuous; elev change
583   3,345 ft.) (F, H); Twentymile Loop Trail (2.8 mi, moderate) (F); Gregory Bald Trail (7.2 mi, strenuous; elev change 1,740 ft.) (F, H); Long Hungry Ridge Trail (4.6 mi, strenuous; elev change 2,240 ft.) (F, H)

Special Features: heath balds, flame azalea, wildlife, historic

Trailhead and Description: (These five trails create two loops and a potential third loop by using a segment of the AT.) From the ranger station parking lot, begin on the Twentymile Trail (a svc road) and pass a park svc barn. Cross a bridge over Moore Springs Branch where the trail forks at 0.5 mi. Wolf Ridge Trail goes L on an old RR bed. Twentymile Trail goes R. At this fork, a loop of 6.6 mi can be made by taking either route to include Twentymile Loop Trail. At either end of the Twentymile Loop Trail either Wolf Ridge Trail or Long Hungry Ridge Trail can be used to ascend and reach jct with Gregory Bald Trail to form a second loop of 14.1 mi.

If following Wolf Ridge Trail, parallel Moore Springs Branch; cross three bridges and make two wadings in the first 1.1 mi to the mouth of Dalton Branch, L. Here is a jct with Twentymile Loop Trail R. (It crosses [must wade] Moore Springs Branch, climbs over Long Hungry Ridge, and descends to wade across Twentymile Creek for a jct with Twentymile Trail at 2.9 mi.) On the Wolf Ridge Trail ascend upstream on Dalton Branch to Dalton Branch backcountry campsite #95 at 2.0 mi. (There have been bear sightings here.) From here, turn E to swing N in a climb up Wolf Ridge. Pass through an open oak-hickory forest. Arrive at Parson Bald among wildflowers, flame azaleas, and grasses at 5.6 mi. For the next 0.8 mi, the crest is generally level with easy treadway to a jct with Gregory Bald Trail R and L. Here is rationed Sheep Pen Gap backcountry campsite #13.

(Half of the Gregory Bald Trail descends L, 4.0 mi, to Sam Gap, its beginning on Parson Branch Rd in TN. The road, closed in winter, is a one-way vehicle route S only, 5.6 mi from Cades Cove. It exits at US-129. The other half of the trail, R, follows the main ridge to end at the AT in Doe Gap at 3.1 mi.

Along the way, it is 0.5 mi to Gregory Bald [4,948 ft.], a grassy field with incredible views and beauty from groves of flame azaleas. They bloom usually from mid- to late June. It is another 0.6 mi to a jct L with the 5.0-mi Gregory Ridge Trail, which descends to Forge Creek Rd, 2.3 mi S of Cades Cove in TN. To the R of the jct is Long Hungry Ridge Trail, described below.)

If following the Twentymile Trail from the fork at Wolf Ridge Tail, parallel the Twentymile Creek upstream in a forest of poplar, maple, oak, hemlock, and rhododendron. Ferns, orchids, and other wildflowers are on the trailside. In a valley of logging history, follow an old RR bed, cross two bridges, and reach Twentymile Creek backcountry campsite #93 at 1.7 mi, near another bridge. Cross Turkey Cove Branch at 2.1 mi. Soon cross a bridge and move away from Twentymile Creek, but follow the N side of Proctor Branch to Proctor Field Gap at 3.1 mi. Reach jct here with Twentymile Loop Trail L. (If hiking the loop, wade across Twentymile Creek, ascend and descend Long Hungry Ridge, and wade Moore Springs Branch to a jct with Wolf Ridge Trail.) Ahead, and also L, at Proctor Field Gap is Long Hungry Ridge Trail.

(Long Hungry Ridge Trail crosses Proctor Branch at 0.1 mi; it goes to a ridge nose to parallel Twentymile Creek upstream. At 1.2 mi, pass Upper Flats backcountry campsite #92, R. Cross Twentymile Creek and another stream on the E slope climb of Long Hungry Ridge to the crest at scenic Rye Patch [4,400 ft.] at 3.5 mi. Reach Gregory Bald Trail L and R at 4.6 mi. To the R, it is 2.0 mi to the AT at Doe Knob. To the L, it is 0.7 mi to scenic Gregory Bald described above.)

To complete the Twentymile Trail from the E end jct of Twentymile Loop Trail, ascend, cross Proctor Branch at 3.3 mi, and follow switchbacks, steeply near the end, to Sassafras Gap (3,653 ft.) at the AT, R and L, at 5.0 mi. To the L, it is 0.9 mi to Birch Spring Gap backcountry campsite #113 (reservations required for usage), and to the R, it is 0.3 mi to a 0.1-mi spur trail at Shuckstack fire tower, where there are magnificent views of Fontana Lake. Ahead (across the AT) begins Lost Cove Trail, described above. (USGS-FS Maps: Fontana Dam, Cades Cove, Calderwood, Tapoco)

Chapter 8

Other Trails in the National Park System

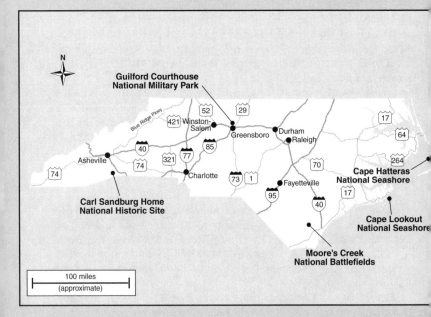

Introductions to Trail Areas

Other Trails in the National Park System

The Outer Banks are made of sand . . . the most tenacious and
resilient ecological community on earth.
—John Alexander & James Lazell, *Ribbon of Sand*

Cape Hatteras National Seashore (Dare and Hyde Counties)

Cape Hatteras, a chain of barrier islands E of Pamlico Sound, has 30,318 acres
of sandy Atlantic beaches, dunes, and marshlands. It is the nation's first
national seashore. Authorized as a park by Congress on August 17, 1937, the
islands are havens for more than 300 species of migratory and permanent
shorebirds. Major shore fish are flounder, bluefish, and spot, and offshore are
marlin, dolphin, mackerel, and tuna. Often referred to as the Outer Banks and
the "Graveyard of the Atlantic," the offshore area has two ocean currents near
Diamond Shoals that are used as shipping lanes and are hazardous for those
navigating the seas. More than 600 ships have fallen victim to the shallow
shoals, winds, and storms over the past 400 years.

For hikers and campers on the string of islands, the NPS permits camping
at designated campgrounds only. Facilities are limited to cold showers, drinking
water, tables, grills, and modern rest rooms. Oregon Inlet, Cape Point, Ocracoke, and Frisco fee campgrounds are usually open from Memorial Day
through Labor Day. Sites are rented as available, except Ocracoke, where sites
may be reserved through BIOSPHERICE; for more information, contact 800-
365-CAMP. Hikers using tents are requested to use stronger tents and longer
stakes than usual for protection against the sand and wind. Protection against
sunburn and insects is essential. Also be aware of strong littoral currents, rip currents, and shifting sand when swimming. Tidal currents near inlets are hazardous, and the NPS recommends swimming only where lifeguards are on duty.

Nature trails are located at the visitor centers at Cape Hatteras, Bodie
Island Lighthouse, and near the campground on Ocracoke Island. The Cape
Hatteras Beach Trail (a route of the MST) follows the park's entire chain of

islands as described below. (It also jointly follows the MST for 70 mi.) In addition to the Cape Hatteras park, the same office administers two other area parks. The Wright Brothers National Memorial (9.0 mi N of the US-64/NC-12 jct at Whalebone Junction) is a 431-acre memorial museum to Wilbur and Orville Wright, who on December 17, 1903, were the first to successfully achieve air flight with machine power. In addition, Fort Raleigh National Historic Site is 8.0 mi W of Whalebone Junction on US-64. Designated a historic site on April 5, 1941, it covers 346 acres and includes parts of the former 1585 and 1587 settlements. The Lindsay Warren Visitor Center displays excavated artifacts, and exhibits tell the story of Sir Walter Raleigh's "lost colony." In addition, the park includes a reconstruction of Fort Raleigh, the Waterside Theatre (which presents Paul Green's symphonic drama of the "Lost Colony" in the summer), an Elizabethan garden maintained by the Garden Club of North Carolina, Inc, and the Thomas Hariot Trail. The trail is a 0.3-mi interpretive loop with signs about the plant life that Hariot found in the area in 1585. It begins at the visitor center.

Address and Access: Cape Hatteras National Seashore, 1401 National Park Dr, Manteo, NC 27954; 252-473-2111. To reach the park headquarters, turn off US-64/264, 3.0 mi W of Manteo at the park sign.

Support Facilities: In addition to the park campgrounds there are commercial campgrounds to choose from, some open year-round. For this and other information, contact the Outer Banks Visitor's Center, 1 Visitor Center, Manteo, NC 27954; 800-446-6262. Open every day 9:00AM–5:30PM.

Cape Hatteras Beach Trail   584
Length and Difficulty: 75.8 mi, moderate
Special Features: lighthouses, wildlife refuge, seashore
Trailhead and Description: (Although the difficulty of this trail is listed as moderate, its classification may be vague. The reasons are miles and miles in sand without refuge from inclement weather, gale winds, hot weather [as much as 10 months of the year], and insects make the hike anything but easy or pleasant.) This unique trail generally follows the beach line, but in shorter sections it climbs dunes with sea oats and beach holly; winds through forests of live and laurel oaks, pine, and sweet bay; passes salt marshes of sedge and cordgrass; and clings to road shoulders. In a given season the hiker will see scores of bird species—swans, geese, ducks, gulls, egrets, terns, herons, songbirds, and shorebirds—migratory and permanent. The trail crosses the Oregon Inlet bridge, passes historic Coast Guard sites, and requires a ferry

ride to pass the wild ponies on Ocracoke Island. (Through-backpackers should plan camping arrangements and shuttle service well in advance; see introduction above.) The trail is not blazed or signed except at a few key points.

Begin the hike at the jct of US-64/264/158/NC-12 at Whalebone Junction in Nags Head and proceed S on NC-12 for 0.1 mi to the Cape Hatteras National Seashore Information Center (252-441-6644) on the R. (It may not be staffed.) (Hatteras and Ocracoke ferries sign is nearby.) Hike the L shoulder of NC-12 by a border of myrtle, beach holly, bayberry, sedge, and cattails. Pass parking areas on the R at 1.5 mi, 3.2 mi, and observation decks at 3.8 mi and 4.4 mi. At 4.7 mi, pass a park maintenance area, L, and at 5.9 mi L is a paved entrance road to a large parking area at Coquina Beach. Area facilities for picnicking and rest rooms are available, with showers during the summer season. Here the Cape Hatteras Beach Trail joins the MST to continue R. (The MST continues L over the dunes where it follows the beach for 11.0 mi to Jockey's Ridge State Park, its eastern trailhead.) Exit the parking area, cross NC-12, and follow a paved entrance road to Bodie Lighthouse Station and Visitor Center (252-441-5711). Reach the parking area for the lighthouse **585** (built in 1871) at 6.9 mi. (Behind the lighthouse is 0.3-mi, round-trip Bodie Island Pond Trail. It enters the wetlands on a boardwalk to an observation deck. Plants include bayberry, Baccharis, salt meadow, salt marsh cordgrasses, and black rush.)

From the lighthouse and visitor center, go to the S end of the parking loop **586** and enter a gated sandy NPS road to the 0.8-mi. Bodie Island Dike Trail, which runs jointly with the MST to NC-12. After 0.2 mi, cross a small cement bridge, and turn L, off the road. Follow a wide trail with numbered markers through wax myrtle, beach holly, cedar, and cordgrasses. Occasional views of the lighthouse and lakes are on the L. Reach jct with NC-12 at 8.0 mi.

Turn R and follow the road shoulder to Oregon Inlet Campground on the L at 8.6 mi. Begin to cross the Herbert C. Bonner bridge on the L, facing traffic at 9.0 mi. Observe traffic carefully because pedestrian walk space on the 2.4-mi bridge is only 45-inches wide. Views from the bridge are spectacular. Reach the end of the bridge at the abandoned Coast Guard station at 11.4 mi and enter the Pea Island Wildlife Refuge. Pass a ferry schedule sign, R, at 12.2 mi, and a parking area for beach access at 13.8 mi (125 yd. to the Atlantic **587** Ocean). At 14.1 mi, turn R off NC-12 to follow a hiking sign, the 2.5-mi North Pond Interpretive Trail, on the N dike of North Pond in the Pea Island National Wildlife Refuge. (The 5,915-acre refuge has 265 species of birds, 24 species of reptiles, and 23 species of mammals. The waterfowl numbers are greater in January, but a greater variety of species can be observed during the fall migration of October–November. For more information, contact the Refuge Manager, Pea Island National Wildlife Refuge, P.O. Box 150, Rodanthe, NC 27968; 252-987-2394.) Reach an observation deck of the impoundment at 14.3 mi. Continue on the trail around the W side of North Pond for 1.7 mi. Turn L at 16.2 mi, pass an observation deck at 16.7 mi, and reach NC-12 parking area. (If the South Pond area is hiked, permission must be granted from the refuge office.) Exit the trail on steps and enter the parking lot of the Pea Island NWR Visitor Center, where hikers will find information, rest rooms, and a book store. Cross NC-12 and return to the beach. At 19.2 mi, an interpretive exhibit area indicates the Pea Island Life-Saving Station was authorized by Congress in 1873. The station's crews rescued more than 600 people by 1915. After a visit to the refuge headquarters return across NC-12 and to the beach at 19.4 mi. For the next 30.0 mi, you will be hiking on the beach.

At 24.8 mi, pass an exit over dunes to a parking area at NC-12, near the end of the Pea Island Refuge. At 25.6 mi, pass dune exit to old Chicamacomico Coast Guard Station, a historic site, on NC-12, 0.5 mi from the beach. A general store, laundry, and private campground are over the dunes at 25.8 mi, 0.5 mi from the beach. The Rodanthe post office is at 26.1 mi, and a restaurant and fishing pier are at 26.3 mi. The original KOA is at 27.7 mi (125 yd. from the beach to the KOA bathhouse and another 0.3 mi to the KOA office near NC-12). Holiday KOA is at 28.1 mi, 125 yd. from the beach. At 29.0 mi is the Salvo/Waves/Rodanthe post office. Salvo NPS campground is closed at 31.0 mi, 0.5 mi from the beach. Instead, it serves as a picnic and day-use area. Beach exit and parking area are at 35.4 mi on off-road vehicle ramp #27. Another beach exit and parking area are at 37.6 mi and another at 41.9 mi. A shopping center is at 43.7 mi, followed by a fishing pier. Another ORV ramp exit, #38, is at 45.9 mi. A parking area and beach exit are also here. At 46.8 mi, cross over the dune for 100 yd. to the parking area at the old beach road; NC-12 is 100 yd. ahead. Follow S on NC-12 for 0.2 mi and take an old jeep trail R. Hike this road for 2.6 mi to near Buxton. Cross over NC-12 to the beach at 49.6 mi, turn R, and after 1.4 mi, arrive at the former site of the historic Cape Hatteras Lighthouse.

Continue straight on the road to Buxton Woods parking area and picnic area at 51.5 mi. Here is the Buxton Woods Nature Trail, R, a self-guided, interpretive, 0.6-mi scenic loop, as well as a parking area for the Cape **588**

Hatteras Lighthouse and Cape Hatteras Visitor Center (252-995-4474). Ahead pass a maintenance area, R, and at 51.9 mi, R, enter the Open Pond Rd where exists the largest forest on Cape Hatteras. (Camp trailers disposal system is L at this point, and the paved road continues L 0.9 mi to ORV ramp #44.) Nearby is the NPS Cape Point Campground, which is closed in winter.

Follow the sandy road and cross a stream at 53.2 mi; reach a Y in the road at 53.3 mi. Take the R fork where a sign restricts ORVs, and follow the S side of the lake at 53.4 mi. Enter an open area of dunes at 53.5 mi and follow the sandy road to NPS Frisco Campground at 55.8 mi. After the campground go to the gate at 56.1 mi, turn L, and follow the ramp to the beach at 56.3 mi. Turn R on the beach, pass a fishing pier, and after 6.0 mi on the beach, turn R at ramp #55 to a parking lot and NC-12. Turn L and after 0.1 mi reach the Hatteras Ferry at 62.6 mi. (From the NPS Frisco Campground it is 1.1 mi on a paved road to NC-12 and the Frisco post office.)

Take the Hatteras Ferry to Ocracoke Island (the time is usually 40 minutes), and after arrival, hike 0.6 mi on NC-12 to a parking area L. Go over the dunes to the beach at 63.3 mi. A parking area for the beach is also at 66.5 mi. **589** (To visit 0.8-mi loop Hammock Hills Nature Trail, leave the beach to cross NC-12 to parking aea. Markers identify sand dune, maritime forest, tidal flats, plants and birds.) At 68.1 mi, cross the dunes from the ocean for 100 yd. to a parking area. A short hike on NC-12 leads to the observation deck for the Pony Pen to view the wild ponies. Return to the beach. At ORV ramp #68, reach NPS Ocracoke Campground at 72.4 mi, R. Follow either the beach or the road to ORV ramp #70 at the Ocracoke airstrip, which is 0.2 mi from the beach, at 75.3 mi. From here follow NC-12 to the town boundary at 75.8 mi, the trail's terminus. Another 1.3 mi goes to the Ocracoke Island Visitor Center (252-928-4531) and Ocracoke Ferry. Toll ferries leave the port to Swanquarter to US-264 or to Cedar Island to US-70 (800-BY-FERRY). The town has motels, restaurants, a marina, and supply stores. (USGS Maps: Roanoke Island, Oregon Inlet, Pea Island, Rodanthe, Little Kinnakeet, Buxton, Cape Hatteras, Hatteras, Green Island, Howard Reef, Ocracoke)

Cape Lookout National Seashore (Carteret County)

Across Ocracoke Inlet SW from the Cape Hatteras National Seashore begins the Cape Lookout National Seashore. These barrier islands are narrow with low dunes, bare beaches at the Atlantic Ocean, and flat grasslands and salt marshes on the sound side. It includes Portsmouth Village (part of the N Core

Banks), S Core Banks from Drum Inlet to Cape Lookout, and Shackleford Banks, W of the cape and ending S of Beaufort. Authorized by Congress in 1966 and established in 1976, the 58.0 mi of islands remain uncommercialized and present a fragile natural resource. Although the islands are best known as a fisherman's haven, hikers, campers, and beachcombers use the beach as a trail. There are not any signs or distance markers or campsites or lifeguard-protected beaches (there are sharks and jellyfish in the Atlantic Ocean).

Choose comfortable packs and shoes. Wear a hat, shirt, and plenty of sunscreen lotion. Take plenty of potent insect repellent (insects are worst May through October). Use a strong tent with fine insect netting and, because of the wind, use foot-long tent stakes. Carry in plenty of food and water. Pets are not allowed on the barrier islands of the park. Only driftwood campfires are allowed. All trash must be carried out.

At Portsmouth Village, the 1.0-mi easy Portsmouth Village Trail goes **590** from the dock to the old schoolhouse, homes, cemeteries, Methodist church, and former US Life-Saving Station. From here it is another 1.0 mi to the beach. Now a ghost town, parts of the village are preserved by the NPS. Portsmouth began in 1753 as a trans-shipment point for goods entering Ocracoke Inlet. Its population reached nearly 600 by 1860, but most of the inhabitants went ashore upon federal occupation during the Civil War. (USGS Maps: Portsmouth, Wainwright Island, Styron Bay, Davis, Horsepen Point, Harkers Island, Cape Lookout, Beaufort)

Address and Access: Cape Lookout National Seashore, 131 Charles St, Harkers Island, NC 28531; 252-728-2250 or www.nps.gov/calo. Access is by private concession ferries that operate from Harkers Island to Cape Lookout and the lighthouse (252-728-3907); from Davis to Shingle Point (252-729-2791); from Atlantic to North New Drum Inlet (252-225-4261); and Ocracoke to Portsmouth Village (252-928-4361). Call for rates and schedules.

Support Facilities: Shopping centers, restaurants, and motels are in Beaufort and Moorehead City. There are at least a dozen commercial campgrounds in the area. Contact the Cape Lookout National Seashore office for a list of the local campgrounds, beach driving permits, fishing information, tide table, and map. Waters forecast can be heard by calling the Coast Guard base at Fort Macon (252-726-7550) or a five-day forecast from the National Weather Service in Wilmington (919-762-3240) or Cape Hatteras (252-223-5122 or 252-223-5327).

Guilford Courthouse National Military Park (Guilford County)

The park was established March 2, 1917, in honor of the 4,300 officers and soldiers of Commanding General Nathaniel Greene's Continental Army in the battle against British Field Commander Lord Charles Cornwallis, March 15, 1781. Although the battle was not a total victory for either side, it was significant in that Cornwallis retreated to Wilmington, practically abandoning the Carolinas. The end of the Revolutionary War came seven months later at Yorktown, Virginia, October 19, 1781. The 220.4-acre park has a museum in the visitor center; there are seven tour stops of historical interest. Camping is prohibited. Open daily except Christmas Day and New Year's Day.

Address and Access: Guilford Courthouse National Military Park, 2332 New Garden Rd, Greensboro, NC 27410; 336-288-1776. Access is 0.5 mi on New Garden Rd from US-220 N 6.0 mi from downtown Greensboro.

591 *Guilford Courthouse Battlefield Trail*

Length and Difficulty: 2.5 mi, easy

Trailhead and Description: From the visitor center, follow the paved trail SW of the parking area through a mature forest of oak, hickory, walnut, and poplar with an understory of dogwood, redbud, and sourwood. The first tour stop, the American first line, is at 0.4 mi. Cross Old Battleground Rd and reach a spur trail, L, to the General Greene monument at 0.6 mi. Continue on trails through open fields of large scattered oak and poplar with senna, milkweed, evening primrose, lobelia, and bur marigold among the wildflowers. At 1.3 mi, reach stop five at the site of Guilford Courthouse. (At a parking area R, a few yards W on the road leads to a 0.2-mi walking/biking trail into the city's Country Park. Here are also connections with the Lake Brandt Greenway and the Bicentennial Greenway; see chapter 13.) Return by stop six, American third line, at 1.9 mi for a return to the visitor center at 2.5 mi.

Moores Creek National Battlefield (Pender County)

The battlefield was established June 2, 1926, by the War Department and transferred to the NPS June 10, 1933. It has 87 acres and is significant because it is where the North Carolina patriots won a victory February 27, 1776, that notably advanced the American cause against the British Loyalists. On April 12, 1776, North Carolina became the first colony whose delegation at the Continental Congress in Philadelphia voted for independence. The 1.0-mi

Moores Creek Trail begins on the Pathway to History Trail, W of the visitor **592-** center, and follows interpretive signs through pine and hardwoods with Span- **593** ish moss to a bridge at 0.4 mi. The nature trail part begins at 0.7 mi in the loop. There are facilities for the physically disabled. Open daily except Christmas Day and New Year's Day.

Address and Access: Moores Creek National Battlefield, 40 Patriots Hall Dr, Currie, NC 28435; 910-283-5591. Access from the jct of US-421/NC-210 is 3.0 mi to Currie on NC-210; follow the signs another 3.0 mi.

Carl Sandburg Home National Historic Site (Henderson County)

Carl Sandburg (1878–1967), poet, author, lecturer, and social philosopher, won the Pulitzer Prize for history in 1940 with his *Abraham Lincoln: The War Years* and the Pulitzer Prize for poetry in 1951 with *Complete Poems.* He lived his last 22 years at "Connemara," a 240-acre farm at Flat Rock. A constant hiker, he refreshed himself by walking the trails designed by the first owner of the property (attorney Christopher G. Memminger of Charleston SC). On October 17, 1968, Congress authorized the farm as a historic site; it acquired the property from the Sandburg family in 1969 for commemorative purposes, and opened to the public in May 1974. It is open daily, 9:00AM to 5:00PM, except Christmas Day.

Address and Access: Carl Sandburg Home National Historic Site, 1928 Little River Rd, Flat Rock, NC 28731; 828-693-4178. Entrance is by Little River Rd (SR-1123) off US-25 (near the Flat Rock Playhouse), 3.0 mi S of the jct with US-64 in Hendersonville.

Memminger Trail (0.7. mi); *Little Glassy Trail* (0.2 mi); *Big Glassy* **594-** *Trail* (1.0 mi); *Spring Trail* (0.3 mi); *Jerusalem Trail* (0.3 mi); *Loose* **600** *Cow Trail* (0.1 mi); *Front Lake Trail* (0.5 mi)

Length and Difficulty: 3.1 mi combined round-trip, easy

Trailhead and Description: From the main building parking lot ascend on a trail to the main house and follow the signs (or use a brochure map) to begin on the Memminger Trail. It connects with, but circles, the Little Glassy Trail, which leads to an outcrop in the circle. From the trail gap and jct with the Big Glassy Trail, go 1.0 mi through oak, hickory, hemlock, and white pine to Big Glassy Mtn., a large rock face with scenic views. Backtrack to the woodshed for the Spring Trail. The Jerusalem Trail, Loose Cow Trail, and Front Lake Trail are all near the main house and are interconnected. (USGS Map: Hendersonville)

Part III

Trails in Other
US Government Properties

Sandy Ridge Wildlife Trail.

Chapter 9

National Wildlife Refuges and the Army Corps of Engineers

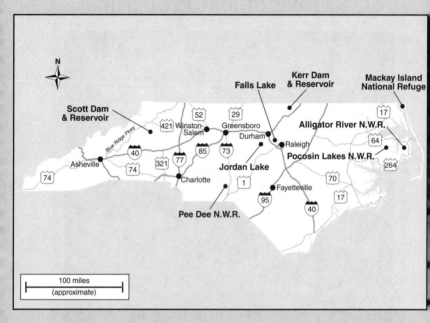

Introductions to Trail Areas

Chapter 9

National Wildlife Refuges and the Army Corps of Engineers

The taking of game has also helped me make peace with the truth of life.
—Chris Powell in "The Arrowhead"
Wildlife in N.C. November 2003

SECTION 1: NATIONAL WILDLIFE REFUGES

The origins of the National Wildlife Refuge System began in September 1937 with passage of the Federal Aid in Wildlife Restoration Act. Its conservationist sponsors were Senator Key Pittman of Nevada and then Representative Willis Robertson of Virginia. It did not come too soon, because the impact of plundered forests and uncontrolled slaughter of wildlife in the early twentieth century had wiped out some species and threatened and endangered others. Some earlier efforts had been made. For example, President Theodore Roosevelt in 1903 signed an executive order protecting wildfowl on Florida's Pelican Island. Later, migratory bird bills were passed in the 1930s, the Fish and Wildlife Act in 1956, and the National Wildlife Refuge System Administration Act of 1966. Other acts have followed, each one a building block of a process to save and protect the nation's native wildlife.

There are more than 520 refuges in the United States and its trust territories that encompass nearly 100 mil acres. They range in size from the smallest, Mille Lacs in Minnesota (less than an acre), to the Yukon Delta (nearly 20 mil acres) in Alaska. All these refuges are under the jurisdiction of the US Fish and Wildlife Service of the Department of the Interior. The regional headquarters for North Carolina is at 1875 Century Blvd, Atlanta, GA 30345; 404-679-7289. There are also many citizen clubs and organizations in the nation whose mission is to conserve natural resources and protect wildlife. One is the National Wildlife Federation, which has 13 regions (Region 3 for North Carolina). Its national headquarters is at 1400 16th St, Suite 501, NW, Washington, DC 20036; 202-797-6800. Other names and addresses of government and citizen groups are listed in the appendix. It is estimated that 28 mil people annually visit the refuges for hunting, fishing, boating, and nature study. In North Carolina there are nine refuges, two of which (Great Dismal Swamp and Mackay Island) are partly in Virginia. Only the refuges with designated trails are described below. The Cape Hatteras Beach Trail passes through the Pea Island National Wildlife Refuge and is described in chapter 8.

A native North Carolinian, Charles Kuralt (1934–97), emphasized the values and splendor of the nation's wildlife refuges in his CBS Sunday Morning program with *On the Road.* Posthumously, he was honored with a distinguished citizen's award by the US Fish and Wildlife Service. Another honor was the establishment of the Charles Kuralt Trail, a routing to 11 of the coastal **601** refuges that have estuarine sounds, bays, and lakes.

At some of the refuges are kiosks with observation towers or decks (Mackay Island and Pungo Lake) or trails (Roanoke River). To access Roanoke River Trail, drive 3.0 mi N on US-13/17 from the US-64 intersection in Williamston and turn R at a parking space. (If arriving S toward Williamston, cross the bridges and turn at the first L [near the Roanoke Landing Shopping Center] to make a U turn, N. It is 2.5 mi, R.) At a gate follow a road on a floodplain that may be partially under water after a nocuous storm or hurricane. Come to Conine Island. Listen to sounds from a mixture of birds, insects, and frogs, all at home among the cypress, sweet gum, and serpentine vines. After 0.6 mi. (it may be farther, depending on floodplain water level), backtrack. (Insect repellent is recommended.)

Alligator River National Wildlife Refuge (Dare and Hyde Counties)

The 150,000-acre refuge is a peninsula between Albemarle Sound and Pamlico Sound. It is a world of pocosins, brackish marshes, white cedar and cypress swamps, and dry lands with hardwoods—all the habitats of a wide range of wildlife and 145 species of birds, mammals, and reptiles. In its center is 46,000 acres owned by the federal government for US Air Force and Navy bombing practice. There are more than 150.0 mi of old logging roads, many too wet and impenetrable for vehicular use or hiking. Other roads (gated or open) are in good condition and popular with hunters and nature enthusiasts. For hunters, a map and brochure on hunting regulations, permits, and list of game animals are essential. Alligator, bear, and red wolf are protected. (Harassing, harming, or possessing a red wolf carries a penalty of one-year imprisonment, $100,000 fine, or both.) Hunting and fishing opportunities are available for the physically disabled. Arrangements can be made in advance by contacting the refuge office.

602   Creef Cut Wildlife Trail is fully handicapped accessible. The wide, paved 0.5-mi trail has boardwalks over freshwater marshes. There are resting benches, interpretive and directional signs, and a fishing dock with priority use for the physically disabled. In addition to a grand pine border on the trail, there are fragrant garlands of yellow jasmine and wild rose, bunches of wax myrtle, and aquatic strands of cattails. Backtrack. The parking access is on the S side of US-64 at the jct with Milltail Rd, 7.0 mi E of Alligator River bridge and 3.0 mi W of the US-64/264 jct. There are 13.0 mi of canoe/kayak trails in a channel to Sawyer Lake and wide Milltail Creek. Access is at the end of Buffalo City Rd described below from the Sandy Ridge Wildlife Trail. (USGS Maps: East Lake; Manns Harbor; Buffalo City; East Lake SE; Wanchese; Engelhard W, E, NW, and NE; Stumpy Point; Fairfield NE)

Address and Access: The refuge can be accessed from Columbia (E) on US-64 and from Engelhard (S) on US-264. The office is at 708 N Highways US-64/264 jct. The mailing address is Alligator River NWF, P.O. Box 1969, Manteo, NC 27954; 252-473-1131 (Wildlife violations: 800-662-7137).

603 *Sandy Ridge Wildlife Trail*

Length and Difficulty: 2.2 mi round-trip, easy

Trailhead and Description: From the Alligator River bridge on US-64, go E 3.8 mi to Buffalo City Rd, and turn R (3.2 mi W on US-64 from Creef Cut Wildlife Trail). Go 1.9 mi to dead-end road to park for both the trail and the canoe/kayak trails. Hike across a channel bridge and follow an old road with soft duff from loblolly pine needles and leaves of cypress, sweet gum, willow, and maple. On the L is a canal (used by canoeists/kayakists). At 0.7 mi, cross a low bridge. Sections of the trail have wooden pallets in wet areas to assist in keeping feet dry. Sphagnum moss beds and the sounds of wildfowl are prominent; carnivorous plants (such as sundew) are infrequent. Backtrack.

Mackay Island National Wildlife Refuge (Currituck County)

The refuge is in the extreme NE corner of the state, with 842 of its 8,055 acres in Virginia. Established in 1960 as a wintering ground for migratory water-fowl, it is at its peak from December to February when flocks of ducks, geese, and swans travel through their Atlantic flyways. The refuge lists 174 species of birds, including many songbirds. Some of the most rare fly-ins are the white ibis, peregrine falcon, red-necked grebe, and cinnamon teal *(Anas cyanoptera)*. There are two designated trails. The 0.3-mi Great Marsh Trail, **604** used heavily by fishermen, leads to a pond where there are excellent views of the marsh and waterfowl. It is on the S side of the Causeway of the Great Marsh, N 4.8 mi on NC-615 from the ferry dock at Knotts Landing. The other trail is described below. There is a kiosk and observation area in honor of Charles Kuralt. Camping is prohibited in the refuge.

Address and Access: Refuge Manager, Mackay Island NWR, PO Box 39, Knotts Island, NC 27950; 252-429-3100. At the jct of NC-168/615 in Currituck, take the free auto ferry to the island. Drive 2.7 mi on NC-615 and turn L on Mackay Island Rd. Go 1.3 mi to the gated entrance.

Mackay Island Trail   **605**
    Length and Difficulty: 3.4 mi, easy

    Trailhead and Description: (The trail is closed from October 15 to March 15 to protect migratory waterfowl.) Begin the hike on an open svc road about 3 ft. above sea level. At 0.5 mi, arrive at a road fork, where either direction completes the loop. If continuing ahead, go through a forest of loblolly pine, yaupon, bays, and cedar, with cordgrass and cattails at the clearings. At the next road jct, turn L and follow a 1.0-mi dike road. Turn L again, go 1.4 mi, and at another road jct take a R; go 0.5 mi to return to the entrance gate. There is evidence of nutria in the refuge, and waterfowl are prominent, particularly egrets, ducks, grackle, and grebe. (USGS Maps: Knotts Island, Barco)

Pee Dee National Wildlife Refuge (Anson and Richmond Counties)

Containing 8,443 acres, this refuge was established in 1965 to protect the habitat of resident wildlife and wintering geese and ducks. It is the state's most inland refuge where the rolling hills of the Piedmont level out to floodplains (mostly on the S side) of the Pee Dee River. More than 175 species of birds have been classified, including Canada geese, mallards, wood ducks, herons, owls, hawks, and songbirds. There are 28 species of mammals and 48 species of amphibians and reptiles. There is a 2.5-mi wildlife drive with interpretive management panels that is open April 1 through October 15. The 0.5-mi Pee Dee Nature Trail has interpretive history signs about flora and fauna. **606** It passes a photo-blind on Sullivan Pond and is open all year. Both routes are located directly behind the refuge headquarters. Camping is prohibited.

Address and Access: Refuge Manager, Pee Dee NWR, Highway 52 North, Wadesboro, NC 28170; 704-694-4424. Access is on US-52, 6.0 mi N of Wadesboro and 3.0 mi S of Ansonville.

Pocosin Lakes National Wildlife Refuge (Hyde, Tyrrell, Washington Counties)

This refuge has 113,000 acres (25,427 of riverine swamp; 50,319 of pocosin wetlands; 25,828 of grass fields; and other acres of lakes and forest). What a remarkable refuge for hungry and weary ducks, geese, tundra swans, and other feathered wildlife on their migratory skyways, some from the neotropics. Already there are deer, black bear, raccoon, rail, snipe, reptiles, and fish, only part of hundreds of species of fauna. There is a cross pattern of roads and canals, of which some roads are open to the public for observing wildlife, fishing, or hunting. The latter has strong regulation; for example, bear hunting is not allowed. At Pungo Lake is a Charles Kuralt Trail observation tower and kiosk. Access from NC-45, 18 mi S of Plymouth, is on Hyde Park Canal Rd for 5.5 mi.

Headquarters for the refuge is in the town of Columbia, where the refuge has 8.61 acres for the Walter B. Jones, Sr. Center for the Sounds. It is an environmental education center that includes a screened outdoor classroom. On **607** the property is also the Scuppernong River Interpretive Trail, a 0.5 mi boardwalk loop through a watery forest. The trail is handicapped accessible. It has exhibit sign about swamps, wildlife, and flora such as cypress, wild pink rose, **608** hibiscus, and scuppernong grape. The trail connects with a 0.2 mi Waterfront Boardwalk, a scenic setting for sunsets. It is part of the town and the distinguished Tyrrel County Visitor's Center that adjoins the refuge headquarters.

Historic Columbia is located on the eastern shore of Scuppernong River. The location was originally Shallop's Landing, a colonial trading post. In 1793 it was incorporated as Elizabethtown, but changed to Columbia in 1801.

Access and Address: If crossing the Scuppernong River Bridge E on US-64, turn at the first street R (Ludington Dr). If going W, turn L before crossing the bridge. Pocosin Lakes National Wildlife Refuge, P.O. Box 329, Columbia, NC 27925; 252-796-3004; fax: 252-796-3010; www.pocosinlakes.fws.gov. (For allied information, contact Partnership for the Sounds, P.O. Box 55, Columbia, NC 27925; 252-796-1000 or www.partnershipforthesound.org.) (Greater Tyrell County Chamber of Commerce, P.O. Box 170, Columbia, NC 27925; 252-796-1996.)

SECTION 2: US ARMY CORPS OF ENGINEERS PROJECTS

Formed during the early years of the nation as part of the Continental Army, the US Army Corps of Engineers had its beginning at West Point, a garrison on the Hudson River. In 1798 the Corps was enlarged, and in 1802 Congress made West Point a military academy for the United States. Since then, Congress has authorized a wide range of Corps projects. Among them have been blazing and building roads, clearing waterways and harbors, building dams for flood control and hydropower, protecting and restoring shorelines, providing natural disaster relief, fish and wildlife development, and multiple recreation opportunities. While emphasizing diversity in recreational usage year-round, the Corps enforces zoning regulations to protect the ecology.

There are four major Corps projects in NC: Falls Lake (Neuse River); Jordan Lake (Haw and New Hope Rivers); Kerr Dam and Reservoir (Staunton/Roanoke and Dan Rivers); and Scott Dam and Reservoir (Yadkin River). All were constructed for the major purpose of preventing downstream flood damage. With the exception of the Scott project, acreage is leased by the state's Department of Environment, and Natural Resources (DENR) for recreational purposes and managed by the Division of Parks and Recreation. These properties are described by the DENR as state recreation areas (SRAs). The Corps also leases acreage to the state's Wildlife Resources Commission for wildlife management and motorboat registration on all four projects. Examples of other types of leases are Wilkes County Park at the Scott Reservoir project and commercial leases (such as marinas) on all the projects (usually subleased by the DENR). All of the projects have trails.

Falls Lake (Durham, Granville, Wake Counties)

The 38,886-acre (11,620 water and 27,266 land) Falls Lake project has 12 public-use sites, 5 of which are SRAs managed by the Division of Parks and Recreation: Beaver Dam, Highway 50, Sandling Beach, Shinleaf, and Rolling View. Boating, water skiing, sailing, fishing, and picnicking are the major activities. Hiking the 26.1-mi Falls Lake Trail, described below, is another significant recreational activity. It is being constructed on the S boundary of the lake as a joint project of the Division of Parks and Recreation, Triangle Greenways Council, Friends of the Mountains-to-Sea Trail, and the Corps of Engineers. The continuation of the trail is proposed from NC-50 to other recreational areas along the Corps property and to Eno River State Park. Falls Lake received its name from the Falls of Neuse, a short section of rapids below the dam.

Address and Access: Falls Lake SRA Management Office, 13304 Creedmore Rd, Wake Forest, NC 27587; 919-676-1027. From the jct of NC-98/50, drive N on NC-50 1.6 mi, R. The Corps of Engineers Resources Manager's Office address is 11405 Falls of the Neuse Rd, Wake Forest, NC 27587; 919-846-9332. Access is 0.9 mi S from the Falls Lake parking area below the dam.

609   ***Falls Lake Trail, Section 1*** (Falls of the Neuse to Six Forks Road) (F)
       Length and Difficulty: 13.2 mi, moderate
       Trailhead and Description: This well-designed and well-maintained trail section was designated a state trail as part of the MST on April 11, 1987. Through a hardwood forest, it weaves in and out of coves and crosses numerous small drainages. It ascends to a number of gentle ridges and offers occasional scenic views of the lake. The mature forest has a few old-growth trees and some specific evidence of succession. For example, a few places have young growth among former tobacco rows. Holly, laurel, loblolly pine, Christmas fern, wild ginger, and running cedar comprise the winter greenery. Among the ferns are royal, cinnamon, sensitive, resurrection, ebony, southern lady, and bracken. Wildflowers include three species of wild orchids, coral bell, squirrel cups *(Hepatica americana),* mandrake, yellow root, and spring beauty *(Claytonia virginica).* Some of the more evident mammals are deer, beaver, fox, squirrel, and raccoon.

       Access to the E trailhead is at Tailwater Fishing Access Area parking lot below the dam on Falls of Neuse Rd (SR-2000) in N Raleigh. (Access from the Wake Forest jct of US-1 and NC-98 is 0.7 mi W on NC-98 to Old US-98 L, then follow the signs 2.4 mi to the parking area.) (Other access points will be described along the trail route.) The trailhead may not have signs or blazes, but it is in front of the rest rooms at a two-car parking space. (Do not go up the path to the dam.) Follow an old svc road where white blazes line the route. Pass through loblolly pine, sweet gum, tulip poplar, and oaks with an understory of holly and dogwood. At 0.1 mi, turn L on a foot trail and after 110 yd. the trail forks near a unique double tulip poplar. Take either route. (The blue-blazed trail, L, goes 0.6 mi to rejoin the main trail.) On the main trail, turn R, cross the paved dam road, and arrive at the parking lot of the Corps's Operational Management Center at 0.3 mi. Follow the lakeside road and after 0.2 mi, reenter the forest that has scattered jessamine and redbuds. Cross a Corps svc road and reach jct with the blue-blazed alternate route at 0.9 mi. Turn R. At 1.5 mi, cross a pipeline right-of-way and a scenic stream area at 2.0 mi. Cross footbridges over streams at 2.3 mi and 2.6 mi. Pass some fine views of the lake between the streams and the arrival at Raven Ridge Rd (SR-2002) at 3.4 mi. (It is 3.9 mi L on Raven Ridge Rd and Falls of Neuse Rd to the E trailhead.) Turn R and cross the Honeycutt Creek causeway to reenter the woods R at 3.5 mi. Enter a clear-cut area at 4.4 mi, followed by a series of small stream crossings and an old power line clearing at the edge of a residential area. At 5.0 mi, pass an old farm pond and old farm area, followed by a cove and large beech trees. Arrive at a residential area and exit to Possum Track Rd at 6.1 mi. (The road R is barricaded, but the road L is a vehicle access back to the trail's origin for 6.2 mi; 1.4 mi to Raven Ridge Rd, L; 2.9 mi to Falls of Neuse Rd, L; and 1.9 mi to the parking lot, L.)

Continuing on Falls Lake Trail, cross the road into a grove of loblolly pine. Cross a paved road at 6.4 mi, and enter another pine forest grove at 6.6 mi. Pass lake views at 7.7 mi. Cross a couple of ravines before crossing a footbridge at 8.5 mi. At 8.8 mi reach an old woods road, turn R, and arrive at Possum Track Rd at 9.0 mi. (It is 0.2 mi L to the Raven Ridge Rd jct.) Turn R and cross the Cedar Creek causeway. At 9.2 mi, turn R into a pine forest with cedar and honeysuckle. Pass remnants of an old homestead, R, at 10.1 mi. Enter a scenic area of large beech trees and cross a footbridge at 10.2 mi. After views of the lake at 10.7 mi, enter a section of laurel for the next 0.6 mi. At 12.0 mi, arrive at Bayleaf Church Rd (SR-2003). (To the R is the Yorkshire Center of Falls Lake Rec Area, and to the L, on the gated road, it is 1.0 mi to Bayleaf Baptist Church and the jct with Possum Track Rd.) Cross the road at the exit sign of the Yorkshire Center and reenter the forest. Cross a number of small streams in rocky areas and arrive at the end of the guardrail on Six Forks Rd (SR-1005), at the Lower Barton Creek causeway, at 13.2 mi. (To the R, it is 2.2 mi to NC-98. To the L, it is 7.9 mi back to the parking lot below the dam. The vehicle route is 0.7 mi on Six Forks Rd where a L turn follows Possum Track Rd and Raven Ridge Rd as described above.) (USGS Maps: Bayleaf, Wake Forest)

Falls Lake Trail, Section 2 (Six Forks Road and Blue Jay Point County Park) (F)

Length and Difficulty: 3.4 mi, moderate

Trailhead and Description: From the trailhead on Six Forks Rd (described above), follow the road R (N) across the Lower Barton Creek causeway for 0.3 mi to the end of the road railing at gravel shoulder parking. Turn R and enter Blue Jay Point County Park through the forest. Follow an old woods road for 0.1 mi before descending on a footpath to cross a footbridge. Here are wildflowers and unique roots to a maple tree. Ascend and descend in and out of coves and crossing footbridges. At 0.9 mi are patches of spicebush, wild ginger, and hepatica. At 1.6 mi is the first of four spur trails, color coded, for the next 0.7 mi. They cross or join Falls Lake Trail from the recreational areas on top of the peninsula. Blue Jay Point Trail (0.2 mi) is the first to cross. Laurel Trail (0.2 mi) follows, the next trail leads to a trail for the physically disabled, and the last trail, Sandy Point Trail (0.2 mi), originates at the park lodge. There are rock piles left by early farmers at 2.0 mi. Come out of the forest at 2.3 mi to a display board and parking lot between a ball field and the park lodge. Cross the paved road and descend to footbridges; follow the undulating trail through hardwoods and loblolly pine to reach Six Forks Rd at 3.4 mi at a trail sign. (To the R, is 1.0 mi to NC-98; to the L, it is 1.3 mi to the W trailhead of Section 1.) (USGS Map: Bayleaf)

610-
612

Falls Lake Trail, Section 3 (Blue Jay Point County Park/Six Forks Road to NC-98) (F)

Length and Difficulty: 2.7 mi, easy to moderate

Trailhead and Description: Turn R on Six Forks Rd and cross the causeway to a roadside parking space, R. At the upper end, enter the forest to follow white blazes at 0.3 mi. Arrive at an overflow parking lot for Upper Barton Creek Boat Ramp and cross straight to the woods on the other side. Enter the forest and cross under a power line at 0.7 mi, where there is a copious variety of wildflowers and berries. Into the forest are large hardwoods and two bridges, one over a stream near a large beech tree. Cross an old road at 1.0 mi. (To the R, it descends to a scenic and sandy beach area.) At 1.2 mi, exit to a power line for a parallel of the forest to descend into a cove. Ahead are wildflowers such as trillium, wild quinine, and blazing star. Arrive at the paved old NC-98 at 2.4 mi. Turn R; after 0.1 mi, turn L into a grove of oaks at an old homesite. Descend to NC-98, turn R and cross the road to a roadside parking space toward the causeway. (It is 1.5 mi, W on NC-98 to the jct with Six Forks Rd.) (USGS Map: Bayleaf)

Falls Lake Trail, Section 4 (NC-98 to NC-50) (F)

Length and Difficulty: 6.8 mi, moderate

Trailhead and Description: From the intersection of Six Forks Rd and NC-98 drive E 1.5 mi on NC-98 to the W edge of the lake bridge. Here is a gravel parking area on the N side of the road. At 0.1 mi, pass under a power line among redbud, sumac, and blackberry. Cross a number of footbridges in coves and at 0.7 mi, enter a grove of large beech and tulip poplar (scattered understory is dogwood, holly, and sparkleberry), where there are views of the lake. At 1.1 mi, there is a scenic area with large beech and wildflowers, and at 1.5 mi, near cove waters, is a skillfully designed footbridge. At another scenic lake area are infrequent tawny pine-sap *(Monotropa hypopithus),* and also at 2.6 mi in the same genus is Indian pipe *(Monotropa uniflora).* After a number of footbridges and hilly climbs reach Shinleaf Rec Area, a walk-in campground with central rest rooms and showers at 3.0 mi. (Access by vehicle is 0.5 mi N on New Light Rd from the NC-98 jct, opposite the N end of Six Forks Rd.) Across the parking area, enter the forest where to the L is Norwood cemetery. Descend steeply and ascend. At 3.5 mi, exit to New Light Rd. (It is 1.5 mi L to NC-98.)

Turn R on New Light Rd and after 0.1 mi turn L up an embankment (watch for sign; may be easy to miss). Enter a low area with large ironwood and spots of yellow root at 3.9 mi. Ascend to cross paved Ghoston Rd at 4.0 mi. Descend to banks of mayapple, foamflower, and crested dwarf iris. Cross the dam of a small pond at 4.6 mi. Pass around a rocky knoll at 5.1 mi; notice former tobacco field ridges on the hillside. At 5.3 mi, pass R of an unnamed cemetery near an old homesite. On an old road of red clay approach a jct with a grassy road at 5.6 mi. Turn L (avoid the extreme L grassy road) and leave the road R at 5.7 mi. Because of logging, the next two turns (L and R) may require alertness. After the R, turn through young pines follow a grassy open road bordered in section with orange cow-itch vine. Cross two paved roads, the latter for the State Management Center, R, at 6.6 mi. Exit at the edge of a highway railing on NC-50 at 6.8 mi. To the R it is 0.1 mi to a gravel road shoulder parking area. (It is 1.6 mi L [S] on NC-50 to NC-98.) (USGS Maps: Bayleaf, Creedmore)

For shorter trails, the Sandling Beach SRA has the Woodland Nature Trail, **613** a 0.7 mi interpretive loop with 24 stations about trees, flowers, and ferns. Other activities include swimming, fishing, boating, and picnicking. Access is off of NC-50, 2.2 mi N from the Falls SRA headquarters sign, and 5.5 mi S of Creedmore. Rolling View SRA offers 3.2 mi of unnamed loop trails that connect the area's facilities, such as a full-service campground, boating, picnicking, and swimming. Access is off of NC-98 near John W. Neal Middle School on Baptist Rd for 4.0 mi. For more information, contact 919-676-1027.

B. Everett Jordan Dam and Lake (Chatham, Durham, Orange, and Wake Counties)

The US Congress instructed the Army Corps of Engineers to study the historic Cape Fear River basin in 1945 for flood control. A lake, known then as New Hope Lake, was authorized in 1963 and constructed in 1967. In 1973, it was named in honor of US Senator B. Everett Jordan. Since then the NC Division of Parks and Recreation manages nearly 14,000 acres of the 46,768-acre project as SRAs. Twelve areas are now developed, some of which have trails. The prominent recreational activities are boating, fishing, water skiing, sailing, windsurfing, camping, and swimming.

There are five campgrounds: New Hope Overlook SRA for tents only; Poplar Point SRA and Crosswinds SRA for tents and RVs (walking trails for registered camper only); Parker's Creek SRA for tents, RVs, and group camps **614** (walking trails for registered campers only, except a 0.5 mi Children's Nature Trail at picnic shelter #3); and Vista Point SRA for group camps and RVs. (See Vista Point SRA ahead for trail information.) Entrance to Parker's Creek SRA is off US-64 (across the highway from Seaforth SRA, described ahead).

Address and Access: Jordan Lake SRA, 280 State Park Rd, Apex, NC 27523; 919-362-0586; fax: 919-362-1621. Access is off US-64 (S), last road before crossing the causeway/bridge, 3.7 mi W from the US-64/NC-751 jct.

At Ebenezer Church SRA are two trails (foot traffic only). Access is off US-64 at the Wilsonville jct with Beaver Creek Rd (SR-1008) S for 2.1 mi, R. After entrance, take the first road R and park on the E side of the parking lot **615** at a trail sign. Hike the easy red-blazed Old Oak Trail past a bamboo grove at sign about puddle and diving ducks at 0.4 mi. Complete a loop of 0.9 mi through a pine forest and tall oaks. Return to the entry road, drive R, and park at the nearest access at the lake on the L at a picnic area. There is a sign about **616** Ebenezer Church. Follow the red-blazed Ebenezer Church Trail (foot traffic only) on an old road. After nearly 0.2 mi is the former site of the historic church, R, but turn L off the road. Walk through a young forest, cross a paved road at 0.4 mi, curve around a tranquil small pond, cross the road again, and return to the parking area at 1.0 mi. (USGS Map: New Hope Dam)

617 At the Seaforth SRA is 1.6-mi Pond Trail (foot traffic only). Access is off US-64, the first L after crossing the lake's causeway/bridge W from Wilsonville. Park near the end of the parking area across from the beach bathhouse. Enter the red-blazed trail through an oak forest that becomes mixed with loblolly pine. At 0.2 mi, cross a boardwalk for an exceptionally beautiful view of the lake. By the boardwalk are lizard's tail, marshmallow, and fragrant buttonbush. Circle L of a pond with a beaver hutch at 0.6 mi. Pass through a field of lespedeza, cross the entrance road, walk through a loblolly pine forest, pass a former pond site with willows, and exit at a picnic shelter. Cross the parking area for a return to the point of origin.

On a return to US-64, drive W 2.5 mi to Griffins Crossroad (5.0 mi E from Pittsboro), and turn L (S) on Pea Ridge Rd (SR-1700) to Vista Point SRA.

After 2.5 mi park on the L before the entrance fee booth. Begin the red-blazed 2.7-mi Vista Point Red Trail (foot traffic only) through a mixed forest of oak, **618** maple, and pine. (At 0.7 mi is a proposed loop extension. At 0.8 mi is a lake view, L, and at 1.1 mi is evidence of former tobacco rows. For the next 1.2 mi, curve in and out of a series of coves, sometimes close enough to view the lake through the trees. Footbridges are over the ravines. Forest growth remains the same with occasional holly, sparkleberry, and fern beds. Pass L of a group RV campground at 2.3 mi and R of a picnic shelter at 2.5 mi. Cross a paved road and at 2.6 mi is a jct with Vista Point Blue Trail, a blue-blazed trail, L. (It is a **619** walk-in route to campsites where a continuance is to an old barn and well house.) Keep R and exit to the parking area where the trail began. Another recreation area is New Hope Overlook, a primitive campground with 24 walk-in campsites. A 5.0-mi New Hope Overlook Trail is under construction. For **620** more information, contact 919-362-0586. Access from US-1 on Pea Ridge Rd, N (S of Apex), is 3.0 mi, L. From US-64 (W of Cary), turn L on Beaver Creek Rd S to Pea Ridge Rd, R at 5.2 mi. (USGS Map: New Hope Dam)

John H. Kerr Dam and Reservoir (Granville, Vance, Warren Counties in North Carolina; Charlotte, Halifax, Mecklenburg Counties in Virginia)

The reservoir of 48,900 acres was completed in 1952 and named for the NC congressman whose leadership made the project possible. More than three-fourths of the area project is in VA. There are 29 rec areas, of which 9 are in NC, including 6,200 land acres leased to the state by the Corps. Chief activities are boating, sailing, skiing, fishing, swimming, picnicking, and camping. There are 700 numbered campsites among the following parks: Bullocksville, County Line, Hibernia, Henderson Point, Kimball Point, Nutbush Bridge, and Satterwhite Point. All campgrounds open April 1 or Easter (whichever comes first) and close the last day of October. Two campgrounds (Cooper Point at Satterwhite, and Nutbush Bridge) are open year-round. All campgrounds have portions with electrical and water hookups. Three commercial marinas offer full svc for fishermen, boaters, and campers. Among the special events in the parks is the Governor's Cup Invitational Regatta in June, 4th of July Celebration, and Labor Day Parade of Lights. Only the rec areas with nature trails are covered below. (See *The Trails of Virginia* by Allen de Hart, published by the University of North Carolina Press, for trails on the Virginia side of the reservoir.) (USGS Maps: Middleburg, Townsville, John H. Kerr Dam, Tungsten)

Address and Access: Kerr Reservoir State Rec Area, 6254 Satterwhite Point Rd, Henderson, NC 25737; 252-438-7791. At the I-85 jct (Exit 217) in North Henderson, take Satterwhite Rd (SR-1319) N 5.8 mi.

621- 622   The 0.4-mi Big Poplar Trail and the 0.6-mi Henderson Nature Trail are at Satterwhite Point; the access is described above. Access to the Big Poplar Trail is in the J. C. Cooper Campground. It is a linear trail between the washhouse (L of the fork) at campsite section 105–123 and the entrance loop, R, of campsite section 1–15. The wide trail in a mature forest could also be called big beech (tree-carving dates are in the late 1800s) or big white oak. A large tulip poplar grows halfway on the trail at a streamlet. On Satterwhite Rd, across the road from the J. C. Cooper Campground entrance, is the entrance to Henderson Nature Trail. It loops from the Henderson kiosk at the Outdoor Lab of the Vance Soil and Water Conservation District sign. The graded interpretive trail is bordered with pieces of old RR cross ties. If following the trail clockwise, enter a hardwood forest. At 0.3 mi is a bed of Christmas ferns, then lakeside views, L. At 0.5 mi is a lighted outdoor stage. From here it is 0.2 mi on paved trail to the area headquarters office.

623   At Bullocksville Rec Area is the 0.5-mi Old Still Trail, a loop trail whose entrance is opposite the baseball field at the ranger sta. At 0.3 mi it turns sharply L to ruins of an old liquor still. Access is 3.3 mi W from Drewry on Bullocksville Rd (SR-1366), and Drewry is accessible 2.3 mi W on Manson Rd (SR-1237) from I-85, Exit 223, or 2.4 mi W on Ridgeway Rd (SR-1224) from I-85, Exit 226. Both I-85 exits are N of Henderson. (To reach County Line Rec Area, use either of the accesses to Drewry and drive N on Drewry Rd (SR-1200) for 3.0 mi. Turn L on Buchanan Rd [SR-1202] and go 2.1 mi to the entrance.)

W. Kerr Scott Dam and Reservoir (Wilkes County)

The project was constructed by the Corps from 1960 to 1962 and named in honor of former US senator and NC governor W. Kerr Scott (1896–1958). There are 16 recreational areas, one of which has been leased to Wilkes County and another to a commercial establishment. The lake contains 1,470 acres and is surrounded by 2,284 land acres. Popular aquatic sports are boating, skiing, swimming, and fishing. Small-game hunting is allowed at selected areas. Land activities are camping (Bandits Roost Park and Warrior Creek Park have electrical and water hookups and hot showers), picnicking, and hik-

624   ing. At the manager's office is a 0.3-mi self-guiding loop, Scott Dam Nature Trail. It has 27 interpretive points for the local trees, flowering shrubs, and ferns. Access is described below. Another short trail is the 0.8-mi Bandits **625** Roost Trail. It goes from the boat-ramp parking lot of Bandits Roost Campground in Area B along the shoreline to a terminus between campsites #25 and #26 in Area A. Access is 1.9 mi W on NC-268 from the dam entrance. A longer trail is described below.

Address and Access: W. Kerr Scott Dam and Reservoir, 499 Reservoir Rd, Wilkesboro, NC 28697; 336-921-3390. The entrance road to the manager's office is on NC-268, 3.0 mi SW from the jct of US-421 in Wilkesboro.

Overmountain Victory Trail   236
Length and Difficulty: 2.7 mi, easy

Trailhead and Description: Now a national historic trail, this trail was formerly called the Warrior Creek Trail. Warrior Creek is historically significant because the mouth of the creek at the Yadkin River (now underwater) was where the Overmountain Men of the Wilkes County militia crossed the Yadkin, September 28, 1780. The army of 350 men continued to Lenoir where it joined the main patriot army (from the mountains of NC, TN, and VA) at Quaker Meadows. Their march to the historic Battle of Kings Mtn. in SC, where Col Pat Ferguson was killed and his Tory army defeated on October 7, 1780, was a turning point in the Revolutionary War. To commemorate this route, the Corps and local citizen groups have established this trail.

From the NC-268 entrance to the dam, continue SW 4.3 mi on NC-268 to Section F, Warrior Creek Park, and turn R. Go 0.6 mi and turn L at the campground sign. (If the campground is open, usually May 1 to September 30, ask for a campground and trail map and drive the 1.0 mi to the trailhead, following the signs. If the campground is closed, park outside the gate and walk to the trailhead.) From the trailhead parking lot descend the steps on a well-graded and well-maintained trail. Pass through a forest of white pine, holly, and tall hardwoods. Galax, yellow root, ferns, and fetterbush decorate the trail and stream banks. Cross two footbridges and arrive at Area C camping road at 0.5 mi. Cross the road; pass through Area E camping at 0.6 mi, and pass a natural spring at 1.1 mi. Pass a picnic area at 1.3 mi. Descend into a lush cove on the lake, and arrive at an abandoned picnic area at 2.0 mi. Ahead, follow an old woods road and ascend to an abandoned parking area at 2.5 mi. Turn L and follow the road to a Corps gate at 2.7 mi. To the L is a parking overlook and picnic shelter with scenic views of the lake. To the R, it is 1.3 mi on the paved campground road to the E trailhead and point of origin. (USGS Map: Boomer)

Part IV

Trails in State Parks and the Recreational System, Forests, Natural Areas, Historic Sites, and Other State Properties

High Shoals Falls Loop Trail.

Chapter 10

The State Parks
and Recreation System

Happily may I walk . . .
May it be beautiful all around me.
—Night Chant (Navaho)

The Department of Environment and Natural Resources (DENR) has seven divisions in Natural Resources: Aquariums, Forest Resources, Marine Fisheries, Museum of Natural Sciences, Parks and Recreation, Soil and Water Conservation, and Zoological Park. The current administrative form was created in 1997, but a number of reorganizations preceded the change. For example, in 1989, the department included Health (DEHNR). In 1977, the state legislature combined a number of agencies under the Department of Natural Resources and Community Development (DNRCD), which included the Division of Parks and Recreation. In 1955, the state legislature transferred all the state historic sites from Parks and Recreation to a new Department of Archives and History.

The state park system is divided into six units of management: state parks, lakes, recreation areas, rivers, trails, and natural areas. All the trails in the parks are covered in this chapter, the natural areas in chapter 11, and the state recreation areas in chapter 9.

Interest and concern about the state's natural resources began in the late nineteenth century. A specific example was the establishment of a state Geological Survey in 1891 to determine the state's mineral and forest resources. State geologist Joseph A. Holmes was appointed to direct and present biennial reports. In 1905, the state legislature reorganized the survey to create the NC Geological and Economic Survey. Its duty was expanded to "all other material resources." When the legislature and Governor Locke Craige learned in 1914 that timber harvesting and forest fires were destroying such valuable areas as Mt. Mitchell, the governor (a strong conservationist) went to the area for a personal inspection. The result was a bill passed in 1915 to create the state's first park (cost not to exceed $20,000). The management of Mt.

Mitchell State Park became the responsibility of the Geological and Economic Survey. The state's second state park, Fort Macon, came in 1924 after director Holmes and the legislature were successful in acquiring the 410-acre Fort Macon Military Reservation from the federal government for one dollar.

In 1925, the legislature expanded responsibility to fire prevention, reforestation, and maintenance of the state parks and forests when the Geological and Economic Survey was phased into the new Department of Conservation and Development. Acquisition was slow; only three of the Bladen Lake areas were added to the list in the 1920s, and unfortunately did not include any land acreage at White Lake. But in the 1930s there was a change when federal assistance programs became available, particularly the CCC. Between 1935 and 1943, the state acquired six new parks: Morrow Mtn., Hanging Rock, Pettigrew, Singletary Lake, Jones Lake, and Crabtree (now Umstead). The congressional Recreation Area Study Act of 1936 became the blueprint for state park systems, but the NC state legislature appropriated only sporadic capital funds. From 1945 to 1961, only Mt. Jefferson was acquired. Five state parks and a natural area were added in the 1960s, and there was a notable increase in the 1970s with 11 new parks, eight new natural areas, and the first state recreation area (SRA) at Kerr Lake (the facilities had been parks since 1951). This decade of growth was under the administrative leadership of governors Bob Scott and James E. Holshouser. Within a three-year period, the park lands nearly doubled (50,000 acres more). Other advances during this period were the beginning of the state zoo, a heritage trust fund (for the natural areas), and in 1973 the State Trails System Act, which created a master plan with procedures for implementing a statewide network of multiuse trails for hikers, bicyclists, equestrians, canoeists, and ORV users. It also created a seven-member citizen's Trail Committee to advise the director of Parks and Recreation.

During the 1980s, three SRAs were opened—Jordan Lake, Falls Lake, and Fort Fisher, and in 1999 a new park, Gorges State Park, was dedicated. In 1987, the legislature passed the State Parks Act, led by Senator Henson P. Barnes. The act would establish a master plan that "firmly defines the purpose of state parks and requires sound strategy in managing the system."

For many years the state has been in the lowest national percentile of funding for park construction, staffing, and maintenance. Voters responded to this neglect by passing a $35 million bond referendum in 1993 to provide funds to improve state park facilities. In July 1994, the General Assembly passed and created the Parks and Recreation Trust Fund—funded by a $1 increase in the excise tax on property transfers. The Trust Fund is the largest single appropriation in the division's history and appropriates 65 percent of available funds to state parks, 30 percent to local parks and recreation agencies and 5 percent to the Beach Access Program. Phil McKnelly, the division's director, stated that trail supporters were among the many groups who made the citizens aware of park system needs.

Among the park system's 28 regular parks, 26 have officially named trails. All the parks are open year-round. An exception is Mt. Mitchell, which has to close when snow closes the Blue Ridge Parkway. Other western parks may close temporarily if there are unusually heavy snowstorms. Parks open daily at 8:00AM and close at 6:00PM November through February; 7:00PM in March and October; 8:00PM in April, May, and September; and 9:00PM June through August (except Carolina Beach at 11:00PM). There are exceptions: Hammocks Beach 8:00AM to 6:00PM year-round; Lake Waccamaw, 9:00AM to 6:00PM; and Singletary Lake, open to groups 8:00AM to 5:00PM. Additionally, the state has four State Recreation Areas, all of which have trails, and 16 Natural Areas, some of which have trails.

Park rules are posted conspicuously in the parks. Alcohol, illegal drugs, and firearms are prohibited. Fishing is allowed but a state license is necessary. Camping facilities for individual parks are described in this chapter. Some of the parks without a campground have the nearest commercial campground listed under support facilities. Descriptions are also made about primitive and youth-group camping. When visiting a park, first go to the park office and request brochure and maps available to make your stay a pleasurable and educational experience.

The state's physiographic regions are divided into mountains (17 western counties in the Appalachian Mtns. chain); Piedmont (42 counties from the Appalachian foothills through the central part of the state to the fall line); and the coastal plains (41 eastern counties from the fall line 150.0 mi E on flatlands to the Atlantic Ocean). (The fall line designates the area that separates the hard, resistant rocks of the Piedmont plateau from the softer rocks and sediments of the coastal plains. This common term also designates where the rivers cease to have falls or rapids.) Geographically, the coastal plains include a series of seven sloping terraces that range in descent from about 275 ft. in elev to sea level at the barrier islands. Because Mt. Mitchell is the state park in the mountain physiographic region, parks in the adjoining counties (with elev ranging from 2,305 ft. to 4,900 ft.) are included in the mountain region for the purpose of this guidebook.

Information: Division of Parks and Recreation, 1605 Mail Service Center, Raleigh, NC 27699 (512 North Salisbury St); 919-733-7275. For information on trails, contact the state Trails Coordinator, Division of Parks and Recreation, 12700 Bayleaf Church Rd, Raleigh, NC 27614; 919-846-9991.

Mountain Region

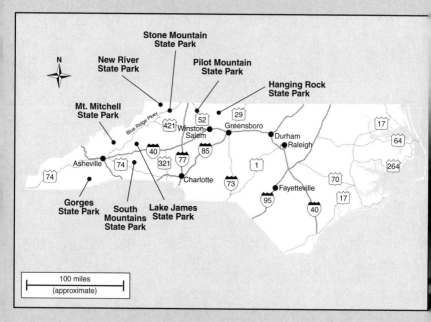

Introductions to Trail Areas

The Mountain Region is described alphabetically rather than for geographical proximity. Three parks are at the edge of the mountains and near the Piedmont Region. Each park has a trail system.

SECTION 1: MOUNTAIN REGION
Gorges State Park (Transylvania County)

The state's most western park is also the newest, dedicated September 3, 1999. It has 7,100 acres, part of a 10,000-acre state purchase from Duke Energy Corp. The other 2,900 acres are managed as game land by the state's Wildlife Resources Commissions. This multi-ridge, peak, outcrop, waterfall, and deep gorge section of the Jocassee Gorges has a major concentration of rare plant and animal species (about 125, of which 2 are Oconee bells *[Shortia galacifolia]* and green salamander *[Aneides aeneus].* There are also 12 endangered species. As the park continues to be developed there will be an office/visitor center, a campground with allied services, picnic areas, maintenance building, and other facilities. Meanwhile, an interim office is located in the same building as the Sapphire post office on US-64 (north side) near the intersection with NC-281. Parking areas have already been completed for six trails, one of which is a multi-use road where motor vehicular traffic is allowed for hunters to pass through to game lands beyond Turkey Pen Gap (no hunting in the park). Backcountry camping for hikers is allowed at the end of Ray Fisher Place Trail and Canebrake Trail. A section of SC's Foothills Trail passes through the park and connects with Canebrake Trail. (USGS Map: Reid)

Address and Access: Gorges State Park, P.O. Box 100, Sapphire, NC 38774; 828-966-9099, gorg@citcom.net, or www.ncsparks.net/gorg.html. Access to the west parking entrance (gated at night) is 1.0 mi S on NC-281 from its jct with US-64 in the community of Sapphire. The east parking entrance (for Auger Hole Trail and Canebrake Trail) from the Sapphire jct is 8.4 mi E of US-64 to a R turn of Frozen Creek Rd (SR-1139). (From Brevard, it is 9.1 mi W on US-64 with a L turn.) After 3.2 mi on Frozen Creek Rd, turn R at sign.

626-629   *Buckberry Ridge Trail* (0.7 mi) (F); *Bearwallow Valley Trail* (1.2 mi) (F); *Bearwallow Falls Trail* (1.7 mi) (F); *Ray Fisher Place Trail* (2.7 mi) (F)

> **Length and Difficulty:** 7.0 mi round-trip on all trails, easy to strenuous
>
> **Special Features:** wildlife, wildflowers, waterfall, and scenic views
>
> **Trailhead and Description:** At the NE corner of the parking area is a signboard and access for the color-coded trails; they begin as a unit. After 0.2 mi, Buckberry Ridge Trail breaks away, L. (Forming a loop, the easy nature trail has 12 signposts to identify flowers, trees, or shrubs. At 0.5 mi, cross a road in a

picnic area and return to the parking area.) Continuing on the other trails, descend gradually, pass under a power line at 0.9 mi, and at 1.1 the red-blazed Bearwallow Valley Trail turns R. (The trail goes 0.1 mi to an observation deck, near the same power line, at the trail's end. Here are expansive views S of Bearwallow gorges, and peaks of Chestnut Mtn. Backtrack and turn R on the other trails.) In a grove of mountain laurel and on an old road, R, the green-blazed Ray Fisher Place Trail turns R at 1.5 mi. (The trail descends moderately on an old road along the side of a ridge and passes under the power line again at 1.9 mi. After a set of curves arrive at the headwaters of Jake's Branch, a backcountry campsite at 2.7 mi. Back track to Bearwallow Falls Trail, R.) The blue-blazed trail descends steeply on four switchbacks to an observation platform at 1.7 mi. Here is a view of Bearwallow Creek Falls in a gorgeous gorge. Signs provide information about the impressive scenery. Backtrack. There are resting benches along the way. (USGS Map: Reid)

Canebrake Trail (5.3 mi) (F); *Auger Hole Trail* (6.0 mi) (F, B, H, A)   **630-**
    Length and Difficulty: 10.6 mi round-trip, strenuous. 12.0 mi round-trip,   **631**
moderate

    Trailhead and Description: (See access above.) The parking lot is not gated and motor vehicles can be parked overnight (no camping here). There is a rest room and picnic tables. These trails are gated forest roads, but differ in usage. Canebrake is for hiking only, and Auger Hole is multiple use that includes motor vehicles. For hikers and bicyclists, begin at the L corner of the parking lot. After 75 yd. on a well designed trail cross a bridge over Frozen Creek Rd; to the R, the road is a 0.6 mi passage for both trails. After crossing a stream on the ascent, turn L at a gap on the yellow-blazed Canebrake Trail.

    (The red-blazed Auger Hole Trail continues R around the curve and soon descends gradually to meander, but parallels the NW side of Auger Fork Creek. After tributaries and a horseshoe, curve near a bend of the Toxaway River, cross the river at 4.4 mi. Begin an ascent to cross Bearwallow Creek, then follow a tributary to reach the park's boundary. If you use this trail watch for traffic at the sharp and narrow curves during hunting seasons.)

    Continuing on the gated Canebrake Trail, follow the pleasant and reposing road among hardwoods, scattered pines, and wildflowers on the road banks. At 1.9 mi, pass a posted road, L. There is a small stream with a rhododendron canopy at 2.9 mi and a change in scenery with a large boulder on a ridge, R, at 3.5 mi. A small spring garnished with fetterbush, partridgeberry, and wild grapes near a ravine is at 3.7 mi. Rockhop another small stream at

4.5 mi where you begin to hear cascading waters on both sides of the road. Some partial view of the waters can be seen at 4.9 mi near a switchback. At the jct with the Foothills Trail at 5.3 mi it is a few yards R to the 75 yd. swinging bridge over Toxaway River. Postcard views are upriver on rock formation and downriver's ending at Lake Jocassee. To the L at the jct of the trail is a bridge over Toxaway Creek for camping under hemlock and picnic tables near **105** the tumbling waters of the creek. Backtrack. (It is 19.1 mi W on the Foothills Trail to SC-130/NC-281 and 13.3 E to US-178.)

Hanging Rock State Park (Stokes County)

Hanging Rock State Park, with 6,921 acres in the Sauratown Mtns., has more than 18.0 mi of named and side trails. They go to scenic heights, waterfall areas, rocky ridges, and caves, and in the process provide the hiker with views of as many as 300 species of flora, including the mountain camelia *(Stewartia ovata)*. Canadian and Carolina hemlock grow together here, a rarity, and a species of lespedeza is found only in this area. Animal life includes deer, fox, skunk, woodchuck, squirrel, raccoon, owl, and hawk. The park has camping (also cabins), picnicking, swimming, fishing, and mountain climbing. All **632** trails connect except the Lower Cascades Trail. It can be reached by going W from the park entrance on Moore's Springs Rd 0.3 mi. Turn L on Hall Rd (SR-2012) and go 0.4 mi to the parking area, R. The 0.6-mi round-trip Lower Cascades Trail descends to the scenic falls and pool under a huge overhang. The park is open year-round. (USGS Map: Hanging Rock)

Address and Access: Hanging Rock State Park, P.O. Box 278, Danbury, NC 27016; 336-593-8480; fax: 336-593-9166. To reach the park, turn off NC-8, 1.5 mi N of Danbury onto Moore's Springs Rd (SR-1001), across the road from Reynolds Hospital. The W entrance route is off NC-66, 0.5 mi N of Gap, on Moore's Springs Rd.

Support Facilities: The park has a campground with 73 tent/trailer campsites (no hookups) and family vacation cabins. The campground is open year-round (water off December 1 to March 15); the cabins are available (with reservations) March 1–November 30. Groceries, restaurant, gasoline, and PO are in Danbury.

633- *Hanging Rock Trail* (1.2 mi); *Wolf Rock Loop Trail* (1.9 mi); *Cook's* **638** *Wall Trail* (1.1 mi); *Magnolia Spring Trail* (0.4 mi); *Chestnut Oak Nature Trail* (0.7 mi); *Moore's Wall Loop Trail* (4.2 mi)

Length and Difficulty: 11.4 mi combined round-trip, easy to strenuous
Connecting Trail: (Tory's Den Trail)
Special Features: geology, wildflowers, scenic views
Trailhead and Description: After passing the park office entrance, L, turn L to a large parking lot at the visitor center. Heavily used Hanging Rock Trail begins on the R at a sign. Descend on wide cement steps and follow a cement tread for 340 yd. before ascending on gravel. At 0.5 mi is a jct with Wolf Rock Loop Trail, R. At Hanging Rock ascend steeply 200 ft. on metamorphic rock to the summit for superb views. Backtrack to form a loop by taking Wolf Rock Loop Trail. Ascend to and remain on a rocky ridge with pine, oak, laurel, and blueberry. Overlooks are L (SE and S). After 1.0 mi is a jct with Cook's Wall Trail which goes ahead on the ridge. Wolf Rock Loop Trail turns sharply R, descends to join the Chestnut Oak Nature Trail, and ends at the swimming lake's bathhouse. From here through the parking lot and entrance road it is 0.4 mi back to the parking lot for Hanging Rock Trail, a loop of 4.2 mi.

If continuing on the ridgecrest for Cook's Wall Trail ascend among a mixture of hardwoods, pine, and laurel with patches of galax, trailing arbutus, and downy false fox glove. After 0.5 mi is a jct with Magnolia Spring Trail, R. (Although this name may not be on the trail signs, the trail is a popular connector between the park's two main ridges. It received its name from the magnolia growing in a damp area of the trial's N end.) Arrive at House Rock at 0.7 mi. Here are excellent views of Hanging Rock (NE) and the vicinity of Winston-Salem (S). At 1.1 mi, reach Devil's Chimney over rocky Cook's Wall for a view of Pilot Mtn. (W). Backtrack, but turn L at Magnolia Spring Trail. Descend steeply through a dense forest to Magnolia Spring at 0.1 mi. Pass through an arbor of rhododendron, cross a footbridge over a clear stream, and reach jct with Moore's Wall Loop Trail, R and L and 0.4 mi. A turn R goes through a bog with boardwalks. Ferns and purple turtleheads grow nearby. Reach jct with Chestnut Oak Nature Trail, arrive at the bathhouse, and return to the Hanging Rock Trail parking lot for a loop of 6.4 mi.

If following the Moore's Wall Loop Trail from Magnolia Spring Trail, follow the sign and after 0.6 mi is a jct with a connector to the former Sauratown Trail and Tory's Den Trail. Turn R and ascend to a rocky area with hemlock, turkey grass, and laurel after another 0.6 mi. An observation tower (2,579 ft.) with spectacular views is reached at 1.9 mi. Descend, pass Balanced Rock and Indian Face on an old road. Cross Cascade Creek at 3.0 mi, pass through the camping area, and rejoin the trail's entrance. Turn L and return to the parking lot at the bathhouse at 3.9 mi. If walking from the parking lot to the Hanging Rock parking lot, the loop is 9.3 mi. (If hiking only the Moore's Wall Loop Trail, it is 4.2 mi if beginning at the parking lot at the bathhouse.)

639-   *Upper Cascades Trail* (0.2 mi); *Indian Creek Trail* (3.7 mi)
640   **Length and Difficulty:** 7.8 mi combined round-trip, easy to moderate
        Special Features: waterfalls, wildlife, cliffs
        Trailhead and Description: From the visitor center parking lot and picnic area access Upper Cascades Trail at the W side of the parking lot. Part of the trail is asphalt for the physically disabled. Backtrack. To access Indian Creek Trail, follow the trail signs at the NE end of the parking lot and picnic area. Descend 0.4 mi to a shady area at Hidden Falls on Indian Creek. Continue downstream, crossing the creek several times. Pass a jct L with a connector trail to a group camping area. Cross the creek to exit at Hanging Rock Rd (SR-1001) at 1.7 mi (0.1 mi E of the park entrance).
        Cross the road, descend on an old farm road, cross a cement bridge, pass L of an old tobacco barn, and descend to the creek. Veer away from the creek, ascend a ridge, follow an old forest road, and descend to a scenic overlook from cliffs at 2.9 mi. Descend to the creek's basin near cliff walls, over mossy banks, and through dense rhododendron. After several creek crossings arrive at an old farm road. Turn R, and cross the creek on a footbridge to the trail's end. Ahead it is 0.1 mi to the Dan River Canoe Trail boat launching and parking area. Backtrack, or use a second vehicle. (Access to the river by vehicle from the park entrance is 0.5 mi E on Hanging Rock Rd to Piedmont Springs Rd [SR-1489], L. After 0.9 mi turn L on NC-8/89, go 0.3 mi, turn L on SR-1482, and go 0.4 mi to the trailhead at the creek. River parking area is R.)

641   *Tory's Den Trail*
        Length and Difficulty: 4.2 mi, easy
        Connecting Trails: (Chestnut Oak Trail); (Moore's Wall Loop Trail)
        Trailhead and Description: From parking lot #2, follow the trail signs on the E side of the bathhouse and lakeshore. Follow the Chestnut Oak Trail, but leave it, R, at 0.3 mi and follow the red-blazed trail. At 0.4 mi, pass a jct R with Moore's Knob Loop Trail. Cross a stream and boardwalk and reach jct L at 1.0 mi with Magnolia Spring Trail (which ascends 0.4 mi to a jct with Cook's Wall Trail). Continue ahead, ascend slightly to a saddle at 1.5 mi, and reach jct with a blue-blazed trail, L. (The trail R is Moore's Wall Loop Trail.) Follow the blue-blazed trail, and after 0.5 mi, reach the crest of Huckleberry

Ridge near a large rock formation. Descend, and reach jct with Sauratown **642**
Loop Trail at 2.4 mi R and L. (The 5.5 mi loop is off the 20.3 mi Sauratown
Trail/MST. See chapter 14.) Turn R, descend, and cross a small stream at 3.5
mi. Ascend to Charlie Young Rd (SR-2028) at 3.6 mi. Cross the road and turn
R. Follow the trail 0.4 mi to Tory's Den parking lot, L. Follow the trail 0.3 mi
to an outcrop, but turn R on the approach. Descend 90 yd. near a small cave
L and turn R. (Ahead L, it is a few yards to a view of Tory's Den Falls.)
Descend 100 yd. on the path to the 30-ft. Tory's Den. Backtrack, or use a second vehicle for the Tory's Den parking lot. Vehicle access is to drive W from
the park entrance on Moore's Springs Rd to Mickey Rd (SR-2011); turn L,
and turn L again on Charlie Young Rd, a total of 4.3 mi.

Lake James State Park (Burke and McDowell Counties)

Named in honor of James B. Duke, founder of the Duke Power Co., Lake
James State Park is one of the state's most recent parks. Established in 1987 by
the state legislature, it became the first park in the state's system to receive
funding for development and operations at the time of its 565-acre acquisition.
The land is at the S side of the 6,510-acre lake where NC-126 runs through it.
The lake impounds the Catawba River, its North Fork, and the Linville River.
From the park launch sites at Hidden Cove and Canal Bridge, fishermen can
use the lake to catch large- and smallmouth bass, walleye, crappie, bluegill,
sunfish, perch, and catfish. (Information about the best time of day to fish for
specific species is at the ranger office.) Other activities include swimming,
boating, camping (backpack tent campsites), picnicking, hiking, and nature
study. Special facilities have been adapted to provide tent camping and pier
fishing for the physically disabled. (USGS Maps: Ashford, Marion East)

   Address and Access: Lake James State Park, P.O. Box 340, Nebo, NC
28761; 828-652-5047; fax: 828-659-8911. From I-40, Nebo/Lake James Exit
90, follow the park signs N to veer R on Harmony Grove Rd for 1.8 mi to
Nebo and US-70 at Kehler's Store. Turn L on US-70, go 0.3 mi, and turn R
on NC-126. Go 2.4 mi to the park entrance L.

Sandy Cliff Overlook Trail (0.5 mi); *Lake Channel Overlook Trail* **643-**
(1.3 mi); *Fishing Pier Trail* (0.1 mi); *Fox Den Loop Trail* (2.0 mi) **646**
   Length and Difficulty: 4.2 mi combined round-trip, easy to moderate
   Trailhead and Description: All trails can be accessed from the parking
lot. The Sandy Cliff Overlook Trail goes N on a peninsula of oak, maple, and
Virginia pine to the edge of the lake for scenic views. Backtrack to a connection

with the Lake Channel Overlook Trail, L. It parallels the lake's edge through white and Virginia pine, rhododendron, and young hardwoods at the base of a N slope. After a short distance on a gravel road toward the tent campsites, follow a gravel foot trail to a scenic point at the end of the peninsula. Backtrack. From the SW corner of the parking and picnic area follow the paved Fishing Pier Trail to a cove. From the pier follow the Fox Den Loop Trail into the cove. At 0.6 mi the trail forks to make a loop on a hilly peninsula. Plant life includes oak, hickory, Virginia pine, hemlock, rhododendron, laurel, and flame azalea. Pink lady slippers bloom in late April or early May, and in rich damp soils are white Indian pipe. Deer, fox, woodpecker, owl, and songbird are residents of the area.

Mount Jefferson State Park (Now a Natural Area. See chapter 11.)

Mount Mitchell State Park (Yancey County)

Mt. Mitchell State Park, extending over 1,855 acres of the Black Mtns. ridge, is the state's highest park (6,684 ft.), and Mt. Mitchell itself is the highest peak east of the Mississippi. This is also the state's oldest park, having been designated in 1915 thanks to the influence of early environmentalists such as Governor Locke Craig and US president Theodore Roosevelt. The park is listed in the National Registry of Natural Landmarks. Mt. Mitchell is named in honor of Elisha Mitchell, a clergyman and University of North Carolina geology professor, who fell to his death in a gorge N of Little Piney Ridge (about 2.0 mi from Mt. Mitchell summit) while on one of his scientific explorations. A creek and waterfall also bear his name. Geologically, the Black Mtn. range is estimated to be more than 1 billion years old, erosion having worn down the summits about 200 million years ago. Fraser fir (damaged by the woolly aphid and acid rain) and red spruce give the crest an alpine look reminiscent of Canada or Maine. Some of the flowering plants are white hellebore, blue-beaded Clinton's lily, and bearberry. Among the forest animals are bear, deer, bobcat, and squirrel. There are 18.0 mi of hiking trails, including Commissary Rd but not including the many connecting trails into the Pisgah NF. The Mountains-to-Sea Trail passes through the park. From the W it enters the park on a short piece of the park's 2.0 mi Commissary Trail (Rd), then a section of Camp Alice Trail before following a section of Old Mt. Mitchell Trail in the steep ascent to the top of Mt. Mitchell. From there it descends on part of the

Mt. Mitchell Trail for a total of 2.3 mi. The restaurant and observation lounge are open May 1–October 31. Park museum and concessions are open May through October, and picnic area is near the summit parking area. (USGS Maps: Montreat, Mt. Mitchell)

Address and Access: Mt. Mitchell State Park, 2388 State Highway 128, Burnsville, NC 28714; 828-675-4611; fax: 828-675-9655. Entrance is from NC-128 off the BRP near map 355, 30.0 mi NE of Asheville and 11.2 mi S from Buck Creek Gap and a jct with NC-80.

Support Facilities: Primitive camping is available year-round; limited facilities in winter months; tents only. The nearest campground is Black Mtn. Rec Area in Pisgah NF. Access is from the BRP, mp 351.9, at Deep Gap. Descend 4.9 mi on FR-472 and turn L at the campground entrance. (There are no hookups.)

Mt. Mitchell Summit Trail (0.2 mi); *Old Mt. Mitchell Trail* (2.0 mi); *Camp Alice Trail* (0.5 mi); *Balsam Nature Trail* (0.7 mi); *Mt. Mitchell Trail* (0.8 mi in state park; 5.6 mi in national forest); *Commissary Trail* (1.5 mi); *Campground Spur Trail* (0.4 mi)   647-653

Length and Difficulty: 6.1 mi combined, easy to strenuous

Special Features: Mt. Mitchell summit, spruce/fir forest

Trailhead and Description: From the summit lower and upper parking area, ascend the wide Mt. Mitchell Summit Trail in a damp forest of conifers and mosses for 0.2 mi to an observation tower and the tomb of the Dr. Elisha Mitchell, who after "39 years a professor at the University of North Carolina lost his life in the scientific exploration of this mountain in his 64th year, June 27, 1857." The magnificent views from the tower are panoramic. Other trails connect along the ascent. To the R is the N trailhead of the yellow-blazed Old Mt. Mitchell Trail, and ahead on the L is the white-blazed Balsam Nature Trail and the blue-blazed Mt. Mitchell Trail. If using the Balsam Nature Trail, a nature trail among Fraser fir, you will see markers with emphasis on flora and fauna, history, ecology, physical geography, and more. On the trail is the highest spring in the eastern United States, with an average temperature of 36 degrees. The Mt. Mitchell Trail/MST descends steeply with switchbacks into the Appalachian Ranger District of the Pisgah National Forest to end at Black Mtn. Campground. (See chapter 3, section 1B, Toecane Station for the trail's description.) If descending on the Old Mt. Mitchell Trail, pass through Fraser fir and rhododendron on a rugged trail. at 0.2 mi is the Campground Spur Trail, R, to walk-in, primitive campsites. Continue L and at a switchback, is a jct with the blue-blazed Camp Alice Trail, L, at 0.4 mi. (A loop can be made here on the Camp Alice Trail for 0.5 mi and join the Commissary Trail (Rd), L and R. It connects L with the Buncombe Horse Range Trail, where a L to Mt. Mitchell Trail will bring the hiker back to the summit of Mt. Mitchell for about 4.1 mi. For a longer loop, continue on the Old Mt. Mitchell Trail past the restaurant and park office to connect with the S trailhead of Commissary Trail, L, and follow routing as above for about 5.8 mi.) Otherwise, arrange a vehicle shuttle at the park office or backtrack on the Old Mt. Mitchell Trail.

654   *Deep Gap Trail*

> **Length and Difficulty:** 6.0 mi round-trip, strenuous
>
> **Trailhead and Description:** This trail is also part of the Black Mtn. Crest Trail described in the Appalachian Ranger District, chapter 3. From the summit parking and picnic area, follow an orange blaze N over rough terrain to Mt. Craig (6,645 ft.) at 1.0 mi; at 1.1 mi, reach Big Tom (6,593 ft.), named in honor of Thomas Wilson (1825–1900), who found the body of Dr. Mitchell. Continue over strenuous treadway to Balsam Cone (6,611 ft.) at 1.9 mi, and reach Cattail Peak (6,583 ft.) at 2.4 mi. Leave the state park boundary and go another 1.5 mi to Deep Gap, the site of a former USFS shelter. Currently there is tent camping space and a spring nearby. (Ahead the Black Mtn. Crest Trail goes to Bowlens Creek Rd [SR-1109] for a total of 12.0 mi.) (See chapter 3, section 1B, Toecane Station.)

New River State Park (Ashe and Alleghany Counties)

New River State Park is a 26.5-mi scenic corridor of a river claimed to be North America's oldest. For 22.0 mi the park is the river's South Fork to where it joins the North Fork 4.5 mi S of the Virginia state line. Headwaters for the South Fork are in the Blowing Rock/Boone area. After convergence of the forks, the New River (named by Peter Jefferson, father of Thomas) winds its way N through VA and into WV before merging with the Kanawha River. This classic and historic river was threatened by the Appalachian Power Co., which was trying to build a dam. In opposition, citizens and government officials prevented it and declared it a state scenic river in 1975. By 1976, it was a national wild and scenic river. The park's forests are mainly oak/hickory communities with some eastern red cedar and yellow pine. The understory has red bud, mountain laurel, and hydrangea. There are 14 species of wildflowers, including Carolina saxifrage *(Saxifrage caroliniana)*. This area is home to animals such as mink, deer, bear, wild turkey, and songbirds. Canoeing and fishing are the river's chief appeal. Permits are required for canoe-in camping. Although canoeing can begin at least 50.0 mi upstream, the park has three major access points, the Wagoner Rd Access Area (with park office and primitive campsites, picnic tables, rest rooms with hot showers, telephone, water, and hiking trails); US-221 Access Area (with community building [reservations required], primitive campsites, picnic tables, rest rooms with hot showers, proposed full-service campground, and hiking trails); and the Alleghany County Access (accessible by canoe only, with primitive campsites, picnic tables, pit toilet, telephone, and hiking trail). (USGS Maps: Jefferson, Laurel Springs, Mouth of Wilson)

Address and Access: Office for both Mt. Jefferson SNA (see chapter 11), 336-246-9653 and New River State Park, P.O. Box 48, Jefferson, NC 28640; 336-982-2587; fax: 336-982-3943. To Wagoner Rd Access Area from Jefferson, E, on US-221, take NC-88/16E. After 3.3 mi, NC-16 breaks away, R, to BRP and onto North Wilkesboro. Continue 1.5 mi on NC-88 to a sharp L at Wagoner Rd (SR-1590) (at Wagoner Missionary Baptist Church) and follow it 1.6 mi to the Park's parking lot near the office.

Wagoner Road Access Area
Running Cedar Trail (1.0 mi); *Fern Trail* (1.0 mi)   **655-**

Trailhead and Description: If hiking the white-blazed Running Cedar   **656**
Trail first, go to the upriver signboard and descend, R. Enter and easily ascend into a white pine grove. Cross a wire fence twice, pass Christmas ferns in and out of hardwood coves to cross the park's entrance road (maintenance nearby) at 0.6 mi. Descend through dogwood and hawthorne; in a L curve, pass a large apple tree. At 1.0 mi is a jct with orange-blazed Fern Trail, R and L. (Because the trail makes a numbered loop, it is recommended to turn L and descend beside a small stream 0.1 mi to acquire a Fern Trail brochure at a box on the svc road. Backtrack.) Continue on the loop and pass #4, the remains of cattle feed tank and followed by a rhododendron slick at #5. At 0.4 mi, make a sharp L and descend to parallel the picturesque riverside and islands. Complete the loop at #19 near a rest room, campsite access, and svc road at 0.7 mi (Brochures may be returned here, to the box.) Follow the road past a picnic area and old chimney to a gravel path with large apple trees, L. Enter the parking lot and complete the double loop at 2.0 mi where the trail began.

US-221 Access Area

To access E of Jefferson at a jct of US-221 and NC-88/16, drive N on US-221/NC-16 for 1.4 mi to sharply turn R onto US-221. Follow the narrow road 7.5 mi to turn R at the park entrance. (If coming from Sparta, go W 0.3 mi on US-21 and turn L onto US-221. Follow for 14.2 mi and turn L at the park **657** entrance.) Arrive at the riverside parking lot after another 1.3 mi. The Hickory Trail sign is R at the parking-lot entrance. Upstream are primitive campsites with a rest room and hot shower, picnic area, and canoe access. Ascend steps on an easy, orange-blazed footpath. Pass through a grove of locust and hawthorne. (After 0.2 mi, a 50-yd. spur trail goes R to entrance road and community building.) Continue to a loop, R and L. If hiking clockwise, enter a mature hardwood forest with an understory of mountain laurel. (At 0.5 mi is a jct with a 0.4-mi white-blazed access to a proposed full-service campground. Backtrack.) On the Hickory Trail, cross the park access road into a white-pine grove. At 0.9 mi, enter a grassy, open path among dogwood and wildflowers and beautiful views of the river area. Cross the park access road again and complete the loop at 1.2 mi.

Alleghany County Access Area

Access by canoe is 15.0 mi downstream from US-221 Access Area. An easy **658** 1.0-mi Farm House Loop Trail passes through a former farm meadow, into hardwood forests and offers impressive views of the cliffs across the river. There are eight canoe campsites, a water pump, telephone, and pit toilets. It is 4.0 mi downriver to the ramp take-out at VA/NC-93 bridge.

Pilot Mountain State Park (Surry and Yadkin Counties)

Pilot Mountain State Park covers 3,703 acres in two sections—Pilot Mtn. and the S and N side of the Yadkin River—and is connected by a 6.5-mi 300-ft.-wide forest corridor for hikers and equestrians. In the park is the Big Pinnacle, rising 200 ft. from its base, 1,500 ft. above the valley floor and 2,420 ft. above sea level. Dedicated as a national natural landmark in 1976, it is geologically a quartzite monadnock. Park activities are canoe camping, picnicking, horseback riding, hiking, and camping. A family type tent/trailer campground is near the base of the N side of the mountain. It has hot showers but no hookups (closed December 1 through March 15). Trails connect easily with the exception of Yadkin River Trail on the S side of the Yadkin River. Sauratown Trail has its W terminus at the park, and the MST may pass from the W through the park to connect with the Sauratown Trail going E to Hanging Rock State Park. (USGS Maps: Pinnacle, Siloam)

Address and Access: Pilot Mountain State Park, 1792 Pilot Knob Park Rd, Pinnacle, NC 27043; 336-325-2355; Fax: 336-325-2751. Entrance to the park is at the jct of US-52 and Pilot Knob Rd (SR-2053), 14.0 mi S of Mt. Airy and 24,0 mi N of Winston-Salem.

Sassafras Trail (0.5 mi); *Jomeokee Trail* (0.8 mi); *Ledge Spring* **659-**
Trail (1.6 mi); *Mountain Trail* (2.5 mi); *Grindstone Trail* (1.6 mi) **663**

Length and Difficulty: 7 mi combined, easy to strenuous

Special Features: Big Pinnacle, scenic ledges

Trailhead and Description: All of these trails connect and can be reached from the parking lot at the top of the mountain. From the parking lot, go past and behind the comfort station to a rocky area and a sign for the Jomeokee Trail. To the L, 30 yd., is the Sassafras Trail. (Follow the Sassafras Trail N on a self-guiding loop. It is an interpretive trail among pitch pine, chestnut oak, laurel, and ground cover patches of galax.) At the Jomeokee Trail sign, descend among rocks and follow a much used access to the Big Pinnacle. (Jomeokee is an Indian word for "great guide" or "pilot.") At 0.2 mi, pass the base of Little Pinnacle and a jct R with the yellow-blazed Ledge Spring Trail. Ahead, after another 0.1 mi, turn R to follow a rocky loop around the Big Pinnacle. The trail walls have caves, eroded rock formations, ferns, wildflowers, lichens, and mosses. Park officials say that ravens nest on the summit. (Climbing or rappelling is prohibited.) On the return from the loop, take the Ledge Spring Trail, L. Descend on a rocky, rough, and sometimes strenuous base of the ledges. At 1.0 mi, reach Ledge Spring, R, 30 yd. from the jct with the Mountain Trail. (Formerly the Mountain Bridle Trail, the Mountain Trail is a rough connector trail to the Corridor Trail described below. Blazed red, it descends through a hardwood forest with scattered patches of laurel and pine in the beginning. At 1.8 mi, it reaches large boulders pushed up in a row from a former clearing. After another 0.4 mi, it leaves the row and follows a footpath to an exit at the Surry Line Rd [SR-2061] to a jct L with the 1.7-mi Grassy Ridge Trail and R with the 6.5-mi Corridor Trail at 2.5 mi). To continue on the Ledge Spring Trail, turn R and begin a steep ascent over the ledges to a jct with Grindstone Trail, L, at 1.3 mi (Grindstone Trail follows first on an easy contour, but soon descends in a rocky area with hardwoods and laurel. It crosses a footbridge and small stream at 1.3 mi, an old road at 1.5 mi, and exits at 1.6 mi between campsites #16 and #17).

Continue the ascent ahead on Ledge Spring Trail, pass R of the picnic area, and return to the SW corner of the parking lot at 1.5 mi.

664-   *Grassy Ridge Trail* (1.7 mi); *Corridor Trail* (6.5 mi); *Horne Creek*
667   *Trail* (1.3 mi); *Canal Trail* (1.0 mi round-trip)

Length and Difficulty: 10.5 mi combined, easy

Trailhead and Description: (With the exception of Canal Trail, these trails are horse/hiker trails.) The N terminus of the white-blazed Grassy Ridge Trail is on Pilot Knob Rd (SR-1151) in Surry County, under the US-52 bridge, 0.2 mi E of the park entrance. (At this trailhead is the W terminus of planned Sauratown Trail). (Vehicular access to the S end of Grassy Ridge Trail and the N end of Corridor Trail from here is E on Pilot Knob Rd, 1.1 mi to a jct with Old Winston Rd [SR-1152]. Turn R, go 0.4 mi, and turn R on Old US-52 [SR-1236]. After another 0.4 mi, turn R across the RR on Surry Line Rd [SR-1148], which becomes Pinnacle Hotel Rd [SR-2061] in Surry County, and drive 1.6 mi.)

Enter Grassy Ridge Trail at a poplar tree and into a hardwood forest. Cross a streamlet at 0.1 mi and reach a jct, R, at 0.2 mi (To the R, it is 0.3 mi on a footpath to the park office.) Continue L, pass an old tobacco barn at 0.4 mi. Cross small streams at 0.5 mi and 1.3 mi. Arrive at Pinnacle Hotel Rd (SR-2061 in Surry County) at 1.7 mi. (To the R, on the road, it is 75 yd. to the S terminus of the red-blazed Mountain Trail.) Cross the road to a road jct with Culler Rd (SR-2063) and a parking area in the corner of Pilot Mtn. State Park Corridor. Here is the N terminus of the Corridor Trail. (Vehicular access to the S terminus of the Corridor Trail is W on SR-2061 for 2.6 mi to a jct with Shoals Rd [SR-2048]. Turn L, and go S 4.0 mi [turning neither R nor L] but partly on SR-2069, also called Shoals Rd, to a fork. Ahead is a dead-end sign. Turn L on gravel Hauser Rd [SR-2072] and go 1.0 mi to the S terminus, L. Ahead it is 0.2 mi, R, to the park's Yadkin River section.)

Begin the yellow-blazed Corridor Trail on an old farm road in a grove of Virginia pine and pass under a power line at 0.1 mi. At 0.3 mi is a view (looking back) of the Pinnacles. Cross two footbridges with a meadow of wildflowers and elderberry in between. At 0.7 mi, leave the forest and enter a field with another good view of the Pinnacles (looking back). After 0.1 mi, enter a forest of pine and cedar. Pass remnants of an old tobacco barn, L, at 1.2 mi. Cross a small stream bordered with pinxter at 1.4 mi, and another stream at 1.5 mi. At 1.6 mi, cross paved Mt. Zion Rd (SR-2064). Follow the trail through areas of old farmland and young-growth forest. Descend to rock-hop a tributary of Grassy Creek at 2.6 mi. Pass patches of yellow root and wood betony among the river birch. Exit from the woods into an open area of honeysuckle, blackberry, and poison ivy, and cross paved Shoals Rd (SR-2048) at 3.0 mi. Follow the woods' edge into the forest, cross a stream, cross a number of old woods roads, and descend gently to another stream with beds of sensitive fern at 4.7 mi. Cross a footbridge constructed by the YACC. Cross paved Stoney Ridge Church Rd (SR-2070) at 5.0 mi. Follow the trail through beautiful routes of alternating pine groves and open hardwoods. At 6.0 mi, cross a rocky tributary of Horne Creek. (Upstream are two large millstones.) Pass under a power line at 6.3 mi and reach the trail's S terminus at 6.5 mi at Hauser Rd (SR-2072). Across the road begins the Horne Creek Trail. (To the L on the road it is 0.2 mi to the entrance, R, of the Yadkin River section of the park at a log shed.) (Vehicular access to US-52 from here is on SR-2072, E, 2.8 mi to Perch Rd [SR-2065]. Turn L, and go 3.5 mi to US-52 in Pinnacle.) (Vehicular access to the S end of the Horne Creek Trail is on the park road. Drive in at the park gate by the log shed, ford the small Horne Creek three times, pass through a picnic area, and reach a cul-de-sac on a bluff by the Yadkin River. The Canal Trail begins here, on the W side of the cul-de-sac at a wide trail opening, and connects with Horne Creek Trail, after 80 yd., at the Southern Railway track.)

At the N end of Horne Creek Trail enter a partial field with walnut trees. After 0.3 mi arrive at the park road, turn R, rock-hop Horne Creek, and at 0.5 mi reenter the woods. Ascend and rejoin the park road in a grove of pines at 0.8 mi. Turn R, follow the road, but leave it after 0.2 mi. Descend to the Southern Railway track and reach jct, L, with the Canal Trail (which begins 80 yd. up the bank to the cul-de-sac). Cross the RR tracks and after 60 yd. reach the Yadkin River, the trail's end. (To the R the Canal Trail crosses a footbridge. It goes upstream 0.5 mi between the river and the RR tracks among sycamore, poplar, and river birch. At 0.2 mi pass a long rock wall, R. Backtrack.) Although Horne Creek Trail ends at the river, horses can ford the river to two islands and to Yadkin River Trail described below.

Yadkin River Trail

668

Length and Difficulty: 0.7 mi, easy

Trailhead and Description: To reach this trail, take NC-67 to East Bend and follow Old NC-67 (SR-1545) into town. Turn NW on Fairground Rd (SR-1541), go 0.5 mi, turn R on Shady Grove Church Rd (SR-1538) for 0.4 mi, and turn R on Old Shoals Rd (SR-1546) for 2.5 mi to the picnic and parking area. Follow the yellow-blazed trail to the river and return on a loop through a pine forest W of the ranger station. (This is also an area for a bridle trail that crosses the Yadkin River N to Horne Creek Trail and Corridor Trail described above.) There are two renovated campsites for individual canoeists on the 45-acre islands in the Yadkin River. Group camping is prohibited.

South Mountains State Park (Burke County)

This remote, rugged, and generally underdeveloped park has about 18,000 acres in a broad range of knobs and ridges, near 3,000 ft. in elevation, and watershed streams for Jacob Fork River. Located in the SW piedmont area of the state, the area is underlain mainly by a mixture of gneiss and granite. The major attraction in the park is the 80-ft.-high Shoals Falls. The park is heavily forested with a mixture of pine, oak, hickory, and poplar. Almost all coves have one or more of the parks three species of rhododendron. Ferns and wildflowers are commonplace. There are more than 60 species of birds, and among the reptiles are copperhead and timber rattlesnake (both poisonous). Wildlife also includes black bear, deer, chipmunk, and raccoon. This is the site of a former CCC camp, where the many back roads were constructed in the 1930s. (At least half of the park has other old roads in a closed environment W into Henry Fork watershed.) Park plans are in process to clear some of these overgrown routes for future trail connections. Park officials are also planning a visitor center.

Current facilities provide equestrians a large parking area, campground, 37-stall barn, washhouse, hot showers, flush toilets, and 29 mi of trails/roads. There are at least 9.6 mi of hiking-only trails/roads, and at least 17 mi of mountain-biking options on multi-use routes. In addition to a family campground (no electricity), there is a group camp (reservations necessary at Shinny Creek [pronounced "Shiny"]) and backpack camping. For the latter option, each backpacker must register on a list beside the park-office door. All supplies, including water, must be packed to the sites. The six campsites are Upper Falls Trail (four sites, 1.5 mi from park office); Shinny Creek Trail (four sites, 1.5 mi from park office); Sawtooth Trail (three sites, 2.5 mi from park office); Fox Trail (three sites, 5.0 mi from park office); Jacob Branch campsites, off of the HQ Trail (three sites, 3.5 mi from park office); Murray Branch campsites, off of the Lower CCC Trail/Rd (three sites, 6.0 mi from park office). Picnic areas are at the Jacob Fork parking lot and Shinny Creek picnic area, 0.4 mi up HQ Trail.

There are three short trails from the Jacob Fork parking lot. Short Trail, a 0.6-mi foot trail, only ascends from the L of the park office up the mountainside for views of Jacob Fork Gorge and a connection to multi-use Little River Trail. The 0.5-mi Jacob Fork River Trail is a linear trail connecting Jacob Fork parking area downstream to Cicero Branch parking lot and family campground. A scenic route among hemlock, rhododendron, and maple, it crosses two bridges over the river rapids. At 0.3 mi, it crosses Raven Rock Trail. The third short trail, the 0.3-mi Hemlock Nature Trail, parallels Jacob Fork River **669** upstream from the Jacob Fork parking lot. Flawlessly crafted, the handicapped-accessible route has display markers and kiosks with information on the riparian environment of salamander and fish, bird habitats, and trees and flowers. Along the way is an amphitheater and resting benches. A return can be made on the connecting HQ Trail.

Other trails in the park are described as loops because trails make a circle around the boundaries of the park, and a combination of inter-circle trails make loops. All of the hiking loops described here are some full lengths of trails and pieces of linear trails to provide the park's trail highlights. They all begin at Jacob Fork parking lot. Rather than follow any of the loops presented here, hikers will find with the park map that other connections and backtracks can be made. Additionally, the park office provides some loop descriptions with maps on request. For hikers on the High Shoals Falls Loop Trail, there are eight numbered posts for a "Geology hike." Request a copy of the guide from the park office. (USGS Maps: Casar, Benn Knob, S Morganton)

Address and Access: South Mountains State Park, 3001 South Mtn. State Park Ave, Connelly Springs, NC 28612; 828-433-4772; fax: 828-433-4778. Access from Morganton is S on NC-18 from its jct with I-40. Go 10.8 mi to the state-park sign at Sugar Loaf Rd (SR-1913), R (opposite a service station), and drive 4.2 mi to Old NC-18 (SR-1924), L. After 2.7 mi, turn R on Ward's Gap Rd (SR-1901), go 1.3 mi, cross Jacob Fork River bridge, and stay R up a hill on South Mtn. State Park Ave (SR-1904). Proceed to park sign across a bridge and bear L into park. The equestrian parking area is 0.1 mi on the L, which also accesses Turkey Ridge Trail (all bridle trails). The parking lot and park office are another 1.7 mi ahead.

Support Facilities: Shopping centers, motels, restaurants, and hospitals are in Morganton.

Loop Trail #1 (2.5 mi round-trip)

670   ***High Shoals Falls Loop Trail*** (2.5 mi, easy to strenuous)

From the Jacob Fork parking lot, enter at the sign board on the paved HQ Trail (or at the corner of the parking lot, take Hemlock Nature Trail). On a wide route, pass a rest room, L, and pass a jct with Chestnut Knob Trail, R, at 0.2 mi. At 0.3 mi, pass a connection with the Hemlock Nature Trail, L. Cross a bridge over Shinny Creek at 0.4 mi. To the L is a numbered post for the "Geology Hike." (See introduction above for a brochure.) At Shinny Creek picnic area are signs; HQ Trail goes R to a jct upstream with Shinny Trail. High Shoals Falls Loop Trail begins here. At 0.5 mi is a fork with steps in each direction. (Backpacking campers: turn R here to follow an old road with switchbacks to a ridge and a jct with Upper Falls Trail where a 0.2-mi L leads to primitive campsites, R.) Continue L on High Shoals Fall Loop Trail. Cross a footbridge and enter a cool misty area among hemlock, fern, trillium, and foamflower. Ascend numerous steps and cross bridges among cascades and large boulders in a couloir. At 0.9 mi, view a waterfall from a deck. (Beware: Here, as at the top of the falls, is hazardous. Stay on the trail and watch steps for slippery surfaces.) Continue ascent on steps and cross a stream on a footbridge at 1.0 mi. Follow old road, and at 1.2 mi is a jct with Upper Falls campsites, L. At 1.4 mi is a jct with Upper Falls Trail ahead and turn R on High Shoals Falls Loop Trail. Descend on old road with switchbacks through a forest of hemlock, black gum, and poplar. Reach the loop connection at 2.0 mi and return to parking area at 2.5 mi.

Loop Trail #2 (4.6 mi round-trip)

671-   ***High Shoals Falls Loop Trail*** (1.4 mi, strenuous); ***Upper Falls Trail***
672   (0.9 mi, moderate); ***HQ Trail*** (2.3 mi, easy to moderate)

Follow High Shoals Falls Loop Trail as described in Loop #1, but continue ascending on Upper Falls Trail, mainly on ridgeline and gaps among hardwoods. At 2.3 mi is a jct with HQ Trail, R and L. (The HQ Trail continues L, ahead, for 2.0 mi to a jct with outer-loop Horseshoe Trail and Lower CCC Trail/Rd.) Turn R on HQ Trail and gradually descend to a scenic cove, R, at 3.0 mi. As the trail (old road) becomes steeper, make a horseshoe curve to level off, and cross a bridge over Shinny Creek at 3.5 mi. Here are hemlock, fetterbush, and rhododendron. To the L is narrow (no horses or bicycles) Shinny Creek Trail. To the R are Shinny Creek primitive campsites in an open meadow. Ascend and descend and cross a bridge over Shinny Creek at 3.9 mi. Pass through a gorge of dense hemlock and rhododendron. Shinny Creek,

deep below, L, has flumes and cascades roaring in a twilight zone. Arrive at
Shinny Creek picnic area to turn L and cross Shinny Creek again near its con-
fluence with Jacob Fork at 4.3 mi. Return to parking area on road or Hemlock
Nature Trail.

Loop Trail #3 (10.1 mi round-trip)

HQ Trail (1.1 mi, moderate); *Shinny Creek Trail* (2.2 mi, moderate   **673-**
to strenuous); *Possum Trail* (1.5 mi, strenuous [3.0 mi for backtrack-   **677**
ing]); *Lower CCC Trail/Rd* (0.4 mi, moderate); *Fox Trail* (1.1 mi,
moderate); *Jacob Branch Trail* (1.2 mi, moderate)

Begin at the Jacob Fork parking area and follow HQ Trail as above back to
Shinny Creek Trail. Turn R on Shinny Creek Trail at 1.1 mi. Follow it
upstream and rock-hop the creek at cascades and pools at 1.3 mi. Cross a
bridge over Shinny Creek again and a jct with Possum Trail, R. (The Possum
Trail ascends steeply from the toe of a ridge to a knob; it then follows the
ridge of oak, hickory, pine, and laurel to a jct with Horseridge Trail at 1.5 mi.
Backtrack. [Horseridge Trail, 3.3 mi, is part of the outer-loop of equestrian
trails.]) Continuing on Shinny Creek Trail, cross the creek again on a bridge
and immediately a second bridge over Dark Creek in a forest of hemlock and
rhododendron. Follow an old RR grade. Turn sharply L at a ridge toe; ascend
steeply, rocky in sections, among hardwoods, yellow pine, and turkey beard.
Reach the ridge crest at 2.8 mi. Follow an old road and arrive at the trail's end;
reach jct with HQ Trail, R and L, at 3.4 mi.

Turn R on HQ Trail. After 0.8 mi is a jct with equestrian Lower CCC
Trail/Rd and turn L. (The Lower CCC Trail/Rd is 2.5 mi in the outer-loop
between Horseridge Trail N and Benn Knob Trail S, which is 3.0 mi on the
park's S rim that passes Benn Knob, elev. 2,894.) After 0.4 mi is a jct L with
Fox Trail (old forest road). Follow for 0.3 mi to the first access R to backpacker campsites in a former wildlife field. After another 100 yd. is a second
access R to campsites. Continue 0.1 mi and pass the gravesite of William
Crotts (Confederate States of America) and unmarked graves, L. Ascend to
Grass Ridge; follow it to a side ridge to a jct with Jacob Branch Trail, L, at
5.7 mi. (Fox Trail continues SE for 2.5 mi to a jct with Dogwood Trail/Rd, a
paved road used by cyclists and horseback riders.) Descend on Jacob Branch
Trail and curve L off of the ridge to cross Jacob Branch at 6.4 mi. Ascend on
the N trailhead of Jacob Branch Trail at 6.9 mi to a jct with HQ Trail. (It is 0.3
mi L to the W trailhead of Shinny Trail.) Turn R on HQ Trail, pass a wildlife
field, R, and at 7.8 mi is a jct with Upper Falls Trail. Stay L and after 1.2 mi,

arrive at a jct with Shinny Creek and Shinny Creek Trail at 9.0 mi, the completion of the loop. A return to the Jacob Fork parking area is another 1.1 mi for a total of 10.1 mi.

Loop Trail #4 (5.9 mi or 6.2 mi, round-trip)

678-682　*HQ Trail* (0.2 mi, easy); ***Chestnut Knob Trail*** (2.1 mi, strenuous); ***Sawtooth Trail*** (1.1 mi, moderate); ***Little River Trail*** (1.2 mi, moderate); ***Short Trail*** (0.6 mi, moderate); ***Jacob Fork River Trail*** (0.4 mi, easy)

From Jacob Fork parking area, follow HQ Trail to Chestnut Knob Trail, R, into a forest of hemlock, white pine, and laurel. (Elevation gain to Chestnut Knob is about 1,000 ft.) Ascend numerous steps and switchbacks. At 1.0 mi, R, is Jacob Fork River Gorge Overlook. Level off and pass an intermittent spring, L, at 1.3 mi. Continue ascent. At 1.9 mi, ascend steeply with more steps. The forest has chestnut, oak, galax, maple, and scattered pine. Arrive at a T jct at 2.0 mi. To the L, it is 0.2 mi to rugged cliffs of Chestnut Knob, elev 2,291. Views are of Shinny Creek hollow and of Kings Mtn. Range, SE. Backtrack, but stay ahead to reach jct with Sawtooth Trail, R and L, 2.5 mi. (To the L, it is 1.4 mi to Horseridge Trail.) Turn R sharply on Sawtooth Trail, and after 0.1 mi, begin descent. At 3.1 mi, turn R sharply and descend steeply; level off on the E side of the ridge. Rock-hop Little River in a scenic area of pools and cascades adorned with rhododendron at 3.4 mi. Ascend among short-leaf pine and reach jct with Little River Trail, R, and Upper CCC Trail, L, at 3.6 mi (The Upper CCC Trail/Rd is 1.6 mi to Horseridge Trail, both part of the outer-loop of equestrian trails.) Turn R into a young forest and make a horseshoe curve at 3.8 mi. Pass running cedar on the L mountainside. At 4.3 mi, cross a wood bridge over a stream laced with fetterbush and sweet pepperbush. Ascend steeply and at 4.9 mi are a jct and signs. Little River Trail goes straight ahead, and Turkey Ridge Trail is L. (Turkey Ridge Trail descends, passes an open grazing field with a few apple trees, and crosses the park road entrance at 1.3 mi. It turns L and parallels the road to its E trailhead at the equestrian parking area at 1.6 mi.) Continuing on the Little River Trail, reach jct with Short Trail, R, and a gate at 5.3 mi. If turning R, follow the 0.6 mi Short Trail down to the park office and parking area for a round-trip of 5.9 mi. (If continuing on Little River Trail, descend on switchbacks and cross the park entrance road to a jct with Jacob Fork River Trail, R and L, at 6.0 mi. (Across the river is 1.9-mi Raven Rock Trail.) (To the L, it is 0.1 mi to Cicero Branch parking lot.) Turn R and follow the Jacob Fork River Trail 0.4 mi upstream to Jacob Fork parking lot at 6.2 mi.

Stone Mountain State Park (Alleghany and Wilkes Counties)

Stone Mountain State Park, with 13,960 acres of forests, trout streams, water-falls, and rugged medium-grained biotite granite domes, borders the eastern edge of the Blue Ridge Mtns. The largest granite area is Stone Mtn., rising in grandeur 600 ft. above its base and 2,305 ft. above sea level. The granite is estimated to be 300 million years old. The park's protected environment provides a habitat for deer, beaver, mink, bobcat, squirrel, bear, and a number of smaller mammals. Spring wildflowers are prominent. The major activities are picnicking, fishing, hiking, climbing, and camping. There is a 37-unit tent/trailer campground (0.8 mi N of the park office) with grills and tables, flush toilets, and hot showers (water off December 1 to mid-March). Walk-in camp- **683** sites are also available in the backcountry at designated areas on Widow's Creek Trail. All walk-in campers must make reservations. Climbing is allowed on the S face of Stone Mtn. Access is by way of Stone Mountain Trail (described below) to the mountain base. The mountain is closed to climbing when the rocks are wet, and all climbers (as well as all hikers) must be out of the area a half-hour before closing. The MST passes through the park for 3.8 mi from the park's Backcountry Parking lot to the BRP boundary. From there it ascends another 2.2 mi to the Devil's Garden Overlook, mp 235.7. (USGS Map: Glade Valley)

Address and Access: Stone Mountain State Park, 3600 Frank Parkway, Roaring Gap, NC 28668; 336-957-8185. The main access is from US-21 in Thurmond. Follow Traphill Rd (SR-1002) W 4.3 mi to a jct with John P. Frank Parkway (SR-1784), and follow SR-1784 N 2.5 mi to the park office, R.

Support Facilities: A grocery store may be open 0.6 mi W on SR-1002 from the park's S entrance (W of Traphill). Shopping centers, restaurants, motels, and other services are in Elkins, 15.0 mi SE on US-21.

Stone Mountain Trail (4.5 mi); *Wolf Rock Trail* (1.2 mi); *Cedar* **684-** *Rock Trail* (0.7 mi); *Blackjack Ridge Trail* (1.4 mi); *Stone Mountain* **690** *Nature Trail* (0.5 mi); *Middle and Lower Falls Trail* (1.6 mi round-trip); *Stone Mountain Connector Trail* (0.5 mi)

Length and Difficulty: 9.5 mi combined, easy to strenuous
Special Features: granite domes, waterfalls

Trailhead and Description: Access to all these trails is at the lower parking lot; they all connect and provide multiple loop options. The longest trail is Stone Mountain Trail. It begins and ends at the parking lot. After 107 yd. it forks to make a loop. The L route follows switchbacks, steeply in places, for the first 1.0 mi. The R route from the fork descends to a footbridge among rhododendron, ascends, and forks again, L, at 0.2 mi. It descends and crosses four more footbridges to enter a large meadow and spectacular view of the S face of Stone Mtn. after another 0.4 mi. (See continued description below.)

(At the second fork, listed above, the R fork is Wolf Rock Trail. From here it ascends on a ridge and switchbacks to a jct with an old road at 0.6 mi. Keep L on the Wolf Rock Trail where it blends R on another old road at 0.7 mi. Ahead pass a long stone wall, L, and a former homestead area. At 1.0 mi, reach a short spur, R, to the pockmarked flat dome of Wolf Rock. Views W are of Little Stone Mtn. and SW of Greenstreets Mtn. After another 0.1 mi is a jct L with a narrow path that ascends 120 yd. to a concrete box spring. Descend, pass a seepage, L, and two old sheds, R. At 1.2 mi is a jct L with Cedar Rock Trail, and end Wolf Rock Trail to begin Blackjack Ridge Trail. At this point you have a choice of two return loops to the parking lot. If taking Cedar Rock Trail, ascend 100 yd. to a granite slope and outstanding view of Stone Mtn. Follow the yellow blaze painted on the rock. Descend to join Stone Mountain Trail, turn L on it, and complete the loop after 2.9 mi. If taking Blackjack Ridge Trail, follow the old road in a forest of oak, laurel, and pine to pass Buzzard Rock, R, at 0.2 mi. Leave the ridge, L, at 0.6 mi [at yellow blazes] and soon descend to rock-hop Cedar Rock Creek. Ascend steeply and terminate the trail at a jct of Cedar Rock Trail at 1.4 mi. Bear R on Cedar Rock Trail to Stone Mountain Trail, where a L for 0.2 mi will complete the loop of 3.8 mi.)

To continue on the Stone Mountain Trail, pass through the grassy meadow for views of the S face of Stone Mtn. A plaque describes the dome as a registered natural landmark. At 0.8 mi (at the edge of the woods) is a jct L with Stone Mountain Nature Trail. (It crosses the meadow, N, to the base of the mountain. Enter the woods, L. Turn R on a yellow-blazed trail with interpretive signs among the boulders. Cross a small stream and return to Stone Mountain Trail after 0.5 mi.) On Stone Mountain Trail, 25 yd. into the woods, is a jct with Cedar Rock Trail. (A sign here may refer to Stone Mountain Trail as Stone Mountain Falls Trail; they are the same.) Cross Big Sandy Creek twice. Continue downstream on the Stone Mountain Trail, and reach jct R with the Middle Falls Trail and Lower Falls Trail at 1.5 mi. (Both of the falls trails dead-end. Rock-hop Big Sandy Creek, follow an old road, and after 0.2 mi is a jct with the Middle Falls Trail, R. Follow it for 0.1 mi to a view of the cascades. For the Lower Falls Trail continue on the old road and rock-hop or wade Big Sandy Creek twice to see the cascade after 0.5 mi. Backtrack.)

Proceed on the Stone Mountain Trail, which becomes a footpath through a rhododendron grove. Arrive at the beautiful 200-ft. tumbling Stone Mtn. Falls (also called Beauty Falls) at 1.8 mi. Climb carefully the stairway to the fall's summit. At 2.1 mi, come to a fork near an old stone chimney. (To the R is Stone Mountain Connector Trail, a 0.5-mi well-designed trail to the picnic area and park office parking lot.) On the Stone Mountain Trail, fork L. Views N are of the Blue Ridge Mtns. and SW of Cedar Rock. Large patches of lichen, mosses, and pine cling to the rocks. Follow the yellow blaze painted on the barren granite and begin the descent at 3.9 mi among chestnut oak, pine, and blueberry patches. Return to the parking lot at 4.5 mi.

Central Piedmont Region

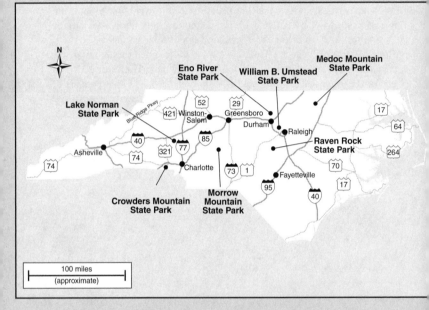

Introductions to Trail Areas

SECTION 2: CENTRAL PIEDMONT REGION
Crowders Mountain State Park (Gaston County)

Crowders Mountain (1,625 ft.) is named for for Crowders Creek, which headwaters in the park. Crowders Mountain, is part of 2,713 acres of Crowders Mountain State Park. In 1987, Kings Pinnacle (1,705 ft.) was acquired. Family and group backpack camping is available in separate camping areas. Registration at the park office is necessary. The park has been designated a natural heritage area; some infrequent plants—ground juniper *(Juniperus communis depressa)* and Bradley's spleenwort *(Asplenium bradleyi)* found in acidic rocks—and a wide variety of flora and fauna make it ideal for natural preservation in the future. Recreational opportunities are picnicking, fishing, camping, rock climbing, and hiking. (USGS Maps: Kings Mtn., Gastonia)

In December 2000, approximately 2000 acres were added to the park, These additional acres contain the Kings Mtn. Ridgeline, where the park now adjoins King Mtn. State Park in SC (which adjoins King Mtn. National Military Park). The combined acreage of the three parks is approximately 15,000 acres. A new hiking trail has been approved to run along the ridgeline and join the parks' trail systems. An access with parking, rest rooms, picnicking, and a contact sta is planned near the South Carolina line, and a backpack camping area will be constructed adjacent to the Kings Mountain Ridgeline Trail.

691

Address and Access: Crowders Mtn. State Park, 522 Park Office Lane, Kings Mountain, NC 28086; 704-853-5375; fax: 704-853-5391. One access from the I-85 jct is US-74/29 (E toward Gastonia). Turn R on Freedom Mill Rd (at sign) and after 2.5 mi, turn R on Sparrow Spring Rd. Reach the park entrance on R after another 0.6 mi.

692-
695

Crowders Trail (3.0 mi); *Backside Trail* (0.9 mi); *Tower Trail* (2.0 mi); *Rocktop Trail* (2.1 mi)

Length and Difficulty: 5.2 mi round-trip, moderate to strenuous

Special Feature: views from Crowders Mtn.

Trailhead and Description: From the park office, follow the signs on a well-graded and well-maintained trail N to a jct with Pinnacle Trail at 0.1 mi. Turn R, follow white-blazed markers through mature hardwood to Freedom Mill Rd (SR-1125) at 0.8 mi. Cross the road, turn L, and skirt the ridge to a jct with Backside Trail at 2.6 mi. Turn R. (The orange-blazed Backside Trail is a 0.9-mi connector trail with Tower Trail, which runs from Linwood Rd Access [SR-1131] to Crowders Mtn. The parking lot for these trailheads is W of Linwood Rd, 200 yd. NE of the trails' intersection. It is 1.8 mi round-trip.

The blue-blazed Tower Trail is 4.0 mi round-trip). At 2.9 mi, climb steps and at 3.0 mi, reach the summit for impressive views from 150-ft. cliffs. Return SW on red-blazed Rocktop Trail, whose jct with Tower Trail loop is at 3.4 mi; continue on rocky quartzite ridge, descend, and reach SR-1125 at 4.4 mi. Return to the park office parking lot at 5.2 mi.

Pinnacle Trail (1.7 mi); ***Turnback Trail*** (1.2 mi); ***Fern Nature Trail*** (0.7 mi); ***Lake Trail*** (1.0 mi) 696-699

   Length and Difficulty: 4.5 mi combined, easy to strenuous
   Special Feature: views from King's Pinnacle
   Trailhead and Description: From the parking lot at the park office go N on a gravel trail 0.1 mi to a jct with the orange-blazed Pinnacle Trail and Crowders Trail. Take the L and at 0.7 mi, pass an access route to walk-in campground. Continue ahead to a rocky ridge treadway and the jct with white-blazed Turnback Trail, L, at 1.1 mi. At 1.3 mi, climb gradually along the eastern slopes of King's Pinnacle to the ridge top at a point 1.6 mi S of the summit. Turn N and continue to the terminus at the summit for scenic views of Crowders Mtn. and pastoral scenes, W. Vegetation has blueberry, scrub oak, pine, sourwood, and sassafras. Backtrack, or take the Turnback Trail, R, at the base of mountain, a portion of red-blazed Fern Nature Trail in a 1.4-mi return to the park office. The Fern Nature Trail is a loop that can be reached either from the office parking area or the picnic parking area for a difference of 0.3 mi. Among the plants are yellow root, sweet pepperbush, pine, and hardwoods. Between the office and the picnic area is a parking lot where 1.0-mi Lake Trail circles the lake.

Lake Norman State Park (Iredell County)

Located on the N shore of Lake Norman, the largest man-made lake in the state, is Lake Norman State Park. It has 1,548 acres (mostly donated by Duke Power Co.) set aside for swimming, boating, fishing, picnicking, camping, and hiking. Norwood Creek and Hicks Creek transect the park. Lake Norman covers 32,510 acres and has a 520.0-mi shoreline. A 33–site campground is open March 15 to November 30 (no hookups) with hot showers, flush toilets, tables and grills, and a sanitary dumping station. The park harbors more than 800 species of plants. The forest is mainly hardwoods with Virginia and loblolly pines. A subcanopy of sweet gum, dogwood, and sourwood tops numerous ferns and wildflowers. Among the waterfowl are green-winged teal, blue heron, wood duck, and osprey. Black crappie, bass, and perch are the

700-
701
chief fish. After entrance into the park is a parking lot L. The 0.8-mi Alder Trail begins at the parking lot of picnic area #1. It loops around the peninsula among stands of wildflowers, willow, and tag alder to picnic tables and to the swimming area. (USGS Map: Troutman)

Address and Access: Lake Norman State Park, 159 Inland Sea Lane, Troutman, NC 28166; 704-528-6350. From the town of Troutman (6.0 mi S of Statesville and 3.0 mi N of I-77 on US-21/NC-115) go 3.6 mi W on State Park Rd (SR-1330).

Support Facilities: Groceries, gasoline, restaurants, and other stores are in Troutman. Statesville has shopping centers, motels, and restaurants.

702- *Lakeshore Trail*
703   **Length and Difficulty:** 6.7 mi round-trip, moderate

Trailhead and Description: Begin at the parking lot of picnic area #2, and follow the sign R of the rest rooms to white blazes. At a jct after 0.5 mi, turn either R or L for a loop. If R, follow to the main park road and cross near a gate. (It is 0.7 mi S on the road to the campground.) At a red-blazed jct, follow ahead by the lakeside to the end of the peninsula. (For a shortcut, the red blazes can be followed for a 3.5-mi loop.) In the process, pass the amphitheater and the campground before continuing around the lakeshore on the return trip.

Eno River State Park (Durham and Orange Counties)

Eno River State Park is a popular hiking and fishing area along 12.0 mi of the river between Hillsborough and Durham. Covering 2,738 acres, the park is segmented into four sections (Few's Ford, Cabe's Land Access, Cole Mill Rd Access, and Pump Station Access), but they are similar, with floodplains, rocky bluffs, and some low-range white water. Remnants of mill dams and rock piles illustrate the settlements of pioneer millers and farmers. Sycamore, river birch, and sweet gum are prominent on the riversides. Wildflowers are profuse; it is a park with a million trout lilies. Among the wildlife are deer, beaver, squirrel, fox, chipmunk, and turkey. Anglers will find Roanoke bass, largemouth bass, bream, redhorse sucker, and catfish. Other activities include picnicking and canoeing. Canoe launching points are below Pleasant Green Dam, Cole Mill Rd, and Few's Ford. Organized group camping is allowed by reservation. All supplies including water and firewood must be packed in for 0.4 mi. Five backpack sites are available on a first-come basis for small groups or individuals. These require a 1.0-mi hike to access. (USGS Maps: Durham NW, Hillsborough)

Address and Access: Eno River State Park, 6101 Cole Mill Rd, Durham, NC 27705; 919-383-1686. One access to the park office is 5.3 mi from I-85 (Exit 173) in W Durham, N on Cole Mill Rd (SR-1401 in Durham County, which becomes SR-1569 in Orange County).

Eno Nature Trail (0.3 mi); *Cox's Mountain Trail* (3.7 mi); *Fanny's Ford Trail* (1.0 mi)   704-706

   Length and Difficulty: 5.0 mi combined round-trip, moderate

   Trailhead and Description: All these trails connect. From the park office, drive to the second parking area, R. Follow a well-maintained trail 0.1 mi to a jct L with the red-blazed Eno Nature Trail. (The trail is also called the Eno Trace; it loops 0.3 mi through large hardwoods.) Continue on blue-blazed Cox's Mountain Trail to cross the swinging footbridge over the Eno River. Reach the Wilderness Shelter campsite, L at 0.3 mi. At 0.7 mi, the trail forks for a loop, L, up the mountain and ahead on the old road. If hiking L, ascend and pass under a power line at 0.9 mi to Cox's Mtn. Descend to a stream at 1.2 mi and follow downstream to the Eno River at 1.6 mi. Turn R and go downriver among river birch and beech. Turn R on an old wagon road at 2.0 mi, pass under a power line, and follow the old road in a forest with beds of running cedar. At 2.8 mi is a jct with Fanny's Ford Trail, L. (Fanny's Ford Trail is a 1.0-mi purple-blazed loop by the riverbank and the pack-in primitive campsite. The trail's name comes from Fanny Breeze, a beloved black midwife and hospitable neighbor to the river community during and after the Civil War.) To complete Cox's Mountain Trail loop, continue on the old road to the fork at 3.0 mi. Backtrack to the parking lot at 3.7 mi.

Buckquarter Creek Trail (1.5 mi); *Holden's Mill Trail* (2.6 mi); *Ridge Trail* (1.3 mi); *Knight Trail* (0.3 mi); *Piedmont Trail* (0.1 mi); *Shakori Trail* (1.0 mi)   707-712

   Length and Difficulty: 6.8 mi combined round-trip, easy to moderate

   Trailhead and Description: From the park office drive ahead to the first parking lot, R. Walk down to the Eno River, turn R, upriver to a fork at 0.1 mi (The first trail with steps is not the trail route.) If hiking R follow an old road and at 0.5 mi is a jct with blue-blazed Ridge Trail ahead. At the Buckquarter Creek Trail, turn L. If following the Ridge trail, reach jct with the Knight Trail at 0.2 mi. It is a red-blazed route up a hill for 0.3 mi to the park boundary. R and L are a few yards to the private property. Backtrack. Continue on the Ridge Trail to rock-hop Buckquarter Creek. After 0.1 mi is a jct with Shakori Trail, a yellow-blazed old road that ascends in a hardwood forest to a ridge-top. Stay

L and rejoin the Ridge Trail at 1.0 mi. Descend to complete the loop, recross the creek, and rejoin the Buckquarter Creek Trail, R downstream. At 0.8 mi is a jct R with yellow-blazed Holden's Mill Trail. (Holden's Mill Trail crosses Buckquarter Creek on a footbridge and after 160 yd. ascends on an old farm road in a hardwood forest. Pass rock piles from early farm clearings. Pass under a power line and descend to the Eno River at 1.0 mi. [On the descent is a 0.6-mi loop upriver.] To the R is the site of Holden's Mill. Return downriver on a scenic path of rocks and wildflowers near occasional rapids. Rejoin the Buckquarter Creek Trail at 2.6 mi.) Continue downriver and complete the trail after another 0.7 mi.

713- 716   *Pea Creek Trail* (1.3 mi); *Dunnagan's Trail* (1.8 mi); *Cole Mill Trail* (1.2 mi); *Bobbitt Hole Trail* (1.6 mi)

Length and Difficulty: 7.0 mi combined round-trip, easy

Trailhead and Description: These trails are at Cole Mill Rd Access, Section 2. Activities are picnicking, fishing, canoeing, and hiking. Access is as described above to the park office, except from I-85, go 3.2 mi and turn L onto Old Cole Mill Rd). The trails connect, may overlap in parts, and are red-blazed. From the lower end of the parking area, follow the sign down to the Eno River at 0.3 mi to blue-blazed Pea Creek Trail, L, and yellow-blazed Cole Mill Trail, R. On the Pea Creek Trail pass under the Cole Mill Rd bridge, and at 0.6 mi under a power line. Reach Pea Creek in an area of wildflowers and ferns. At a footbridge is a jct with red-blazed Dunnagan's Trail. Across Pea Creek turn R along the Eno River. Turn L at the river and follow the bank downstream. Just after the stone wall of the old pump station is visible across the river, turn L. Go uphill and circle back to Pea Creek on a ridge above the river and pass through two old homesites. Complete the Pea Creek Trail on a return to Cole Mill Trail.

Hike upriver on the Cole Mill Trail, and at 0.6 mi is a jct with red-blazed Bobbitt Hole Trail, which continues upriver, but Cole Mill Trail turns R under a power line. This route rejoins Bobbitt Hole Trail, L, after 300 yd. (From here, R, it is 0.4 mi on Cole Mill Trail to the upper parking lot and picnic area.) If taking the higher elev of Bobbitt Hole Trail, follow a beautiful wide trail through pine, oak, and holly on the approach to the river. To the R for a few yards is to a sharp curve in the river and the large scenic pool called Bobbitt Hole after 0.9 mi. Return downriver, and after 0.6 mi is a jct with Cole Mill Trail for a return to the parking area.

Old Pump Station Trail
717

Length and Difficulty: 1.5 mi, easy

Trailhead and Description: This red-blazed loop trail is the Pump Station Access, Section 4. Access is as above, except after I-85, go 2.3 mi and turn R on Rivermont Rd (SR-1402). Drive 0.6 mi to Nancy Rhodes Creek and park, L. Follow the trail sign downstream to remains of the old Durham Pump Station at 0.4 mi. (To the R is access to Laurel Bluff Trail [2.4 mi, moderate] **718** along the Eno River to Guess Rd bridge.) On Old Pump Station Trail curve L upriver to maker a loop.

Cabe Lands Trail
719-721

Length and Difficulty: 1.2 mi, easy

Trailhead and Description: This loop trail is at Cabe's Land Access, Section 3. Access is as above, except after I-85, go 2.3 mi and turn L on Sparger Rd (SR-1400). Go 1.3 mi, turn R on Howe St (Howell Rd on county maps), and after 0.5 mi, reach parking space on R. Follow an old service road to the Eno River, passing carpets of periwinkle, ivy, and running cedar. Reach the river at 0.4 mi, turn L, pass beaver cuts and old mill foundations at 0.4 mi. Cross a small stream and ascend to the point of origin.

Falls Lake State Recreation Area (SRA), Jordan Lake SRA, and Kerr Lake SRA (See chapter 9, section 2, US Army Corps of Engineers.)

Medoc Mountain State Park (Halifax County)

The 2,286-acre park is on the granite fall line of the Piedmont where the coastal plain zone begins. The area was named Medoc, for a grape-producing region in France, when a large vineyard was operated here in the nineteenth century. Although locally called a mountain because of its higher than usual elev in the area, it is more a low ridge with the summit at 325 ft. above sea level. Winding through the park is Little Fishing Creek with bluegill, large-mouth, and Roanoke bass; redbreast sunfish; and chain pickerel. Plant life is diverse; it is unusual for laurel to be this far E. Activities include fishing, picnicking, hiking, and tent camping. Camping facilities include tables, grills, tent pads, a central water source, and hot showers. Camping facilities for groups and families are available mid-March through November (reservations for groups required). (USGS Maps: Hollister, Aurelian Springs, Essex) Of the

34 campground sites, 12 have electric hook-ups and 2 are handicapped accessible and are open year-round.

Address and Access: Medoc Mtn. State Park, 1541 Medoc State Park Rd, Hollister, NC 27844; 252-586-6588; fax: 252-586-1266. Park office is on Medoc State Park Rd (SR-1322) 1.2 mi from NC-561. Access from Hollister is on Medoc Mtn. Rd (SR-1002) for 2.8 mi, L, and go 1.6 mi to park office. If from NC-48/4 W go 3.8 mi and turn R.

Support Facilities: Groceries and gasoline are in Hollister.

722-   ***Summit Trail*** (2.9 mi); ***Dam Site Loop Trail*** (0.9 mi)
723   **Length and Difficulty:** 3.8 mi combined round-trip, easy
        Trailhead and Description: From the park office parking lot follow the trail sign, and after 125 yd. turn L to begin the loop of Summit Trail. At 0.5 mi, cross Rocky Spring Branch, and reach the E bank of Little Fishing Creek at 0.7 mi. Turn R and go upstream. Pass a large granite outcropping, the core of the summit, at 1.4 mi. After a few yards the trail ascends R 0.1 mi to the peak, but to include the Dam Site Loop Trail continue ahead, N, and pass an artesian well. Pass the ruins of a dam built by the Boy Scouts in the early 1920s, and the ruins of another dam upstream. Circle back to the Summit Trail through groves of laurel at 2.5 mi. Follow a gravel road, but turn from it at 3.1 mi. Pass an old cemetery, L, and return to the parking lot.

724-   ***Stream Trail*** (2.2 mi); ***Discovery Trail*** (0.1 mi); ***Bluffs Trail*** (2.8 mi)
726   **Length and Difficulty:** 5.1 mi combined, easy
        Trailhead and Description: Access to these connecting trails is 2.2 mi W from the park office on SR-1002 to Medoc State Park Rd (SR-1322). Turn R and follow the park signs 1.0 mi to the picnic parking area. From the parking area go 60 yd. R of the picnic shelter to the trail sign. Stream Trail is L. (The Bluffs Trail is R.) Stream Trail is a beautiful, well-designed, and carefully maintained trail. It passes through a forest of loblolly pine, oak, and beech with laurel, holly, and aromatic bayberry part of the understory. Rattlesnake orchid, partridgeberry, and running cedar are part of the ground cover. At 0.2 mi, arrive at Little Fishing Creek and go upstream. At 0.4 mi is a jct with Discovery Trail, proceed 0.3 mi L to exit to picnic and parking area. To include the Discovery Trail, turn R. At 1.2 mi is a confluence with Bear Swamp Creek. Enter an open area with kudzu and trumpet vine at 1.6 mi. Exit the forest at 2.0 mi and cross the picnic grounds to the parking area at 2.2 mi. On Bluffs Trail, pass through an old field on a wide manicured trail into a forest. At 0.4 mi, turn R downstream by Little Fishing Creek. Pass through large

loblolly pine, beech, river birch, and oak. Climb to a steep bluff at 1.0 mi. Reach the highest bluff (over 60 ft.) at 1.4 mi. Descend, bear R on a return ridge, cross a stream at 2.6 mi, and return to the parking lot at 2.8 mi.

Morrow Mountain State Park (Stanly County)

This 4,742-acre park is in the heart of the lower Piedmont region and in the ancient Uwharrie range. More than 500 million years ago it was covered by a shallow sea in which volcanic islands developed; they later became the hard basalt and rhyolite deposits of this area. Established in 1935, the park is adjacent to the Pee Dee River and Lake Tillery. Some of the park's facilities were constructed by the CCC and WPA between 1937 and 1942. Named after J. M. Morrow, a former landowner, the park is scenic and historic. It offers a nature museum, picnicking, boating, fishing, nature programs, swimming, hiking, equestrian trails, and camping. Family camping, with 106 tent/RV campsites, is open year-round with water, showers, and rest rooms (no hookups). Backpack camping and youth-group tent camping are also provided, but advance registration is necessary. Rental cabins, available from March 1 through November, also require advance registration. All trails are hiking trails, including the 16-mi. Bridle Trail that circles the park, but horse traffic must only use the Bridle Trail. (USGS Maps: Badin, Morrow Mtn.) **727**

Address and Access: Morrow Mtn. State Park, 49104 Morrow Mtn. Rd, Albemarle, NC 28001; 704-982-4402; fax: 704-982-5323. An access route from Albemarle is 1.8 mi NE on NC-740 (from the jct with NC-24/27/73) to Morrow Mtn. Rd (SR-1798) and 2.5 mi to the park entrance.

Laurel Trail (0.6 mi.); *Morrow Mountain Trail* (3.0 mi); *Quarry Trail* **728-**
(0.6 mi); *Hattaway Mountain Trail* (2.0 mi) **731**
    Length and Difficulty: 6.2 mi combined, easy to moderate
    Trailhead and Description: Park at the Natural History Museum and begin the Laurel Trail behind the museum. If going clockwise, stay on the main trail through a mature forest of hardwoods, pine, laurel, and pink azalea for a loop of 0.6 mi. (After 0.2 mi is a jct L with Morrow Mountain Trail, which goes to the top of Morrow Mtn. Ascend W of Sugarloaf Creek and reach jct with Sugarloaf Mountain Trail at 0.7 mi. Follow the Sugarloaf Mountain Trail for 0.6 mi and turn L. Cross a small stream and arrive at the E side of Morrow Mtn. at 2.5 mi. Ascend steeply on switchback to a jct with the Mountain Loop Trail. Exit at either the overlook or the picnic area to the Morrow Mtn. parking area.)

For the Quarry Trail, hike NW from the museum, past the swimming pool, to the picnic area (or drive to the picnic parking area). The loop of 0.6 mi reveals a belt of argillite. On the Hattaway Mountain Trail, begin at the pool bathhouse and follow the 2.0-mi loop trail up and over dry, rocky Hattaway Mtn., the park's third highest. The mature forest has oak, sourwood, maple, and laurel.

732-   *Three Rivers Trail* (0.6 mi); *Fall Mountain Trail* (4.17 mi)
733   **Length and Difficulty:** 4.7 mi combined, easy to moderate
     Special Features: Kron House, river views, rhyolite
     Trailhead and Description: Park at the boathouse near the boat launch. The Fall Mountain Trail begins at the S end of the parking lot. If taking the W route, reach jct L with Three Rivers Trail. (Three Rivers Trail is a 0.6-mi, self-guiding interpretive trail that crosses the boat-launch road and loops by an open marsh of swamp rose and arrowwood. It passes through a damp forest area and to the riverside for views of the Yadkin, Pee Dee, and Uwharrie Rivers.) Continuing on Fall Mountain Trail, twice cross an access path to the youth-group tent campsites. At 1.2 mi, pass the historic Kron House, L. (Dr. Kron, physician, lived here from 1834 until his death in 1883. His 6,000-acre farm was used for numerous horticultural experiments.) Ascend N to cross the Fall Mtn. ridge in a forest of oak, laurel, and scattered pine at 1.7 mi. Descend on a rough area of rhyolite and volcanic outcroppings. There are excellent views of the Falls Dam and the Yadkin River. Silverbell, coneflower, and lip fern are among the flowering plants and ferns. Descend and cross a small stream, for a loop of 4.1 mi. Deer and squirrel may be seen in these areas.

734 *Rocks Trail*
     Length and Difficulty: 2.6 mi round-trip, easy
     Trailhead and Description: Park at the administrative building and begin at the rear of the building, hiking E. Arrive at the family campground and follow the blue blazes on Rocks Trail (which has parts of a bridle trail). At 0.2 mi from the campground, turn L. (Because of numerous campground trails and extra lead-in trails to Mountain Creek Bridle Trail, the hiker may need to watch carefully for the blue blazes.) Pass R of a jct with the bridle trail at 0.6 mi. Continue ahead to an excellent view of the Pee Dee River. Descend over a rock area to trail's end at 1.3 mi. Return by the same route.

Sugarloaf Mountain Trail (2.8 mi); *Mountain Loop Trail* (0.8 mi)   735-
  Length and Difficulty: 3.6 mi combined, moderate   736

  Trailhead and Description: (These trails connect with the Morrow
Mountain Trail, bridle trails, and Morrow Mtn. Rd.) Park at the parking lot R
(E) of the park gate. Follow the trail sign for hikers, bearing L from the bridle
trail. Cross two small streams and Morrow Mtn. Rd. Ascend and follow the
NW ridge side of Sugarloaf Mtn.(858 ft). Reach jct L with Morrow Mountain
Trail at 1.4 mi. Turn R (jointly with Morrow Mountain Trail) and after 2.0 mi,
continue R (Morrow Mountain Trail goes L in its ascent to the top of Morrow
Mtn.), cross Morrow Mtn. Rd at 2.2 mi, cross a stream at 2.7 mi, and enter a
field near the parking lot to complete the loop. For the Mountain Loop Trail,
drive to the top of Morrow Mtn. The trailhead can be found at the picnic shelter or the overlook. It leads to a loop around the peak (936 ft.). The trail is
graded, with bridges over the ravines. It also connects on the E side with Morrow Mountain Trail, described above. From Morrow Mtn. are views E to Lake
Tillery and Dennis Mtn. (the route of the Uwharrie Trail) in the Uwharrie NF
(see chapter 4).

Raven Rock State Park (Harnett County)

Established in 1970, Raven Rock State Park is a large 3,780-acre wilderness-
type forest. The Cape Fear River runs through its center. A major geological
feature of the area is the 152-ft-high crystalline rock jutting out toward the
river. Ravens once nested here; thus the park's name. It is unusual for rhododendron and laurel to grow this far E with a diverse and long list of Piedmont
and coastal-plain plants. Some of the wild animals and birds are osprey, eagle,
owl, squirrel, raccoon, salamander, and deer. Prominent fish are largemouth
bass, catfish, and sunfish. Activities are picnicking, hiking, fishing, and primitive backpack camping. (All gear, including water, must be carried to the
camps. Registration is required at the park office.) There are two equestrian
trails (3.5-mi East Loop Horse Trail and 3.5-mi West Loop Horse Trail) off
River Rd (SR-1418) on the N side of the river; directions and regulations are
available from the park office. (USGS Map: Mamers)

  Address and Access: Raven Rock State Park, 3009 Raven Rock Rd,
Lillington, NC 27546; 910-893-4888; fax: 910-814-2200. Access to the park is
3.0 mi off US-421 on Raven Rock Park Rd (SR-1314), 6.0 mi W of Lillington.

737-   ***Raven Rock Loop Trail***
741   **Length and Difficulty:** 2.1 mi, easy
         Connecting Trails: American Beech Nature Trail (0.5 mi, easy); Little
Creek Loop Trail (1.4 mi, easy); Fish Traps Trail (1.2 mi round-trip, easy);
Northington's Ferry Trail (2.2 mi round-trip, easy)
         Special Feature: Raven Rock overhang
         Trailhead and Description: From the parking lot follow the Raven Rock
sign on the E side of the lot. Reach jct R with the American Beech Nature
Trail. (The nature trail descends and crosses a small stream through poplar,
sweet gum, red maple, beech, sweet bay, laurel, and oak. It returns on the E
side of the picnic area.) At 0.8 mi reach the Raven Rock Loop Trail jct R with
Little Creek Loop Trail. (It descends downstream by Little Creek for 0.7 mi
to a canoe camp.) Downriver it is another 0.5 mi to a group backpack campsite. Reach scenic Raven Rock at 0.9 mi. Descend on stairways to the riverbank and rock overhangs. Return on the steps, but take a turn R at the top.
Arrive at a scenic overlook of the Cape Fear River at 1.1 mi. Reach jct sharply
R with Fish Traps Trail and Northington's Ferry Trail at 1.7 mi. (Fish Traps
Trail leads to a rock outcropping at 1.1 mi beside the river. [Indians placed
trap baskets at the rapids to catch fish. Backtrack.] Northington's Ferry Trail
follows a wide, easy route to the mouth of Campbell Creek [also called
Camels Creek], site of the Cape Fear River crossing. The ferry served as a
crossing between Raleigh and Fayetteville as early as 1770. Backtrack.) Continue on the Raven Rock Loop Trail on an old woods road to the parking area.

742-   ***Campbell Creek Loop Trail*** (5.1 mi); ***Lanier Falls Trail*** (0.4 mi)
743   **Length and Difficulty:** 5.5 mi combined round-trip, easy to moderate
         Trailhead and Description: At the parking lot, follow the old svc road N
45 yd. and turn L into young growth that enters an older forest. Descend gradually in an oak-hickory forest to a footbridge over Campbell Creek at 0.7 mi.
Here the trail loops R or L. To the L route, ascend and descend on low ridges
through sections of laurel to a jct with the former Buckhorn Trail at 2.1 mi
(The Buckhorn Trail has been abandoned.) A park svc road comes in from the
L and joins Campbell Creek Loop Trail R. Descend to the primitive campsites
at 2.3 mi, L, and Lanier Falls Trail, L, at 2.5 mi. (The 0.2-mi Lanier Falls Trail
leads to a scenic rock outcropping at the Cape Fear River. Backtrack.) Continue the trail to the mouth of Campbell Creek and follow upstream to rejoin
the access route at the bridge at 4.4 mi.

Umstead State Park (Wake County)

William B. Umstead State Park covers 5,480 acres: 4,026 in the Crabtree Creek section (N) and 1,454 in the Reedy Creek section (S). Crabtree Creek, which runs W to E through the park, separates the two sections. Among the largest state parks, Umstead is a valuable oasis in the center of a fast-developing metropolitan area. Adjoining on the W is the Raleigh-Durham International Airport, on the N is US-70, and on the S is I-40. A former CCC camp, the park's original 5,088 acres were deeded to the state by the US government in fee simple of one dollar in 1943. It was designated Crabtree Creek State Park, but in 1955 it was named in honor of the former governor. In the Reedy Creek section is Piedmont Beech Natural Area, a 50-acre tract with American beech *(Fagus grandifolia),* some of which are more than 300 years old. The tract is included in the National Registry of Natural Landmarks. Access is allowed by permit only from park officials.

In addition to Crabtree Creek, Sycamore Creek also runs through the park from the NW to the SE to empty into the Crabtree. The park is hilly and rocky with tributaries such as Pott's Branch, Reedy Creek, and Turkey Creek flowing into the main creeks. Quartz rock piles indicate the presence of farmers in the last century and the early part of the 1900s. There are three lakes: Big Lake, Sycamore Lake, and Reedy Creek Lake. Fishing for bass, bluegill, and crappie is allowed, but swimming is allowed only at the park's group campsites: Crabtree, Lapihio, and Whispering Pine. Large stands of mature oak, poplar, and loblolly pine provide a canopy for dogwood, redbud, laurel, and sourwood. Beaver, deer, squirrel, and raccoon are among the mammals found in the park. Recreational activities include fishing, camping, hiking, picnicking, horseback riding, bicycling, boating, and nature studies. There are three organized group camps and a lodge. In both park sections are equestrian and hiking trails for 10.0 mi on gated park gravel roads. Their access points are off Ebenezer Church Rd from US-70 (N), from Reedy Creek Rd off Ebenezer Church Rd (SE), and Old Reedy Creek Park Rd from Weston Pkwy (SW).

In both park sections the management has pragmatically provided a network of bridle and bicycle (B&B) trails, and reconstructed some of the separate hiking/walking nature trails. (The B&B trails are listed ahead and they are also open to hikers and runners.) In the Crabtree Section is Big Lake Trail, a **744** 0.2 mi one-way paved ADA trail for the disabled. It crosses the dam and spillway of Big Lake to the boathouse, and provides scenic beauty and fishing. (This trail is also accessible by a steep trail from the parking lot at the end of

Umstead Park Rd.) Access by vehicle is to turn L on Maintenance Rd after going S of the park office and visitor center. Take the first R on Group Camp Rd and after crossing a bridge below the dam, park R at the dam's edge.

745   Another singular foot trail is 2.5 mi Sal's Branch Trail, an orange-blazed path accessed from the N side and behind the park office and visitor center. The trail goes through a hardwood forest with spots of pine. If making a counterclockwise loop, descend 110 yds to cross Sal's Branch. At 0.3 mi is a short connector, R, to the park's campground. (Access to the campground is first R after entering from US-70.) At 0.9 mi is a dry ravine, followed by mounds of quartz on former farmland. There are views of Big Lake at 1.6 mi, and the trail's forest highlight is from a high embankment at 2.3 mi.

746   The 6.0 mi Loblolly Trail is a linear trail with 2.7 mi in the park and the other miles under supervision of the Raleigh Division of Parks and Recreation. In the park the NW trailhead is near a signboard in the NE corner of the parking area of the Reedy Creek Section. The trail crosses the Reedy Creek (B&B) Trail and the South Turkey (B&B) Trail before leaving the park boundary. (See Reedy Creek Section access below.) The trail's SE trailhead is at a special parking area near entrance D off Trinity Rd at the RBC Center (formerly Carter/Finley Stadium). (See Raleigh in chapter 13.)

Address and Access: William B. Umstead State Park, 8801 Glenwood Ave, Raleigh, NC 27617; 919-571-4107; fax: 919-571-4161. Access to the Crabtree Creek section entrance is on US-70, 6.0 mi W of the jct with I-440-US-1. To reach the Reedy Creek section entrance from the Crabtree Creek entrance on US-70, drive W 1.5 mi to I-540 (Northern Wake Expressway) and turn L. Drive 4.7 mi to I-40 (Exit 283). Turn L (E) and drive 4.9 mi to Harrison Ave (Exit 287) to Reedy Creek entrance. If from I-440, reach jct at Wade Ave in Raleigh drive W 4.0 mi on Wade Ave and I-40 to exit 287 R.

747-749   *Potts Branch Trail* (1.4 mi); *Oak Rock Trail* (0.6 mi) *Sycamore Trail* (7.0 mi)

Length and Difficulty: 9.0 mi combined round-trip, easy to moderate

Trailhead and Description: These trails are individual loops, but the Sycamore Trail cuts across the center of orange-blazed Potts Branch Trail, making the latter a double loop of either 0.6 or 0.7 mi each, depending on where you parked in the parking lot. From the visitor's center drive 0.6 mi to the lower end of the parking area loop. Here is the Potts Branch Trail, R. Descend 120 yd. and turn L from a jct. (To the R is a descend to Big Lake Trail. [See park introduction above.] Arrive at the banks of Sycamore Creek at 0.2 mi and turn L among tall sycamores and uphill oaks and pines. Parallel the stream among Christmas ferns, wildflowers, and rock ledges. At 0.5 mi is a cross trail with Sycamore Trail, L up steps to picnic and parking area, and R across the creek bridge. Continuing on the Potts Branch Trail, pass cascades, a former dam, and uphill to an outdoor stage at 0.8 mi. Near the upper parking lot, turn L to follow a paved path to complete the loop at 1.4 mi.

If choosing the white-blazed Oak Rock Trail, enter at the corner of the upper parking lot. This popular interpretive trail has signs identifying the trees. After 30 yd. fork R and descend 0.1 mi to the Rock Tree, R, a red oak that has sealed its roots in a rock shaft and made a natural work of art. Follow the path upstream beside Potts Branch. Cross a rock bridge at 0.3 mi and circle back to origin. (It is 0.2 mi to the lower parking lot.)

The blue-blazed Sycamore Trail is accessed at the lower parking area up steps to a paved trail and picnic area. Turn L on the pavement, then the first R to pass picnic shelters #2 on the L and #1 ahead, R. Descend on wide steps to cross Potts Branch Trail and a bridge over the branch. Follow upstream to cross Sycamore Lake Rd at 0.5 mi. Easily ascending pass through a forest of oak, maple, sweet gum, and pine. At 1.5 mi on the top of a ridge, enter a former homesite and grove of huge oaks; these and a healthy honey locust are entwined with wisteria. After a few yards, cross Sycamore Road (B&B) Trail, **750** R and L. (To the R, it descends to a circular parking area accessed at the end of Sycamore Rd. To the left, it is 32 yd. to Graylyn [B&B] Trail, an access L **751** to gate at Graylon Drive. On the access is King Cemetery.)

Continuing on the Sycamore Trail, descend, then curve into a cove for an ascent to the trail's loop, L, and ahead at 2.1 mi. If going ahead, descend on two switchbacks and arrive beside Sycamore Creek at 2.2 mi. Cross under a power line, ascend to 2.4 mi at a fenced and scenic cliff overlook. Descend past a large bed of Christmas fern, and arrive at a crossing of Graylyn (B&B) Trail at 3.0 mi. (To the L, the B&B route ascends to the location mentioned above. To the R, it crosses a CCC-built stone bridge to connect with Reedy **752** Creek [B&B] Trail. Also on this trail and across the bridge, R, is the 90-yd. Company Mill Spur Trail to Company Mill Trail, a hiking-only trail described **753** ahead.) Continuing on the Sycamore Trail, descend on steps and parallel the creek. Large boulders and high banks make this a scenic area. Undulate on a few ridges before leaving the creek to turn L at a tributary. At 4.0 mi cross a bridge over a brook (so attractive it needs a name). Criss-cross the rocky stream where in the springtime is a wildflower garden of wild orchids, crested dwarf iris, trailing arbutus, and ferns. At the last crossing among boulders, 4.2

754   mi, there is a view upstream of a bridge for North Turkey Creek (B&B) Trail. Ascend and cross the Graylyn (B&B) Trail at 4.8 mi. Slightly descend to complete the loop at 4.9 mi. Turn R and return 2.1 mi to the parking lot.

755-   *Company Mill Trail* (5.8 mi); *Inspiration Trail* (0.3 mi); *Beech Trail*
757   (0.4 mi)

Length and Difficulty: 6.1 mi combined round-trip, easy to moderate

Trailhead and Description: From the Reedy Creek section parking lot go to the NW corner and descend to a display board at the edge of the woods. At 0.1 mi is a large stone picnic shelter in the picnic area. (This 0.1 mi is counted in the total distance of the Company Mill Trail.) The orange-blazed trail descends on steps to a jct with blue-blazed Inspiration Trail, L, at 0.2 mi. (The 0.3-mi loop trail has interpretive signs with names of the trees.) The Company Mill Trail continues to ascend and descend to the Crabtree Creek steel footbridge at 0.9 mi. On the way, observe quartz rock piles made by pioneer farmers on the rocky slopes. After crossing the footbridge, turn R or L for a loop. If hiking R, descend between rock ledges, L, and the creek, R. At 1.0 mi are rapids and remnants of the dam. A millstone is L of the trail. Turn L at 1.5 mi and follow a tributary, crossing it a number of times among tall trees, many of them beech. Cross the Reddy Creek (B&B) Trail. Descend from the ridge to the S bank of Sycamore Creek and turn L at 2.4 mi. (To the R is the 90-yd. Company Mill Spur Trail to the Graylyn [B&B] Trail and L over a bridge to a jct with the Sycamore Trail, R and L.) Stay near the creek side, partly on a rim of a former millrace. Maidenhair fern, buckeye, and black cohosh adorn the trail. There are rock remnants of the George Lynn Mill Dam to the R. Leave the creek on switchbacks at 2.5 mi to a ridge. Then descend on switchbacks to a small stream. Ascend; reach the top of the ridge at 3.0 mi. Cross Reedy Creek (B&B) Trail at 3.4 mi, and gradually descend to the creek bank of Crabtree Creek at 4.5 mi. Pass R of a rock slope and complete the loop at 5.0 mi. Cross the high footbridge over the creek and ascend to the picnic shelter at 5.8 mi.

Coastal Region

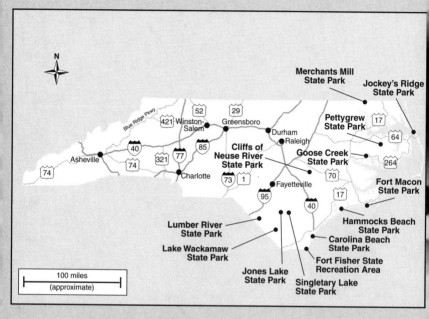

Introductions to Trail Areas

The Coastal Region State Parks are widely scattered on the coastal plains. All have natural lakes or rivers, or bays, or are near the saltwater of the Atlantic Ocean. Here they are listed alphabetically from S and SW to N and NE.

SECTION 3: COASTAL REGION
Carolina Beach State Park (New Hanover County)

The 761-acre Carolina Beach State Park is considered a naturalist's delight with more than 50 species of flora (including the rare Venus's-flytrap and four other insectivorous plants native to the coastal environment). Its trail system enables the hiker to study salt marshes, sandhills, rainwater ponds, and swamplands. One historic sandhill, Sugarloaf, was the settlement area of the Cape Fear Indians up to 1725 and a navigational landmark as early as 1663. Park facilities include a tent/trailer campground, picnic area, marina to the Cape Fear River for fishing and boating, and hiking. (USGS Map: Carolina Beach)

Address and Access: Carolina Beach State Park, P.O. Box 475, Carolina Beach, NC 28428; 910-458-8206 (office), 910-458-7770 (marina); fax: 910-458-6350. From Greenfield Park in Wilmington, go S 12.0 mi on US-421 to entrance R, at a jct with Dow Rd (SR-1573).

758-
763

Sugarloaf Trail (3.0 mi); *Swamp Trail* (0.8 mi); *Fly Trap Trail* (0.5 mi); *Campground Trail* (1.0 mi); *Snow's Cut Trail* (0.45 mi); *Oak Toe Trail* (0.25 mi)

Length and Difficulty: 6.1 mi combined, easy

Trailhead and Description: Trailheads are at Fly Trap parking area, the campground, the picnic area, parking lot, and the marina parking area. (If Fly Trap parking is chosen, take the first paved road L after the park entrance. The campground trailhead is the second paved road, R, but parking is allowed only for registered campers.) Follow the road signs to the marina parking area. From here enter the looped orange-circle-blazed Sugarloaf Trail at the trail sign and follow it through a forest of pine, oak, and yaupon. At 0.2 mi, the red-circle-blazed Swamp Trail is L. Continue ahead along the riverbank to 0.6 mi and turn L in a forest of live oak, pine, moss, and pink spiderwort *(Tradescantia rosea)*. At 0.7 mi, L, is a jct with Oak Toe Trail that goes 0.25 mi to Swamp Trail. Follow the trail on white sandhills to Sugarloaf, a 65-ft. relict sand dune, at 1.0 mi. Turn sharply L, pass the Cypress Pond, and make another sharp L at the Lily Pond at 1.7 mi. Pass a jct with the Campground Trail, R, and at 2.3 mi is a jct with the red-blazed Swamp Trail, L. Continue ahead, cross paved road, pass a jct R with the blue-circle-blazed Campground Trail, and reach the Fly Trap parking area at 2.8 mi. The Fly Trap Trail (blazed with orange circles) begins here near a kiosk that describes the Venus's-flytrap *(Dionaea muscipula)*. Charles Darwin described it as the "most wonderful plant in the world." Protected by law, it is found only in SE NC and NE SC. After the 0.5-mi loop on the Fly Trap Trail, return on the Sugarloaf Trail, continue about 20 yd. N of the road, and hike NW. Cross a boardwalk, pass through a mixed pine and hardwood forest to the trail's end at the marina parking lot.

If going to the campground from the Fly Trap Trail parking area, backtrack on the Sugarloaf Trail 0.4 mi and turn L. Blue lupine *(Lupinus perrennis)* grows here. At the N side of the campground loop road enter the woods toward Snow's Cut, and curve L on the red-diamond blazes on Snow's Cut Trail for 0.45 mi to a picnic area located along the main park road.

Cliffs-of-the-Neuse State Park (Wayne County)

Cliffs-of-the-Neuse State Park covers 751 acres, chiefly of forests, on the W bank of the Neuse River. The park's most extraordinary attraction is the 90-ft. cliff carved over thousands of years to show countless fossil shells (not for public collection), the remains of other marine species, and sedimentation at what was once the Atlantic shoreline. Spanish moss drapes the oaks and pines. Galax, a more mountainous plant, grows on the N bank of Mill Creek. Picnicking, swimming and boating (in the lake), fishing, and hiking are the activities. Family camping is provided at tent/RV sites that have water, flush toilets, tables and grills, and hot showers (no hookups) March 15–November 30. Tent camps for youth groups are available. Reservations are required. (USGS Map: Seven Springs)

Address and Access: Cliffs-of-the-Neuse State Park, 345A Park Entrance Rd, Seven Springs, NC 28578; 919-778-6234; fax: 919-778-7447. Entrance to the park is on SR-1743, E 0.5 mi from NC-111, 13.0 mi SE of Goldsboro.

Spanish Moss Trail (0.5. mi); *Galax Trail* (0.5 mi); *Bird Trail* (0.8 mi)   **764-766**
    Length and Difficulty: 1.8 mi combined, easy
    Trailhead and Description: From the parking area, follow the trail signs R and descend to a scenic area by the riverbank and Mill Creek. Turn L on red-blazed Bird Trail to loop across Still Creek and reach the jct with a yellow-blazed loop, the Galax Trail, at 0.8 mi. Follow the Galax Trail 0.5 mi and return to the parking lot. The Spanish Moss Trail is L of the parking lot but R of the Interpretive Center. Descend and circle back to the parking lot after 0.5 mi. (Campers have made numerous connecting trails in this area.)

Fort Fisher State Recreation Area

The park is located on a scenic island S of Wilmington with the Cape Fear River on the W and the Atlantic Ocean on the E. Recreational opportunities include seven miles of beach for swimming and sunning. For fishing, there are bluefish and Virginia mullet from the shoreline (where ORVs are allowed) and in the estuary, there are spot and flounder. Other activities are the study of the maritime forest, wildlife, and nesting birds. For hiking, there is the 1.0-mi

767 Basin Trail to Basin Overlook. From the visitor center parking area, follow the trail sign. In the forest is a spur trail to the beach, L, and a connector trail, R, near a pond to the NC Aquarium (accessible via vehicle when staying R from the recreation area parking lot.) Cross a boardwalk among yaupon, catbrier, and wax myrtle to a marsh meadow. At 7.0 mi, pass a World War II bunker. (It's called Hermit's Bunker, because George Harrill lived off of the land and water in this salt marsh for many years.) Loggerhead turtles use the beach as a nesting habitat. Among the birds are brown pelican, gull, gannet, and loon. After the overlook, backtrack for a total of 2.0 mi (USGS Map: Kure Beach)

Address and Access: Fort Fisher State Recreation Area, P.O. Box 243, Kure Beach, NC 28449; 910-458-5798; fax: 910-458-5799. South of Wilmington on US-421, pass Carolina Beach State Park, R, and after 5.6 mi, pass Fort Fisher State Historic Site, R. Fort Fisher State Recreation Area parking lot is 1.0 mi ahead, L.

Fort Macon State Park (Carteret County)

The Fort Macon State Park is best known for its restored fort at Beaufort Inlet. Emphasis is on its Civil War history. Facilities and services in the 389-acre park include ocean swimming (June 1 through Labor Day), fishing, picnicking, and hiking. A short nature trail and beach hiking provide more than 2.0

768 mi of walking. The 0.4-mi Fort Macon Nature Trail begins R between the parking area and the fort's covertway. Follow the signs on a loop trail through a shrub thicket to Beaufort Inlet and back. Some trees and shrubs are live oak, black locust, Hercules' club *(Zanthoxylum clava-herculis),* and yaupon. Camping is not allowed in the park. (USGS Map: Beaufort)

Address and Access: Fort Macon State Park, Box 127, Atlantic Beach, NC 28512; 252-726-3775 (office) or 252-726-8598 (fort); fax: 252-726-2497. To reach the park (which is on the E tip of Bogue Banks), turn S off US-70 in Morehead City to cross the bridge to Atlantic Beach. At the jct with NC-58 turn L on Fort Macon Rd (SR-1190), and go 2.2 mi.

Goose Creek State Park (Beaufort County)

Goose Creek State Park is a coastal park that covers 1,665 acres on the N side of the Pamlico River. Special features are the tall loblolly pines and live oaks draped with ghostly gray Spanish moss and both freshwater and saltwater fishing. Primitive camping, picnicking, swimming (Memorial Day to Labor Day), fishing, boating, and hiking are provided in this sandy wilderness. The primitive camping can be used by families and groups, and a boat ramp and canoe trail is at the end of the campground road. (Canoes are not provided by the park.) Swamps and marshes are accessible by boardwalks; natural sandy beaches; excellent freshwater fishing for bass, bluegill, and perch; and saltwater fishing for bluefish and flounder (spots and croakers in brackish water) are features of a distinctive recreational area. Native mosquitoes and ticks welcome visitors; a maximum-strength repellent is advisable. In 1998, the Environmental Education & Visitor Center opened with a park office; interactive exhibits and displays, such as taxidermied mounts of animals found in the park; and an auditorium for educational purposes. A special interpretive trail, the 0.7-mi Palmetto Boardwalk Trail, handicapped accessible, begins here S from the parking area. The trail is numbered and a brochure guide is available for enhancing the trail's appeal. Pass a screened picnic shelter and enter the forest. After 0.1 mi, cross a boardwalk. There are dwarf palmetto palm, ash, sweetleaf, bay, and red maple. Wildlife includes pilated woodpecker, beaver, frog, skink, and owl. At 0.5 mi, leave the boardwalk and after 0.2 mi farther exit at a parking space on the main road. The Ivy Gut Trail is across the road. Backtrack. (USGS Map: Blounts Bay) **769**

Address and Access: Goose Creek State Park, 2190 Camp Leach Rd, Washington, NC 27889; 252-923-2191; fax: 252-923-0052. Access from Washington at a jct of US-264/17 is 9.0 mi on US-264 and a R turn on Camp Leach Rd (SR-1334) for 2.4 mi to park entrance.

Support Facilities: Shopping centers, motels, and restaurants are in Washington. A nearby private campground is Whichard's Beach campground, Box 746, Washington, NC 27889; 252-946- 0011. From the jct of US-264/17, go 1.7 mi S on US-17 and turn SE on Whichard's Beach Rd (SR-1166) for 3.0 mi. Full svc, rec fac. Open year-round.

Mallard Creek Trail (1.3 mi); *Love Oak/Cemetery Loop Trail* (0.8 mi); *Goose Creek Trail* (1.9 mi); *Flatty Creek Trail* (1.0 mi); *Ivy Gut Trail* (2.0 mi) **770-774**

Length and Difficulty: 7.0 mi combined, easy

Trailhead and Description: These trails connect the picnic area on the E side of the park and the campground on the W side. If backtracking on the linear trails, add 4.0 mi or more. If beginning with the Mallard Creek Trail, drive E on the main road to the last parking lot and follow signs. After 95 yd., the trail forks for a loop. Either direction provides a scenic overview of the Pamlico River from a side trail and along the banks of Mallard Creek. Returning to the parking lot after 1.3 mi, cross to the W side and enter the forest on a paved access to a rest room and picnic area at 0.2 mi for the Live Oak/Cemetery Loop Trail. Pass a cemetery (dated 1880s) and arrive at the Pamlico River among live oaks at 0.3 mi. (A longer Live Oak Trail was once here until hurricanes destroyed the routing.) Pass a nice beach area and begin to curve R in the loop. In the process connect with the Goose Creek Trail at 0.5 mi. Complete the loop at 0.6 mi, pass the rest rooms and return to the parking area at 0.8 mi.

If hiking the Goose Creek Trail, hikers will continue to see Spanish moss draped from the trees and shrubs. At 0.9 mi, there are boardwalks over Black Gum Swamp and Cypress Swamp. If you have a brochure, match the interpretive numbers to identify plant and animal life. There are at least five species of singing frogs here. (To the R, it is a 0.2-mi access from a parking space on the main road, 1.2 mi S from the visitor center.) At 1.9 mi, arrive at the trail's W terminus and a jct with the campground road. Ahead, L, is the E trailhead of Flatty Creek Trail. Across the campground road is the W trailhead of Ivy Gut Trail. If hikers choose Flatty Creek Trail, continue W and at 0.3 mi, turn L. Cross two boardwalks with higher ground in between. Ascend an observation tower for views of waterfowl in Flatty Creek. Red cedar and black needle rush grow nearby. Return to main trail (where ahead is 0.1 mi to campsite #7), or turn L and end the trail at 1.0 mi, which is also the end of the campground road at Goose Creek. (For campers there is a courtesy landing here for canoeing Goose Creek. All others may use Dinah's Landing across the river. It is accessible by using the Goose Creek Rd [SR-1332] that turns L after 2.0 mi W from the park entrance on Camp Leach Rd [SR-1334].)

For the Ivy Gut Trail hikers have a choice of the one-way route to the main road (across from the Palmetto Boardwalk Trail or taking a shortcut for the 1.2 mi Ivy Gut loop that brings hikers back to the campground. The Ivy Gut Trail meanders partially near Goose Creek through a mixture of hardwoods and evergreens (including pine). On the forest floor are prickly pear, blue flag iris, blueberry, wax myrtle, and sweet bay. Lizard's tail and marsh pennywort have damp or wet areas. (There is a folk legend that the ghost of a Goose Creek pirate walks through these woods after dark looking for a cache of gold.) Arrive at the main road parking space at 2.0 mi.

Hammocks Beach State Park (Onslow County)

Hammocks Beach State Park's 892 acres occupies all of Bear Island SE of Swansboro. The island is reputed to be one of the most unspoiled and beautiful beach areas on the Atlantic coast. For the hiker there are 3.8 mi of a wide beach trail from Bear Inlet to Bogue Inlet. It is an unmarked trail whose sandy tread-way shifts with each change of the tide. There are high dunes; one in the SW section of the island is 60 ft. In addition to hiking, other activities are fishing, swimming, and birding. Vegetation is sparse, but there are sea oat, croton, elder, yaupon, cordgrass, and near the marsh side some live oak and cedar. A few deer, rabbit, and raccoon live on the island. It is also the nesting ground of the log-gerhead sea turtle. The park has a seasonal bathhouse, refreshment stand, and picnic tables. There are three group campsites and 10 other campsites on the beach. A fee passenger ferry operates daily (9:30AM–6:00PM) from Memorial Day through Labor Day, but the park is open year-round. The distance to the park is 2.5 mi through a web of marshy islands. Visitors using private boat ser-vice for day use or overnight camping must contact the park office to register for a permit. There is a designated route through the marshes for canoeists and kayakers to Bear Island. (USGS Maps: Hubert, Brown's Inlet)

Address and Access: Hammocks Beach State Park, 1572 Hammocks Beach Rd, Swansboro, NC 28584; 910-326-4881; fax: 910-326-2060. From the W edge of Swansboro on NC-24, take Hammocks Beach Rd (SR-1511) S to the ferry landing.

Jockey's Ridge State Park (Dare County)

Jockey's Ridge State Park, better known as a center for hang gliding than for hiking, covers 426 acres of "marching" sand dunes adjacent to Nags Head Woods, a maritime forest of 1,980 acres. Jockey's Ridge is named, according to one among a number of local stories, for its use as a natural grandstand for races of Banker ponies. It has a 90-ft.-high dune, the largest and highest on the Atlantic coast. A hike to the top of the ridge presents an outstanding view of both the Atlantic Ocean and Roanoke Sound, particularly at sunset. Activities include hiking, nature study and photography, hang gliding, and kite flying. Contact the park ranger for information concerning hang glider takeoff and landing zones. Facilities include a park office, nature displays, rest rooms, vis-itor center, and picnic shelters with tables and grills. Camping is not available at the park. The park has two trails. The 1.5-mi round-trip Tracks-in-the-Sand **775** Trail is a nature path with 14 numbered stations. (Request a brochure at the visitor center.) The trailhead is at a shelter in the SE corner of the parking lots (near the visitor center). Pass through a live oak passageway, and follow the numbers. After station #5 the trail forms a loop, part of which is by the shore of Roanoke Sound. Topics are about sand formations, animal tracks in the sand and their habitats, and trees and shrubs. Return, or consider hiking the last mile of the Mountains-to-Sea Trail. Start at the pedestrian entrance at the park gate and follow the MST signs of the serpentine cement walk. Pass by live oak, the edge of parking lots, and into a live oak forest to reach the shelter mentioned above at 0.3 mi. From there follow the Tracks-in-the-Sand Trail to station #3 at 0.5 mi. Turn abruptly L and ascend to the top of the highest dune at 0.7 mi. The other trail is Southside Nature Trail. It is accessed from the park entrance S on Croatan Highway (US-158) for 0.9 mi to turn R on West Sunnyside Rd. Drive 0.5 mi to the road's end and turn R to the far end of the parking lot. This 0.7-mi loop with impressive scenery has boardwalks, sand dunes, beach, and markers about beach heather, cotton bush, red bay, and birdlife such as Carolina chickadee. (USGS Maps: Manteo, Roanoke Island NE)

776

> **Address and Access:** Jockey's Ridge State Park, Box 592, Nags Head, NC 27959; 252-441-7132; fax: 252-441-8416. Access is from US-158 W of Nags Head on West Carolista Dr.

Jones Lake State Park (Bladen County)

Jones Lake is an example of the Bay Lakes area, where shallow depressions (none deeper than 10 ft.) are filled with cool, dark water. Geologically, it is thought that the oval depressions were formed by wind and wave action following a receding Ice Age. Other theories are the ancient ocean springs theory and the ancient ocean lagoons theory. These formations are also found in coastal SC and NE GA. The Bay Lakes area is also known for a wide variety of bay trees and shrubs. The park covers 2,208 acres with facilities for camping, picnicking, swimming, boating, fishing (mainly for yellow perch and blue-spotted sunfish), hiking, and guided nature study (in the summer). The campground has tent/RV sites with drinking water, flush toilets, tables and grills, and hot showers (no hookups). Open March 15–December 1. (Bladen Lakes State Forest is across the road from the park. See chapter 11.) At the time of this writing, a wet section of the 2.8-mi Jones Lake Trail has been closed. A new loop trail is being planned for construction to provide a 5.0-mi dry routing. (USGS Map: Elizabethtown)

777

> **Address and Access:** Jones Lake State Park, 113 Jones Lake Dr, Elizabethtown, NC 28337; 910-588-4550; fax: 910-588-4322. Access is from the jct of NC-53/242 and US-701 on NC-242 N for 4.0 mi.

Lake Waccamaw State Park (Columbus County)

The park has 10,670 acres (1,732 land; 8,938 water). The lake is named for the Waccamaw Indians and is one of the geologically mysterious Carolina Bays, some of which are White Lake, Bay Tree Lake, and Singletary Lake to the N. But this lake is different: limestone bluffs at the N shore neutralize the water. At least 53 species of game and non-game fish inhabit the lake. Among them, the NC Wildlife Resources Commission stocks largemouth bass, bluegill, shellcracker, and redbreast sunfish. Fishing is regulated by state laws. Although there is no boating access on park land, there are two free public boat launch areas. The Columbus County launch area is nearby on the access road to the park entrance, and the second launch area is NW on the lake's Canal Cove Rd. It is maintained by the NC Wildlife Resources Commission. (For canoeing the Waccamaw River, request information from the park office about access at the W side of the dam.) The parks comprises three vegetative communities: white-sand ridge, pocosin, and cypress-gum swamp. Among the flora are a variety of pine and oak, hickory, sweet gum, cypress, Carolina ipecac, queen's delight, Spanish moss, bay, and a number of endangered species. Some of the wildlife are bear, swamp rabbit, fox, deer, mink, snake, wild turkey, and many species of birds.

Facilities in the park are an outstanding visitor center with displays on natural and human history, flora and fauna, and unique qualities of the lake. Walk-in camping (individually or in groups) is primitive, with pit toilets and picnic tables at four sites in a forest of pine and oak. Water and supplies must be packed in. Registration at the visitor center is required; park at the picnic area, which has tables, a rest room with water, telephone, and a soft-drink machine, a service also available to walk-out campers. Two boardwalks with piers into the lake are available for fishing and sunbathing. Small beach areas are available on the W side section of Lakeshore Trail. Nearly 10 mi of trails, hiking only, are described below. (USGS Maps: Whiteville, Bolton, Juniper Creek)

Address and Access: Lake Waccamaw State Park, 1866 State Park Dr, Lake Waccamaw, NC 28450; 910-646-4748; fax: 910-646-4915. From US-74/76 (W 3.0 mi from Bolton) on NC-214, turn L on Jefferson Rd (SR-1757). After 1.2 mi, turn L on Bella Coola Rd (SR-1947) and after 2.5 mi, turn L again for park entrance. If heading from Whiteville, it is 12 mi with a R turn off of NC-214. There is also a park sign on US-74/76 into the town of Lake Waccamaw.

778- *Pocosin Trail* (0.2 mi); *Loblolly Trail* (1.0 mi); *Pines Wood Trail* (2.5
782 mi); *Sand Ridge Nature Trail* (0.7 mi); *Lakeshore Trail* (4.7 mi one-
way and 5.0 mi including Pocosin Trail/boardwalk access at visitor
center)

Length and Difficulty: 9.2 mi combined (or 14.2 with Lakeshore Trail
backtrack), easy

Trailhead and Description: All of these trails connect and some provide
loops either with each other or park roads and can be accessed at either the visitor center or the picnic parking lot. They are color-coded with a hiker symbol
on blazes. All pets must be on leash. After entering the park to the visitor center, acquire a park brochure and visit the exhibits. Begin at the L side facing the
building at trail signs. Enter a pine grove. The red-blazed Loblolly Trail and
yellow-blazed Pine Woods Trail go ahead. For blue-blazed access to the
Lakeshore Trail and the Pocosin Trail, turn R. If following the Loblolly Trail,
cross the park road, enter the pine forest, and make a loop by returning on the
park road. If hiking farther on the Pine Woods Trail, meander through a variety
of pine, bay, and oak. After 1.6 mi, cross park road; follow for 0.1 mi S and reenter the forest. Reach the picnic lot and sign at 2.5 mi. A loop can be made by
taking boardwalk access, R, to the lake and the Lakeshore Trail, R. Follow it N
and return to the visitor center for a total of 5.0 mi. If hiking the red-blazed Sand
Ridge Nature Trail, begin at the picnic parking lot and follow the sandy road
toward primitive campsites. Turn L at the trail sign. On a path of white sand,
notice live and turkey oak, reindeer moss, longleaf and pond pine, and wildflowers. Exit on the campsite road; turn R to return to the parking lot.

The long, blue-blazed Lakeshore Trail begins at the visitor center, follows
the Pocosin Trail on a scenic boardwalk to make a L turn at the lake and pier.
It parallels the lake on a sand ridge among pine and hardwoods. At 2.3 mi, it
intersects with Woods Trail.) Cross the boardwalk and at 2.8 mi, pass R of
campsites #2 and #4. You are now entering the most adventurous and exciting
part of the trail. On this appealing pathway of grasses, white sand, leaves, and
pine needles from the trees (pine, hickory, sweet gum, oak, leatherwood) are
intervals of sandy beaches (two of which are 3.7 mi and 4.4 mi), splendid
views of the lake, and Spanish moss swaying in the breeze. At 3.2 mi, cross a
short boardwalk, followed by a stately grove of cypress, L, in the massive
Green Swamp. On the lapping lake, waters are sculptured by cypress knees.
Pass an old road, L, at 4.2 mi. At 4.9 mi is a marsh, L, and at 5.0 mi is the
lake's low dam for the brackish Waccamaw River. Backtrack.

Lumber River State Park (Hoke, Scotland, Roberson, Columbus Counties)

In 1989 a 115-mi section of Lumber River became a state park and a national wild and scenic river. Winding through a wild and dense forest of bald cypress, river birch, sarvis holly, and water elm, its calm black water provides adventure for canoeing and fishing. Among the fish are black crappie, red breast, and large mouth bass. Facilities at park headquarters provide picnicking, primitive camping (permits required), and group camping (reservations available). From the parking area at the park office are accesses to Griffin's Bluff Trail (0.7 mi), Mill Hole Trail (0.5 mi) (both moderate), and Naked Landing Trail (0.4 mi with backtrack) (easy).

783-785

Address and Access: Lumber River State Park, 2829 Princess Ann Rd, Orrum, NC 28369; 910-628-9844; fax 910-628-1181. From NC-130 in Orrum (E of Fairmont), drive 3.0 mi S on Creek Rd (SR-2225) to Princess Ann Rd (SR-2246) L, then 2.0 mi to park office, L.

Merchant's Millpond State Park (Gates County)

Merchant's Millpond State Park is home for more than 200 species of birds in its 3,252 acres. Warblers stop over in their fall and spring migrations and a large number of waterfowl make this their winter home. Wildlife includes deer, raccoon, turtle, beaver, mink, river otter, and snake. The major fish are largemouth bass, bluegill, chain pickerel, and black crappie. The luxuriant park is a rare ecological community with huge bald cypress and tupelo gum trees in the 760-acre millpond and Lassiter Swamp. The trees are draped with Spanish moss and resurrection fern. Large beech groves, oaks, pines, and holly are in the forest surrounding the wetlands. Activities include fishing, hiking, nature study directed by park staff, canoeing (with rentals), and camping (family tent/RV, group, and primitive). The family campsites contain drinking water, a picnic table and grill, flush toilets, and hot showers (no hookups). Hikers should be alert to a heavy infestation of ticks in the forest during warm-weather months. (USGS Map: Beckford)

Address and Access: Merchant's Millpond State Park, 71 US-158 East, Gatesville, NC 27938; 252-357-1191; fax: 252-357-0149. Park entrance is on US-158, 6.0 mi NE of Gatesville, immediately NE of Merchant's Millpond Rd (SR-1403).

786- *Lassiter Trail* (6.7 mi); *Cypress Point Trail* (0.3 mi); *Coleman Trail*
788 (2.0 mi)

        Length and Difficulty: 6.8 mi, easy

        Special Feature: ecological study of plant life

        Trailhead and Description: All trails are white-blazed and for hiking only. Begin the loop trail NW from the parking lot on Merchant's Millpond Rd (SR-1403). After hiking 0.3 mi across the bridge, turn R at the trailhead and enter a forest of cypress, maple, oak, and pine. At 0.6 mi is a jct L, with a 0.5-mi access route to the family campground. Cross a boardwalk at 0.8 mi and ascend to a division of the loop at 0.9 mi. Turn R, skirt the millpond, and pass a family canoe camp at 1.2 mi. Pass through a longleaf pine restoration near a fire road, and cross it at 2.4 mi. Reach the backpack primitive camp near Lassiter Swamp at 3.8 mi. Turn L on the return trail and pass through a carpet of running cedar. Cross the park fire road at 4.6 mi. Complete the loop at 6.0 mi, reach jct R with the family campground at 6.2 mi, and return to the road at 6.7 mi. (Cypress Point Trail, a 0.3-mi loop trail, extends to a peninsula with picnic tables below the canoe rental building and parking area on SR-1403.) Also at the parking area for the short loop and the Lassiter Trail is another loop in the opposite direction with Coleman Trail. It parallels the road for 0.2 mi before a fork. Its vegetation is similar to Lassiter Trail, and it returns to the parking area at 1.6 mi.

Pettigrew State Park (Washington and Tyrrell Counties)

Pettigrew State Park covers 17,873 acres, the state's largest. Of this acreage, Lake Phelps has 16,600 acres; it is the second largest natural lake in the state. The lake is unique because it is not fed by any known surface streams; thus it may be the cleanest lake in the state. Its origin may date to 38,000 years ago, and in 1775 the area was called the "haunt of the beasts" by hunters. Archaeologists have discovered such artifacts of Native Americans as more than 30 canoes, one 37-ft. long. The lake has bass, catfish, pumpkinseed, yellow perch, bluegill, and shellcracker. Ducks, swans, and other waterfowl winter here. Exceptionally large cypress, poplar, sweet gum, shagbark hickory, swamp cottonwood, coastal plain willow, and sycamore are in the 1,273 land acres of the park. Another part of history in the park is a state historic site, Somerset Place, the nineteenth-century plantation estate of the Josiah Collins family (named for Somersetshire, Collins's home county in England), and Bonarva, home of Confederate General James Johnston Pettigrew (for whom the park is named). The Pettigrew family cemetery is here. Activities at the park are picnicking, fishing, boating, hiking, bicycling, and camping. The

campsites are tent/RV with table and grill, water, flush toilets, and hot showers (no hookups). The park's longest bicycle trail is Morotoc Trail, a 4.2-mi **789**
bicycle route (also open to hikers) from Moccasin Overlook W to Cypress
Point. Along the way you may see otter, quail, and rabbit among other animals. Near the canal edges are large redbay and sweetbay (both either a state
or national champion), cypress, and Spanish moss. At Cypress Point is a fishing pier, picnic facilities, rest rooms and drinking water (March–November).
In addition to this trail, bicyclists may use Lakeshore Drive from the campgrounds W to Weston Rd for about 3.0 mi and another unnamed trail 7.0 mi
from Cypress Point S to loop roads in the Pocosin Lakes National Wildlife
Refuge. Sunscreen and insect repellent are recommended in warm/hot
months. Vehicular access from the park office to Cypress Point is W 2.1 mi on
Lakeshore Dr to turn R on Weston Rd (SR-1164). Go 2.3 mi to Newland R,
turn L, and after 4.9 mi turn L on Shore Dr (Keep Rd). Drive 2.7 mi to the
access area L. (USGS Maps: Creswell, Roper S, New Lake NW)

Address and Access: Pettigrew State Park, 2252 Lake Shore Rd,
Creswell, NC 27928; 252-797-4475; fax: 252-797-7405; Somerset Place
State Historic Site, 2572 Lake Shore Rd, Creswell, NC 27928; 252-797-4560.
(Adjoining Pocosin Lakes NWR address is P.O. Box 329, Columbia, NC
27925; 252-796-3004.) Access to Pettigrew SP is off US-64 in Creswell for
6.0 mi following park signs, and the same for Somerset.

Moccasin Trail/Carriage Trail (2.7 mi); *Bee Tree Trail* (1.3 mi); **790-**
Cemetery Trail (0.3 mi) **792**

Length and Difficulty: 8.6 mi round-trip, easy

Special Features: Somerset Place, scenic carriage route, overlooks

Trailhead and Description: From the parking lot near the park office follow the old carriage road W on a level, wide, grassy trail through virgin stands
of cypress, sycamore, and poplar bordered with willow, papaw, and honeysuckle. Views of the lake, through patches of wildflowers such as wood sorrel,
are found on the L at 0. 4 mi, 0.6 mi, and 1.2 mi. Reach the Western Canal at
2.2 mi, and the trail terminus at Moccasin Canal at 2.7 mi. Here is a boardwalk
where winter waterfowl such as American coot, green-winged teal, tundra swan,
hooded merganser, and pintail may be seen. For the E section, hike past the historic Collins House—Somerset Place—at 0.4 mi on the Bee Tree Trail. Pass the
Bonarva Canal at 0.7 mi and at 1.1 mi is a jct L, with the Cemetery Trail, a side
trail to the burial place for the Pettigrew family. Continue ahead, R, to the Bee
Tree Canal and overlook at 1.3 mi. Return by the same route.

Singletary Lake State Park (Bladen County)

Singletary Park Office is headquarters for the state lake operations of White, Bay Tree and Singletary lakes. The major activity of the 1,221-acre park is organized group camping. Of the two camps, one is open year-round. Facilities provide a mess hall and kitchen, campers' cabins, and washhouses. Swimming, fishing, and boating are activities open to the group campers. The group camp facility is open by reservation only. If the camps are unoccupied, the general public may enter the park and access the hiking trail after checking-in at the park office. The easy 1.0-mi CCC-Carolina Bay Loop Trail makes a loop on the E side of the lake. It goes 290 yd. from the main road to the lake and follows into a forest, R, with cypress, bayberry, gum, yellow poplar, and juniper. Spanish moss is prominent. At 0.4 mi, it crosses a svc road, follows green blazes through groves of scrub oak and longleaf pine, and returns to the point of origin. (USGS Map: White Lake)

793

Address and Access: Singletary Lake State Park, 6707 NC-53 Highway, Kelly E, NC 28448; 910-669-2928; fax: 910-669-2034. Access is 12.0 mi SE of Elizabethtown on NC-53.

Chapter 11

Natural Areas, State Forests, Historic Sites, and Other State Properties

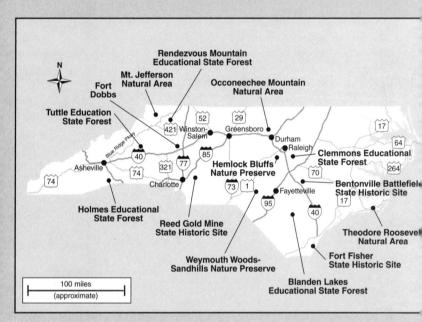

Introductions to Trail Areas

These 14 special places are scattered from near the Tennessee state line to the Atlantic Ocean, and are under the supervision of the state's Department of Environment and Natural Resources. They are listed alphabetically in the order of natural areas, forests, and historic sites.

Chapter 11

Natural Areas, State Forests, Historic Sites, and Other State Properties

Nature speaks various languages.
—William Cullen Bryant

In addition to the state parks, the Division of Parks and Recreation in the Department of Environment and Natural Resources (DENR) administers 16 natural areas, 5 of which have designated trails. They are described ahead. An increase in public pressure to preserve the natural areas prompted the state in 1963 to adopt principles for the natural area system. Among the principles are to preserve, protect, extend, and develop the natural areas of scientific, aesthetic, and geological value.

The Division of Forest Resources (another division of the DENR) administers five educational state forests. They are designated with trails and described ahead. The locations are diverse, but their purpose and facilities are generally the same. For example, they all have interpretive displays and trails, primitive walk-in campsites, and picnic areas. They serve as outdoor-living and environmental centers that teachers and other group leaders use as classrooms. Arrangements can be made with each ranger station for ranger-conducted programs. Campsites are free but require permits. Open season is March 15 to November 30 with the exception of Bladen Lakes, which is open March 1. All are closed on Mondays and Tuesdays.

There are 28 state historic sites, administered by the Historic Sites Section, Division of Archives and History, Department of Cultural Resources. The sites provide visitor centers with artifacts, exhibits, and multimedia programs about historic places. Four with trails are described ahead. The majority of the sites do not have admission charges. For more information, contact the Department of Cultural Resources, 4620 Mail Svc Center (mailing) or 430 N Salisbury St (physical), Raleigh, NC 27601; 919-733-7862 or www.ah.dcr.state.nc.us/sections/hs. Although the majority of trails in this chapter are short, they are ostensibly important walks for educational and cultural purposes.

Hemlock Bluffs Nature Preserve (Wake County)

This 150-acre preserve received its name from eastern hemlock *(Tsuga canadensis),* a conifer usually not naturally found farther east than Hanging Rock State Park, 100.0 mi NE from Cary. In both locations the ingredients of damp, cool N bluffs favor its survival from the Ice Age period of 10,000 to 18,000 years ago. In varying sizes there are more than 200 of these beautiful evergreens, easily viewed from a trail network with observation decks near Swift Creek. (The 0.8-mi Swift Creek Trail on the N side of the stream is part of the Cary greenway system and not part of the Hemlock Bluffs trail network.) The hemlocks, some as old as 400 years, are surrounded by other Appalachian Mountains plant species. Examples are yellow orchid, trillium, and chestnut oak, sometimes found in the western Piedmont.

This valuable and unique preserve was purchased by the state in 1976. Adjoining property is owned by the town of Cary, whose Parks and Recreation Department has developed and managed the entire preserve. Some project assistance has been received by the Wake County Grant-in-Aid Program. At the entrance to the trail system is the Stevens Nature Center, completed in 1992 and named in honor of Col W. W. Stevens and his wife, Emily. The center has a park office, exhibit and classroom space, and a developed wildflower garden. Preserve hours are 9:00AM to sunset daily; center hours vary according to seasons. The exceptionally well designed and maintained trail system is described below. (USGS Map: Apex)

Address and Access: Hemlock Bluffs Nature Preserve, 2616 Kildaire Farm Rd, Cary, NC 27512 (mailing address: P.O. Box 8005); 919-387-5980. To access from the jct of US-1/64, go NE on Tryon Rd for 0.6 mi and turn R on Kildaire Farm Rd. After 1.4 mi, turn R at the preserve entrance.

East Bluff Trail (0.3 mi); *West Bluff Trail* (0.7 mi); *Swift Creek Trail* 794-
(0.8 mi); *Beech Tree Cove Trail* (0.4 mi); *Chestnut Oak Trail* (1.2 mi) 798
    Length and Difficulty: 2.1 mi combined round-trip, easy to moderate
    Trailhead and Description: The trail's entrance is behind the Stevens Nature Center where signboards provide trail information on distance (including overlap), direction, and blaze colors. Hiking from one to the other in two main loops, the distance is reduced. There are two trail brochures keyed to post numbers for the E and W trails. If following the East Bluff Trail, markers 1 through 4 are about the bluffs and 5 through 14 describe the floodplain/Swift Creek area, wildlife, and wildflowers. The trail guide for the W trail grouping is about the history of the upland forest, biological diversity, forest succession,

and ecosystems. Quartz rocks are part of the ground cover and chestnut oak is predominant among the trees. If making a R turn in the W trails, West Bluff Trail comes first.

Mount Jefferson State Natural Area (Ashe and Alleghany Counties)

Mt. Jefferson Natural Area covers 541 acres and includes the summit (4,900 ft) of Mt. Jefferson; it is halfway between the towns of Jefferson and West Jefferson. Now a natural area, the park was initially a state forest wayside in 1952. Later, citizens were successful in obtaining funding and acreage to make it a state park in 1956. Panoramic views from the fire tower reveal other mountain ranges in a three-state area—Whitetop Mtn. in VA, Grandfather and Pilot Mtns. in NC, and Cherokee NF Mtns. in TN. The park has a wide variety of trees, shrubs, and flowers. Its chestnut-oak forest is considered to be one of the finest in the Southeast. In addition, there are maple, ash, oak, black locust, bigtooth aspen, and poplar. Rhododendron, laurel, and flame azalea are also prominent as are banks of galax and scattered wood lilies and Dutchman's-breeches. Animal life includes fox, groundhog, chipmunk, raccoon, songbirds, and red and gray squirrel. Picnicking and hiking are the major activities;

799 camping is prohibited. From the parking lot the Summit Trail passes through the picnic ground and ascends 0.2 mi to a lookout tower for majestic vistas.

800 Near the top the self-guiding Rhododendron Trail makes a 1.1-mi lofty sweep on a horseshoe-shaped ridge to Luther Rock. Here is a scenic outcrop of black volcanic amphibolite. A trail booklet at the trailhead provides information on the preserve's history, geology, plant life, and wildlife. The peak season for purple rhododendron blooming is early June. (USGS Map: Jefferson)

  Address and Access: Mt. Jefferson Natural Area, P.O. Box 48, Jefferson, NC 28640; 336-982-2587 or 336-246-9653. Access is from US-221 between Jefferson and West Jefferson; turn on Mt. Jefferson Rd (SR-1152) for 3.0 mi to the summit.

  Support Facilities: The nearest campground is Greenfield Campground at the base of the park, 0.7 mi SW on Mt. Jefferson Rd (SR-1149 from the park road). Address is West Jefferson, NC 28694; 336-246-9106. Open March 1 to December 1. Full svc, rec fac. Shopping centers, restaurants, and motels are in nearby Jefferson/West Jefferson.

Occoneechee Mountain State Natural Area (Orange County)

With 124 acres on a forested hill, this is a prized natural are between the noise of busy I-85 and solitude of the Eno River W of Hillsborough. Although the elevation is only 867 ft., there are species common to some of the state's western mountains. To hike its trails, begin at the parking-lot signs. Follow the red-blazed Occoneechee Mountain Loop Trail past a fishing pond at a grassy field **801** bordered with blackberry bushes. At 0.2 mi, enter the forest. At 0.5 mi is a jct with 0.2-mi blue-blazed Brown Elfin Knob Trail. (It ascends L to a rocky **802** knob among chestnut, oak, moss, and lichen before descending to the main loop. A turn L for 0.1 mi to the parking area makes a short loop of 0.8 mi.) Continue on the main loop among patches of mountain laurel and huckleberry. Pass power lines to an overlook of Eno River at 1.0 mi, where there are steps down to an abandoned quarry. (Caution signs indicate danger leaving the trail.) Ascend to a jct with a spur; backtrack. Follow yellow-blazed Overlook **803** Trail to the gravel road, R and L. (To the R, it is 0.3 mi to the non-view summit at the park's boundary.) Descend and in a swag at 1.9-mi pass, jct with Brown Elfin Knob Trail, L. Continue descent to parking and picnic area at 2.0 mi. (For more information, contact Eno River State Park [919-383-1686].)

Access: At a jct of I-85 (Exit 164), drive N onto Churton St. Turn L at stoplight at Mayo St. Drive 0.2 mi and at stoplight turn L onto Orange Grove Rd. After 0.5 mi, turn R on Virginia Cates Rd to parking lot.

Theodore Roosevelt State Natural Area (Carteret County)

This natural area of 265 acres on the island of Bogue Banks is set aside to preserve a maritime forest of laurel oak and live oak, red bay, red cedar, swamp red maple, and red ash, especially in the swales. Other plant life includes eight species of fern, wild olive, and the toothache tree *(Zanthoxylum americana)*. There are marshes (freshwater, brackish, and saltwater) and bird sanctuaries, particularly for warblers. The Hoffman Trail, a 0.4-mi loop, provides a visit **804** over the dunes by the swales and the East Pond. The trail entrance is at the SE corner of the Marine Resources Center. The property was established in 1971 from a gift by the grandchildren of President Theodore Roosevelt. Also here is the NC Aquarium at Pine Knoll Shores. It houses exhibits, aquariums, a public library, and meeting facilities. Field trips, boat trips, workshops, multimedia programs, and more are presented. Admission is free; it is open year-round. (USGS Map: Mansfield)

Address and Access: Theodore Roosevelt Natural Area, c/o Fort Macon State Park, P.O. Box 127, Atlantic Beach, NC 28512; 252-726-3775. NC Aquarium at Pine Knolls Shores, Atlantic Beach, NC 28512; 252-247-4003. Access is on NC-58, 5.0 mi W of Atlantic Beach.

Weymouth Woods–Sandhills Nature Preserve (Moore County)

The 515-acre woodland preserve is E of the city limits of Southern Pines. Most of the acreage was donated by Mrs. James Boyd in 1963. (The preserve has another 383 acres in two undeveloped satellite tracts.) There are more than 500 species of plants (including 135 species of wildflowers), including French mulberry, longleaf pine, turkey oak, and bay. Among the wildlife are deer, squirrel, raccoon, beaver, owl, and numerous songbirds. Butterflies are prominent, for example, palamedes swallowtail, American lady, and hairstreak. The sandy ridges, popularly known as the Sandhills Region, were formed from sediments of clay, sand, and gravel deposited by streams in the region millions of years ago when the area was part of an inland sea. The preserve has a Natural History Museum, and naturalists provide illustrated lectures and tours. Open daily, seven days a week. (USGS Maps: Southern Pines, Niagara)

Address and Access: Weymouth Woods–Sandhills Nature Preserve, 1024 N Fort Bragg Rd, Southern Pines, NC 28387; 910-692-2167. In S Southern Pines, turn off US-1 at Magnolia Drive (SR-2053) and go 1.2 mi to a jct with Fort Bragg Rd (SR-2074). Turn L and go 1.7 mi to entrance, L.

805-810   *Bowers Bog Trail* (0.3 mi); *Lighter Stump Trail* (0.5 mi); *Pine Barrens Trail* (1.0 mi); *Gum Swamp Trail* (0.5 mi); *Holly Road Trail* (1.8 mi); *Pine Island Trail* (0.5 mi)

Length and Difficulty: 4.6 mi combined, easy

Trailhead and Description: Bowers Bog Trail is a loop nature trail E of the museum and parking area. On the N side of the loop is Lighter Stump Trail, a connector between Bowers Bog Trail and Pine Island Trail. Begin the Pine Barrens Trail W of the museum and follow the white blazes through prominent displays of longleaf pine, turkey oak, bracken, and blueberry. The Gum Swamp Trail loop joins it at the N side, but it contains chiefly hardwoods. From the Gum Swamp Trail, begin the 1.8-mi Holly Road Trail. After crossing James Creek at 40 yd., turn L or R at 0.1 mi on the yellow-blazed trail. If you turn R, reach a jct with the Pine Island Trail loop at 0.2 mi, R. (This area is lush with plant life in a swampy area of James Creek. The trail crosses James Creek twice and some tributaries. On the S side of the loop, it comes to jct with Lighter Stump Trail.) Continue on Holly Road Trail, cross a stream and soon a fire road. At 1.4 mi, pass L of a spring. Complete the loop at 1.8 mi, and return on the E or W side of the Gum Swamp Trail loop and the Pine Barrens Trail loop.

Bladen Lakes Educational State Forest (Bladen County)

The 32,237-acre coastal forest is spread between South River and the Cape Fear River in the bay lakes area. Within the general boundaries are Salters Lake, Singletary Lake, and Jones Lake, but the forest office, exhibits, trails, and picnic areas are concentrated near the jct of NC-242 and Sweet Home Rd (SR-1511), across the road from Jones Lake State Park. The primitive walk-in campsites are 3.7 mi SE on Sweet Home Rd. Smith Swamp Trail is a slow 3.5-mi auto tour (14 mph) past exhibit stations, and the 0.4-mi Turnbull Creek Trail is a manicured interpretive foot trail. An approach to them is on Sweet Home Rd, 0.2 mi E from the forest office. If the gate to the road is locked, walk the sandy road and at 0.2 mi pass the Naval Stores Industry exhibit, L. Turn L at the fork in a pine plantation and reach the picnic area (with exhibits and kiosk), R. Turnbull Creek Trail is L, opposite the picnic area. The trail dips to a natural spring and circles through Spanish moss, water and turkey oak, fetterbush, and fragrant nettle *(Cnidoscolus stimulosus)*. Turnbull Creek is on the N side. Fox squirrels (which feed on the large seed cones of the longleaf pine) may be seen here. (USGS Map: Elizabethtown N) **811-812**

Address and Access: Bladen Lakes Educational State Forest, 4470 Highway 242, North Elizabethtown, NC 28337; 910-588-4964; fax: 910-558-4101. The office is on NC-242, 4.0 mi N of Elizabethtown (0.6 mi N of Jones Lake State Park) and 9.0 mi S of Ammons.

Clemmons Educational State Forest (Johnston County)

A forest of 512 acres between Clayton and Garner, it has study sites for rocks, trees, wildlife, watersheds, and forest management. Opened in 1976, it represents a transitional zone between the Piedmont and coastal plain. A forestry center and exhibits explain the varied facilities of the area. Picnicking and primitive group camping facilities are available, and sections of the trails can be used by the physically disabled. There are 20 ranger-conducted programs for visiting groups to choose from. The 2.2-mi Clemmons Forest Demonstration Trail begins at the parking lot. Follow the signs 100 yd. to a forest information board and another 100 yd. to the forestry center and trail signboard. **813**

814   Turn R, and follow the red blazes. At 0.2 mi cross a stream near Geology Trail, a path with talking rocks and yellow diamond blazes for 0.8 mi. At 0.3 mi pass a shortcut trail and pass it again at 1.3 mi. The 0.6-mi green-blazed
815   Clemmons Talking Tree Trail loops from the trail signboard. An exceptionally well designed trail, it provides push-button devices for recorded botanical information. All trails have easy treadway. (USGS Map: Clayton)

   Address and Access: Clemmons Educational State Forest, 2411 Garner Rd, Clayton, NC 27520; 919-553-5651; fax: 919-550-8050; email: clemmonsesf@mindspring.com. Access is on Old US-70 (SR-1004), 1.5 mi N of Clayton city limits and 4.2 mi N of US-70.

Holmes Educational State Forest (Henderson County)

The forest named in honor of Canadian-born John S. Holmes (1868–1958), who served as the state's first forester from 1915 to 1945. The forest covers 231 acres, 25 of which are rich bottomland and 206 on steep mountainsides and rounded summits. It was a CCC camp in the 1930s, and a seedling nursery until it became a state forest in 1972. More than 125 species of flowering plants have been identified. Facilities are available for picnicking, hiking, and nature study. Group camping is provided on the mountaintop; it has road access and requires a reservation. Approach to the trailheads is 0.1 mi from the main parking lot to the forestry center and trail-system signboard. The
816   exception is the unblazed 0.5-mi Crab Creek Trail. Access is W at the parking area where it goes to a tree plantation zone near Crab Creek. (USGS Map: Standing Stone Mtn.)

817-   *Forest Demonstration Trail* (3.0 mi); *Holmes Talking Tree Trail* (0.5
820   mi); *Wildcat Rock Trail* (0.7 mi); *Soil and Water Trail* (0.3 mi)

   Length and Difficulty: 4.5 mi combined round-trip, moderate to strenuous

   Trailhead and Description: From the forestry center, hike E on the red-blazed Forest Demonstration Trail with study sites through hardwoods and white pines on switchbacks. Reach the campground shortcut trail at 1.0 mi. Keep L, pass a small pond, cross a forest road, and reach jct with the shortcut, R, again. Pass a scenic overlook, L, and begin a descent on switchbacks for a return to the forestry center via Wildcat Rock Trail. Also starting L at the forestry center is the green-blazed Holmes Talking Tree Trail, which has push-button devices for information on forest history, use, growth, and values. Cross cascades at 0.4 mi. On the W side of the loop is a jct with Wildcat Rock Trail, a steep climb on switchbacks to an overlook with superb views of the Crab

Creek basin and W to the Blue Ridge Mtns. Additionally, from the forestry center W to the amphitheater is short unblazed Soil and Water Trail loop.

Address and Access: Forest Supervisor, Rte 4, Box 308, Hendersonville, NC 28739; 828-692-0100. Access is from Penrose on US-64. Take Featherstone Creek Rd (SR-1528) for 2.6 mi to Little River. Turn L on Crab Creek Rd, which becomes Kanuga Rd (SR-1127), and go 4.2 mi to entrance, R. Another route is from downtown Hendersonville. From the jct of US-64E and US-25S go S 0.5 mi on US-25S to a jct R with Caswell St, which becomes Kanuga Rd (SR-1127), and go 10.0 mi.

Rendezvous Mountain Educational State Forest (Wilkes County)

In 1926 Judge Thomas Finely donated the 142-acre Rendezvous Mtn. to the state as a park, but the state never developed it. Thirty years later it became a state forest. It is a scenic hardwood forest with rugged terrain at the foothills of the Blue Ridge Mtns. There are facilities for picnicking, hiking, and nature study (primitive camping is planned). After entering the gate, park at the first parking lot, R. Cross the road (R of the picnic area), and follow the 0.2-mi Table Mountain Pine Sawmill Trail. The loop has historic exhibits of timber-cutting equipment, logging methods, and a sawmill from the 1950s. At the second parking lot, R, the 0.6-mi Rendezvous Mountain Talking Tree Trail loops through a beautiful forest of hardwood, laurel, pinxter, and flame azalea with scattered rhododendron. Descent is moderate to steep. Also, from the parking lot is the 275-yd Firetower Trail, which ascends N past the forest office to the old fire tower (2,445 ft.) with scenic views. (USGS Map: Purlear) **821 822 823**

Address and Access: Rendezvous Mtn Educational State Forest, P.O. Box 42, Purlear, NC 28665; 336-667-5072. From NC-16 in Millers Creek (5.3 mi NW of Wilkesboro), turn W on Old US-421 (SR-1304) and go 2.8 mi to a jct with Purlear Rd (SR-1346). Turn R on Purlear Rd and go 1.8 mi, turn L on Rendezvous Mtn. Rd (SR-1348), and ascend to the forest entrance after 1.3 mi.

Tuttle Educational State Forest (Caldwell County)

The forest honors Lelia Judson Tuttle (1878–1967), a teacher and missionary whose property was deeded to the state in 1973. In the 170-acre forest are facilities for picnicking, hiking, nature study, and primitive camping. An original old schoolhouse called Lingle School is part of the emphasis on education. As at the other state forests, ranger programs are designed for groups

from kindergarten to adults. Also, workshops are provided for continuing-education credit. Trail access is from the parking and picnic area. The easy
824 1.9-mi Tuttle Demonstration Trail follows signs past the forestry center to a signboard at 0.1 mi. Turn L on the red-blazed trail through pines (white, Virginia, and shortleaf) and hardwoods. At 0.7 mi is a jct with a shortcut, R. Pass Sleepy Hollow School site and go through the campsites for a return to the
825 parking area. Tuttle Talking Tree Trail loops 0.6 mi on a green-blazed interpretive trail from the forestry center. The audio devices play recordings about forest succession and species of trees. (USGS Map: Morganton N)

Address and Access: Tuttle Educational State Forest, 3420 Playmore Beach Rd., Lenoir, NC 28645; 828-757-5608. Access is on Playmore Beach Rd (SR-1331), 0.8 mi off NC-18 (near the Burke/Caldwell county line), 6.0 mi SW of Lenoir.

Bentonville Battleground State Historic Site (Johnston County)

After the capture of Savannah December 20, 1864, General William T. Sherman's troops turned N to join General U. S. Grant's troops in VA. On the way General Sherman continued a swath of destruction, particularly in Columbia SC, the capital city and seedbed of the Secessionist movement. Every public building in the city was destroyed (whether by accident or design) on February 17, 1865. The Battle of Bentonville is significant because it was the last major Confederate offensive and the largest ever fought in NC. General Joseph E. Johnston's troops, with less than half the number of Union troops, fought bravely but lost during March 19 to 21. They withdrew toward Smithfield with plans to protect Raleigh, the state's capital city, but the Union forces did not pursue them.

Address and Access: Bentonville Educational State Historic Site, Box 27, Newton Grove, NC 28366; 910-594-0789. Entrance is 1.4 mi off US-701 on Cox Mill Rd (SR-1008), 3.0 mi N of Newton Grove.

826- *Bentonville Battleground History Trail* (0.2 mi); *Bentonville Battle-*
827 *ground Trail* (13.4 mi)

> **Length and Difficulty:** 13.6 mi combined, easy.
>
> **Special Features:** 27 history stations.
>
> **Trailheads and Description:** The Bentonville Battlefield History Trail is a self-guiding walk that begins near the field fortifications exhibit and leads to the original trenches dug by Union forces on the first day of the battle. From

the historic Harper House, begin the longer route by crossing Cox Mill Rd (SR-1008) between trail markers #3 and #4 and follow the public road. At 0.6 mi turn L on SR-1192. Reach a jct with SR-1008, turn R, and at 2.7 mi see the United Daughters of the Confederacy (UDC) monument to the Confederate soldiers. Turn L on SR-1194, which later merges with Devils Race Track Rd (SR-1009), and arrive at the Bentonville Community Building at 5.6 mi. Continue to marker #23 at 5.8 mi; here Confederate cavalry was halted by the flooded Mill Creek. Return to the Community Building and take the road L, following 0.1 mi and turning R at marker #24. At 7.1 mi turn L at marker #25, pass markers #26 and #27, and turn R on a private dirt field road near a feed bin at 7.9 mi. Continue by the field's edge for 0.7 mi to a paved road and turn L at marker #28. Reach SR-1008 at 9.0 mi; turn R and go 0.6 mi to Ebenezer Church to a jct with SR-1009. (A country store is across the road.) Turn R and go 0.5 mi to marker #20, return to SR-1008 at 10.6 mi. Follow it to the UDC marker at the SR-1194 jct at 11.6 mi. Return on SR-1008 to the starting point for a total of 13.4 mi. (The management is in the process of purchasing more land on the battlefield area and constructing roadside pull-offs at the markers.)

Fort Dobbs State Historic Site (Iredell County)

Named for Royal Governor Arthur Dobbs, the fort was built (ca 1750s) during the French and Indian War to protect the settlers. Excavations of the vanished fort show a moat, cellar, magazine area, and well. A pioneer cottage has exhibits of the period. The 0.5-mi Fort Dobbs Nature Trail goes through a **828** hardwood forest with footbridges over small ravines. Ferns and wildflowers are prominent among the spicebushes.

Address and Access: Fort Dobbs State Historic Site, 438 Fort Dobbs Rd, Statesville, NC 28625; 704-873-5866. From the jct of I-40 and US-21 in Statesville, go N 1.2 mi on US-21, turn L on Fort Dobbs Rd (SR-1930), and go 1.3 mi to entrance, R.

Fort Fisher State Historic Site (New Hanover County)

This historic fort was constructed in 1861 for the purpose of defending the City of Wilmington as a port of trade in the Civil War. The protection lasted until early 1865 when the Confederate protection failed from a powerful bombardment by a large fleet of Union ships, which was followed by a land assault with more than 3,000 infantry. The result was the last major stronghold of the Confederacy. The visitor center has a fiber-optic map detailing the battle and other video presentations. Guided tours are available daily, and there is no admission fee. Exterior exhibits consist of about 10 percent of the **829** original fort. There is a 0.5-mi Fort Fisher Loop Trail in and around the battery. There is also a walkway and kiosks across the road at Battery Acre. Open April through October, Monday through Saturday 9:00AM to 5:00PM, Sunday 1:00PM to 5:00PM; November through March, Tuesday through Saturday 10:00AM to 4:00PM; closed Sunday and Monday; closed on holidays.

Address and Access: Fort Fisher, P.O. Box 169 (mailing) or 1610 Fort Fisher Blvd (physical), Kure Beach, NC 28449; 910-458-5538; fax: 910-458-0477. Access is S of Wilmington on US-421, 5.6 mi S past Carolina Beach State Park, and N 1.0 mi of Fort Fisher State Recreation Area.

Reed Gold Mine State Historic Site (Cabarrus County)

Gold was discovered here, accidentally, when in 1799 Conrad Reed, son of John Reed, found a 17-pound yellow rock while fishing in Little Meadow Creek, which flowed through the family farm. This was the first documented discovery of gold in the United States. A silversmith in Concord, 10.0 mi away, could not identify the rock, so the Reeds used it as a doorstop. In 1802, a Fayetteville jeweler recognized the rock and purchased it from John Reed for $3.50, a week's pay. The Reeds began surface, or placer, mining that year, forming partnerships with other area miners. Underground or lode mining began in 1831 and lasted until 1912. The state purchased the property in 1971 and developed a large visitor center with mining exhibits, orientation film, and guided tour of the underground. The mine trail goes 50 ft. below the surface and through 400 ft. of tunnel. Self-guided tours are available around the **830** Upper Hill archaeological area and the Lower Hill Nature Trail. It is an easy 0.4-mi loop, which starts from the Upper Hill mining area, goes by the restored Stamp Mill, around Lower Hill, and back to the visitor center. Along the way markers indicate sites of mining shafts and adits. Vegetation includes oak, maple, holly, cedar, fern, and crane fly orchid. The historic site is open 9:00AM–5:00PM Tues–Sat, Apr 1–Oct 31, 10:00AM–4:00PM Tues–Sat, Nov 1–Mar 31. Panning is available during spring and summer for a nominal fee. There is no admission charge.

Address and Access: Reed Gold Mine State Historic Site, 9621 Reed Mine Rd, Midland, NC 28107; 704-721-4653. From the jct of US-601/NC-200, 6.0 mi S of Concord, take NC-200 E 3.5 mi. Turn R on Reed Mine Rd (SR-1100) and go 2.0 mi. From Locust at NC-24/27, take NC-200 W 4.5 mi and turn L.

Part V

Trails in Counties and Municipalities

American Tobacco Trail.

Chapter 12

County Parks and
Recreation Areas

I measure your health by the number of shoes . . .
you have worn out.
—Ralph Waldo Emerson

Seventy-two percent of the state's 100 counties have parks and recreation departments, but not all have trail systems. They operate as a separate public unit in each county, usually under a county board of commissioners. A few counties and cities combine their departments or resources to provide joint services or special projects. Cooperation between counties and cities also is provided with long trails such as the Mountains-to-Sea Trail and the American Tobacco Trail. A few counties have joint partnerships, such as Forsyth and Guilford counties. With their county line dividing 426 acres, the Triad Park is developing into a regional centerpiece for park facilities. (See Forsyth County in this chapter.) The 391-acre Little River Regional Park and Natural Area is a similar cooperative in Durham and Orange Counties. (Call 919-245-2660 or 919-560-7956 for trail information.) Official reports from state and local government agencies indicate that with an increase in population, there is a greater demand for open-space preservation. Greenways have become a common issue in park planning, even for small towns and less populated counties. More populated counties, such as Haywood County (with many USFS trails nearby), are considering hiring greenway coordinators for their needs. This chapter details varied examples of what each county has and what is in development stages. Almost all county (and city parks) have sport-facility basics such as ball fields and courts, picnic areas, and playgrounds. It is not unusual for these areas to be near or adjacent to public schools. Paved walkways are often standard. Buncombe County Sports Park's walkway (1.0 mi) circles the facility. Although walkways can be called nameless trails, the emphasis in this guidebook is on named trails with educational and/or cultural value in addition to physical exercise. Stanley County has community walking routes in

partnership with Albermarle, Badin, Norwood, Oakboro, Richfield, and Stan-
field (call 704-984-9560 for a map). The town of Pittsboro has the Jaycee Park **831**
Trail of 1.0 mi beside a lake and bridge over a dam, but it is under the supervision of Chatham County (919-542-8252).

There are about 17 rail-trails (and a few more in planning/development
stages) in the state. More of them are sponsored by towns/cities and North
Carolina Rail-Trails than by counties. One exception is the American Tobacco
Trail, which involves Durham (city also), Chatham, and Wake counties. (See
City of Durham in chapter 13.) A few counties in the state have grouped to
feature historic walks/trails for tourism value. An example is Scenic Sou-
journs of Beaufort, Bertie, Hyde, Tyrell, and Washington counties (including
some historic towns described ahead). For more information, contact Partnership for the Sounds, P.O. Box 55, Columbia, NC 27925; 252-796-1000 or
www.partnershipforthesounds.org. For the addresses and telephone numbers
of the state's counties and cities with parks, contact the Recreation Resources
Services, NC State University, Campus Box 8004, Raleigh, NC 27695; 919-
515-7118.

County Parks and Recreation Areas: Western Half of the State

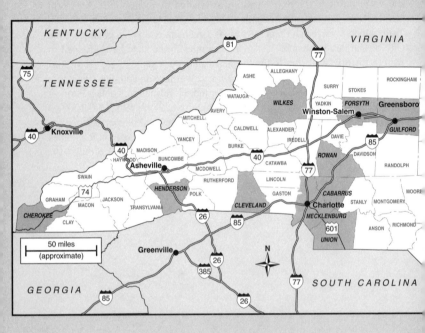

Introductions to Trail Areas

The following counties have parks and allied areas with official and designated trails. The western half of the state is represented here and the eastern half ahead. The listing is alphabetical rather than geographical to conform to the text.

Historic in location and design, a unique greenway circles a lake to refurbished landmarks such as a farm barn.

This historic trail runs through a former Native American settlement.

This area is home to Broad River Greenway, with its river and Jolly Mtn. scenery.

With elaborate design, the 426-acre Triad Park has vast sport options and a network of trails in meadows and forests. The park is a joint project with Guilford County.

Jackson Park has a remarkable nature trail with honeybees, birds, butterflies, berries, and flowering bushes.

What a choice! There are 175 parks with options among greenways and paths to hike or bike by streams, meadows, and residential complexes.

Dan Nicholas Park has a lake trail and skillful hillside loop trails. Eagle Point Nature Preserve has nature trails as well.

Cane Creek Park (1,051 acres) has multiple trails, many with circles for all ages.

This area is home to the Scenic River's Edge Trail, which is on an old airport runway.

SECTION 1: WESTERN HALF OF THE STATE
Cabarrus County

The county has two parks with trails. At North Cabbarus Park in Concord is a new 1.2-mi trail surfaced with recycled steel slag, and a nature trail is planned. For more information, contact 704-920-3350. Bakers Creek Park has 37 acres with picnic shelters, lighted ball fields, tennis and volleyball courts, primitive camping for organized groups, and the 1.0-mi Science Trail. Paved 1.0-mi Bakers Creek Greenway Trail connects with Village Park.

832-
833

     Address and Access: Kannapolis PRD, P.O. Box 1199, Kannapolis, NC 28082; 704-938-5133, but the park location is off I-85, Exit 63, W into Kannapolis on Lane St. Cross US-29 and US-29A. At the first traffic light past US-29A, turn R on West A St, and go 1.0 mi to park entrance, L.

     Another park, Frank Liske Park, consists of 220 acres. Fishing and paddle boating are allowed in the 9.2-acre lake, and a refurbished barn provides facilities for group picnics and social gatherings. There is also a complex of lighted fields and courts for baseball, softball, soccer, tennis, miniature golf, and an amphitheatre. Trails include a 2.0 perimeter trail, 1.0-mi Liske Park Nature Trail with markers identifying plant life in its circle around the lake, and a fitness trail.

834

     Address and Access: Cabarrus Co PRD, 2323 Concord Lake Rd, Concord, NC 28025; 704-920-3350. Frank Liske Park, 4001 Stough Rd, Concord, NC 28027; 704-782-0411. Access from I-85, Exit 58, is S on US-29 to Roberta Church Rd, L. At Roberta Mill Rd, turn R and then L on Stough Rd; park entrance is L.

Cherokee County

835

In the state's most western county is Konechette Park, with 1.0-mi (easy) Valley River Trail. Located in the town of Murphy, the county seat, the park is a wide meadow on the W side of Valley River. The park has ballfields, courts and an indoor swimming pool. The paved trail begins from the parking lot at the park office and edges the scenic river flanked with river birch and sycamore trees. Curve L toward the entrance road for a loop in return to the parking lot.

     Address and Access: Cherokee County Rec, 699 Conaheeta St, Murphy, NC 28906; 828-837-6617; fax: 828-835-9737. If arriving on US-64 at the jct of US-74/19/NC-129 (N-S), cross the highway into downtown Murphy. Turn R onto Hill St and follow it to cross a bridge. Turn L on Conaheeta St.

Cleveland County

Broad River Greenway   836

The former and famous Old College Farm Trail has been resurrected as the Broad River Greenway by new owners. It was not a sudden surprise; the born-again blessing has had plenty of brain-storming. With its new life, the potential is more than 15 mi, 7 mi more than the original hill and dale adventure. It has plenty of parents: NC Dept of Transportation, government leaders of Cleveland County, and the college town of Boiling Springs, plus devoted councils, scout troops, clubs, paper and electric companies, the county trail association, and lovers of the Rubber Ducky Regatta. A county staff member described the boundary lines of the 1,400 acres as an abstract amoeba. Others have stated that it was a priceless pattern that included fantastic views of the river rapids, the joy of Jolly Mtn., and as fragrant as the jessamine on the layers of the ledges. There will be new routes, and some of the old routes, E and W of NC-150, will remain. Oak, pine, mountain laurel, river birch, senna, and blueberry now have a permanent home and memories of the past will have an 1850 log cabin, much like the originals near crystal-clear Jolly Branch.

Address and Access: Broad River Greenway, P.O. Box 2626, Shelby, NC 28151; 704-434-2357, 704-434-0040, or www.broadrivergreenway.com; fax: 704-434-2358.

Forsyth County

This county has a system of 18 parks, one of which is Triad Park, a partnership park with Guilford County. All parks are open year-round and some have named trails or walkways. The smallest is 1.6-acre Old US-421 River Park for canoe access to the Yadkin River Trail. (Access W of Winston-Salem is on   837
Yadkinsville Rd (SR-1525) into the Lewisville area. After turning S, reach jct with Conrad Rd, where a R turn is on Old US-421. After 0.2 mi and before the bridge, turn R.) Another small park, Joanie Moser Memorial Park, has ball fields, courts, a picnic area, and the 236-yd. Nature Trail. (It is located from   838
Exit 242 on US-421 on Styers Ferry Rd N and immediately at the W ramp, take Lewisville-Clemmons Rd 1.3 mi to park, R.) The 70-acre C.G. Hill Memorial Park has a fishing lake (bass, bluegill, catfish) and fountain, a picnic area, and the following trail system: Rockdust Loop Trail (0.16 mi), Upper   839-
Loop Trail (0.4 mi), and Lower Loop Trail (0.3 mi.). All are accessible from   841
the parking lots. On the latter trail, there is a yellow poplar tree with an exciting history of more than 500 years.

Address and Access: County of Forsyth Parks and Rec, 500 W. Fourth St, Suite 103, Winston-Salem, NC 27101; 336-703-2500 or www.co.forsyth.nc.us/PARKS/ParksRec.htm. Access is off NC-67 (Reynolda Rd) W of Bethania is on Transou Rd, S, 1.2 mi to Balsom Rd for a R turn, then 1.0 mi to park, L.

Triad Park

The concept for this superb park was proposed in 1996, with the hope of acquiring 6,000 acres to serve as a natural area—a type of buffer—between two large metropolitan areas. After years of delay and high increase in land value, plus a bond referendum in Forsyth and Guilford counties, a portion of the dream came true: 414 acres. The county lines are N/S and Reedy Fork flows W to E. Development is in 13 phases, some of which are completed at the time of this writing. They include large picnic shelters, playgrounds, ball fields and courts, and a multi-purpose community center. An 18-acre lake with a lakeside amphitheatre, a campground, and 8 mi of trails are also planned. Some of the trails will be paved, while others will retain a natural forest floor. For more information, contact 336-703-2500.

Address and Access: 9652 E. Mountain St, Kearnersville, NC 27284. From Winston-Salem on I-40 Bus, E, take Colfax, Exit 16, L. Stay on Mountain St, E (formerly US-421), for 1.8 mi and turn L at park entrance. From Greensboro on I-40, W, take Sandy Ridge Rd, Exit 208, R. Drive 0.5 mi and turn L on Mountain St (formerly US-421). After 2.0 mi, turn R into park.

Horizons Park

The 492-acre park is one of 10 county rec areas and historic sites that encircle the city of Winston-Salem. The county and the city have been leading the state in parks and recreation with 20 acres per 1,000 citizens. Horizons Park is an example of how well they are serving the public. The facility has a large picnic area (with shelters), a playground, a softball field, 18-hole flying-disc golf course (the state's first), and hiking trails. (USGS Map: Walkertown)

Address and Access: Parks and Rec, 500 W. 4th St, Winston-Salem, NC 27101; 336-727-2946; fax: 336-727-2164. One access is from the jct of US-52 and NC-8 (N of the city). Follow NC-8 4.2 mi and turn R on Memorial Industrial School Dr (SR-1920) 1.1 mi to the entrance, R.

842   *Horizons Hiking Trail (2.5 mi)*

Length and Difficulty: 2.5 mi combined, easy

Trailhead and Description: From the parking area, go to the picnic shelter and locate the trail signs. After 110 yd. the Horizons Hiking Trail goes R and L for a shorter loop (B) and a longer loop (A). If going R, cross a stream at 0.3 mi and reach a jct with loop B, L, at 0.4 mi. If going R, go through a field, cross a bridge (one of a number on the trail), and follow the white blazes. Pass a tree nursery, cross another bridge, and begin ascending and descending on rolling hills in a young forest. Redbud, Virginia pine, dogwood, and red cedar coexist with the major hardwoods. At 1.1 mi, cross a boardwalk in a damp area. Arrive at the loop-B jct at 2.1 mi, L and R. If continuing R, there is a huge holly tree at 2.3 mi, R. Here also is a nineteenth-century grave-yard. Return to the nature trail and complete the loops at 2.5 mi.

Tanglewood Park

Tanglewood is the William and Kate B. Reynolds Memorial Park, an outstand-ing Piedmont recreation and leisure resort. Facilities include the elegant manor house and lodge, rustic vacation cottages, tennis courts, swimming pool, golf (36-hole championship course and driving range), lake for paddleboats and canoes, picnic areas, arboretum and rose garden, deer park, horse stables and steeplechase course, 0.8-mi exercise-walking trail, professional summer-stock theater, and the Walden Nature Center. There is also a 4-mi tract for the Festi-val of Lights, a holiday spectacular usually held from the second week in November to the first week in January. (USGS Maps: Clemmons, Advance)

Address and Access: Tanglewood Park, 4061 Clemmons Rd, Clemmons, NC 27012; 336-778-6319 or www.tanglewoodpark.org; fax: 336-778-6322. From the I-40 jct (Clemmons), go S 0.9 mi on Middlebrook Dr (SR-1103) to US-158. Turn R, go another 1.7 mi, and turn L (park office is L at 1.3 mi.).

Walden Nature Trail   843

Length and Difficulty: 1.5 mi combined, easy

Trailhead and Description: From the park entrance, go E on US-158 0.4 mi to the park office, R (opposite Harper Rd, SR-1101, and service sta-tion) for the Walden Nature Center. Approach the Walden Nature Trail behind the park office and acquire a brochure at the signboard or from the park office. The trail has three sections, each consecutively increasing in dif-ficulty and species variety. Little Walden Trail (sec 1,195 yd.) has audio sta-   **844** tions for the visually handicapped around a small pond (service by advance reservations); Emerson's Walk (sec 2, 0.7 mi round-trip) is a paved old road   **845** with 18 tree-interpretive markers and is accessible for the physically disabled; and Thoreau's Woods Trail (sec 3, 0.7 mi round-trip) has 28 interpretive   **846** markers about the trees. The trail is named after Thoreau's Walden Pond and was completed in 1982 as a memorial to the NC Wildlife Enforcement Officers who have died in the line of duty since 1947. Little Walden was built entirely by volunteers and through donations. Major contributors were the Reader's Digest Foundation, Winston-Salem Host Lions Club, AT&T Pioneers, and Girl Scout Troop 437. (There is an exhibit of live wildlife L of the main trailhead.)

Henderson County

847

Henderson County's Parks and Rec Dept office is at Jackson Park where there are expansive recreation facilities: lighted basketball and baseball fields, tennis courts, picnic shelters, an amphitheatre, and the exceptionally beautiful 1.5-mi Jackson Park Nature Trail. After entering the park, drive to the office and main building parking lot on the hilltop and acquire a map of the garden trail. (There is a special parking lot near the creek's bridge and a paved route into the garden part of the trail for the physically disabled.) Markers at the stops, plus the brochure, provide information on the flora and fauna. The natural sounds are chickadees, titmice, scarlet tanagers, and warblers. Begin the hike L of the office among hardwoods on the hill, descend to a wide old road, and turn L alongside the stream. Cross the paved road at the sign for the disabled and turn R across a footbridge at 0.3 mi. There are fragrant white and pink wild roses (at their peak in May), buttercup, fire pink, and ferns. Surrounding the trail are hundreds of species of plants, some in wet or boggy areas that a number of vocally active frog species inhabit. At marker #16, ascend up a ridge to the entrance road for a crossing to the point of origin.

Address and Access: Henderson County Rec and Park Dept, 801 Glover St, Hendersonville, NC 28792; 828-697-4884; fax: 828-697-4886. Access from I-26, Exit 18, is on Four Seasons Blvd (US-64) W. At the seventh traffic light, turn L on Harris St. Descend 0.1 mi to curve L for park entrance.

Mecklenburg County

Mecklenburg County is rapidly developing into an urbanized county. In 1977, a 10-year park plan was begun; in 1982, a park's bond master plan set a goal of 9,250 acres; and in 1986, a $15 million park bond was passed by county referendum. Then in 1992, the city of Charlotte Park and Rec Dept merged with the county's system. A model for cities and counties planning cooperative efforts, the Mecklenburg County Park and Rec Dept operates and maintains more than 16,000 acres of suburban and urban parkland with more than

175 parks and eight greenways. In 1989, the city/county master plan and the 1990s acquisition assessment called for developing another 24 parks. Presently, a visitor will need to visit 3 different parks a week to see them all within a year.

The recreation and cultural diversity of the parks is divided into nature preserves, recreation centers, community parks, golf courses, district parks, aquatic centers, neighborhood parks, greenways, lake and river accesses, historic sites, and other facilities such as arts and athletic arenas, an equestrian center, and a stadium. Nature preserves encompass the largest parks (usually 1,000-plus acres) designed to serve all the metropolitan area. Ninety percent of these properties are restricted to passive recreation because of the natural qualities. Three of the preserves have trail networks and are described below. Community parks are designed for serving the public within a 5.0-mi radius and usually have between 300 to 500 acres. They are known for their wide range of athletic activities and tournaments. District parks best serve a closer community with less than 200 acres. They are likely to have athletic fields, picnic shelters, playgrounds, small lakes, pools, and fitness/walking connector trails. An example is East District Park, with 1.5-mi Idlewild Nature Trail. **848** It is located at 10512 Idlewild Rd, Charlotte, NC 28212; 704-545-9486. McAlpine Creek Park, also in the East District, has multiuse trails. It is described in more detail below.

The 76 neighborhood parks serve local areas almost within walking distance. They provide the usual playgrounds, ball fields, tennis courts, picnic shelters, and concessions. Some have fitness or short walking trails.

Lake and River Access areas provide water-based sports at Lake Norman, Mountain Island Lake, and Lake Wylie. Six aquatic parks serve the metropolitan area. A flagship facility for aquatic sports is the Mecklenburg County Aquatic Center. It features a world-class swimming and diving pool. A new $7.5 million state-of-the-art indoor water park, Ray's Splash Planet, opened in 2002 and provides family fun and fitness opportunities. Among the historic sites is McIntyre Nature Trail, which passes a pioneer gold mine and Revolu- **849** tionary War site. It is located at 4801 McIntyre Ave, Huntersville, NC 28078; 704-336-3854. Visitors unfamiliar with the city/county should purchase a street/road map and request a free copy of *Mecklenburg County Park and Rec Directory of Facilities* and *Mecklenburg County Greenways* booklet. (USGS Maps: Lake Norman N & S, Mooresville, Mtn. Island Lake, Derita, Harrisonburg, Charlotte W and E, Mint Hill, Midland, Lake Wylie, Fort Hill, Weddington, and Matthews)

Address and Access: Mecklenburg County Park and Rec, 5841 Brookshire Blvd, Charlotte, NC 28216; 704-336-3854 or www.parkandrec.com; fax: 704-336-5472.

Latta Plantation Nature Preserve

The 1,290-acre nature preserve is named for James Latta, merchant and planter, who with his wife, Jane Knox, lived in a handsome Federal-period plantation house in the early nineteenth century. The house, near the Catawba River (Mtn. Island Lake), is restored and open afternoons Wednesday–Saturday (704-875-2312). The preserve also has a nature center (with live native animals and exhibits on the preserve's flora and fauna), equestrian center (with two arenas and 80 permanent stalls) and 13.0 mi of bridle trails, canoe access to the lake, picnic areas (with shelters), the 55-acre Carolina Raptor

850   Center, and hiking trails. Entrance to one of the hiking trails, Beechwood Trail, is at the horse-trailer parking area, the fourth R after entering the preserve. The footpath circles the headwaters of a stream that flows into Beechwood Cove. Tall beech, oak, and poplar are predominant in the 1.1-mi loop. Fragrant honeysuckle and cedar are near the entrance. At the Raptor Center is

851   the 0.3-mi Raptor Trail for viewing live birds of prey, such as eagles, owls, hawks, falcons, and vultures, in a pine forest. The center is open weekends 12:00AM–5:00PM; it is a nonprofit tax-exempt public corporation for rehabilitation, research, and conservation of raptors. (USGS Map: Mtn. Island Lake)

Address and Access: Latta Plantation Nature Center, 622 Sample Rd, Huntersville, NC 28078; 704-875-1391. Carolina Raptor Center Inc, Box 16443, Charlotte, NC 28297; 704-875-6521. Access from the S: At Exit #38 on I-85 in Charlotte, take Beatties Ford Rd (SR-2074) N 7.3 mi to Sample Rd (SR-2125) (opposite Hopewell Presbyterian Church), and go 0.7 mi to the preserve entrance. From the N: Turn off I-77 at Huntersville on Gilead Rd; go W 0.9 mi, turn L on McCoy Rd (SR-2138), and go 1.6 mi to a jct R with Hambright Rd (SR-2117). After 1.7 mi on SR-2117, turn L on Beatties Ford Rd and go 0.8 mi to Sample Rd, R.

852-   *Audubon Trail* (1.0 mi); *Cattail Trail* (1.0 mi)
853   **Length and Difficulty:** 2.0 mi, easy

Trailhead and Description: From the picnic area parking lot, locate the central signboard on a paved route. For the Audubon Trail go L, and enter the woods on a trail of natural turf. At 0.2 mi is a scenic area of the lake. Curve around a peninsula (a side trail L leads to a gazebo) and reach a fork at 0.3 mi.

(A turn R leads 0.3 mi on a spur trail through a dense grove of young hard-woods, papaw, and grapevine to a floating dock and boat-access parking lot. Backtrack.) The L fork is a return to the picnic area after another 0.2 mi. From the signboard follow the paved route R, pass the rest rooms, and enter the forest to the Cattail Trail. After 0.1 mi, turn R at a fork on a treadway of wood chips into a mixture of sweet gum, Virginia pine, and cedar. Muscadine grapes hang from some of the trees and yellow senna borders open areas. After the trail makes its final turn, L, at 0.6 mi, there is a side trail, R, to the tip of the peninsula where a large rock faces the lake. Here is a beautiful view of the lake, particularly at sunset. Complete the loop by passing a pier at the picnic area.

McAlpine Creek Park and Greenway

The 350-acre McAlpine Creek Park and Greenway was the first purchase for the greenway system. It has mature forests, floodplains, and open meadows along McAlpine Creek. Facilities include soccer fields, picnic areas, and well-designed biking and hiking rails. (USGS Maps: Charlotte East, Mint Hill)

Address and Access: Park District Supervisor, McAlpine Creek Park and Greenway, 8711 Old Monroe Rd, Charlotte, NC 28212; 704-568-4044. The park is in SE Charlotte, near Matthews and between Independence Blvd (US-74) and Sardis Rd. If in Matthews, take John St W (which becomes Monroe Rd) and go NW 5.0 mi to the Seaboard RR overpass, R. If downtown, take East 7th St (which becomes Monroe Rd) SE 7.3 mi to the above address, L.

McAlpine Creek Greenway (3.1 mi); *Cottonwood Trail* (1.0 mi round-trip); *McAlpine Creek Nature Trail* (1.7 mi round-trip)   **854-856**

Length and Difficulty: 4.7 mi combined and round-trip, easy

Trailhead and Description: At the parking area (N of the RR bridge) follow the signs to McAlpine Creek Greenway (a bikeway for bikers and hikers), R of the soccer field. Cross a weir at McAlpine Creek, R, and go under the RR at 0.2 mi. Pass under the Monroe Rd bridge, downstream, where the trail becomes compacted pit gravel in an open meadow. At 0.9 mi a paved jct, R, is an access trail that crosses McAlpine Creek on a concrete weir. (Ahead, McAlpine Creek Greenway goes another 1.0 mi to Sardis Rd, and en route passes through a marsh.) On the access trail it is 0.2 mi to Tara Dr. Along the way, R, after 125 yd. is Cottonwood Trail, and after another 120 yd., L, is the trailhead of McAlpine Creek Nature Trail. The Cottonwood Trail is a 0.5-mi interpretive path through a floodplain dominated by large cottonwood trees. (Plans are to extend the trail to Monroe Rd.) The McAlpine Creek Nature

Trail is a footpath through tall sycamore, cottonwood, elm, sweet gum, and oak. A 300-yd. boardwalk covers a low area. Wildflowers, raccoon, squirrel, and owl are part of the preserved area. The trail ends at the McAlpine Creek bank at 0.9 mi. Backtrack.

McDowell Park and Nature Preserve

The preserve is named in honor of John McDowell, a leader of the county's recreation program in the 1960s and 1970s. The initial rolling land on the E side of Lake Wylie was a 150-acre gift to the county from the Crescent Land and Timber Corp, a subsidiary of Duke Power Co, in 1976. Now with 1,108 acres, the preserve is among the county's largest; it is open year-round. It has a nature center that emphasizes natural history with exhibits and hands-on nature displays. Activities include camping (full service), fishing, picnicking, hiking, and boating (rentals also). (A hiker symbol is on the park's entrance sign, and another sign on the main road cautions vehicular traffic that hikers have the right-of-way—a distinctive characteristic of the preserve.) The preserve is also good for birders; more than 85 species of birds have been catalogued. All the trails can be hiked from the nature center, either directly by access trails, or by connecting trails. (USGS Map: Lake Wylie)

Address and Access: McDowell Park Nature Center, 15222 York Rd, Charlotte, NC 28278; 704-588-5224. From the jct of I-77 and Carowinds Blvd, go on the blvd for 2.4 mi. Turn L on NC-49 and go 4.2 mi to the preserve entrance, R.

857-
865   *Creekside Trail* (1.2 mi round-trip); *Sierra Trail* (0.3 mi); *Four Seasons Trail* (0.4 mi); *Pine Hollow Trail* (0.9 mi); *Cedar Ridge Trail* (0.5 mi); *Cove Trail* (0.8 mi); *Shady Hollow Trail* (0.6 mi); *Kingfisher Trail* (0.9 mi); *Chestnut Trail* (1.2 mi)

Length and Difficulty: 6.4 mi combined and round-trip, easy

Trailhead and Description: Park at the nature center parking area and enter the trail network on the L side of the nature center. Immediately reach jct L with the Pine Hollow Trail, and R with the Sierra Trail. (The Sierra Trail is a sensory-interpretive loop on a hillside of hardwoods. From its loop is a connector trail to the Chestnut Trail.) If taking the Pine Hollow Trail, descend gradually 0.3 mi to a parking area and reach jct, L, with the Cove Trail. Turn R on a wide paved trail, cross a bridge over Porter Branch, and go upstream to follow the looped Four Seasons Trail. (The trail has benches, displays, side trails [one to the water's edge of Porter Branch], wildflowers [including the cardinal flower], and a huge white oak.) Pass a footbridge R and reach jct with the S terminus of Pine Hollow Trail and Creekside Trail. (Pine Hollow Trail crosses the bridge into mixed hardwoods and pine, crosses a marshy area and tributary to Porter Branch, and ascends to connect with the Sierra Trail after 0.5 mi.) At 0.5 mi on the Creekside Trail, is a jct with the Cedar Ridge Trail, L. (The Cedar Ridge Trail ascends slightly to pass under a power line at 0.1 mi. Ahead is a kudzu path and a forest of cedar, pine, and some large oaks near former homestead sites. Running cedar and periwinkle are ground cover. Pass a deep ravine, R, and descend to rejoin the loop end of the Creekside Trail at 0.6 mi.) To continue on the Creekside Trail, cross the footbridge, R, ascend to pass under the power line, and descend to the creek where the trail forks for a loop at 0.8 mi. If going L, cross the branch on a footbridge and go upstream to a jct L with the Cedar Ridge Trail at 1.0 mi. Continue upstream through a beautiful forest of tall hardwoods, redbuds, and spring wildflowers such as trillium and bloodroot. Curve around a steep slope to rejoin the creekside at 1.3 mi. Backtrack to the parking area at the Cove Trail, or return L to the nature center.

The Cove Trail begins downstream at the Four Seasons Trail parking area and follows a slope on a well-graded trail. At 0.2 mi, approach Porter Cove in an area of wild ginger, ironwood, and sugar maple. Follow the waterfront to a peninsula ridge and a paved road. Turn R on the road and descend through the L corner of the picnic area to end the Cove Trail at 1.0 mi. Continue ahead and after 75 yd. is a jct L with the Shady Hollow Trail. (The Shady Hollow Trail is a 0.6-mi access route through a mixed forest to the nature center.) Follow ahead 0.3 mi on the Kingfisher Trail to the rest rooms, another picnic area, gazebo on the edge of Lake Wylie, and pedal-boat dock.

Continue the Kingfisher Trail near the rest rooms and follow it to cross a gravel road. At 0.2 mi is a jct with a connector to Chestnut Trail. If going R, cross a footbridge (where a R turn is an access trail to the campground), turn L, and at 0.7 mi is a jct with an access R. (It is a 0.1-mi spur to the campground information station.) At 0.9 mi is a jct R with a connector trail to the nature center. The Chestnut Trail, among beech, oak, dogwood, and hickory, curves L and descends to rejoin its access at the gazebo for a total of 1.6 mi. (The 0.2-mi connector trail to the nature center from the Chestnut Trail crosses the main road and descends to the Sierra Trail for a return to the nature center.)

Reedy Creek Park and Nature Preserve

Situated in the central NE of the county, this remarkable park/preserve is near the Cabarrus County line. The park has 116 acres with recreational facilities and 727 acres for a natural environment of forests, lakes, streams, and open spaces. Its facilities, open daily, include picnic shelters, ball courts, a nature center (with exhibits, classrooms, and many educational programs), nature gardens, playgrounds, and a fishing pier. Hiking trails are described ahead.

Address and Access: Reedy Creek Park and Nature Preserve, 2900 Rocky River Rd, Charlotte, NC 28215; 704-598-8857 or www.parkandrec.com/nature. From I-85, NE of the city limits, take Exit 42 NE to the jct of US-29/NC-49 for a L (N). After 2.0 mi, turn R on Rocky River Rd and drive 2.2 mi to sign and entrance, R. (If driving S on I-85, take Exit 45 [Harris Blvd] and go E 0.3 mi to US-29; turn R and after 1.0 mi, turn L onto Rocky River Rd.)

866-872 *Dragonfly Pond Trail* (1.0 mi); *Umbrella Tree Trail* (1.0 mi); *Big Oak Trail* (1.0 mi); *Sassafras Trail* (0.6 mi); *Sierra Loop Trail* (1.5 mi); *Robinson Rockhouse Trail* (0.5 mi); *South Fork Trail* (0.25 mi)

Length and Difficulty: 5.9 mi (not counting backtracks), easy to moderate

Trailhead and Description: All trails are part of a connecting system for making loops (except the linear Robinson Rockhouse Trail). A map from the Nature Center is recommended. There are many unnamed trails that connect with the picnic areas and athletic fields and S to another picnic area where contact can be made with the named loop trails. The third area with parking space is farther S at the Nature Center where they are described clockwise for continuity. Follow the graveled green legend Dragonfly Pond Trail from the parking lot to Dragonfly pond. At the dam, turn L for longer loops or stay R for a return to the parking lot. If heading L, reach jct with black legend Sassafras Trail, which leads to picnic site #6. Continuing R on undulating trails in hardwood and pine forests, reach jct with yellow legend Sierra Loop Trail, the group's longest and most remote route (1.5 mi.). From there, connect with Robinson Rockhouse Trail (1.0 mi round-trip), a historic location where archaeologists think it may have been constructed in 1790. After backtracking to the Sierra Loop Trail, turn L, then L again to follow the short South Fork Trail. After 0.25 mi is a jct with red legend Umbrella Tree Trail. A turn R is the shortest route back to the parking lot; heading L, cross a number of Reedy Creek tributaries. At a jct of blue legend Big Oak Trail, the shortest way back the parking area is R for 0.4 mi. Turning L will make the hike back about 1.0 mi.

Greenway Systems

873-875 Other greenway systems (in addition to McAlpine Creek Greenway) are Little Sugar Creek Greenway, which has completed 1.1 mi of Upper Little Creek

Greenway and 1.3 mi of Lower Little Creek Greenway. The former can be accessed at the jct of Davidson St and Parkwood Ave E across the creek to a parking lot in Cordelia Park. From here the greenway follows Sugar Creek S to Alexandria Park at Alexander St and 16th St. The latter greenway is from Queens Rd through Freedom Park to Princeton Ave. Little Sugar Creek Greenway will eventually be 15 mi to meet SC trail efforts at the state line.

Mallard and Clark's Creek Greenway (3.6 mi) is NE of the city. Parking is **876** provided for Clarks Creek Greenway at Mallard Creek Elementary School off of Colvard Parkway. The greenway is NW to Fair Lea Dr and SE 3.5 mi (toward downtown to a jct with Mallard Creek Greenway at the confluence of the streams). Mallard Creek Greenway goes E and W. To the E, it extends to University Research Park (on the W side of I-85 S to W.T. Harris St. Plans are prepared to extend the Mallard Creek Greenway to the UNC-C campus, Mallard Creek Rec Area, and the Blockbuster Pavilion at the jct of US-29 and I-485.

McMullen Creek Greenway is in the SE corner of the county. Trailhead **877** access parking is on the S side of the 3000 block of Pineville-Matthews Rd (NC-51). (Across the road on the N side is McMullen Creek Market.) Follow the 1.5 mi McMullen Creek Greenway downstream and parallel to the creek. There are four side trails to residential areas along the way. Pass under I-485 and soon reach jct with the 2.2 mi Lower McAlpine Creek Greenway. Continue on it to **878** parallel upstream on McAlpine Creek. Pass under I-485 and conclude the route at Johnson St Backtrack, or go 1.5 mi L on Johnston St to Pineville-Matthews Rd, L, and parking area. (Plans are to continue the greenway farther NE. (Call 704-336-3854 for updated information, and/or see www.parkandrec.com.)

The 1.8-mi Torrence Creek Greenway follows Torrence Creek from Cedar **879** River Rd W to Bradford Hill N to Gilead Rd. Access is I-77 Exit 23 W on Gilead Rd to Bradford Hill Lane. The 2.0-mi Campbell Creek Greenway is off **880** of NC-24/27 between W.T. Harris Blvd and Central Ave. (Call 704-336-3854 for updated information on Irwin Creek and Six Mile Greenways.) **881-** **882**

Rowan County

This county has two outstanding locations for hikers and nature lovers. The first, Dan Nicholas Park, is described ahead, and the second is Eagle Point **883-** Nature Preserve. For the latter, there are two trails: Plant Loop Trail (0.75 mi, **885** easy) and Goldeneye Trail (1.5 mi, easy). Both exist within 100 acres donated to the county by Land Trust for Central NC. Plans are for more trails after an additional 100 acres is acquired. Preserve is open daily. For more information, contact (toll-free) 866-767-2757. From Dan Nicholas Park, continue E on Bringle Ferry Rd 3.0 mi to cross High Rock Lake, then 2.5 mi to Black Rd, L, to preserve after 0.7 mi.

Dan Nicholas Park

The park has 435 acres, 330 of which were donated to the county by philanthropist Dan Nicholas in 1968. Facilities include fishing and paddle-boating access, full-service camping, picnicking (with shelters), hiking trails, nature center, small zoo, ball fields, and T.M. Stanback Theatre. The park is open daily. (USGS Map: Salisbury)

   Address and Access: Rowan County Parks and Rec, 6800 Bringle Ferry Rd, Salisbury, NC 28146; 704-636-2089 or www.co.rowan.nc.us/parks; fax: 704-636-0947. At the jct of I-85 and E Spencer, take Choate Rd (SR-2125) 1.1 mi E. Turn L on McCandless Rd, which becomes Bringle Ferry Rd (SR-1002) after 0.5 mi. Continue E 4.8 mi to the park entrance, L.

886-   *Persimmon Branch Trail* (2.3 mi); *Lake Trail* (1.0 mi); *Volksmarchers*
888   *Trail* (1.4 mi)

   Length and Difficulty: 4.7 mi combined, easy

   Trailhead and Description: From the concession stand at the dam, walk to the opposite side of the lake and turn R at 0.2 mi on the Persimmon Branch Trail. Follow the 32 interpretive markers that identify trees such as oak, pine, ash, elm, and hornbeam, as well as moss and fern. Cross Persimmon Branch at 0.4 mi. turn L, and begin the return loop at 1.0 mi. From the dam the Lake Trail circles the lake along its edge through a picnic area and large campground. The lake has a large variety of ducks and other waterfowl. To hike the Volksmarchers Trail, begin from the campground store and make a loop.

Union County

Cane Creek Park

This is one of the state's largest county-owned natural environment parks; it has 1,050 acres (including a 350-acre lake). It has a large family-oriented campground (full svc), a group camp, a primitive tent camping area, and a camp store. In addition to camping, there is picnicking (with shelters); fishing (a trophy largemouth bass lake with bluegill and crappie); mountain biking; horseback riding; boating (also rentals for sailboats, canoes, pedal-boats and rowboats); and lake swimming. Almost at the South Carolina state line, the park was constructed as a joint project by the county and the US Soil Conservation

Service for recreation, watershed protection, and flood control of Cane Creek. The park is open year-round, and a small entrance fee is charged for each car or other vehicle. A fee is also charged for riding horses or bicycles. The park has about 10.9 mi of multi-use trails. Although pedestrians may use the trails, the only exclusive pedestrian trails are marked with yellow blazes and located in recreational and camping areas. Horse trailers must be parked in the gravel lot at the ball field, and equestrians are not permitted to ride along roadways, picnic areas, or in family camping areas. All trails interconnect (may be unnamed) and are color coded. A 3.4-mi loop blazed red is located on the day-use side of the park. An orange-blazed and blue-blazed trail provide shortcuts if the hiker wishes to reduce the distance. A 1.5-mi red-blazed loop and a 1.8-mi green-blazed loop are on the campground side of the park. A 3.2-mi purple-blazed trail connects the trails on the day-use side of the park to the campside trails. All trail users must enter the park on the day-use side, obtain permits, and pay fees before accessing trails. (USGS Map: Unity)

Address and Access: Cane Creek Park, 5213 Harkey Rd, Waxhaw, NC 28173; 704-843-3919 or www.co.union.nc.us; fax: 704-843-4046. In E Waxhaw on NC-75, take Providence Rd (SR-1117) S 6.7 mi (crossing NC-200 at 5.8 mi) to Harkey Rd (SR-1121), turn L, and go 0.8 mi to park entrance R. (Providence Rd crossing is 11.0 mi S of Monroe on NC-200.)

Wilkes County
Park at River's Edge
This scenic park offers an old 1.0-mi airport runway and a grassy plain available for ball games. A rock-dust trail connects the riverside area and the runway. From the parking lot, the 2.0-mi easy River's Edge Trail follows a loop through a grassy field to the bank of the Yadkin River, where it curves L. It then follows the river among shady sycamore, river birch, and walnut. After 1.0 mi, it curves L to reach the old runway at 1.2 mi for another L and returns to the parking area.

889

Address and Access: From jct of US-421 Byp and NC 268 (River St) drive 0.7 mi SW to Stokes St and turn R near the James Wellborn historical marker and the E end of Wilkes County Industrial Park. After 0.2 mi turn L onto the old runway. After 0.1 mi park near trail, R. Wilkes County Parks and Rec, 110 North St, Wilkesboro, NC 28697; 336-651-7355; fax: 336-651-7344.

Chapter 12, Section 2

County Parks and Recreation Areas: Eastern Half of the State

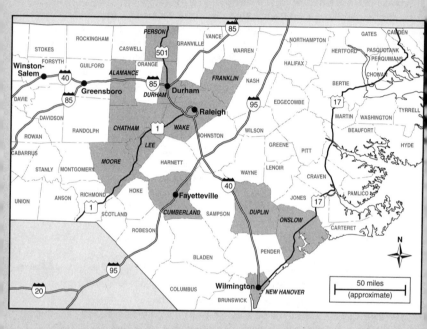

430

Introductions to Trail Areas

The following counties in the eastern half of the state includes some of the central (Piedmont) region and all of the coastal region. They are listed in alphabetical order to conform to west to east in the text.

SECTION 2: EASTERN HALF OF THE STATE
Alamance County
Cedarock Park

The 414-acre park contains the Cedarock Park Center (for conferences and workshops in the Paul Stevens homestead); Cedarock Historical Farm (1830s); ropes obstacle course, horseshoe courts; disc golf course; basketball courts; picnic area; playgrounds; fishing; horseback-riding trails; walk-in campsites (primitive with permits); and hiking trails. The trails are color-coded and create interconnecting loops. There is also a mountain-bike trail that begins at picnic shelter #3. The park is open year-round. (USGS Map: Snow Camp)

Address and Access: Alamance County Rec and Parks Dept, 217 College St, Graham, NC 27253; 336-570-6760 or 336-570-6759; fax: 336-570-6358. From the jct of I-85/40/NC-49 in Burlington (Exit #145A from the W, #145 from the E), go 6.0 mi S on NC-49 to a jct with Friendship-Patterson Mill Rd, and turn L. Go 0.3 mi to Dean Coleman Rd, L. The park office is on the L approximately 1.0 mi from Friendship-Patterson Mill Rd.

890-
895
Cedarock Trail (2.2 mi); *Ecology Trail* (0.5 mi); *Nature Trail* (0.8 mi); *Green Trail* (0.13 mi); *Red Trail* (0.16 mi)

Length and Difficulty: 3.9 mi combined, easy; hiking only

Trailhead and Description: From the picnic area, begin at shelter #3 at the trail signboard. (To the R is white-blazed Mountain Bike Trail.) Follow the yellow-blazed Cedarock Trail and descend to cross a narrow footbridge over Rock Creek at 0.1 mi in a meadow. Enter the forest and reach jct with brown-blazed Ecology Trail, L, that runs jointly with Cedarock Trail to 0.4 mi where it turns L to complete its loop. To the R is blue-blazed Nature Trail. If following it, look for Green Trail to the R after a few yards; Green Trail makes a short curve among fern, wild azalea, and rock formations beside a cascading stream. Turn L and return to Nature Trail. (In the short distance between the trailheads Green Trail, Nature Trail intersects with the western trailhead of Red Trail, a connector.) Continue upstream on Nature Trail and pass through an oak/hickory forest among scattered pine. Ferns, hepatica, and wild orchid are prominent near the stream. At 0.4 mi, leave the scenic stream and ascent gently over a ridge. Reach jct with Red Trail to a walk-in campsite at 0.6 mi, then cross a small footbridge and rejoin Cedarock Trail at 0.7 mi. If heading L, approach a stream to rock-hop and reach jct with Ecology Trail for a return to the signboard. If continuing to the R on Cedarock Trail, leave the forest, cross through a meadow near a tent campground, and reach an old mill dam, L. Cross Equestrian Trail and a bridge at Elmo's Crossing. Enter a meadow at 2.0 mi, cross a bridge, and return to the parking lot at 2.2 mi. **896**

Cumberland County
Lake Rim Park

The 30-acre park has lighted outdoor facilities that include fields, courts, picnic areas, playgrounds, a visitor information center, and hiking trails. Three short trails connect the facilities: Border Trail (0.3 mi), North Sports Field Trail (0.2 mi), and Spring Crossing Trail (0.1 mi). The Wetlands Trail (0.1 mi) is accessed from the parking lot near the playground. An interpretive trail and ADA accessible, it has 50 markers on the route and passes the unique Pine Tar Kiln, which is planned for restoration. At the end of the boardwalk in a marsh is an observation deck of Bone Creek. The park is open daily, except major holidays. **897-900**

Address and Access: Cumberland Parks and Rec, 2165 Wilmington Highway, Fayettevelle, NC 28306; 910-321-6505 or 910-864-3882. In W Fayetteville at the jct of US-401Byp and US-401Bus, go W on US-401 (Old Raeford Rd) 3.3 mi to park, L (across from Lake Rim).

Duplin County
Cabin Lake County Park

The park is 15 mi E of historic Kenansville, the county seat and famous Liberty Hall Plantation and the home of the prestigious Kenan family. The park has a full-service campground, a beach for swimming, piers for fishing, picnic areas, and the 2.4-mi Cabin Lake Trail. From the parking lot, R, after entry, follow the trail sign counterclockwise to cross the dam and curve L from the spillway. In an open area with lake breezes are orange sedum, yellow jasmine, and purple passion at 0.5 mi. Pass a deck, enter a forest, and cross a bridge in a cove. With the pine and oak are bay trees. At 1.2 mi are impressive views from the lake to end at arched bridges near the parking lot at 2.4 mi. The park is open daily April through October and weekends November through March. **901**

Address and Access: Duplin County Parks and Rec, P.O. Box 950, Kenansville, NC 28349; 910-296-2335; fax: 910-296-2107, or Cabin Lake Park, 220 Cabin Lake Rd, Pink Hill, NC 28572; 910-298-3648. Access is 5 mi N of Beulaville on NC-111 and 5.8 mi S of Kornegay on NC-111.

Franklin County
Franklinton Area County Park

This 25-acre park has lighted ball fields, group picnic shelters and individual picnic facilities, a large playground, a lighted all-weather track and walk-
902 ways, and the Running Cedar Trail. To access the 0.4 mi nature trail park inside, head to the park entrance and descend to cross a footbridge. Continue uphill at the loop jct and pass through a carpet of dense running cedar. On the loop's descent among tall hardwoods, there are streamside spring wild-flowers and ferns.

Address and Access: Franklin County Parks and Rec, 1638 M.C. Wilder Rd, Louisburg, NC 27549; 919-496-6624; fax: 919-496-7656. On NC-56 in E Franklinton, turn N on Burlington Mill St and cross the old RR track. Turn L on Mason St, then immediately R on Second St to stop sign at park entrance.

Lee County
San-Lee Park

The park is composed of 160 acres of forest, lakes, old waterworks, trails, pic-nic areas, family (RV) and group campgrounds. There is also an amphitheatre, boat launch (and rentals), volleyball court, and other rec facilities. All the trails are well designed and maintained. The park is open year-round; for more information, contact 919-776-6221. (USGS Map: Sanford)

Address and Access: Parks and Rec Dept, Box 698, (225 S. Steele St) Sanford, NC 27330; 919-775-2107; fax: 919-775-1531. At the jct of US-1Bus and Charlotte Ave (US-421/NC-87/42), take Charlotte Ave E 1.2 mi to Grapeviney Rd (also called San-Lee Dr, SR-1509) and turn R. After 2.2 mi, turn R on Pumping Station Rd (SR-1510) and go 0.6 mi to park entrance, R.

903- *Muir Nature Trail* (1.1 mi); *Gatewood Trail* (0.8 mi); *Hidden Glen*
906 *Loop Trail* (0.2 mi); *Thoreau Trail* (0.9 mi)

Length and Difficulty: 3.0 mi combined, easy

Trailhead and Description: From the parking lot by Miner's Creek, cross the bridge, turn R, and follow the Muir Nature Trail signs into the woods (there is a choice of an upper or lower loop). At 0.5 mi, turn L at the lake's edge at the steps. Follow through rocks, hard- and softwoods, and wildflowers on the return. Hike a few yards or park at the refreshment stand to hike the other trails. Follow the campground road to Colter amphitheatre signs. Turn R on Gatewood Trail and at 0.3 mi is a jct with Thoreau Trail, R. Turn L and reach jct with Hidden Glen Loop Trail at 0.5 mi. Pass Aldo Leopold Wilderness group campground on the return. The Thoreau Trail begins at the boat launch near the bridge over Moccasin Pond. Cross the bridge and follow the shoreline, L. Cross a bridge over Crawdad Creek and reach jct with Gatewood Trail at 0.6 mi. Return either L (shorter) or R.

Moore County
Hillcrest Park
This park has ball fields, courts, playgrounds, concession stands, and a nature walk (ADA accessible). The 1.5-mi Hillcrest Trail makes a loop through a   **907** long-leaf forest with sparse understory and two foot bridges. Among the wildlife are gray fox and squirrel, deer, opossum, and endangered red-cockaded woodpecker.

   Address and Access: Moore County Parks and Rec, P.O. Box 905 Carthage, NC 28327; 910-947-2504; fax: 910-947-1627. South of Carthage at the jct of US-15/501 and NC-22, go L (S) on NC-22, then L into Hillcrest Park.

New Hanover County
Among the beautiful trails in the Wilmington area is 0.9-mi Summer Rest   **908** Trail. It is a wide asphalt passage through a hardwood forest of oak, maple, holly, sweet gum, and scattered pine. Ostrich ferns and fragrant wax myrtle add to the forest floor landscape. The trail ends at a street cul-de-sac at the bay. Backtrack. Access is from the jct of US-74 and US-17 E 3.2 mi on US-74 (Eastwood Rd) (past Landfall Golf Course) to a small parking area on the L (N) side of the highway (which is 0.3 mi before the Intercoastal Waterway bridge to Wrightsville Beach). Almost W of Wrightsville Beach is a unique trail at the Senior Dept of Aging. There is a paved 0.7-mi Hugh MacRae   **909** Nature Trail that circles a natural pond. It is ADA compliant, crosses a 200-ft. wooden bridge, and offers scenic views of pond and native wildlife. If entering Wilmington on I-40, follow NC-132 (College Rd) into the city, cross US-76 (Oleander Dr), and approach the center at the jct of Shipyard Ave. Another unique trail is 1.5-mi Castle Hayne Park Trail. The nice option is to meander   **910** on a natural ground cover in a forest with a disc-golf course. At the S edge of Castle Hayne on US-117/NC-133, cross a bridge over Prince George Creek and turn L on Parmele Rd. Then turn R on Old Avenue to Castle Hayne Park. (USGS Map: Wrightsville Beach)

Address: New Hanover County Parks Dept, 414 Chestnut St, Wilmington, NC 28401; 910-341-7198; fax: 910-341-7194.

Onslow County

911

Among the parks in Onslow County are two with nature trails. One is Onslow County Pines Park with a 0.4-mi Bicentennial Nature Trail. It is a wide, smooth, carefully designed route through a forest of bay, pine, oak, holly, and small shrubs such as inkberry *(Ilex glabra).* Completed and dedicated in 1976 (with the assistance of Raymond Busbee of East Carolina University), it has 18 interpretive sites. A major unique site is that of plant succession. The beautiful park has ball fields, tennis courts, an arena, and picnic areas with a shelter. From the jct of US-258 and US-17 in Jacksonville, drive 3.0 mi S on US-17 to Onslow Pines Rd (SR-1116). Turn R; go 0.7 mi and turn R.

912

Another park, Hubert By-Pass Park, is at the corner of Hubert Blvd and NC-24, 5.3 mi E on NC-24 from the main entrance to Camp Lejeune Marine Corps Base. After a turn on Hubert Blvd (SR-1745), go 0.3 mi and turn R. The park is clean and well maintained. It has picnic areas, a soccer field, a 0.7-mi jogging trail, and a nature trail. The 0.5-mi Mitchell Swamp Trail begins at the most E parking area. There are 27 interpretive sites with the common name, botanical species name, and descriptions on a permanent sign. After 0.2 mi, reach a rain shelter at the scenic swamp, a major focus point. Eight species of oak are on the trail; other plants include wax myrtle and sweet leaf *(Symplocos tinctoria).*

913

Another impressive place is the 56-acre Stump Sound Park, open daily from 10:00AM to dark. Secluded, it has athletic fields, picnicking, a playground, and the Stump Sound Nature Trail. The trail's double loops are accessible from the first parking lot, L, after park entry. Examine the signboard. The trail, W, crosses a boardwalk, then forks and, on a path of white sand, makes a loop among young loblolly pine, blueberry, and scattered hardwood for 0.4 mi. After returning to the parking lot, cross the road and follow the nature-trail sign with markers of red bay, bamboo brier, and pond pine to exit after 0.2 mi at the playground. At the jct of NC-172 and NC-210, W of Sneads Ferry, go W on NC-172 for 1.0 mi and turn R to park entrance. If going E from US-17 on NC-172, it is 2.9 mi, L.

The 55-acre Onslow Pines Park has the dept administrative office, lighted ball fields and courts, a little league baseball field, senior citizens' outdoor rec area, numerous picnic facilities, playgrounds, a 0.9-mi jogging trail, and the

0.4-mi Pines Park Nature Trail. The trail has 20 interpretive markers about **914** indigenous plants and information on plant succession. From the jct of US-17 and US-258 in Jacksonville, go S on NC-17 for 3.0 mi to Onslow Pines Rd (SR-1116), R. (USGS Maps: Jacksonville S, Hubert)

Address and Access: Onslow County Parks and Rec Dept, 1244 Onslow Pines Rd, Jacksonville, NC 28540; 910-347-5332; fax: 910-347-4492. Access is off NC-172, 1.0 mi W of its jct with NC-210 at Sneads Ferry.

Person County

The Mayo Park is on a penisular of the Mayo Reservoir in the NE corner of Person County. Mill Creek and May Creek, E of Roxboro, are two headwater streams for the 2,800-acre Mayo Lake system. Parts of the Person Game Land surround Mayo Lake. A boat launch is operated by the NC Wildlife Resources Commission. Facilites include RV campsites, platform and primitive tent sites, cabins, picnic shelters, a playground, bath houses, and an amphitheatre. A network of hiking trails make loops within park facilities. Annual events include the Fish for Fun Derby; Canoe and Kayak Festival, tours, nature classes, and Cross County 5K. The park is open year-round. (USGS Map: Roxboro). (The county has paved and lighted walking tracks at eight county athletic facilities: Allensville; Bethel Hill; Bushy Fork; Helena; Hurdles Mills; Mt. Tirzah; Olive Hill; and Sansbury. Each track is about 0.3 mi. Contact the county office for more details and calendars of events.)

Address and Access: Person County Parks and Rec. Dept., 425 Long Ave., Roxboro, NC 27573; 336-597-7806 (park office) or www.personcounty.com; 336-597-1755 (main office); fax: 336-597-1754. If leaving N Roxboro from US-501, drive NE on NC 49 for 9 mi to Neals Store Rd, L. (It is 0.7 mi farther NE on NC-49 to Triple Springs and another 5.5 mi to the Virginia state line at Virginia and NC-96.) On Neals Store Rd pass the main park entrance and park at the NW corner of the boat launch parking area for access to the trail system.

Lake View Trail (0.3 mi); *Wild Turkey Trail* (0.5 mi); *Bridge Trail* **915-** *Loop* (0.25 mi); *Eagle Trail* (0.2 mi); *Red Tail Hawk Trail* (1.9 mi); **922** *Beaver Trail* (1.1 mi); *Rocky Trail* (0.9 mi); *Sappony Spring Trail* (0.1 mi)

Length and Difficulty: 5.35 mi combined (including backtrack of Sappony Spring Trail), easy to moderate

Trailhead and Description: All trails are well designed with wraparound color blazes on the trees, and numerous educational markers about plants and animals. Begin at a display sign near a rest room at the boat launch parking area. Follow direction for Lake View Trail loop and Bridge Trail loop. The forest has hardwoods of oak, yellow poplar, sweet gum, hornbeam, holly, and pine. At the E end of the parking area choose either direction of the Eagle Trail loop. A family cemetery is on the side nearest the parking area.

To connect with other trails cross the main park road to the 0.2 -mi lavender-blazed Eagle Trail. It descends into a hollow of tulip poplar and ground cedar before ascending to cross a park road. (Picnic shelters are to the L.) Connect with the red-blazed Red Tail Hawk Trail, which makes a complete loop S with yellow-blazed Beaver Trail, and N with gray-blue Rocky Trail. If following the Red Tail Hawk Trail, R, descend and cross a footbridge over a stream. At 0.2 mi, pass through a beech grove near the lake, R, park cabins, L. Ground cedar is on a slope and at 0.6 mi is a patch of ebony spleenwort, L. After a clear understory of a hardwood forest, pass an educational sign of the red-tail hawk at 0.8 mi. Pass through scattered wildflowers and wild quinine at a power line at 0.9 mi. A primitive campground is L at 1.4 mi. Cross park office road at 1.0 mi, followed by the brown-blazed Sappony Spring Trail, L. After backtracking, turn L and complete the loop at 1.9 mi. A return to the parking area is another 0,5 mi by using the Eagle Trail and the Wild Turkey Trail.

Wake County

Wake County has three major park areas with pedestrian trails. The newest park, Harris Lake County Park, is located in the SW area of the county. Progress Energy (formerly Carolina Power and Light) owns the lake and the park land. The county leases 680 acres on a peninsula section. It has day-use facilities with bicycle and hiking trails, and a group campground is planned. For more information, contact 919-387-4342. The two other parks are described ahead. In addition, the county is constructing and maintaining 3.7 mi of the American Tobacco Trail, which passes into Wake County from Chatham County. (For more information, see chapter 13 for Durham).

Address: Harris Lake County Park, 2112 County Park Dr, New Hill, NC 27562.

Blue Jay Point County Park

This park is leased on property owned by the Corps of Engineers for Falls Lake. Located on a peninsula, it has ball fields, a playground, picnic areas, a lodge, and an environmental-education center. The latter was established

school visits and training programs. Part of the Falls Lake Trail (also part of the Mountains-to-Sea Trail) passes around the park's lake boundary (see chapter 9). Short connector trails Blue Jay Point Trail (0.2 mi); Sandy Point **923-** Trail (0.2 mi); Laurel Trail (0.2 mi); and a paved trail for the physically dis- **925** abled descend to meet the 3.1-mi Falls Lake Trail.

Address and Access: Blue Jay Point County Park, 3200 Pleasant Union Church Rd, Raleigh, NC 27614; 919-870-4330. Access is off Six Forks Rd, 1.5 mi S from its jct with NC-98 and 1.5 mi N from its jct with Possum Track Rd. Wake County Parks and Rec, Box 550, Suite 1000, Wake County Office Bldg, Raleigh, NC 27602; 919-856-6670.

Lake Crabtree County Park

Bordering I-40 at the W edge of the county, this 212-acre park adjoins 520-acre Lake Crabtree. The park provides picnic areas with shelters, playgrounds, fishing piers, and boat rentals and ramps. It has 0.6-mi Old Beech **926** Nature Trail with markers in a damp area, where boardwalks are among oak, pine, sweet gum, and maple (one with three legs at 0.3 mi.). Access is at the first parking lot, R, after entry to the park. Also here, across the road, is a foot route with switchbacks up the hill to Highland Trail. It has four loops, three **927** of which are L (loop #2 is 0.5 mi, and farther W is loop #3 with 1.3 mi (connecting #2 and #3 is loop #4 for 1.0 mi), and the other is R (loop #1 with 1.3 mi.). Biking is allowed in each of the loops. Three access points exist: (1) off Old Reedy Creek Rd at the dam; (2) in the park road from the open play area; and (3) at the far end of th park as hikers exit the boat launch parking lot. The sound of traffic from I-40 and the Raleigh-Durham International Airport is prominent. The park's longest hiking trail is Lake Crabtree Trail, described below. (USGS Map: Cary)

Address and Access: Lake Crabtree County Park, 1400 Aviation Pkwy, Morrisville, NC 27560; 919-460-3390. Access is from I-40, Exit 285, S on Aviation Pkwy 0.3 mi and turn L.

Lake Crabtree Trail **928**

Length and Difficulty: 5.2 mi, easy to moderate

Trailhead and Description: (Hiking only on this trail.) If parking at the trailhead for the nature trail (the closest to the W trailhead of Lake Crabtree Trail) and entering first the E trailhead, walk E on the main park road for 0.3 mi to the road R to the boat rental and fishing dock. At the first parking lot notice the trailhead and signboard L. At 0.2 mi, cross a footbridge and turn R on the blue-blazed trail. Among the young pine and oak forest pass through redbud, hazelnut, sumac, and witch hazel. At 0.4 mi is an observation deck. Stay near the lake's edge and avoid routes to the L (which connect with the Highland Trail). At 0.8 mi parallel I-40, where cow-itch vine hugs the rocks on the lakeside, and pass through a gated fence at 1.0 mi. Ascend to the top of Lake Crabtree Dam. Here is a signboard of information and to the L is a gate at Old Reedy Creek Rd. (Access to Old Reedy Creek Rd is off I-40, Exit 287, S on Harrison Ave for 0.4 mi, turn R on Weston Pkwy, go 0.5 mi, turn R, and go 0.8 mi to shoulder parking at the dam.)

929   Continue on the trail by following asphalt-surfaced Black Creek Trail on top of the dam (part of the Cary greenway system). Uplake views are scenic. (At 1.2 mi is a signpost of the 2.5-mi Black Creek Trail. The dam, built in 1987, is part of the Crabtree Watershed Project to create a drainage area of 33,128 acres.) Pass the grassy overflow area, go through a gate, and reach an observation deck for scenic views of the lake at 1.5 mi. At 1.6 mi, L, is an emergency phone and access up the hill to an IBM building, part of the Research Triangle Park. Watch for a sudden turn R leaving the paved trail (may be a white blaze instead of blue) at 1.8 mi. (The Black Creek Trail continues upstream, underneath Weston Pkwy, on its meandering route to exit at West Dynasty Dr, off N Harrison Ave. See Cary in chapter 13.)

Cross Black Creek footbridge and begin to ascend and descend along the S edge of the lake. On a narrow treadway in and out of coves and past close points to the lake are large hardwoods with buckeye (a species in alluvial wood and swamp forests), lavender monarda, and false foxglove. Cross a wet area at 2.6 mi, enter an easement with a thin passage through grasses and shrubs, and at 3.2 mi use the cement footing for a passage through a swamp. Here are cattails, willows, and a cacophony of frogs. Reach Evans Rd at 3.4 mi and walk on the narrow trail at the base of the road shoulder. Cross a steel arched footbridge over Crabtree Creek at 3.6 mi and turn R (though there may not be signs or blazes for direction). Stay R on an easement, perhaps seeing blue blazes near the lake, and pass through a swampy area to exit at Aviation Pkwy, near an undeveloped parking area at 4.6 mi. Turn R across the causeway and reenter the forest at the edge of the shoulder railing at 5.0 mi. Poison ivy is prominent in the woods. Enter a field of tall grasses and shrubs (wet after rains), then approach a manicured lawn of the park. Complete the loop at the Old Beech Nature Trail parking lot at 5.4 mi.

Chapter 13

Municipal Parks and Recreation Areas

*Every urban transportation plan should
put the pedestrian at the center of proposals.*
—Lewis Mumford

More than 160 cities and towns in the state have departments of parks and recreation. Some towns whose boundaries join have formed a joint department, and other cities have teamed with the counties for financial reasons and cooperative services. A few cities are continuing with their long-range master plans for greenway systems that will not only serve the inner city but connect with other cities and into the counties. An example is the Raleigh/DurhamChapel Hill/Cary/Research Triangle greenway plan, influenced strongly by a citizens' group, the Triangle Greenways Council. Winston-Salem has a plan to connect with other towns and counties. Other cities with plans are Charlotte/Mecklenburg County and High Point/Jamestown/ Greensboro/Guilford County. Urban trails are usually multiple-use for walking, jogging, biking, and in-line skating. They frequently follow streams, city utility routes, nonmotorized roads, recreational parks, and historic areas. The urban trails provide opportunities for appreciating the city's heritage and culture at a relaxed pace, for meeting neighbors, and for physical and spiritual health. Urban walking clubs are being organized, and books and magazines on urban trails are increasing. "Trails for day use must be developed in and near urban areas," stated the National Park Service in 1986 when it was developing a national trails system plan.

On the following pages are examples of diverse trails whose treadways is city soil, asphalt, brick, and concrete that lead into history and remind us that urban trails are heritage trails. Although hundreds of paved and unpaved walkways across the state in cities and towns are called "trails," many of them are unnamed. They may serve only as connectors in campgrounds or athletic areas or for fitness or tract. Unless such "trails" have names or signs or have scenic, geographical, or botanical significance, they are unlikely to be described here. Some town rec departments have proposed or planned parks with trails. Examples are Benson Parks and Rec, P.O. Box 69, Benson, NC 27504; 919-894-5117 (Benson Middle School); Fletcher Parks and Rec, 4005 Hendersonville Rd, Fletcher, NC 28732; 828-687-0751 (proposed master plan for a greenway system from community park to downtown); Hope Mills Parks and Rec, 5770 Rockfish Rd, Hope Mills, NC 28348; 910-424-4500 (Little Rockfish Creek); Kernersville Parks and Rec, P.O. Box 728, Kernersville, NC 27285; 336-992-0804; Wendell Parks and Rec, P.O. Box 828, Wendell, NC 27591; 919-366-2266 (proposed greenway network with Zebulon); Zebulon Parks and Rec, 202 E Vance St, Zebulon, NC 27597; 919-269-8265.

The following town and city parks host "nature trails" that have special scenic or educational value.

- *Carrboro:* At the jct of NC-54 Byp and West Main St (at Carrboro Plaza Shopping Center), go W 0.7 mi on NC-54 and turn R into Carrboro Community Park (with lighted facilites). Walk partly into the forest on a 0.4-mi nature trail that circles the lake, home to duck, geese, and songbirds (919-918-7364).

- *Clayton:* On US-70 in Clayton, take Amelia Church Rd, S, 1.2 mi to entrance, L, of Clayton Community Park. From the parking area near a playground, follow the paved trail to a scenic 0.5-mi nature trail that circles a small lake. There are markers identifying some of the forest's trees. Clayton's Parks and Rec has planned more trails to an amphitheatre and perhaps to a community greenway (919-533-5777).

- *Columbia:* If going E on US-64, cross the Scuppernong River bridge, turn R onto Ludington Dr, and park R at Tyrell County Visitor Center (252-796-1996 or www.albermarle-nc.com/columbia). Walk out to the waterfront boardwalk where the sunset views are spectacular. (This boardwalk trail connects with the 0.5-mi Scuppernong River Interpretive Trail of the Pocosins Lakes NWR described in chapter 9.)

- *Lexington:* On I-85, Exit 94 (driving S), turn R onto Raleigh Rd to a L turn onto Paul Beck Rd to Finch Park. There is a scenic walk around the lake and a "stroll through the nature trail" (336-248-3960).

- *Madison/Mayodan:* On S Second St in Mayodan is a 0.25-mi crushed-stone walkway which is available to all, including the physically disabled and senior citizens (336-548-9572).

Municipal Parks and Recreation Areas: Western Municipalities

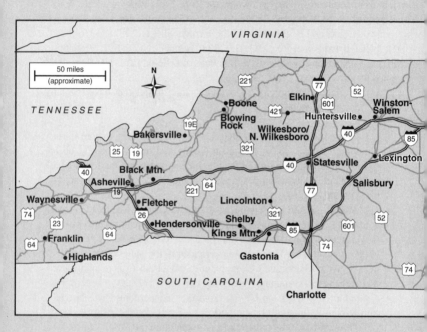

Introductions to Trail Areas

Cities are listed alphabetically to conform to the order they appear in the text.

SECTION 1: WESTERN MUNICIPALITIES
Asheville (Buncombe County)

930 The state's largest city in the mountains has a downtown walk through time on the distinguished Asheville Urban Trail. The 1.7-mi sidewalk trail has thirty stations divided into five periods of history: Frontier Period (1784–1880), Guilded Age (1880–1930), Times of Thomas Wolfe (1900–1938), Era of Civic Pride and Age of Diversity to current times. Each division has a pink granite symbol in the sidewalks. (For example, there is a horseshoe for the Frontier Period.) Realistic sculptures of people and animals grace the grand passageways among historic buildings and sites. It is a "walk to health, history, and art." The trail is owned by the city and maintained by the city's parks and rec department. Visitors may choose a self-guided tour by picking up a brochure at Pack Place (near the Vance Monument at the Circle in Pack Square), the Asheville Area Arts Council at 11 Biltmore Ave, the Chamber of Commerce at 151 Haywood, or places such as hotels, businesses, or galleries. A guided tour (for a small fee) is available Saturdays at 3:00PM from April through November at the front desk of Pack Place.

Address and Access: For more information and reservations, contact 828-258-0710. The city is also in the process of developing Glenn's Creek Greenway to include Weaver Park. For an update on the progress of this and other greenways, contact the Asheville Area Arts Council, 11 Biltmore Ave, Asheville, NC 28801; 828-258-0710. From I-40, Exit 50, drive N on Biltmore to Pack Square, R. From I-240, Exit 5A, drive S on US-25 to a L on Patton Ave to Pack Place.

French Broad River Parks

931 Asheville Parks and Rec is developing a park system in phases along the French Broad River. For phase I and II, the park has a gazebo, picnic tables, restrooms, and a dog park. There is a 0.5-mi paved greenway loop, French Broad River Trail, on a meadow among shade trees of sycamore, river birch, ash, and honey locust. The system's phase IV park has ball fields, courts, tracks, and two unnamed trails. One is a 0.8-mi linear paved route and the other is a 1.5-mi mulch loop. Plans are to connect the two parks with a riverside greenway.

Address and Access: Asheville Parks and Rec, P.O. Box 7148, Asheville, NC 28802; 828-259-5800; fax: 828-259-5606. Access from I-40, Exit 50, is N on US-25. Descend to cross a bridge and turn L on Meadow Rd. Follow it to the second traffic light and turn L for crossing a bridge over French Broad

River to Amboy Rd. Immediately turn R to park's entrance. To the system's phase IV park, continue on Amboy Rd about 1.0 mi near a split-rail fence and turn L into the park (the location of a former NASCAR speedway). If going E on I-240, turn R at Exit I-C off the ramp to Amboy Rd for a R turn.

Bakersville (Mitchell County)

The county seat, this friendly small town is the state's gateway to famous Roan Mtn. Gardens on NC-261. The town is famed for its Rhododendron Festival, founded by O.D. Calhoun, which is usually held the third week of June. Its 0.3-mi Bakersville Greenway is a classic example of how a short trail can be **932** beautiful. Bordered with flowers, the trail is paved, lighted, and easily accessible to the physically disabled. It parallels clean, clear, and cascading Cane Creek with occasional observation decks. Sycamores and willows provide summer shade. Gracing the trail's S wall are rocks and ferns, a natural spring, and ceramic panels of children's art from the local elementary school. There is an arched bridge and playground. Designed by Joe and Nell Young, the town has now planned another 0.3 mi downstream. (USGS Map: Bakersville)

Address and Access: Town Hall, P.O. Box 53, Bakersville, NC 28705; 828-688-2113. Driving W on NC-226 from Spruce Pine, slow down at the town's edge and park at the sign, L, or continue downstream to a narrow bridge, L, for parking near the new section.

Black Mountain (Buncombe County)

At Lake Tomahawk Park, 0.6-mi Lake Tomahawk Trail circles the lake. Wide **933** and easy, the trail is accessible to the physically disabled. From the picturesque path are views of Black Mtn. range, including the "Seven Sisters." The park also has picnic facilities, senior citizens center, lighted tennis court, and outdoor swimming pool.

Address and Access: Off I-40, Exit 64. Go N on NC-9 to third traffic light at US-70. Turn L, go to second traffic light, turn R on Cragmont Rd; take R fork on Rhododendron Ave to parking lot, L. Black Mtn. Rec and Parks, 101 Carver Ave, Black Mtn., NC 28711; 828-669-2052.

Blowing Rock (Watauga County)

The 2.4-mi round-trip Glen Burney Trail is a scenic, strenuous descent into the **934** Glen Burney Gorge. From the parking lot observe the trail description board, descend into the gorge, cross New Years Creek twice among rhododendron, hemlock, ferns, witch hazel, and wildflowers. At 0.8 mi is an observation deck at Glen Burney Falls. Descend to the falls' base on a rough and sometimes slippery treadway. Descend to the base of beautiful Glen Marie Falls at 1.2 mi. Backtrack. The more-than-100-year-old trail is on property donated to the town in 1906 by Emily Puruden. (USGS Map: Globe)

Address: Blowing Rock Parks and Rec Dept, Box 47, Blowing Rock, NC 28605; 828-295-5222; fax: 828-295-5223. Access is off Main St (US-221) W on Laurel Lane 0.1 mi to Ann L. Cannon Memorial Garden and parking lot, L.

Boone (Watauga County)

Boone is county seat, home to Appalachian State University, and the historic site of an outdoor drama on the life of its namesake, Daniel Boone. Nestled in Boone Creek Valley at 3,266 ft. elev, it is only 1.0 mi E of the Tennessee Valley Divide at the base of magnificent Howard Knob (4,420 ft.). To the E of this enchanting town is South Fork of the New River. On its floodplains is an appealing greenway system. The S access is 1.0 mi off of US-221 (between US-421 and US-321) on State Farm Rd to Hunting Hills Lane L and the Watauga Swim Complex, L. A parking lot is near the basketball court. For the N access turn off of US-421/221 on Daniel Boone Dr for 1.0 mi to turn R on Casey Lane; go 0.1 mi to a parking lot near Humane Society Shelter.

If going downriver from Hunting Hills Lane, walk 0.2 mi to a large parking area for Appalachian State University at a concrete-lane road, R. Cross the
935   river on a covered bridge. Follow the wide asphalt South Fork Trail (for hikers, bikers, skaters, and joggers) through meadows on the R and hardwoods
936   on the riverside, L. At 1.1 mi is a bridge over the river, where Oakwood Trail begins L. (It ascends 0.6 mi up the hill on an old cattle path of a former farm. Its N access is at Oakwood Dr in a residential area. Access here is from US-421 on Forest Hills Dr, then R on Appalachian Dr.) At 1.4 mi pass a historic
937   dam site. Reach jct with proposed Daniel Boone Trail, L, up Rocky Knob Creek. Cross the river again on a bridge at 1.6 mi, turn L, exit from the woods, and arrive at the parking lot at 1.9 mi. A 0.4 addition to the greenway at Hunting Hills Lane is a paved route past the parking lot, across the street to a field and picnic area, and over an arched bridge at Winklers Creek. From there the greenway parallels Winklers Creek to become part of a loop around a meadow at the confluence of East Fork and Middle Fork for another 0.4 mi. Near the scenic streams are locust and wild cherry, tag alder, and wildflowers.

Address and Access: Vehicular access to the loop's parking area is SE on State Farm Rd to a L on Deerfield, then L to the parking area. (USGS Map:

Boone) Planning and Inspections, Town of Boone, 567 W. King St, Boone, NC 28607; 828-262-4540/4560.

Elkin (Surry County)

At Elkin Municipal Park there is 0.8-mi (roundtrip) Big Elkin Nature Trail. **938**
Access to it is from the most NW parking area of the park. First follow the paved walking/jogging trail in the park upstream to W Spring St (NC-268) bridge. Go underneath the bridge, pass rapids and the site of an old dam, L, at 0.3 mi. Follow the curve of Big Elkin Creek and cross a bridge. (Parks and Rec plans to extend the trail for about 3.0 mi upstream. Plans are also for an extension downstrean to Yadkin River for an undetermined distance on the river. Call for an update.) Backtrack. Flora on the trail include sycamore, walnut, cherry, rhododendron, trout lily, and blackberry.

Address and Access: Elkin Rec and Parks Dept, Box 345, Elkin, NC 28621; 336-835-9814; fax: 336-835-8908. Also, Foothills Nature Science Society, Box 124, Elkin, NC 28621. Access from I-77, Exit 82, is W on NC-67 1.6 mi to US-21. Turn R, follow US-21 0.7 mi to a jct L with W Spring St (NC-268) and go 0.8 mi to park, L.

Franklin (Macon County)
Little Tennessee River Greenway

939

This first-class greenway has 3.0 mi completed, another 0.6 mi partially completed, and plans for an additional 2.4 mi. More advanced than any other greenway system in the state's SW corner, it is designed and constructed to parallel the river. It partially follows an old RR bed; it has three major bridges; it has five parking areas, one with a playground another the future home of an amphitheatre; picnic areas, restrooms, resting benches, and a number of markers and kiosks. Day-use only; camping is prohibited. Dogs must be leashed and accompanied by a scooper. This project has been made possible by the town's government, grants, businesses, Friends of the Greenway, Inc., and many volunteers. Most of the names along the trail represent Native American culture.

Trailhead and Description: Begin hiking or bicycling at the downstream trailhead parking lot at Riverview Dr and Arthur Drake Rd. (It is accessible from Bryson City on NC-28 where it turns R at its jct with Riverview Dr.) If approaching from US-23-441, turn onto E Main St to cross the river and turn onto the first R, Depot St Ext. Drive 1.0 mi to the parking area. At a sign, go 130 yd. through Suli Marsh to Morris Trace, a wide trail, R, and named for **940**

Gideon Morris. (To the L is a short spur to view the river [Lake Emory].)
Under a power line, follow the open greenway past marshes and swamps with
cattails, willows, aqueous flowers, tadpoles, frogs, and birds. At 0.6 mi, R, is
a large area of abandoned heavy industrial equipment. (Perhaps the town or
private owners could create a "heavy metal park," similar to farm or timbering museums, for the equipment to be preserved with fresh paint, placed on
gravel or concrete pads, and adorned with descriptive markers.)

Arrive at Big Bear playground, picnic shelter, rest rooms, parking lot, floral garden, and kiosk beside Main St at 1.0 mi. A temporary route continues
by crossing the street then L to cross the river bridge, where a turn R is behind
East Franklin Shopping Center. Go behind Franklin Central Storage building
to enter the forest at 1.3 mi. Cross a bridge over Cat Creek. Ahead are large
sycamores. (Here is a site for a future bridge to span the river, thus avoiding
the traffic of Main/E Main.) Enter a manicured green meadow with a paved
941 loop (Old Airport Trail) among walnut and locust. Pass a gazebo and savor the
perfumed honeysuckle entwined with river cane and infrequent princess trees.
Reach a parking area accessible from Highlands Rd and Fox Ridge. Cross a
bridge over the river at a confluence with the Cullasaja River and arrive at
Tassee Park at 2.0 mi. It has a picnic shelter, a kiosk, rest rooms, and a
942 boat/canoe ramp. The greenway now becomes Tallulah Falls RR Trail,
because this route was that of a former rail line to Cornelia GA.

Across the river is a large timber-processing company. At 2.7 mi, cross the
river on the Nickajack Bridge to the Nikwasi Center (a future amphitheatre).
943 Here is the short Traders Path, named for an early trading post. (Access here
is from US-64-441 at Oak Forest Lane (SR-1702) to Wiggins Rd (SR-1700).
At 2.8 mi, cross over the river again via the arched and covered Nonah Bridge,
an architectural tour de force. Descend on a gravel passage and pass under
944 US-64-441 at 3.0 mi. From here is a future greenway, the Tartan Trail, but currently easy to follow. The trail curves R and goes around the field to hug the
forest line on the R. At 3.5 mi is a scenic view of the confluence of Little Tennessee River, L, and the Cartoogechaye Creek, R. (To the R, the future greenway will follow the creek to Recreation Park at US-23-441.) Backtrack.

Addresses: Macon County Recreation Park, 1288 Georgia Hwy,
Franklin, NC 28734; 828-349-2090; fax: 828-349-2090. Friends of the
Greenway, Inc., 23 Macon Ave, Franklin, NC 28734; 828-369-7331,
frogs@LittleTennessee.org, or www.LittleTennessee.org.

Gastonia (Gaston County)

The city's Parks and Rec Dept provides seven lighted walking/jogging tracks throughout the city. (For safety's sake the city requests no dogs or bicycles on the trails.) Each track is 1.0 mi. In addition, the city has Avon Creek and Catawba **945** Creek Greenway. The 2.2-mi main trail begins at Lineberger Park, travels within the floodplain of Avon and Catawba Creeks, and ends at the Southeast Rec Center on Robinwood Rd. The 10-ft.-wide asphalt trail crosses the creeks several times, underpasses all of the major streets, and is surrounded by a 10-ft. vegetated buffer in most areas. The trail provides a natural connection between older established neighborhoods and multi-family developments, office parks, a school, restaurants, retail shops, the main branch of the Gaston County Public Library, and the Schiele Museum of Natural History.

Address and Access: Gastonia Parks and Rec, P.O. Box 1748, Gastonia, NC 28053, 704-866-6838; fax: 704-842-5104. If approaching from I-85, take New Hope Rd S for 1.1 mi and turn R on Garrison Blvd for 1.5 mi. Parking is at Lineberger Park.

The Schiele Museum of Natural History and Planetarium is a facility of the city of Gastonia. The 28-acre park is an example of how history can be preserved. Habitat settings in the museum show more than 25,000 mounted birds, mammals, and reptiles. The wide, well-groomed, 0.7-mi Trail for All Seasons **946** introduces the visitor to natural and human history through the colonial period. There is a smokehouse, molasses boiler, log cottage, sorghum cane press, mill, and barn. The exceptional trail crosses Kendrick Creek (also known as Slick Rock Branch) twice, and passes 19 markers. The markers indicate the process of forest succession, wildflowers, shrubs, wildlife, and pioneer history.

Address and Access: Schiele Museum of Natural History, 1500 E Garrison Blvd (P.O. Box 953), Gastonia, NC 28054; 704-866-6041. If approaching from I-85, take New Hope Rd S for 1.1 mi, and turn R on Garrison Blvd for 0.7 mi to the 1500 block.

Hendersonville (Henderson County)

Northeast of Jackson Park, a Henderson County park described in chapter 12, is Mud Creek Wetlands Nature Trail. An asphalt surface accessible to all, it is 1.0 **947** mi, of which 235 yd. is boardwalk through a swamp. In an appealing 40-acre preserve, the major emphasis is on environmental education. Unique to the area is the large wood duck population. Other wildlife are teal, owl, hawk, turtle, and chipmunk. Plant species are identified. Dogs must be kept on a leash.

Address and Access: City of Hendersonville, Box 1670, Hendersonville, NC 28793; 704-697-3079. From I-26, Exit 18, go W on US-64 to Duncan Hill St; turn R, go one block, and turn L on 7th Ave E to parking area near Mud Creek.

Highlands (Macon County)

One of the most unforgettable towns in the state, Highlands, the "Land of the Sky," is 4,118 ft in elev. It is encompassed by cool fresh air and water and many magnificent wonders: spectacular waterfalls, rocky overlooks, wilderness whitewater, precious gems, and vascular floral gardens. Its accommodations, dining, fishing, cultural activities, and hiking options make it a desirable place for a vacation. Its nearby USFS trails are described in chapter 2, section 2; and its Sunset Rocks Trail and the Highlands Biological Station in chapter 14. Within the village, Highlands Rec Park is developing a trail between 4th

948 St and Oak St, and the Highlands Greenway Trail is already established.

Like a string of jewels it is from Sunset Rocks to Mirror Lake, partly on clean highways and streets, gravel and earthy roads, and soft pathways. The distance is 2.0 mi unless you include the round-trip 1.4 mi of Sunset Rocks Trail and 1.0 mi of trails at the biological station. If a second car is used to avoid backtracking, follow US-64 W on Main St and descend to Mirror Lake Rd, R. If beginning at Sunset Rocks return to Horse Cove Rd and the Highlands Biological Station at Ravenel Lake. Follow Horse Cove Rd W to Hudson Library, then an art gallery at the corner of Main St and 5th St. Turn R (N) on 5th St and after two blocks turn L on Pine St to the Chamber of Commerce (where you may receive further descriptions of this walk). From here turn R on N 4th St, but watch for a foot trail, L, after crossing Mill Creek. The trail passes behind the Civic Center, crosses the creek again, and comes out on Oak Lane among hemlock and rhododendron. Follow Oak Lane to Raoul Rd, follow it N to an unpaved road to Mirror Lake Rd and Thorne Park. Here are wood duck, mallard, and heron and the end of the hike. (USGS Map: Highlands)

Address and Access: Highlands Park and Rec Dept, Box 460, Highlands, NC 28741; 704-526-3556. Park office is on Cashiers Rd (US-64) W across from Laurel St at Highlands Rec Center.

Lincolnton (Lincoln County)

949 In this historic town, Betty G. Ross Park hosts the 0.5-mi South Fork Nature Trail. It was made possible with donated funds from the Timken Foundation in 1982. The easy and wide loop trail is mainly on a floodplain bend of South Fork of Catawba River. (A primitive campsite is in the loop's center; reservations are required.) Tall oak, green ash, sycamore, and river birch are on the riverside. (A physical-fitness trail adjoins the trail in a grassy meadow.) Access in downtown Lincolnton from the courthouse is W on W Main St (NC-27) and turn L at the first traffic light. Turn R to park off of S Madison St.

The town's 0.4-mi Marcia H. Cloninger Rail Trail is named in honor of **950** the city council member. Constructed and landscaped on an old railroad grade, it was dedicated in 1998. Access is off of E Main St on N Poplar St to parking space in front of the old depot. Walk up R of the depot to turn L on the wide asphalt trail. A granite marker about council member Cloninger is before a tunnel under E Main St. English ivy, kudzu, and planted hardwoods and shrubs line the trail. At 0.2 mi is a 90-yd. spur, L, that ascends to S Poplar St. Cross S Academy St, parallel and active RR grade at 0.3 mi, cross under a bridge, then arrive at the end at S Government St. (Plans are to extend the greenway from here.)

Address: Lincolnton/Lincoln County Rec, P.O. Box 25 (800 Madison St), Lincolnton, NC 28093; 704-735-2671; fax: 704-735-1662.

Salisbury (Rowan County)

The city was founded in 1753 and has a 23-block historic district that is listed in the National Register of Historic Places. It is through this area and 20 other blocks that the Historic Salisbury Trail loop covers 3.9 mi of industrial, com- **951** mercial, and residential historic sites. A national recreation trail, it is a grand tour past tall trees and nineteenth-century architecture. It reflects the pride of the Historic Salisbury Foundation and its dedication to preserve the city's heritage. A map and individual site description can be obtained from the address below. Otherwise, a description of the route and a few buildings is as follows: Begin at the NE corner of N Bank St and S Jackson St (two blocks W of Main St) at the Josephus Hall House, a large antebellum house (1820) with Federal, Greek Revival, and Victorian features. Proceed N on Jackson St to the Rowan Museum (1819), which is open for guided tours. After five blocks, turn L on W Kerr St to Water St R, and to the Waterworks Gallery. Turn R on W Cemetery St one block to Church St, turn L one block, and turn L again on W Franklin St to the Grimes Mill (1896). After two blocks turn L on Fulton St, go six blocks, turn R on W Fisher St, go one block, and then turn L on S Ellis St to the Governor John Ellis House (1851). Go two blocks to the R on Horah

St, go one block, turn R for three blocks on S Fulton St, and turn L on Thomas St. Go three blocks to Main St and turn L. To the R is Military Ave and the Salisbury National Cemetery. (Monuments honor the nearly 5,000 Union soldiers who died here in the Civil War.) Continue N on Main St on wide sidewalks for six blocks (passing such sites as the Empire Hotel and the former courthouse square.) Turn L on W Council St for one block to pass L on S Church St for three blocks (to pass Andrew Jackson's well), and R on N Bank St to the point of origin.

Address and Access: Salisbury Parks and Rec, P.O. Box 4053, Salisbury, NC 28145; 704-638-5291; fax: 704-638-8557. From I-85 jct with US-52 in Salisbury, go NW 1.0 mi to Main St (US-29/70). Continue ahead on W Innes St two blocks and turn L on S Jackson St two blocks to Hall House at 226 S Jackson.

Shelby (Cleveland County)

952   The 3.3-mi urban Historic Shelby Trail. The downtown area reflects architectural history of pre–Civil War, Colonial Revival, and Gothic styles. Additionally, there is the history of one of the state's most powerful political influences, beginning with Max Gardner as governor in 1928 and lasting until the death of US Senator Clyde R. Hoey in 1954 (a former governor).

The walk in Shelby Central Historic District begins at the former Cleveland County Courthouse on S Washington St, and in a counterclockwise route to Marion St at the Colonial Revival home of Governor Hoey. One block N on Sumter St is the Blanton House, an example of Gothic Revival. A return on Marion St includes historic homesites, markets, and commercial places on W Warren and N Lafayette Sts to S Washington St. The walk then follows S Washington St S in a clockwise manner to Gidney St before returning to Courtsquare, covering a total of 38 sites. Landscaped lawns and floral gardens enhance this stimulating walk. (A detailed map is available.)

Information: Historic Shelby Foundation, 704-481-1842. Cleveland County Chamber of Commerce, 200 S Lafayette St, Shelby, NC 28150; 704-487-8521.

Statesville (Iredell County)

953   The 25-acre Lakewood Park has 1.6-mi Lakewood Nature Trail. To access the park for I-40, Exit 150, drive S on NC-115 (North Central St) and turn L onto

Hartness Rd. After 0.3 mi, turn L onto Lakewood Dr and proceed to the parking area. From there, follow the trail signs onto a paved and interconnecting trail system in a forest of oak, pine, and yellow poplar.

There are two trails in Mac Anderson Park. To access the park form I-40, Exit 150, go 0.3 mi S on NC-115 and turn R onto Race St. Cross Ridgeway Ave to enter the park, located on the R at 0.6 mi. From the parking lot near the rest rooms, begin the paved 1.0-mi Mac Anderson Walking Trail at the **954** signboard. If going N and W among large hardwoods and pines, make a sweeping curve and a gentle descent to a footbridge at 0.7 mi for a jct. Take a L to Iredell Memorial Trail, donated by Iredell Memorial Hospital in 1989. **955** On this 1.0-mi paved trail, gradually ascend a serpentine loop on a grassy knoll. After passing through part of a forest, return to the first trail, cross a footbridge, and ascend to the parking lot.

Address: Statesville Parks and Rec, P.O. Box 1111 (Signal Hill Dr), Statesville, NC 28677; 704-878-3429; fax: 704-871-0008.

Waynesville (Haywood County)

This ideal historic town is in a scenic valley N of the Blue Ridge Parkway's Balsam Gap on US-23/74 and S of Lake Junaluska and I-40. Its quality of life is demonstrated in immaculately clean Main St and sparkling business windows. Friendly, cultural, environmentally concerned, and lovers of the outdoors, its people welcome visitors. The town reflects Haywood County's charm and beauty, which has 19 mountain peaks above 6,000 ft., streams for fishing, and forests for multiuse trails. Local citizens have produced the detailed color-coded Haywood County Trail Map, which reveals nearly 50 hiking, biking, equestrian, cross-country skiing, and canoeing trails. In Waynesville, the county seat, is the 6.2-mi Volkswalk. It loops through downtown **956** between historic sites, country club, and residential areas. Additionally, there is 0.5-mi Richland Creek Trail in Recreation Creek Park. The linear 8-ft.-wide **957** trail is part rock dust and pavement for the physically disabled. The paved section leads to a fishing/observation deck with two fishing pads. The trail is also open to bicycles and skates. Other park facilities are ball fields and picnic shelter. Access is off Main St on Vance St toward the Southern Railway line.

Address: Waynesville Parks and Rec Dept, 550 Vance St, Waynesville, NC 28786; 828-456-2031. For additional information on Volkswalk: Tarheel State Walkers, American VolksSport Assoc, Box 15013, Winston-Salem, NC 27113.

Wilkesboro/North Wilkesboro (Wilkes County)

958 These twin towns have nine recreational parks, few of which have walking paths without signs. For example, VFW Trail in North Wilkesboro's VFW Park is suitable for walking and running. The trail goes behind the park building to the Yadkin River and passes between the baseball field and tennis courts to from a loop. Park facilities include rest rooms and a playground. Access to the park form the jct of US-421 Bus and NC-18-268: Drive 0.3 mi E on US-421 Bus, then turn N onto Beech St. Another walk is on the scenic, shady, and

959 linear 1-mi Reddies River Trail. It borders Reddies River among rhododendron, mountain laurel, white pine, and wildflowers. Access is off of US-421 Bus on 13th St for 0.15 mi to park at Riverside Medical Associates.

960 The city also has a Yadkin River Greenway master plan in progress, which is managed by the Yadkin Greenway Council with help from local government and citizens. One section follows Reddies River S to its confluence with Yadkin River, where it turns W. A phase in the plan is to eventually make contact upstream with the Overmountain Victory Trail in W. Scott Reservoir and downstream with Smoot Park in North Wilkesboro. A suggested parking location is as follows: From the jct of US-421 Byp and US-421 Bus at the W side of the Yadkin River Bridge, turn NE on US-421 Bus to West Park Medical Complex and park in the Wellness Center parking lot. Access to the greenway is downstream on the W side Reddies River, then the N side of Yadkin River to a parking area on West Fork Dr. (For more information, contact Yadkin River Greenway Council, 717 Main St [P.O. Box 191], North Wilkesboro, NC 28659; 336-651-8967.)

961 Downtown Wilkesboro has a historic walking tour along Club Creek. the 13 buildings on the Old Wilkes Walking Tour are located on Main and North Sts between Woodland Blvd on the W and Corporation St on E. Among the oldest structures is the Old Wilkes Jail, completed in 1860. (One of the first inmates was Tom Dula [Dooley in the song].) The restored jail is now a museum. Guided tours can be arranged by calling 336-667-3712 or request a brochure at the Wilkes County Courthouse on Main St.

962 The largest and most developed park in the Wilkesboro area is the impressive Cub Creek Park. It is accessed by following Bridge St off of Main St to a parking area near the creek. The park offers picnic shelters, restrooms, and resting benches beside the water. A 1.0-mi loop, Mile Walk Track passes around five ball fields, two playgrounds, and five tennis courts. On the S part of the trail are large sycamore and river birch. For more information, contact 336-667-8804.

Westwood Hill Park has Westwood Hill Nature Trail, a 0.3-mi loop. To **963** access the park, take Westwood Rd off of US-421 Byp for 0.4 mi to West Field, R. After ascending the 0.1 mi, turn R to the parking lot. Walk around the tennis courts to the W side and descend through white pine. After crossing a footbridge, ascend to point of origin. A short 0.1-mi trail, School Street **964** Park Nature Trail is located across the street from Wilkesboro Elementray School. It makes a circle on a hillside of pine and hardwoods. For access, follow NC-268 W off of US-421 Byp. After 1.0 mi, turn L before crossing the bridge over Moravian Creek and drive 0.6 mi to the school's parking lot.

Addresses: Wilkesboro Parks and Rec, 203 W Main St, Wilkesboro, NC 28697; 336-667-8804; fax: 336-838-7616. North Wilkesboro Parks and Rec, P.O. Box 218 (801 Main St), North Wilkesboro, NC 28659; 336-838-3359; fax: 336-838-1779.

Winston-Salem (Forsyth County)

A city and county planning board has established a growth-strategy program that encourages the development of greenway networks for rec and land-use development. An example is the city's major trail system of Salem Lake Trail and Salem Creek Trail at Salem Lake, described below. (A loop extension is proposed at the lake's NE cove of Lowery Creek.)

Other metropolitan trails are at Winston Lake, where an easy 0.7 mi is between the Winston Lake swimming pool parking lot and the picnic shelter. From the swimming pool it passes through a playground and gate to enter a mature forest of pine, oak, and poplar near the creek. At 0.3 mi it passes a physical-fitness sta. (No camping.) Access: From I-40 (Bus), go on US-311 N for 1.9 mi to turn R on Winston Lake Rd. Go 0.2 mi to Waterworks Rd, turn R, and immediately turn L to Winston Lake swimming pool.

The easy 0.8-mi Silas Creek Trail is a wide greenway from the parking lot **965** at Schaffner Park. Access: Off Silas Creek Parkway turn E on Yorkshire Dr for a few yards to the parking lot, R. To the L the trail parallels a stream and Silas Creek Parkway. In a mature forest with honeysuckle and wild roses, the trail crosses a footbridge at 0.4 mi. The N trailhead does not have a parking lot. Backtrack, or go E 250 yd. on Robinhood Rd to a parking lot at a church.

At Bethabara Park is a longer greenway, Bethabara Trail, and side trails **966** to historic sites of the pioneer Moravian settlement. Access: Off Silas Creek Parkway, go W on Bethabara Rd, past the Bethabara Park to a parking lot at the jct of Bonbrook Dr, L. (Mill Creek is nearby.) To access the SE trailhead turn off Silas Creek Parkway E on Bethabara and R on Hayes Forest Dr (a retirement settlement). Descend to the hollow; the gated trail is R and the only parking lot is L (for residential space). If walking the trail from here, ascend ahead 100 yd. to a gate R. Descend on the Bethabara Trail; cross a culvert into a mature forest. At 0.4 mi pass through a tunnel under Silas Creek Parkway. Ascend on steps, then follow a narrow foot trail to skirt a residential area. Descend through beech grove, and ascend steps to Old Town Rd at 0.9 mi. Turn R for 0.1 mi to turn L. Pass through prominent sycamore and poplar at

967   1.1 mi Parallel Monareas Creek and at 1.5 mi, L, is God's Acre Nature Trail. (It ascends steeply 0.1 mi to a historic hilltop cemetery. Backtrack.) To the R are access points to the meadows of Bethabara Park. Continue downstream to end the trail at Bonbrook Dr at 1.8 mi and the parking lot R.

968   The city's most urban trail is the downtown 1.2-mi linear Strollway Trail. Parking at either end is street or business parking. Access: Corner of Salem Ave and Liberty St for S trailhead where it connects with Salem Creek Trail (see below), and the N trailhead is on 4th St between Cherry St and Liberty St. If starting from the S trailhead follow the sign at the W side of Liberty St and go N. Called "super greenway," this classic metropolitan trail is landscaped with trees, shrubs, flowers, and bridges. Part of its wide treadway is a mixture of asphalt and pea gravel. Pass by Old Salem, R, and then under I-40 (Bus) at 0.7 mi; reach a drinking fountain at 0.9 mi. To the R are glistening skyscrapers. Reach the N trailhead at a large archway at downtown 4th St. (Plans are to extend the trail S from Salem St to the NC School of the Arts.)

Address: Rec and Parks Dept, Box 2511, Winston-Salem, NC 27102; 336-727-2063.

Salem Lake Park

The park is a 365-acre city reservoir surrounded by 1,800 acres of land. Activities are picnicking; fishing (bass, bluegill, catfish, crappie); boating (rentals also); horseback riding; biking; birding; and hiking (no skiing or swimming). Open daily, except Thursdays; 910-788-0212.

Access: From I-40 (Bus), go S on US-311/NC-209 at Claremont Ave (which becomes Martin Luther King St). After 0.8 mi, turn L on Reynolds Park Rd (SR-2740) and go 1.9 mi to Salem Lake Rd, L.

969-   *Salem Lake Trail* (6.9 mi); *Salem Creek Trail* (4.5 mi)
970   **Length and Difficulty:** 11.4 mi combined, easy to moderate
           Trailhead and Description: Park R on the approach to the second entrance gate. For hiking Salem Lake Trail, counterclockwise, begin R (NE)

on a wide svc road through poplar, oak, beech, Virginia pine, and sweet gum. Fern, yellow root, sweet pepperbush, sensitive briar, and wild rose grow in the open coves and lakeside. At 0.9 mi cross a cement bridge and at 2.7 mi a causeway where kingfisher and wild duck frequent the marsh, R. Arrive at Linville Rd (SR-2662) at 3.4 mi. (To the L it is 0.7 mi to I-40 (Bus), exit 10.) Continue on the trail by crossing the causeway L to a reentrance in the woods. Follow the svc road under a power line at 3.9 mi and to a scenic view by the lake at 5.0 mi.

At 6.0 mi is a jct L with a causeway and arched bridge over the lake. (To the R is a gravel svc road 0.3 mi to a gate and parking lot at the end of New Greensboro Rd. It goes E 1.2 mi to a jct with Linville Rd and its jct with I-40 [Bus], Exit 10.) Cross the bridge to a resting bench and scenic view of the lake. Follow near the shoreline to descend at the base of the dam at a jct with Salem Creek Trail, R, at 6.5 mi. If making a loop, cross a low-water bridge, ascend to gate and W end of parking lot. (If the gate is locked, follow the paved trail around the fence to the point of origin at 6.9 mi.)

To follow the Salem Creek Trail, parallel Salem Creek downstream through tall poplar, river birch, pine, wild grapevine, and wildflowers. Kudzu is smothering trees and shrubs at a few dense sections. Pass a picnic table at a cascade (called gorge by the city) at 0.9 mi. Pass R of Reynolds Park Golf Course and rest rooms at 1.4 mi. Go under Reynolds Park Rd, pass under M. L. King, Jr Dr bridge at 2.0 mi. To the L is the Civitan Park with ball fields and a spur footbridge over the creek to Anderson Center, R. For the next 0.3 mi is a powerful reminder of urbanization: noise from overhead Vargrave St and US-52, high and huge Southern RR trestle, and glimpses of the city skyline.

At 3.0 mi enter the edge of Happy Hills Park, but cross the creek on a footbridge to wide meadows of Central Park ball fields. Cross Waughtown Rd (which goes L to NC School of Arts) and reach jct with Strollway Trail at 3.4 mi, R. Follow the sidewalk past a minimart and turn off R from Broad St into the woods. Come out of the woods at 3.9 mi to a jct with a fitness trail. Ball fields are on both sides of the creek in Washington Park. Cross an arched footbridge at 4.0 mi and reach the parking lot at the NW corner of the Marketplace Mall at 4.5 mi (It is 0.2 mi farther to Peters Creek Parkway and its jct with Silas Creek Parkway.) Backtrack, or have a second vehicle.

There are a number of unnamed short walks at some of the city parks. Examples are those at Old Town Park (0.5 mi), Piney Grove Park (0.5 mi), Skyland Park (0.3 mi), and Speas Park (0.4 mi). Longer trails are at Hanes Park, where a popular route runs 1.2 mi on the sidewalk and another 1.2 mi through the park's center. There are multiple tennis courts and ball fields and grassy area scattered with sycamore, oak, and willow. Miller Park has trails of 1.0 mi and 0.5 mi Little Creek Park has a 0.5-mi walk. A delightful, unnamed 0.2-mi trail is downtown at Spring St, where the trail meets a huge oak, passes a picnic table, and crosses two footbridges. They and others are part of at least 20 other city parks with physical-fitness walks. There is a new park being constructed near the intersection of Yorkshire Rd and Stiles Creek Parkway. As of this writing, the trail distance had not yet been determined. For more information, contact the marketing coordinator at 336-727-2063.

Municipal Parks and Recreation Areas: Central Piedmont Municipalities

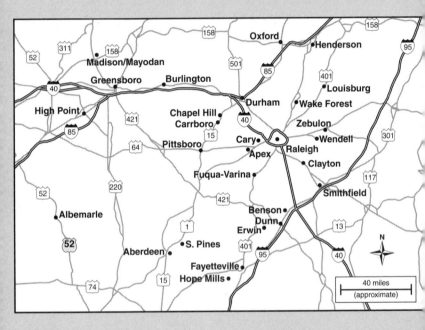

Introductions to Trail Areas

This list of cities that lie in Central Piedmont counties is arranged alphabetically to conform to the order they appear in the subsequent text.

SECTION 2: CENTRAL PIEDMONT MUNICIPALITIES

971   ## Aberdeen (Moore County)

Aberdeen park system has three parks, one of which is Aberdeen Lake Park, with a trail network. In addition to the trails, there are picnic areas, a boat ramp and dock, a playground, lighted tennis courts, and a community center. The park is open daily 7:00AM to dusk. Only walking and bicycling are allowed on the trails. The lake trailhead begins at the lakeside gazebo.

Aberdeen Lake Park

972-   *Cedar Trail* (0.09 mi); *Maple Trail Loop* (0.2 mi); *Pine Trail Loop*
975   (0.7 mi); *West Trail* (0.2 mi)

> **Length and Difficulty:** 1.9 mi round-trip (depending on backtracks), easy
> **Trailhead and Description:** Begin the Cedar Trail at the lakeside gazebo and go L on the walkway past the community center to the dam. After crossing, stay R and near the lake. The trail weaves through small marshes with boardwalks and groves of Atlantic white cedar. The understory is mainly fetter-bush and cane. At 0.5 mi is a trail jct. To the L is a sign with above trail names. To the R is a bridge across the lake. If following the other trails, hikers will notice picnic tables, bluebird houses, and markers to identify shrubs and trees in a loblolly-pine area. Backtrack to bridge at 1.5 mi and continue on Cedar Trail across the 380-ft. bridge over the lake. Halfway across is a shelter and benches for scenic lake views. On the N side of the lake, cross a bridge over a small stream to stay R and complete the loop at 1.9 mi near the gazebo.
> **Address and Access:** Aberdeen Parks and Rec, 107 N Poplar St (P.O. Box 785, Aberdeen, NC; 910-944-5902; fax: 910-944-7459. On US-1, drive S 1.4 mi from the jct of US-15-501 to Maple Ave, R. If coming N on US-1 from jct of NC-5, turn L at Maple Ave after 0.3 mi.

Albemarle (Stanly County)

The city has two trails, one in Rock Creek Park and another in Chuck More-head Memorial Park. Access to Rock Creek Park is immediately R after turn-
976   ing S on US-52 at the jct of NC-24/27/73. Begin Rock Creek Trail at the far end of the parking area and pass a number of park buildings, R. Follow a wide, easy, old RR grade 1.0 mi to a dead end. Tall pine and hardwoods comprise a canopy over shrubs and honeysuckle. Rock Creek, R, partially parallels the rail. Backtrack.

To reach Chuck Morehead Memorial Park, take US-52 from Rock Creek Park N to US-52 Bypass at 2.2 mi. Turn R, go 1.3 mi; turn R onto Northeast

Connector and turn L immediately. Park at the swimming pool parking lot. Begin the unnamed trail at the edge of the hardwood forest and follow a path for a loop of 1.5 mi in either direction. The trail ascends and descends in a hilly area, both on old woods roads and through a section with physical-fitness stations. The Dept of Transportation has paved a greenway from Salisbury Ave S to Montgomery Memorial Park. The city has received a grant to add 1.5 mi to it. (USGS Maps: Albemarle SW and NW)

Address: Director, Parks and Rec Dept, P.O. Box 190, Albemarle, NC 28001 704-984-9560; fax: 704-982-0199.

Apex (Wake County)

In the town's 160-acre community park is Apex Reservoir (not part of the town's drinking water). Circling the lake among pine is the 2.1-mi (easy) paved Apex Reservoir Greenway. Along the pleasant trail are resting benches. **977** The park also has facilities for picnicking, ball fields, a playground, and opportunities for fishing, and boating (no swimming). (The town's parks department is planning a 4.5-mi greenway W to connect with the American Tobacco Trail.)

Address and Access: Apex Parks, Rec, and Cultural Resources, P.O. Box 250, Apex, NC 27502; 919-496-3419 or www.apexnc.org/parks; fax: 919-249-3419. On US-64, 2.4 mi W from US-1. Turn R onto Laura Duncan Rd and drive 0.6 mi to Community Park Dr, R.

Burlington (Alamance County)

The Burlington Rec and Park Dept and the Burlington Women's Club sponsor the Town and Country Nature Park with its easy 1.5-mi Town and Country Nature Trail. Access to the park is from I-85/40 and NC-87 (Exit 147) N **978** on S Main St in Graham. Turn R onto NC-49, follow it to US-70 to Church St, and turn L. Go 0.9 mi; turn R on McKinney St for 0.3 mi, R on Berkley Rd, and go 0.2 mi to Regent Park Lane. Park at the end of the street. Follow the trail signs W on a well-graded trail (with picnic areas at intervals) through oak, birch, Virginia pine, black willow, and wildflowers. Cross bridges at 0.3 and 0.7 mi. Pass the S side of the Haw River at 0.9 mi Side trails go up and down the river. (USGS Map: Burlington)

Address: Rec and Parks Dept, Box 1358, Burlington, NC 27216; 336-222-5030; fax: 336-229-3106.

Cary (Wake County)

The Cary Greenways system, begun in 1980, continues to expand within town limits and to connect with greenways elsewhere in the county. Parks and trail systems are dispersed throughout the area with greenways frequently follow-

979   ing streams. Examples of greenway diversity are the short 0.4-mi Higgins Trail along Swift Creek between Danfort Dr (crescent off W Chatham St) (N) to W Maynard Rd (S) and a 7.0-mi trail system in Bond Park Community Center. Unless otherwise marked at the trailheads, all trails are for walkers and bikers. Paved trails are open to skaters. Camping is prohibited.

980   Black Creek Greenway is an exceptionally scenic 2.5-mi asphalt linear trail from Lake Crabtree County Park (N) to Maynard Rd (NC-54), 0.1 mi off N Harrison Ave (S). Access to its N trailhead is off of Weston Pkwy on Old Reedy Creek Rd for 1.3 mi to a gate at Lake Crabtree Dam, L. From here the trail jointly follows Lake Crabtree Trail for 1.0 mi. At 0.5 mi is a sandy beach at the lake. Seats are arranged to provide rest, watch the birds and sunsets, or listen to the lake lapping the shoreline. There is an observation deck, R, at 0.7 mi and an emergency telephone, L, at 0.8 mi. At 1.0 mi the trail divides. Lake Crabtree Trail turns sharply R on a bridge over Black Creek to a dirt path (see Wake County, chapter 12). Black Creek Greenway continues ahead under Weston Pkwy and later under Cary Pkwy. The trail parallels the creek through a hardwood forest (elm, poplar, oak, black walnut) and wildflowers (cardinal flower, jewelweed). It leaves Black Creek and veers L up a tributary before crossing the last creek bridge at 2.4 mi and parking space at W Dynasty Dr. (To the L, it is 0.1 mi to N Harrison Ave.) Continue on the greenway, R, by ascending and descending a ridge on W Dynasty for 0.2 mi. Turn at the stream and bridge onto an asphalt greenway. Cross Black Creek on a bridge (and six other times upstream). Under the forest Canopy are patches of running cedar and pinxter. After a scenic criss-crossing of the stream, pass soccer and track fields. At 3.4 mi is a drinking fountain and a fork in the middle of the greenway system. (To the R, partially on asphalt and on steps, it is 0.2 mi to Cary Middle School and another 0.1 mi to Evans Rd.) Continue L on the Black Creek Greenway, cross a bridge, and arrive at the S trailhead at 3.5 mi to a large (28 car capacity) parking lot on NW Maynard Dr (NC-54). (Godbold Park is across the road.) It is 0.3 mi R (W) to Evans Rd and 0.4 mi L (E) to N Harrison Ave, where a L is 2.0 mi to I-40, Exit 287.

981   At McDonald Woods Park is 0.8-mi Hinshaw Greenway. Access is off of Cary Pkwy on Seabrook Ave for 0.35 mi, R, for street-side parking. At the park sign are steps for a descent to a playground, grassy meadow, and svc road to a gate for 0.2 mi. Across the street from the park sign is the asphalt trail. It weaves through an almost all hardwood forest (elm, poplar, beech, oak, hickory) to parallel Lynn's Branch, a tributary to Lochmere Lake. The trail's N terminus is at the jct of SE Maynard Rd and Greenwood Cir at the parking lot of Cary Church of Christ. Nearby the McDonald Woods Park is 0.6-mi Pirates **982** Cove Greenway. Also a N-S greenway, its N access is off Seabrook Ave on Greenwood Cir E 0.1 mi to the street's dead-end. Its S trailhead is a dead-end of Kildonan Ct, which is off of the crescent-shaped Glenary Dr off of Seabrook Ave. This access is between McDonald Woods Park and Glenwood Cir. The trail's treadway is gravel in a hardwood forest and parallels Straight Branch. (Be alert to fenced-in dogs that may lunge at pedestrians.)

Panther Creek Greenway is a paved, 1.5-mi circle around a lake in a W **983** suburb of Cary. Shrubbery and wildflowers are part of the landscape. Waterfowl are present. For access for NC-55 (between Alston Ave and Good Hope Church Rd), turn W on Cary Glen Blvd. Cross Carpenter Fire Sta Rd at 1.5 mi, and after 0.3 mi, cross Green Level Durham Rd to descend at the lake. Hikers may need to park by the curb, but a 0.5-mi second loop is being constructed E toward Green Level Durham Rd.

Swift Creek Greenway is unique, not because of plant life or history, but **984-** because of the composition of its treadway. The wide smooth trail looks like **985** asphalt, but as part of the Swift Creek Recycled Greenway it contains ash from coal-powered electric-generating plants, recycled old asphalt, rubber tires, roof shingles, and plastics. There are descriptive signs. Perfectly landscaped, the 0.8-mi trail crosses three bridges and is from Regency Pkwy W to Kildaire Farm Rd E. A place to park is in the center of the route at Ritter Community Park. Access from Kildaire Farm Rd is 0.2 mi W on W Lochmere Dr, L. The trail goes under Kildaire Farm Rd bridge to a T jct. (A turn R crosses a footbridge over Swift Creek to connect with hike/bike trails in Loch Highland residential development.) A turn L connects with a trail at Lochmere Golf Club, where it parallels Kildaire Farm Rd to Lochmere Dr, R (E), for 2.5 mi. It is a serpentine design to Cary Pkwy. (The trail around Lochmere Lake has a No Trespassing sign; usage is for Lochmere residents only.) Symphony Lake Greenway can be accessed from US-64/US-1, Exit 98, on Tyron Rd, E, but **986** immediately turn R onto Regency Pkwy. At 0.5 mi, pass Swift Creek Greenway W access and continue 0.3 mi to Symphony Lake parking, L. Hike past an amphitheatre for a 1.2-mi paved circle around the lake.

987   White Oak Creek Greenway, 1.7 mi and paved, crosses four pedestrian bridges. It links David Drive Park (1610 Davis Dr, with ball fields, picnic shelters, and a playground), a connector trail to Middle and Elementray Davis Dr schools, and W to White Oak Park (9216 Jenks Carpenter Rd with ball fields, picnic shelters, and a playground).

Address and Access: Cary Parks and Rec & Cultural Resources, 111 James Jackson Ave (P.O. Box 8005), Cary, NC 27512; 919-496-4061 or www.townofcary.org; fax: 919-469-4344. From US-64 on Salem Church Rd N to Davis Dr, L, drive 1.3 mi N to Davis Park, R. If taking Park Village Rd, L, to Jenks Carpenter Rd, turn R to White Oak Creek Park.

Annie Jones Park

Located in the SW part of the city, Annie Jones Park serves a residential area with Scottish Hills swimming pool, playground, tennis courts, and a lighted athletic field. Nearby is a small tributary to Swift Creek shaded by young and mature hardwoods (sweet and black gum, maple, poplar, and loblolly pine) over ferns and spicebush. Access: From a jct of Cary Pkwy go three blocks N on Lake Pine Rd, turn L (W) to 1414 Tarbert St for 0.5 mi to parking lot, R.

988-   From the park follow 0.2-mi McCloud Court Trail (part asphalt and gravel)
989   upstream to McCloud Ct. Backtrack. Downstream is 0.5-mi. Coatbridge Trail (natural treadway and gravel), which makes a horseshoe shape in returning to Tarbert Dr between Wishaw Ct, R (E), and Brodick Ct, L (W). Across Tarbert
990   Dr is 0.2-mi asphalt Tarbert-Gatehouse Trail. It passes a playground to end at Gatehouse Dr. Backtrack. On the horseshoe curve of Coatbridge Trail is a side
991   trail, 0.2-mi Lake Pine Trail. It continues downstream to end at the corner of Cary Pkwy and Lake Pine Rd (diagonally opposite a minimart).

Bond Park Community Center

On the W side of Cary is Wake County's largest municipal park, 360-acre Fred G. Bond Metro Park, named in honor of a former Cary mayor. A 42-acre lake provides fishing and boating (including boat rentals). Swimming and wading are not allowed. Designed to preserve the environment, the recreation areas are separated within the forest and scattered parking areas. There are four lighted athletic fields and two large picnic shelters, one large enough to accommodate 200 people. There is also a playground. The Sertoma Amphitheatre is arranged on a natural slope to seat an audience of more than 350. A color-coded network of trails for hikers and bikers provides multiple loops (described below). For guided nature tours throughout the year call 919-387-5980; for reserving the athletic facilities call 919-469-4062; for reserving picnic shelters call 919-460-4965.

Access: From downtown go W on Old Apex Rd to High House Rd and turn L off High House Rd at the park entrance. From the S follow Cary Pkwy off US-1 to High House Rd, turn R and then R again at the park entrance.

Lake Trail (2.5 mi); *Loop Trail* (2.0 mi); *Bond Nature Trail* (0.5 mi); **992-**
Parkway Greenway (0.8 mi); *Oxxford Hunt Greenway* (1.5 mi) **996**

Length and Difficulty: 7.3 mi combined, easy

Trailhead and Description: The trailheads are accessible from any of the interconnected parking areas. None of the trails is paved and camping is prohibited. The trail system is designed to provide short loop walks or longer combinations. Linear trails (Parkway Greenway and Oxxford Hunt Greenway) can be backtracked or a second vehicle used. An example of a loop arrangement is to begin at the parking area near field #1. Enter the woods at Par exercise #5 on the physical-fitness course (may be yellow blazed), which at this point runs R and L with the red-blazed Loop Trail. Turn L and after 0.2 mi cross the park's entrance road. At 0.4 mi join the Bond Nature Trail, which has markers about the variety of plants, such as blackjack oak *(Quercus marilandica)*, whose wood is used commercially for charcoal.

Cross a paved road (which leads R to Pkwy Athletic Complex) at 0.6 mi. At 0.8 mi come out of the woods to a field at the base of the dam, but stay L until the trail markers show a R turn. Reach a jct with the blue-blazed Lake Trail, R and L, at 1.1 mi (The Loop Trail [red] and Bond Nature Trail [green] goes L.) Turn R on the Lake Trail across the dam, one of the most scenic views of the hike. At the other end of the dam to the R are steps that descend to white-blazed Parkway Greenway. (It follows downstream to cross under Cary Pkwy and end in a private greenway open to the public.) Turn L and continue around the lake. For the next 1.2 mi the trail dips into ravines and over bridges and boardwalks, sometimes close to the lakeshore. On the hillside slope it meanders into the backyards of residents who may watch you pass by their azalea beds and lawn decks. Cross a footbridge over a stream at 2.6 mi and reach jct with white-blazed Oxxford Hunt Greenway near another bridge. (It follows 1.5 mi upstream and across W Chatham St to a private greenway open to public use.) Continue L on a svc road. At 2.9 mi rejoin the yellow and red markers R and L. Turn R and notice Par #17. Pass athletic fields #3 and #2, and return to Par #5, the point of origin, L, at 3.4 mi. (USGS Map: Cary)

Chapel Hill (Orange County)

Chapel Hill Parks and Rec Dept has a comprehensive master plan for its greenway system to provide more than 38 mi of multi-use trails on paved and unpaved trails. The master plan shows corridors mainly alongside creeks and branches, some of which will extend beyond current trails. New trails are designed in phases. From N to S, they are Booker Creek (six phases), Cedar Fork (completed), Dry Creek (five phases, two completed), Bolin Creek (seven phases, three completed), Little Creek (two phases), Battle Creek (completed), Morgan Creek (four phases), and Fan Branch and Wilson Creek (four phases and four tributaries). Other proposed trails near or crossing a stream are Old Field Creek Trail, North Trail, and Rail Trail.

997-
1000   An older trail, the 0.4-mi Tanyard Branch Trail, is accessed from Airport Rd (NC-86) on Umstead Dr, 0.9 mi N from downtown Franklin St, L (W). From the parking lot it follows R of the former rec center along Bolin Creek that leads to Caldwell St. For another 0.2 mi, it goes along Mitchell Ln to Har-
1001   graves Community Center. For 10-ft paved Fan Branch Trail, 1.1 mi of 1.9 mi is complete. Access is at the SW corner jct of Culbreth and Mt. Carmel Church Rd. on US 15-501 S across Morgan Creek Bridge. The professionally land-scaped and clean greenway crosses two arched bridges, the latter at 0.35 mi before slightly ascending to a subdivision. Open for sunshine it passes large homes and has a children's playground at 0.9 mi. It accesses Scroggs Elementary School. Other trails are described ahead. (USGS Map: Chapel Hill)

Address and Access: Chapel Hill Parks and Rec, 200 Plant Rd, Chapel Hill, NC 27514; 919-968-2785; fax: 919-932-2923.

Bolin Creek Greenway

1002-
1003   At the Community Center Park (the N terminus of Battle Branch Trail) is the E terminus of the paved and easy 1.5-mi Bolin Creek Greenway. From the parking area, begin between the playground and the resting seat shaped like human hands. Pass a gazebo and floral garden, enter a street cul-de-sac, and pass under E Franklin St bridge. Near the weaving greenway and creekside are sycamore, beech, and hornbeam. Uniquely interpretive are the elevated manholes painted with green tree leaf designs and titles. At 0.7 mi is paved access, L, to Elizabeth St. Cross scenic bridges at 0.8 mi and 1.4 mi. Arrive at Airport Rd at 1.5 mi. Backtrack or arrange a shuttle.

1004 ### Booker Creek Greenway (Lower)

This easy serpentine greenway parallels Booker Creek for 0.8 mi from East Gate Shopping Center on N Franklin Street. With a 10-ft. wide cement base the route has grassy sides through a hardwood forest and floodplain. In the springtime are wild white roses and in the summertime are jeweled and water hemlock *(Sium cicutaefolium),* whose small white flowers form domed clusters. (According to legend, the poisonous roots of this plant killed Socrates.) At 0.6 mi is an arched bridge over Booker Creek. The trail ends at Booker Creek Road. Backtrack. (At the East Gate Shopping Center the greenway continues at an angle between the shopping center and Village Plaza backsides for 0.3 mi to a parking area near the jct. of Elliott Rd and US-15-501 [Fordham Blvd]. Along the way, near Booker Creek, is landscaped Linear Park. Plans are for the greenway to continue SE down Booker Creek to connect with future Little Creek Trail. For more information, contact 919-968-2787.) **1005**

Access: Parking is available at East Gate Shopping Center. (Near a service station of North Franklin Street cross the highway at a traffic light and follow the sign north a few yards on the sidewalk for a turn.)

Cedar Fall Park

The park has three baseball fields, a picnic area, a playground, and tennis courts. Among the city's oldest parks, it has large hardwood forest on the hills and valleys. The understory has virbinum, crane-fly orchid, wild ginger, and muscadine grape. The park's trail system is a maze that has increased the number of loops with short cuts and spur trails from residential areas.

After entering the parking area drive to the S side parking lot (L of a yellow gate to the ballfields). Follow the paved trail to a signboard. The original trail construction has yellow, blue, and white blazes. The 0.7-mi yellow blazed loop is the Jo Peeler Nature Trail, named in her honor: "because of her love **1006** for natural beauty, encouraged the town to acquire land as an open space for others to enjoy." Numbered posts identify plant life. At 0.6 mi pass through a grove of large white pines, the old and former homesite of Jesse Johnson.

For the Blue Trail follow a wide paved trail toward the tennis court, but **1007** after 125 yd. turn R on an earthen trailbase. After partially circling the tennis court turn R to cross the Jo Peeler Nature Trail for a fork at 0.3 mi. Turn R at the fork and later descend. The curve R to a ridge. (To the L is a side trail to a scenic rock outcropping at Cedar Creek. Wildflowers and wild pink azalea are on the descent to the cascades. From this area is a 0.1 mi access route to Lakeshore Lane, but no parking is allowed there.) Continue the loop by ascending the ridge and staying loft from other loops that may have red or white blazes. At 0.9 mi, exit at the ballfield; keep right to pass the rest room and return to the parking area near the yellow gate.

Access: From I-40, Exit 266, drive 0.4 mi S on NC-86 (Airport Rd.) to Weaver Dairy Rd., L. After 1.5 mi turn R into entrance of the park. If approaching from US 15-501, turn W on Erwin Rd (1.2 mi S from I-40 crossing), and drive 0.5 mi and turn L on Weaver Dairy Rd. After 1.2 mi, turn L at park entrance.

1008   *Dry Creek Trail*

Across Weaver Dairy Rd. from Cedar Fall Park is the W trailhead of Dry Creek Trail at East Chapel Hill High School. If hiking from the park, follow an entrance road with a bicycle route for 0.2 mi to the parking area of the football stadium, or drive through the main entrance of the school and park at the north end of the parking lot. At that point descend R for 260 yd., partially on asphalt (which ends at a lake) and old road to a sharp R turn up a bank into the woods. (If you go under a power line you have gone too far on the old road.) Through the woods the trail crossed Dry Creek four times among scenic rocky sections. Crested dwarf iris, hepatica, and wild ginger are on the stream banks. At 0.3 mi, cross San Juan Dr, then descend on steps into the forest. At 0.5 mi cross Silver Creek Rd, and descend on steps. Parallel the creek and cross a boardwalk in a flood plain and ascend steps to Perry Creek Dr. at 0.9 mi. Backtrack. (Plans are to extend the trail another 0.4 mi to Erwin Road, another 0.6 mi to Providence Rd, and a joint project with Durham Open Space and Trails Commission for another extension of 1.0 mi to Mt. Moriah Church Rd.)

1009   *Battle Branch Trail*

This trail is 1.6 mi, easy to moderate. The W trailhead is at Country Club Rd at the University of North Carolina, Chapel Hill (no parking except a pull-off at picnic tables), and the NE trailhead is at Sugarberry Rd (street-side parking only). Parking may be more practical at the Community Ctr Park parking area, off E Franklin St on Plant Rd. If beginning from the W (across the street from Cobb dormitory), descend by the Forest Theatre to Battle Branch. After 0.2 mi, there is a jct L with the corner of Boundary and Park Sts. The rocky and rooty double trails (one following a city waste system road and the other a pathway) crisscross each other and a stream. Towering loblolly pine, oak, and poplar are the principal trees, some of which are entangled with wisteria. Ground beds of ivy and fern provide diversity in the subcanopy. At 0.5 mi is a steep bluff and **1010**   at 0.7 mi is a jct with an access R to Sandy Creek Trail (street) and Greenwood Rd. Cross a branch bridge at 1.0 mi near an access L to Glendale Rd. A number of boardwalks, steps, and bridges follow where a path stays close to the stream and a city svc road parallels on a higher contour. At 1.5 mi the trail forks. A turn L is to Valley Park Dr where a turn L at 0.2 mi accesses Community Ctr Park. On the R, fork cross a boardwalk among honey locust and privet to ascend steps at Sugarberry Rd at 1.6 mi. (USGS Map: Chapel Hill)

Address: Parks and Rec Dept, 200 Plant Rd, Chapel Hill, NC 27514; 919-968-2785; fax: 919-923-2923.

Dunn and Erwin (Harnett County)
Dunn-Erwin Rail-Trail
The historic towns of Dunn and Erwin are separate but connected by US-421/NC-55 and a former railroad. Now the former railroad is a 5.0-mi hiking and bicycling trail that ties the towns even closer. The rail corridor was made possible by the NC Rails Trails Land Trust, and supported by Dunn and Erwin governments, chambers of commerce, and other local citizens. Usage is allowed in daylight only, and with a request to stay on the trail, not walk alone, have pets on a leash, and use caution at vehicular crossings.

Access: To the E terminus of Dunn-Erwin Rail-Trail in Dunn is from I-95 (Exit 73) W on US-421/NC-55 (Cumberland St) 1.2 mi to McKay Ave, R. After 0.4 mi (5 blocks) park across the RR tracks, L, at Sunbeam Bread Bakery. For access to the W terminus drive 3.5 mi W on US-421/NC-55 and turn off, L, on NC-82 (13th St). Downtown, park R in a parking space of former but famous textile Erwin Mills. Walk across the street to the old RR track and between a cluster of historic and orderly shops. Pass a sign of the Centennial Walk and notice there are mile markers in the center of the trail. On a gravel trail bed cross under US-421 at 0.8 mi and at 1.0 mi is a pond, R. For the next mi there are large oaks and sweet gums along the corridor. Outside are fields of cotton and soybean. At 2.0 mi the trail curves R, in a more open space and away from a wye of the original RR. At 2.3 mi cross busy Old Field Church Rd. (Six other roads are crossed before crossing Watauga Ave in Dunn.) Pass under a powerline at 2.9 mi and at 3.0 mi cross a bridge over wild Black River. Here is a place to stop and absorb the beauty of the swamp, home to peepers and beavers. At 4.3 mi is a spur trail. R, where John Haywood Byrd, a confederate soldier, is buried. Arrive at McKay Ave at 5.0 mi. (Ahead, 0.3 mi, are old RR tracks to RR jct at Railroad Ave.)

Address: For information: Dunn Area Tourism Authority, P.O. Box 310, Dunn, NC 28325; 910-892-3282, and NC Rail-Trails, P.O. Box 61348, Durham, NC 27715; 919-542-0022.

Durham (Durham County)

Among some of the city's developed parks are single or combination trails with current or planned greenway systems, but central to the city's planning is the N-S Greenway Project. It begins at the West Point Park amphitheatre area parking of West Point on the Eno Park and heads S through the heart of the city to connect with the American Tobacco Trail (ATT) at Durham Bulls Athletic Park. From there, the ATT completes the greenway project through the city and through Durham County. Farther S, the ATT has sections in Chatham and Wake counties to end near Bonsal. In addition to the N-S plans, there is the Eno River Greenway, an E-W Greenway route E from West Point Park to connect with Penny's Bend Trail to Old Oxford Rd. (East of this point is West Falls Lake Trail/East Falls Lake Trail of the Mountains-to-Sea Trail in N Raleigh.) West from West Point Park are plans for the Eno River Greenway/Mountains-to-Sea Trail to connect with Laurel Bluff Trail through Eno River State Park.

In the city's N-S Greenway are spurs and potential connections en route. They are described in that order ahead with proposed or unfinished pockets listed along the way. These (plus other plans from a master plan first approved in 1985) may result in about 25 mi for the future. (For an update on progress or completion, contact the sources listed below.)

Address: Durham's Dept of Parks and Rec, 101 City Hall Plaza, Durham, NC 07701; 919-560-4355; fax: 919-687-0896.

West Point on the Eno Park

This 373-acre city park emphasizes the history and environmental value of the West Point Mill community that existed between 1778 and 1942. The mill, the McCown-Mangum farmhouse, the blacksmith shop, and the garden have all been restored or reconstructed. (The old Roxboro road passed the E side of the mill and forded the Eno River where the current bridge is located.) Facilities in the park allow picnicking, fishing, rafting, canoeing, and hiking. (Camping and swimming are prohibited.) The Festival of the Eno is held annually during the weekend of the 4th of July; for more information, contact 919-620-9099 or Friends of West Point, 919-477-2442.

Address: West Point on the Eno Park, 5101 N Roxboro Rd, Durham, NC 27704; 919-471-1623.

South River Trail (0.5 mi); *Laurel Cliffs Nature Trail* (0.4 mi); *Buf-*   **1011-**
falo Trail (0.4 mi); *Buffalo Spur Trail* (0.15 mi); *Sennett Hole Trail*   **1016**
(0.15 mi); *Eagle Trail* (1.8 mi)

    Length and Difficulty: 3.4 mi combined one-way, easy to moderate

    Trailhead and Description: If parking near the West Point Mill, walk
across the Millrace bridge toward the dam. Ascend L on the South River Trail.
(Part of this trail is also the Laurel Cliffs Nature Trail that has interpretive
markers. Maps and marker brochures are available at the park office and trail
sign entrance boards.) On a rocky bluff are views of the dam and passage
through mountain laurel, wintergreen, and galax. Pass a jct with Laurel Cliffs
Trail, L, and at 0.5 mi is a jct with Buffalo Trail. Turn R, cross a bridge over
Warren Creek on Sennett Hole Trail, and stop at the riverbank. Here are great
views of rapids, rock formations, and an island. Backtrack; if using the Buffalo Trail, hikers can use Buffalo Spur Trail, or exit near the picnic shelter at
the S end of the circle road.

    For access to blue-blazed Eagle Trail, pass the mill downstream to a hik-
ing/bicycling bridge over Eno River to access the trail, L. (To the R is the proposed trail to connect with Penny's Bend Trail. See chapter 15.) Ahead is 0.1
mi to a parking area for West Point Park amphitheatre. (This is accessible
from the main park entrance 5.0 mi N on Roxboro Rd [US-501] and turn L at
park sign.) Follow the Eagle Trail upstream, cross a bridge or rock-hop
Crooked Creek, and ascend to an old road jct near the amphitheatre at 0.2 mi.
Turn L on the old road, pass an old gate, and at 0.45 mi, curve R in a floodplain. At 0.65 mi, pass the rapids and rocky area of Sennett Hole. At 1.2 mi,
turn away from the river, reach jct with Lochaven Hills access, turn L, and
complete the trail at a gate near Guess Rd. Backtrack or arrange a shuttle.
(USGS Map: Durham NW)

Upper Warren Creek Trail   **1017**

From the parking circle near the entrance to the tennis courts at Whippoorwill
Park, follow the sidewalk past the rest rooms and descend 105 yd. To the
asphalt greenway trail entrance, R. Cross an arched bridge and downstream.
The mixed forest has flowering shrubbery and wildflowers, some of which are
commercial. A patch of wild blackberries is near the end of the trail at 0.8 mi
at Horton St. (Call 919-560-4355 for an update on the proposed greenway
from here along Warren Creek to West Point on the Eno Park.) Backtrack.
From the SW corner of the park, between the tennis courts, the N-S Greenway project continues into the forest on asphalt. Wildflowers, green and gold,

are here. Cross a cement bridge. Exit the forest at Stadium Dr at 0.2 mi, turn
1018   R on a wide sidewalk. (Plans are to provide a Stadium Drive Trail to Connect
with Ellerbee Creek Trail.)

    Access: In N Durham from the jct of NC-157 (Guess Rd) and Carver St,
drive N 0.4mi on NC-157 to Kirkwood Dr, R. After 0.2 mi, turn L onto Britt
St, then after another 0.1 mi, turn R onto Rosemont St to the park entrance, L.

1019   *West Ellerbee Creek Trail*

(This trail is part of a SW spur from the planned Stadium Drive Trail and
Ellerbee Creek Trail.) From the parking space at the trailhead, follow the sign
on the asphalt greenway. The open scenic route parallels Ellerbee Creek, and
tall forest trees are on both sides. Along the trail are mulberry trees (ripe fruit
in mid-May), jewelweed, and milkweed. At 0.3 mi is a garden of wildflowers
with a unique trail developed by the Ellerbee Creek Watershed Association
from a former city trash pile. Turn right and cross a bridge over the creek to
Indian Trail Park, which has a playground and picnic area. The 0.7-mi trail
ends at the parking area.

    Access: At Exit 175 of I-85, drive south 0.5 mi on guess Rd to Wagoner
Forest Rd, R, at Westover Park and R again to the parking area. Or, from I-85,
Exit 174, go S for 0.2 mi; turn L onto Indian Trail (St) to Indian Trail Park.

1020-   *Ellerbee Creek Trail* (1.3 mi); *South Ellerbee Creek Trail* (1.2 mi);
1022   *Rock Quarry Trail* (0.4 mi)

    Length and Difficulty: 2.5 mi combined one-way, easy

    Trailhead and Description: If beginning N to S, leave I-85, Exit 176, and
drive Non Duke St 0.9 mi to turn R on Stadium Dr. (The W Stadium Dr. is the
proposed NC Greenway route.) At this street corner is the N trailhead of Ellerbee Creek Trail (greenway) that follows a wide sidewalk. Parking is 0.1 mi on
Stadium Dr, R, next to the National Guard Armory. (If hiking the Rock Quarry
Trail, drive 0.2 mi farther on Stadium St to Rock Quarry Park to parking lot,
R.) At Ellerbee Creek Trail, descend on a paved trail through a forest of large
trees, cross a bridge, and parallel Ellerbee Creek to Murray Ave at 0.5 mi (To
the L is the S terminus of Rock Quarry Trail.) Turn R on Murray Ave; after 170
ft., cross the street into Glendale Heights Park, followed by lighted Jaycee ball
field in scenic Northgate Park. At 1.3 mi, arrive at Club Blvd, the end of Ellerbee Creek Trail and the beginning of South Ellerbee Creek Trail.

    Turn R on the sidewalk. Cross Glendale Ave, pass Club Blvd Elementary
School, and go under US-15/70Byp/I-85. At the Washington St. traffic light,
cross to the SW corner of the jct at 1.7 mi. On a curvy route, parallel a tribu-

tary, upstream, of Ellerbee Creek. Cross Knox St at 2.0 mi near residences, R. Wild roses grow near the trail and stream. Cross an arched bridge, then cross other streets. Cross under a power line on the approach to cross Dacian St at 2.3 mi. Cross a culvert bridge, turn L, then R to end at 2.5 mi at Trinity Ave. To the L, over Trinity, is abandoned RR, and to the R is a parking lot on the E side of Duke University Diet & Fitness Center. It is one block W to Duke St. Heading N, it goes to a jct with Stadium Dr, R. Backtrack or arrange a shuttle. (Plans are to extend the greenway system to the N terminus of the ATT at Durham Bulls Athletic Park.)

For the Rock Quarry Trail at Stadium Dr, follow the paved trail beside the rest rooms S through the forest. Pass the Vietnam War Memorial, R, at 0.2 mi. The Edison Johnson Rec Center is L. Descend to Murray St and turn R to connect with Ellerbee Creek Trail at 0.4 mi. Backtrack or make a loop for the return to Stadium Dr. (USGS Map: Durham)

American Tobacco Trail   1023

The multi-use, 22-mi American Tobacco Trail is described briefly here because its N terminus is in Durham, where the longest section is in both the city and county of Durham. It is also partly in Chatham and Wake counties, in Jordan Lake property of US Army Corps of Engineers, and can have connections to nearby towns and cities. The ATT is a rail-trail, formerly constructed as the New Hope Valley Railroad and later the Durham & South Carolina Railroad. The ATT has become possible from the influence of the Triangle Rails-to-Trails Conservancy, a volunteer nonprofit organization, and the Durham Parks and Rec Dept. At press time, nearly 10 mi had been completed in Durham (city and county), 3.7 mi of 6.5 mi in Wake County, and Chatham County's section was in planning stages. (For more information, contact 919-545-9104, 919-560-4355, or www.triangletrails.org/.)

Access to the N trailhead is in downtown Durham at Durham Bulls Athletic Park. A suggested parking space is at the corner of Morehead St and Blackwell St. (Durham Freeway is overhead.) Begin S at the trail sign. Cross a wide steel bridge over Lakewoods Dr at 0.2 mi Kudzu and honeysuckle garnish the trailside. At 0.8 mi, go under Roxboro St bridge and cross Otis St at 1.4 mi. Sweetgum and mimosa can be found in the forest. Cross Fayetteville St (near a mini-mart across the street at Pilot St.) At 2.0 mi is a plaque honoring a local popular bluesman, "Blind Boy Fuller," a.k.a. Fulton Allen buried nearby. (A few feet ahead, L, is 0.7 mi Rocky Creek Trail that parallels Third   **1024** Fork Rock Creek to Elmira Park upstream to Dakota St and NC-55. Forking

1025 off the trail after 0.15 mi is 0.9-mi Pearsontown Trail. It also passes Elmira Park going N and crosses eight streets in a residential area. At 0.6 mi, it passes through Shady Oaks Park and at 0.9 mi it stops at Nelson St Campus Ministry Building in NC Central University.)

A proposed greenway is to follow Third Fork Rock Creek along the stream SW to Woodcroft Pkwy and New Hope Rd (NC-751). Cross Third Fork Rock Creek bridge into a forest for the next 0.3 mi. Pass Hillside High School, R, at 2.9 mi, and follow L on an access road to Riddle Rd at 3.0 mi. (Roadside parking, but a better place is at the high-school parking area.) Cross Riddle Rd and **1026** after 30 yd. is a jct with spur trail, L, Riddle Rd Spur Trail. (It goes through a forest for 0.5 mi then crosses Riddle Rd. It also crosses NC-55 at 0.8 mi, S Alston St at 1.2 mi and ends at Bridges Ave parking lot at 1.5 mi.)

Continuing on the mainline trail, cross Cornwallis Rd at 3.2 mi. Along the greenway are wild red roses, Queen Anne's lace, and mullen. At 3.8 mi, cross **1027** Martin Luther King Parkway. (At this jct, the MLK, Jr. Pkwy Street Trail uses sidewalks and bike lanes for 3.1 mi E to NC-55 and W to Hope Valley Rd.) Cross United Dr at 3.9 mi, Belgreen Rd at 4.1 mi, and Fayetteville Rd after another 55 yd. Pass by basketball courts and a playground, R, with princess trees. In the community of Arborfield, pass Southwest Elementary School, R, at 5.0 mi. After more street crossings and sections of forest on the railroad bed, pass under a power line at 6.0 mi. Turn off of the old railroad track at 6.4 mi, R, to follow the sidewalk behind Southpoint Crossing Shopping Center, but on the residential-housing sidewalk. Stop at NC-54 at 6.7 mi. Parking is available at the shopping center. (The next section is in the process of development.)

To continue S on the mainline greenway, drive across NC-54 and I-40 on Fayetteville Rd, S, for 1.2 mi to Massey Chapel Rd, R. (Along the way is Southpoint Mall and Massey Chapel.) After 0.6 mi, the ATT is L. Park on roadside. The ATT follows a gravel-grassy route among pines. Pass a housing development, L, at 0.3 mi, followed by a water treatment plant. At 0.7 mi, pass under Fayetteville Rd bridge, then after 0.3 mi, cross a bridge over Crooked Creek. Cross under a power line at 1.6 mi and arrive at Scott King Rd, R and L, at 1.8 mi (From here it is 0.9 mi R [W] to Fayetteville Rd.) To complete this section, cross the road where an informational kiosk sits. On a gravel-grassy treadway, pass under a power line and soon enter a deep forest. After 1.0 mi, arrive at a RR bridge (partial frame) over Northeast Creek near Durham/Chatham county line. Backtrack to Scott King Rd. (For more information, contact NC Rail-Trails at 919-545-9104.)

For the S end section of the ATT in Wake County, park at the Wimberley Access parking area. Access it from US-64 W of the jct with NC-55; turn R on Jenks Rd. Drive 0.6 mi and turn L on Wimberley Rd. After 1.1 mi, park R at the ATT sign. Cross the road and enter the forest. On the wide, smooth greenway, there are resting benches along the way. Pass a gate at 0.1 mi followed by a bridge. At 1.4 mi, enter a tunnel under US-64, after which there is a caution sign about stray golf balls from a nearby driving range. At 2.2 mi, pass under a power line and by a scenic stream area. There may be high water in a few places of the hardwood and pine forest below the RR grade. Cross a bridge at 2.9 mi. Turn R to access the parking area at 3.7 mi. Backtrack or arrange a shuttle 0.2 mi out to NC-751 (New Hill–Olive Chapel Rd) and turn R. After 2.2 mi, turn R onto US-64. Drive 1.7 mi to a L on Jenks Rd as described above. (More details about the ATT and other triangle trails will be in the second edition of *Trails of the Triangle,* by Blair Publisher.) (USGS Maps: SW Durham, Green Level, New Hill)

New Hope Bottomland Trail

(This trail and Sandy Creek Greenway are not connected with the N-S Greenway at this time.) From the Githens Middle School parking area, walk to the NE corner and go around the track to its NE corner steps at 0.2 mi. Turn L on an old water-treatment space road. (Notice white arrow blazes; they are the school's running trails.) At 0.3 mi, pass the last white arrow, and at 0.6 mi, turn R into the woods. After 130 yd., the trail divides. If heading R, proceed on an outstanding example of bottomland with tall hardwoods. Some sections of dense forest undergrowth are entangled with honeysuckle and wild-grape vines. At 0.8 mi, cross the first of at least 15 footbridges or boardwalks. There are two underpasses of a power line. At 1.2 mi is a scenic of New Hope Creek. Ahead is the sound of traffic on Durham/Chapel Hill Blvd. Between 1.4 mi and 1.9 mi is a low area subject to flooding with 11 boardwalks. (At 2.1 mi, there is a 0.1 mi side trail, R, to Hopedale Ave in a private housing development and public Wilkins Rd.) Continue on the main trail and arrive at the loop at 2.8 mi and to the school parking area at 3.4 mi.

1028

Access: From the jct of Old Chapel Hill Rd (US-15-301[Bus]) and Watkins Rd, drive NE 0.2 mi on Old Chapel Hill Rd and turn L to Githens Middle School.

Sandy Creek Park

This restored park has picnic and restroom facilities near a few large willow oaks, a walk around the pond, and a 0.5-mi paved Sandy Creek Greenway

1029

along Sandy Creek N to Pickett Rd. On the greenway are wildflowers, and a wetland N of the pond has an usually large display of button bush. Backtrack. (A Sandy Creek Environmental Education Center is planned for the park.)

Access: At the jct of Pickett Rd and Nello Teer Senior Highway (US-15-501Byp), go a few yd. And quickly turn L on Sandy Creek Rd for 0.6 mi to dead-end at the park.

Rock Quarry Park

The park is on Stadium Dr, 0.3 mi from N Duke St (0.9 mi from I-85). It has athletic fields and tennis courts. From the parking lot at the softball field, begin the Rock Quarry Trail at the woods' edge. Turn L at the first fork, pass the old rock quarry, and reach at 0.3 mi a 90-yd. side trail L to the Edison Johnson Rec Ctr. Cross the Ellerbee Creek bridge on Murray St and make an immediate L on a wide paved trail. After 125 yd., pass a replica of a brontosaurus, L (part of the NC Museum of Life and Science). At 0.7 mi, pass the Jaycee softball field. Cross Lavender St and reach jct L with a side trail and footbridge over Ellerbee Creek to a picnic and parking area of Northgate Park. The trail ends at Club Blvd at 1.2 mi. (Plans are to join the trail with the 0.5-mi Pearl Mill Trail for connections downtown.)

1022

1030

Fayetteville (Cumberland County)

Clark Park was established in 1959. It is best known for the J. Bayard Clark Nature Center with its nature exhibits and live animals. (A historical center is proposed.) The park is 70 acres between a RR and the Cape Fear River. A waterfall on a tributary is near the center. The park has three nature trails: 0.3-mi Laurel Trail among hardwoods, loblolly pine, and laurel; 0.6-mi Bear Trail, which loops to a river overlook among tall trees; and 0.4-mi Wetlands Trail, which crosses two streams among sweet gum, pine, fern and swamp cane. Cape Fear River Trail (3.5 mi, easy, multi-use) goes N in scenic river area. After 700-ft. boardwalk cross Eastwood Ave. Access N is at Methodist College soccer field and parking area. (See chapter 15.) All trails are accessible from the parking area toward the center.

1031-
1034

Address and Access: Access to the park is off US-401 on Sherman Dr (E), two blocks S of Veterans Hospital. Clark Nature Center, 631 Sherman Dr, Fayetteville, NC 28301; 910-433-1579. Also, Fayetteville Parks and Rec Dept, 433 Hay St, Fayetteville, NC 28301; 910-433-1547.

Fuquay-Varina (Wake County)

Some towns have recreation departments that provide additional activities. This town's park management sets a good example by having concerts, drama programs, arts and crafts, dances, and a biological education program in a community center. Adjoining the center is South Park, which emphasized physical recreation. There are three ball fields, other sports facilities, and a 0.6-mi paved track and walking trail. Described below is a special 28-acre forest park that features educational trails, a picnic area, an amphitheatre, overlooks, bridges, resting benches, and rest rooms. The park is open daily 7:00AM to dusk. Horses and ATVs are prohibited from the trails.

Carroll Howard Johnson Environmental Education Park

Honeysuckle Lane Trail (92 yd.); *Holly Ridge Trail* (0.3 mi); **1035-** *Loblolly Loop Trail* (165 yd.); *Laurel Lane Trail* (0.17 mi); *Creek-* **1046** *side Trail* (0.15 mi); *Willow Way Trail* (82 yd.); *Hickory Hollow Loop Trail* (0.3 mi); *Whitetail Trail* (141 yd.); *Heritage Trail* (0.3 mi); *Kenneth Crossing Trail* (60 yd.); *Hummingbird Lane Trail* (0.12 mi); *Persimmon Trail* (90 yd.)

Length and Difficulty: 1.7 mi or 2.0 mi (more if backtracking), easy

Trailhead and Description: From the cresent-shaped parking area with huge oaks, examine the park's signboard near the rest rooms and amphitheatre. Hikers will see a labyrinth of multiple color-blazed trails. Once on them, hikers will see markers with an aggregation of natural history and vascular plants. If going to the picnic shelter or to use a clockwise approach, choose a L entrance. This would include such trails as Honeysuckle Trail and Holly Ridge Trail because it is 0.2 mi to the picnic shelter on Loblolly Loop Trail. Both the Holly Ridge Trail and Laurel Lane Trail take hikers along the hillside, under a power line, and to a meeting place beside the stream (Kenneth Branch). These trails also connect with Creekside Trail, which leads to bridges for the Heritage Trail and other trails on a hillside. The shortest trail to arched Kenneth and the Heritage Trail is on 90-yd. Persimmon Trail, R of the amphitheatre and trail map. The Heritage Trail meanders upstream beside Kenneth Branch. Open areas under the power line have wildflowers, birds such as cardinal, bluebird, and towhee, and shrubs such as sparkleberry and titi. After crossing Wagstaff Rd at 0.3 mi, the trail follows upstream for another 0.3 mi to the third (lowest) baseball field at South Park.

Address: Fuquay-Varina Parks, Rec, and Cultural Resources Dept, 820 S Main St, Fuquay-Varina, NC 27526; 919-552-1430; fax: 919-557-3112.

Greensboro (Guilford County)

The city of Greensboro operates 170 parks and rec areas. The city has a 70-mi labyrinth of bicycle trails (some of which are used for hiking, birding, skating, and jogging). A number of parks have unnamed paths (such as Fisher Park Circle, traditional and beautiful), and others only physical-fitness courses. Some areas, such as Hamilton Lake, may have a path nearby, but not **1047** around the lake. The 0.9-mi Hamilton Lake Trail begins at the corner of Starmount Dr and E Keeling Rd at Lake Hamilton. It follows R of Starmount Dr on pea gravel through an open forest of tall and magnificent hickory, oak, poplar, pine, and beech—excellent to view for autumn foliage. The trail ends at the corner of Kemp Rd and Starmount.

Barber Park is an ultramodern and spaciously landscaped facility with an Indoor Sports Pavilion for tennis and volleyball. It has sheltered picnic plat-**1048** forms, athletic fields, and remarkable 1.0-mi Barber Park Trail. The cement loop is designed for the physically disabled. It passes through the forest on the NW side and sweeps around a grassy area elsewhere. Wild rose, cow-itch vine, wild grapevine, and honeysuckle garnish the E fence line. Access is off I-40, Exit 128, W on E Lee St to Florida St L, and park entrance L.

Bur-Mil Park is an expansive and popular facility of 247 acres in the NW edge of the city. The park is off US-220 on 5834 Owl's Roost Rd E, where the entrance is L (N). It is bordered on the N side partly by Lake Brandt and Brush Creek from Lake Higgins on the NW. Facilities include an indoor and outdoor swimming pool, golf courses, tennis courts, two fishing ponds, picnic shelters, athletic fields, volleyball courts, playground, clubhouse, and two multi-use trails. They are connected by 0.4 mi of the Lake Brandt Greenway. The park's **1049** 2.0-mi Big Loop Trail makes a circuit on the W side of the park. The most convenient access is either at the swimming pool parking lot or the golf driving-range parking lot. Follow the trail into the forest of tall hardwoods, pine, and a groundcover patch of running cedar. Cross a number of bridges over small streams, the last of which is 0.2 mi before a jct with Lake Brandt Greenway. (To the L on Lake Brandt Greenway is a bridge over a narrow part of the lake and on to Strawberry St.) Turn R on the greenway and follow it to a fishing pier, L, and access to a parking lot, R., near picnic shelter #6. (If hik-**1050** ers wish to include the 1.0-mi Little Loop Trail, continue ahead on the greenway 65 yd. To pass Owl's Roost Trail, L, and continue on the greenway to a jct with Little Loop Trail, R. Both loops provide access to the clubhouse and parking lots. For more information, contact 336-373-3800.

Country Park, also in the NW part of the city, adjoins Science Center/ Planetarium on the NW (only 110 yd. between their parking lots), Lewis Rec Center on the S, and Guilford Courthouse National Military Park on the N. Access is off US-220 on Pisgah Church Rd, R, for four blocks to turn L on Lawndale Dr N. Turn L on Nathanael Greene Dr to park's parking area and office. Facilities include a lake for fishing, picnic shelters, volleyball courts, and a special 0.5-mi trail for the visually impaired. Another trail, 1.6-mi **1051** Country Park Trail, is a paved loop around the park. (The Bicentennial Greenway, a regional trail, which upon its completion, will connect to High Point's Gibson Park, begins here just W of Lewis Rec Center at Country Park.) There is also a trail for mountain bikes. One of the city's oldest parks (1924), it has an impressive history. Some of the special events are Carolina Cup Bicycle Road Race (one of the largest cycling events in the US) and the Wild Turkey Fat Tire Festival (mountain-bike race). Park office phone is 336-545-5342/5343, and shelter reservations is 336-335-6495.

Oka T. Hester Park is a more recent facility SW in the city E of the Sedgefield Country Club. The park has a large center for community activities, a lake, picnic area, playground, tennis and volleyball courts, and a physical-fitness trail. The 1.3-mi Hester Park Trail loops the beautiful lake. Access from **1052** I-40 and US-29A/70A, Exit 217, is 1.8 mi W on US-29A/70A to Groometown Rd. Turn L, and after 0.9 mi turn L to Ailanthus St and Hester Park.

Lake Daniel Park has Lake Daniel Trail, an easy 3.5-mi concrete biking, **1053** hiking, and exercise trail between Lake Daniel Park complex and Latham Park. On Lake Daniel Trail the mileage is marked. Entry can be made at a number of streets between the points of origin. To walk the distance given above, begin on Lake Dr near Battleground Ave and proceed W (near an E-flowing stream) to N Elam Ave near Wesley Long Community Hospital. Meadows are open and grassy, with scattered trees of oak, ash, poplar, and pine. (A city bike map is advisable.)

With Guilford County, the city has an expansive long-range plan to have greenways, bike trails, and hiking trails to encompass the entire county. The bike trails currently within the city proper will have at least 10 new access routes to connect with the Mountains-to-Sea Bicycle Route #2, which passes through the S side of the county. When completed, the outstanding Bicentennial Trail will be the longest trail in the state to connect multiple cities. Currently, a 7.0-mi section is completed as a greenway from High Point Lake at High Point/Jamestown N to Gallimore Dairy Rd near I-40 (see High Point in this chapter). Currently there are 3.8 mi of this trail on the ground at the N end and beginning from Country Park/Lewis Rec Center area. It then extends to Horse Pen Creek Rd. The N section will cross I-40, pass E of the Piedmont Triad International Airport, go NE near Horsepen Creek, turn E, then SE along Old Battlefield Rd, and reach jct with existing greenways at Guilford Court House National Military Park. From there it connects with Jaycee Park and Country Park. A master plan shows the potential for its route N to connect with the lake system of trails, including the MST foot trail.

Address: Parks and Rec Dept, Box 3136, Greensboro, NC 27402; 336-373-2574.

Gardens of Greensboro

The city has three major gardens: Bicentennial Garden, Arboretum, and Bog Garden, all in the heart of the city within a few blocks of, or adjoining, each other. The day-use gardens are open year-round and admission is free. They are made possible by the partnership of Greensboro Parks and Rec Dept and Greensboro Beautiful, a nonprofit organization of volunteers affiliated with Keep America Beautiful Inc. Brochures as elegant as the gardens are available on location. Visits to these parks lift the human spirit. Address: Greensboro Beautiful Inc, 501 Yanceyville St, Greensboro, NC 27402; 336-373-2199 (other visitor information, 800-344-2282).

The Greensboro Arboretum is located within Lindley Park, accessed off W Market St on Green Valley Rd (S), then immediately R on one-way Starmount Dr to a parking area. From the end of the parking area (near a basketball court), walk to an arched bridge over a stream. A 1.1-mi Greensboro
1054 Arboretum Trail loop can be made, but the distance is longer if using spur trails for closer examination of the collection areas and off the trail to the dancing fountain. Hundreds of species in such collections as conifers, sun shrubs, wildflowers, small trees, hydrophytic plants, vines, shade shrubs, and ground covers make this an alluring horticultural delight. Birds and butterflies are prominent visitors.

To locate the Bicentennial Garden turn off Friendly Ave N to 1105 Hobbs Rd. The park is meticulously maintained and specializes in mass regimented
1055 plantings of bulbs, annuals, perennials, and roses. Follow the 0.8-mi Bicentennial Garden Trail to the bridge over a small stream and into a lightly wooded garden where more than 100 plants are found in a fragrance garden and herb garden. (Labels are also in braille). The area is part of the Caldwell

Memorial Park, in honor of David Caldwell (1725–1824), patriot, statesman, clergyman, physician, and founder of Caldwell Log College in 1767.

Nearby the Bicentennial Garden is Bog Garden, E of Hobbs Rd between Starmount Farm Rd (N) and Northline Ave on the S side. It features aquatic plants (such as cattail, iris, lilies, sedge, arum) that need wet, spongy, acidic soil. Additionally, the bog entices duck, geese, and heron. Paved Bog Garden Trail, usable by visitors with wheelchairs, is around the lake for a total of 0.7 mi. There are boardwalks and a hillside path for a total of 0.7 mi.   **1056**

Hagan-Stone Park

The park has 409 acres of forest, fields, and developed areas. Facilities include a tent/RV campground (with full svc), hot showers, picnic tables, and public phone. (Among the rec activities are swimming at Camp Joy Pool, fishing, picnicking, nature study, and hiking. There are two unique historic structures: one for tobacco and the other is Oakgrove School House.

Access: From the jct of I-85 and US-421, go SE on US-421 for 3.4 mi to NC-22 jct. Turn R and go 4.1 mi on NC-22 to Winding Rd (SR-3411). Turn L and go 0.4 mi to entrance, L.

Louise Chatfield Hiking Trail (3.4 mi); *Dogwood Trail* (0.5 mi); *Harold Draper Nature Trail* (1.5 mi); *Schoolhouse Trail* (0.3 mi); *Ridge Trail* (0.8 mi)   **1057- 1061**

Length and Difficulty: 6.5 mi combined round-trip, easy

Trailhead and Description: When entering the park, turn L to a parking area near the trail center. Descend to the lake and begin the trail clockwise. The red-signed Louise Chatfield Trail connects with all other trails. If following this trail, enter an old forest road that is also the blue-signed Dogwood Trail and part of the circle of the yellow-signed Harold Draper Nature Trail. After 1.0 mi is a hardwood forest; turn off of the old road on a foot trail. Descend to cross a small bridge and go upstream to a jct where Dogwood Trail turns R at 0.3 mi. (Dogwood Trail crosses a footbridge over a small stream and ascends in a rocky area for 0.1 mi to a jct with Harold Draper Nature Trail, R and L. If heading R, hikers will descend near a parking area, a picnic area, and lake #2. Cross a stream at the upper edge of the lake and follow a forest road back to the trail center.)

If continuing on the Louise Chatfield Hiking Trail and the Harold Draper Nature Trail, you will ascend slightly on a rocky area to pass L of the primitive tent and group campgrounds. At 0.7 mi, the Louise Chatfield Hiking Trail turns L at a signpost and Harold Draper Nature Trail turns R. (A return can be made here on Harold Draper Nature Trail. Cross an old forest road and gently descend to cross a footbridge at 0.2 mi. At 0.3 mi, curve R at the headwaters of lake #4. Enter a grassy field; pass L of the RV campground and R of a restored tobacco barn. In this area, hikers will see connecting routes of the 8K cross-country route. At 0.55 mi, cross the campground road and connect with Dogwood Trail, R and L. Stay L to return to the trail center.)

After leaving Harold Draper Nature Trail, the Louise Chatfield Hiking Trail curves E and reaches the Oak Grove Schoolhouse at 1.3 mi. (Here the short Schoolhouse Trail loops to connect with a softball field and picnic shelter #4.) On Louise Chatfield Hiking Trail, hikers will soon enter an open field with yellow pine and cedar borders, pass a 5K–8K route on the R that leads to orange-signed Ridge Trail. (The Ridge Trail passes to the R of lake #1 and follows an old straight fence lined with cedar and pine. At 0.4 mi, reach an intersection with the 5K–8K route. Go straight; at 0.7 mi is a jct with an access leading L to rest rooms and picnic shelter #5. Cross a gravel road, pass L of a tennis court, and reach jct with the Louise Chatfield Hiking Trail at 0.8 mi.)

To complete the Louise Chatfield Hiking Trail, continue and pass through groves of dogwood by an open field. Pass twice under a power line. At 2.7 mi, make a jct with Ridge Trail, R. Continue ahead and at 3.0 mi is a jct with a service-road access. Pass L of lake #3 to reach the park office. Across the entrance road is the trail center parking lot at 3.4 mi.

Greensboro Watershed Trails

Lake Brandt, between Lake Higgins and Lake Townsend, is one of the city's watershed lakes. It has a marina on the S side that provides fishing and boating (no swimming). Cooperative efforts between the city, county, and private citizens have created and maintain the six trails at Lake Brandt, three trails at Lake Higgins, and three trails at Lake Townsend. The trails are described ahead in that order.

Address and Access: Lake Brandt Marina, 5945 Lake Brandt Rd, Greensboro, NC 27455; 336-545-5333. From the NW section of the city at the jct of US-220 (Battleground Ave) and Lawndale Dr, follow Lawndale Dr (which becomes Lake Brandt Rd) 5.3 mi N to the S end of the dam and park L at entry space (or onto available side-road space) for Nat Greene Trail. (See other parking spaces ahead.)

Lake Brandt

Nat Greene Trail (3.4 mi); *Lake Brandt Greenway* (3.5 mi); *Owl's Roost Trail* (4.1 mi); *Piedmont Trail* (3.0 mi); *Reedy Fork Trail* (3.7 mi); *Laurel Bluff Trail* (3.5 mi)

1062-1067

Length and Difficulty: 21.2 mi combined, easy

Connecting Trails: (Little Loop Trail, Big Loop Trail, Peninsula Trail at Lake Townsend)

Trailhead and Description: Two loops (8.1 mi and 15.2 mi) can be made of these trails. The Nat Greene Trail is part of the MST and is for hiking only. The trail was named to honor Nathanael Greene, who led the colonial army against Lord Cornwallis at Guilford Courthouse, March 15, 1781, and for whom the city is named. After entering a forest of oak, yellow poplar, beech, and Virginia pine, pass the parking area of Lake Brandt Marina at 0.1 mi. Weave in and out of coves for periodic views of the lake. Cross a small stream at 1.5 mi and reach jct with paved multi-use Lake Brandt Greenway, R and L, at 2.7 mi. (To the L, the greenway ascends 1.0 mi to Lake Brandt Rd near the corner with Old Battlefield Rd. To the R, the greenway's N trailhead is at Strawberry Rd.) Continue ahead on the Nat Greene Trail and enter a marsh at 2.9 mi. Follow a 153-yd. boardwalk through a floodplain and reach Old Battleground Rd and multi-use Bicentennial Greenway, L and R.

(To the L, it follows a sidewalk 0.4 mi to Lake Brandt Rd, through Guilford Courthouse National Military Park, and to a parking area accessible off of Pisgah Church Rd and on Jaycee Park Dr, its N terminus. To the R, it crosses a trail bridge over Horse Pen Creek, and after 0.1 mi turns L across Old Battleground Rd to continue into a forest. [Old Battlefield Rd goes 0.7 mi to US-220.] The greenway is 3.8 mi and currently ends at Horse Pen Creek Rd. Future plans are for the greenway to continue SW paralleling the creek until crossing Ballinger Rd, then S to cross W Market St, I-40, and join the Chimney Rock Rd section. From there it follows the completed section to High Point Lake. For more information, contact 336-373-3816.)

To continue the loop, backtrack on the Nat Greene Trail to Lake Brandt Greenway (also the MST route) and turn L. Cross a new bridge (honoring Michael Weaver) of an old RR crossing at 0.1 mi. At 0.4 mi is a jct with Owl's Roost Trail, R. (The Owl's Roost Trail is a multi-use trail designed for mountain-bike enthusiasts as well as hikers. The trail passes through both hardwoods and pine. It winds through fallen pine from storms and has irregular turns over banks and logs for leaps by mountain bikers. At 2.0 mi is a view (mainly wintertime) of the lake's dam and marina. There is a hilly area at 2.4 mi and a boardwalk at 3.6 mi. It returns to the greenway at 4.1 mi.)

If following Lake Brandt Greenway from Weaver Bridge, pass a second jct with Owl's Roost Trail, R, at 0.6 mi. At 0.9 mi, cross Owl's Roost Rd subdivision and for a short distance on a concrete treadway into a forest of tall trees. Pass L of a small pond to a jct with Bur-Mill Park's Little Loop Trail at 1.3 mi. At the N end of the pond an access goes straight ahead to a parking lot near a park office, but the trail curves R to rejoin the RR bed. Turn L and at 1.6 mi reach jct R with N access to Owl's Roost Trail. Continuing 65 yd. is a pier, R, and to the L up an embankment is access to a Bur-Mill Park parking lot. At 1.9 mi is a jct L with Big Loop Trail. (See Bur-Mill description above.)

Continuing on the Lake Brandt Greenway, cross an old 295-ft. RR bridge, where highway traffic can be seen L on US-220. Enter a pastoral area and reach jct with the Piedmont Trail, R, at 2.3 mi. Ahead it is 0.2 mi to a small roadside parking space on Strawberry Rd (SR-2321), the N end of Lake Brandt Greenway. (It is 0.2 mi L to US-220.) (Work has begun on extending a greenway across Strawberry Rd on the old RR grade N toward Summerfield.)

To continue the loop, backtrack to Piedmont Trail and follow it into a combination of grassy fields, cedar, and wild plum. After 0.5 mi, descend into a seepage area near the lake. Cross streams at 1.0 and 1.2 mi, then a boardwalk at 1.6 mi. Cross a bridge at 2.6 mi and at 2.8 mi, arrive at Lake Brandt Rd. Turn R and cross a bridge at the dam for 0.3 mi to complete the loop.

A longer loop can be made by taking the Reedy Fork Trail across the road from Piedmont Trail. After a forest of hardwoods, cross a gas pipeline at 0.5 mi. Cross a footbridge and enter a mountain-laurel grove. At 1.3 mi, turn L from Reedy Creek. To the R, briefly join an old woods road at 2.1 mi. In this area are multiple wildflowers. Arrive at Plainfield Rd (SR-2324) at 3.2 mi near a guardrail. Turn R on the road to cross a marsh causeway frequented by waterfowl. At 3.7 mi, reach a jct with Church St (SR-1001). Turn R and cross the bridge. After 0.1 mi, reach a jct to the R with Laurel Bluff Trail. To the L across the road is the N trailhead of Peninsula Trail. (Both are part of the MST route.)

The Laurel Bluff Trail passes through the Roger Jones Bird Sanctuary and into a river birch grove at 0.1 mi. Follow an old woods road for a short distance and at 0.6 mi, pass a field boundary. Among the shrubs are filbert, beauty-bush, and redbud. Pass the edge of a lake at 2.0 mi, followed by a wet area. At a fork, stay R and pass a spur to the L at 2.7 mi. After crossing a pipeline at 3.1 mi, exit to follow woods edge and return to Lake Brandt Rd at 3.3 mi. The Nat Greene Trail is across the road, L, for a loop of 15.2 mi.

Lake Higgins

The lake is a product of a dam on Brush Creek NW of Greensboro. The dam is near the W side of US-220, and its outlet is under the highway from which point waters flow E to join Reedy Creek on the way into Lake Brandt. Access is 0.9 mi N on US-200 from Bur-Mill Park entrance to a L turn onto Hamburg Mill Rd. After 0.4 mi, turn L to a marina parking area. At the SW corner is Lake Higgins Nature Trail (0.4 mi, easy). It makes a loop among hardwoods **1068-** by the lake. For multi-use Bald Eagle Trail (4.0 mi, easy), drive a few yards **1069** farther on Hamburg Mill Rd to parking lot, L. The white-blazed trail is predominantly used by mountain bikers and is sponsored by the Greensboro Fat Tire Society. Generally on flat terrain, it passes through a forest of hardwoods and pine. Cross Carlson Dairy Rd at 1.6 mi and a natural gas pipeline at 2.4 mi. Cross a paved road at 2.9 mi. After wet or damp areas, cross a sewage line at 3.6 mi. Arrive at Long Valley Rd at 4.0 mi. (To the L is 110 yd. to Brass Eagle Loop Rd.) Backtrack. To reach Beech Bluff Trail (1.0 mi, easy) at the **1070** end of Bald Eagle Trail, turn L on Brass Eagle Loop Rd, cross the bridge over Brush Creek, go 90 yd. and turn L into the woods to follow a blazed foot trail. Ascend on a hillside, and at 0.5-mi a descent to cross a sewage line. After a floodplain area, follow a svc road to Lewiston Rd at 1.0 mi. Backtrack.

Lake Townsend

Lake Townsend is fed by Lake Higgins, Lake Brandt, and Richard Lake. All waters flow E, and at the E end of Lake Townsend is its dam. Adjoining the lake/dam area is Bryan Park, one of the city's largest and known for its golf courses. Three Lake Townsend area trails are described below.

Peninsula Trail (1.2 mi); ***Osprey Trail*** (2.5 mi); ***Townsend Trail*** (4.2 mi)   **1071-**
    Length and Difficulty: 7.9 mi combined, easy   **1073**
    Connecting Trail: (Laurel Bluff Trail)
    Trailhead and Description: From the jct of Pisgah Church Rd (its NE end where it becomes Lees Chapel Rd) and Church St (Rd) (N), go 2.0 mi to a roadside parking area R, for the Osprey Trail, R. Ahead, across the causeway, it is 1.0 mi to the N trailhead of Peninsula Trail. Across the road, L, is the trailhead for Laurel Bluff Trail. For the E trailhead of Osprey Trail, it is 2.1 mi N on Yanceyville Rd from Lees Chapel Rd. Here is the W trailhead of Townsend Trail. Its E trailhead is accessed by taking Lees Chapel Rd NE to Southshore Rd L at the Townsend Rd jct. (The Osprey Trail and Townsend Trail are part of the MST route.)

Enter the white-blazed Peninsula Trail through young Virginia pines. At 0.6 mi is an observation spot of Lake Townsend. After a wet runoff area is a mixed pine and magnolia grove at 0.9 mi. Exit at N Church Rd at 1.2 mi, turn L, and cross the causeway for 300 yd. to a roadside parking area, L (E). The Osprey Trail begins here. Follow the white-blazed trail past remains of an old cabin at 0.2 mi. At 0.3 mi, pass close to the lake's lapping shoreline. Ascend a slight ridge of oak and pine and descend to parallel a cove before rock-hopping a stream at 0.8 mi. Return to the lake's edge, then cross under two power lines to follow a rim of a former pond. At 2.1 mi is an excellent view of the lake. Arrive at Yanceyville Rd at 2.5 mi. Backtrack, or have a second vehicle. It is 5.9 mi on the roads for a return to the point of origin.

The white-blazed Townsend Trail begins across the road at a gate opposite the Osprey Trail. Pass through a grassy slope by the lake for 113 yd. to enter the forest at a berm. At 0.4 mi, L, is an old well in a forest of oak, beech, and dogwood. Curve around a long cove, cross a stream, and return to the lakeside at 1.0 mi. At 1.6 mi, walk on the sandy edge of the lake to avoid dense growth under a power line. Here are buttonbush, filbert, and tag alder. Reenter the forest and follow the edge of another cove. Cross a footbridge, enter a grove of Virginia pine and club moss. At 2.7 mi are ridges on the treadway, indicating a former tobacco field. Pass under a power line at 3.1 mi and 3.4 mi. Curve R of a farm pond to ascend at 3.7 mi. Cross a small stream and ascend slightly. At 3.8 mi arrive at a parking lot on Southshore Rd. (From here it is 0.4 mi R to a RR crossing, where a R on Lees Chapel Rd is 3.7 mi to Church St, and R for 2.0 mi on Church St to Osprey Trail.) (USGS Maps: Lake Brandt, Browns Summit)

Henderson (Vance County)

Fox Pond Park has lighted tennis courts, picnic area with shelters, playground, youth baseball field, fishing (no swimming), and trails. From the parking lot near the tennis courts, begin the 1.4-mi Fox Pond Trail on the E side of the lake and go counterclockwise. Cross a floating bridge at the lake's headwaters at 0.5 mi. Cross a svc road near a cement bunker at 0.9 mi, cross over the stream (near the dam) on a bridge at 1.3 mi, and return to the parking lot. E of the parking lot is the 0.6-mi Conoconors Trail, which loops through sweet gum and poplar trees around the tennis courts. Park is open year-round.

1074

1075

Address and Access: Rec and Parks Dept, Box 1556, Henderson, NC 27536; 252-431-6090; fax: 252-492-1229. On NC-39 (0.4 mi E of Bypass US-1) turn on Vicksboro Rd (SR-1533) and go 0.5 mi to the park, L.

High Point (Guilford County)

The city is following the trend of its triangle cities, Greensboro and Winston-Salem, in long-range plans for a greenway system. At present a 1.4-mi section of Boulding Branch Trail is completed. Access to its SW trailhead is off N **1076** Main St E on Farris Ave to its jct with Forest St. Follow an asphalt trail downstream and go through a cement tunnel at Centennial St at 0.2 mi. Pass through High Point University campus between W College Dr and E College Dr at 0.5 and 0.6 mi. At 1.2 mi, reach E Lexington Ave, where to the L is High Point Museum and Historic Park. Ahead and R of the trail is the Little Red Schoolhouse, built in 1930 at Ray Street Elementary School downtown, and moved here in 1987. At 1.3 mi is access W to Welborn Middle School across a footbridge. Continue R on the main trail and exit at the jct of Woodruff and Wiltshire Sts. When the trail (about another 3.0 mi) is completed downstream to Deep River and connected with the Bicentennial Greenway Trail at Penny Rd, High Point and Jamestown will be joined by a greenway system. The city also contributes approximately 65 percent of the funding for the Piedmont Environmental Center at High Point City Lake, a 200-acre preserve for natural-science study. It provides an outdoor classroom program for public schools, and it has a wildflower garden with emphasis on plants from the Piedmont. Picnicking is allowed but no camping or swimming. The center is open daily.

Address and Access: Piedmont Environmental Center, 1228 Penny Rd, High Point, NC 27260; 336-883-8531. From the jct of US-29A/70A and Penny Rd (W in Jamestown), go N 1.1 mi on Penny Rd and turn R at the center's entrance. From Greensboro, at the jct of Wendover Ave and I-40, Exit 214, go SW on Wendover Ave 4.5 mi to the jct with Penny Rd (at the Deep River intersection). Turn L and go 2.0 mi to the center, L. (The Parks and Rec Dept address is 221 Nathan Hunt Dr, High Point, NC 27260; 336-887-3477.)

Bicentennial Greenway

Bicentennial Greenway Trail 1077

Length and Difficulty: 6.2 mi, easy to moderate

Trailhead and Description: The N access is off I-40, Exit 210, on NC-68 S for 0.4 mi. Turn L (E) on Regency Dr and park on the R at a parking space (may become another street). Walk 290 yd. farther on Regency Dr to trailhead R(S). The S trailhead is at the N end of Deep River bridge on Penny Rd where parking is available 0.35 mi N on Penny Rd to the Piedmont Environmental Center.

Throughout the trail are tall mixed hardwoods of oak, yellow poplar, sycamore, and river birch. Virginia pine thrive on the slopes, mixed with loblolly pine. Grassy trail shoulders are frequently mowed and the width of the landscape provides a flow of breezes. Wild roses, muscadine grape, blackberry, and August olive are prominent. Ferns and wildflowers border the woods' edges.

The multiuse trail is open for bikers, pedestrians, skaters, and joggers. Horse traffic and motorized vehicles are not allowed; neither is camping. Dogs must be on a leash. Some sections are easy for the physically disabled.

If beginning at Regency Dr at Piedmont Centre Office Park, follow the signs on a wide asphalt trail. After steps and a boardwalk in a forest arrive at a meadow of blackberry and honeysuckle. At 0.6 mi is a parking area. A sign indicates the first 2.8 mi of the trail opened in November 1989. Continue along the side of the East Fork of Deep River, occasionally crossing it on concrete bridges. Cross a bridge over a stream from Davis Lake, R, at 1.1 mi. At 1.3 mi is a small cascade, L. Cross W Wendover Ave at 2 mi. (The access is under construction, and the trail may go under the road beside the river.)

At 2.5 mi pass through Gibson Park. To the R is Deep River Cabin (ca. 1830), rest rooms, and an access on Park Entrance Rd to W Wendover Ave. On the trail is a plaque honoring the history and craftsmanship of the Jamestown Long Rifles. (Here is also a 1.0-mi-loop trail. It has a spur trail to a bluff and cascade.) One of the most scenic areas of the trail is at 3.0 mi where an observation deck juts into a swamp, an excellent retreat for birders. Cattail, arrow arum, buttonbush, swamp buttercup, and willow provide plant diversity. At 3.4 mi is a patch of wild plums. Reach a svc road (Sunnyvale Dr) **1078** at 3.5 mi and turn R. After 80 ft. red-blazed, 4.6-mi Deep River Trail (for pedestrians only) crosses the road, L and R. (To the R it follows up a small stream and returns after a crescent to join the main trail. To the L it enters a floodplain and meanders near the W bank of High Point Lake until it rejoins **1079** the main trail at E Fork Rd. Along its route it makes a loop, Hollis Rogers Pine Woods Trail [under construction] in a loblolly pine forest.)

Continuing on the main trail, follow the road for another 150 yd. and turn L, steeply uphill. Cross a pipeline, then under a power line, and arrive at Jamestown Park at 4.4 mi. Here are rest rooms and parking facilities, R, across E Fork Rd. Parallel the road; reach jct L with the Deep River Trail at 4.7 mi. Cross the E Fork Rd. For the next 0.2 mi are a number of boardwalks, bridges, and steps. Enter the Piedmont Environmental Center trail network (see above). At 5.8 mi arrive at the parking area of the center. Beyond the center's entrance the trail descends steeply to High Point Lake and its S end at Penny

Rd. Backtrack to the center's parking area. (USGS Maps: Guilford, High Point E)

Louisburg (Franklin County)

The historic town of Louisburg has a historic district of heritage homes that includes Louisburg College, the oldest two-year college (1787) in the nation. There are two parks, one mainly as a picnic area, on the E side of Tar River, downtown, and another, the Joyner Park, upstream on the W side of the river. Access to the latter from S Main St is 0.5 mi on West River Rd to the park's entrance R. In Phase I there is a sports field, sheltered picnic areas, a children's playground, and 0.4 mi paved River View Loop Trail on a bluff. From 1080 it is a 2.0 mi Cypress Scout Trail that follows an easy contour on a N slope, 1081 under a powerline, and into a deep forest where near the river is a scenic cypress grove. Along the way are ferns, blood root, dotted horsemint, and cranefly orchids. After a loop, backtrack. Access to the trails is from the E side of both parking lots. In addition a 2.2 mi section of Louisburg-Franklinton 1082 Rail-Trail is being constructed from S Main St near the Tar River bridge W to Vance-Granville Community College, Franklin County Campus.

Address: Louisburg Parks and Rec, 110 W Nash St, Louisburg, NC 27549; 919-496-4145; fax: 919-396-6319.

Oxford (Granville County)

Lake Devin is also called City Lake. Originally constructed for Oxford's water supply the 196.6-acre lake now serves as a recreational site for boating and fishing (with permits). Swimming is not allowed, but picnicking (tables on trails and a large picnic shelter) is authorized.

Address and Access: Oxford Parks and Rec Dept., P.O. Box 506, Oxford, NC 27565; 919-603-1135; fax: 919-603-1138. From I-85, Exit 204, drive 1.0 mi W on Linden Ave (NC-96) to Hillsboro St S (US-15). After 0.2 mi, stay straight (do not follow US-15), cross RR track on Providence St, pass Industry Rd, and at traffic light turn R on Old NC-75. After 0.3 mi, turn R on Lake Devin Rd. Drive 0.4 mi slowly and watch for small sign, R, to Lake Devin. If accessing from the N on US-158 follow Industry Drive S and turn R on Providence St (as above).

Spillway Trail (1.3 mi); *Pine Grove Trail* (0.7 mi); *Peninsula Trail* 1083-
(2.0 mi) 1085

Length and Difficulty: 4.7 mi round trip and backtracking, easy

Trailhead and Description: From the gravel parking area walk to and cross the pastoral dam among yellow buttercup on Spillway Trail. Cross a footbridge over the spillway at 0.3 mi. After 70 yd. cross under a power line to enter the forest. Follow the signs on a wide trail to make a loop. If turning R pass a picnic site. At 0.6 mi are Solomon seal and whorled loosestrife. Complete the loop and return. At the parking area the Pine Grove Trail begins N of the picnic shelter. Unsigned and possibly unmaintained the old road enters the forest beside a fence with honeysuckle. In tall grass the route may be damp. Turn L under a power line and into a field to a large water pump, L. Re-enter the forest in a mature stand of loblolly pine. Curve sharply L in a cove at 0.4 mi. Arrive at Hillsboro St Ext and trail sign at 0.5 mi. Turn L, cross causeway and at 0.7 mi turn off road to sign L, and being Peninsula Trail. After 100 yd. bear R of an observation site and picnic table. Old directional signs indicate the trail route on a peninsular and coves among hardwoods and pine. Wood duck and Canadian geese are on the lake; wild turkey and raccoon in the woods. Ridges in pathway indicate tobacco rows of a former farm field. At 0.4 mi ascend steps to an open field. Back in the woods are tall blueberry bushes and pink orchids. At 1.0 mi is open area and a view L of the "Red Barn," a preserved property of the town. Backtrack. (USGS Maps: Berea, Oxford)

Raleigh (Wake County)

Raleigh's sytem of more than 149 parks, recreation areas, and greenways/trails is diverse and expansive. Its greenway system is planned to circle within the city to make a connection with other triangle cities in the future. City residents approved a bond issue of $47.2 million (if it incures no tax increase) for expansion of parks and recreation. In addition, the Congressional Omnibus Appropriations provided $500,000 for a greenway section along Neuse River. The city currently has three major loop trails: Shelly and Lyn Lakes in the N half and Lake Johnson in the S. Another loop trail (unpaved) and lake are in Durant Nature Park, in N Raleigh. Until more connections can be made, the majority of the remaining trails are linear and on riparian land. Described ahead are some of the singular or isolated trails, then followed by small or large groups of trails. (Due to space constraints, descriptions are limited. Readers may find more specifics and maps in the author's *Trails of the Triangle* [John F. Blair Publishers]. Readers are advised to have a city map, as well as a map from Raleigh's Parks and Rec.)

Address: Raleigh Parks and Rec, 222 W Hargett St (P.O. Box 590), Raleigh, NC 27602; 919-890-3285; fax: 919-890-3299.

Border Trail (2.2 mi, moderate) is the longest trail in Durant Park. (also **1086** called Camp Durant and Durant Nature Park, but not to be confused with residential subdivision Durant Trails or nearby Durant Greenway. See Durant Trail ahead.) It begins at the parking area, accessible from US-1 (Capital Blvd) W 1.1 mi on Durant Rd to a small sign, L. From the map kiosk, the Border Trail, R, makes a loop around Upper and Lower Lakes. Along the way, it passes "whale rocks" by a stream at 0.3 mi, crosses a footbridge at 1.0 mi to enter a boggy area, and enters an old home site where a massive display of wisteria smells as fragrant as a perfume factory in the springtime. Intersect with numerous side trails and cross the dam at 2.0 mi to a jct with the N side Lakeside Trail (1.3 mi, easy), L. (It connects with Nature Trail, which ascends **1087-** with a bicycle trail to the parking lot.) Secret Trail (0.7 mi, moderate) (not a **1089** secret anymore) is E of the park office.

Buckeye Trail (2.5 mi, easy) is a paved greenway that meanders through **1090** a forest of river birch, yellow poplar, oak, and loblolly pine. It passes a picnic area at 0.2 mi, a playground at 1.4 mi, and a creek observation deck (ADA accessible) at 1.9 mi. Its E trailhead is at Crabtree Park off of Milburnie Rd, R, from US-64 (New Bern Rd) and W of I-440 (Exit 13). Upstream access is on Crabtree Blvd parking lot near the Raleigh Blvd jct.

Falls River Trail (1.2 mi, easy) is a suburban asphalt trail in the Falls River **1091** subdivision. It weaves among tall trees behind private homes and out to open spaces among wildflowers and flowering shrubs. If hiking from N to S, the trail crosses Falls River Ave at 0.9 mi and curves under a power line to exit at Walkertown Dr. **Access:** From the jct of US-1 and Durant Rd, drive W 1.8 mi on Durant Rd and turn R onto Falls River Ave. Drive 1.2 mi N and turn R on Farmington Grove Dr. If access is from Falls of Neuse Rd, drive E 0.8 mi on Durant Rd to L at Falls River Ave entrance.

Durant Trail (1.5 mi, easy) is a paved greenway paralleling a stream **1092** where the SE terminus is at Durant Park and the NW terminus is near Durant Rd Middle School. For access parking, choose parking lot at top of hill at Durant Park (See Border Trail above) and walk back 0.1 mi to greenway at bottom. Hiking SE 0.1 mi near end of road, residents are using spur routes to cross to Secret Trail in Durant Park. Pass the "whale rocks" at 0.3 mi, cross Hiking Trail (street) at 0.7 mi, a small natural waterfall at 1.0 mi, pass W of the school, and arrive at Durant Rd at 1.5 mi. Backtrack.

1093   Gardner Street Trail (0.8 mi, easy) is at Rose Garden and Raleigh Little Theatre. It begins at Gardner and Everett Sts. Follow the sign into the forest of hardwoods and loblolly pine to end at Jaycee Park on Wade Ave.

1094   Beaver Dam Trail (1.4 mi one-way, easy) follows Beaver Dam Creek partly in Hymettus Woods Park and on sidewalks. Access is corner of Lake Boone Trail (St) and Brooks Ave.

1095   Lake Johnson Trail (5.5 mi, moderate) makes a loop around the lake. Access from Western Blvd is on Avent Ferry Rd, 3.2 mi to park, L, across the causeway. It winds through a hardwood forest where coves have ferns and wildflowers and the pathway provides two small loops. Pass a waterfall at 0.6 mi and cross the lake's spillway at 1.6 mi. Continuing L, it arrives at the lake office, picnic area, and boathouse parking lot at 2.6 mi. Cross a long causeway for a visual display of the lake and return to the trailhead. Across the road, upstream, is a non-paved trail that makes a loop of the upper lake. Return across the causeway after 2.5 mi.

1096   Lake Lynn Trail (2.1 mi, easy) is a paved loop around a scenic lake. The main loop has six boardwalks, the longest of which leads across the marshy N end of the lake, a watery respite for turtles and waterfowl. Every 0.25 mi there are distance markers. If walking clockwise, cross the first boardwalk at
1097   0.4 mi in a cove; one of the longest (238 ft.) begins at 0.8 mi. At 1.0 mi, Lake Lynn Park Trail (0.3 mi, easy) goes R to exit at a parking area near a tennis court where the exit is to Bay Rd. Backtrack to complete the W side of the lake. Access from the W to the main entrance is off of US-70 on Lynn Rd for 1.3 mi to parking lot, L, near the base of the dam.

746   Loblolly Trail (6.0 mi, moderate) is diverse and unique with two lighted tunnels, through an experimental forest, by two lakes, across hills, and sandy footing on a floodplain. A special parking place is at Gate E (W) at the RBC Center (former site of Carter-Findley Stadium). Access is from I-440, Exit 4, W on Wade Ave for a R ramp turn to Edwards Mill Rd, L, and under a bridge. After 0.4 mi, turn L at Gate E (W) and go 100 yd. to parking, L. (If entering from Blue Ridge Rd on Trinity Rd, turn R at Gate D to four-way stop. Turn L and immediately turn R to parking lot.) Ascend bank to short descent of pavement and follow L of a fence to cross a small stream. Advance to crossing under Edwards Mill Rd, then downstream to enter tunnel under Wade Ave. Exit R, at 0.5 mi, then L to wide and grassy passage downstream. Enter Schenck
1098   Memorial Forest and reach jct with Frances Liles Interpretive Trail (1.2 mi, easy), R. Pass lake and exit forest at Reedy Creek Park Rd at 2.4 mi. Turn R and after 150 yd., turn L off of the road to border the lake, L, and a housing

development, R. Cross the dam halfway at 3.0 mi; descend R. At the base, enter the woods and follow the sign L. Enter Umstead State Park at 3.4 mi. Ascend and descend, pass a small lake (favored by beavers) and pass under a power line at 5.7 mi. Arrive at Reedy Creek parking lot for Umstead State Park at 6.0 mi. Access here is 0.3 mi from I-40 (see chapter 10, section 2).

Brentwood Greenway (0.6 mi, easy) in Brentwood Park. Located near the **1099** Brentwood Community Center off of Brentwood Rd, it parallels the stream to cross a bridge at the end of Glenraven Dr.

Museum Park Trail (0.9 mi, easy) and Upper Woodland Trail (0.7 mi, **1100** easy) are part of the NC Museum of Art open space. The trails connect and **1101** are part of a loop. The Museum Park Trail begins at a sign near the far L end of the parking area. It descends gently and passes a lake in a meadow. At 0.4 mi, the Upper Woodland Trail goes L. It rambles into the forest and passes an atronomy art chamber. After 1.1 mi, return to the paved loop, ascend, and pass through three Gyre ellipses of concrete, colored with iron oxide. Windmill art is also on display. At 1.5 mi, arrive at Blue Ridge Rd, circle the museum, and return to point of origin at 1.6 mi. (This area is part of the 2.0-mi Reedy Creek **1102** Greenway from Museum Park Trail, spanning a 660-ft. truss bridge over I-440, and through the campus of Meredith College to the corner of Hillsborough and Faircloth Streets.) Access from I-440, Exit 4: take Lake Boone Trail (St) W 0.8 mi, turn L on Blue Ridge Rd, and after 0.4 mi, turn L at Art Museum.

Neuse River Trail (4.0 mi) is a linear path paralleling Neuse river. The S **1103** access is off of US-64 (0.9 mi E of New Hope Rd) on Rogers Lane. After 1.4 mi, turn L into a parking lot. Follow a wide grassy road with trees such as beech and willow and shrubs such as wax and myrtle. At 1.1 mi is a long boardwalk near wetlands. Pass under US-64 bridge at 1.5 mi. At 2.1 mi, make a L, the R shift onto Raleigh Beech Rd. At 2.7 mi is a bridge near a wet area with water hyacinth. Pass L of a swamp at 3.3 mi. Leave the river, ascend and exit at the parking lot. Access here from US-64 is 0.9 mi N on New Hope Rd with a R turn onto Southall Rd. After 0.8 mi, turn R onto Castlebrook Dr, go 0.5 mi and turn R onto Abington Lane to its end.

Shelley-Sertoma Park/Crabtree Greenway Area

This combination of connecting trails provides the longest arrangement in the city at the time. The trails go out in three prongs, N, W, and E. Future plans are to connect the Shelley Lake area N to Honeycut Creek, and Crabtree Creek W to Umstead Park and E to Neuse River.

1104-   *Shelley Lake Trail* (2.2 mi); *Snelling Branch Trail* (0.6 mi) *Bent*
1113   *Creek Trail* (1.0 mi); *Sawmill Trail* (1.0 mi); *Ironwood Trail* (1.2
            mi); *Crabtree Valley Trail* (1.4 mi); *North Hills Trail* (1.0 mi);
            Alleghany Trail (2.4 mi); *Fallon Creek Trail* (0.5 mi); *Crabtree-Oak*
            Park Trail (1.6 mi)

Length and Difficulty: 12.9 mi (without backtracking), easy

Trailhead and Description: A suggested central parking area is Shelley-
Sertoma Park. the popular Shelley Lake Trail provides bicycling, hiking,
strolling with baby carriages, and roller skating. Access is the jct of US-70 and
NC-50 at Crabtree Valley Mall. Take NC-50 N 0.8 mi to Millbrook Rd (SR-
1812) and turn R to drive 1.0 mi at parking, L. Another option is 1.3 mi W on
Millbrook Rd from Six Forks Rd to the park, R. Parking is below the lake's
dam. Follow the paved trail to top of the dam and go R or L. If heading R,
enter a forest at 0.2 mi. At 0.7 mi is an alternate trail, L, to a wildlife observation deck. Reach jct with Snelling Branch Trail. (It goes 0.6 mi to cross
North Hills Dr and end at Optimist Club parking lot.) Backtrack.

Continuing on Shelley Lake Trail among sweet gum, oak, river birch, and
yellow root. Cross a bridge over Lead Mine Creek at 0.9 mi. (To the L, the
loop of Shelley Lake Trail continues.) To the R is Bent Creek Trail, which parallels Lead Mine Creek. The trail passes through a tunnel of North Hills Rd
and Lynn Rd, after which it divides with Sawmill Trail. Backtrack on both for
a return to Shelley Lake Trail. At 1.6 mi on the Shelley Lake Trail is a support
wall, observation area, and a long bridge over a lake cove for duck and geese
watching. Pass an access trail, R, to a residential area. to the L are rest rooms.
Return to the dam and descend to the parking lot.

From here at the far end of the parking lot, descend on Ironwood Trail and
hike under Millbrook Rd bridge on an asphalt treadway. The trail parallels,
and occasionally crosses, Lead Mine Creek 1.2 mi to a jct with North Hills
Trail. In the process, an access spur is L at 0.6 mi to North Hills Rd. At 0.8 mi
is a scenic rock bluff at the creek, L. A boardwalk is at 1.0 mi and access to
North Hills Rd is at 1.2 mi. (No parking here.) Turn L and for a few yds follow the sidewalk to cross the street and reenter the forest onto North Hills
Trail. Along the way is an arched bridge and tall hardwoods and loblolly
pines, some dressed in ivy that also covers sections of the forest floor. At 1.6
mi jct with Crabtree Valley Trail, R. If hiking L cross a bridge over Mine
Creek near its confluence with Crabtree Creek. After 0.1 mi jct with the
Alleghany Trail ahead and where the North Hills Trail goes L. (Trail users
may be confused on trail names because there are not any specific signs, only

Capital Area Greenways signs on most of the accesses. Some park listings have part of the North Hills Trail as Ironwood Trail Extension. The Parks and Rec trail planners may change some of the multiple names to a singular name such as Crabtree Trail for any section that follows Crabtree Creek.) If continuing on the North Hills Trail pass through a forest of large elm, ash, and yellow poplar to an ascent. At the top of the ridge pass the tennis court to the parking lot. Access here from Yadkin Dr is on Currituck Dr, L. **1114**

If continuing downstream on the Alleghany Trail pass under Benson Beltline (I-440/US-1) bridge with its noisy traffic sounds. Immediately turn R to cross an arched bridge over Crabtree Creek to a side access trail, R, at 0.2 mi. (The paved access trail goes 110 yds. to Alleghany Dr and jct with Alamance Rd R.) The main Alleghany Trail curves L to parallel the stream for more than 2.0 miles to connect with Middle Crabtree Trail. It passes under Wake Forest **1115** Rd and US-1/401. When completed, this section will cross a marsh on a 0.4 mi boardwalk to Raleigh Boulevard. From here it joins the 2.5 mi Buckeye Trail to Milburnie St. (Call 919-890-3293 for updated information.)

To hike Crabtree Creek upstream on paved Crabtree Valley Trail from the North Hills Trail, begin at the bridge jct mentioned above. Parallel the creek; apartment buildings are R. At 0.2 mi is a scenic rock overlook, L, and at 0.3 mi is a 30-yd. access to North Hills Rd (no parking here). At 0.5 mi is a short access of steps to a parking lot created for trail users. For vehicular access from the jct of busy US-70 (Glenwood Ave) and Lead Mine Rd (at Crabtree Valley Mall) take Lead Mine Rd and immediately turn R on Century Dr, then L to parking area. This parking retreat is also accessible for traffic off I-440 (Exit 7) W on US-70, R lane into access for Holiday Inn, then turn L on Century Dr.

Continuing on Crabtree Valley Trail cross an arched bridge where to the L are steps up to a svc station. Pass under US-70 bridge and follow a regal example of greenway engineering on a concrete base. At 0.8 mi concrete ends and asphalt begins. To the L is a parking area and restaurant (off Blue Ridge Rd and Crabtree Valley Rd). There is an access bridge, R, over the creek to the shopping mall at 1.0 mi, and 1.2 mi. At 1.4 mi is a greenway sign before going under Creedmoor Rd to Crabtree–Oak Park Trail. Pass a parking area used for overflow parking from a commercial area, R, at 0.1 mi. From here the character of the greenway changes to a gorge-like atmosphere with more natural areas in a dense hardwood forest. There are 9 bridges or boardwalks. Cross under a powerline at 0.9 mi. At 1.1 mi is an outstanding display of mountain laurel on the high slope across the creek. The trail currently ends at 1.6 mi, but a clearing is upstream for another 0.5 mi to see the high Duraleigh Rd bridge. There is a proposal to not only construct a greenway on this site but to extend beyond to Umstead State Park. Backtrack.

Walnut Creek Greenway Area

1116-
1117
1118

The following trails are in southside Raleigh. The first three are under construction with intent to connect. Two other greenway sections (Walnut Creek Eliza Pool Trail and Walnut Creek–City Farm Road Trail) are in a planning stage to connect with the other three. Little Rock Trail is separate and closer to downtown. The 1.2 mi paved Upper Walnut Creek Trail begins at the dam of Lake Johnson, goes downstream among tall trees and trailside wildflowers, crosses a 100-ft. boardwalk, and stops at Trailwood Rd. Access at the dam is from the parking lot off of Lake Dam Rd where it is 0.2 mi across the dam

1119

and arched bridge on Lake Johnson Trail to the trailhead, L. The paved Lower Walnut Creek Trail begins downstream near a bridge at Garner Rd. After passing through The Legacy Garden of wild plants with markers, the greenway goes under bridges, passes swamps, and parallels the creek to end at Rose

1120

Lane after 2.5 mi. The Rocky Creek Trail can begin at Western Blvd and Nazareth St jct (near the WRAL-TV Station). Turn L on Crusader Drive at Nazareth St and walk E to parallel Western Blvd. (At 0.5 mi Pullen Park is L across the boulevard.) Pass the entrance to Dorethea Dix Hospital, R, at 1.3 mi. After passing swamps, crossing arched bridges, and hiking under street bridges, exit at Wilmington St (near City Farm Rd) at 2.8 mi. Roadside parking is possible.

1121

Little Rock Trail is a 0.7-mi paved route at Chavis Park. (Park on Chavis Way.) From the corner of Lenoir and Chavis Way, cross the Garner Branch footbridge, pass two picnic areas, cross Bragg St at 0.5 mi, and end at McMackin St. Tall elm, ash, and sycamore shade the trail.

Smithfield (Johnston County)

Town Common Park

1122

The city's Parks and Rec Dept maintains the easy 0.8 mi roundtrip Neuse River Nature Trail, on the E side of the Neuse River. From the parking lot at the end of Front St, N, descend to the asphalt trail beside the river. Turn L. Mulberry trees ripen with fruit in mid-May. Cross a footbridge and pass under US-70 bridge at 0.1 mi Neuse Little Theater and outdoor stage are L. Enter a pristine forest of large sweet gum, sycamore, oak, and green ash. Reach the end of the trail at 0.4 mi and return. The park authority reports that plans are to extend this trail upriver for nearly 3.0 mi as Buffaloe Creek Greenway to Smithfield Community Park and Smithfield Senior School. (USGS Maps: Selma, Four Oaks)

Address and Access: Parks and Rec Dept, 200 South Front Street (or P.O. Box 2344), Smithfield, NC 27577; 919-934-2148; fax: 919-934-6554. Access is on N Front St, one block from E Market St. (US-70) at the bridge.

Smithfield Community Park

This 43-acre park (of which 14 acres are wetlands) is an outstanding example of how a town can combine its public service plans for educational, sports, and aesthetic values. Here are sports fields and a high school with plenty of parking space and Long Haul Trail, a curving cement route with border night **1123** lighting. Begin on the W side of the park entrance and follow the edge of the forest. There are interpretive sign along the way. Pass a pavilion at 0.2 mi, then a soccer field, L. Enter a forest and wetlands at 0.4 mi for a short distance. There are color coded connector trails at 0.5 mi and 0.6 mi. At 0.7 mi in the loop there is an access to the school, R. Pass a tennis court and playground to complete the circle at 1.1 mi. (Address as above)

Access: From the jct of US-70 and US-301/96, turn S on the latter, pass under bridge, pass Center Pointe Shopping Center, and drive 1.1 mi to a Texaco station R, on Booker Dairy Rd. After 1.3 mi, pass Smithfield Senior School and 0.2 mi farther to park entrance, L.

Southern Pines (Moore County)

The town of Southern Pines has a trail system in 165-acre Reservoir Park. Its central 2.0-mi loop, Reservoir Park Trail, around the lake, has connective **1124-** trails to Sandhills Community College, NW, and to Whitehall Trail at White- **1125** hall Center, NE. (An additional connection is planned to include 3.0 mi of trails S in the Talamore Country Club area.) Forest trees in the park include longleaf pine, sweet gum, maple, and turkey oak.

From the parking lot begin by crossing the arched bridge over the spillway, cross the dam, and turn L at 0.1 mi. (Sharply R is an unmarked 0.8-mi connector on an old road by twin lakes to a gate at the Sandhills Community College Horticultural Gardens. See chapter 15.) Follow the wide-screened gravel trail by the lake, cross a boardwalk in a sphagnum bed at 0.3 mi, and a boardwalk over a stream at 0.6 mi. Cross another boardwalk over a stream at 0.9 mi. Pass L of a golf course and lake to reenter the woods at 1.2 mi. Enter a clearing that exists for 0.4 mi to provide excellent views of the lake. There are spur trails for closer lakeside viewing. Pass through a picnic area and return to the parking lot at 2.0 mi. (From the parking lot is 2.0-mi Whitehall Trail loop on private property open to the public. See chapter 14.)

Address and Access: Southern Pines Rec and Parks Dept, 482 E Connecticut Ave, Southern Pines, NC 28387; 910-692-2463. From US-1 turn W on Midland Rd, go 0.2 mi, turn R on NC-22. After 1.6 mi, turn L at the park entrance.

Wake Forest (Wake County)

1126   The H.L. Miller Park, downtown, has paved Miller Park Nature Trail (0.3 mi, easy) accessible to users with physical disabilities. The trail loops among loblolly pine and hardwoods. There are three bridges over a stream, picnic tables, and benches for relaxation. To access from NC-98 turn S on Franklin St for one block, then R on East Elm St. After 0.1 mi turn R to the Town Hall parking area to enter the park behind the building. Another short asphalt trail,
1127   the Kiwanis Park Greenway (0.2 mi, easy) is at the end of Franklin St, S, in front of the EMS building. The west end is on White St behind the post office. The trail weaves through a forest of tall trees and is bordered with fragrant white wild roses that bloom in the month of May.

1128   The Smith Creek Trail is a paved greenway. Its north entrance is from a residential area, Burlington Mill Rd, S to the Neuse River, with a spur to Ligon Mill Rd. If beginning at Burlington Mill Rd the trail has houses up an embankment, L, and the floodplain of Smith Creek is to the right. Most of the trees are sweet gum, sycamore, river birch, and scattered pine. Wild grape vines are frequent. At 0.5 mi is a small pond, R, and views of the creek at 0.6 mi. The asphalt ends and a water treatment plant is at 0.7 mi. Toward the R is access to the creek and near its confluence with Neuse River. (In a curve L an old road in a forest is another 0.9 mi to a gated end at Ligon Mill Rd.) Backtrack. To access from US-1 drive E 0.7 mi on Burlington Mill Rd and park immediately after crossing the Smith Creek bridge. The greenway sign is a few yds ahead with trail access, R.

Address: Parks and Rec Dept, 401 Elm Ave, Wake Forest, NC 27587; 919-554-6180.

Municipal Parks and Recreation Areas: Coastal Municipalities

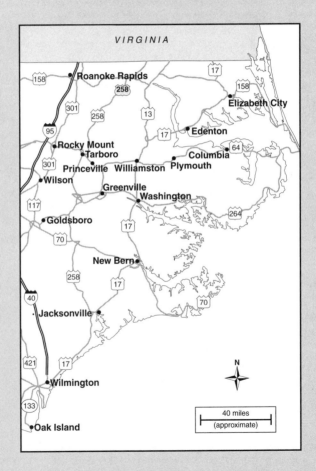

Introductions to Trail Areas

This list of cities that lie in coastal counties is arranged alphabetically to conform to the order they appear in the subsequent text.

SECTION 3: COASTAL MUNICIPALITIES

Edenton (Chowan County)

The town of Edenton, surveyed in 1712 and incorporated in 1722, is one of the state's oldest communities. It is often referred to as a "stroller's paradise." Three centuries of outstanding architecture (particularly Georgian, Federal, Greek Revival, and Queen Anne) make this national recreational trail a unique educational experience.

1129   *Edenton Historic Trail*

Length and Difficulty: 1.5 mi, easy

Trailhead and Description: The visitor center is open April–October: Mon–Sat 9:00AM–5:00PM, Sun 1:00–5:00PM; November–March: Tues–Sat 10:00AM–4:00PM, Sun 1:00–4:00PM, closed Mon. Maps are available at the visitor center, but if you do not have a map, the following will guide you past the 28 designated sites. From the visitor center, go L (S) on Broad St, turn R onto W Church St. Pass St Paul's Episcopal Church (begun 1736) R, before turning L on S Granville St. Turn R on W Eden St, but L after one block on Blount St (which becomes W King St). At the jct with S Broad St turn R. Pass the Cupola House (1758) R. Proceed to the waterfront where the Barker House (ca 1782) is located. From the Barker House go R on E Water St to the cannons of Edenton Bay and turn L on the Courthouse Green. Pass the Tea Pot, which commemorates the Edenton Tea Party of October 25, 1774, one of the earliest political actions by women in the American colonies, before turning R on E King St. Pass the Chowan County Courthouse (1767) L, but backtrack after the Coffield House to S Broad St and turn R. Turn R on E Church St. Pass the James Iredell House State Historic Site (1800) L, but backtrack after the Blair House (ca. 1775). Turn R on N Broad St for a return to the Historic Edenton Visitor Center.

Address and Access: Historic Edenton Visitor Center, 108 N Broad St, Box 474, Edenton, NC 27932; 252-482-2637; fax 252-482-3499. Parking available at the visitor center. (Edenton-Chowan Parks and Rec, 252-482-8595.)

Elizabeth City (Pasquotank County)

Settled in the 1660s, the town, like Edenton described above, has numerous historic buildings. Its 30-block historic district contains the state's largest number of antebellum commercial buildings. A sidewalk trail offers unforgettable views of vintage homes with marble window sills, stained glass windows, aesthetic woodwork, and spacious gardens. In contrast, a nature trail in Knobbs Creek Park shows the unchanged swamp.

Elizabeth City Historic Trail 1130
Length and Difficulty: 1.6 mi, easy

Trailhead and Description: Access is from US-158 (Elizabeth St) on Water St, S (at the W end of the Pasquotank bridge). Park at the riverfront of the Pasquotank River (corner of Water and Fearing Sts). This is the former site of Elizabeth "Betsy" Tooley's Tavern (ca. 1790). (If you do not have a guide map the following will direct you past the 32 historic sites.) Follow Fearing St for six blocks, passing Christ Episcopal Church (ca. 1856). At the jct of Fearing and South Rd, turn L at the Grice-Fearing House (ca. 1800), R (probably the oldest structure on the hike). Turn R on Church St, and after another six blocks turn R on the original brick pavement of Selden St to Main St. Turn R and pass 19 historic buildings (including the courthouse) on your return to Water St. Turn R, one block to the point of origin.

Address and Access: Chamber of Commerce, 502 E Ehringhaus St (P.O. Box 426), Elizabeth City, NC 27909; 252-335-4365.

Knobbs Creek Park
From US-17 Bus (near the N Bypass jct), take E Ward to the park entrance, L. At the parking area follow the trail sign. The 0.7-mi Knobbs Creek Nature 1131 Trail meanders through a dark watery area of cypress, black cherry, sweet gum, and beech. A group of Alabama supplejack (*Berchemia scandens*) hangs like lengthy jungle serpents over the cypress knees. Boardwalks built by the YCC in 1976 offer observation decks. Backtrack, or make a loop on the park meadow.

Address: Director, Park and Rec Dept, 200 E Ward St, Elizabeth City, NC 27909; 252-335-1424; fax: 252-338-2018.

Goldsboro (Wayne County)
A combination of city parks and greenway planning provides a route for the Stoney Creek Trail to begin at Quail Park and eventually extend to the Neuse 1132 River. To approach Quail Park, turn off Bypass US-70/13 at Wayne Memorial Dr, S, to the first street L, Newton Dr. Turn L again on Quail Dr to the park. Walk past the picnic shelter to Stoney Creek and turn downstream through the Kemp Greenway. Trail blazes may be yellow or white. Plant life includes tall 1133 river birch, poplar, maple, laurel oak, ironweed, cardinal flower, day flower,

beauty bush, and sensitive fern. (This trail is also good for bird watching.) Cross Royall Ave and go under the RR trestle at 0.3 mi. At 1.1 mi, cross Ash St and enter Stoney Creek Park. At 1.8 mi, cross Elm St (entrance gate L to Seymour Johnson Air Force Base). Go 130 yd. to a dead-end street for parking space. (See appendix A for MST continuance downstream.) (USGS Maps: Goldsboro NE and SE)

Address: Director, Parks and Rec Dept, Drawer A, Goldsboro, NC 27533; 919-739-7480; fax: 919-734-6201.

Greenville (Pitt County)

The city operates 19 parks, and at least 2 have trails. The city is currently constructing the first phase of a greenways corridor. Eventually it will follow Green Mill Run through most of the city. (For an update call 252-329-4567.) Another park, River Park North, has nature trails.

Address: Parks and Rec Dept, Box 7207, Greenville, NC 27834; 252-329-4567; fax: 252-329-4062 (252-758-1230 at River Park North).

River Park North

The park was opened to public use in 1983 and currently has 324 acres, with at least 190 acres of rich bottomland forest by the Tar River. It has four lakes for fishing, rental boats, boat ramp, organized group camping area, picnic shelter, and a natural science center with an aquarium, theater, and classroom. The park is open daily except Mondays and major holidays.

1134- **Willow Branch Trail** (0.3 mi); **Old Eason Run Trail** (0.2 mi); **Parkers**
1136 **Creek Tail** (1.1 mi)

Length and Difficulty: 2.7 mi round-trip combined, easy

Trailhead and Description: Access to the park from downtown at 5th St and Green St is to go N on Green St 1.5 mi (across the Tar River bridge) and take a R on Mumford Rd for 0.8 mi to the park, R. From the parking area follow the wide svc road S toward the lakes. Near the picnic shelter a L beyond the pedal-boat dock is the trailhead for the 0.3-mi Willow Branch Trail. It follows the lake bank among water oak, red mulberry, and black willow. It has a forest observation deck. It rejoins the svc road in an open area with swamp rose, passion flower, rose mallow, and pinkweed. Connect with the Old Eason Run Trail. The Parkers Creek Trail follows the svc road, passes between the lakes and under a power line at 0.3 mi and 0.5 mi. In a scenic forest of tall river birch, ash, cypress, and sycamore turn L at 0.6 mi. This route forms a loop, and bridges and boardwalks were donated by Contentnea Creek Ducks Unlimited. At 1.0 mi reach a tributary and turn R to rejoin the svc road at 1.2 mi. Turn R, follow the Tar River among cottonwood and water and willow oaks. Return to the parking lot at 2.2 mi if following only Parkers Creek Trail.

Jacksonville (Onslow County)

In the city's park system are a few named trails, such as Chaney Creek Power-line Trail (0.5 mi, easy). Access from Marine Blvd (US-17) is 0.6 mi NW on Onslow Dr to the corner of Henderson and River Streets. The trail begins under the powerline and exits NW at Brook Valley Park off of Estate Dr. (If driving from the corner of River St and Henderson Dr, use Henderson Dr NW for 1.1 mi to turn R on Doris Ave. After 0.4 mi is Brook Valley Park off of Estate Dr.) **1137**

The city's major trail is Jacksonville Rails-to-Trails Greenway (5.2 mi, easy). A completed section, Chaney Creek Trail (0.8 mi, easy) is from War-lick St (two blocks S of NC-24) NE on the edge of US-17 to Onslow Dr inter-section. The section under construction continues NE in front of some stores. After crossing Thompson St, begin to curve R into the forest at 0.6 mi. From here, go SE mainly though a forest other than a few open spaces and road crossings. Some of the flowers along the way are aster, thistle, and goldenrod. Cross busy NC-24 at 2.4 mi and begin to parallel it through Camp Johnson. Pass an elementary school and kindergarten. Along the RR edge are large anthills at 3.4 mi. At 4.4 mi is a scenic RR bridge crossing (420 ft.) over a bay of White Oak Creek. Arrive at Camp Lejeune visitor center at 5.2 mi (Ahead is a connection to the Camp Lejeune greenway system.) Parking for this access is at the visitor center, R, after approaching the military base on Hol-comb Blvd form NC-24. **1138-1139**

Address: Jacksonville Parks and Rec, P.O. Box 128 (100 Recreation Lane), Jacksonville, NC 28541; 910-938-5313; fax: 910-938-9520.

New Bern (Craven County)

New Bern, "the land of enchanting waters," is a historic river port at the con-fluence of the Trent and Neuse Rivers. Settled in 1710 and named for the city of Bern, Switzerland, it is one of the most elegantly restored cities in the state. The colonial assembly met here as early as 1737, and after the completion of Tryon Palace in 1770 it was the colonial capital and the state capital until 1794. After the Revolutionary War there was a dramatic development of

Federal-style architecture. Examples are the Stevenson House (ca. 1805); First Presbyterian Church (1819); and the New Bern Academy (1806). On the

1140 New Bern Historic District Trail are 67 historic buildings (business, government, homes, and churches) within a walking (or auto) route of 4.5 mi. Because the route is divided into four sections (1.2 mi in the palace area; 1.1 mi in the Johnson St area; 1.2 mi in the E Front St area; and 1.0 mi in the downtown area) that may begin or end in irregular patterns (such as in the middle of a block), it is essential that you have a tour map to know which building is in which tour section. Maps are available free of charge from the Craven County Convention and Visitors Center (address below). There are guided tours sold through a tour agency or a taped walking tour can be rented from the center. Most buildings on the tour have a steel shield (yellow, black, and red) with a bear logo. The center is open Monday through Friday 8:00AM to 5:00PM and Saturday 10:00AM to 4:00PM. Call for tours and information.

Address and Access: Craven County Convention and Visitors Center, 203 S Front St (P.O. Box 1713), New Bern, NC 28563; 252-637-9400 or 800-437-5767. From US-70/17, which passes through on Broad St, turn S on E Front St and go two blocks to SW corner of E Front St and S Front St.

Oak Island (Brunswick County)

1141 Oak Island Nature Center has a 0.5-mi Talking Tree Trail, a butterfly garden, a small zoo, and picnicking and fishing facilities. There are outstanding

1142 views of Intercoastal Waterway. The town also has Beaver Pond Trail, with boardwalks to the beach and observation decks for bird watching. In the bays of the Long Island area is the 17.7-mi Cone Canoe Trail.

Address and Access: Oak Island Parks and Rec, P.O. Box 280 (4601 E Oak Island Dr), Oak Island, NC 28465; 910-278-4747 or www.oakisland. nc.com. For access to Oak Island Nature Center, cross the island on NC-133, near Southport, and drive to the corner of 52nd St and Yatch Dr. For access to Beaver Pond Trail, drive to the corner of Island Dr and Seashore 30th St.

Plymouth (Washington County)

The town of Plymouth traces its history to 1584 when the governor of the first English Colony, Robert Lane, came ashore from the Roanoke River (initially the Moratucke River). To house the town's history and its significant role in the civil War, the Washington County Historical Society established the Port O'Plymouth Museum in 1988. In a 1996 article about the town's history the

Charlotte Observer stated that the town was "one of the top ten Civil War sites in the two Carolinas." The museum is at the old RR sta and is the main trailhead for the Roanoke River Trail. Forming a long loop of 2 mi and shorter **1143** loops if 1 mi or less, the color-coded trail can begin down river on a gravel passage into a dense forest. It soon leaves the river to access Martin Lane. From there it returns to the museum area for a route of history along Main Street, past the county courthouse, and a long side trip on Washington St to Eight St for a backtrack.

Address and Access: Port O' Plymouth Museum, 302 E Water St, Plymouth, NC 27962; 252-793-1377. At the jct of US-64/NC-32, turn NW on Washington St. After 1.5 mi, turn R on Main St and drive 0.4 mi to the museum, L.

Princeville

Among historic trails is 1.0-mi Princeville Heritage Trail at the E edge of the **1144** town of Tarboro. As a partial greenway on a levy of the Tar River it passes through parks, a business section, and by cemeteries. Princeville, the oldest chartered African-American town in the U.S., was founded by ex-slaves in 1885.

Address and Access: Town Hall, 201 South Main St, Princeville, NC 27886; 252-823-1057. Access is Exit 486 off US-64 Bypass, N on US-258/NC-111/122, 0.2 mi to NC-33 R and L. Turn R on South Main St to Town Hall, L.

Roanoke Rapids (Halifax County)

The city has three parks: Emery, Chockoyotte, and Tinsley. Emery Park Trail **1145** is a wide and neatly groomed 0.5-mi loop. From the parking lot it follows the sign clockwise through a forest of willow, white oak, and loblolly pine. Leaving the forest it passes a lighted athletic field, tennis courts, and a playground. Access is from the jct of US-158/NC-48 on NC-48 (Roanoke Ave) N to Ninth Ave and a turn L to the park. Chockoyotte Park Trail is a 0.7-mi smooth- **1146** surface loop similar to Emery. An easy route, it circles all the athletic facilities and can be used for physical fitness. Access is off US-158 on Chockoyotte St for 0.3 mi to a turn L on Third Ave. Tinsley Park Trail will be a 0.5-mi **1147** nature trail when completed. It is in a natural urban forest island between W and E Arbutus Dr and between Holly Rd and Fifth St. The city's major trail is Roanoke Canal Trail, described below.

Address: Parks and Rec Dept, P.O. Box 38, Roanoke Rapids, NC 27870; 252-533-2847 or www.roanokerapids.nc.com.

1148 *Roanoke Canal Trail*

Length and Difficulty: 7.7 mi, moderate

Special Features: wildlife, river views, Roanoke Aqueduct

Trailhead and Description: The NW trailhead is at a parking lot at Roanoke Rapids Lake Dam and end of Oakwood Ave, off Fifth St, and the SE trailhead is at the Wildlife Landing parking area beside US-301 in Weldon. The trail has four accesses along the way. Listed on the National Register of Historic Places, the trail is a joint project of the city and the Roanoke Canal Commission. The canal was begun in 1819 and completed in 1823 by hand. Hamilton Fulton, an English engineer, was hired to supervise the construction of the canal around Great Falls. On a natural surface treadway the trail follows the towpath of an old navigational canal. The trail stays on the N side of the canal most of the distance, but crosses many footbridges and ascends and descends steps. It does not have blazes, but has frequent title and distance markers. Principal trees are hardwood, and wildlife includes deer, turkey, fox, beaver, squirrel, and waterfowl.

If beginning at the NW terminus follow the trail's slight descent under power lines in and out of the woods on the L rim of the canal. At 0.6 mi, pass the base of Rochelle Pond. At 0.9 mi, R, is an exceptionally large wild grapevine attached to a poplar. Here is also the Roanoke Canal Museum at the jct with Jackson St. To the L are remains of a river lock. Cross NC-48 at 1.6 mi. Here is a minimart, perfect for thirsty summer hikers. To the L are more locks and the International Paper plant. For a while parallel a RR and go under or near power lines. At 2.8 mi, L, is a bog with arrow arum and white marsh mallow, followed by a dry area with a papaw patch and anise root. Arrive at River Rd E at 3.2 mi. To the L is a parking lot; beyond is a residential area.

Cross the road and after 0.3 mi there are water hemlock in the canal, followed by steps to a footbridge over a stream. At 4.1 mi, cross an immaculate lawn between the river and a magnificent home. Within 0.2 mi, follow a fence channel to pass under I-95 at the riverbank, then ascend to continue on the canal towpath. At 4.8 mi, begin a curve around a pond. After returning to the canal the sound and sight of huge Roanoke Valley Energy Facility is noticeable to the R. Pass a water infiltration plant at 6.1 mi. At 6.2 mi, arrive at Aqueduct Rd. (To the R it is 0.3 mi to Ponderosa Campground.)

Follow the canal rim, which parallels a smooth canal base to scenic area of Roanoke Canal Aqueduct at 6.3 mi. An observation deck is at the base of the arch and near Chockoyotte Creek. Continue for a few yards on the canal to return to the canal rim, where the trail goes straight for 0.6 mi to Weldon water treatment plant. Follow the exit road past a warehouse to Walnut St, turn R, and reach First St at 7.2 mi. Turn L, cross the RR, and turn L at an angle on a former RR bed. Pass under a RR bridge among sneezeweed, senna, and wisteria to make a sharp R at the Weldon RR Museum and Weldon Memorial Library at 7.4 mi. At another RR crossing and Washington Ave, turn L on First St. Follow it to the edge of US-301 where a L turn on a sidewalk proceeds to a tunnel under US-301. Exit to the Wildlife Landing and parking area. Complete the trail at an observation platform by the river at 7.7 mi. (USGS Maps: Roanoke Rapids, Weldon)

Rocky Mount (Nash County) 1149

The city has proposed the development of a Tar River Greenway. It would connect several major parks and recreational facilities such as City Lake, Sunset Park, Battle Park (see below), Tom Stitch Park, and Talbert Park. (Call Parks and Rec Dept for an update.) Battle Park is a 54-acre recreation park, a gift from the Battle family of Rocky Mount Mills. It has a picnic area with shelters, playground, a boat ramp to the Tar River, and a history trail. After parking, follow Battle Park Trail on a paved and easy 1.6-mi loop. Pass the 1150 Donaldson Tavern site, a stagecoach station from an overland route. (Near here the Marquis de Lafayette was entertained while on his Southern tour in 1825.) At 0.2 mi, turn R to the waterfall overlook on the Tar River. Proceed to the playground through a picnic area with pine, birch, oak, elm, and dogwood. Cross the driveway at 1.3 mi and pass the site of the first Rocky Mount post office on the return. (The trail is accessible to the physically disabled.)

An additional 0.6-mi paved trail has been added that extends from the loop trail to Church St. Along the way are two fishing piers and overlooks, a boat launch, and several historic sites, including a turn-of-the-century bridge site, a Tuscarora Indian site, and an old dam site.

Address and Access: Parks and Rec Dept, PO Drawer 1180, Rocky Mount, NC 27801; 252-972-1151. Access is from the jct of US-64 Byp and NC-43/48. Take NC-43/48 (Falls Rd) SE 0.5 mi to the parking area near the Confederate monument.

Tarboro (Edgecombe County)

1151   The Tarboro Historic District Trail is a remarkable adventure into history. It is a trail of beauty any season of the year. A national recreation trail, it is a 2.4-mi walking or driving tour within a 45-block area of beautiful downtown Tarboro. More than 100 homes, gardens, churches, and government and business structures are designated as historically or architecturally significant. The trail begins at the tour headquarters on Bridgers St at the Blount-Bridgers House (ca. 1808). (A trail map is advisable and is available here. The building is open Monday–Friday, 10:00AM–4:00PM; Saturday and Sunday 2:00–4:00PM [April–November]; and by appointment, 919-823-4159.) In case you do not have a map, brief directions follow: Within the Bridgers St block, go N (R side of the Blount-Bridgers House) and pass the Pender Museum (ca. 1810). Turn R on Philips St; L on St Patrick St; L on Battle Ave; L on Main St; R on Porter St; R on Trade St; R on Baker St; R on St Patrick St (by the Town Common [1760] at 0.9 mi); L on Church St; R on St David St; (by the Calvary Episcopal Church); R on St James St; R on St Andrew St; L on Wilson St; and L on Main St. At 1.8 mi is a jct with Granville St; turn R and backtrack on Main St to R on Park Ave; turn L on St Andrew St and return to the Blount-Bridgers House. The Main St section of the trail has received national recognition for expansive restoration.

   Address and Access: Tarboro Dept of Planning and Economic Development, 500 Main St (P.O. Box 220), Tarboro, NC 27886; 919-641-4249. (Chamber of Commerce; 919-823-7241.) Access: turn E on Bridgers St from Main St (NC-33), and go one block.

1152   Another trail is 0.6-mi Indian Lake Nature Trail in 52-acre Indian Lake Park. The trail has interpretive stations about the vascular flora. The park also provides a picnic area, fishing, boat rentals, nature tours, and camping for special groups or organizations.

   Address and Access: Tarboro Parks and Rec Dept, 305 W Baker St, Tarboro, NC 27886; 919-641-4263. Access to the park is on Western Blvd (US-64A), 0.5 mi S from its jct with N Main St.

Washington (Beaufort County)

The "original Washington, 1776," is the first town in the US to be named for George Washington. Settlements at this jct of the Pamlico and Tar Rivers began as early as the 1690s, but the origin of the present city is traced to the early 1770s. The city's earliest buildings of historic and architectural significance were mainly destroyed by fire, first in 1864 by federal forces and again in the business district in 1900 by an accidental fire. A remarkable restoration and preservation has created a historic district of at least 29 historic buildings and special sites in the downtown area. They can be seen on the 2.0-mi Washington Historic District Trail (a national recreation trail), a walking tour among homes, businesses, churches, by the old courthouse, and along streets of magnolia and crepe myrtle. Parking is available at the corner of Gladden St and Stewart Parkway. A map of the tour is available from addresses below, but without a map the following description will assist. Also, the trail sign, a colorful shield with directional arrows, serves as an excellent guide at each turn.   **1153**

Begin the trail at the NW corner of Gladden and Main Sts at the renovated Seaboard Coastline RR Depot. On Main St walk W three blocks and turn R on Pierce St. Go one block, turn L on W 2d St for one block, and turn L on Washington St back to W Main St at 0.5 mi. Turn R to see (halfway down the block) the stately 1820s "Elmwood." Return on Main St to pass the Havens Warehouse and Mill to the parking lot at 1.0 mi. Walk R along the Stewart Parkway waterfront pavilion. After passing three eighteenth-century houses on Water St, go N two blocks on Bonner St (passing the 1860s St Peter's Episcopal Church). Turn L for one block on E 2d St, turn L one block to Main St, and turn R for the return.

Address and Access: City of Washington, P.O. Box 1988 (310 W Main St), Washington, NC 27889; 252-975-9367. For access to the trailhead, follow US-70 N or S to Main St. Turn E two blocks to the corner of Gladden St.

Williamston (Martin County)
Skewarkee Trail
This greenway trail plan follows an old CSX RR bed that parallels Main St. from downtown to the Roanoke River. The first phase of the Skewarkee Trail (0.9 mi, easy) is an asphalt passage within visiting distance of historic buildings, such as the county courthouse (1885) and the county government center. Future planning will include riverfront camping facilities, interpretive overlooks, Moratoc Park, a fishing pier, and boating access to Roanoke River.   **1154**

Address and Access: Williamston Parks and Rec, P.O. Box 6, Williamston, NC 27892; 252-792-7042; fax: 252-792-2509. Access parking is off of NC-125 downtown, a block S of Main St.

Wilmington (New Hanover County)
Greenfield Gardens Park

Greenfield is a magnificent 200-acre city park with trails, tennis courts, picnic areas, rental boats, amphitheatre, rec center, nature study area, and fragrance garden. Millions of azalea blossoms provide a profusion of color in April. Additional color and greenery come from camellia, yaupon, magnolia, bay, live oak, crepe myrtle, water lily, dogwood, and Spanish moss draped on cypress. (The park is popular during the city's annual NC Azalea Festival [first or second weekend in April].) Open daily. No camping or swimming.

Address: Public Services and Facilities Dept, Box 1810, Wilmington, NC 28402; 910-341-7852. The park office is located at 1702 Burnette Blvd, Wilmington, NC 28401.

1155-   *Rupert Bryan Memorial Trail* (4.5 mi); *Greenfield Nature Trail* (0.3 mi)
1156   **Length and Difficulty:** 4.8 mi combined, easy

Trailhead and Description: The trail (also called Greenfield Gardens Trail) is a paved loop for hiking, jogging, and bicycling around the lake and over bridges. (It parallels, with little exception, the auto route on W and E Lakeshore Dr.) If you follow the trail R from the parking area, pass the amphitheatre and rec center at 0.9 mi. At 2.4 mi, jct L with the Greenfield Nature Trail boardwalk, which has interpretive signs. Among the plants are fern, swamp rose, and Virginia willow. Continue ahead to Jackson Point picnic area, Indian sculpture, and a return to the parking area.

Wilson (Wilson County)

There are more than 26 parks in the city, and many others are proposed. Unnamed walkways are prominent; three areas have designated trails. The
1157   wide Hominy Canal Trail is a 0.9-mi path between Ward Blvd and the jct of Kincaid Ave and Canal Dr. Tall loblolly pine, willow and live oak, sweet gum, and river birch shade the trail. Access to parking can be had at Williams Day
1158   Camp on Mt Vernon Dr. The 1.2-mi Toisnot Lake Trail circles the lake; it also extends 0.6 mi into the hardwood forest downstream to the Seaboard Coast RR. Access to Toisnot Park is on Corbett Ave, N, near its jct with Ward Blvd (NC-58/42). Corbett Ave is also the 3.8-mi access route to Lake Wilson and the Lake Wilson Trail. Go N 3.3 mi, turn L on Lake Wilson Rd (SR-1327) at Dunn's Cross Rd, and go 0.5 mi to the lake, R.

Lake Wilson Trail 1159

Length and Difficulty: 2.3 mi, easy

Trailhead and Description: From the parking lot go either R or L on the dam. If L, cross the dam/spillway and follow an old road through a forest of river birch, alder, sweet gum, and holly. At 0.8 mi bear R, off the old road, and enter a swampy area to follow the yellow blazes. (Beavers may have dammed the area and prevented crossing.) Cross a bridge on the feeder stream to an old road at 1.3 mi. Among the swamp vegetation are buttonbush and swamp candle *(Lysimachia terrestris)*. Turn R and follow the old road (damaged by jeeps and 4WDs) to complete the loop at 2.3 mi. (This is a good bird-watching trail.)

Address: Wilson Parks and Rec, P.O. Box 10, Wilson NC 27894-0010; 252-399-2262; fax: 252-399-2196.

Part VI

Trails on Private and Commercial Properties, Including College and University Trails

Grandfather Trail.

Chapter 14

Private and Commercial Trails

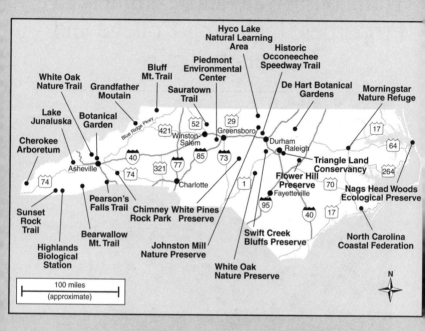

Introductions to Trail Areas

These special trails represent the diversity of trails other than federal, state, county, and city public properties. Some of these require permission or fees for use. They are listed alphabetically without geographic order.

522

Chapter 14

Private and Commercial Trails

Walk amidst beautiful things
That adorn the world.
—George Santayana

Some land owners have been and are reluctant to open their properties for trails because of liability and trail abuse. To alleviate at least some of the concern, the state legislature passed a bill (Act to Limit the Liability of Landowners to Persons Using Their Land in Connection with the Trails System) in 1987. Most private summer retreats and conference centers with trail systems allow only paying guests of the sponsoring agencies to use the trails. A few allow specific trail(s) if the owners are open year-round. An example of such is Montreat Conference Center (a 4,500-acre compound owned by the Presbyterian Church). Within the trail system, Lookout Trail (0.8 mi, moderate) is **1160** open to the public. If only visiting, request a map at the ranger station or the Assembly Inn, and request to park at the Lookout Trail parking lot. The summit's elev is 3,760 ft. with 360-degree views. Access is from I-40, Exit 64, at Black Mt. Drive N on NC-9 for 3.1 mi through town to the ranger station, R. For more information, contact 828-669-2911.

Nevertheless, corporate and individual landowners have a long history of cooperation with Scout troops, schools, nature-oriented groups, and hunting or fishing clubs to use their properties. Examples are in this chapter. Most private trails are not publicized and the majority have never been named. If all the pathways through farm woodlands, or those favorite forest fishing and hunting routes, or those walks to points of meditation were all counted, they would number in the thousands. There are also private resorts, retreats, and special camps where only paying or invited guests may walk the trails. A popular hiking pastime in the mountain area is to ascend highly publicized mountain peaks (particularly those with a view) on both public and private properties. Some private peak owners object and have placed No Trespassing signs at appropriate places. If you see such signs, they may apply mainly to vehicles. An inquiry to the owners would show respect for their property rights. Frequently, private owners will given an individual, or a small group, permission to walk a path or roadway if the purpose is for education or aesthetics. Access to some mountain peaks requires passage over lands of multiple owners. Bushwhacking or random cross-country hiking on these premises can result in trespassing on one piece of property but not on others. Examples are Blackrock Mtn. near Sylva, Sandymush Bald S of Luck, Snake Mtn. near Boone, and Wesner Bald near Balsam Gap. Some commercial properties require an entrance fee; for example, Chimney Rock Park and Grandfather Mtn.

1161   Bearwallow Mountain Trail (Henderson County)

Length and Difficulty: 2 mi round-trip, moderate

Trailhead and Description: From the jct of US-74 and Bearwallow Rd (SR-1594) in Gerton (5.0 mi NW on US-74 from the jct of NC-9 in Bat Cave), go 2.1 mi on SR-1594 (mostly on a gravel road) to Bearwallow Gap. Park away from the L gate. (No dogs, unless on a leash.) Ascend on a moderate-grade pasture road through oak, hickory, locust, and maple to the fire tower (leased by the state) on Bearwallow Mtn. (4,232 ft.) at 1.0 mi. Scenic views from the tower are of Sugarloaf Mtn, Bat Cave area, and Little Pisgah Mtn. Flowering plants include bellflower, turtlehead, and phlox. Backtrack. For more information contact the property owner at 704-685-7371. (USGS Map: Bat Cave)

1162   Bluff Mountain Trail (Ashe County)

West of West Jefferson is the spectacular Bluff Mtn. (5,100 ft.), part of a 2,000-acre controlled-access preserve held by the NC chapter of The Nature Conservatory, a private organization. Visitation is allowed only with the accompaniment of an authorized guide on the rugged 2.0-mi one-way climb to Perkings Rock. A naturalist's dream, the diverse scenery is unforgettable. The hike is confined to good weather and from springtime through autumn. Reservations are required and a fee is required. Guided trips are also made on nearby Three Top Mtn.

Address: Doug Munroe, 415 Waterfall Mtn., Warrensville, NC 28693; 336-385-6507. The Nature Conservatory: 919-484-7857.

Botanical Gardens at Asheville (Buncombe County)

The gardens were founded in 1960 and designed by Doan Ogden. Covering 10 acres, it is a community of more than 600 species of perennials, shrubs,

and trees native to the southern Appalachian Mountains. To see this remarkable display of flora, walk the Botanical Gardens at Asheville Trail (0.6 mi, **1163**
easy). From the parking lot, follow the gravel routes through meadows and
forest. On the trail is an original dog-trot mountain cabin that honors Hubert
H. Hayes, author and playwright. History buffs can view the original earth-
works of the Battle of Asheville, a Civil War site. The trail also passes by
Glenn and Reed creeks with magnificent boulders for dramatic photographic
shots. The Gardens are open daily from dawn till dusk free of charge. The
Garden Path gift shop is open from March through mid-December from
9:30AM to 4:00PM.

Address and Access: The Botanical Gardens at Asheville, 151 W.T.
Weaver Blvd, Asheville, NC 28804; 828-252-5190, botgardens@main.nc.us,
or www.ashevillebotanicalgardens.org. From the jct of I-240 and US-19/23/70
in Asheville, drive N on the latter toward Weaverville and Marshall. Go 2.0 mi
and turn R off of the expressway and R onto Broadway. Go 0.5 mi to the second traffic light and turn L at W.T. Weaver Blvd. Entrance is 0.1 mi on the L.

Cherokee Arboretum (Swain County)

Cherokee Arboretum Trail (0.5 mi); *Mt. Noble Trail* (4.6 mi round-trip) **1164-**
    Length and Difficulty: 5.1 mi combined round-trip, easy to strenuous **1165**

    Trailhead and Description: From the jct of US-19 and US-441 in
Cherokee, turn N on US-441 and go 0.6 mi to a sign for Oconaluftee Indian
Village, L. Follow the road to a parking area and locate the trail sign for the
Cherokee Arboretum Trail near the stockade gate. On an easy loop pass
through a forest of pines and hardwoods where more than 150 species of
plants are labeled. On the trail are a restored Indian log cabin, a stream, small
pool, and an herb garden. A national recreation trail, it is maintained by the
Cherokee Historical Association. Access to the Mt. Noble Trail is from the
upper parking lot on the R (E) side. On a moderate to strenuous climb, ascend
in and out of hardwood coves, first to the W and then N to headwaters of Owl
Branch at 1.4 mi. After curving around a ridge ascend more steeply to the
summit of Mt. Noble (4,066 ft.) and a fire tower at 2.3 mi. (elev gain 1,666
ft.). Outstanding views are of the Cherokee area (E, SE), GSMNP (NW, N),
and Nantahala NF (S). (The village is also home for the Cherokee outdoor
drama "Unto These Hills.") (USGS Map: Whittier)

    Information: Cherokee Historical Association, Box 398, Cherokee, NC
28719; 828-497-2111.

Chimney Rock Park (Rutherford County)

Chimney Rock Park (2,280 ft.) is a 1,000-acre scenic private nature preserve with commercial comforts. The first developer was J. B. Freeman in the late 1800s, but the first extensive developers were three brothers, Lucius, Asahel, and Hiram Morse, from Missouri in the early 1900s. The park continues to be operated by their descendants. One of the park's outstanding features is the giant granite monolith, Chimney Rock, which rises sharply to 315 ft. It is a remnant of 500-million-year-old igneous rock. Another major feature is Hickory Nut Falls, which plummets 404 ft. into the gorge before it cascades another 900 ft. There are a number of special annual events, among them an Easter sunrise service, rock-climbing exhibitions, guided tours, concerts, and workshops. Open daily from 8:30AM to 4:30PM year-round (except Thanksgiving, Christmas, and New Year's Day); an entry fee is charged. There is a large picnic area with a pavilion and nature center. (USGS Maps: Bat Cave, Lake Lure)

Address and Access: Chimney Rock Park, P.O. Box 39, Chimney Rock, NC 28720; 828-625-9611. Entrance is on US-74A/64/NC-9 in Chimney Rock.

1166-
1169

Skyline Nature Trail (0.9 mi); *Cliff Trail* (0.6 mi); *Woodland Trail* (0.6 mi); *Four Seasons Trail* (1.2 mi)

Length and Difficulty: 3.2 mi combined round-trip, moderate to strenuous

Trailhead and Description: After entry to the park, drive 1.5 mi to the Ticket Plaza parking area, another 1.5 mi to the Tunnel parking lot and the tunnel to the 258-ft. elevator to the Sky Lounge or use the steps on a route past Vista Rock or Needle's Eye. Follow the signs for Skyline Nature Trail (and use a brochure for the 28 interpretive stops). Among the trees and shrubs are table mountain pine, wafer ash *(Ptelea trifoliata),* chestnut oak, laurel, and rhododendron. Wildflowers include windflower, wild orchid, and shooting star *(Dodecatheon meadia).* Reach spectacular Hickory Nut Falls at 0.9 mi. Backtrack, or return on the precipitous Cliff Trail (which was constructed by Guilford Nanney, a local resident who also designed the intricate series of stairways in the park). Pass Inspiration Point where both Hickory Nut Falls and Lake Lure can be viewed. For the Four Seasons Trail, leave the parking area and walk to the rest rooms on steps to a fork in the trail. Left goes through a forest of hemlock, oak, and laurel to the base of a waterfall. Backtrack. Or if taking a R at the steps, descend to the Meadows by the Four Seasons Trail or take a R along the way to the Woodland Trail.

De Hart Botanical Gardens (Franklin County)

The 83-acre preserve is part of another 178-acre preserve in Patrick County VA. The purpose of both preserves is to protect a natural environment with limited facilities. On the NC preserve, more than 500 species of vascular plants have been identified. A prominent species is wild pink *(Silene caroliniana)*. Flame azalea and commercial azalea are near the lake area. Hiking and picnicking are allowed. Weddings are allowed by the lake and guided nature tours are provided with advanced notice. Smoking and alcohol are prohibited on the preserve, and all dogs must be leashed. The preserve is free and open to the public from sunrise to sunset, but visitors should sign the registry at the parking lot gazebo upon entry. With a map and taking the Lake Trail first, there is a fork after a bridge. To the R is Rock Trail (0.3 mi, easy) and L **1170-** is Trail for Handicapped (90 yd., easy). Both reach the Lake Trail (0.3 mi, **1175** easy) and from it the Crane Fly Orchard Trail (0.5 mi, easy) makes a loop near a bridge across the lake. Below the dam is Children's Bamboo Trail (75 yd., easy). The waterfall access is at the N edge of the parking area. The Waterfall Trail (1.8 mi, moderate) makes a loop among and old and new forest, rocky granite areas, past historic sites, and wildflowers.

Address and Access: De Hart Botanical Gardens, 3585 US-401 South, Louisburg, NC 27549; 919-496-4771. From the jct of US-401 and NC-56 in Louisburg, drive S 5.5 mi on US-401 to sign and parking lot, L. From Raleigh on US-401, drive 4.5 mi after the traffic light at NC-98 and turn R.

Grandfather Mountain (Avery, Caldwell, and Watauga Counties)

Grandfather Mountain is a popular commercial tourist attraction and nature preserve with its mile-high swinging bridge over an 80-ft. couloir (dedicated in 1952); natural wildlife habitats (dedicated in 1973); plant and mineral exhibits; hiking trails over rugged terrain; and unspoiled natural beauty (such as the world's largest gardens of pink-shell azalea, *Rhododendron vaseyi*). Geologically, the mountain is unique; its metamorphic sandstone is distinct from all other surrounding mountains. "We have made it inoffensively accessible," said Hugh Morton, whose family has owned the property since his MIT-graduate grandfather, Hugh MacRae, bought it in 1885. Among the annual events are the Highland Games (more than 100 Scottish clans represented in traditional sports and arts) held the second weekend in July; "Singing on the Mountain" (a modern and traditional gospel concert) the fourth Sunday in June; and the Nature Photography Weekend (with contests and lectures) in late May. (Photography is a special interest of Morton, who was a combat newsreel photographer in the Philippines in WWII, and who is internationally known for his filmed wildlife series.) Campground facilities are not available, but picnic facilities are set up at scenic overlooks. An entrance fee is required at the gatehouse on US-221.

One of the reasons Grandfather Mtn. is so impressive is because it towers high, 2,100 ft., above the valley floor. The mountain received its name from pioneer settlers who saw a grandfatherly profile northwest of Calloway Peak. The image is of a face looking skyward with a long forehead and a thick beard. It is most recognizable on NC-105 in the community of Foscoe, looking S, between Boone and Linville.

There are 9 trails on the mountain that are a part of other connecting trails.
1176   Two trails are separate. One is Woods Walk Nature Trail (0.4 mi loop, easy) 0.1 mi after entry from the entrance gate. The trail markers are about ecology. The other separate trail, Black Rock Nature Trail, is described ahead. Six accesses provide convenient trail-length options—one on NC-105, one from BRP, one from US-221, one at the visitor center, and one on the entrance road. The access to the visitor center and entrance road is for day hikes only. The
1177-   short Bridge Trail was constructed in 1995, and a new Grandfather Trail
1178   Extension has been made. (The original Grandfather Trail still starts at the visitor center. The Grandfather Extension starts at the Black Rock parking area and end/intersects the Grandfather Trail just below the patio view of MacRae Peak.) Both trailheads originate at the Grandfather Mtn. Visitor Center. Overnight parking or walking up or down the entrance road is prohibited. Daily permits (unless hikers purchase a season hiking pass) and small fees are required on all trails and for camping at the designated campsites. Permits are available at the Grandfather Mtn. gatehouse; at Foscoe Fishing Co., and the McDonalds/Exxon Complex at the jct of NC-105 and NC-184; Grandfather Market on US-221 (6.4 mi S of Blowing Rock); at Footsloggers store, Main St, in Blowing Rock; and at Footsloggers, 139 S. Depot St, in Boone. Contact the backcountry manager for a list of additional permit outlets. Permits are also available by mail, directly from the backcountry manager. Before a trip is planned, it is essential to contact the manager and request the free Trail Map of Grandfather Mountain, and a flyer on preparation for what to pack and what to do after arrival at the mountain. Examples of the regulations are: the limitations of groups to not exceed 12, campfires are not permitted at Hi-Balsam

shelter and all high elevation campsites, and no alcoholic beverages are allowed on Grandfather Mtn. The trail map shows all trailheads, campsites, altitudes of the peaks, trail routes, and access points. Other information on the map is about the severe weather condition of the preserve. (Fees for hiking permits are used for trial maintenance, protection and conservation of the ecology, safety, and security patrol.)

Grandfather Mtn. is a wilderness area. Some of its 3,087 acres are exceptionally fragile and are protected from visitor exploration. With the cooperation of the NC Natural Heritage Area and The Nature Conservancy, there are adjoining areas also protected. In addition, Grandfather Mountain Inc. is a member of the Southern Appalachian and the Biosphere Reserve. Among the biosphere's objectives is "to build a harmonious relationship between man and the environment." (USGS Maps: Grandfather Mtn., Valle Crucis).

Address and Access: Grandfather Mtn., Box 129, Linville, NC 28646; office, 800-468-7325; gate, backcountry manager, 828-737-0833; maintenance, 828-733-8820. Gatehouse entrance on US-221, 2.0 mi NE from Linville, 1.0 mi W from the BRP.

Grandfather Trail (2.4 mi); *Underwood Trail* (0.5 mi); *Black Rock Nature Trail* (1.0 mi)   1179-1181

Length and Difficulty: 3.7 mi combined, strenuous

Trailhead and Description: From the visitor center parking area locate the trail signs, N, on a high embankment and follow the blue-blazed Grandfather Trail through dense rhododendron. At 0.4 mi reach a gap, and at 0.5 mi jct L with the yellow-blazed Underwood Trail. (The Underwood Trail, which rejoins the Grandfather Trail after 0.5 mi, passes Raven's Nest Spring on a rocky treadway. Its purpose is for a route less arduous than the rough climbs of Grandfather Trail.) Continuing on the Grandfather Trail, ascend steeply and climb ladders to scenic MacRae Peak (5,939 ft.). Continuing on the Grandfather Trail reach the Attic Window Peak (5,949 ft.) at 1.1 mi, and the Indian House Cave (200 ft. off the trail, R) at 1.2 mi. At 1.9 mi is a jct with the red-blazed Calloway Trail, L (described below), and reach a spur trail to Watauga View at 2.2 mi. Entrance to the Black Rock Nature Trail is on the main entrance road at the Black Rock parking area, near the visitor center. For the first 0.4 mi the yellow-blazed trail is on a level grade. The next 0.4 mi leads to the Black Rocks, and a view of Grandmother Mtn., the visitor center, and swinging bridge.

1182-   *Profile Trail* (2.7 mi); *Calloway Trail* (0.3 mi)
1183   **Length and Difficulty:** 3.0 mi combined, moderate to strenuous
        Trailhead and Description: Access to the Profile Trail is 0.6 mi N of the
jct of NC-105 and NC-184 on NC-105. From the parking lot, cross the
Watauga River on huge flat boulders and follow a skillfully designed trail on
a slope through cherry, maple, birch, beech, Fraser's sedge, fern, and Indian
pipe. Pass benches of impressive stonework. At 0.8 mi, cross Shanty Spring
Branch in a beautiful area. Pass through a large rock formation at 0.9 mi and
begin an ascent on Green Ridge switchbacks to a good view of Snake Mtn.,
Seven Devils, and the Foscoe Valley at 1.7 mi. At 2.0 mi is the Profile Campsite (50 ft., L) with intricate rock work for a fireplace and bench, almost under
the chin of the Grandfather profile. With good views NW, pass R of Haystack
Rock at 2.2 mi. At 2.7 mi is a jct with the former Shanty Spring Trail, R,
which is closed. (Here is the last dependable source of water for any of the
campsites on the main ridge ahead.) The Profile Trail ends at the spring, and
the red-blazed Calloway Trail begins. After a 0.3-mi climb to the top of the
ridge, reach jct with the blue-blazed Grandfather Trail, R and L. (To the R it
is 1.9 mi to the visitor center parking area, and L it is 0.3 mi to Calloway Peak,
the end of the Grandfather Trail, and the beginning of the Daniel Boone Scout
Trail. The latter trail descends the E side of the mountain to jct with the
Tanawha Trail, the BRP, and US-221.)

1184-   *Daniel Boone Scout Trail* (2.6 mi); *Nuwati Trail* (1.2 mi); *Cragway*
1186   *Trail* (1.0 mi)
        Length and Difficulty: 4.8 mi combined, strenuous (elev change 2,082 ft.)
        Trailhead and Description: These trails can be accessed either from US-
221 (1.6 mi S from the Grandfather Market, and 7.4 mi NE from the Grandfather gatehouse entrance) or from the BRP. The recommended route for
overnight parking is from US-221. Begin the hike on the Asutsi Trail and after
0.4 mi is a jct with the Tanawha Trail after passing under the BRP Boone Fork
bridge. Turn L. (To the R across the Boone Fork footbridge, are two trail
accesses to the BRP. The nearest is to Boone Fork parking after 260 yd. [mp
299.9], and the other access is at the BRP Calloway Peak Overlook parking
1187   area [mp 299.7] on the Upper Boone Fork Trail for 0.5 mi. Continue L on the
Tanawha Trail and go 0.2 mi to a jct, R, with the Nuwati Trail. Ahead on the
Tanawha Trail it is 255 yd. to a jct where the Daniel Boone Scout Trail begins
R. (See chapter 6 for the details of the Tanawha Trail.)

If hiking the Nuwati Trail follow the old woods road 0.6 mi to a jct L with the Cragway Trail. (The 1.0-mi Cragway Trail ascends, steeply in sections, to upturned cliffs that offer magnificent views of a geographical cirque, the Boone Fork Bowl. Other views are of the Blue Ridge Mtns. and their foothills, NE. Rhododendron, red spruce, Allegheny sand myrtle, and blueberry landscape this beautiful route. It connects with the Daniel Boone Scout Trail.) Continue ahead, upstream on the Nuwati Trail and cross Boone Fork at 1.0 mi. Ascend to Storyteller's Rock, L, at 1.2 mi for a view of the Boone Fork Bowl and the end of the trail. Nearby are two campsites. Backtrack to either Cragway Trail or Tanawha Trail.

If continuing on the Daniel Boone Scout Trail from the Tanawha Trail, ascend on a ridge, eroded in sections, to a campsite L, and reach jct R with the Cragway Trail at 1.3 mi. (A dependable spring is 145 yd. to the L.) It is 85 yd., R on the Cragway Trail to the first of its major scenic views—Flat Rock View.) In a forest of spruce, mountain ash, rhododendron, birch, striped maple, galax, and fern, ascend on a narrow, rough treadway to Hi-Balsam Shelter, L at 2.3 mi. (The shelter sleeps six; no campfires.) A few yards below the shelter from here is a view of the Linn Cove Viaduct on the BRP. Continue a steep ascent to the Calloway Peak (5,964 ft, the highest elev of the Blue Ridge Mtn. range) at 2.7 mi. (Calloway Peak is named for Ervin and Texie Calloway, proprietors of the Grandfather Hotel on the W side of the mountain at the turn of the century.) Panoramic scenery from large boulders provides an awesome view of Beach Mtn. and Tennessee (W); Mt. Rogers in VA (N); Mt. Mitchell (SW); and Table Rock (S). (From here it is 2.2 mi on the Grandfather Trail to the visitor center.)

Highlands Biological Station (Highlands)

Founded in 1927, the Highlands Biological Station in the small town of Highlands (Macon County) is presently an interinstitutional center of the University of North Carolina system. Its primary mission is to promote research and education about the habits and organisms of the Southern Appalachians. A total of 34 colleges and universities throughout the Southeast are formally affiliated with the station and send faculty and students there to study. Public education and outreach are handled through the Highlands Nature Center, located in the newly remodeled Clark Foreman Museum Building. The Nature Center offers programs for K–12 and adults year-round and maintains exhibits of local flora and fauna, archaeological artifacts, and geological specimens.

1188   The Highland Botanical Station Trail is on the shores of the 5-acre Lake Ravenel. The main purpose of the garden is to display native plants in a natural setting. A second goal is to demonstrate how to landscape and garden in an ecologically sustainable way using plants native to the Southern Appalachians. The garden includes more than 500 labeled specimens of native plants, including some rare and endangered species. (Sunset Rock Trail is across the road from the Nature Center. See description ahead.) (USGS Map: Highlands)

Address and Access: Highlands Biological Station, P.O. Box 580 (265 Sixth St), Highlands, NC 28741; 828-526-2602. From the jct of US-64/NC-28 in Highlands, go 0.5 mi E on Main St (Horse Cove Rd) to the Nature Center. Park in the Sunset Rock Trail lot. Cross the street and follow the trail and signs down to the Botanical Garden.

Historic Occoneechee Speedway Trail (Orange County)

This walking trace winds through a 44-acre preserve at the former NASCAR Speedway (1948–68). Once a place for cheering and revving, it is now quiet except for the peaceful sound of songbirds. Yet with only slight imagination, you can smell the gasoline fumes mixed with dust and the screams of joy for favored racers. It was also once used for football games and other community events. At the trailhead is a kiosk with brochures on the speedway's natural and cultural history. Placed on the National Register of Historic Places in 2002, its soil may someday be part of the Mountains-to-Sea Trail. User restrictions: daylight use only, no bicycles or motorized vehicles, no dogs without leashes, no smoking, no drugs, hunting, or fishing.

1189-   Follow the trail through a forest of cedar and hawthorne to an open space
1194   of wild rose, then a pine forest and kiosk at 0.15 mi. Ahead is the option to go R or L on the Speedway Trail (0.6 mi round-trip, easy). If heading to the far R, hikers will pass side trails, R, such as Big Bend Trail (0.6 mi round-trip, easy). It provides a scenic edge to the river. Another sidetrail, Beech Bluff Trail (0.2 mi, moderate, sits on a bluff with tall trees by the river. Other trails are Wolf Tree Trail (0.5 mi, easy) on top of a ridge, Terrance Trail (0.2 mi, easy) leading to concrete seating for spectators, and Spectator Trail (0.25 mi, easy) for a completion of the circle. Allowing for some backtracking, the total distance may be 2.7 mi.

Address and Access: Preservation North Carolina (PNC), P.O. Box 27644, Hillsborough, NC 27278; 919-832-3652 or www.presnc.org. CAHPT, 376 St. Mary's Rd, Hillsborough, NC 27278; host@nc.rr.com.

Hyco Lake Natural Learning Area (Caswell County)

The 65-acre Hyco Park, started in 1965, is on a peninsula of Hyco Lake, a reservoir of 3,750 acres, NW of Roxboro. The major reservoir headwaters are Hyco Creek and Hyco Creek South flowing north. The park has facilities for camping, picnicking, swimming, boating, fishing, and a network of educational trails. There is also a Natural Learning Area, conceived by the Person-Caswell Lake Authority. The park is open year-round. (USGS Map: Olive Hill)

Address and Access: Person-Caswell Lake Authority, 205 Kelly Brewer Rd, Leasburg, NC 27291; 336-599-4343, 336-597-1755, or www.person-county.com. From Roxboro, it is 10 mi NW on NC-57 to a turn L. After 0.8 mi, turn R, enter L of a gate, and curve L to ascend at a parking lot for hikers. (It is 6.5 mi N on NC-57 to Milton near the Dan River and Virginia state line.)

From the parking area, walk to the edge of the woods information booth. Enter the woods and descend on Beaver Trail (0.5 mi, easy) Along the way are **1195-** short-leaf pine, black gum, and dogwood. In open areas are blackberry, **1199** sumac, and cedar. Pass Campfire Trail (0.2 mi, easy) at 0.1 mi, R, followed by Rockpile Trail (0.2 mi, easy). (If following it, ascend to a colorful design for observing birds such as titmouse, nuthatch, junco, wren, and bluejack. Descend to rejoin Beaver Trail at 0.3 mi but soon after take the Ridge Trail (250 yd.), R. At 0.6 mi is a 28–step descent to a scenic picnic area by the lake. Return to Campfire Trail and follow it to connect with Shore Trail (0.3 mi, easy). At 1.2 mi, ascend R on a svc road for a return to the parking area at 1.4 mi.

Lake Junaluska (Haywood County)

Adjoining the mountain town of Lake Junaluska, Lake Junaluska Assembly is the 1,200-acre conference and retreat complex of the Southeastern Jurisdiction (SEJ) of the United Methodist Church. Named for the Cherokee Indian peace-leading chief, Junaluska, the 200-acre lake covers an area once known as Tuscola. Surrounding the lake and valley are mountain ranges. Conference facilities can accommodate individuals, families, and church or educational groups up to 2,500. Recreational activities include ball fields and courts, biking, canoeing, fishing, golf, swimming, and more. The SEJ's Commission on Archives and History and the Boy Scouts of America have a cooperative project for hiking the 27.0-mi Asbury Trail. The journey is between Mt. Sterling community (accessed on Waterville Rd, off I-40, Exit 451) and Cove Creek jct of old NC-284 and US-276 (accessed from I-40, Exit 20). The trail route is mainly on the ancient Cataloochee Trail and honors the clergyman Francis

Asbury, who covered 275,000 mi as a circuit rider in 45 years. (See chapter 7, Asbury Trail.)

1200   Lake Junaluska Trail is a 2.3-mi easy loop that circles the lake. Upon entry to the assembly grounds, park at the second parking lot, R, near the swimming pool. Begin clockwise; pass the Paul Kern Youth Center and parallel the rose walk to the Methodist World Council. After passing the Harroll Center Audi-

1201 torium and Memorial Chapel, enter a gate at 0.6 mi to the Francis Asbury Trail. It runs jointly with the main trail for 0.2 mi. Here are large pine, oak, cultivated flowers, and markers honoring distinguished humanitarians. At 0.7 mi, cross the dam and bridge. From grassy manicured lawns are scenic views of the luminescent lake. Cross a boardwalk-bridge at 2.0 mi, and return to the parking lot at 2.3 mi.

Information: Lake Junaluska Assembly, P.O. Box 67, Lake Junaluska, NC 28745; 800-222-4930/828-452-2881; (SEJ Commission on Archives and History, P.O. Box 1165, Lake Junaluska, NC 28745).

Morningstar Nature Refuge (Martin County)

The 20-acre sanctuary for plants and animals has 5 acres open to the public.
1202- In a beautiful biological refuge is a 1.6-mi network of trails: Morningstar
1211 Trail, Holly Ridge Trail, Blue Heron Trail, Buckskin Beech Trail, Eagle Spirit Trail, Sacred Circle Trail, Moon Feather Trail, Marsh Trail, Black Bear Trail, and Fern Valley Trail. Access from the jct of US-17 and US-64 Bypass in Williamston is 4.0 mi S on US-17, turn L (E) on Mill Inn Rd (SR-1521), go 2.0 mi, and turn L on Meadow Branch Rd (SR-1526). (Call Gail Roberson for appointment.)

Information: Morningstar Nature Refuge, 1967 Meadow Branch Rd, Williamston, NC 27892; 252-792-7788.

Nags Head Woods Ecological Preserve (Dare County)

This maritime forest of more than 1,200 acres is an outstanding biological resource for hikers and students of nature. There are more than 300 species of plants and 50 species of birds, plus amphibians and mammals. Protected by The Nature Conservatory, the public is free to follow the trails without a guide. Your self-guided adventure (hiking only) is confined to daylight hours. Stay on the trails, and do not bring domestic animals on them. Picnicking, smoking, and alcohol are prohibited. If beginning S from the parking area and
1212 the office/gift shop, cross bridge to a fork for the Center Trail (0.25 mi, easy)

and make a loop among red bay and sparkleberry. Cross two arched bridges for a return and continue S on Sweetgum Swamp Trail (2.2 mi, easy). Ascend **1213** steps on a dune. At 0.1 mi is a preserve sign and at 0.2 mi, turn R to follow under a power line. After more dunes and bridges, arrive near a pond at Blue- **1214** berry Ridge Trail (3.7 mi round-trip, moderate), L. (If returning, R, it is 1.3 mi to the office.)

Continuing SE, pass swamps, cross footbridges, and take a break at some of the resting benches. After making a loop, return to Sweetgum Swamp Trail and stay L. Follow it and at the loop again, stay L for a return to the power line. After returning to the office and parking lot, turn L on the entrance road and after 120 yd., turn R to pass under a power line briefly. At an old road crossing, hikers will see Discovery Trail (0.5 mi, easy), L, and Roanoke Trail **1215-** (1.5 mi with backtracking, moderate), R. If heading R, cross a boardwalk at **1216** 0.5 mi, pass site of former building, cross more boardwalks, and reach a beach at Roanoke Sound at 0.7 mi. On the return, turn R on Discovery Trail for a return to the parking lot. A separate trail, Nags Head Town Trail (1.6 mi, mod- **1217** erate), requires a drive back to US-158. Turn R, and after 1.2 mi, turn R at the traffic light on Barnes St. Drive 0.3 mi and turn L to the town park. Follow trail signs from far R of the parking lot. Ascend and descend dunes and at 0.8 mi, reach the Roanoke Sound. In the process, hikers are likely to see water-fowl. Backtrack.

Address and Access: Nags Head Woods Ecological Preserve, 701 Ocean Acres Dr, Kill Devil Hills, NC 27948; 252-441-2525 or www.nature.org. On US-158, turn W on Ocean Acres Dr for 1.0 mi to the parking lot and office, L.

North Carolina Coastal Federation (Atlantic Beach)

The Hoop Pole Creek Nature Trail (0.5 mi round-trip, easy) is a project of the **1218** NC Coastal Federation and the NC Clean Water Management Trust Fund. Hoop Pole Creek is a natural refuge for fish, wildlife, and plant communities. On the trail are 18 interpretive markers to illustrate the value of a maritime forest. Part of the trail is on an old road and under a majestic spread of live oak. The forest also has pennywort, red bay, devilwood, and salt shrub. There is a viewing platform of Bogue Sound at the trail's terminus. Open daily and free of charge. Call in advance if a large group or for a guided tour.

Address and Access: NCCF, 3609 Highway 24, Newport, NC 28570; 252-393-8185 or www.nccoast.org. Follow NC-58 onto Emerald Island and into Atlantic Beach. Park at Atlantic Station Shopping Center, L. Trail entrance is E at the forest.

1219   **Pearson's Falls Trail** (Polk County)

Pearson's Falls Trail (0.3 mi) is part of a 268-acre nature preserve maintained and financed privately by the Tryon Garden Club (organized in 1928). Open year-round, there is a small fee to view the beautiful 90-ft. cascades and botanical display of more than 252 species (one of which is the rare broadleaf coreopsis, *Coreopsis latifolia*). (The club purchased the property in 1931 from the Charles W. Pearson family.) Access to the property is 4.0 mi N of Tryon on US-176; turn L on SR-1102 (3.0 mi S from Saluda). Follow the signs 1.0 mi.

Information: Tryon Garden Club Nature Preserve, P.O. Box 245, Tryon, N.C. 28782; 828-749-3031

Piedmont Environmental Center

1220-   *Lakeshore Trail* (1.8 mi); *Fence Row Trail* (0.1 mi); *Wildflower Trail*
1227   (0.2 mi); *Fiddlehead Trail* (0.4 mi); *Dogwood Trail* (0.6 mi); *Pine Thicket Trail* (0.3 mi); *Raccoon Run Trail* (0.7 mi); *Chickadee Trail* (0.1 mi)

Length and Difficulty: 4.2 mi round-trip combined, easy

Trailhead and Description: All trails can be accessed from the Lakeshore Trail (white), which begins at the parking lot or the back porch of the center. If beginning from the parking lot, enter at the S side (near the driveway entrance and crossing of Bicentennial Greenway Trail). Immediately L is a connector to Fence Row Trail (tan), L, and Chickadee Trail (green), R. Either way, they connect with the Lakeshore Trail after 0.1 mi. If following L, pass behind the parking lot and buildings, turn R, and after a few yards jct with the Wildflower Trail (purple). (The Wildflower Trail has double loops, connects with the Bicentennial Greenway Trail, and has a mixed forest of pine and hardwoods, ferns, and wildflowers.)

Continuing on the Lakeshore Trail, reach a jct with 0.4-mi Fiddlehead Trail (yellow), R. (It descends to jct with Pine Thicket Trail [red], L, and down to a cove in High Point City Lake. Here is jct R and L with Lakeshore Trail. A turn R on the floating bridge will make a return to the parking lot for a 1.0-mi loop.) If passing by the Fiddlehead Trail, go past a spur connector L to the Bicentennial Greenway Trail, followed by a R jct with the Dogwood Trail (orange). (The Dogwood Trail goes through the heart of the Lakeshore Trail loop, exposing oak, pine, poplar, and cedar. Along the way it jct R with Pine Thicket Trail.)

Staying on the Lakeshore Trail, pass through a forest of large trees and arrive at the lake at 0.8 mi. Curve around the peninsulas, where to the interior of the loop is kudzu. Pass the jct R with Dogwood Trail at 1.0 mi, and at 1.3 mi is a jct with Raccoon Run Trail (blue), L. (Raccoon Run Trail goes briefly on a linear trail before a scenic circle on the peninsula.) Finish the Lakeshore Trail by crossing the floating bridge and ascending to the parking lot at 1.8 mi. (Three miles of the Bicentennial Greenway Trail are within the center's preserve [see section 2 in chapter 13].) (USGS Maps: High Point E, Guilford)

Address and Access: Piedmont Environmental Center, 1220 Penny Rd, High Point NC 27260; 336-883-8531 or 8533. From the jct of US-29A/70A and Penny Rd (W in Jamestown), go N 1.1 mi on Penny Rd and turn R at the center's entrance. From Greensboro, at the jct of Wendover Ave and I-40, Exit 214, go SW on Wendover Ave 4.5 mi to a jct with Penny Rd (at the Deep River jct). Turn L and go 2.0 mi to the center.

Sauratown Trail (Stokes and Surry Counties)   1228

This historic trail is a remarkable example of how a dedicated team of equestrians (Sauratown Trails Association) can plan, construct, and maintain a 20.3-mi section on private properties. Although the credit list is long for making the trail possible, R.M. Collins has received considerable recognition for it becoming a reality. On June 1, 2002, when the state officially designated the trail as part of the MST, Collins was presented with a prestigious award: the Order of the Long Leaf Pine Award, from Gov. Mike Easley. The trail connects two state parks, Pilot Mtn. in the W and Hanging Rock in the E. A condensed description follows in that order. (The trail is 21.7 mi when the 1.45 mi. Grassy Ridge Trail in Pilot Mtn. State Park is included, and if three private property connecting loops are included, the distance is 33.1 mi. Described here is only the section designated by the state as part of the MST.)

At the W terminus, near the entrance to Pilot Mtn. State Park, is roadside parking near the W side of US-52 (I-74) bridge on Pilot Knob Park Rd. Hike E under the expressway bridge. After 1.0 mi, turn L at a private road (New Pilot Knob Lane) and immediately L into a meadow. Enter a hardwood forest to parallel a stream. Ascend and cross Pilot Knob Park Rd at 0.6 mi, then descend in a forest among quartz rock. Rock-hop Grassy Creek where hillsides have acres of running cedar and spots of mountain laurel. Ascend. At 1.0 mi is an open space, and at 1.4 mi is a prominent view of Pilot Mtn. Descend; after crossing a small stream, ascend to a house and barn where a gravel road exits to Old Winston Rd at 2.0 mi. Across the road to the R is a large parking space.

Continue by crossing the RR on Coon Rd and promptly turn R into a forest. After 108 yd., cross old US-52 and enter another forest for a descent with switchbacks. Rock-hop a stream at 2.5 mi and cross Bradley Rd at 2.8 mi. Cross three more streams between uphills and downhills. At 4.0 mi, wade or rock-hop Mill Creek. The forest has mountain laurel and ironwood. At 4.3 mi, enter a farm field and pass an old tobacco barn at 4.6 mi. After a mixture of forest, fields, and old roads, cross a culverted stream at 5.0 mi. Return to scenic Mill Creek and follow it upstream at 5.3 mi. After crossing two small bridges, leave the creek and parallel Coon Rd. Cross Volunteer Rd at 6.0 mi; descend on a private gravel road between farm buildings. Access Brims Grove Rd at 6.4 mi where a short descent to the L is a parking space.

If not stopping, stay R, leave the road, and descend 160 yd. To wade the West Prong of the Yadkin River. For the next 1.0 mi, pass in and out of forest and field before descending on switchbacks to the scenic side of West Prong. Tall trees, including beech, are here. After frequent stream crossings, arrive at Old Mill Rd at 8.2 mi. Turn R onto the road and after 0.2 mi, turn L on a private farm road (Mazie's Lane). If looking back, there is a distant view of Pilot Mtn. At 806 mi, leave the road and follow a grassy route between fence and forest. Turn R for a descent into the forest at 8.7 mi. The next 3.0 mi is the most strenuous and wild part of the trail. There are 16 switchbacks in the ascent and descent of the N side of Sauratown Mtn. in a forest of hardwoods, pine, and groves of mountain laurel and rhododendron. Rock formations and streams add scenic quality to the route. At 10.2 mi, cross a paved, private access road (Makay Rd) to Mtn. Top Youth Camp. After a descent, wade or rock-hop South Double Creek at least 11 times through a forest with dense rhododendron. Cross a power line and exit to Flat Rock Rd at 11.6 mi. (Flat Rock Rd continues R to Rock House Rd. On the way, it passes a rock house, some of which is still standing, on the L.)

To the L and ahead, the trail descends on Thore Rd, past a well-groomed clearing at a waterfall. After 1.0 mi, ascend the steep road (may be gravel) to Rock House Rd, R and L, at 13.0 mi. (To the L, Rock House Rd is 0.7 mi to NC-268.) Across the road is Marshall Ridge Rd (private), but enter the Sauratown Trail R of the road. The trail undulates and partially parallels the road before descending to a ridge. At 14.1 mi is a jct with a trail sign. On a ridge, descend on six switchbacks to wade or rock-hop South Double Creek at 15.1 mi. (To the R is a trail jct for a 0.7-mi access to parking at Sauratown Trail Center on Rock House Rd.) Pass through a rhododendron grove; parallel and cross a stream with a waterfall. Pass an old tobacco barn and field at 15.5 mi.

Ascend to Taylor Rd at 15.9 mi. Cross and descend and shortly cross NC-66. Descend on switchbacks and rock-hop Vade Mecum Creek. Pass 3.2-mi Tucker Loop Trail, L, at 18.2 mi and Moores Springs Rd (SR-100) at 18.4 mi. **1229** Ascend to cross Mickey Rd (SR-1481) at 19.8 mi. Ascend and pass 2.7-mi Booth Loop Trail, L. Ascend to a trail jct where to the L, a foot trail ascends **1230** to Tory's Den parking lot in Hanging Rock State Park at 20.3 mi. (At jct, R and ahead cross Charlie Young Rd to continue into the forest on the Tory's Den Trail and pass two access points 5.3-mi Sauratown Loop Trail, an equestrian trail. See Hanging Rock State Park for the continuance of Tory's Den Trail and other connecting trails in the park.) (USGS Maps: Pinnacle, Pilot Mtn., Hanging Rock)

Address: Sauratown Trails association, 1045 Mallard Lake, Pinnacle, NC 27104; 336-351-4402 or lgreeves@surry.net.

Sunset Rock Trail (Macon County)   1231
Length and Difficulty: 1.4 mi round-trip, easy
Trailhead and Description: From the jct of US-64 and NC-28 in Highlands, proceed on E Main St 0.4 mi and park opposite the Highlands Nature Center. Follow the sign and turn R at 0.2 mi over rock slabs through pine, rosebay, rhododendron, hemlock, and locust. At 0.6 mi an 1879 rock engraving indicates that the park area is a memorial to Margaretta A. and S. Prioleal Ravenel. To the R is a large rock outcropping that provides a magnificent view of the Nantahala NF and the town of Highlands. From here, hikers can also see Satulah Mtn. (4,542 ft.) about 1.0 mi S, a property owned by the same corporation that owns Sunset Rock, Satulah Summit–Ravenel Park Inc. Backtrack.

Address: Highlands Visitor Center, Town Hall, Box 404, Highlands, NC 28741; 828-526-2112.

Triangle Land Conservancy
Since 1983 the Conservancy has preserved its mission to preserve natural areas that have biological, historical, scenic, and water quality value. In 2004, the non-profit land trust was in six counties: Chatham, Durham, Johnson, Lee, Orange, and Wake with more than 4,539 acres. The four preserves described ahead are open to the public daily, and some others are open for special causes.

Address: Triangle Land Conservancy, 1101 Haynes St., Suite 205, Raleigh, NC 27604; 919-833-3662, www.tlc-nc.org, or info@tlc-nc.org.

Flower Hill Preserve (Johnson County)

This 10-acre site, purchased in 1989, is on a high bluff bordered by NC 231 on the N side and Moccasin Creek on the E side. Among its shrubbery and wildflowers is a grove of *Rhododendron catawbiense,* farthest E in the state. The **1232** Flower Hill Trail stays on the rim of the bluff for 0.3 mi. It then descends 165 yd. on Kenneth Narrow property to a spring near Moccasin Creek. Backtrack.

Access: From the jct of US-264 and NC-39 (E of Zebulon), drive S on NC-39 for 6.0 mi and turn L (E) on NC-231. If from Selma drive N on NC-39 for 14 mi and turn R (E). After 3.0 mi on NC-231 is Flower Hill Road, R. It is 0.1 mi up the hill to the trail entrance, L, but the road shoulder parking is narrow. More space is on the shoulder of NC-231, 90 yd. E of the jct with Flower Hill Road.

Johnson Mill Nature Preserve (Orange County)

The 296-acre preserve has markers of honor to those who made it possible. **1233** Usage is for hiking only. If entry is on Mt. Sinai Rd, follow Johnson Mill Trail beside New Hope Creek among tall hardwoods, spice bush, and sugar hackberry. At 0.3 mi are stream rapids, followed by a pass under a power line. On a resplendent floodplain, cross a footbridge over Old Field Creek near it confluence with New Hope Creek at 0.6 mi. On the creek bank are natural but gnarled sculptures of sycamore roots. Approach a four-way jct. If heading R, make a loop on a hillside and return at 1.3 mi to continue downstream. In a riparian laboratory, there are resting benches, some close to the scenic streamside. At 1.8 mi, arrive at Turkey Farm Rd parking space. Backtrack or arrange a shuttle.

Access: From I-85, Exit 165, drive 5.3 mi S on NC-86 to a L turn on Mt. Sinai Rd (SR-1718) and go 1.0 mi to a parking space, R. To Turkey Farm Rd, continue ahead 0.9 mi for a R turn and 0.8 mi for a parking area, R.

Swift Creek Bluffs Preserve (Wake County)

This preserve has bottomlands with profuse spring wildflowers in alluvial woods. An example is pink wild geranium. Hikers pass through a grove of it after beginning the trail. Along the way, R, is a plaque expressing appreciation to donors who made the preserve possible for perpetuity. After 75 yd., fork R to parallel the creek. At 0.6 mi is the creekside end, where there is a large beech tree, ferns, and mossy forest floor. Backtrack 0.1 mi, turn R and ascend on 74 steps, with resting benches, to the summit of the bluffs. There is an overlook at 0.9 mi. Songbirds are prominent in spring and summer. If you continue you will descend to Lochmere Golf Course at 1.0 mi. (A 0.2 mi asphalt greenway ascends L to a residential area.) Backtrack.

Access: From the intersection of US-1 and Cary Parkway in S Cary, drive 2.0 mi E on the Parkway to Holly Springs Drive, R. After 1.6 mi. (across Swift Creek bridge), make an immediate R to a parking area for about six cars.

White Pines Preserve (Chatham County)

Like Flower Hill and Swift Creek Bluffs, this preserve has high bluffs facing north where the shade and moisture from creeks or rivers influence the botanical diversity. In this 258 acres of hardwoods are scattered Eastern white pine *(Pinus strobes),* the easternmost stand of the nation's Southeast. From the parking space begin the descent on the River Trail at the sign on an old road. **1234** Pass under a powerline and enter the gate at 0.1 mi. The remains of an old chimney are R. At 0.2 mi, L, is a rough road to Rocky Creek. If continuing ahead you will see a sign, L, Overlook Trail at 0.4 mi. If following the River **1235** Trail continue R, descend to a floodplain and bank of Deep River. Curve L among large sycamores. At 7.0 mi, curve L at the confluence of Rocky Creek with Deep River. Pass through spice bush and notice mountain laurel on the L side. At 0.9 mi is a jct with Comet Trail, L, that ascends 0.3 mi to a loop with **1236** Overlook Trail, and to a plaque in memory of David H. Howells (1920–95), professor emeritus of NC State University. Continuing on the River Trail leave the floodplain and ascend L on an old road. The forest is dense with mountain laurel and white pine are among the hardwoods. After 0.3 mi, return to the entrance road and turn R to exit.

Access: From Courthouse Circle in Pittsboro, drive S on US-15/501/NC-87 for 8.2 mi to River Forks Rd, L. Immediately turn R. After 1.7 mi, turn R at a stop sign, then turn L after another 0.5 mi. After 0.4 mi is a preserve property sign and parking space. Access from the jct of US-1 and US-15/501/NC-87 north of Sanford is 6.2 mi to River Forks Rd.

Whitehall Circuit Trail (Moore County) 1237

Length and Difficulty: 2.0 mi round-trip, easy

Trailhead and Description: If beginning at Reservoir Park and hiking counterclockwise, walk up the steps on the bank, W, and turn sharply L on an old road. Follow a white disc through longleaf pine, turkey oak, and scattered patches of goat's rue and tufts of wire grass. At 0.8 mi arrive at a vehicle gate (described above near entrance to the center). At 0.9 mi turn on a road that may announce it as a farm entrance. Leave the road to a footpath at 1.2 mi for a gentle descent to a small bridge over a streamlet. Here is a grove of magnolia bay at 1.5 mi. Complete the loop on a grassy area at the opposite side of the parking lot. The trail is monitored in perpetuity by the Sandhills Area Land Trust. (At the parking area is a 2.0-mi loop trail around Reservoir Lake, described in chapter 13, and a connector trail at the N end of the dam to Sandhill Community College trails described in chapter 15.)

Address and Access: Sandhills Area Land Trust, 140A Southwest Broad St, Southern Pines, NC 28387; 910-695-4323. In Southern Pines turn off US-1 W onto NC-2 (Midland Rd), drive 0.2 mi for a R turn on NC-22. After 1.1 mi turn L on Pee Dee Rd; then 0.4 mi to Whitehall Center sign, R. The trail begins here, but ahead on the entrance road at a fork, L is a place to park. (Another place to park is at Reservoir Park. Access is to continue on NC-22 past Pee Dee Rd for 0.6 mi for a L turn to the parking lot.)

1238 White Oak Nature Trail (Wake County)

White Oak Nature Trail is an easy 1.5-mi double loop at Carolina Power and Light Harris Nuclear Power Plant. The skillfully designed and color-coded blazed route begins at a parking and picnic area at the Harris Plant Visitor Center/Energy and Environmental Center. There are interpretive markers about wildlife, trees, ferns, and flowers. The longer part of the loop has boardwalks on the approach to Big Branch, a scenic wetland. (Proposed plans are to have talking-tree markers like those at the state forests' educational centers.) A trail brochure is available either at the trailhead or the visitor center.

Address and Access: Harris Energy Visitor Center, 3932 New Hill-Holliman Rd, New Hill, NC 27562; 919-362-3261 or 1-800-452-2777. From US-1 (S of Apex), turn off at New Hill sign to New Hill–Holleman Rd (SR-1127) and drive 1.5 mi SE.

Chapter 15

College and University Trails

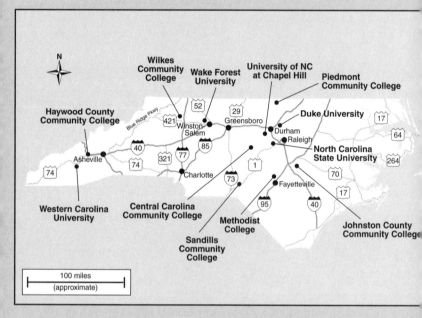

Introductions to Trail Areas

This listing of Colleges and Universities includes only educational institutions where there are trails associated with their biological research, preserves, gardens, arboretums, or forests. They are listed alphabetically rather than geologically.

Chapter 15

College and University Trails

*A book that says anything about walking
has a ready passage to my inmost heart.*
—Christopher Morley

Physical education and recreation are part of the academic life of colleges and universities. In 32 of the senior institutions, the curriculum offers degrees in forestry, parks and recreation management, environmental fields, or health and physical education. A few offer degrees in recreation therapy. Fourteen community colleges offer preliminary degree programs in recreation, two of which offer therapeutic recreation. Because campus life has such a strong emphasis on physical education, it is not surprising that if trails are not on the campus property, there are organizations and clubs to sponsor field trips elsewhere. A few colleges have made track runs and sidewalks part of the "trail" system. An example is Elon University where logos indicate loops of 1.0 mi (white), 2.0 mi (black), and 3.4 mi (yellow) route options for both physical exercise and seeing the landscape and historic buildings on the campus (336-278-7529). Described ahead is coverage of academic institutions that responded to the author's statewide invitation.

Central Carolina Community College (Pittsboro Campus)

The college is a branch campus of Central Carolina Community College in Sanford. Distinctive to this campus is the easy 1.0-mi Thanks Trail ellipse around an expansive and scenic lawn. ("Thanks" stands for Trail for Health, Art, and Nature for Kids to Seniors.) Floral displays are along the way. From the parking lot begin clockwise to a picnic table under a large sweet gum and pass a physical fitness stop at 0.4 mi. A grove of walnut trees hover over dense and heavy burdock before on a hill top. There is a shortcut route to the campus buildings at 0.5 mi. Pass a picnic table at an old bridge (built in 1921). Stop for views at the agriculture nursery at 0.9 mi before returning to the parking lot.

1239

Address and Access: Central Carolina CC, Pittsboro Campus, 424 West St, Pittsboro, NC 27312; 919-542-6495. From downtown courthouse in Pittsboro, drive W on West St (US-64Alt) 0.8 mi to college entrance, R. (On the way was a jct with NC-902, L.)

Duke University (Durham, Chatham, Alamance, and Orange Counties)

The university, a private institution, has two major areas of natural resources open to the public. One area is the 55-acre Sarah P. Duke Memorial Gardens and the other is the vast 7,700-acre Duke Forest composed of six main divisions in four counties. To protect these remarkable properties, the university has provided guidelines and regulations described ahead. The gardens have at least 2,000 species of vascular plants among three main areas of local, national, and foreign collections. A network of trails has special landscaping for easy viewing. Open daily from 8:00AM to dusk, visitation is free. The Doris Duke Center is located centrally in the gardens. Its office is open from 9:00AM to 5:00PM daily and has an amphitheatre, White Garden, Water Garden, and East-West Garden. For information about reserving space for weddings, educational tours, assistance to the physically disabled, or botanical information, call the number below. Garden guidelines prohibit damage or taking samples of the plants; dogs must be on a leash and are not permitted on narrow pathways or in Blomquist Garden of Native Plants, and supervision of children is required. Hiking only.

Address and Access: Sarah P. Duke Memorial Gardens, P.O. Box 90341, Duke University, Durham, NC 27708; 919-684-3698 or www.hr.duke.edu/ dukegardens. The main entrance is at 426 Anderson St (between Campus Dr and Erwin Rd) to a parking lot. Parking is not allowed on Flowers Dr (on the NW border of the gardens).

The Duke Forest property is managed as an outdoor laboratory for teaching and forestry research, and because of the nature of the research, some tracts are not open to the public. Permissible recreational activities are hiking, bicycling, and horseback riding (on graded and fire roads only), picnicking, and fishing. Camping is prohibited. In the entrances of the trail networks, a large sign lists restrictions. Group activities must be approved in advance by the forest resource manager.

Address: Duke Forest Resource Manager, School of the Environment, Room A116, Levine Science Research Center, P.O. Box 90332, Durham, NC 27708; 919-613-8013 or www.dukeforest.duke.edu/.

Because the tracts are so widely located and the trail systems involve more than 40 trails, an abbreviated introduction is described here. For full details and maps see the author's guidebook *Trails of the Triangle,* published by Blair Publisher, 1406 Plaza Drive, Winston Salam, NC 27103; (800-222-9796 for credit card orders or available at bookstores).

Durham Division

1240-1254

This tract has 24 gated roads, nine fire trails and an interpretive trail. The trails are Duke Cross Country Trail (2.9 mi, easy); Fitness Trail (0.6 mi, easy); Gate #2 to Gate #4 Road (1.0 mi, easy); Old Oxford Road (0.6 mi round-trip, easy); Cotton Mill Fire Trail (0.6 mi round-trip, easy); Mud Creek Fire Trail (0.4 mi round-trip, easy); Gate #3 Road to Gate #7 Road (2.6 mi round-trip, easy); Gate C Road and Shepard Nature Trail (1.0 mi, easy); Gate #9 Road (0.4 mi round-trip, easy); Gate #14, Kinsman Fire Trail (0.4 mi round-trip, easy); Gate D Road and Picnic Area (0.2 mi round-trip, easy); Gate #10 Road to Gate #13 Road (1.9 mi, easy); Gate #11 Road to Gate #12 Road, Couch Mountain Fire Trail (3.2 mi or 5.4 mi round-trip, moderate). (USGS Maps: Durham NW and Hillsborough)

Access: All trails are accessible on NC-751 with the exception of gated road #14 on Kerley Rd, 0.1 mi off NC-751. The gates are numbered 2 through 13; some on each side of NC-751. It is 2.85 mi W from gate #2 to US-70. If going W on NC-751 from the jct with US-15-501 Byp, Exit 107, drive 0.3 mi and park near gate #2 for first selection.

Korstian Division

1255-1270

This 1,950-acre track has Gate #25 Concrete Bridge Road and Gate #24 Wooden Bridge Road (10.3 mi, moderate); Concrete Bridge Road (1.8 mi, easy); Hard Climb Road (1.2 mi round-trip, moderate); Midway Fire Trail (0.6 mi round-trip); Thrift Fire Trail (0.4 mi round-trip, easy); Echinata Fire Trail (0.5 mi round-trip, easy); Big Bend Fire Trail (0.2 mi round-trip, easy); Wooden Bridge Road (1.9 mi, easy to moderate); Dead End Fire Trail (0.4 mi round-trip, easy); Land's End Fire Trail (0.4 mi round-trip, easy); Bluff's End Fire Trail (0.5 mi round-trip, easy); West Road Trail (0.6 mi, round-trip, easy); Unnamed Fire Trail (0.4 mi round-trip, easy); Gate #26 Laurel Hill Fire Trail, Slick Hill Fire Trail (1.0 mi round-trip, moderate); Gate #21 Piney Mountain Fire Trail (1.0 mi round-trip, easy). (USGS Map: Chapel Hill)

Access: The tract is SW of the Durham tract and between Mt. Sinai Rd on the N and Whitfield Rd on the S. Access from US-15-501 Byp, Exit 107, drive W 0.3 mi on Cameron Blvd, then turn L on Erwin Rd at the Duke Forest sign. Follow Erwin Rd 3.1 mi (you will pass a jct with Mt. Sinai Rd at 1.75 mi) and turn R on Whitfield Rd. Drive 0.85 mi to Gate #25 Concrete Bridge Rd, R. To access the other end of the loop drive 0.5 mi farther on Whitfield Rd to a narrow entrance on the R and Gate #24 Wooden Bridge Rd. (From that point on Whitfield Rd, it is 2.05 mi to a jct with NC-86 and I-40, Exit 266. The N access of Concrete Bridge Rd is 2.05 mi W on Mt. Sinai Rd from Erwin Rd, or 3.0 mi E on Mt. Sinai Rd from NC-86.)

Eno Division
This 519-acre track is SE of Hillsborough and W of Eno River State Park, between I-85 and I-40. Gate #28 Eno Road (1.4 mi, easy); Flat Rock Fire Trail (0.7 mi round-trip, easy); Stone Wall Fire Trail (1.3 mi round-trip, easy); Bivens Fire Trail (0.8 mi round-trip, easy); Oak Hill Fire Trail (0.7 mi round-trip, easy); Slick Rock Fire Trail (0.4 mi round-trip, easy). (USGS Map: Hillsborough) **1271-1276**

Access: If driving W in Durham on I-85, turn off at Exit 172 onto US-70. After 1.3 mi turn L immediately past the traffic lights onto Old NC-10 (SR-12710). Drive 3.75 mi to the jct with New Hope Church Rd and turn L. After 0.4 mi, reach Gate #28, R.

Hillsborough Division
In the 645-acre track is only one trail, Gate #31 Wagon Fire Trail (1.2 mi round-trip, easy). (USGS Map: Efland) **1277**

Access: In Hillsborough at a jct of NC-86 and US-70, drive W 1.5 mi on US-70 to Gate #31 on the N side.

Blackwood Division
This area's 998 acres has the forest's highest hill (Bald Mtn., 762 ft. elev) and part of a swamp known as Meadow Flats. Bald Mountain Fire Trail (2.2 mi round-trip, easy). USGS Map: Chapel Hill) **1278**

Access: At I-85, Exit 261 drive S on NC-86 for 4.1 mi Roadside parking; refrain from parking in a private driveway.

Haywood County Community College (Clyde)
Landscaping of the woodlands on a gentle slope, manicured lawns in the meadow, a mill pond near the entrance, and multiple gardens makes the entire campus an arboretum. An easy 1.0-mi Haywood CCC Trail loop pro- **1279** vides the visitor an opportunity to see it all. If parking at the first parking lot, L, after entry to the campus on Freedlander Dr, cross the street and descend

on a paved trail to circle the pond and behind a waterwheel. Enter the Nix Horticultural Complex with its special display of the Freedlander Dahlia Garden. Ascend to recross Freedlander Dr to a double loop among a variety of trees and shrubs, including rhododendron, where it can connect with College Drive. Return toward the Student Center but curve R to stay in the forest. Follow the trail that exits the forest near an athletic field. From here return to where you parked.

Address and Access: HCCC, 185 Freedlander Dr, Clyde, NC 28721; 828-627-2821, main switchboard; 828-627-4699, campus tours; 828-627-4640, campus arboretum; www.haywood.edu. On US-19/23 take Exit 107 if arriving from Asheville, and Exit 105 if from Clyde onto Jones Cove Rd; turn L on Freedlander Drive.

Johnston County Community College (Smithfield)

Located in an urban area, this large college serves the area with basic educational curricular, a varied and expansive cultural arts program, and an expanded biological science program with the Howell Woods Environmental Learning Center near the Neuse River. The center is part of a 2,856-acre donation by Rudolph Howell in 1993 and located about 11 mi S of the college. **1280** Additionally, plans are for construction of the 9.0-mi Native Woodlands Trail to connect areas and the college in the city. Known within the Woods Center property are 58 species of butterflies, 62 species of dragon and damsel flies, 43 species of reptiles and 42 mammals, and 165 species of plants. There are more than 30 trails and roads, some of which are not open to the public. Of that number, a staff official at the Woods Center has provided a list of 16 trails where either the passage is mowed or has a sand/gravel base. The preserve is open daily, but the office is open 8:00AM–5:00AM M–F. Hiking is free, but there is a fee for $5 for either mountain biking or fishing, and $10 for horseback riding. Camping is prohibited. In heavy rains or flooding, all routes may be closed. Insect repellent is recommended in warm/hot seasons.

The following trails are near the office, except Howell Drive and Plantation Rd that begin near the office but extend deeper into the preserve. Inquire about the condition of River Loop West and East Rd through wetlands near **1281-** the river: Bartram Trail (0.2 mi, easy; mowed); Box Turtle Trail (0.3 mi, easy; **1295** mowed); B.W. Wells Trail (0.24 mi, easy; mowed); Cornell Rd (0.5 mi, easy; sand/gravel); Diversity Trail (0.7 mi, easy; sandy); Fox Squirrel Trail (0.3 mi, easy; sandy/mowed); Howell Drive (2.5 mi, easy; improved gravel); Leopold

Trail (0.4 mi, easy; mowed); Loblolly Lane Trail (0.6 mi, easy; mowed); Longleaf Lane (0.25 mi, easy; sandy); Outside Slough Trail (0.2 mi, easy; mowed); Owl Box Trail (0.1 mi, easy; mowed); Plantation Rd (1.6 mi, easy; improved gravel); Smokey Trail (0.2 mi, easy; mowed); Thoreau Trail (0.6 mi, easy; mowed); Wild Turkey Lane (0.25 mi, easy; sandy).

Address and Access: Howell Woods Environmental Learning Center, 6601 Devil's Racetrack Rd, Four Oaks, NC 27524; 919-938-0115 or www.johnstoncc.edu/information/howellwoods/. From Smithfield drive S on I-95 to Exit 90 and S on US-701, but immediately L on the access to return N on I-95, then quickly R on Devil's Racetrack Rd. After 0.8 mi, turn L at sign.

Methodist College (Fayetteville)

The Neuse River is part of the E boundary of Methodist College, and on the river's high embankment to gentle slopes is an academic network of hiking trails. Sponsored by faculty and students in botany and biology the main trail access is at the SE corner of Shelley Field, an athletic parking lot. Named the Pauline Longest Nature Trail (2.0 mi, easy to moderate), it has subtitle trails **1296** as different classes have added trail options to expand academic knowledge of the terrain. A signboard lists the usage guidelines; hiking only. At the trail entrance, cross a RR grade to enter the forest. (At 0.1 mi an unnamed old road passage is L. It dead-ends at a residential area.) At 0.2 mi, hikers have a choice to descend ahead for a loop trail or take a sharp R to a waterfall. (If taking the 0.5-mi L trail, it extends into a forest of tall trees and returns near impressive high bluffs to the main trail.) If choosing the Waterfall Trail, descend to a sur- **1297** prisingly attractive water flow over colorful shades of tan, brown, and orange siltstone. From here you have options to incorporate 1.3 mi of scenic river views and upland mixture of hardwood and pines. Routes will include a passage above the waterfall, steps, and over bridges. The trails are Mountain Laurel **1298-** Trail, Upper and Lower Atamasco Trail, Sourwood Trail, Pawpaw Trail, and **1302** Sweetgum Trail. Among the wildflowers are galax, may apple, and dog-tooth violets. Return to the main trail. (There is a proposal to extend the trail system downriver to connect with Clark Park and perhaps other areas.)

Address and Access: Methodist College, Dept of Science, 5400 Ramsey St, Fayetteville, NC 28311; 919-630-7163. Enter the campus at 5400 Ramsey St (US-401) and follow the athletic facilities signs and/or the nature trail signs. Descend to pass Golf and Tennis Learning Center, R, and arrive at Shelley Field parking lot. Enter the trail at the SE corner.

North Carolina State University (Wake, Durham, and Moore Counties)

The Carl A. Schenck Memorial Forest is a research laboratory of conifers and broadleaves on the university property between Wade Ave and Reedy Creek Park Rd (SR-1650) in Raleigh. The 6.0-mi Loblolly Trail (see chapter 10)

1098 goes 1.5 mi through the forest, and the 1.2-mi Frances Liles Interpretive Trail is in the forest interior. It has ten stops that describe the multiple benefits derived from forest land. Redbud groves and pine grafting are prominent on

746 the S side of the loop. Access is either from the Loblolly Trail or the picnic shelter. To reach the picnic shelter, take Reedy Creek Park Rd off Blue Ridge Rd (1.0 mi N of the state fairgrounds) and go 0.9 mi to the forest entrance sign L. Go 0.1 mi to the entrance gate and park to avoid blocking the gate. Walk on the gated road 0.1 mi to the picnic shelter, R, and the trailhead. (USGS Map: Raleigh W)

The Hill Forest is in Durham County and has a network of single-lane access roads that provides 10.5 mi of unnamed trails. Permission for hiking in the forest is required; contact the address below. The forest is on both sides of Flat River, which has some exceptionally steep banks. Dial Creek also flows S through the forest. To reach the forest from I-85 and US-501 in Durham, go 12.5 mi N on US-501 to Quail Roost and turn R on Moores Mill Rd (SR-1601), immediately turning R on State Forest Rd (SR-1614) after crossing the N & W RR. Go 1.0 mi to the forest entrance. (SR-1614 also goes through the forest to jct at 2.2 mi with Wilkins Rd [SR-1613] and Hampton Rd [SR-1603] for a route E to Hampton.) The George K. Slocum Forestry Camp is on the L of the entrance. (USGS Maps: Rougemont, Lake Michie)

Goodwin Forest is in Moore County. Although there are no developed trails, there are 4.1 mi of single-lane access roads open to hikers. If approaching from Carthage, go W 1.3 mi on NC-22/24/27 to a jct with Bethlehem Church Rd (SR-1261), L. After 1.5 mi enter Goodwin Forest. Follow the first road L or go straight ahead. Permission for the hike is required from the office listed below. (USGS Map: Carthage)

Information: College of Forest Resources, Dept of Forestry, NCSU, Box 8002, Raleigh, NC 27695; 919-515-2891.

Piedmont Community College (Roxboro)

1303 The PCC Nature Trail (2.0 mi, easy to moderate) has color-coded sub-titles. The major one is red-blazed General Trail that makes a loop on a hardwood hillside with boulders and near Marlowe Creek. The other trails connect to the L within the loop except Wild Flower Trail. If beginning counterclockwise from the entrance, descend to a grassy ridge and turn R. At 0.1 mi are Conservation Trail and Observation Trail, L. Geology Trail branches from Conservation Trail to connect with General Trail. Pass Wildlife Trail on a descent, and after Forestry Trail an amphitheater is L at 0.7 mi. Arrive at the creek bank for a parallel upstream. Cross a small footbridge. At 1.0 mi turn L at a scenic area with large boulders, cascades, and pools. After crossing the small stream above the cascades, temporarily leave the creek, but return before making a steep ascent to pass Connector Trail and Spring Connector Trail. A completion can either end where you started or exit to the parking lot on a R spur. The trail is free and open to the public during daylight hours. If a large group is visiting an advance notice should be made to the college's director of physical facilities.

1304-1310

1311

Address and Access: On US-501 N in Roxboro, drive 1.0 mi from jct of NC-49 and turn L (W) on Memorial Dr. After 0.5 mi turn R and go 0.7 mi to the college and to the NW end of parking lot #4 near sign. PCC, P.O. Box 1197, Roxboro, NC 27573; 336-599-1181; fax: 336-597-3817.

Sandhills Community College (Moore County)

The Sandhills Horticultural Gardens and the Landscape Gardening School (established in 1968) at Sandhills Community College are rare among two-year colleges. A coordinator of the Gardens stated there were about 1,500 species at the sites. A citizens support group is the Sandhills Horticultural Society. Hundreds of graduates have brought honor and recognition to the college as horticulturists, landscape designers and architects, nurserymen, and managers worldwide.

From the garden's entrance it is 1.5 mi to walk all the circuits and backtracking walkways within the varied collections of the Sandhills Horticultural Gardens Trail. The first garden, R, is the Conifer Garden, with such striking species as weeping blue Atlas cedar, blue weeping juniper, and weeping red pine. The Sir Walter Raleigh Garden is a formal English garden, followed by an herb garden, and the remarkable collection in the Ebersole Holly Garden. To the L of these areas are the Hillside Garden with pools, cascades, and flowers, a rose garden, and even a vegetable and fruit garden. To the L of this is the Hackley Garden, featuring azalea, camellia, rhododendron, and many other shade loving plants. In the cove of twin lakes is the 0.1-mi Desmond Native Wetland Trail, a boardwalk through indigenous species and bird sanctuary. An

1312

1313

upland garden has been constructed nearby. It depicts the native Sandhill Savannah. The gardens are open daily without charge; docents for tours are **1314** available by appointment. (An 0.8-mi unmarked Connector Trail goes beyond the gate at the end of the Ebersole Holly Garden to connect with the 2.0-mi Reservoir Lake Trail described in chapter 13. Along the way the connector passes R of the twin lakes, follows part of the college's fitness trail, staying L, and connects at the W end of the reservoir dam.)

Address and Access: Sandhills Horticultural Gardens, Sandhills Community College, 3395 Airport Rd, Pinehurst, NC 28374; 910-695-3882. From US-1 turn W on NC-2 for 0.2 mi, turn R on NC-22, drive 2.3 mi to Airport Rd, turn L and go 1.0 mi to the college, L. Park at the C. Victor & Margaret Ball Visitor Center.

Southeastern Community College (Whiteville)

At the N parking lot behind the Allied Health Bldg is the access to SCC Nature Trail (0.5 mi, easy). Constructed and maintained by students, the emphasis is on general biology. Their effort is to identify and place markers at each species. In the learning process the college also involves community groups in conservation and knowledge of plants and animals. In those groups are Scouts, 4-H Clubs, and participants in Earth Day events. Some of the plants are by streams in the forest, home to pond pine, blackjack oak, horse sugar, sweet pepper bush, and dwarf white azalea. A Butterfly Garden, a.k.a. "Bird Lane" is being added.

Address and Access: Southeastern CC, 4564 Chadbourn Highway, Whiteville, NC 28472; 910-642-7141 or www.southeastern.cc.nc.us. On US-74-76 Byp, halfway between Chadbourn W and Whiteville E, exit at Union Valley Rd, S. Cross US-74/76/NC-130 Bus. After 1.5 mi from the Bypass jct with Chadbourn Highway. Turn R and after 0.1 mi turn R into the campus and stay R to reach the parking lot listed above.

University Of North Carolina (Chapel Hill) (Orange County)
North Carolina Botanical Garden

The 600-acre NC Botanical Garden is a botanical preserve of southeastern trees, shrubs, plants, ferns, wildflowers, and herbs. Its nature trails are open daily, and the administrative offices are open Mon through Fri. Guided tours of the garden are offered by prior arrangement to groups of 10 to 60. From the

parking lot follow the signs on the NC Botanical Garden Nature Trail (a self-   **1315**
guided interpretive trail). Cross a bridge at 0.2 mi and turn R. (Another trail
ascends L to connect with other unnamed trails.) Follow a combination of
trails under a subcanopy of flowering trees such as dogwoods and return to the
parking lot after 1.5 mi. (The Totten Center is across the street.)

Address and Access: NC Botanical Garden, UNC-CH, CB# 3375 Totten
Center, Chapel Hill, NC 27599; 919-962-0522. In E Chapel Hill the location
is at Laurel Hill Rd (SR-1901), 0.7 mi S of the US-15/501 and NC-54 jct.

Penny's Bend Nature Preserve (Durham County)

This 84-acre nature preserve is managed by the NC Botanical Garden under a
long-term lease from the US Army Corps of Engineers. It is upstream from
Falls Lake on the N side of Eno River. The preserve has a diabase of unerod-
able igneous rock. As a result the Eno River has formed an oxbow shape.
Many of the preserve's wildflowers are more common to the prairies of the
nation's Midwest. From the parking area enter the preserve where names of
wildflowers are on signs. Hike L toward and along the riverbank on River   **1316**
Bend Trail (1.8 mi, easy). Part of the forest has dense oak, walnut, and
sycamore. After passing some river rapids turn R to a slope with wildflowers
at 1.4 mi. At 1.6 mi, reach a jct with Ridge Trail (0.7 mi, easy), R. (It forms a   **1317**
loop toward the river.) Continuing on the main trail for the next 0.2 mi return
to the parking lot. (USGS Map: Durham NE)

Access: From the jct of I-85 and US-15 Bus (Exit 177B if going W, exit
177C if going E), and drive N on Roxboro Rd for 1.3 mi. Turn R on Old
Oxford Rd. At 3.3 mi cross Eno River bridge, and turn immediately L to the
parking lot on Snow Hill Rd.

Wake Forest University

The 129-acre Reynolda Gardens are part of a 300-acre gift to the university
from the estate of Richard Joshua Reynolds and Katherine Smith Reynolds.
Reynolda Gardens Trail access begins from the parking lot behind Reynolda   **1318**
Village at former Lake Katherine. (No bicycling or picnicking on the trail, and
pets must be on leashes.) Enter the forest by large trees and follow upstream
among large oaks and hickories, many of which are enshrouded with English
ivy. Under the canopy are redbud, dogwood, and many other planted shrubs.
At 0.5 mi turn L, then immediately R to pass through wild rose and scattered
pine. After entering a meadow curve R and follow the rim of the manicured

meadow. Join an entrance road and at 1.4 mi pass a grove of tall trees, including stately cedars. (A loop can be made here by taking the paved trail R to enter the forest R for a return to the 0.5 mi point described above. A turn L here for a return to the parking lot would be 2.1 mi.) Continuing on the entrance road pass L of the Reynolda House Museum of American Art and enter L into the Formal Gardens. In the gardens are hundreds of plants and elegant patterns in the rose gardens. Exit to the Reynolda Village entrance road, turn R and descend to the parking lot for a loop of 1.8 mi. (At the parking lot a paved 0.4 mi trail goes L to the marsh, crosses a dam and enters the university campus.)

Address and Access: Reynolda Gardens of WFU, 100 Reynolda Village, Winston Salem, NC 27106; 336-758-5593 or www.wfu.edu/gardens. Reynolda Village (of shops and restaurants), 336-758-5584; Reynolda House Museum of American Art, 336-725-5325. From I-40 Bus, Exit 2, take Silas Creek Parkway N (NC-67) 3.8 mi to a fork R that becomes Wake Forest Rd. After 0.3 mi to a traffic light turn R on Reynolda Rd. Drive 0.2 mi and turn L into Reynolda Village Shopping Center. Stay ahead to descend an embankment to the parking lot.

Western Carolina University (Jackson and Macon Counties)

The university has a 300-acre preserve and NC Natural Heritage Area in the Wolf Creek watershed, a state natural heritage area N of Brown Mtn. Access paths are also on private and Nantahala NF properties. One access, frequently used by the university's Biology Club, is 5.4 mi S from the campus. From the jct of the main campus entrance on NC-107 in Cullowhee, go S on NC-107 for 1.3 mi to a jct with Speedwell Rd (SR-1001). Turn R and drive 1.1 mi to Cullowhee Mtn. Rd (SR-1157) at the bridge over Tilley Creek. Drive 3.5 mi (along Cullowhee Creek, R) to a switchback curve in the road and park on a large grassy area beyond the curve. Follow USFS Cherry Gap Rd (off-road vehicles) to the preserve entrance. Oak, birch, maple, hemlock, and rhododendron are common along the slope as the road leads to the watershed. Ahead upstream are the university preserve lands and an extended pathway. Backtrack, or follow Cherry Gap Rd out to SR-1157, turn R, and descend 0.6 mi to where you parked. To hike the university and private properties, request permission from the address below. (USGS Map: Glenville)

Address: Dept of Biology, WCU, Cullowhee, NC 28723; 828-227-7244.

Wilkes Community College (Wilkesboro)

Located in Wilkesboro, there are two trails. From the campus parking lot walk the (1.0 mi, easy) Walking Trail clockwise. Wide, smooth, and lighted, pass a **1319** pond, then curve R beside the bank of Moravian Creek. Resting benches are along the way. At 0.7 mi pass R of a RR caboose and complete the loop. Near the caboose is Woodland Trail (0.2 mi, moderate). It follows a street toward **1320** the Continuing Ed Bldg, but turns up a hill, L, to a parking lot. Turn L to Whitley Cabin and complete the loop.

Address and Access: Wilkes CC, P.O. 120, Wilkesboro, NC 28697; 910-651-8642. Follow NC-268 W, off US-421 Byp. After 2.0 mi, turn L on South Collegiate Ct. Drive 0.4 mi and turn L at the campus parking area.

Mountains-to-Sea Trail

*On the trail I always feel a quiet excitement
in anticipation of what awaits me around
the bend, into the next mile.*
—Bob Benner

The Mountains-to-Sea Trail (MST) is currently about 935 mi from Clingmans Dome and the Appalachian National Scenic Trail in the Great Smoky Mountains National Park in the west, to Jockey's Ridge State Park at the Atlantic Seashore in the east. Almost 430 mi are complete. The MST follows many established hiking trails, other newly constructed hiking trail sections, and parts of the Department of Transporation's official bicycle routes on backcountry roads. It passes through 37 counties and 38 towns and cities, crosses hundreds of streams and rivers, ascends scores of mountain peaks (including the state's highest, Mount Mitchell at 6,684 ft.), and encounters such spectacular places as Craggy Gardens, Linville Gorge, and Cape Hatteras National Seashore. A state trail, it is supported by more than 50 task forces whose volunteer work assists in design, construction, and maintenance. In 1997 the Friends of the Mountains-to-Sea Trail (FMST) was incorporated with the purpose to "promote the concept, research and provide information, advocate cooperative efforts among allied government offices and citizens, and assist task forces and trail organizations. . . ."

Because there is not space in this guidebook for descriptions of the MST (though you will notice sections of its location throughout this book) it is recommended that interested hikers secure *Hiking North Carolina's Mountains-to-Sea Trail* at a bookstore, or call the publisher at 1-800-848-6224. For FMST information call 919-496-4771; web: www.ncmst.org.

Appendix B

Conservation and Recreation Organizations

US SENATE COMMITTEES

Senate Committee on Agriculture,
Nutrition, and Forestry
US Senate
Washington, DC 20510
Tel: 202-224-2035

Senate Committee on Energy
and Natural Resources
US Senate
Washington, DC 20510
Tel: 202-224-4971

Senate Committee on Environment
and Public Works
US Senate
Washington, DC 20510
Tel: 202-224-6176
Web: epw.senate.gov

US HOUSE COMMITTEES

House Committee on Agriculture
(Resource Conservation)
US House of Representatives
Washington, DC 20515
Tel: 202-225-2171

House Committee on Resources
US House of Representatives
Washington, DC 20515
Tel: 202-225-2761
Web: resourcecommittee.house.gov

US FEDERAL GOVERNMENT AGENCIES

Advisory Council on Historic
Preservation
1100 Pennsylvania Ave., NW
#809, Old P.O. Bldg
Washington, DC 20004
Tel: 202-606-8503
Web: www.achp.gov

Appalachia Regional Commission
1666 Connecticut Ave., NW, Suite
700 Washington, DC 20009
Tel: 202-884-7700
Web: 222.arc.gov

Council on Environmental Quality
722 Jackson Place, NW
Washington, DC 20503
Tel: 202-456-6224
Web: www.eop.gov/ceq

Department of Commerce
(Global Warming)
1100 Wayne Avenue
Silver Spring, MD 20910
Tel: 301-427-2089
Web: www.ogp.noaa.gov

Environmental Protection Agency
1200 Pennsylvania Ave., NW
Washington, DC 20460
Tel: 202-260-2090
Web: www.epa.gov

and

Environmental Protection Agency
Region IV (NC included)
61 Forsyth St., SW
Atlanta, GA 30303
Tel: 404-562-9900
Web: www.epa.gov/region04

Migratory Bird Conservation
Commission
1849 C St., NW (Arl Sq. 622)
Washington, DC 20240
Tel: 703-358-1716

US Department of Agriculture
(National Forests and Grasslands)
P.O. Box 96090
Washington, DC 20090
Tel: 202-205-8333
Web: www.fs.fed.us

and

US Forest Service
Southern Research Station
P.O. Box 2750
Asheville, NC 28802
Tel: 828-257-4832
Web: www.cs.unca.edu/nfsnc

US Department of Agriculture
Natural Resources Conservation
Services

14th and Independence Ave., SW
Washington, DC 20013
Tel: 202-720-3213
Web: www.nrcs.usda.gov

and

NC Public Affairs Specialist
4405 Bland Rd., Suite 205
Raleigh, NC 27609
Tel: 919-873-2107

US Department of the Interior
(GSMNP, BRP, & National
Trail System)
1849 C St., NW
Washington, DC 20240
Tel: 202-208-6843
Web: www.nps.gov

and

Bureau of Land Management
1849 C St., NW
Tel: 202-208-3801
Web: www.blm.gov

and

Fish and Wildlife Service
Tel: 202-208-5634
Web: www.fws.gov

and

Southeast Regional Office #4
Fish and Wildlife Service
1875 Century Blvd.
Atlanta, GA 30345
Tel: 404-679-4000
Web: www.fws.gov

US Army Corps of Engineers
Wilmington District
P. O. Box 1890
Wilmington, NC 28402
Tel: 910-251-4501
Web: www.saw.usace.army.mil

NORTH CAROLINA GOVERNMENT AGENCIES

NC Department of Environment &
Natural Resources
1601 Mail Services Center
Raleigh, NC 27699-1601
Tel: 919-733-4984
Web: www.enr.state.nc.us

NC Cooperative Fish and
Wildlife Research
201 David Clark Lab
Raleigh, NC 276-95
Tel: 919-515-2631
Web: www.4.scsu.edu:8010/
nccoopunit

NC Division of Soil & Water
Conservation Commission
1614 Mail Service Center
Raleigh, NC 27699
Tel: 919-733-2302
Web: www.dem.com

NC Wildlife Resources Commission
1701 Mail Services Center
Raleigh, NC 27699
Tel: 919-733-3391
Web: www.ncwildlife.org

NON-GOVERNMENT ORGANIZATIONS

American Association for Leisure
and Recreation
1900 Association Drive
Reston, VA 20191
Tel: 703-476-3472

American Birding Association
P.O. Box 6599
Colorado Springs, CO 80934
Tel: 719-578-9703
Web: www.americanbirding.org

American Camping Association
5000 State Rd., 67N
Martinsville, IN 46151
Tel: 765-342-8456
Web: www.acacamps.org

American Fisheries Society
5410 Grosvenor Ln., Suite 110
Bethesda, MD 20814
Tel: 301-897-8616
Web: www.fisheries.org

and

NC Wildlife Resource Commission
1721 Mail Center Service
Raleigh, NC 27699
Tel: 919-362-3557
Web: www4.ncsu.edu/unity/users

American Forests
P.O. Box 2000
Washington, DC 20013
Tel: 202-955-4500
Web: www.americanforests.org

American Hiking Society
1422 Fenwick Lane
Silver Spring, MD 20910
Tel: 301-565-6704
Web: www.americanhiking.org

Appalachia Mountain Club
5 Joy Street
Boston, MA 02108
Tel: 617-523-0636
Web: www.outdoors.org

Appalachian Trail Conference
P.O. Box 807
Harpers Ferry, WV 25425
Tel: 304-535-6331
Web: www.appalachiantrail.org

Audubon Naturalist Society of
Central Atlantic States
8940 Jones Mill Road
Chevy Chase, MD 20815
Tel: 301-652-9188
Web: www.audubonnaturalist.org

Audubon Society, NC Office
123 Kingston Dr., Suite 206A
Chapel Hill, NC 27514
Tel: 919-929-3899

Camp Fire USA
4601 Madison Avenue
Kansas City, MO 64112
Tel: 816-756-1950
Web: www.campfireusa.org

Clean Water Action
4455 Connecticut Ave., NW, Suite A300
Washington, DC 20008
Tel: 202-895-0420
Web: www.cleanwateraction.org

Conservation Council of NC
Raleigh, NC 27605
Tel: 919-839-0006
Web: www.serve.com/ccnc

Cousteau Society, Inc.
870 Greenbriar Circle
Chesapeake, VA 23320
Tel: 757-523-9335
Web: www.cousteausociety.org

Defenders of Wildlife
1101 14th St., NW, Suite 1400
Washington, DC 20005
Tel: 202-682-9400

Environmental Defense
NC Office
2500 Blue Ridge Rd., Suite 330
Raleigh, NC 27607
Tel: 919-881-2601
Web: www.environmentaldefense.org

Environmental Educators of NC
P. O. Box 4901
Chapel Hill, NC 27515
Tel: 919-250-1050
Web: www.eenc.org

Izaak Walton League of America, Inc.
707 Conservation Lane
Gaithersburg, MD 20878
Tel: 301-548-0150
Web: www.iwla.org

National Audubon Society
700 Broadway
New York, NY 10003
Tel: 212-979-3000
Web: www.audubon.org

National Parks and Conservation Association
1300 19th St., NW, Suite 300
Washington, DC 20036
Tel: 800-628-7275
Web: www.npca.org

and

NPCA Southeast Regional Office
101 South Main St., Suite 322
Clinton, TN 37716
Tel: 865-457-7775
Web: www.npca.org

National Wildlife Federation Hq.
11100 Wildlife Center Drive
Reston, VA 20190
Tel: 703- 438-6000
Web: www.nwf.org

The Nature Conservancy
Mid-Atlantic Division Office
4705 University Dr., Suite 290
Durham, NC 27707
Tel: 919-403-8558

North Carolina Museum of Natural Science
(11 W Jones St.) P.O. Box 29555
Raleigh, NC 27626
Tel: 919-733-7450

NC Recreation and Park Society, Inc.
883 Washington Street
Raleigh, NC 27605
Tel: 919-832-5868
Web: www.ncrps.org

NC Watershed Coalition, Inc.
P.O. Box 337
Colfax, NC 27035
Tel: 336-992-8734
Web: www.ncwatershedcoalition.org

NC Wildlife Federation
P.O. Box 10626
Raleigh, NC 27605
Tel: 919-833-1923
Web: www.ncwildlifefed.org

Scenic North Carolina, Inc.
P.O. Box 628
Raleigh, NC 27602
Tel: 919-832-3687
Web: www.scenicnc.org

The Sierra Club, NC Chapter
112 South Blount Street
Raleigh, NC 27601
Tel: 919-833-8467
Web: www.sierraclub-nc.org

The Wilderness Society
1615 M St., NW #100
Washington, DC 20036
Tel: 202-833-2300
Web: www.wilderness.org

and

The Wilderness Society
NC Chapter
2279-13 Lystra Road
Chapel Hill, NC 27514
Tel: 919-968-1575

Appendix C

Family Day Hikes

The following trails are but a few of the state's offerings appropriate for parents who wish to plan fun and educational outdoor trips for their children. These trails will give you access to natural areas that include forests, waterfalls, lakes, overlooks, boardwalks, islands, arboretums, historic and military sites, rock formations, outstanding scenic views, and nature/interpretive trails of flora and fauna. At many parks and natural areas listed in the book you may find that all trails are appropriate for children. Examples include the Johnson Environmental Education Park, Piedmont Environmental Center, and North Carolina Educational State Forests.

Trails Recommended for People with Disabilities

This is a list of trails suitable for wheelchairs or walkers—usually these have paved surfaces. Also note that "greenways" listed in the book will offer a choice of trails within its network system. Examples include the following greenways: Charlotte (Mecklenberg County); Greensboro (Guilford County); Durham (Durham County); Cary and Raleigh (Wake County).

Appendix E

Leave No Trace

The Appalachian Mountain Club is a national educational partner of Leave No Trace, a nonprofit organization dedicated to promoting and inspiring responsible outdoor recreation through education, research, and partnerships. The Leave No Trace Program seeks to develop wildland ethics—ways in which people think and act in the outdoors to minimize their impacts on the areas they visit and to protect our natural resources for future enjoyment. Leave No Trace unites four federal land management agencies—the U.S. Forest Service, National Park Service, Bureau of Land Management, and U.S. Fish and Wildlife Service—with manufacturers, outdoor retailers, user groups, educators, organizations such as the AMC and the National Outdoor Leadership School (NOLS), and individuals.

The Leave No Trace ethic is guided by these seven principles:

- Plan ahead and prepare
- Travel and camp on durable surfaces
- Dispose of waste properly
- Leave what you find
- Minimize campfire impacts
- Respect wildlife
- Be considerate of other visitors

The AMC has joined NOLS—a recognized leader in wilderness education and a founding partner of Leave No Trace—as a national provider of the Leave No Trace Master Educator course. The AMC offers this five-day course, designed especially for outdoor professionals and land managers, as well as the shorter two-day Leave No Trace Trainer course, at locations throughout the Northeast.

For Leave No Trace information and materials, contact:
Leave No Trace Center for Outdoor Ethics, P.O. Box 997, Boulder, CO 80306
Toll Free: 800-332-4100, or locally, 303-442-8222; Fax: 303-442-8217
www.lnt.org

Trail Index

Each trail's designated number, which appears in the margin near the trail's description in the book, is listed here in parentheses. For example, the A. Rufus Morgan Trail, the first entry in the index, appears on page 102 and is trail number 172.

General Index

About the Author

Allen de Hart has been hiking, designing, constructing, maintaining, and writing about trails for six decades. When only five years old, his 17-year-old brother, Moir, took him on a hiking, camping, and fishing trip to Smith River Falls, a few miles from their home in Patrick County, Virginia. The experience made an indelible impression and enhanced his interest in natural science and outdoor sports. His first childhood hikes in North Carolina were at Hanging Rock and Pilot Mountain (before they became state parks). In the 1930s he and his two younger brothers, Dick and Willie, built trails on their large farm, and the Bobwhite Trail to Woolwine School, a shortcut from a long school-bus ride. With the Appalachian Trail being constructed by the CCC at Rocky Knob, he and his brothers were among the first local users, but it was not until 1978 he hiked the entire length of the Appalachian Trail.

De Hart has a master's degree in American history and doctoral courses from the University of Virginia in Charlottesville. He also did additional doctoral work at North Carolina State University and received two National Science Foundation grants in psychology, one at Florida State University and the other the University of Georgia. He is a graduate of the Adjutant General Corps of the US Army and served overseas during the Korean War. He is a history professor emeritus at Louisburg College, Louisburg, NC, where he and his wife, Flora (whose discipline was English), began teaching in 1957. He also served as director of public affairs for 27 years and has taught courses in outdoor recreation for 22 years. Active in state and community service organizations, he has received three Governor's Awards.

He has hiked in 46 states and 18 foreign countries. By 2003 he had measured more than 49,000 miles of trails. From his journals he has authored eight books and trail guides for West Virginia, Virginia, North and South Carolina, Florida, and the sea islands of Georgia. Other outdoor sports in which he participates are mountain climbing, whitewater rafting, biking, canoeing, hunting and fishing, diving, water skiing, and spelunking. He and his wife created the De Hart Botanical Gardens in Virginia and North Carolina in 1969. The North Carolina preserve is 5.0 mi south of Louisburg on US-401.